Edmund Spenser

an

Annotated Bibliography

Philological Series
Volume Seventeen

EDMUND SPENSER

an

Annotated Bibliography

1937—1972

By

Waldo F. McNeir
and
Foster Provost

DUQUESNE UNIVERSITY PRESS, PITTSBURGH
Distributed by Humanities Press, Atlantic Highlands

First Printing

Printed in the United States of America

Library of Congress Cataloging in Publication Data

McNeir, Waldo F
   Edmund Spenser: an annotated bibliography, 1937-1972.

   (Duquesne studies: Philological series; v. 17)
   First ed. (1962) published under title: Annotated
bibliography of Edmund Spenser, 1937-1960.
   Includes Index.
   1. Spenser, Edmund, 1552?-1599—Bibliography.
I. Provost, George Foster, 1925-   joint author.
II. Series.
Z8830.8.M33 1975   [PR2363]   016.821'3   75-33311
ISBN 0-391-00395-X

TABLE OF CONTENTS

PREFACE TO THE SECOND EDITION

A resurgence of interest in Edmund Spenser as a subject of scholarship and criticism has occurred since the first edition of this bibliography was published in 1962, a development which has been noticed by students of the English Renaissance and which we take pleasure in recording in this second edition. The rediscovery of Spenser, hoped for but hardly foreseen fifteen years ago, is gratifying to those who know his work as a mirror in which many facets of the many-faceted Renaissance are both reflected and refracted.

It is significant, we think, that in recent times the two reference works which our own followed have been reprinted: Frederic Ives Carpenter's *A Reference Guide to Edmund Spenser*, in 1969; and Dorothy F. Atkinson's *Edmund Spenser: A Bibliographical Supplement*, in 1967. The first edition of our bibliography was reprinted in 1967. Not unrelated is the fact that the great Variorum edition of Spenser's works, together with A. C. Judson's *Life of Edmund Spenser*, first published by the Johns Hopkins Press from 1932 to 1949, has been reprinted by the same press several times. With evidence of renewed interest in Spenser, a revised and enlarged edition of this bibliography became a desideratum.

Some comparisons of our first edition with the one now being offered may be in order. Our Bibliography of Sources in the first edition listed seventy-six works; the Bibliography of Sources in this edition lists one hundred seventeen works. The list of Serials and Abbreviations in our first edition contained about two hundred titles; the same list in this edition contains about three hundred fifty titles. When specialized bibliographical tools and outlets for publishable work on Spenser have increased to such an extent, the advent of a non-verbal culture would not seem to be dangerously imminent. The Shakespeare industry which we noted somewhat ruefully in the Preface to our first edition continues unabated as a multinational enterprise, and modern men of the Renaissance accept it as the way of the world. Spenserians may take heart, however, from the fact that the present edition of this bibliography, which adds only twelve years (1961-1972) to our previous coverage of the twenty-four years from 1937 to 1960, contains more than twice as many entries as the first edition—more than 2600 compared to not quite 1200. Clearly, Spenser's position as a great figure of the English Renaissance and a premier poet of the Elizabethan age is once again widely recognized.

Perhaps our obvious satisfaction will be pardoned if we present further evidence of a Spenser revival. Many articles, dissertations, and books on Spenser in recent years have followed established lines of investigation, while some others have signaled new directions. Of continuing interest are Spenser's relations to earlier writers—medieval romancers and allegorists, the *stil novisti*, Petrarch, Langland, and Chaucer; his connections with figures of the Continental Renaissance—Ficino, Bembo, Pico, and other Neoplatonists, with Ariosto, Tasso, and the Pléiade; his resemblance or contrast to his English contemporaries—Shakespeare and other dramatists, Nashe and the satirists, Sidney and the members of his circle, and Drayton and Donne; his influence on poets of the seventeenth century—the Spenserians, and writers as different as Knevet, Marvell, Butler, Fanshawe, Milton, Bunyan, and Waller; his influence on his eighteenth-century imitators—Pope, Thomson, and Collins, and his effect on his eighteenth-century defenders—Hurd and the Wartons; his impact on the English romantic poets and on Tennyson; and his stimulation of American writers such as Hawthorne and Melville. Studies of these and other familiar topics have continued, with fresh insights and emphases. New studies of Spenser have been devoted to his work in terms of Renaissance theories of allegory, myth and archetype, imagery, history, and the history of ideas. Newer approaches have studied Spenser's iconography, rhetoric, etymology, emblems, and prosody. The newest approaches have been concerned with Spenser's numerological structures, with his humor and playfulness, and with the relation between Spenser, his personae or voices, and the reader. These studies will continue, inviting new ways of reading Spenser.

In reviewing the first edition of our bibliography in *Seventeenth-Century News*, 21 (1963), 3-4, Kathrine Koller said: "The most interesting bibliographical items in many respects are the dissertations. There are thirty-eight doctoral dissertations which are relevant to Spenser, and sixty-eight which deal with Spenser specifically." Within the new period covered by this edition, 1961-1972, we have listed about one hundred twenty doctoral dissertations which are relevant to Spenser, and about one hundred five more which deal with Spenser specifically. "The prince of poets in his time" is not being neglected in the graduate schools, for these two hundred twenty-five dissertations were produced at some seventy American universities and at ten or more foreign universities. The leader was Yale University with fifteen dissertations on Spenser, second was Columbia University with fourteen, and third was Harvard University with twelve. A reader who compares these figures with those presented in our entry number 892 will observe a difference which might have been expected, given a Spenser revival in progress in the 1960's. It might not have been expected that in the same period between 1961 and 1972, five or more dissertations dealing with Spenser would be written at eleven other American universities: the University of California at Los Angeles, Princeton University, Duquesne University, the University of North Carolina at Chapel Hill, Brown University, Michigan State University, Stanford University, the University of Minnesota, Vanderbilt University, the University of Texas, and Indiana University.

A good many studies of Spenser which began as doctoral dissertations have been published as books, sometimes soon after the dissertation was completed, sometimes more than a decade later. In either case we have annotated the book, noting its inception as a dissertation by a reference to *Dissertation Abstracts* or *Dissertation Abstracts International* (the "international" added in July of 1969 is for the most part a joke), or else by a reference to the university at which the dissertation was written, and when. If an abstract of an unpublished dissertation was not available in DA or DAI, as with dissertations written at Harvard, British universities, and a few others, we have usually been able to obtain the manuscript through interlibrary loan service. A small number of dissertations not available in other form were obtained on microfilm. The only dissertations which remain unannotated are those about which we have been unable to get substantive information.

The listing of several sources of a dissertation title or abstract in our first edition has been abandoned. If the abstract was published in DA, before the publication of abstracts became standard practice, we give no other source for it in the present edition, thus eliminating some of the clutter in older dissertation entries. Another change affects M. A. theses. We have kept the listings and annotations of British M. A. theses which appeared in our first edition, but we have not added more recent M. A. theses, either British or American. With the increasing popularity of an "All But Dissertation" degree in American universities, the M. A. with or without an accompanying thesis approaches desuetude in this country at universities which offer the doctorate.

In these days of proliferating paperbacks and rampant reprints, two phenomena that were unforeseeable in the 1950's when the first edition of this bibliography was in the making, we have found it impossible to keep track of these developments in the book trade. We hope that users of this bibliography will overlook our failure to give the titles of publishers' reprint series or to designate paperbacks as such. Although the reprint publishing houses do not account for all the paperbacks that stream forth, it is well known that many reprint publishers are on the scene. We have tried to perform a service to Spenser scholars by noting reprints of works of special importance, including those of older works that were listed in the bibliographies of Carpenter or Atkinson but were not included in our first edition because they were published before 1937. A good many entries of this kind will be found. We have noted reprints of some works that may be of special usefulness to students of the Renaissance, but we have made no effort to note all reprints of general works in the period.

A different policy has been followed in the listing of reviews. In our first edition we listed many reviews of books on Spenser, and also of books on the Renaissance that were not primarily concerned with Spenser. The result was inflation of some entries in which the list of reviews occupied as much space as the annotation. The listing of reviews in a bibliography may be considered a kind of lagniappe. Our policy on reviews in the present edition has been conservative. We have eliminated reviews of books published before 1960, in the belief that reviews of more recent books, together with separate entries for review articles dealing with many of these, would provide a valuable index to the present state of Spenser studies. At the same time, we have limited the important reviews of any book to five or six, and we have not listed the important reviews which a librarian would naturally consult in *Choice* and *Library Journal*, or those which a student or scholar would naturally consult in the annual surveys of recent work in the Renaissance appearing in *The Year's Work in English Studies* and in *Studies of English Literature, 1500-1900*. We note in passing and with regret the discontinuance of the bibliography of recent studies in the Renaissance, with reviews listed, which was formerly published as a supplement to *Studies in Philology*. Finally, in listing reviews in this edition we give a page reference only to the page on which the review begins. For review articles we give a complete page reference.

The bibliographical style of our entries is the same as before. It seems to be easily decipherable; at least, we have had no complaints about it from reviewers or users of the first edition. The new annotations, like the old ones, are descriptive and not evaluative, or not conspicuously so. They are intended to show in concise form the chief points of a study in its bearing on Spenser. Much valuable criticism of Spenser has been published; yet the annotation of diffuse, technical, poorly written, pretentious, or complex studies has sometimes been difficult. In some of our annotations, always with an acknowledgment, we have relied on *The Year's Work in English Studies*, *Abstracts of English Studies*, the author's idea of what he said in *MLA Abstracts*, and especially the notices of work on Spenser which have been appearing in the *Spenser Newsletter* since its beginning. Although each of these sources of information has been indispensable, we alone are responsible for our annotations describing the content of a study as we understand it.

Users will wish to note that it is our policy to record the names of the authors of our various entries exactly as these names are given on the title page of the work (or at the foot of some articles). In most instances any confusion in identity which might derive from variant forms of an author's name—e.g., Alastair Fowler, entry number 1367, A. D. S. Fowler, entry number 1917—can be resolved quickly by consulting the Index.

Numerous cross-references appear in this edition, a feature made necessary by the publication of several anthologies of critical essays on Spenser, as well as by the interrelatedness of much Spenser scholarship and criticism. We hope the system of cross-references will facilitate the use of our bibliography in various ways. The first edition was not without cross-references, as one reviewer claimed, but this edition contains many more.

The Index, we believe, will be a valuable supplement to the cross-references, since it contains about 200 subject-topic headings, as well as extensive lists of references to characters, incidents, and locales in *The Faerie Queene* and to characters and individual poems in *The Shepheardes Calender*. It also lists the authors and the editors named in the titles and the annotations of the more than 2600 works which we have recorded; it lists the persons other than authors and editors named in the titles and annotations; and it lists the authors of the non-Spenserian literary and historical works mentioned in titles and annotations, and the reviewers named in the annotations.

The subject-topic entries constitute a new feature in this second edition. We must acknowledge, however, that not even this large list of subject headings will obviate scholarly diligence on the user's part, since many subjects and authors treated in the books we have listed cannot be identified through our Index. We have indeed indexed "Ariosto" for C. S. Lewis's *The Allegory of Love* (item 1513), though the name "Ariosto" does not appear in our annotation; but it has been impossible to index the huge variety of material which Lewis treats in passing. In such instances the only safe procedure for the searcher is to consult the index of the book in question.

Again, it has not been practicable to make as many categories as we should have liked in such nebulous areas as "Myth and archetype" and "Rhetoric and the rhetorical tradition," since the boundaries of "archetypal" and "rhetorical" criticism are exceedingly flexible, and to say that this item is or is not "rhetorical" criticism and this other is or is not "archetypal" criticism is to risk injustice to the authors of the studies involved, who might not agree at all with this labeling. We have made it our policy to list in the rhetoric category, for example, any items which under the broadest definitions of the words in the heading might be included. A reader looking for items containing the recent "rhetorical criticism," usually understood to treat of Spenser's manipulation of the reader's response, will find less help than he might wish in the "rhetoric" listing, which contains many other items as well. He still is not helpless, however; he can use another listing, "Reader's response to Sp's poems," which will help identify the particular items that he wishes to examine. A little practice in using our headings will, we believe, enable the user to find what he needs.

Finally, after due consideration we have decided not to present three or five indexes but to gather all items (subjects treated, works treated, authors treated, persons treated other than authors, and authors and editors of studies and works listed) into a single main list, with only two sublists under *The Faerie Queene* and *The Shepheardes Calender*. With only one Index to consult, the user will not be constantly wondering whether the item he wants is in a separate index.

Once again it is a pleasant duty to speak of the assistance we have received, individually and as collaborators. Fellow-bibliographers will believe us when we say that work on this second edition has been in mind, if not actually in progress, since the first edition was published. Together we thank all the reviewers of our first edition (see entry number 70), especially those who called attention to several prominent omissions, all of them corrected in this edition with the exception of a few items of which no trace could be found.

The western and eastern branches of our operation have been in regular communication with each other, sometimes in personal contact at national and regional meetings, and they were in conjunction in Eugene for six weeks in the early summer of 1974. It was during this last period that Harrison T. Meserole, Bibliographer of the Modern Language Association, kindly sent to us the page proofs of the Spenser listings and the Spenser cross-references in the *1972 MLA International Bibliography*, Vol. 1, in advance of publication. It was then that A. C. Hamilton kindly sent to us the galley proofs of the revised Spenser section of the new *Cambridge Bibliography of English Literature*, Vol. 1. It was then that both members of the partnership experienced the long-continued courtesies of Roland Bartel, Head of the English Department at the University of Oregon; of Myrna Lassiter, Secretary of the English Department, and her assistants; and of the librarians and staff members of the University of Oregon Library, especially Robert R. McCollough, Head Humanities Librarian, Reyburn R. McCready, Head Reference Librarian, and Clair Meyer, Interlibrary Loan Librarian. It was then that A. Kent Hieatt, of the University of Western Ontario, and William Nelson, of Columbia University, graciously agreed to serve as readers of our book in manuscript, a fortunate development indeed, for the book has benefited enormously from the scrupulous attention of these two scholars.

The western partner wishes to thank his graduate students for their steady help, particularly Robert Fraser, Louise Westling, Joe Smith, T. A. K. Thomason, Peter Mortenson, Arthur Amos, Michael Payne, William Kelly, James Reither, and Robert Wilson. He was greatly aided by an Academic Year Research Award from the Graduate School of the University of Oregon in 1973-1974, an award which subsidized several capable assistants, Stephen Murakami, Scott Sloan, and notably Clifford Cuniff. He wishes to acknowledge the invaluable services of Owen Daly as research assistant in the final phases. Finally, his share of this arduous task could not have been completed without the active help and constant encouragement of Corinne C. McNeir, Documents Librarian Emeritus of the University of Oregon.

At the eastern end of our operation, we are deeply indebted to James P. Beymer, Chairman of the English Department at Duquesne University, who supported the project with funds and with other tangible aid at crucial moments; to Richard Benzinger of the English Faculty for important help in assembling scattered items; to Paul Pugliese, Head Librarian at Duquesne, Marian Thomson of the Acquisitions Department, and Erica Strasser of the Reference Department, all of whom provided extensive aid; and to Susan Corliss, English Department secretary, and her assistants, especially Cheryl Porpora.

The eastern partner wishes to thank his graduate students generally and to single out those who helped most: Sylvia Denys, Alfred Hanley, Henry Kielarowski, and Raymond Riehl, all of whom did important spadework, and most notably Thomas R. Biagini, whose devotion to the task was extraordinary. Thanks are also due to the Duquesne English Department library secretaries Deborah R. Katz, Jo Ann Wheeler, and especially Pamela Wood and Hari H. N. Vishwanadha. A further special word of thanks goes to Jo Ann Wheeler, whose remarkable drawing, undertaken in sheer exuberance upon reading *The Faerie Queene* for the first time, is the fold-out frontispiece for this volume.

A checklist of criticism of *The Faerie Queene* prepared by Carolyn Burgholzer and Bernard J. Vondersmith has been most useful to us. Most important of all to the eastern partner has been the willingness of his wife, Rina, and his three children to share their claim on him with Edmund Spenser.

A work such as this could not be undertaken without drawing on the resources of many libraries and their services. These are now easier of access than they were a few years ago. Besides the many favors we have received from the libraries of our own universities, we are indebted to the Center for Research Libraries in Chicago, the Pacific Northwest Bibliographic Center in Seattle, the Widener Library of Harvard University, the Joseph Regenstein Library of the University of Chicago, the Fondren Library of Rice University, the Fred Lewis Pattee Library of the Pennsylvania State University, the Hillman Library of the University of Pittsburgh, the Carnegie Library of Pittsburgh, and the libraries of the University of California at Berkeley, Los Angeles, and Santa Barbara; of Yale University, Portland State University, Oregon State University, the University of Cincinnati, Princeton Theological Seminary, Washington State University, the University of Illinois at Urbana, Louisiana State University, and the University of British Columbia. In addition, we are grateful for the assistance in German libraries received from Dr. Hans Otto Thieme, of the Gesamthochschule Wuppertal.

Waldo F. McNeir   Foster Provost
University of Oregon, Emeritus   Duquesne University

PREFACE TO THE FIRST EDITION

This bibliography of Edmund Spenser has two predecessors: Frederic Ives Carpenter's *A Reference Guide to Edmund Spenser* (University of Chicago Press, 1923) and Dorothy F. Atkinson's *Edmund Spenser: A Bibliographical Supplement* (Johns Hopkins Press, 1937). Carpenter's work was a fine product of the early modern period of historical scholarship which saw invaluable additions to the *apparatus criticus* of Chaucer, Shakespeare, Milton, and many later and lesser poets. Spenser received his share of this attention, significantly from the school of American Spenserians active under the leadership of Edwin Greenlaw, Frederick M. Padelford, Charles Grosvenor Osgood, and others. Their devoted interest culminated in the great Variorum edition of Spenser's works published at Johns Hopkins between 1932 and 1949. Miss Atkinson's bibliography, designed as a supplement to Carpenter's pioneering effort, was another result of this interest. We have begun where she left off, with work published in 1937, and have carried the bibliography of Spenser through 1960, wishing to supply a need long felt by students of the Elizabethan period and to show, in doing so, the range, the emphasis, and the state of Spenserian studies during the past two decades. We hope this bibliography will prove a useful successor to the two works it follows.

Miss Atkinson's bibliography is principally devoted to the period from 1923 through 1936, and it contains about 1750 entries. Despite the fact that these include numerous entries of the same work in more than one place, the output of Spenser scholarship in the fourteen years covered by Miss Atkinson was indeed substantial. This bibliography covers the following twenty-four years and contains about 1200 entries. A considerable decline in Spenserian studies is registered; it would seem that "the prince of poets in his time" has not been drawn into the main currents of contemporary criticism to the extent that he deserves. Milton studies, one may feel, have been prosecuted with some vigor in recent years; yet Calvin Huckabay's *John Milton: A Bibliographical Supplement, 1929-1957* (Duquesne

University Press, 1960), covering nearly thirty years, lists 1960 entries, some of which appear more than once. Milton, then, has also been relatively neglected. Of Shakespearian studies, in contrast, there is apparently no end. Paul A. Jorgensen, reviewing *The Year's Work in English Studies* for 1956, notes that "Shakespeare covers twenty-eight pages, the Renaissance eight." He thoughtfully adds, "A survey such as this, then, tells us quite factually and beyond argument what subjects have presently the most vitality as fields for scholarship. The results are not necessarily pleasant even to devout Shakespearians, most of whom would be troubled by the little more than a page devoted to poets like Spenser and Donne (a proportion which makes the total poetical output of these men carry approximately the same weight as a play like *Henry IV*)."[1] Devout Shakespearians of this persuasion may be further troubled by the fact that *PMLA*'s bibliography for 1960 contains 296 entries on Shakespeare, twenty-three on Spenser, and twenty-five on Donne.[2] Clearly, an imbalance of scholarly attention prevails among the major poets of the English Renaissance. We hope this bibliography and guide to recent work on Spenser will fertilize the interest of students and scholars by revealing what remains to be done, so that scholarship and criticism on one of the most important of English poets, and through him on the whole period of the Renaissance in England, will be continued and expanded in a fruitful way.

Our relation to earlier Spenser bibliographers and our general aims having been stated, we may now explain the particular nature of the present work. Comprehensiveness is an ideal of every bibliographer; he hopes nothing will elude him. His users have the same hope. M. A. Shaaber has said of the compilers of the annual bibliography of Renaissance literature appearing in *Studies in Philology*, "What we hope for from them is accuracy and completeness."[3] But omissions are inevitable in a work of such wide scope as ours, drawn from the most diverse sources of information. Our Bibliography of about seventy-five sources includes, not all the likely and unlikely ones that have been examined, but only those in which Spenser items have been found. The List of Serials and Abbreviations, modeled on the one accompanying the annual bibliography in *PMLA* and using the same abbreviations whenever possible, contains more than two hundred titles, approximately twenty per cent as many as the "basic

---

[1] SQ, 10 (1959), 610.
[2] Annual Bibliography for 1960, PMLA, 76 (1961), 158-63, 164, 166.
[3] Recent Literature of the Renaissance, RN, 2 (1949), 42.

master list of about 1,060 periodicals" used in the compilation of that bibliography.[4] Since Spenser is a central figure of the English Renaissance, he reflects many aspects of the culture of the period and has connections with other literary figures. We have therefore included, mainly in the section on General Criticism, a good many publications which, while not primarily concerned with Spenser, serve to show in some significant way this centrality and these connections. Inclusiveness rather than exclusiveness has been one guiding principle. Where this is so, what to put in and what to leave out sometimes require rather nice judgment, and decisions in both directions have been made on the basis of what we hope are valid reasons. One class of items we have omitted is American Masters' theses; they did not seem worth the effort.[5] On the other hand, we have included British Masters' theses, far fewer in number and generally of higher quality. More than one hundred doctoral dissertations, both American and foreign, are listed. We trust that users of the bibliography will be happy to find in it perhaps more, rather than less, than they expected. Yet no allegedly comprehensive bibliography, especially one of a major English poet like Spenser, ever contains everything that everybody might look for in it. We are conscious of our shortcomings. And we are conscious above all of the worst occupational hazard of bibliographers who are not merely current: their work is no sooner completed than it is out-of-date.

Next to the listings themselves, the most important single feature of this bibliography is the annotations. A few items—those we have been unable to see, including some doctoral dissertations to which we did not have access—remain unannotated. Most of the dissertations, incidentally, have been annotated from the original typescript of an abstract, when one was available, or a preface describing the author's procedure, or a conclusion stating the author's findings. Despite the wide use of *Dissertation Abstracts*, a majority of the dissertations listed in this bibliography have not been abstracted in it. Our brief analyses are descriptive, not critical; indicative, not evaluative. They are usually written in a synoptic, note-taking style that is intended to show at a glance the substance of the study in its relevance to Spenser.

Our bibliographical style will be readily apparent, but perhaps it deserves a comment. It is simpler than most: italics and quotation

---

[4] PMLA, 76 (1961), 94.
[5] See Robert F. Stephens, A Check List of Masters' Theses on Edmund Spenser (93), through 1949.

marks which would otherwise appear as a result of editorial copy editing are eliminated, but they are retained in quotations, whether author's or editor's; Arabic numerals are used for volume numbers, although some Roman numerals will be found in the annotations, for example, those designating books of *The Faerie Queene;* the year of a periodical is enclosed in parentheses; the shortest possible indication is given of the pages devoted to an article or a passage on Spenser in a book; reviews are put in block form, and separated by semicolons, after the annotation. A word about reviews. Our aim was not to list every review. For example, we omit those in *The Year's Work in English Studies* as too obvious. We include reviews of the more important works, and we have not intentionally omitted any which have significance in regard to Spenser.

Although this is a continuation of Carpenter's guide and Atkinson's bibliography—in a sense, a "sequel" to the latter reference work—our system of organization is different from theirs. Miss Atkinson, who followed Carpenter's scheme, has only five main divisions but sixty-one subheadings in her bibliography. This makes for a great deal of repetition, because she lists each work or part of a work under all the appropriate subheadings. To take an extreme example, H. S. V. Jones's Spenser handbook is entered in twenty-five different places; it is not exceptional for the same work to appear two, three, or even four times. Each item in this bibliography is entered only once, under one of the fifteen main divisions; there are no subheadings. Studies which concern more than one of Spenser's works, except for a few that call for more specific classification, will be found under General Criticism; those which concern more than one book of *The Faerie Queene* will be found under The Faerie Queene: General Criticism. The arrangement in each division is alphabetical.

It is a pleasant duty to acknowledge the assistance we have received. For a number of years before our collaboration began, the elder member of the partnership occasionally induced graduate students in his courses in Elizabethan literature at Louisiana State University to undertake a segment of post-Atkinson Spenser bibliography as a special project. These students, whose spadework has been incorporated into the finished product, he now wishes to thank for their help: Ray W. Miller, Sue K. Wiseman, William C. Carloss, Jack G. Gilbert, James V. Holleran, Hugh K. Johnson, and Jack N. Renfrow. More recently, he has received useful aid from the graduate students in his Spenser course at the University of Oregon. His friend and former colleague, Professor Thomas A. Kirby, gave him tangible support at critical times. He received help from another former colleague, Professor Melvin R. Watson, who happened to be in London on sabbatical leave and looked at several items in the British Museum that were not available in the United States. A grant from the Louisiana State University Research Council enabled him to devote the summer of 1958 to this work, and one from the University of Oregon Graduate School was of much help in the final stages. The younger partner received substantial assistance, for which he is grateful, from the following students at Duquesne University: Eugene Blair, John Krnacik, Mildred B. Krnacik, Sister M. Patricia Meszesan, D. D. R., and Margaret Parker; Joan Connors, Elizabeth Carney, Robert Carmack, Lois Fitzgerald, Charles Roggemann, John Yarnovic, Sister M. Celestine Blazowski, C. S. S. F., Sister M. Sheila Curran, O. P., Sister M. Mary Golias, C. S. A., Sister M. Kenneth Hodge, R. S. M., Sister M. John Berchmans Misko, V. S. C., Sister M. Catherine Paff, O. S. F., Sister M. Philomena Rak, C. S. S. F. Both of us are especially indebted to Joe Max Braffett, whose unpublished Master's thesis, The Last Twenty Years of Spenserian Scholarship: A Bibliographical Study, completed at the University of Oklahoma in 1956, he turned over to us a check on our own work, and for that purpose it proved very valuable. Our book was read in manuscript by Professor Rudolf B. Gottfried, of Indiana University, and by Professor Roland M. Smith, of the University of Illinois. It has benefited much from the acumen and thoroughness of these two scholars, and we are especially grateful to Professor Smith for his extraordinary interest in this undertaking.

No work of this kind could be done without constant reliance on the good offices of capable librarians. We have been fortunate in having the unflagging aid of two of the best: Mrs. Corinne C. McNeir and Mrs. Anne Jane Dyson, formerly Head of the Humanities Division and still Interlibrary Loan Librarian, respectively, of the Louisiana State University Library. We deeply appreciate their patience and counsel. Other professional librarians of the Duquesne University Library who helped were Eleanor McCann, Emma Smith, Mary Beck, and Carol Stephen.

Nor could any such work as this be done without drawing on the resources of many libraries. For this reason we are in debt for various favors to the libraries of Princeton University, Duke University, the University of North Carolina, Tulane University, the University of Texas, Harvard University, the University of Chicago, Yale University, Rice University, Loyola University in New Orleans, the University of South Carolina, the University of Kentucky, Ohio State University, Oberlin College, Texas Agricultural and Mechanical College, New York University, the University of Illinois, the University of California at Berkeley, Oklahoma State University, the Carnegie Library of Pittsburgh, the University of Pittsburgh, the University of Oklahoma, St. Louis University, Johns Hopkins University, the University of California at Los Angeles, the University of Virginia, the University of Kansas, Fordham University, the University of Florida, the Catholic University of America, the Library of Congress, the University of Toronto, the University of London, the University of Nottingham, the University of Reading, the University College of Wales, the University of Mainz, the University of Erlangen, the University of Vienna, the University of Graz, and the University of Innsbruck. Specialized help was received from Philip L. Miller, Chief of the Music Division, New York Public Library; Professor Georg Buhtz, of the University of Hamburg; and Dr. Bernhard Fabian, of the University of Marburg. Great courtesy and cooperativeness have been shown by all those to whom we have appealed, from time to time, for aid, comfort, and advice. We thank them.

The errors in what we have done are of course ours.

Waldo F. McNeir   Foster Provost
University of Oregon   Duquesne University

LIST OF SERIALS AND ABBREVIATIONS

AAAPSS	Annals of the American Academy of Political and Social Sciences
AB	Art Bulletin
ABC	American Book Collector
ABR	American Benedictine Review
ACF	Annali di Ca' Foscari (Venezia)
Accent	
Acta et Commentationes Universitatis Tartuensis (Dorpatensis)	
Ad Interim	
ADUC	Abstracts of Dissertations . . . in the University of Cambridge
AES	Abstracts of English Studies
AHR	American Historical Review
AJP	American Journal of Philology
AL	American Literature
AN&Q	American Notes and Queries (New Haven, Conn.)
AnM	Annuale Mediaevale (Duquesne University)
Anglia	
Arcadia	
Archiv	Archiv für das Studium der neueren Sprachen und Literaturen
Arethusa	A Journal of the Wellsprings of Western Man
Ariel	Ariel: A Quarterly Review of the Arts and Sciences in Israel
ASch	American Scholar
Atkinson	Dorothy F. Atkinson, Edmund Spenser, A Bibliographical Supplement
AULLA	Australasian Universities Language and Literature Association
AUMLA	Journal of the Australasian Universities Language and Literature Association
BA	Books Abroad
Baconiana	
BAGB	Bulletin de l'Association Guillaume Budé
BB	Bulletin of Bibliography
BC	Book Collector
Beiblatt	Beiblatt to Anglia

BFLS   Bulletin de la Faculté des Lettres de Strasbourg
BHM   Bulletin of the History of Medicine
BHR   Bibliothèque d'Humanisme et Renaissance
BHS   Bulletin of Hispanic Studies
BJA   British Journal of Aesthetics (London)
BJRL   Bulletin of the John Rylands Library
BNYPL   Bulletin of the New York Public Library
BSE   Brno Studies in English
BSUF   Ball State University Forum
BuDE   Bulletin of the Department of English (Calcutta University)
BuR   Bucknell Review
BUSE   Boston University Studies in English
CamJ   Cambridge Journal
Canadian Forum
CanHR   Canadian Historical Review
CanL   Canadian Literature
CathHR   Catholic Historical Review
CathW   Catholic World
CBul   Classical Bulletin
CE   College English
CentR   Centennial Review
CH   Church History
CHEL   Cambridge History of English Literature
Cithara   Cithara (St. Bonaventure University)
CHR   Catholic Historical Review
CL   Comparative Literature
CLAJ   College Language Association Journal (Morgan State Coll.,
              Baltimore)
Classical Weekly
CLS   Comparative Literature Studies (U. of Ill.)
ConP   Concerning Poetry (West. Wash. State College)
ConR   Contemporary Review
ConTM   Concordia Theological Monthly
Conradiana: A Journal of Joseph Conrad
Conv   Convivium
Costerus: Essays in English and American Language and Literature
CP   Classical Philology
CQ   The Cambridge Quarterly
Crit   Critique: Studies in Modern Fiction
Criterion
Criticism (Wayne State)
CritQ   Critical Quarterly

CS	Cahiers du Sud
CSE	Cornell Studies in English
CUAT	Cornell University Abstracts of Theses
CUDD	Columbia University Masters' Essays and Doctoral Dissertations
CUSECL	Columbia University Studies in English and Comparative Literature
DA	Dissertation Abstracts
DAI	Dissertation Abstracts International
DDAAU	Doctoral Dissertations Accepted by American Universities
Descant	
Deutsche Zukunft	
DLit	Deutsche Literaturzeitung
DM	The Dublin Magazine (formerly The Dubliner)
DQ	Denver Quarterly
DR	Dalhousie Review
DSPS	Duquesne Studies, Philological Series
DubR	Dublin Review
DUJ	Durham University Journal
DVLG	Deutsche Vierteljahrsschrift für Literaturwissenschaft und Geistesgeschichte
EA	Études anglaises
E&S	Essays and Studies by Members of the English Association
EASG	English and American Studies in German
EETS, OS	Early English Text Society, Original Series
EHR	English Historical Review
EIC	Essays in Criticism (Oxford)
EIE	English Institute Essays
EigoS	Eigo Seinen [The Rising Generation] (Tokyo)
Éigse: A Journal of Irish Studies	
EIUES	English Institute of the University of Uppsala: Essays and Studies on English Language and Literature
ELH	Journal of English Literary History
ELN	English Language Notes (U. of Colo.)
ELR	English Literary Renaissance
EM	English Miscellany
Encore	
English (London)	
Era	
ErasmusR	Erasmus Review: A Journal of the Humanities
ES	English Studies
ESA	English Studies in Africa (Johannesburg)

ESQ   Emerson Society Quarterly
ESRS   Emporia State Research Studies
EStud   Englische Studien
EUPLL   Edinburgh University Publications, Language & Literature
Expl   Explicator
ForumH   Forum (Houston)
FUD   Fordham University Dissertations
GaR   Georgia Review
The Gate
Genre (U. of Ill. at Chicago Circle)
GRM   Germanisch-romanische Monatsschrift, Neue Folge
GSLI   Giornale storico della letteratura italiana
HAB   Humanities Association Bulletin (Canada)
HHM   Harvard Historical Monographs
History
HLB   Harvard Library Bulletin
HLQ   Huntington Library Quarterly
HPCS   High Point College Studies
HR   Hispanic Review
HRDP   Harvard University and Radcliffe College Doctors of Philoso-
             phy with the Titles of Their Theses
HSCL   Harvard Studies in Comparative Literature
HSE   Harvard Studies in English
HudR   Hudson Review
Huntington Library Bulletin
HUST   Harvard University Summaries of Theses
IADD   Index to American Doctoral Dissertations
IF   Indogermanische Forschungen
IHS   Irish Historical Studies
IJES   Indian Journal of English Studies (Calcutta)
IllQ   Illinois Quarterly
Illustrated London News
Indiana University Studies
Ingiliz Filolojisi Dergisi
IQ   Italian Quarterly
Isis
ISLL   Illinois Studies in Language and Literature
Italica
ITGBI   Index to Theses Accepted for Higher Degrees in the Universi-
             ties of Great Britain and Ireland
IUPHS   Indiana University Publications, Humanistic Series
JAAC   Journal of Aesthetics and Art Criticism

JAE	Journal of Aesthetic Education
JAF	Journal of American Folklore
JC	Journal of Communication
JdH	Jahresverzeichnis der deutschen Hochschulschriften
JEGP	Journal of English and Germanic Philology
JHAM	Johns Hopkins Alumni Magazine
JHI	Journal of the History of Ideas
JMH	Journal of Modern History
JMRS	Journal of Medieval and Renaissance Studies
JNT	Journal of Narrative Technique
JR	Journal of Religion
JWCI	Journal of the Warburg and Courtauld Institute
KR	Kenyon Review
KSJ	Keats-Shelley Journal
LAC	Lehrgangsvorträge der Akademie Comburg
L&I	Literature and Ideology (Montreal)
LCUT	Library Chronicle of the University of Texas
Library	The Library
Literaturblatt	
LJ	Library Journal
Llên Cymru	
LM	Language Monographs
London Mercury	
LonM	London Magazine
LQ	Library Quarterly
LR	Les Lettres Romanes
LRin	La Rinascita
LSUSHS	Louisiana State University Studies, Humanities Series
LT	Levende Talen
MA	Microfilm Abstracts
MAE	Medium AEvum
Manchester Guardian Weekly	
M&H	Medievalia et Humanistica (Case Western Reserve Univ.)
M&L	Music and Letters (London)
Manuscripta	
McNR	McNeese Review (McNeese State University, La.)
MdF	Mercure de France
Merc	London Mercury
MHRev	Malahat Review
MiltonN	Milton Newsletter
MiltonQ	Milton Quarterly (Formerly MiltonN)
MLJ	Modern Language Journal

MLN   Modern Language Notes
MLQ   Modern Language Quarterly
MLR   Modern Language Review
MLS   Modern Language Studies
Month
Mosaic   A Journal for the Comparative Study of Literature and Ideas
MP   Modern Philology
MQR   Michigan Quarterly Review
MSE   Massachusetts Studies in English
Mythlore (Maywood, Calif.)
N&Q   Notes and Queries
Nation
NatR   National Review
NCF   Nineteenth-Century Fiction
Neophil   Neophilologus (Groningen)
NEQ   New England Quarterly
New Statesman and Nation
NHJ   Nathaniel Hawthorne Journal
NLH   New Literary History (U. of Va.)
NM   Neuphilologische Mitteilungen
NMQ   New Mexico Quarterly
NR   New Republic
NS   Die Neueren Sprachen
NUSDD   Northwestern University Summaries of Doctoral Disserta-
               tions
NYH-TBR   New York Herald-Tribune Book Review
NYRB   New York Review of Books
NYT (D)   New York Times (Daily)
NYTBR   New York Times Book Review
NYUB   New York University Bibliography
OeB   Oesterreichische Bibliographie
OJES   Osmania Journal of English Studies
OSUADD   Ohio State University Abstracts of Doctors' Dissertations
Paunch (Buffalo, N.Y.)
PBA   Proceedings of the British Academy
PBSA   Papers of the Bibliographical Society of America
PCP   Pacific Coast Philology
PCSM   Publications of the Colonial Society of Massachusetts
Peabody Abstracts of Dissertations
Person   The Personalist
PhR   Philosophical Review
PLL   Papers on Language & Literature

PMLA   Publications of the Modern Language Association of America
Poetry
PoR   Poetry Review
PoetryR   Poetry Review (London)
PP   Philologica Pragensia
PQ   Philological Quarterly (Iowa City)
Proverbium (Helsinki)
PSCS   Pennsylvania State College Studies
PSE   Princeton Studies in English
PSQ   Political Science Quarterly
PUASAL   Proceedings of the Utah Academy of Sciences, Arts, and
              Letters
PULC   Princeton University Library Chronicle
QJS   Quarterly Journal of Speech
QQ   Queen's Quarterly
QR   Quarterly Review
RBPH   Revue Belge de Philologie et d'histoire
RDUM   Register of Ph.D. Degrees Conferred by the University of
              Minnesota
REL   A Review of English Literature (Leeds)
RenD   Renaissance Drama (Northwestern U.)
RenP   Renaissance Papers
RenQ   Renaissance Quarterly
RES   Review of English Studies
RevAng-am   Revue Anglo-américaine
RG   Revue Germanique
RHD   Revue d'histoire diplomatique
RIB   Revista Interamericana de Bibliografía
RIP   Rice Institute Pamphlet
Rising Generation
RLC   Revue de Littérature Comparée
RMS   Renaissance & Modern Studies (University of Nottingham)
RN   Renaissance News
Rom   Romania
RomN   Romance Notes (U. of N.C.)
RORD   Research Opportunities in Renaissance Drama
RPh   Romance Philology
RQ   Riverside Quarterly (U. of Saskatchewan)
RR   Romanic Review
RS   Research Studies (Wash. State U.)
RSSCW   Research Studies of the State College of Washington
RTP   Revue de théologie et de philosophie (Genève)

SAB	Shakespeare Association Bulletin
SAQ	South Atlantic Quarterly
SatRL	Saturday Review of Literature
SB	Studies in Bibliography: Papers of the Bibliographical Society of the University of Virginia
SCB	South Central Bulletin
SCN	Seventeenth-Century News
Scrutiny	
SEL	Studies in English Literature, 1500-1900
SELit	Studies in English Literature (Eng. Literary Soc. of Japan, Univ. of Tokyo)
SF&R	Scholars' Facsimiles and Reprints
SFQ	Southern Folklore Quarterly
ShakS	Shakespeare Studies (U. of Cincinnati)
SHR	Southern Humanities Review
ShS	Shakespeare Survey
ShStud	Shakespeare Studies (U. of Tokyo, Japan)
SJH	Shakespeare-Jahrbuch (Heidelberg)
SJW	Shakespeare-Jahrbuch (Weimar)
SLUB	St. Louis University Bulletin
SN	Studia Neophilologica
Societas Scientiarum Fennica, Commentationes Humanorum Litterarum	
SHR	Southern Humanities Review
SoQ	The Southern Quarterly (U. of So. Miss.)
SoRA	Southern Review: An Australian Journal of Literature Studies (U. of Adelaide)
SoR	Southern Review (Louisiana State U.)
SP	Studies in Philology
Spectator	
Speculum	
SPET	Society for Pure English Tracts
SpN	Spenser Newsletter
SQ	Shakespeare Quarterly
SR	Sewanee Review
SRen	Studies in the Renaissance
SSL	Studies in Scottish Literature (U. of S. C.)
SSLL	Stanford Studies in Language and Literature
STBILP	Sir Thomas Browne Institute, Leiden Publications
Stratford-upon-Avon Studies	
SWL	Studies in Western Literature
SWR	Southwest Review
T&T	Time and Tide

Thoth (Dept. of English, Syracuse U.)
Thought
TLS   London Times Literary Supplement
TQ   Texas Quarterly (U. of Texas)
Travaux du Cercle linguistique de Copenhague
TSE   Tulane Studies in English
TSL   Tennessee Studies in Literature
TSLL   Texas Studies in Literature and Language
TWA   Transactions of the Wisconsin Academy of Sciences, Arts,
                and Letters
TxSE   Texas Studies in English
UCPE   University of California Publications in English
UCSD   University of California Programs of the Final Examinations
                and Summaries of Dissertations . . . Doctorate Degrees
UDQ   University of Denver Quarterly
UIDDAR   University of Iowa Doctoral Dissertations, Abstracts and
                References
UKCR   University of Kansas City Review
ULSD   University of London Subjects of Dissertations
UMSE   University of Mississippi Studies in English
UMST   University of Minnesota Summaries of Ph.D. Theses
UNCSCL   University of North Carolina Studies in Comparative Litera-
                ture
University of Toronto Final Oral Examinations for the Degree of Doctor of
Philosophy
UOB   University of Oklahoma Bulletin
UR   University Review (Kansas City)
UTDEMS   University of Tulsa Dept. of Eng. Monograph Ser.
UTQ   University of Toronto Quarterly
UVS   University of Virginia Studies
UWAT   University of Washington Abstracts of Theses
UWSDD   University of Wisconsin Summaries of Doctoral Dissertations
VdD   Verzeichnis der . . . Dissertationen. Universities of Vienna
                and Innsbruck
VP   Victorian Poetry (W. Va. U.)
VQR   Virginia Quarterly Review
VUAT   Vanderbilt University Abstracts of Theses
VUSH   Vanderbilt University Studies in the Humanities
WascanaR   Wascana Review (Regina, Sask.)
WBEP   Wiener Beiträge zur Englischen Philologie
WCR   West Coast Review
Western World Review

WHR	Western Humanities Review
WSUSB	Wichita State University Studies Bulletin
WVUPP	West Virginia University Philological Papers
XUS	Xavier University Studies
Yenitürk	
YES	Yearbook of English Studies
YIS	Yearbook of Italian Studies
YR	Yale Review
YSE	Yale Studies in English
ZAA	Zeitschrift für Anglistik und Amerikanistik (East Berlin)

SPENSER ABBREVIATIONS

Amor	Amoretti
Astro	Astrophel
CCCHA	Colin Clouts Come Home Againe
Daph	Daphaida
Epith	Epithalamion
4 Hymns	Fowre Hymnes
FQ	The Faerie Queene
HHOB	An Hymne in Honour of Beautie
HHOL	An Hymne in Honour of Love
HOHB	An Hymne of Heavenly Beautie
HOHL	An Hymne of Heavenly Love
Lay	The Lay of Clorinda
Ltr	A Letter of the Authors . . . To . . . Sir Walter Raleigh
MHT	Prosopopoia, or Mother Hubberds Tale
Muiop	Muiopotmos, or The Fate of the Butterfly
Proth	Prothalamion
RR	Ruines of Rome
RT	The Ruines of Time
SC	The Shepheardes Calender
Theatre	A Theatre for Worldlings
TM	The Teares of the Muses
VB	The Visions of Bellay
VG	Virgils Gnat
View	A View of the Present State of Ireland
VP	The Visions of Petrarch
VWV	Visions of the Worlds Vanitie

An Annotated Bibliography

BIBLIOGRAPHY OF SOURCES

Abstracts of Dissertations Approved for the Ph. D., M. Sc., and M. Litt. Degrees in the University of Cambridge. 1936-1959. Cambridge: University Press, 1937-1959. **1**

No longer published.

Abstracts of English Studies. 1 (1958)-16 (1972-1973). Washington, D.C.: National Council of Teachers of English, 1958-1973. **2**

Altick, Richard D., and Andrew Wright, eds. Selective Bibliography for the Study of English and American Literature. 4th ed. New York: Macmillan, 1971. **3**

Arms, George, and Joseph M. Kuntz. Poetry Explication: A Checklist of Interpretation since 1925 of British and American Poems, Past and Present. New York: Swallow Press and William Morrow, 1950. 188 pp. Sp, pp. 140-1. Kuntz, Joseph M. Rev. ed., 1962. Denver: Alan Swallow, 1962. 332 pp. Sp, pp. 240-1. **4**

Association of Research Libraries. A Catalogue of Books Represented by Library of Congress Printed Cards. Issued to July 31, 1942. Ann Arbor, Mich.: Edwards Bros., 1942-1946. 167 vols. Supplement. Cards Issued Aug. 1, 1942-Dec. 31, 1947. Ann Arbor, Mich.: J.W. Edwards, 1948. 42 vols. **5**

Atkinson (Evans), Dorothy F. Edmund Spenser: A Bibliographical Supplement. Baltimore: Johns Hopkins Press, 1937; repr. New York: Haskell House, 1967. 242 pp. **6**

Supplements and continues Carpenter's Reference Guide to Edmund Spenser, 1923. Follows the organization of Carpenter's work, having five main sections: I. The Life (pp. 1-48); II. The Works (pp. 49-162); III. Criticism, Influence, Allusions (pp. 163-91); IV. Various Topics (pp. 193-213); V. Addenda (pp. 215-20). Full Index, pp. 221-42.

Baldensperger, Fernand, and Werner P. Friederich. Bibliography of Comparative Literature. Chapel Hill, N. C.: University of North Carolina Studies in Comparative Literature, 1950. UNCSCL, 1. 701 pp. **7**

Bateson, F.W. A Guide to English Literature. 2nd ed. Chicago: Aldine, 1968. 258 pp. **8**

First pub. 1965. Handbook of "principal editions and commentaries" through 1966 dealing with major English writers. Sp (pp. 71-2).

Bell, Inglis F., and Jennifer Gallup. A Reference Guide to English, American, and Canadian Literature: An Annotated Checklist of Bibliographical and Other Reference Materials. Vancouver: University of British Columbia Press, 1971. 139 pp. **9**

Sp, pp. 110-1. Also, see Index.

"Biblio." Catalogue des Ouvrages Parus en Langue Français dans le Monde Entier. 1937-1968. Paris: Hachette, 1938-1969. Bibliographie . . . 1969-1970. Paris: Hachette, 1970-1971. **10**

Bibliographic Index. A Cumulative Bibliography of Bibliographies. 1937-1972. New York: H.W. Wilson, 1945-1973.   11

Bibliographie der an Deutschen und Österreichischen Universitäten 1939-1951 Angenommenen Anglistischen Dissertationen. Anglia, 70 (1952), 454-60; 71 (1952), 127-8; 71 (1953), 249-56, 376-83, 498-515.   12

Discontinued.

Bibliographie der Deutschen Zeitschriften-Literatur. 78 (1936)-128 (1964). Leipzig and Osnabrück: Dietrich, 1936-1964.   13

Combined with 14. Vols. 95 (1945) and 96 (1946) not published.

Bibliographie der Fremdsprachigen Zeitschriften-Literatur, 1937-1960. Leipzig and Osnabrück: Dietrich, 1937-1961. N.S. 51 (1964)-.   14

Bibliographie Internationale de l'Humanisme et de la Renaissance. Geneva: Droz, 1966-1970.   15

1-5 (1965-1969).

Bibliotheque d'Humanisme et Renaissance. Paris: Droz, 1941-1965.   16

Successor to 53. Notes bibliographiques, 2 (1942), 196-219; 10 (1948), 209-27; Isadore Silver, Ronsard Studies (1936-1950), 12 (1950), 332-64, and Ronsard in European Literature: A Synoptic View of Scholarly Publications, 16 (1954), 241-54; bibliography of humanism and the Renaissance, 1956-1964, 20-27 (1958-1965).

Biography Index. A Cumulative Index to Biographical Material in Books and Magazines. 1946-1972. New York: H. W. Wilson, 1949-1973.   17

Book Review Digest, 1961-1973. New York: H.W. Wilson, 1962-1973.   18

Book Review Index. 1965-1968, 1969-1971 still to be published, 1972-1973. Detroit: Gale Research Company, 1966-1970, 1972-1973.   19

Bradner, Leicester. The Renaissance: 1939-1945, M&H, 5 (1948), 62-72.   20

A survey of Renaissance studies published in the United States during World War II. Sp, pp. 67-8.

British Museum General Catalogue of Printed Books: Ten-Year Supplement, 1956-1965. London: Trustees of the British Museum, 1968. 50 vols. Five-Year Supplement, 1966-1970. 1971. 26 vols.   21

British National Bibliography. 1950-1972. London: Council of the British National Bibliography, 1951-1973.   22

Bulletin Bibliographique de la Société Internationale Arthurienne. Bulletin of the International Arthurian Society. Paris, 1949-1972.   23

Vols. 1-4 (1949-1952) repr. Amsterdam: Swets & Zeitlinger, 1972. Vols. 19 (1967)—, titles reversed in order on title-page.

The Cambridge Bibliography of English Literature, ed. F. W. Bateson. 4 vols. New York: Macmillan, 1941.   24

Edmund Spenser, I, 417-9. Lists nothing later than 1936, Atkinson's terminal year.

The Cambridge Bibliography of English Literature, Vol. V, Supplement: A.D. 600-1900, ed. George Watson. Cambridge: University Press, 1957.   25

"As nearly as possible sections have been brought down to the beginning of the year 1955" (p. xi). Edmund Spenser, pp. 205-10.

Carpenter, Frederic Ives. A Reference Guide to Edmund Spenser. New York: Peter Smith, 1950; Kraus, 1969. 333 pp.   26

Repr. of 1923 ed. A pioneer work which is still valuable.

Columbia University Library. Masters' Essays and Doctoral Dissertations. 1952-1971. Morningside Heights, N. Y.: Columbia University Libraries, 1952-1971. 27

Cooperating with DA and DAI since 1952.

Comprehensive Dissertation Index 1861-1972. Vol. 30, Language and Literature, M-Z. Ann Arbor, Mich.: Xerox University Microfilms, 1973. 28

Spenser, pp. 556-7.

Cornell University Abstracts of Theses. 1937-1947. Ithaca, N. Y.: Cornell University Press, 1938-1949. 29

Cooperating with DA and DAI since 1952.

Craig, Hardin. Recent Scholarship of the English Renaissance: A Brief Survey, SP, 42 (1945), 498-529. 30

Deals with the period since the end of the first World War. Notes the decline since 1918 of English scholarship on the major figures, such as Shakespeare, Sp, Marlowe, Jonson, Donne, and Milton, much of it now being devoted to details or speculations, partly because of "the lack of fresh factual material bearing on the great Elizabethan writers." Special section on Sp, 3c., pp. 509-10. Sp scholarship has reached a stage of advanced development, with a machinery of research and study that puts it in a fortunate position. Available are bibliographies, a concordance, a subject-index, two elaborate editions (Renwick's and the Variorum) nearing completion, and other formal works. The flood of research, criticism, and controversy continues to the present day.

Cumulative Book Index. A World List of Books in the English Language. 1933-1972. New York: H.W. Wilson, 1938-1973. 31

Delattre, Floris. Émile Legouis et la Renaissance anglaise, EA, 3 (1938), 240-57. 32

Reviews Legouis' Spenserian scholarship. See also Liste des Publications d'Émile Legouis, ibid., pp. 271-88.

Deutsches Bücherverzeichnis. 1936-1959. Leipzig: Buch- und Bibliothekswesen Leipzig, 1942-1960. 33

Dissertation Abstracts: Abstracts of Dissertations and Monographs in Microform. (DA). Ann Arbor, Mich.: University Microfilms, 1961-June 1969. Dissertation Abstracts International: Abstracts of Dissertations Available on Microfilm or as Xerographic Reproductions. (DAI). Ann Arbor, Mich.: Xerox University Microfilms, July 1969-1972. 34

Dissertation Abstracts International. Cumulated Keyword and Author Index. Indexes to vols. 21-32. Ann Arbor, Mich.: Xerox University Microfilms, 1961-1972. 35

Doctoral Dissertations Accepted by American Universities. New York: H. W. Wilson, 1935-1955. 36

First volume covers academic year 1933-34. Continued as IADD.

Edwards, Sara Scott, comp. Ed. Pauline Cook. Theses and Dissertations Presented in the Graduate College of the State University of Iowa, 1900-1950. Iowa City, Iowa: State University of Iowa, 1952. 37

English and American Studies in German. Summaries of Theses and Monographs. A Supplement to Anglia. Ed. Werner Habicht. I (1969)-V (1973). Tübingen: Max Niemeyer, 1969-1973. 38

English Association. The Year's Work in English Studies, 1937-1971. Oxford: University Press, 1939-1961; London: John Murray, 1962-1973.   39

Vols. 18-52.

Eppelsheimer, Hanns W., and Clemens Köttelwesch, eds. Bibliographie der deutschen Literaturwissenschaft. 12 vols. Frankfurt: Vittorio Klostermann, 1957-1973.   40

Vol. 1 (1945-1953, 16 Jahrhundert, pp. 122-9)-12 (1972, 16 Jahrhundert, pp. 183-8).

Essay and General Literature Index. 2 (1934-1940)-7 (1965-1969). New York: H.W. Wilson, 1941-1973.   41

The vols. covering the period of this bibliography are an index to more than 150,000 essays and articles in collections of essays and miscellaneous works.

Fordham University Dissertations. 1937-1972. New York: Fordham University Press, 1938-1973.   42

Cooperating with DA and DAI since 1961.

Golden, Herbert H., and Seymour O. Simches. Modern French Literature and Language: A Bibliography of Homage Studies. Cambridge, Mass.: Harvard University Press, 1953. 158 pp.   43

Lists and analyzes contents of 309 homage volumes. Sixteenth century, pp. 27-47.

Granger, Edith. Index to Poetry. 5th ed. Ed. William F. Bernhardt. New York: Columbia University Press, 1962. 2123 pp.   44

Gray, Richard A., and Dorothy Willmow. Serial Bibliographies in the Humanities and Social Sciences. Ann Arbor, Mich.: Pierian Press, 1969. 345 pp.   45

Gray, Richard A., comp. A Guide to Book Review Citations: A Bibliography of Sources. Columbus: Ohio State University Press, 1969. 221 pp.   46

Gregory, Winifred, ed. Union List of Serials in Libraries of the United States and Canada. 2nd ed. New York: H. W. Wilson, 1943. Supplement 1941-1943; Second Supplement 1944-1949.   47

Griffith, Dudley D., et al. Frederick Morgan Padelford, MLQ, 3 (1942), 517-24.   48

Bibliography of Padelford's writings, pp. 519-24. Between 1913 and his death in 1942, he published some 30 studies dealing specifically with Sp.

Guffey, George R. Elizabethan Bibliographies Supplements VII: Samuel Daniel 1942-1965; Michael Drayton 1941-1965; Sir Philip Sidney 1941-1965. London: Nether Press, 1967. 52 pp.   49

Harvard University. Summaries of Theses. 1937-1945. Cambridge, Mass.: The University, 1938-1947.   50

Discontinued. English Department does not cooperate with DA and DAI.

Harvard University and Radcliffe College. Doctors of Philosophy with the Titles of Their Theses. 1945-46 to 1956-57.   51

Discontinued. English Department of neither institution cooperates with DA and DAI.

Huckabay, Calvin. John Milton: An Annotated Bibliography 1929-1968. Pittsburgh: Duquesne University Press, 1969. 392 pp.   52

Humanisme et Renaissance. Paris: Droz, 1936-1940.   53

Bibliographies in 3 (1936), 115-40, 340-63; 4 (1937), 98-108, 429-50; 5 (1938), 341-84; 6 (1939), 114-33, 245-6.
Succeeded by 16.

Index to American Doctoral Dissertations. Ann Arbor, Mich.: University Microfilms, 1957-1964. 54

> A continuation of DDAAU. Appeared annually as a separate number of DA. Included Canadian dissertations.

Index to Book Reviews in the Humanities. 1961-1972. Williamston, Mich.: Phillip Thomson, 1961-1973. 55

> Vols. 6-13.

Index to Theses Accepted for Higher Degrees in the Universities of Great Britain and Ireland. London: Aslib, 1950-1971. 56

International Index to Periodicals. A Quarterly Guide to Periodical Literature in the Social Sciences and Humanities. Vol. 7, July 1934-June 1937 to vol. 60, Dec. 1972. New York: H. W. Wilson, 1937-1973. 57

Internationale Bibliographie der Zeitschriften-Literatur. 1 (1965)-7 (1972). 58

Jackson, William A., and Emma V. Unger. The Carl H. Pforzheimer Library, English Literature, 1475-1700. New York: Privately Printed, 1940. 3 vols. 59

> Sp, III, 994-1016; Spenseriana, III, 1017-22.

Jahresverzeichnis der Deutschen Hochschulschriften. Leipzig: Deutsche Bücherei, 1937-1969. 60

> First vol. with this title covers 1936.

Johnson, Francis R. A Critical Bibliography of the Works of Edmund Spenser Printed before 1700. London: Dawsons, 1966; Folcroft, Pa.: Folcroft Press, 1969. 60 pp. 61

> Reprints of 1933 ed. In Atkinson, p. 49.

Jones, Buford. A Checklist of Hawthorne Criticism 1951-1966, With a Detailed Index. ESQ, 3 (1968), 5-91. 62

Kujoth, Jean S. Subject Guide to the Periodical Indexes and Review Indexes. Metuchen, N.J.: Scarecrow, 1969. 129 pp. 63

Library of Congress. A List of American Doctoral Dissertations Printed in 1937, 1938. Washington: U.S. Government Printing Office, 1938, 1939. 64

> Discontinued.

Library of Congress Author Catalog. A Cumulative List of Works Represented by Library of Congress Printed Cards 1948-1952. Ann Arbor, Mich.: J.W. Edwards, 1953. 24 vols. New York: Rowman and Littlefield, 1964. 65

> Reprint of 1953 ed.

Library of Congress Catalog. Books: Subjects. A Cumulative List of Works Represented by Library of Congress Printed Cards, 1961-1972. Washington, D.C.: Library of Congress, 1962-1972. 66

Libri d'Italia. 1947-1958. Florence: Sansoni, 1948-1959. 67

Lievsay, John L. The Sixteenth Century: Skelton through Hooker. Goldentree Bibliographies. New York: Appleton-Century-Crofts, 1968. 132 pp. 68

> Sp, pp. 89-98. See Index.

McNamee, Lawrence F. Dissertations in English and American Literature. Theses Accepted by American, British, and German Universities, 1865-1964. 1124 pp. Supplement 1, 1964-1968. 450 pp. New York: R.R. Bowker, 1968, 1969. 69

> Lists dissertations dealing with Sp's minor works, SC, prose, FQ, influences on Sp, Sp's influence and Sp scholarship, and general studies.

McNeir, Waldo F., and Foster Provost. Annotated Bibliography of Edmund Spenser, 1937-1960. Pittsburgh: Duquesne University Press, 1962; repr. New York: AMS Press, 1967. 255 pp.
                                                    70

First edition of this bibliography. Rev: Hermann Heuer, SJH, 99 (1963), 232; Michel Poirier, EA, 16 (1963), 276; Isabel E. Rathborne, RN, 16 (1963), 337; Kathrine Koller, SCN, 21 (1963), 3; Jack W. Jessee, PBSA, 57 (1963), 243; Lillian Herlands Hornstein, MLR, 59 (1964), 453; Millar MacLure, UTQ, 33 (1964), 311; Kathleen Williams, RES, 15 (1964), 418; George Burke Johnston, SQ, 16 (1965), 270.

Microfilm Abstracts. Ann Arbor, Mich.: University Microfilms, 1938-1951.   71

Succeeded by DA in 1952.

Modern Humanities Research Association. Annual Bibliography of English Language and Literature, 1936-1971. Cambridge: University Press, 1938-1961; Cambridge: Modern Humanities Research Association, 1964-1973.   72

Vols. 17-46.

Modern Humanities Research Association. The Year's Work in Modern Language Studies, 1937-1972. Cambridge: Cambridge University Press, 1938-1963. London: MHRA, 1964-1973.   73

Vols. 8-34.

Modern Language Association of America. MLA Abstracts of Articles in Scholarly Journals, Vol. I (1970-1972). New York: Modern Language Association of America, 1972-1974.   74

Modern Language Quarterly. Bibliography of Critical Arthurian Literature, 1936-1962. Ed John J. Parry, et al.   75

Annually in June issue, ending 1963.

National Union Catalog. A Cumulative Author List Representing Library of Congress Printed Cards and Titles Reported by Other American Libraries. 1953-1957; Ann Arbor, Mich.: J. W. Edwards, 1958. 28 vols. 1958; Washington: Library of Congress, 1959. 5 vols. 1959; Washington: Library of Congress, 1960. 5 vols. 1958-1962; New York: Rowman and Littlefield, 1963. 54 vols. 1963-1967; Ann Arbor, Mich.: J. W. Edwards, 1969. 72 vols. 1968-1971; Washington: Library of Congress, 1969-1972. 24 vols. 1968-1972; Ann Arbor, Mich.: J. W. Edwards, 1973. 84 vols. 76

New Serial Titles. A Union List of Serials Commencing Publication After December 31, 1949. 1950-1970; New York: R. R. Bowker, 1973. 1971-1972; Washington: Library of Congress, 1973.   77

New York University. University Bibliography. 1937-1955. Washington Square, New York: New York University, 1938-1955.   78

Cooperating with DA and DAI since 1952.

Nicoll, Allardyce (1948-1965), and Kenneth Muir (1966-), eds. Shakespeare Survey: An Annual Survey of Shakespearian Study and Production. Vols. 1 (1948)-26 (1973). Cambridge: University Press, 1948-1973.   79

Northwestern University Summaries of Doctoral Dissertations, 4 (1936)-20 (1952). Chicago and Evanston, Ill.: Northwestern University, 1936-1953.
                                                    80

Cooperating with DA and DAI since 1952.

Oesterreichische Bibliographie: Verzeichnis der Oesterreichischen Neuerscheinungen. 1945-1971. Vienna: Oesterreichische Buchhändler, 1946-1972.   81

Ohio State University Abstracts of Doctoral Dissertations, No. 21 (1936)-No.

67 (1950-1951). Columbus, Ohio: Ohio State University, 1937-1957.   82

> Cooperating with DA and DAI since 1954.

Pollard, A. W., G. R. Redgrave, and others. A Short-Title Catalogue of Books Printed in England, Scotland, & Ireland and of English Books Printed Abroad 1475-1640. London: Bibliographical Society, 1946. 609 pp.   83

> Reprint of the first edition of 1926. "Spenser, Edmund," Nos. 23076-23095, pp. 537-8.

Publications of the Modern Language Association of America.   84

> American bibliography for 1936-1955, annually in supplementary issue, 1936-1948; May number, 1949; April number, 1950-1956. Annual bibliography for 1956-1960, international coverage, in April number, 1957-1958; May number, 1959-1966; June number, 1967-1969; MLA International Bibliography, Vol. I, 1970-1972.

Reader's Guide to Periodical Literature. An Author and Subject Index. 1961-1972. New York: H.W. Wilson, 1961-1973.   85

> Vols. 22-32.

Register of Ph. D. Degrees Conferred by the University of Minnesota 1938 Through June 1956. Minneapolis, Minn: University of Minnesota, 1957.   86

> See 107. Cooperating with DA and DAI since 1952.

St. Louis University Bulletin. Publications and Research in Progress by Faculty Members and Students, 50, No. 13 (1953-1954)-52, No. 13 (1955-1956). St. Louis: St. Louis University, 1954-1956.   87

> Cooperating with DA and DAI since 1952.

Schutz, Alexander H., ed. The Sixteenth Century, Vol. 2 of A Critical Bibliography of French Literature. D. C. Cabeen, General Editor. Syracuse, N. Y.: Syracuse University Press, 1956. 365 pp.   88

> See Index for Sp references.

Shakespeare Association Bulletin. Bibliography of Shakespeare and His Contemporaries, 12 (1937)-23 (1948). Ed. Samuel A. Tannenbaum, et al.   89

> Annually in January issue. Succeeded by SQ.

Shakespeare Quarterly. 1 (1950)-24 (1973).   90

> Successor to SAB. Annual annotated Shakespeare bibliography in Spring issue. Shakespeare: An Annotated World Bibliography, beginning in 17 (1966).

Social Sciences and Humanities Index. 1965-1973. New York: H.W. Wilson, 1965-1973.   91

> Vols. 18-26.

Spenser Newsletter, Vol. 1, No. 1 (Winter 1970)-Vol. 5, No. 1 (Winter 1974).   92

Stephens, Robert F. A Check List of Masters' Theses on Edmund Spenser. Charlottesville, Va.: Bibliographical Society of the University of Virginia, 1950. 16pp.   93

> Mimeographed pamphlet. 170 titles, 1902-1949. Not listed herein.

Studies in Bibliography. A Selective Check List of Bibliographical Scholarship, 1961-1971. Charlottesville: University of Virginia, 1963-1973.   94

> Vols. 16-26.

Studies in English Literature 1500-1900. 1 (1961)-12 (1972). Recent Studies in the English Renaissance. Houston: Rice University, 1961-1972.   95

> Annually in Winter issue.

Studies in Philology. 33 (1936)-66 (1969). Recent Literature of the English Renaissance, 33 (1936)-35 (1938); Recent Literature of the Renaissance, international coverage, 36 (1939)-66 (1969).   96

Bibliography discontinued.

Subject Guide to Books in Print: An Index to the Publishers' Trade List Annual. 2 vols. New York: R.R. Bowker, 1962, 1965, 1968, 1971.   97

Sullivan, Majie Padberg. Standard Editions of the Complete Works of the Major Figures of English Literature. Los Angeles: Loyola University of Los Angeles, 1950. 60pp. Mimeograph.   98

Lists 10-volume Variorum, 1-volume Oxford, and 1-volume Cambridge editions (p.50).

Thomson, S. Harrison. Progress of Medieval and Renaissance Studies in the United States and Canada. No. 15 (1940)-No. 25 (1960). Boulder, Colo.: University of Colorado Press, 1940-1960.   99

Successor to Progress of Medieval Studies in the United States and Canada, 1923-1939.

Tonkin, Humphrey. Sir Walter Raleigh, 1900-1968. Elizabethan Bibliographies Supplements, XVII. London: Nether Press, 1971. 79 pp.   100

Tosello, Matthew. The Relationship Between Dante Alighieri (1265-1321) and Edmund Spenser (1552-1599). DAI, 31 (1970), 2357A. Duquesne University, 1970. 358 pp.   101

An annotated bibliography of 246 items published between 1750 and 1968, inclusive, relating Dante and Sp. Ten appendices providing bibliographical and historical information related to Sp's possible use of Dante; indexes of authors and of the two poets' works in parallel.

Tuve, Rosemond. A Critical Survey of Scholarship in the Field of English Literature of the Renaissance, SP, 40 (1943), 204-55.   102

One of a series of articles published in various journals 1940-1944. Also appears in Surveys of Recent Scholarship in the Period of the Renaissance. Compiled for the Committee on Renaissance Studies of the American Council of Learned Societies. First Series, 1945. Sp scholarship reviewed passim in both text and footnotes.

Universities of Vienna and Innsbruck. Verzeichnis der 1934 bis 1937 an der philosophischen Fakultät der Universität in Wien und der 1872 bis 1937 an der philosophischen Fakultät in Innsbruck eingereichten und approbierten Dissertationen. Vol. 4. Vienna: Philosophische Fakultäten der Universitäten in Wien und Innsbruck, 1937.   103

University of California Programs of the Final Examinations and Summaries of Dissertations . . . Doctorate Degrees, 1940-1959. Berkeley: University of California, 1941-1959.   104

Various branches cooperating with DA and DAI: Berkeley, 1962; Davis, 1964; Irvine, 1967; Los Angeles, 1962; Riverside, 1964; San Diego, 1964; San Francisco, 1964; Santa Barbara, 1965; Santa Cruz, 1970.

University of Iowa Doctoral Dissertations, Abstracts and References, 1 (1900-1937)-10 (1952). Iowa City, Iowa: University of Iowa Press, 1940-1954.   105

Cooperating with DA and DAI since 1952.

University of London. Subjects of Dissertations, Theses and Published Works presented by Successful Candidates at Examinations for Higher Degrees. 1937-1958. London: University of London, 1944-1958.   106

University of Minnesota Summaries of Ph. D. Theses, prior to 1937-1942. Minneapolis, Minn.: University of Minnesota, 1939-1951.   107

See 86. Cooperating with DA and DAI since 1952.

University of Washington Abstracts of Theses, 1 (1931)-10 (1949). Seattle, Wash.: University of Washington Press, 1931-1949.   108

Covers 1914-1946. Cooperating with DA and DAI since 1952.

University of Wisconsin Summaries of Doctoral Dissertations, 1 (1935-1936)-16 (1954-1955). Madison, Wis.: University of Wisconsin Press, 1937-1956. 109

Cooperating with DA and DAI since 1954.

Vanderbilt University Abstracts of Theses. Aug., 1937-1972. Nashville: Vanderbilt University, 1937-1972.   110

Cooperating with DA and DAI since 1952.

Vesenyi, Paul E. European Periodical Literature in the Social Sciences and the Humanities. Metuchen, N. J.: Scarecrow, 1969. 226 pp.   111

Walcutt, Charles Child, and J. Edwin Whitesell, eds. The Explicator Cyclopedia. Vol. II, Traditional Poetry: Medieval to Late Victorian. From The Explicator, I-XX (1942-1962). Chicago: Quadrangle Books, 1968. 387 pp.   112

Washington, Mary A. Sir Philip Sidney: An Annotated Bibliography of Modern Criticism, 1941-1970. Columbia: University of Missouri Press, 1972. 199 pp.   113

Continuation of Samuel A. Tannenbaum's Sir Philip Sidney (A Concise Bibliography), 1941.

Watson, George. The English Petrarchans: A Critical Bibliography of the Canzoniere. London: Warburg Institute, 1967. 47 pp.   114

Williams, Kathleen. The Present State of Spenser Studies, TSLL, 7 (1965), 225-38.   115

Critical survey of Sp scholarship. Spenserian criticism, especially of FQ, has moved from misplaced emphasis on style begun by Romantics to the newest studies exemplified in 1367. Has become scholars' poet rather than poet of ordinary reader.

Wurtsbaugh, Jewel. Two Centuries of Spenserian Scholarship (1609-1805). New York: AMS Press, 1970; Port Washington, N. Y.: Kennikat Press, 1970. 174 pp.   116

Reprints of 1936 ed. Listed in Atkinson, p. 57.

Yearbook of Comparative and General Literature, vols. 1-9. Ed. Werner P. Friederich, et al, 1952-1960. Vols. 10-18. Ed. Horst Frenz, et al, 1961-1969. Vols. 19 (1970)-21 (1972), in collaboration with MLA bibliographers.   117

Each vol. contains bibliography of Comparative Literature.

LIFE

Anonymous. The Grave in Valhalla, Newsweek, Nov. 14, 1938, p. 20.   118

News item on the opening of Sp's tomb in Westminster Abbey. See 119.

Anonymous. The Search for Spenser's Tomb, Baconiana, 23, No. 92 (1939), 22-5.   119

The search was unsuccessful. It was made on Nov. 2-3, 1938, in an effort to confirm Camden's statement in his Annals that when Sp was buried in Westminster Abbey, elegies with the pens that wrote them were cast by contemporary poets into the grave.

Anonymous. The Spenser Mystery, Baconiana, 23, No. 92 (1939), 26-31. 120

Who was Sp? He was one of the many Elizabethan authors whose works were really written by Francis Bacon.

Aubrey, John. Brief Lives. Ed. Oliver Lawson Dick. London: Secker and Warburg, 1949. 419pp.   121

Aubrey's brief life of Sp, pp. 282-3. See 173.

Aubrey, John. Brief Lives and Other Selected Writings. Ed. Anthony Powell. New York: Scribner's, 1949. 409pp.   122

Aubrey's brief life of Sp, pp. 51-2. See 173.

Banks, Theodore H. Spenser's Rosalind: A Conjecture, PMLA, 52 (1937), 335-7.   123

Translates "altera Rosalindula" in one of Harvey's letters in Three Proper and Wittie Familiar Letters as "a changed little Rosalind," which may mean that she relented and became Sp's first wife (see Atkinson, p. 144; and 171, pp. 44-5).

Bennett, H.S. English Books & Readers 1558-1640: Being a Study in the History of the Book Trade in the Reign of Elizabeth I, James I and Charles I. 2 vols. Cambridge: University Press, 1965, 1970. 320, 253 pp.   124

Countess of Pembroke as patroness of Breton, Daniel, and Sp, as well as lesser-known writers who were members of her household; William Ponsonby's publication of Sp's Complaints (1591); Sp as a "needy professional" wrote 17 dedicatory sonnets to leading courtiers for 1590 FQ (I, 40-1, 24-5, 46-7). In 17th century Skelton, Wyatt, and Surrey were neglected, "while even Spenser failed to receive anything like his due" (II, 190).

Bennett, Josephine W. Did Spenser Starve? MLN, 52 (1937), 400-1.   125

No. A few days after his arrival in London in December, 1598, he received a payment of £8 (see 171, p. 202). See 126.

Berry, Herbert, and E.K. Timings. Spenser's Pension, RES, 11 (1960), 254-9.   126

Technicalities of the pension—whether or not he received it, when it was discontinued, how often he collected it—are discussed. Refutes Jonson's statement to Drummond that

Sp died of starvation (see 125). Evidence from Exchequer accounts and Audit Office books in London.

Bradbrook, Muriel C. No Room at the Top: Spenser's Pursuit of Fame, in Elizabethan Poetry, pp. 91-109. Stratford-upon-Avon Studies, 2. London: Edward Arnold, 1960. 224pp.   127

Traces Sp's early quest for fame and preferment, his lack of success, and his "exile" to Ireland where, in the wisdom derived from bitter experience, he wrote no longer for preferment but for himself and posterity.

Bradner, Leicester. Spenser's Connections with Hampshire, MLN, 60 (1945), 180-4.   128

Supports the belief that Sp spent some time in Hampshire and wrote some verses there. He could have had connections with Hampshire through Andrew Reade, from whom he obtained Kilcolman, Sir Henry Wallop, and Sir Nicholas Dawtrey, among others.

Brooks, E. St. John. Edmund Spenser's Brother-in-Law, John Travers, N&Q, 179 (1940), 139, 211.   129

Further details on the husband of Sp's sister Sarah; see also ibid., 74-8, 92-6, 112-5.

Brooks, Eric St. John. Sir Christopher Hatton, Queen Elizabeth's Favourite. London: Jonathan Cape, 1946. 408pp.   130

Two chapters on Hatton's relations with literary men; only Churchyard, Riche, and Dee had any close relations with him (pp. 124-44). Sp addressed him in an introductory sonnet to FQ (p. 139). Hatton's Holdenby estate in Northamptonshire (pp. 153-66) adjoined Althorp, seat of the Spencers (see 1587 map from Finch-Hatton Collection facing p. 162). Hatton and Ireland: his relations with

Lord Grey of Wilton, Sp's patron, his Irish estates from part of the Earl of Desmond's lands, like Ralegh's and Sp's grants (pp. 139, 203, 320-3).

Bryskett, Lodowick. A Discourse of Civil Life. Ed. Thomas E. Wright. Northridge, Cal.: San Fernando Valley State College, 1970. 215 pp.   131

Intro. (pp. vii-xxiii) sketches Bryskett's life, and for his career in Ireland refers to 413, 171, and 174; sketches meeting at his cottage near Dublin when "Master Spenser" invited to discourse on moral philosophy but begged to be excused, saying "I have already undertaken a work tending to the same effect, which is in *heroical verse*, under the title of a *Faerie Queene*, to represent all the moral vertues, assigning to every vertue, a Knight to be the patron and defender of the same." See pp. 21-3, this ed.

Cartier, Général. Le Secret du Cercueil de Spenser, MdF, May 15, 1939, pp. 207-10.   132

Discusses burial place of Sp in Westminster Abbey and its location.

Chamberlin, Frederick. Elizabeth and Leycester. New York: Dodd, Mead, 1939. 487pp.   133

Quotes Dictionary of National Biography article on Sp: Gabriel Harvey brought Sp to notice of Leicester, etc.; Sp became "one of the closest friends of Philip Sidney"; SC and FQ were finished and begun, respectively, at Leicester House. VG dedicated to Leicester, and he is praised in RT. He was Sp's patron (pp. 399-401, 415).

Delany, Paul. Edmund Spenser, the Younger, N&Q, 13 (1966), 259.   134

Note by Brian Bentley on title-page of Epith bound with copy Sp's collected works (1617) says "I knew this author's grandson in Ireland; his name, also, was Edmunde Spenser."

De Robles, Federico Carlos Sainz. Ensayo de un Diccionario de la Literatura. 3 vols. Madrid: Aguilar, 1950. 135

Sp, III, 1435-6. Thumbnail sketch of Sp's life and a partial list of his works.

Disher, M. Willson. The Trend of Shakespeare's Thought—III, TLS, Nov. 3, 1950, p. 700. 136

Sp is the rival poet of Shakespeare's sonnets. Finds uncomplimentary references to Sp and Sp's poetry in sonnets 136, 106, 130; and Sp's retorts in Amor 85 and FQ, VI, x. See letters headed The Rival Poet by J.M. Murry, ibid., Nov. 17, p. 727 (Chapman is the rival poet); by A.S. Cairncross, ibid., Dec. 1, p. 767 (objects to Murry's proposal of Chapman); and by Lynette Feasey, ibid., Dec. 8, p. 785 (Marlowe is the rival poet). See 152.

Dodds, M.H. Chaucer: Spenser: Milton in Drama and Fiction, N&Q, 176 (1939), 69. 137

Sp and Ralegh appear together in Ireland in a scene in Charles Kingsley's novel, Westward Ho! (1855), debating hexameters.

Eagle, R.L. Spenser's Tomb, Baconiana, 23, No. 89 (1938), 122-4. 138

Quotes two notes from Henry Keepe's Monumenta Westmonasteriensa (1682), and compares them with the engraving of Sp's monument in the edition of 1679. Doubts any connection between Sp and Essex, who paid for Sp's funeral.

Eagle, Roderick L. The Search for Spenser's Grave, N&Q, N.S. 3 (1956), 282-3. 139

Answers query of R., ibid., p. 7, reviewing the unsuccessful search

made November 2, 1938 (see 119). See also G. W. Wright's reply to R.'s query, ibid., p. 407.

Eccles, Mark. Elizabethan Edmund Spensers, MLQ, 5 (1944), 413-27. 140

At most twelve and at least seven Edmund Spensers were in London when one of them married Machabyas Childe in 1579. Only the poet, however, then lived in Westminster, where the marriage occurred. It is improbable that another Edmund Spenser married at that place during that period.

Editor. Editorial, Baconiana, 23, No. 92 (1939), 1-2. 141

On the disappointment of the Bacon Society at the failure to find Sp's grave in Westminster Abbey, and the wide publicity before the excavation in press and newsreel.

Edwards, Philip. Sir Walter Ralegh. London: Longmans, Green, 1953. 184 pp. 142

Ralegh's visit to Sp in Ireland 1589; his intellectual associations with Sp, Marlowe, and Jonson; his poems in commendation of FQ; composition of The Ocean to Cynthia in relation to CCCHA, Ralegh's introduction of Sp and FQ to Queen Elizabeth (pp. 12-3, 50-2, 90-2, 96-7).

Falls, Cyril. A Window on the World, Sir Philip Sidney and his Age, Illustrated London News, July 10, 1954, p. 54. 143

A picture of Sidney and the Elizabethan age. Remarks, in passing, that Sidney is an amateur poet compared with Sp.

Fleming, David A. Spenser, Edmund, McGraw-Hill Encyclopedia of World Biography, 10, 156-60. New York: McGraw-Hill Book Company, 1973. 144

Sp's life and works.

Flower, Desmond, and A.N.L. Munby, eds. English Poetical Autographs. London: Cassell, 1938. 25pp.   145

Amor 1, Happy ye leaves when as those lilly hands, in Sp's handwriting (p. 3). "Spenser's autograph in any form is extremely rare, and the poem reproduced here is the only one in his hand which is known. It is the first sonnet of *Amoretti* written out on the fly-leaf of a copy of the *Faerie Queene* which he presented to Elizabeth Boyle, whom he married in 1594" (p. 15). See 2424.

Forster, Leonard. The Translator of the "Theatre for Worldlings," ES, 48 (1967), 27-34.   146

Hypothesizes that while Sp was at Merchant Taylors' School Richard Mulcaster was asked by Emanuel van Meteren, a Dutch friend, if he could recommend "a gifted pupil who would be able to help by translating the verses from French" in Theatre being published by Van der Noot. So Sp became involved in project. Close examination reveals Dutch influence on English verse translations.

Fuller, Thomas. The Worthies of England. Ed. John Freeman. London: Allen and Unwin, 1952. 716pp.   147

Abridged ed. Fuller's Life of Sp, pp. 365-6. See 173.

Geimer, Roger A. Spenser's Rhyme or Churchyard's Reason: Evidence of Churchyard's First Pension, RES, 20 (1969), 306-9.   148

Lines attributed to Sp by John Manningham in Diary (1602) as evidence Sp failed to receive pension promised by Queen probably written by Thomas Churchyard in 1593 concerning pension he finally received in 1597. (See 1190, p. 90).

Goetz, Wolfgang. Das Geheimnis eines Sarges. Sendschreiben an den Dekan

von Westminster, Deutsche Zukunft, 6 (Dec. 4, 1940), 10.   149

Humorous treatment of Baconian theory, inspired by opening of "Sp's" tomb in Westminster Abbey. See 119.

Gordon, George. The Discipline of Letters. Oxford: Clarendon Press, 1946. 207pp.   150

Chapter II, "Virgil in English Poetry" (reprinted from Proceedings of the British Academy, 1931), discusses the effect on Sp of the humanists' making Virgil's life the model of what a poet's life should be (pp. 25-8).

Graham, Rigby. Edmund Spenser's Castle at Kilcolman, ABC, 22 (Oct., 1971), 13-7.   151

Discusses the present state of the ruins and the difficulties of getting past the keepers of the nearby bird sanctuary in order to see Sp's property. Provides a brief account of Sp's life, speculations on relation between his residence at Kilcolman and his writings, sketches of Kilcolman and Dun an Ofr at Smerwick Harbor (by the author), and a print of an engraving of Kilcolman after W. H. Bartlett.

Gray, Henry David. Shakespeare's Rival Poet, JEGP, 47 (1948), 365-73.   152

Argues against other poets, especially Chapman, in favor of Sp. See 136.

Halliday, F. E. The Life of Shakespeare. Baltimore: Penguin Books, 1963. 299pp.   153

Repr. of 1961 ed. Brief mention of Sp's exit from Ireland and his funeral (p. 178). Sp listed among elite frequenters of Wilton House (p. 222). Other Sp references, see Index.

Halliday, F. E. Shakespeare: A Pictorial Biography. Illus. New ed. New York: Viking Press, 1964. 147pp.   154

First ed. 1956. Chronological relation of Sp and Shakespeare noted by simultaneous incidents in their careers. See Index.

Hamer, Douglas. Edmund Spenser's Gown and Shilling, RES, 23 (1947), 218-25.   155

Discusses disbursements of money left by Robert Nowell, and their bearing on Sp's supposed poverty while at Merchant Taylors' School.

Hamer, Douglas. Some Spenser Problems, N&Q, 180 (1941), 165-7, 183-4, 206-9, 220-4, 238-41.   156

These articles deal, respectively, with (1) John and Giles Spenser; (2) Sp's first marriage; (3) Sp's first wife, and Rosalind and the Drydens; (4) Silvanus and Peregrine Spenser, and Edward Kirke; (5) the separate identities of "E. K." and Sp.

Hamilton, A. C. Spenser and Tourneur's "Transformed Metamorphosis," RES, 8 (1957), 127-36.   157

Supports Dorothy Pym's identification of Mavortio as Sp, and tries to clarify the meaning of the poem by showing "how its form is gained through Tourneur's imitation of Spenser." See 195, 199.

Harder, Kelsie B. Nashe and Spenser, in Essays in Honor of Walter Clyde Curry, pp. 123-32. VUSH, 2. Nashville: Vanderbilt University Press, 1955. 298pp.   158

Denies that Nashe always put Sp on a pedestal. "Whether through envy, petulance, pure maliciousness, or merely a natural aversion, Nashe seems to have expressed a certain impertinence toward Spenser."

Harder, Kelsie B. Nashe's Rebuke of Spenser, N&Q, 198 (1953), 145-6. 159

Nashe was not serious in rebuking Sp for failing to honor Lord Strange with a dedicatory sonnet in FQ, 1590; Sp could not have afforded to

honor a possible claimant to the throne.

Hawkes, A.J. An Edmund Spenser in Lancashire in 1566, N&Q, 196 (1951), 336.   160

The Edmund Spenser who in 1566 sold cattle at Wigan market may have been a relative of the poet.

Heffner, Ray. Edmund Spenser's Family. HLQ, 2 (1938), 79-84.   161

Establishes Sp's kinship with the Spencers of Althorp in Northamptonshire. Elizabeth Boyle was also a relative of the Spencers, and Sp may have met her through them during his visit to England in 1590. Reproduces photostatic facsimile of the Spencer pedigree in Huntington Library manuscript EL 1046.

Henley, Pauline. Spenser in Ireland. New York: Russell & Russell, 1969. 231pp.   162

Repr. of the 1928 edition. Listed in Atkinson, pp. 13-4. Accuses Sp of viewing Ireland as an Englishman infected with ethnocentricity. Hence in Sp's writing "both the people and the historical events of his time appear . . . in a false light."

Hogan, Patrick G., Jr. Sidney/Spenser: A Courtesy-Friendship-Love Formulation, ForumH, 9 (1971), 65-9.   163

Sidney and Sp had in common certain ideas which make their relationship not only intellectual but spiritual.

Irwin, Margaret. That Great Lucifer: A Portrait of Sir Walter Ralegh. New York: Harcourt, Brace, 1960. 320pp.   164

Ralegh's friendship with Sp, his visit to Kilcolman, Sp's views on governing the Irish (pp. 65-6). Sp's praise of Ralegh as "the Summer's nightingale," Ralegh's sonnet prefatory to

FQ, his influence in getting FQ into print, his championing of Sp at court (pp. 69-70). For other references to Sp, see Index.

Jenkins, Raymond. Spenser: The Uncertain Years 1584-1589, PMLA, 53 (1938), 350-62.   165

Identifies four additional documents in Sp's secretary hand in the State Papers for Ireland. The careers of Sir John and Sir Thomas Norris in Ireland are traced as clues to Sp's experiences. Effect of these experiences on View. "Considering that Spenser during these hectic years was both witness and actor in some of the world's sternest work, we marvel that the poet in him was never killed."

Jenkins, Raymond. Spenser with Lord Grey in Ireland, PMLA, 52 (1937), 338-53.   166

Identifies thirty-four additional documents in Sp's secretary hand, and supplies details of Sp's movements and activities while in Ireland with Lord Grey.

Judson, A.C. Another Spenser Portrait, HLQ, 6 (1943), 203-4.   167

Adds to the supposed Sp portraits another possibility: the Plimpton Library portrait at Columbia University.

Judson, A.C. Spenser: Two Portraits, N&Q, 182 (1942), 64.   168

FitzHarding miniature, Dupplin Castle portrait.

Judson, Alexander C. A Biographical Sketch of John Young, Bishop of Rochester, with Emphasis on his Relations with Edmund Spenser. Indiana University Studies, 21 (1934), 1-41. 169

Listed in Atkinson, p. 148.

Judson, Alexander C. The Eighteenth Century Lives of Edmund Spenser, HLQ, 16 (1953), 161-81.   170

John Hughes (1715), George Vertue (1731), John Ball (1732), Thomas Birch (1751), Cibber or Shields (1753), John Upton (1758), an anonymous friend of Ralph Church (1758), and the anonymous author of the life in Biographia Britannica (1763). These show a growing sense of the biographer's responsibilities, but tend to neglect new research. Defects come from unavailability of documentary sources, willingness to make unproved and unqualified statements, and lack of intense interest in Sp the man.

Judson, Alexander C. The Life of Edmund Spenser. Baltimore: Johns Hopkins Press, 1966. 238pp.   171

Repr. of 1945 ed. Designed as a supplementary and companion volume of the Variorum edition of Sp's works. This definitive biography gives detailed information on the interrelations between Sp's life, official career, literary activities, and the history of his time as it affected him. Illustrated with photographs, photographic reproductions of portraits, woodcuts, engravings, etc. Bibliography (pp. 213-23) and Index (pp. 225-38).

Judson, Alexander C. Notes on the Life of Edmund Spenser. Bloomington, Ind.: Indiana University Press, 1949. IUPHS, 20. 30pp.   172

Notes and photographs from a Spenserian tour of Ireland in 1947, intended as a sheaf of footnotes to Judson's Variorum Life of Sp. See 171.

Judson, Alexander C. The Seventeenth-Century Lives of Edmund Spenser, HLQ, 10 (1946), 35-48.   173

Camden, Ware, Fuller, Aubrey, Phillips, 1679 anonymous biographer, and Winstanley. All are superficial and inadequate. Gabriel Harvey, Lodowick Bryskett, or Sir Walter Ralegh, three friends who survived Sp by many years, could have written a fascinating biography of the poet.

Judson, Alexander C. Spenser and the Munster Officials, SP, 44 (1947), 157-73.   174

Brief accounts of ten men who held offices in Munster, especially from 1584 to 1589, when Sp was most active as deputy clerk of the Munster council. "This study . . . will, it is hoped, enlarge a little our conception of Spenser's Irish life."

Judson, Alexander C. Thomas Watts, Archdeacon of Middlesex (and Edmund Spenser). Bloomington: Indiana University Press, 1939. IUPHS, No. 2. 26pp.
                                                    175

A biographical sketch of Watts, who may possibly have sent Sp to Pembroke. Bishop John Young was in close contact with Watts's circle, and through an understanding of Watts's ecclesiastical position we may be better able to understand Sp's.

Judson, Alexander C. Two Spenser Leases, MLQ, 5 (1944), 143-7.   176

Sp's early business ventures in Ireland. The two leases were a manor at Enniscorthy and a dissolved Augustinian monastery at New Ross, both in County Wexford.

Kunitz, Stanley J., and Howard Haycraft, eds. British Authors before 1800: A Biographical Dictionary. New York: H. W. Wilson, 1952. 584pp.   177

Sp, pp. 486-8. Portrait. Bibliography.

Laffitte, Susan Cameron Miller. The Literary Connections of Sir Thomas Egerton: A Study of the Influence of Thomas Egerton Upon Major Writers of Renaissance Literature. DAI, 32 (1972), 6935A. Florida State University, 1971. 189 pp.   178

Egerton had connections by politics, friendship, and marriage with Earls of Derby, and through them with Sp. Also influenced Donne, Jonson, and Bacon, illustrating "the interdependence of renaissance England."

McCracken, Eileen. The Woodlands of Ireland circa 1600, IHS, 11 (1959), 271-96.   179

On the wooded areas, cut over in the seventeenth century, of Kilcolman and Sp's rivers.

McLane, Paul E. "Private Personage Unknowne" of Spenser's Letter to Harvey, MLN, 76 (1961), 5-7.   180

The "private Personage Unknowne" referred to in Sp's letter to Gabriel Harvey (October, 1579) is more likely to be Machabyas Chylde, his future wife, than Rosalind, as is commonly believed.

McLane, Paul E. Spenser's Chloris: The Countess of Derby, HLQ, 24 (1961), 145-50.   181

Chloris, "the chiefest Nymph of al" in the April eclogue of SC (ll. 118-123), is probably Lady Margaret, Countess of Derby, granddaughter of Mary Tudor, and first lady of the court next to Elizabeth herself.

Maclean, Hugh. Fulke Greville and "E.K.," ELN, 1 (1963), 90-100.   182

Deals with re-opened argument concerning identity of E.K. and rebuts evidence of Paul E. McLane (2273, pp. 280-95). Attacks that evidence and supports own view that Fulke Greville is not E.K.

MacLure, Millar. Edmund Spenser: An Introductory Essay, QQ, 73 (1966), 550-8.   183

A resumé of Sp's life, with a concluding section on autobiographical hints in the poetry touching on Colin

Clout, Sp's concern with mutability and time, the erotic aspects of his imagination, his melancholy, and his Christianity and apocalyptism.

Magill, Frank N., ed. Cyclopedia of World Authors. New York: Harper, 1958. 2 vols.   184

Sketch of Sp, pp. 1009-12. Bibliography.

Michael, Robert Erlking. *Two Bokes of the Histories of Ireland* by Edmund Campion. DA, 28 (1968), 2651A. Indiana University, 1967.   185

An edition of Campion's work, first English history of Ireland, written 1571, published in part by Richard Stanyhurst in Holinshed's Chronicles of 1577, and in complete form in 1633 by Sir James Ware. Literary worth of Campion's Histories has long been recognized; never finished, but has passages of fine English prose. Long believed Sp owned manuscript of Histories and used in View; but despite fact both Campion and Sp touch on many of same topics, no evidence of direct borrowing. Commentary notes topics Sp mentions in View also found in Histories.

Millican, C. Bowie. A Friend of Spenser, TLS, Aug. 7, 1937, p. 576.   186

Robert Salter, chaplain to Edmund Sheffield, first Earl of Mulgrave, is proposed as the author of the verses signed "R. S." in the 1590 edition of FQ.

Millican, C. Bowie. Notes on Mulcaster and Spenser, ELH, 6 (1939), 211-6. 187

Entries concerning Mulcaster and his family from the parish register of St. Lawrence Pountney, parish church of the Merchant Taylor's School. On March 12, 1564, a son of Mulcaster's was christened Sylvanus.

Millican, C. Bowie. The Supplicats for Spenser's Degrees, HLQ, 2 (1939), 467-70.   188

Unpublished letters concerning Sp's admission to final candidacy for B.A. and M.A. degrees transcribed and explained.

Moore, Marianne. What Are Years. New York: Macmillan, 1941. 54pp.   189

Spenser's Ireland, pp. 34-6. Notes on the poem, pp. 52-3.

Mounts, Charles E. "Sooth" in De La Mare, Keats, and Milton, MLN, 62 (1947), 271-2.   190

Suggests that Meliboeus, "the soothest shepherd that ever piped on plain" in Milton's Comus, is intended to represent Sp.

Newdigate, B.H. Some Spenser Problems: Sylvanus Spenser, N&Q, 180 (1941), 120.   191

Sp's elder son.

Noel, Bernard. Dictionnaire Biographique des Auteurs de Tous les Temps et de Tous les Pays. 2 vols. Paris: Laffont-Bompiani, 1956.   192

Sp, II, 563. Life sketch, followed by a few panegyric quotations and a brief bibliography.

Nosworthy, J. M. Shakespeare's Occasional Plays: Their Origin and Transmission. New York: Barnes & Noble, 1965. 238 pp.   193

In Chap. 11, *Hamlet:* The Occasion and the Folio Text, discusses Cambridge performance referred to on title-page of Q_1. Argues this was 1602-1603, notwithstanding Gabriel Harvey's note in his copy of Speght's 1598 edition of Chaucer, which refers to Shakespeare's "tragedie of Hamlet, Prince of Denmarke," and to Sp and Watson as among "owr florishing metricians." Harvey knew Watson had died 1592 and Sp in January 1599, but "florishing" refers to their works and not to the men.

Perkinson, Richard H. *Volpone* and the Reputation of Venetian Justice, MLR, 35 (1940), 11-8.   194

Sp's commendatory sonnet prefixed to Lewis Lewkenor's translation of Cardinal Gaspero Contarini's The Commonwealth and Government of Venice (London, 1599) may have been written when Sp was in London in 1595-1596, for the translation seems to have been in circulation then (See 171, p. 185; 412, p. 508).

Peter, J. D. The Identity of Mavortio in Tourneur's "Transformed Metamorphosis," N&Q, 193 (1948), 408-12. 195

Dismisses identifications of Mavortio with Essex, Sir Francis Vere, Marlowe, Sp, or Sidney. He is Henry VIII. See 157, 199.

Phillips, James E. Daniel Rogers: A Neo-Latin Link Between the Pléiade and Sidney's "Areopagus," in Neo-Latin Poetry of the Sixteenth and Seventeenth Centuries, pp. 5-28. Los Angeles: William Andrews Clark Memorial Library, 1965. 53 pp.   196

New light on group that involves Sp, Philip Sidney, Gabriel Harvey, Edward Dyer, Fulke Greville, and others. All we know about "Areopagus" in Sp-Harvey letters of 1579-1580. Usually thought group was devoted to classicizing English prosody, but Harvey's reference to "my good friend *M. Daniel Rogers*" in letter to Sp dated April 23, 1580, suggests much broader interests. New biographical material about Rogers in manuscript in own hand (see 1161). In Paris 1561-1570 Rogers associated with members of Pléiade, shared their broad, humanistic concerns. Returned to England 1580 and lived in London

till death in 1591. Knew Sidney and must have communicated to "Areopagus" intellectual spirit of avant-garde in France, far more significant than classicizing English meters. Regrettably, Rogers never mentions Sp in his 561 Latin poems in manuscript.

Pongs, Hermann. Das kleine Lexikon der Weltliteratur. Stuttgart: Union deutsche Verlagsgesellschaft, 1954. 1456 cols.   197

Sp, col. 1269. Biographical sketch and list of works.

Preston, John. Here Is the Place (Spenser's Seat Near Hurstwood), The Gate, 2 (1948), 43.   198

A sonnet. I find the essence still of his soul's great awareness, / The fanciful leaf-hand lacework grown to a picture / Of what he believed it . . . .

Pym, Dorothy. A Theory on the Identification of Cyril Tourneur's 'Mavortio,' N&Q, 174 (1938), 201-4.   199

Identifies "Mavortio" in Tourneur's Transformed Metamorphosis as Sp. See 157, 195.

Ringler, William. John Stow's Editions of Skelton's *Workes* and of *Certaine Worthye Manuscript Poems*, SB, 8 (1956), 215-7.   200

The "I. S." who edited Certain Worthye Manuscript Poems of great Antiquitie Reserued long in the Studie of a Northfolke Gentleman (London, 1597) was probably the historian John Stow. It is dedicated "To the worthiest Poet Maister Ed. Spenser," a tribute from one antiquarian to another. Stow praised Sp in his Annales of England (1615).

Ringler, William A., ed. The Poems of Sir Philip Sidney. Oxford: Clarendon Press, 1962. 578 pp.   201

Section on Influences and Sources in Introduction discusses Sidney's "personal acquaintances most likely to have influenced him as a poet": Thomas Drant, Daniel Rogers, Fulke Greville, Edward Dyer, and Sp. Sidney and Sp had not met before autumn of 1579, when many of Arcadia poems completed, "and the two men do not appear to have become intimately acquainted." Sp at first intended to dedicate SC to Earl of Leicester, but at last minute decided on Sidney. They differed on principles of quantitative verse. Sp later overestimated his indebtedness to Sidney, nor did he influence Sidney in significant way. "Their greatest mutual influence was to encourage each other to be themselves" (pp. xxviii-xxxiv).

Ringler, William A., Jr. Spenser, Shakespeare, Honor, and Worship, RN, 14 (1961), 159-61.   202

Although Sp dedicated SC to Sidney, use of the address "his honor," rather than "his worship," indicates that dedication was originally intended for a nobleman, probably Earl of Leicester.

Roberts, S. C. Adventures With Authors. London: Cambridge University Press, 1966. 276 pp.   203

Sp mentioned in Pembroke historical records (pp. 95, 191).

Roberts, S. C. A Cambridge Sexcentenary: Pembroke College, 1347-1947, Illustrated London News, June 28, 1947, pp. 694-5.   204

Sp mentioned among distinguished alumni. Reproduction of Benjamin Wilson's portrait of Sp, made from a lost original.

Rosenberg, Eleanor. Leicester, Patron of Letters. New York: Columbia University Press, 1955. 395pp.   205

Considers Sp, along with Gabriel Harvey and John Florio, as one of three writers Leicester is alleged to have "neglected" (pp. 323-53). Denies that Sp was sent to Ireland as punishment for embarrassing Leicester by over-zealous partisanship or Puritanism in MHT or SC; rather, Leicester recommended him to Lord Grey for preferment. Sp continued loyal to his patron throughout his life. Leicester in allegory of FQ; as Lobbin in CCCHA. See also Index.

Rowse, A.L. An Elizabethan Garland. London: Macmillan. 1953. 162pp.   206

A collection of informal essays. Chapter 7, In Pursuit of Elizabethan Ireland, pp. 93-7. Takes Sp's Kilcolman as a symbol of the little left of it. "This was the place to which Spenser brought home a bride, Elizabeth Boyle—sooner or later, it seems, everybody married a Boyle—and for whom he wrote his wonderful 'Epithalamion' with its celebration of the countryside. . . . Here, in this stripped shell, within these four walls open to the winds, was written much of that fabulous poem of the age, the *Faerie Queene.*"

Sargent, Ralph M. The Life and Lyrics of Sir Edward Dyer. Oxford: Clarendon Press, 1968. 229 pp.   207

Repr. of 1935 ed. Discusses Areopagus group including Dyer, Sidney, and Greville, knowledge of it in five letters between Gabriel Harvey and Sp in 1579-1580, and Sp's possible association with it (pp. 58-65). Sp mentioned several times in Appendix On the Poetry of Dyer (pp. 165-73).

Saunders, J.W. The Profession of English Letters. London: Routledge and Kegan Paul, 1964. 266 pp.   208

Sp on fringe of Renaissance amateur authors and courtly system as Sheriff of Cork, writer of ceremonial verse, too involved in government service to concentrate on literature, member of congenial circle experimenting in metrical devices, but claim of immortality for SC no courtier would have immodestly made for own work (pp. 31-48). Theatre brought wide public in contact with good literature; nothing equivalent in printed book market. Sp's poetic career illustrates failure to create wide readership for published work. Yet because of "the pioneering work of writers like Spenser and Milton, a literary profession . . . had begun to take root" in England, preparing way for professionals in 18th century (pp. 49-92, especially 80-5). Traces literary professionalism to present. See Index for Sp references.

Saunders, J.W. The Social Situation of Seventeenth-Century Poetry, in Metaphysical Poetry, Stratford-upon-Avon Studies, 11, ed. D. J. Palmer and Malcolm Bradbury, pp. 237-59. London: Edward Arnold, 1970. 280 pp.   209

Compares failure of Michael Drayton to win recognition and status he wanted with Sp's similar failure and Samuel Daniel's. Ultimately, it was Milton who professionalized poetry and "set about creating the very audience they lacked. . . . Before Milton, Ben Jonson, rather than Spenser, is the poet who concerns himself most with literary elites . . . he was luckier than most with his social context." See 208.

Schoenbaum, S. Shakespeare's Lives. Oxford: Clarendon Press, 1970. 838 pp.
                                    210

Francis Meres in Palladis Tamia (1598) effusively praises Sp (see 913), as well as Shakespeare (pp. 53-4). Edmond Malone in Supplement (1780) to edition of Shakespeare's plays by Samuel Johnson and George Steevens (1778) added the Sonnets; in annota-

tions imagined rival poet to be Sp (p. 173). Malone in posthumous life of Shakespeare (1821) devoted 112 pages to whether "pleasant Willy" in Sp's TM is Shakespeare, rejected identification; and whether Aetion in CCCHA (11. 444-447) is Shakespeare, accepted identification. Scholars today consider Drayton more likely (pp. 241-3). John Payne Collier in Life of Shakespeare (1844) accepted both Willy in TM and Aetion in CCCHA as Shakespeare, also "proposes that Spenser at one time resided in Warwickshire and there befriended Shakespeare, twelve years his junior" (pp. 344-4). Alexander Dyce in Memoir of Shakespeare (1832) denies Shakespeare is Willy in TM, accepts allusion in CCCHA (pp. 433-4). Sidney Lee in biography of Shakespeare in DNB confidently asserts Shakespeare is Aetion in CCCHA (p. 513). For other references to Sp's connections with Shakespeare, see Index.

Shaheen, Naseeb. Spenser and the New Testament, AN&Q, 10 (1971), 4-5. 211

Queen's edict of 1559 that clerical Masters of Arts must be examined on the New Testament did not apply to Sp, for no evidence he ever took holy orders. [SpN, Vol. 2, No. 3 (1971), 8.]

Sheavyn, Phoebe. The Literary Profession in the Elizabethan Age. Manchester: Manchester University Press, 1967. 248 pp.   212

Revision by J.W. Saunders of 1909 ed. Sp's patrons, all his works except SC published by William Ponsonby, his literary associates in Ireland. Most popular poet in Robert Allot's anthology, England's Parnassus (1600), with 386 quotations from his poetry. Of 17 sonnets prefixed to FQ, two addressed to Court ladies; response to moral criticism in FQ, IV, Proem;

HOHL and HOHB written to atone for HHOL and HHOB, "though rather perfunctorily." Sp "earned next to nothing as a professional writer; his main support came from the various appointments held in Ireland." Sp listed in Appendix II, An Analysis of the Social Status of 200 Renaissance Poets. See Index for references to Sp.

Sherbo, Arthur. Fielding and Chaucer—and Smart, N&Q, N. S., 5 (1958), 441-2.   213

Christopher Smart may have written Some Account of the Life of Edmund Spenser in second number (February) of the Universal Visiter, periodical edited in 1756 by Smart and Richard Rolt. That Smart knew Sp's poetry shown in his Secular Ode.

Simonini, R. C., Jr. Italian Scholarship in Renaissance England. UNCSCL, 3. Chapel Hill: UNCSCL, 1952. 125pp.   214

"By the Elizabethan Age, Italian had become a recognized part of the education of the nobility and gentry." A number of courtiers, members of the nobility, "and the poets Spenser, Sidney, Daniel, and Lyly are only a few of the many distinguished Elizabethans who knew Italian well" (p. 20). John Florio, "the representative humanist of the Elizabethan Age . . . was the friend of Ben Jonson, Nicholas Breton, Richard Hakluyt, Theodore Diodati, Gabriel Harvey, Edmund Spenser, and Giordano Bruno" (pp. 55-6). He refers to "Curteous Spenser" in epistle of Second Frutes (1591) (p. 60).

Strathmann, Ernest A. Ferdinando Freckleton and the Spenser Circle, MLN, 58 (1943), 542-4.   215

Since there were several Ferdinando Freckletons in Sp's day, all the references to persons of this name do not necessarily refer to Elizabeth Boyle's step-father.

Thompson, Edward. Sir Walter Ralegh, Last of the Elizabethans. New Haven: Yale University Press, 1936. 416pp. 216

Ralegh and Sp at Smerwick; Sp on conditions in Ireland in View (pp. 20-2). Chapter 9, Poet; and Friend of Poets, pp. 69-83, on Sp's relations with Ralegh.

Thomson, Patricia. The Literature of Patronage, 1580-1630, EIC, 2 (1952), 267-84.   217

Discusses Sp, among others, in a study of the effects of patronage on poets of the periods surveyed.

Tuve, Rosemond. "Spenserus," in Essays in English Literature from the Renaissance to the Victorian Age Presented to A. S. P. Woodhouse, 1964, ed. Millar MacLure and F. W. Watt, pp. 3-25. Toronto: University of Toronto Press, 1964. 339 pp.   218

Attributes two lines from Ovid's Tristia written in Bodleian manuscript of Gower's Confessio Amantis to Anne Russell, Lady Warwick, dedicatee with her sister Margaret Lady Cumberland of RT and 4 Hymnes, though inscription may be in Sp's hand. Develops Sp's associations with powerful Dudley, Sidney, Bedford, and Russell families, appearance of several members in his poems, e. g., CCCHA, and effect of their ill fortunes on his hopes and ideals.

Untermeyer, Louis. Lives of the Poets: The Story of One Thousand Years of English and American Poetry. New York: Simon and Schuster, 1959. 757 pp.   219

Sketch of Sp, pp. 65-7.

Vallese, Tarquinio. Politics and Poetry. Milan: Società Anonima Editrice Dante Alighieri, 1937. 111pp.   220

On political influence on English poetry. Chapter II: The Renaissance, pp. 25-47. Sees Sp as an interpreter of political events. MHT was meant to prevent the Queen from marrying Alençon (following Greenlaw); VG alludes to the consequent punishment by exile to Ireland. View shows strong political interest in affairs of state. In FQ "we see shadowed forth the most important personages and events of Elizabeth's reign." Necessary to remember Sp was an active man of affairs.

W., E. G. Some Spenser Problems, N&Q, 180 (1941), 304.   221

Christian name Sylvanus is from the New Testament.

Wallace, Willard M. Sir Walter Raleigh. Princeton, N.J.: Princeton University Press, 1959. 334pp.   222

Ralegh's visit to Sp at Kilcolman in 1589, the exchange of eulogistic sonnets, and Sp's reference to Raleigh's Cynthia in CCCHA. For other references to Sp, see Index.

Warner, Oliver. English Literature: A Portrait Gallery. London: Chatto & Windus, 1964. 205 pp.   223

Chronology of English literary figures from Chaucer into 20th century. For each, one page outline of figure's life and accomplishment with authenticated portrait opposite. Sp (pp. 14-15) with portrait by unknown artist.

Welply, W. H. Edmund Spenser and Alton, Hants, N&Q, 180 (1941), 260. 224

Query on the legend that Sp lived there in 1590.

Welply, W. H. Edmund Spenser's Brother-in-Law, John Travers, N&Q, 179 (1940), 74-8, 92-6, 112-5.   225

Facts and suggestions about the husband of Sp's sister Sarah.

Welply, W. H. John, Baron Lumley, 1534?-1609, N&Q, 181 (1941), 86-8.
226

Possible family connection with Sp indicated by the genealogy.

Welply, W. H. John Travers—A Correction and Some Additions, N&Q, 187 (1944), 143-4.   227

The John Travers of a will dated 20 January 1604/5 is not the John Travers who was Sp's brother-in-law.

Welply, W. H. Some Spenser Problems, N&Q, 180 (1941), 56-9, 74-6, 92-5, 151, 224, 248, 436-9, 454-9.   228

Discusses a variety of biographical problems, e. g., Sp's early marriage and the possibility that Harvey cooperated in editing SC, drawing upon the minor poems, documentary evidence, and genealogical research.

Welply, W. H. Spenser-Tynte Genealogy, N&Q, 186 (1944), 128-9.   229

Elizabeth Boyle married Sir Roger Tynte, her third husband, in 1612. Her son Peregrine and only child by Sp married a step-daughter of his mother's, Dorothy Tynte.

Welply, W. H. Spenser's Two Marriages, N&Q, 188 (1945), 147.   230

Suggests that Amor 39 refers to Sp's widowerhood.

Whitmore, J. B. Some Spenser Problems, N&Q, 180 (1941), 120.   231

Giles Spenser of North End, Burton Dassett.

Whitmore, J. B. Some Spenser Problems, N&Q, 181 (1941), 14.   232

Agrees with Douglas Hamer, ibid., 180 (1941), 166 (see 156), on his construction of Giles Spenser's pedigree.

Williams, Franklin B. Index of Dedications and Commendatory Verses in English Books before 1641. London: Bibliographical Society, 1962. 256 pp.
233

Books cited by STC number in Personal Index; Sp, pp. 174-5. Sp associated with Lewkenor's trans. of Contarini's Commonwealth . . . of Venice (1599); Gabriel Harvey's Foure Letters (1592); Z. I.'s trans. of La Vardin's Historie of George Castriot . . . (1596); Jones's trans. of Neanna's Treatise of Nobility (1595); William Smith's Chloris (1596—see 2295 and 2515); Thomas Lodge's A Fig for Momus (1595).

Williams, Franklin B., Jr. An Initiation Into Initials, SB, 9 (1957), 163-78. 234

Identifies "Z. I.," translator of The Historie of George Castriot (1596), for which Sp wrote a commendatory sonnet, as Zachary Jones, a Lincoln's Inn barrister who was contemporary with Sp at Cambridge, and whom "we may add to the circle of Spenser's friends" (pp. 163-4). See 235.

Williams, Franklin B., Jr. Spenser, Shakespeare, and Zachary Jones, SQ, 19 (1968), 205-12. 235

The "Z. I. Gentleman" to whom Sp dedicated a sonnet in his translation of Vardin's The Historie of George Castriot, surnamed Scanderbeg, was the barrister Zachary Jones, who was a friend of Sp and perhaps also of Shakespeare. See 234.

Williams, Norman Lloyd. Sir Walter Raleigh. London: Eyre and Spottiswoode, 1962. 295 pp. 236

Presents Raleigh as far as possible in own words and those of contemporaries (p. vii). Sp's View quoted on Raleigh at Smerwick (pp. 36-7). CCCHA quoted on Raleigh and Sp at Kilcolman; Raleigh as Timias in FQ, III, v, IV, vii; "Raleigh presented [Sp] and The Faerie Queene to Elizabeth who, in abounding health, was dancing six or seven galliards in a morning, and playing on the virginals and singing. She liked the poem" (pp. 94-7). In 1599: "In Munster the peasantry had wiped out, with much burning and de-gutting, the litigation-ridden English settlements, including Raleigh's and Spenser's" (pp. 152-3).

Williamson, Hugh Ross. Sir Walter Raleigh. London: Faber and Faber, 1951. 215pp. 237

Chapter 7, The Shepherd of the Ocean, pp. 50-5, chiefly on Raleigh's relations with Sp.

Winstanley, William. The Lives of the Most Famous English Poets (1687). Gainesville, Fla.: Scholars' Facsimiles and Reprints, 1963. 221 pp. 238

William Riley Parker in Introduction (pp. v-viii) refutes allegation Winstanley merely plagiarized from Edward Phillips' Theatrum Poetarum (1675), lists among accounts "that add more than they borrow" those of Donne, Drayton, Greville, Jonson, Shakespeare, Sidney, Sp, and others. Winstanley's sketch of Sp (pp. 88-93) mentions SC and Sidney's censure of its rustic language, VG, RR, offense given Lord Cecil by MHT so that he withheld pension granted by Queen Elizabeth until Sp complained and she commanded delivery of it, praise of Sidney in RT, unhappy years in Ireland with Lord Grey, death in poverty in 1598 of "a deep Melancholy" and burial at Essex's expense, unjust treatment of "so great a Poet."

Wraight, A. D., and Virginia F. Stern. In Search of Christopher Marlowe: A Pictorial Biography. Illus. New York: Vanguard Press, 1965. 376 pp. 239

Discussion of supposed portrait of Marlowe found at Cambridge 1953, says Sp had portrait (on p. 154) hung in university library (p. 71). Sp was Cambridge "new Poete" under patronage of Sidney; but Marlowe ignored Sidney's neoclassical tenets in drama (pp. 82-3). Sp member of Sidney's Areopagus group, which first met at Leicester House 1578-1579, "founded largely at the instigation of Gabriel Harvey," who befriended Sp at Cambridge, "assisting him materially in preferment to Leicester's household." Harvey met Marlowe in Raleigh's "School of Night" at some time in London, "but he disliked Marlowe's arrogance." Sp accepted Harvey's friendship. When Sp in London 1589-1590 at Raleigh's invitation, probably met Marlowe. Lines in Tamburlaine echoing passages in FQ before publication "suggest an intimate knowledge of each other's works" (pp. 155-8).

Wright, Celeste Turner. Anthony Mundy, "Edward" Spenser, and E. K., PMLA, 76 (1961), 34-9. 240

Edward Knight, possibly a mutual friend of Mundy and Sp, may have been the author of E. K.'s glosses to SC. Edward Knight wrote verses prefixed to Mundy's Mirrour of Mutabilitie (1580). There are stylistic similarities between the glosses on SC and Knight's book, The Trial of Truth.

WORKS: EDITIONS AND SELECTIONS

Abrams, M. H., and Others, eds. The Norton Anthology of English Literature. 2 vols. New York: Norton, 1962. 1766, 1694 pp.   241

October from SC; Letter to Raleigh, FQ, I, Proem, i, ii, xi, II, xii, 42-87, III, vi, 30-50, VII; 6 sonnets from Amor; Epith; HHOB, 11. 1-161 (I, 444-541).

Adams, Hazard, ed. Poetry: An Introductory Anthology. New York: Little, Brown, 1968. 394pp.   242

January and March from SC; Proth; Amor 75, 10 (pp. 10-21).

Aldington, Richard, ed. The Viking Book of Poetry of the English-Speaking World. Rev. ed. New York: Viking Press, 1958. 1297pp.   243

Sp, pp. 98-120. Two stanzas from lay of Eliza in April of SC; 3 sonnets from Amor; Proth; Epith; selections from FQ, I, v, and II, vii and xii.

Altenbernd, Lynn, ed. Exploring Literature: Fiction, Poetry, Drama, and Criticism. New York: Macmillan, 1970. 702 pp.   244

Six sonnets from Amor (pp. 284-6).

Altenbernd, Lynn, and Leslie L. Lewis, eds. Introduction to Literature: Poems. New York: Macmillan, 1969. 487 pp.   245

First ed. 1963. Epith; Amor 19, 26, 34, 67, 75 (pp. 80-91).

Anderson, George K., and William E. Buckler, eds. The Literature of England: An Anthology and a History. 2

vols. 5th ed. Glenview, Illinois: Scott, Foresman, 1966. 1848 pp.   246

First ed. 1949. Sp in vol. 1. Intro., pp. 480-2. Letter to Raleigh; FQ, I, i-iv, vi, viii, xi-xii; II, vii, xii; III, vi (pp. 482-619). CCCHA, Epith (pp. 619-45).

Anderson, George K. and William E. Buckler, eds. The Literature of England: An Anthology and a History. Rev. single vol. ed. Glenview, Ill.: Scott, Foresman, 1967. 1287 pp.   247

First published 1953. Introduction to FQ; letter to Raleigh; FQ, I, i; II, xii; III, vi; 9 sonnets from Amor; Epith; Proth (pp. 217-54).

Auden, W. H., and Norman Holmes Pearson, eds. Poets of the English Language. 5 vols. Viking Portable Library. New York: Viking Press, 1950.   248

Vol. 1. Langland to Spenser. Sp, pp. 523-614. April and November from SC; 2 sonnets from Amor; Epith; FQ, II, vii and xii, and selections from III, vi and xii, VII, vii and viii.

Ault, Norman, ed. Elizabethan Lyrics. 3rd ed. New York: William Sloane, 1949; repr. New York: Longmans, 1960. 560 pp.   249

Roundelay from August of SC; Iambicum Trimetrum from Two Other Very Commendable Letters; FQ, II, vi, (3 stanzas); and IV, x (4 stanzas); 7 sonnets from Amor; Epith; Proth. Biographical note, pp. 537-8. See Index of Authors, p. 542.

Ault, Norman, ed. A Treasury of Unfamiliar Lyrics. London: Gollancz, 1938. 672pp.   250

FQ, II, vi (3 stanzas); 3 sonnets from Amor; Verses upon the Earl of Cork's Lute, from View.

Baugh, Albert C., and George William McClelland, eds. English Literature: A Period Anthology. New York: Appleton-Century-Crofts, 1954. 1480pp.   251

Introduction to 16th century, Matthew W. Black, pp. 189-205. Introduction to Sp, pp. 221-2. June from SC; Letter to Ralegh; FQ, I, Proem, i-ii; 6 sonnets from Amor; Proth (pp. 223-48).

Bayley, P. C., ed. The Faerie Queene, Book I. London: Oxford University Press, 1966. 344 pp.   252

Critical introduction, explanatory notes.

Bayley, P. C., ed. The Faerie Queen, Book II. London: Oxford University Press, 1965. 345 pp.   253

Critical introduction, explanatory notes.

Bender, Robert M., and Charles L. Squier, eds. The Sonnet: A Comprehensive Anthology of British and American Sonnets from the Renaissance to the Present. New York: Washington Square Press, 1965. 544 pp.   254

Intro. contains paraphrase of Amor 1 (pp.3-4). Section on English Renaissance has biographical note; unrhymed versions of two sonnets, "It was the time . . . " and "I saw the bird . . . " from Theatre followed by rhymed versions from VB; FQ dedicatory sonnets to Ralegh and Countess of Pembroke; 24 sonnets from Amor (pp. 87-103).

Benét, William Rose, and Conrad Aiken, eds. An Anthology of Famous English

and American Poetry. New York: Modern Library, 1945. 951pp.   255

Proth; 2 sonnets from Amor.

Beum, Robert, ed. Edmund Spenser, Epithalamion. Columbus, Ohio: Charles E. Merrill, 1968. 139 pp.   256

A casebook. Text of Epith, with notes (pp. 3-22). Criticism arranged under General, Origins or Genre, Philosophy, Imagery and Symbolism, Language or Style, and Versification. Criticism after 1960: Robert Kellogg and Oliver Steele (333), Hallett Smith (1091), Robert Beum (522).

Black, Matthew W., ed. Elizabethan and Seventeenth-Century Lyrics. Chicago: J. B. Lippincott, 1938. 624pp.   257

Section on The Pastoralists includes Lay of Fair Eliza (April, SC), Perigot and Willie's Roundelay (August, SC), and Proth (pp. 114-25); section on The Sonneteers includes 5 sonnets from Amor (pp. 188-90). Critical comments on Sp's sonnet form, metrics, pastoralism; see Index.

Bloom, Edward A., Charles H. Philbrick, and Elmer M. Blistein, eds. The Variety of Poetry: An Anthology. New York: Odyssey Press, 1964. 220pp.   258

Proth (pp. 132-36).

Bottrall, Margaret, and Ronald Bottrall, eds. Collected English Verse. London: Sidgwick & Jackson, 1947. 586 pp. 259

Repr. of 1946 ed. SC, April, 11. 36-153; Epith, 11. 296-353; Amor 68; FQ, II, xii, 70-80; FQ, VII, viii, 1-2 (pp. 61-72).

Bradbrook, M. C., comp. The Queen's Garland. Verses Made by her Subjects for Elizabeth I, Queen of England Now Collected in Honour of Her Majesty Queen Elizabeth II. London: Oxford University Press, 1953. 74pp.   260

Preface states reliance on 1204 and 1762. Sp represented in 4 of 6 sections: description of Mercilla from FQ, V, ix in Gloriana, the Royal Queen and Empress (pp. 18-9); description of Belphoebe from FQ, II, iii in Belphoebe, the Virtuous and Beautiful Lady (pp. 25-6); description of Cynthia from CCCHA in Diana, Goddess of Woods and Springs, also called Cynthia, as Goddess of the Moon and Seas (pp. 39-40); song of Eliza from April of SC in Flora, the Lady of May and Queen of Shepherds (pp. 45-8).

Brooks, Cleanth, and Robert Penn Warren, eds. Understanding Poetry: An Anthology for College Students. Rev. ed. New York: Holt, 1950. 727pp. 261

First published 1938. Proth (pp. 479-83).

Brower, Reuben A., Anne D. Ferry, and David Kalstone, eds. Beginning With Poems: An Anthology. New York: Norton, 1966. 379pp. 262

Amor 13, 23, 35, 70, 75 (pp. 5-7); Epith (pp. 7-17).

Brown, Harry, and John Milstead. What the Poem Means: Summaries of 1000 Poems. Glenview, Ill.: Scott, Foresman, 1970. 314 pp. 263

4 Hymns; Epith; Proth; Amor 75 (pp. 215-220).

Bullett, Gerald, ed. The English Galaxy of Shorter Poems. Everyman's Library, 959. London: Dent, 1939. 511pp. 264

First published 1933. Amor 89, 87, 72 (pp. 76-8).

Bushnell, Nelson S., Paul M. Fulcher, and Warner Taylor, eds. Literary Masters of England. Rev. ed. New York: Rinehart, 1950. 1158pp. 265

First published 1936. Introduction to Sp; April and October from SC; FQ, I, Proem, i, 29-41, ix, 21-36; II, xii, 42-62; VI, Proem, i-iii, 1-28, xii, 1-2, 23-41; Amor 33, 66, 78, 80 (pp. 132-75).

Calderwood, James L., and Harold E. Toliver, eds. Forms of Poetry. Englewood Cliffs, N.J.: Prentice-Hall, 1968. 598 pp. 266

Proth (pp. 57-61); March eclogue from SC (pp. 184-187); FQ, Letter to Raleigh; I, i-ii, xi-xii (pp. 344-92).

Campbell, Oscar James, Hardin Craig, and others, eds. Great English Writers. 2 vols. New York: Crofts, 1938. 267

English Poetry from Chaucer to Spenser (I, 143-4); Introduction to Spenser (I, 145-7). Letter to Ralegh and FQ, Proem, Book I; Upon a Day from Anacreontics (I, 148-236).

Carpenter, Frederic Ives, ed. English Lyric Poetry, 1500-1700. Freeport, New York: Books for Libraries Press, 1969. 276 pp. 268

Repr. of 1906 ed. Intro., pp. xix-lxv. Unidentified excerpts from FQ, I, ix; Daph; Amor; Proth and Epith, complete; HHOB, in part; few lines of HOHB (pp. 13-43).

Chambers, Edmund K., ed. English Pastorals. Freeport, N. Y.: Books for Libraries Press, 1969. 280 pp. 269

Repr. of 1906 ed. Introduction distinguishes between two "partly opposed waves" of poetry which "coexisted and interpenetrated each other in a hundred ways" 1558-1642, one tendency dominated by "Spenser the musical," other by "Donne the imaginative"; pastoral province of poets associated with Sp; traces development of genre from classical antiquity, mixing of pastoral with other literary forms, efforts to overcome artificiality and convention, for "pastoral is not the poetry of country life, but the poetry of the townsman's dream of country life" (pp. xv-xlvii). Note on Sp, and January, April, May, June, and December from SC (pp. 10-29).

Church, Richard, ed. A Selection of Poems by Edmund Spenser. Crown Classics. London: Grey Walls Press, 1953. 63pp.   270

Introductory essay.

Clark, David Lee, William Bryan Gates, and Ernest Erwin Leisy, eds. The Voices of England and America. 2 vols. New York: Nelson, 1939.   271

The Period of the Renaissance, I, 180-5. Introduction to Sp, I, 185-7. Fable from February of SC; Letter to Ralegh: FQ, I, Proem, i-ii; Epith; Proth (I, 187-216).

Clark, Donald L., and others, eds. English Literature: A College Anthology. New York: Macmillan, 1965.   272

Repr. 1960 ed. Short biography of Sp; Epith; Proth (pp. 152-162).

Coffin, Charles M., and Gerrit Hubbard Roelofs, eds. The Major Poets: English and American. 2nd ed. New York: Harcourt, Brace, 1969. 581 pp.   273

First published 1954. November from SC; seven sonnets from Amor; Epith (pp. 41-68).

Collins, A. J. F., ed. The Faerie Queene, Book II. London: University Tutorial Press, 1942. 247pp.   274

Introductory essay.

Collins, A. S., ed. The Faerie Queene, Book I. London: University Tutorial Press, 1937. 228pp.   275

Introduction, notes, and glossary.

Crinò, Anna Maria, ed. Amoretti and Epithalamion. Florence: Editrice Universitaria, 1954. 195pp.   276

Introduction and notes. English text with Italian translation on facing pages.

Crinò, Anna Maria, ed. Antologia Spenseriana. Verona: Fiorini Ghidini, 1966. 328 pp.   277

Introduction discusses Sp's works in relation to Continental literature of Renaissance (pp. 9-54). Bibliographical note lists no item later than 1962, and Italian translations of Sp's works 1826-1957 (pp. 57-60). Most selections prefaced by introductory note and followed by explanatory notes: October from SC; MHT, ll. 717-814; 12 sonnets from Amor; Epith; CCCHA, ll. 56-155; HHOL; Proth; FQ, I, xii, II, xii, III, vi, IV, x, V, Proem and i, VI, x, VII, vi. English-Italian glossary (pp. 307-26).

Crinò, Anna Maria, ed. Colin Clouts Come Home Againe. Presentazione di Allan Gilbert. Rome: Gismondi Editore, 1956. 112pp.   278

Introduction and notes. English text and Italian translation on facing pages.

Crinò, Anna Maria, ed. Prosopopoeia, or Mother Hubberds Tale. Florence: Olschki, 1957. 129pp.   279

Introduction and notes. English text and Italian translation on facing pages.

Crinò, Anna Maria, ed. The Shepheardes Calender. Florence: Sansoni, 1950. 357pp.   280

Illustrated with the original woodcuts. Introduction and notes. English text and Italian translation on facing pages.

Cunliffe, John W., Karl Young, and Mark Van Doren, eds. Century Readings in English Literature. 5th ed. New York: Appleton-Century, 1940. 1105pp.   281

First published 1910. Introduction to Sp; February and October (without glosses) from SC; FQ, I, i-ii; Epith; Proth (pp. 191-218).

Cunningham, J. V., ed. The Renaissance in England. New York: Harcourt, Brace & World, 1966. 274 pp.   282

Intro. (pp. xiii-xliii) speaks of The Revolution in Style in vein of 1213 (listed in Bibliography, p. 274): "the ornate style of Spenser, and the new plain style . . . imitated by Campian [sic] and Donne, perfected by Jonson." Proth (pp. 146-51).

Daiches, David, and William Charvat, eds. Poems in English 1530-1940. New York: Ronald Press, 1950. 763pp.   283

Sp, pp. 28-36. Roundelay from August of SC; 4 sonnets from Amor; Proth.

Danziger, Marlies K., and Wendell Stacy Johnson, eds. A Poetry Anthology. New York: Random House, 1968. 618pp.   284

Amor 34, 75; Proth (pp. 90-6).

Davenport, William H., Lowry C. Wimberly, and Harry Shaw, eds. Dominant Types in British and American Literature. New York: Harper, 1949. 2 vols. in 1.   285

Vol. I, Part 1, Narrative and Lyric Poetry. Introduction to Sp; FQ, I, Proem, i (pp. 78-87).

Dean, Leonard, ed. Renaissance Poetry. Vol. 3 of English Masterpieces, 7 vols. 2nd ed. Ed. Maynard Mack. Englewood Cliffs, N. J.: Prentice-Hall, 1961. 342 pp.   286

FQ, I, x, II, xii, III, vi, VI, x; Epith; Proth (pp. 52-115).

De Bruin, H., trans. Uit de "Amoretti" van Edmund Spenser, Ad Interim, 4 (1947), 340-1.   287

Amor 25 and 29 in Dutch translation.

De Sélincourt, Aubrey. The Book of the Sea. New York: Norton, 1963. 375 pp.   288

FQ, II, xii, 23-25 (p. 39); VI, xii, 1 (p. 63); II, xii, 10, 1-4 (p. 73); xii, 19 (p. 75). For other scraps on sea from FQ, see Index.

De Selincourt, Ernest, ed. Spenser's Minor Poems. Oxford: Clarendon Press, 1966. 528 pp.   289

Repr. of 1910 ed. Reprinted in 1960 and 1966 from corrected sheets of the 1910 edition.

Dickson, G. S., ed. The Faerie Queene, Book I. London: Nelson, 1937. 195pp.   290

Introductory essay.

Dixon, C. J., ed. Selections from *The Faerie Queene*. London: Heinemann, 1965. 277 pp.   291

Duhamel, P. Albert, and Richard E. Hughes, eds. Literature: Form and Function. Englewood Cliffs, N.J.: Prentice-Hall, 1965. 635 pp.   292

FQ, I, iv, 15-37 (pp. 146-9); August from SC (pp. 286-8).

Eastman, Arthur M., and others, eds. The Norton Anthology of Poetry. New York: Norton, 1970. 1231pp.   293

FQ, III, ix-x; 12 sonnets from Amor; Epith; Proth (pp. 127-61).

Eastman, Arthur M., and others, eds. The Norton Anthology of Poetry: Shorter Edition. New York: Norton, 1970. 622 pp.   294

Amor 67, 68, 70, 75; Epith; Proth (pp. 60-73).

Elledge, Scott, ed. Milton's "Lycidas" Edited to Serve as an Introduction to Criticism. New York: Harper & Row, 1966. 330 pp.   295

Prints nine Renaissance pastorals by Petrarch, Boccaccio, Castiglione, Marot, Ronsard, Sp (November and part of May from SC, pp. 82-94), and Lodowick Bryskett. Sp frequently cited by old and modern critics of Lycidas in Commentaries and Notes on the poem (pp. 251-316).

Feist, Hans, ed. and trans. Ewiges England: Dichtung aus Sieben Jahrhunderten von Chaucer bis Eliot. Zürich: Amstutz, Herdeg, 1944. 591pp.   296

English and German on facing pages. Amor 8, 75; Epith stanzas 1-2, 5-10, 12-14, 16-18, 21, 23, and tornata; FQ, II, xii, 70-75 (pp. 90-115). Notes on selections, pp. 573-4.

Fifteen Poets. Oxford: Clarendon Press, 1941. 503pp.   297

A sample—about 1000 lines of each—of the great English poets from Chaucer to Arnold. Sp, with a short introductory essay by C. S. Lewis, pp. 40-68; January from SC, Epith, Daph, a sonnet from Amor, Invocation and four abbreviated episodes from FQ.

Frank, Joseph. Hobbled Pegasus: A Descriptive Bibliography of Minor English Poetry, 1641-1660. Albuquerque: University of New Mexico Press, 1968. 482 pp.   298

Item 373, The Fairie Leveller, pamphlet of 1648, attributed to Sp. Prints FQ, V, ii, 29-54 (Giant with "An huge great paire of ballance in his hand").

Gardner, Helen, ed. The New Oxford Book of English Verse 1250-1950. New York: Oxford University Press, 1972. 974 pp.   299

Sp, pp. 59-89. Lay of Eliza from April of SC; "Most glorious Lord of Lyfe" from Amor; from FQ: The Cave of Despair (I, ix, 33-44), The Bower of Bliss (II, xii, 70-75), The Garden of Adonis (III, vi, 30-42), The Masque of Cupid (III, xii, 7-18), The Hill of the Graces (VI, x, 10-16), Nature's Reply to Mutability (VII, vii, 57-59), end (VII, viii, 1-2). See Notes and References (p. 947).

Gilbert, Allan H., ed. Literary Criticism, Plato to Dryden. New York: American Book Co., 1940. 704pp.   300

Introductory comment on Sp's poetic theory, and Letter to Sir Walter Ralegh (in part), with notes (pp. 462-5). Sp cited in critical notes throughout the book; see Index.

Goudge, Elizabeth, ed. A Book of Comfort: An Anthology. New York: Coward-McCann, 1964. 384 pp.   301

Proth (pp. 60-1); Muiop, ll. 17-21, 89-96, 161-8, 177-84 (pp. 67-8); Amor 68 (p. 193); FQ, II, viii, 1-2 (p. 319).

Gransden, K. W., ed. Tudor Verse Satire. London: Athlone Press, 1970. 182 pp.   302

From Skelton to Jonson, 1510-1616. Intro. (pp. 1-29) sketches classical and medieval backgrounds of English Renaissance satire; associates Sp's MHT with George Orwell's Animal Farm, calls MHT "homiletic and un-Horatian . . . neo-medieval." Third section of MHT, against the court, ll. 581-942 (pp. 65-74); ll. 652-790 of CCCHA (pp. 74-7), "the most autobiographical of Spenser's poems."

Gray, Douglas, ed. The Faerie Queene, Book I. London: Macmillan, 1969. 246 pp.   303

Introduction (pp. i-xxvi). Old-spelling edition based on 1596 text.

Grebanier, Bernard D. N., Samuel Middlebrook, and others, eds. English Literature and Its Backgrounds. 2 vols. Rev. ed. New York: Dryden Press, 1949. 304

First ed. 1939. Biographical sketch of Sp; introduction to SC, April eclogue; introduction to FQ, Letter to Ralegh, Bk. I, i and xi; Amor 1, 34, 72, 75, and 79; Epith and Proth (I, 286-318).

Grebanier, Bernard, and Seymour Reiter, eds. Introduction to Imaginative Literature. New York: Thomas Y. Crowell, 1960. 969 pp.   305

Amor 1, 75, 79; Epith, Proth (pp. 276-84).

Greenfield, Stanley B., and A. Kingsley Weatherhead, eds. The Poem: An Anthology. New York: Appleton-Century-Crofts, 1968. 420 pp.   306

Amor 1, 34, 45, 79; Epith (pp. 44-58).

Gregory, Horace, and Marya Zaturenska, eds. The Mentor Book of Religious Verse. New York: New American Library of World Literature, 1957. 238 pp.   307

Amor 68; HOHB, ll. 84-105 (pp. 121, 127-8).

Gwynn, Frederick L., and others, eds. The Case for Poetry: A Critical Anthology. 2nd ed. Englewood Cliffs, N.J.: Prentice-Hall, 1965. 361 pp.   308

First ed. 1954. Proth and explication (pp. 266-272).

Hamilton, A.C., ed. Edmund Spenser: Selected Poetry. New York: New American Library, 1966. 548 pp.   309

Introduction (pp. vii-xxix). January, October, December, and Epilogue from SC; Epith; Letter to Raleigh; FQ, I; II, i: opening episode, vii-ix, xii: Bower of Bliss; III, Prologue, i: opening episode, vi: Garden of Adonis, xii; IV, Prologue, x, xii; V, i: opening stanzas, vii; VI, Prologue, ix-x; VII, vi, 1-36, vii.

Hardison, O. B., Jr., ed. English Literary Criticism: The Renaissance. New York: Appleton-Century-Crofts, 1963. 337pp.   310

Part II: The Defense of Poetry includes Sidney, brief Introduction (pp. 98-9) and Apologie for Poetrie, with reference to SC (p. 137). Part III: Practical Criticism includes Sp, brief Introduction (pp. 185-6), "general argument" of SC, October, and Letter to Raleigh (pp. 187-203).

Harrison, G. B., general ed. Major British Writers. 2 vols. New York: Harcourt, Brace, 1954.   311

C.S. Lewis author intro. essay on Sp, I, 91-104, and ed. Sp selections, I, 104-81; Epith; FQ, I, i, ii, iii, vi, vii, viii, ix; II v, vi, vii, xii; III, i, iv, vii, viii, x, xi, xii, IV, v, xi, xii; V, vii; VI, Proem, 1, iv, v, vi, viii, ix, x; VII, vi, vii, viii. No canto given in complete form.

Harrison, Thomas P., Jr. The Pastoral Elegy: An Anthology. New York: Octagon Books, Inc., 1968. 312 pp.   312

Repr. of 1939 ed. Development of the type illustrated in representative work of twenty-two poets from Theocritus to Arnold. Sp's November from SC and Astro, with The Lay of Clorinda appended to the latter, are included (pp. 174-92). See also Introduction, section on The Later Renaissance Pastoral, pp. 15-6; and Commentary and Notes, pp. 283-7.

Haydn, Hiram, ed. The Portable Elizabethan Reader. New York: Viking Press, 1946. 688pp.   313

Sp's letter to Ralegh (pp. 409-14); "The Bower of Bliss," FQ, II, xii, 72-75 (pp. 623-4); Epith (pp. 624-37).

Hayward, John. English Poetry: A Catalogue of First & Early Editions of Works of the English Poets from Chaucer to the Present Day Exhibited by the National Book League at 7 Albemarle Street, London 1947. National Book League: Cambridge University Press, 1947. 141pp.   314

(1) FQ, 1590; (2) FQ, 1596; (3) Complaints, 1591, bound with SC, 1597 (5th ed.), 4 Hymns, 1596, Proth, 1596, and Sidney's Defense of Poesie, 1595; (4) Proth, 1596. All lent by the Duke of Devonshire (pp. 13-4).

Hayward, John, ed. The Faber Book of English Verse. London: Faber and Faber, 1958. 484 pp.   315

First ed. 1956. FQ, I, ix, 33-42; II, xi, 22-25, xii, 70-75; VII, vii, 18-25; Amor 63 and 70; Proth (pp. 14-26).

Hayward, John, ed. The Penguin Book of English Verse. Harmondsworth: Penguin Books, 1956. 484pp.   316

Sp, pp. 14-26. FQ, I, ix, 33-42, II, xi, 22-25, xii, 70-75, VII, vii, 18-25; Amor 63 and 70; Proth (pp. 14-26).

Henderson, Philip, ed. The Shepherd's Calendar and Other Poems. Everyman's Library. London: Dent, 1965. 376 pp.   317

Reprint of 1932 ed.

Heninger, S. K., Jr., ed. Selections from the Poetical Works of Edmund Spenser. Boston: Houghton Mifflin, 1970. 821 pp.   318

General introduction with general bibliography (pp. vii-xii). SC complete with E. K.'s dedicatory epistle and general argument; TM, MHT, Muiop; CCCHA; 31 sonnets from Amor, Epith; 4 Hymnes; Proth; letter to Raleigh and FQ, I, II, VI, and VII; glossary of archaisms. Each major selection has own brief introduction, often with specific references to important studies supplementing general bibliography. Glosses and notes on the page they elucidate.

Hepburn, James G., ed. Poetic Design: Handbook and Anthology. New York: Macmillan, 1966. 362 pp.   319

Proth (pp. 192-196).

Herbert, David, ed. The Penguin Book of Narrative Verse. Harmondsworth, Middlesex, England: Penguin Books, 1960. 462 pp.   320

FQ, I, viii, 2-25.

Herrington, H. W., ed. English Masterpieces, 700-1900. 2 vols., revised ed.

New York: Norton, 1937. Vol. 1, 952 pp.   321

First ed. 1931. Sp in vol. 1. Intro. (p. 242). Intro. to FQ, I, i-iii; Epith (pp. 242-97).

Hibbard, Addison, ed. Writers of the Western World. Boston: Houghton Mifflin, 1942. 1261pp.   322

Part 2, The Romantic Mood, includes an introduction to Sp; Letter to Raleigh; FQ, I, Proem, i-ii (pp. 534-49).

Hieatt, A. Kent, and Constance Hieatt, eds. Edmund Spenser: Selected Poetry. New York: Appleton-Century-Crofts, 1970. 155 pp.   323

Intro. (pp. vii-xvii). October from SC; 7 sonnets from Amor; Epith; FQ, I, ii, 7-45, II, xii, 42-87, III, vi, 4-53, ix, 1-36, 52-53, x, xi, 1-3, 7-55, xii, IV, i, 1-4, x, VI, ix, 5-45, x, 1-29; Bibliography (pp. 153-5).

Hieatt, A. Kent, and William Park, eds. The College Anthology of British and American Verse. Boston: Allyn and Bacon, 1964. 631 pp.   324

Six sonnets from Amor; Proth (pp. 21-29).

Hobsbaum, Philip, ed. Ten Elizabethan Poets: Wyatt, Chapman, Marston, Stanyhurst, Golding, Harington, Raleigh, Greville, Sidney, Spenser. London: Longmans, 1969. 199 pp.   325

Intro. to each poet. Finds Greville superior to Sidney and Sp.

Honey, William Bowyer, ed. The Broadway Book of English Verse. London: Routledge, 1940. 488pp.   326

First published in 1939 under title The Sacred Fire. Introduction in two parts: nature of poetry (pp. 1-12), historical periods in English poetry (pp. 12-25). December from SC, pp. 45-52; Epith, pp. 64-75; Amor 34, 73, 68, 67, pp. 89-91.

Honig, Edwin, ed. Spenser. New York: Dell, 1968. 366 pp. 327

Intro. (pp. 7-19). FQ, I, Two Cantos of Mutabilitie, Letter to Raleigh (pp. 27-220). SC, April, August, October (pp. 221-46). MHT, Muiop, 21 sonnets from Amor, Epith, 4 Hymns, and Proth (pp. 221-356).

Hopkins, Kenneth, ed. The English Lyric. Brussels: Editions de Visscher, 1945. 272pp. 328

For Belgian students and readers; glossarial footnotes in French. Includes only short lyrics that can be printed on one page. Amor 75 (p. 68).

Inglis, Fred, ed. English Poetry 1550-1660. London: Methuen, 1965. 242pp. 329

Perigot's and Cuddy's Roundelay from Aug. of SC; a sonnet, "sweet is the rose, but grows upon a briar," attributed to Sp in England's Helicon; Amor 75 (pp. 60-63). Glosses to Roundelay (p. 214); biographical note (p. 231).

Irwin, John, and Jocelyn Herbert, eds. Sweete Themmes: A Chronicle in Prose and Verse. Foreword by W. J. Brown. London: Max Parish, 1951. 272pp. 330

An anthology on the Thames. Proth, pp. 27-32.

Jeffares, Alexander Norman, ed. Seven Centuries of Poetry: Chaucer to Dylan Thomas. New ed. London: Longmans, 1960. 463 pp. 331

First ed. 1955. Proth; Amor 67, 75; FQ I, xi, 10-14; ix, 39-40 (pp. 38-45).

Judson, Jerome, Ed. Poetry: Premeditated Art. Boston: Houghton Mifflin, 1968. 542 pp. 332

Short discussion of English sonnet forms, including Spenserian (p. 173). Amor 67, 75 (p. 473).

Kellogg, Robert, and Oliver Steele, eds. Edmund Spenser: Books I and II of The

Faerie Queene, the Mutability Cantos, and Selections from the Minor Poetry. New York: Odyssey Press, 1965. 542 pp. 333

Intro. to Bks. I and II of FQ with summary of plot and allegory of each book (pp. 1-73). FQ, I and II, with explanatory notes (pp. 79-398). Intro. and Mutability Cantos; Intro. to SC, and November; Intro. to Amor, and 26 sonnets; Intro. and Epith; Intro. and 4 Hymns; Intro. and Muiop (pp. 399-538).

Kermode, Frank, ed. Edmund Spenser: Selections from the Minor Poems and *The Faerie Queene*. London: Oxford University Press, 1965. 233 pp. 334

Intro.; chronology of Sp's life; bibliography (pp. 1-30); October from SC; CCCHA, 11. 835-94; Epith; Letter to Raleigh; FQ, I, i, 1-27, ii, 20-26, iv, 17-37, vii, 29-33, ix, 45-54, x, 46-68, xi, 29-34, 46-48; II, vii, xii, 70-87; III, vi, 26-52; IV, x, 23-52; V, vii, 1-23, ix, 27-50; VI, x, 10-28; VII, vii, 3-27, 47-59.

Kermode, Frank. English Pastoral Poetry from the Beginnings to Marvell. New York: Barnes & Noble, 1952. 256 pp. 335

First requirement of pastoral difference between two ways of life, rustic and urban. Pastoral is "urban product." Golden Age theme in Virgil, taken over by pastoral in Christian era. Primitive resentment at struggles of life vitalizes myth of heroic age in relation to other primitive myths in "almost every recorded culture from Mycenaean to American Negro" (pp. 14-5). Common ground between satire, another urban genre, and pastoral (p. 16). Behind attitude toward Nature as uncomplicated and contemplative is its opposite, knowledge that Nature is rough, "and the difference between the cultivated and the natural is the difference between Ferdinand and Caliban" (pp. 17-8). Section on Renaissance Theories of Pastoral: Mantuan one of Sp's models in SC; Art-Nature antithesis philosophical basis of pastoral literature; relation between Nature and Art and Grace deeply examined in FQ. "In Spenser alone one may study almost every aspect of Renaissance Pastoral" (pp. 37-42). Prints August, October, and November from SC, Astro, FQ, VI, ix (pp. 90-131).

Kirk, Rudolf, and Clara Marburg Kirk, eds. Types of English Poetry. New York: Macmillan, 1940. 663pp.   336

Sp as narrative poet: selections from FQ, I, i (pp. 42-3); as lyric poet: selections from Proth and Epith (pp. 266-7).

Kirschbaum, Leo, ed. Edmund Spenser: Selected Poetry. Rev. and enl. New York: Holt, Rinehart and Winston, 1966. 677 pp.   337

Intro. (pp. vii-lvii). FQ, Letter to Raleigh, I (complete), selections from other books (omitted parts in synopsis form); August from SC; MHT (1. 943 to end); Muiop; 9 sonnets from Amor; Epith; Proth; HHOB and HOHL.

Kobler, Donald G., and Bertrand Evans, eds. Spenser to Goldsmith. New York: Macmillan, 1964. 387 pp.   338

Amor 37, 75, 79, and 26, with study questions (pp. 12-16).

Kroeber, Karl, and John O. Lyons, eds. Studying Poetry: A Critical Anthology of English and American Poems. New York: Harper, 1965. 605 pp.   339

Amor 62 (p. 14), 75 (p. 58), 70 (pp. 379-80), 37 (p. 392); FQ, VI, ix, 1-46 (pp. 82-94); Astro (pp. 193-9); Proth (pp. 399-400).

Lamson, Roy, and Hallett Smith, eds. The Golden Hind. New York: Norton, 1942. 846pp.   340

Elizabethan prose and poetry. Sp (pp. 117-9); April, August, and October from SC; 21 sonnets from Amor; Epith; HHOB; Proth (pp. 120-67). Rev. ed. 1956, includes same Sp selections (pp. 310-59) and adds Mutability Cantos (pp. 360-90).

Leavenworth, Russell E., ed. Poems From Six Centuries. San Francisco: Chandler, 1962. 309 pp.   341

Contains FQ, II, xii, 74 ("Ah see the Virgin Rose")-75 (p. 6).

Lieder, Paul Robert, Robert Morss Lovett, and Robert Kilburn Root, eds. British Poetry and Prose. Rev. ed. 2 vols. Boston: Houghton Mifflin, 1938.   342

The Elizabethan Period, I, 205-8. Introduction to Sp, I, 219-20. Letter to Ralegh; FQ, I, Proem, i-iv, x-xi; Amor 1, 34, 79, 82; Proth (I, 222-74).

Locke, Louis G., William M. Gibson, and George Arms, eds. Introduction to Literature. 4th ed. New York: Holt, 1962. 826pp.   343

First published 1948. Amor 34, 70, 75 (pp.19-20).

Lowry, Howard Foster, and Willard Thorp, eds. An Oxford Anthology of English Poetry. 2nd ed. New York: Oxford University Press, 1956. 1356pp.   344

August from SC; 7 sonnets from Amor; Upon a Day; Epith; Letter to Ralegh and FQ, Proem, Book I (pp. 100-231).

Lucie-Smith, Edward, ed. The Penguin Book of Elizabethan Verse. Baltimore: Penguin Books, 1965. 288 pp.   345

Intro., p. 249. Amor 67, 75, 84; Proth; HOHL, ll. 22-35; FQ, III, vi, 43-48; Iambicum Trimetrum (pp. 249-62).

McClure, Norman E., ed. Sixteenth-Century English Poetry. Harper English Literature Series. Karl J. Holzknecht, general ed. New York: Harper, 1954. 623pp.   346

Introduction to Sp; April and October eclogues from SC; 21 sonnets from Amor; Epith; HHOB; Proth; Mutability Cantos from FQ (pp. 235-303).

McCollum, John I., Jr., ed. The Age of Elizabeth. Boston: Houghton Mifflin, 1960. 152 pp.   347

Selected source materials in Elizabethan social and literary history. Intro. to Sp (p. 115), abridgments of E.K.'s letter to Gabriel Harvey prefacing SC, Sp's letters to Harvey of Oct. 1579 and Apr. 1580, Letter to Raleigh (pp. 116-25).

Mack, Maynard, gen. ed. English Masterpieces: An Anthology of Imaginative Literature from Chaucer to T.S. Eliot. 8 vols. New York: Prentice-Hall, 1950.
                                              348

Vol. 3, Renaissance Poetry, ed. Leonard Dean. Bower of Bliss, FQ, II, xii, 42-87; Garden of Adonis, FQ, III, vi, 26-52; The Graces of Courtesy, FQ, VI, x, 1-29; The House of Holiness and The New Jerusalem, FQ, I, x; Epith; Proth (pp. 52-115).

Maclean, Hugh, ed. Edmund Spenser's Poetry: Authoritative Texts; Criticism. New York: Norton, 1968. 662 pp. 349

FQ: Letter to Raleigh; I; II, i, 1-34, vii, viii, 1-9, xii; III; VI, Proem, ix, x, 1-30; Cantos of Mutabilitie; Editor's Note (pp. 399-406). SC: April, October; Editor's Note (pp. 424-7). Fifteen sonnets from Amor, Epith; Editor's Note (pp. 445-8). 4 Hymns; Editor's Note (pp. 483-6). Contemporary and 17th-century criticism: E. K.'s Dedicatory Epistle to SC to John Dryden (pp. 499-510). Criticism in

the 18th and early 19th centuries: John Hughes to William Hazlitt (pp. 511-39). Twentieth-century criticism: prints in part works listed herein by Douglas Bush (560), Kathleen Williams (1740), Paul J. Alpers (1230), Graham Hough (1449), Northrop Frye (1378), S. K. Heninger, Jr. (1820), A. S. P. Woodhouse (1752), Thomas P. Roche, Jr. (2049), William Blissett (2170), Hallett Smith (1091), J. W. Lever (2437), Louis Martz (2451), Thomas M. Greene (2382), and William Nelson (961). Selected Bibliography (pp. 659-62).

Magill, Frank N., ed. Masterpieces of World Literature in Digest Form. First Series. New York: Harper, 1949. 1144pp.   350

FQ "digested," pp. 264-6.

Masefield, John, ed. My Favorite English Poems. Freeport, N. Y.: Books for Libraries Press, 1969. 310 pp.   351

Repr. of 1950 ed. Snippets from October of SC; and from FQ, I, iv, 33-35, ix, 40, xii, 42, II, vii, 29-30, vi, 31, 42, xii, 23, 47, 71, 75, III, xi, 28, 50-55 (pp. 37-43).

Miles, Josephine, ed. The Poem: A Critical Anthology. Englewood Cliffs, N.J.: Prentice-Hall, 1959. 553 pp.   352

Amor 1; Epith (pp. 145-57).

Miles, Josephine, ed. The Ways of the Poem. Englewood Cliffs, N.J.: Prentice-Hall, 1961. 440 pp.   353

Intro. to chap. 3, "Tone of Exclamation and Invocation," briefly compares Sp's Amor and Epith with Milton's Lycidas (pp. 119-20). Amor 1; Epith (pp. 122-134).

Miller, James E., Jr., and Bernice Slote, eds. The Dimensions of Poetry: A Critical Anthology. New York: Dodd, Mead, 1962. 742pp.   354

Amor 34 (p. 65), 69 (p. 200).

Millet, Fred B., Arthur W. Hoffman, and David R. Clark, eds. Reading Poetry. 2nd ed. New York: Harper, 1968. 510pp.   355

> First printed 1950. Proth (pp. 444-449).

Morgan, Edwin, ed. Collins Albatross Book of Longer Poems: English and American Poetry from the Fourteenth Century to the Present Day. Freeport, New York: Books for Libraries Press, 1969. 736 pp.   356

> Repr. of 1963 ed. CCCHA, Epith (pp. 97-133).

Muir, Kenneth, ed. Elizabethan Lyrics. Life, Literature, and Thought Library. London: Harrap, 1952. 219pp.   357

> See introductory section on sonnets, pp. 14-28. Five sonnets from Amor; Lay of Eliza from April of SC.

Mutter, R. P. C., ed. Spenser's Minor Poems: A Selection. Methuen English Classics. London: Methuen, 1957. 147pp.   358

> Introduction, pp. vii-ix; Chronological Table, pp. xi-xii; February, April, May, August, October, November from SC; ll. 65-88 from VG; ll. 1-342 from MHT; I, II, IV, VII from VB; I, III, V, VI from VP; ll. 200-289 and 835-955 from CCCHA; Astro; 40 sonnets from Amor; Epith; Proth; notes, pp. 105-28; glossary, pp. 129-47.

Myers, Catherine, ed. Edmund Spenser: *The Faerie Queene.* New York: Barnes & Noble, 1969.   359

Nelson, William, ed. Edmund Spenser: Selected Poetry. New York: Random House, 1964. 612 pp.   360

> Intro.; biographical note; publicaton dates of Sp's works; selected bibliography (pp. vii-xxxvii); FQ, I; II, Proem, xi-xii; III; IV, Proem, x; V,

Proem, vii, 1-24; VI, Proem, ix, x, 1-30; Mutabilitie Cantos; Letter to Raleigh (pp. 5-453); January, April, May, June August, October, and December from SC; MHT: Muiop; CCCHA (abridged); 11 sonnets from Amor; Epith; Proth; 4 Hymns; glossary (pp. 456-612).

Osgood, Charles G., Compiler. A Concordance to the Poems of Edmund Spenser. Gloucester, Mass.: Peter Smith, 1963. 997 pp.   361

> Repr. of 1915 ed.

Osgood, Charles G., and Marvin T. Herrick, eds. Eleven British Writers: Beowulf to Arnold. Boston: Houghton Mifflin, 1940. 1396pp.   362

> Introduction to Sp, pp. 177-88. April, June, October, and November from SC; Letter to Ralegh and FQ, Proem, I, i-x, xii; CCCHA; 20 sonnets from Amor; Epith; 4 Hymns; Proth (pp. 189-327).

Owen, Charles A., Jr., ed. Discussions of the Canterbury Tales. Boston: Heath, 1961. 110 pp.   363

> Quotes FQ, IV, ii, 32-34 (pp. 1-2).

Palgrave, Francis Turner, comp. The Golden Treasury of the Best Songs & Lyrical Poems in the English Language. With a fifth book selected by John Press. London: Oxford University Press, 1964. 615 pp.   364

> First pub. 1861. Proth (pp. 32-7).

Pasinetti, P.M., ed. Masterpieces of the Renaissance, from Literature of Western Culture Through the Renaissance, pp. 1135-1694. Vol. 1 of World Masterpieces. Rev. ed. Ed. Maynard Mack and others. New York: Norton, 1965. 1704 pp.   365

> Intro. to FQ (pp. 1158-1160); biography of Sp (pp. 1180-81); FQ, II, xii, 42-87 (pp. 1334-1345).

Peacock, William, ed. English Prose. London: Oxford University Press, 1944-1945. 5 vols.   366

Reprint of edition of 1921-1922. Vol. 1, Wycliffe to Clarendon, includes Sp's letter to Ralegh, pp. 232-7.

Perrine, Laurence, ed. Poetry; Theory and Practice. New York: Harcourt, 1962. 233 pp.   367

Proth (pp. 183-5).

Peterson, Houston, and William S. Lynch, eds. Poet to Poet: A Treasury of Golden Criticism. New York: Prentice-Hall, 1945. 368pp.   368

Poems on poets. Sp on Chaucer, FQ, IV, ii, 32 (p. 50); Gabriel Harvey, Walter Ralegh, and Leigh Hunt on Sp (pp. 62-4); Sp's sonnet to Ralegh (p. 65).

Poirier, Michel, ed. La Reine des Fées (The Faery Queene). Collection Bilingue. Paris: Edition Montaigne, 1950. 369

Introduction and notes.

Pratt, Robert A., D. C. Allen, and others, eds. Masters of British Literature. 2 vols. Boston: Houghton Mifflin, 1958.   370

Edmund Spenser, ed. D.C. Allen. Introduction; January and December from SC; 18 sonnets from Amor; Epith; FQ, II, i-ix, xi-xii (I, 149-259).

Quintana, Ricardo, ed. Two Hundred Poems. Freeport, N. Y.: Books for Libraries Press, 1969. 393 pp.   371

Repr. of 1947 ed. Introduction: Poetry and the Everyday Reader (pp. xvii-xxxii). Amor 3, 9, 18, 34, 67; Proth (pp. 22-31).

Read, Herbert, and Bonamy Dobrée, eds. The London Book of English Verse. Rev. ed. New York: Macmillan, 1952. 891pp.   372

First published 1949. Sp represented in 4 of 10 sections. Songs and Incantations: roundelay from August of SC (pp. 85-7); The Poetry of Sentiment: 2 sonnets from Amor (pp. 165-6); Descriptions and Observations: Cave of Despair (FQ, I, ix), Bower of Bliss (FQ, II, xii), and Amor 64 (pp. 348-55); The Symphonic Poem: Proth (pp. 738-43). See Index of Authors.

Reeves, James, ed. The Cassell Book of English Poetry. New York: Harper & Row, 1965. Unpaged. 1002 numbered poems.   373

Amor 75 (#161).

Ribner, Irving, and Harry Morris, eds. Poetry: A Critical and Historical Introduction. Chicago: Scott, Foresman, 1962. 521pp.   374

Amor 68, 75, 81; Proth (pp. 72-78).

Rollins, Hyder E., and Herschel Baker, eds. The Renaissance in England. Boston: Heath, 1954. 1014pp.   375

Introduction to Sp (pp. 330-2); prefatory matter and January, April, July, and October from SC with glosses; MHT (in part); CCCHA (in part); 19 sonnets from Amor; Epith; Proth; HHOL and HOHL (pp. 332-79).

Ruoff, James E., ed. Major Elizabethan Poetry and Prose. New York: Thomas Y. Crowell, 1972. 993 pp.   376

Intro. to Sp and FQ (pp. 283-95). Twenty-four sonnets from Amor; Epith; Letter to Raleigh; FQ, I, Proem, i-ii, iii, 1-15, iv, 1-5, vii, 7-16, viii, 29-50, ix, 21-54, x, 1-30, 53-68; III; VI, x, 5-30; VII, viii.

Russell, H. K., William Wells, and Donald A. Stauffer, eds. Literature in English. New York: Holt, 1948. 1174pp.   377

April from SC; Letter to Raleigh; FQ, I, Proem, i and iv; 5 sonnets from Amor (pp. 72-109).

Rhys, Ernest, ed. The Golden Treasury of Longer Poems. Everyman's Library, 746. New and enl. ed. London: Dent, 1950. 405pp.   378

First published 1921. Proth, pp. 66-70.

Sanders, Charles, Robin R. Rice, and Walt J. Cantillon, eds. Synthesis: Responses to Literature. New York: Knopf, 1971. 750 pp.   379

Amor 77; Epith (pp. 516-23).

Schmidt, Karlernst, ed. Spenser's Epithalamion und Hymnen. Hamburger Hochschultexte, 1. Hamburg: Hansischer Gildenverlag, 1948. 55pp.   380

Schneider, Elizabeth W., ed. Poems and Poetry. New York: American Book Co., 1964. 510pp.   381

Amor 34, 75 (pp. 186-7).

Seymour-Smith, Martin, ed. Longer Elizabethan Poems. New York: Barnes & Noble, 1972. 261 pp.   382

Includes Proth.

Shafer, Robert, ed. From Beowulf to Thomas Hardy. New ed. 2 vols. New York: Odyssey Press, 1939-1940.   383

First published 1924. Introduction to the Renaissance and the Protestant Revolt, 1485-1660 (I, 251-92; SC and FQ, 277-9); introduction to Sp, letter to Ralegh, FQ, I, and Epith (I, 352-443).

Shaw, Charles Gray, ed. The 101 World's Classics. Garden City, N. Y.: Doubleday, Doran, 1937. 823pp.   384

Proth, pp. 407-12. One of the 15 poems in the book.

Shumaker, Wayne, ed. An Approach to Poetry. Englewood Cliffs, N.J.: Prentice-Hall, 1965. 443 pp.   385

October from SC; seven sonnets from Amor; Proth (pp. 136-50).

Sillar, Frederick Cameron, and Ruth Mary Meyler. The Symbolic Pig: An Anthology of Pigs in Literature and Art. Illus. Edinburgh: Oliver and Boyd, 1961. 193 pp.   386

FQ, II, xii, 86-87 (p. 98).

Simpson, Louis, ed. An Introduction to Poetry. New York: St. Martin's Press, 1967. 420 pp.   387

Epith (pp. 72-84).

Singh, J. B., ed. The Faerie Queene, Book First. Agra: Nav Jeevan Prakashan, 1962. 255 pp.   388

Sitwell, Dame Edith, ed. The Atlantic Book of British and American Poetry. Boston: Little, Brown, 1958. 1092pp.   389

Introductory note on Sp, p. 133. Song of Eliza from April and elegy from November of SC; Amor 64; Proth; 10 stanzas from Epith; 4 stanzas from FQ, II, xii (pp. 133-50).

Smith, A. J. M., ed. Seven Centuries of Verse: English and American. 3rd ed., rev. and enl. New York: Scribner's, 1967. 818 pp.   390

First published 1947. Amor 68, 70, 75; Epith (pp. 77-89).

Smith, Lewis Worthington, Lawrence L. Smith, and Harold Francis Watson, eds. Types and Times in English Literature. 4 vols. Oklahoma City: Harlow Publishing Corp., 1940.   391

Introduction to 16th century literature, I, 287-90. Introduction to Sp; Amor 3, 21, 51; Letter to Ralegh; FQ, I, Proem, i, 1-28; Epith (I, 322-41).

Snyder, Franklyn Bliss, and Robert Grant Martin, eds. A Book of English Literature. 4th ed. 2 vols. New York: Macmillan, 1942.   392

First published 1916. Introduction to The Elizabethan Age, ed. and rev. by Roy Lamson, Jr., I, 238-79. Introduction to Sp; introduction to FQ; Letter to Ralegh; FQ, I, Proem, i-ii, xi-xii; Epith; 8 sonnets from Amor; Proth (I, 296-346).

Sowton, Ian C., ed. Edmund Spenser: A Selection of his Works. New York: Odyssey Press, 1968. 457 pp.　　393

Intro. includes sections on Sp's life, SC, FQ and influences on it, the allegory, and minor poems; historical and biographical data (pp. vii-lxxxix). Epistle dedicatory and Generall Argument to SC, February, April, and December (pp. 1-56). FQ, I, Two Cantos of Mutabilitie, Letter to Raleigh (pp. 57-331). Fifty-four sonnets from Amor and Epith; Proth; 4 Hymns (pp. 333-453).

Spencer, Hazelton, ed. British Literature: *Beowulf* to Sheridan. 2nd ed. Boston: Heath, 1963. 992 pp.　　394

Intro. to Sp (pp. 299-300). Letter to Raleigh; FQ, I, i-ii, iii, 1-37, vii, 1-18, 43-52, ix; Amor 1, 70, 75, 82; Epith (pp. 301-36).

Spencer, Hazelton, Walter E. Houghton, and Herbert Barrows, eds. British Literature. 2 vols. Boston: Heath, 1951. 395

Vol. 1, Beowulf to Sheridan, ed. Hazelton Spencer. Introduction to Renaissance, I, 213-30. Introduction to Sp; Letter to Raleigh; FQ, I, Proem, i-ii, 1-8; Amor 1, 70, 75, 82; Epith (I, 289-307).

Spenser, Edmund. Amoretti and Epithalamion, 1595. Menston, England: Scolar Press, 1968. 139 pp.　　396

Facsimile repr. of 1595 ed.

Spenser, Edmund. Amoretti and Epithalamion. 1 vol., unpaged. New York: Da Capo Press, 1969.　　397

Facsimile reproduction of the copy (1595) in the John Rylands Library.

Spenser, Edmund. The Complaints. Ed. W. L. Renwick. St. Clair Shores, Mich.: Scholarly Press, 1970. 273 pp.　　398

Repr. of 1928 ed.

Spenser, Edmund. Complete Poetical Works of Edmund Spenser. Ed. R. E. Neil Dodge. Cambridge Editions of the Poets. Boston: Houghton Mifflin, 1947. 852pp.　　399

Reissue of edition of 1908. A standard one-volume edition.

Spenser, Edmund. The Faerie Queene, Disposed into Twelve Books Fashioning xii Morall Vertues. 2 vols. Oxford: Oxford University Press, 1953.　　400

Printed for members of the Limited Editions Club. Introduction by John Hayward, decorations by John Austen, and illustrations engraved in wood by Agnes Miller Parker.

Spenser, Edmund. The Faerie Queene. Illus. by John Austen and Agnes Miller Parker. Coronation Edition. 2 vols. New York: Heritage Press, 1953.　　401

Spenser, Edmund. The Faerie Queene. Intro. by J. W. Hales. 2 vols. New York: Dutton, 1962.　　402

Repr. of original 3 vol. ed., 1897. In Everyman Library since 1910.

Spenser, Edmund. The Faerie Queene, Book III. Epithalamion. Phonodisc. Caedmon TC 1126, 1962.　　402A

Two sides, 12 in., 33 1/3 rpm. Read by Micheál MacLiammoir. Program notes.

Spenser, Edmund. Of the Brood of Angels. Foreword by Sarah A. Davies. Madison, N. J.: Golden Hind Press, 1939. 32pp.　　403

A sonnet sequence from Amor.

Spenser, Edmund. The Poetical Works of Edmund Spenser in Three Volumes. Ed. J. C. Smith and E. de Selincourt. Oxford: Clarendon Press, 1964.   404

Repr. of 1909-1910 ed.

Spenser, Edmund. La Regina delle Fate. Ed. and trans. Carlo Izzo. Florence: Sansoni, 1954. 519pp.   405

FQ, I, with English text and Italian translation on facing pages. Long introduction presents a detailed study of Book I. Notes selected from Variorum and recent periodicals.

Spenser, Edmund. The Shepheardes Calender. Intro. by Oskar Sommer. New York: Burt Franklin, 1967. 112 pp.
        406

Facsimile of first ed. of 1579.

Spenser, Edmund. The Shepheardes Calender, 1579. Menston: Scolar Press, 1968. 128pp. (Facsimile reprint of First Edition.)   407

Spenser, Edmund. A View of the Present State of Ireland. Ed. W. L. Renwick. Illus. Oxford: Clarendon Press, 1970. 230 pp.   408

Repr. of 1934 ed. in modern spelling.

Spenser, Edmund. The Works of Edmund Spenser. Variorum Edition. Ed. Edwin Greenlaw, Charles Grosvenor Osgood, and Frederick Morgan Padelford. 11 vols. Baltimore: Johns Hopkins Press, 1966.   409

Repr. of original ed. (1932-1949), including A.C. Judson's Life of Spenser. See 171.

Spenser, Edmund. The Works of Edmund Spenser. A Variorum Edition. Index. Compiled by Charles Grosvenor Osgood. Baltimore: Johns Hopkins Press, 1957. 125pp.   410

Spenser, Edmund. The Works of Edmund Spenser. A Variorum Edition. The Minor Poems, vol. 1. Ed. C. G. Osgood and Henry G. Lotspeich. Assisted by Dorothy E. Mason. Baltimore: Johns Hopkins Press, 1943. 734pp.   411

Texts (pp. 3-230) and commentary (pp. 231-570): SC, Daph, CCCHA, Astro, Doleful Lay, and 4 Hymns, with critical appendices on first and last named works. Those on SC: General Criticism, Pastoral Sources, The Moral Eclogues, Date and Composition; Language and Style; Design; Metre; Early Fame; Identity of E. K.; Rosalind. Those on 4 Hymns: General Criticism; Date and Retraction; Sources; Form; Style. Index of sources and analogues, Textual Appendix of variant readings and critical notes on texts, and Bibliography (pp. 725-34).

Spenser, Edmund. The Works of Edmund Spenser. A Variorum Edition. The Minor Poems, vol. 2. Ed. C. G. Osgood and Henry G. Lotspeich. Assisted by Dorothy E. Mason. Baltimore: Johns Hopkins Press, 1947. 745pp.   412

Texts (pp. 3-269) and commentary (pp. 271-520), poems in Theatre, Complaints, Amor and Epith, Proth, commendatory sonnets, and fragments. Titles of "lost" works and sources of allusions to them (p. 270). Critical appendices deal with general criticism, date and composition, sources, influences, form and style, allegory, etc. of poems in Complaints (RT, TM, VG, MHT, Muiop, VB and VP), and with biographical significance of Amor, Epith, and Proth. Textual appendix of variant readings and critical notes on texts, Index of sources and analogues, and Bibliography (pp. 735-45).

Spenser, Edmund. The Works of Edmund Spenser. A Variorum Edition. The Prose Works. Ed. Rudolf Gottfried. Baltimore: Johns Hopkins Press, 1949. 570pp.   413

Texts (pp. 5-245) and commentary (pp. 247-440): Letters, Axiochus, View, and A Brief Note of Ireland. Appendices on each of these, and Verse in Spenser's Prose (pp. 441-538); Bibliography (pp. 539-46); Index (pp. 547-70).

Spenser, Edmund. The Works of Edmund Spenser. A Variorum Edition. Vol. 4, The Faerie Queene, Book 4. Ed. Ray Heffner. Baltimore: Johns Hopkins Press, 1935. 357pp.   414

Listed in Atkinson, p. 55.

Spenser, Edmund. The Works of Edmund Spenser. A Variorum Edition. Vol. 5, The Faerie Queene, Book 5. Ed. Ray Heffner. Baltimore: Johns Hopkins Press, 1936. 375pp.   415

Text (pp. 1-152) with commentary (pp. 153-268) and critical appendices: The Virtue of Justice and the Plan of Book V, Historical Allegory, The Political Allegory of Canto II, The Italian Romances, and Index of Sources and Analogues. Textual appendix gives critical notes (pp. 366-73) by James G. McManaway. Bibliography (p. 375) supplements bibliographies in vols. 1-4 of Variorum FQ.

Spenser, Edmund. The Works of Edmund Spenser. A Variorum Edition. Vol. 6, The Faerie Queene, Books 6 and 7. Ed. C. G. Osgood, F. M. Padelford, and Ray Heffner. Assisted by James G. McManaway, Dorothy E. Mason, and Brents Stirling. Baltimore: Johns Hopkins Press, 1938. 506pp.   416

Texts of Book VI (pp. 1-149) and Cantos of Mutabilitie (pp. 151-81), commentary (pp. 183-316), critical appendices, index of sources and analogues, textual appendix including variant readings, critical notes on the text, and a study of punctuation of FQ. Appendices to Book VI: The Plan and Conduct of Book VI. The

Prototype of Sir Calidore, and The Historical Allegory; to Book VII: The Sources and Philosophical Significance, and The Date of the Cantos and their Relation to FQ. Bibliography (pp. 505-6) supplements bibliographies in vols. 1-5 of Variorum FQ.

Spenser, Edmund, trans. Axiochus. Ed. F. M. Padelford. Baltimore: Johns Hopkins Press, 1934.   417

Listed in Atkinson, p. 63. See 658, 2605, 2608.

Stageberg, Norman C., and Wallace L. Anderson, eds. Poetry as Experience. New York: American Book Co., 1952. 518pp.   418

In Part I: The Essentials of Poetry in section on Alliteration and Assonance, Amor 47, p. 126; in section on Cultural Background, Amor 55, pp. 232-3. In Part II: Poems for Study, FQ, II, xii, 70-76, and Proth, pp. 272-9. Notes on Sp, pp. 463-4, 471.

Stallman, R. W., and R. E. Watters, eds. The Creative Reader: An Anthology of Fiction, Drama, Poetry. New York: Ronald Press, 1962. 992 pp.   419

Amor 30 (p. 725); notes and questions (p. 963).

Steele, Oliver L., and Robert L. Kellogg, eds. The First Book of Spenser's Faerie Queene. Charlottesville: Dept. of English, University of Virginia, 1961. 150 pp.   420

Steele, Oliver L., and Robert L. Kellogg, eds. The Second Book of Spenser's Faerie Queene. Charlottesville: Dept. of English, University of Virginia, 1962.   421

Strode, Hudson, ed. Immortal Lyrics: An Anthology of English Lyric Poetry from Sir Walter Ralegh to A. E. Housman. New York: Random House, 1938. 326pp.   422

Introduction, pp. 1-27. Amor 89 (p. 41).

Swallow, Alan, ed. The Rinehart Book of Verse. New York: Holt, Rinehart and Winston, 1965. 364 pp.   423

Repr. of 1952 ed. Amor 19, 72, 67; Proth; FQ, VI, x, 6-16 (pp. 34-44).

Taylor, Walt, ed. English Sonnets. London: Longmans, 1947. 195pp.   424

Sp, pp. 6-18. Twenty-four sonnets from Amor. Ralegh's A Vision upon the Faery Queen, p. 18.

Taylor, Warren, and Donald Hall, eds. Poetry in English. 2nd ed. New York: Macmillan, 1970. 758pp.   425

First published 1963. Amor 34, 55, 67; Proth (pp. 72-77).

Thomas, R. S., ed. The Penguin Book of Religious Verse. Baltimore: Penguin Books, 1963. 192 pp.   426

Headings: God, Self, Nothing, It, and All. Under All appears FQ, I, ix, 43 (p. 165).

Thomas, Wright, and Stuart Gerry Brown, eds. Reading Poems: An Introduction to Critical Study. New York: Oxford University Press, 1941. 781pp.   427

Part I. Lyric Poems, Group Five has Proth, pp. 46-50; Part II. Sonnets has Amor 21, 23, 34, 62, 75, pp. 157-9.

Thompson, Stith, and John Gassner, eds. Our Heritage of World Literature. Rev. ed. New York: Holt, Rinehart and Winston, 1964. 1432 pp.   428

Repr. of 1938 ed. Proth (pp. 1142-44).

Thomson, Patricia, ed. Elizabethan Lyrical Poets. London: Routledge and Kegan Paul, 1967. 219 pp.   429

Intro. includes discussion of SC, Amor, and Proth (pp. 1-22). Selections from Sp: roundelay from August of SC, Up, then Melpomene

from November of SC; song, "Ah see, whoso fair thing" (FQ, II, xii, 74-75); 5 sonnets from Amor; Proth (pp. 23-38).

Tobin, James Edward, Victor M. Hamm, and William H. Hines, eds. College Book of English Literature. New York: American Book Company, 1949. 1156pp.   430

Introduction to Sp; 6 sonnets from Amor; Proth; Letter to Ralegh; FQ, I, i and vii (pp. 233-53).

Trilling, Lionel, ed. The Experience of Literature. Garden City, N.Y.: Doubleday, 1967. 1320 pp.   431

Epith (pp. 978-89).

Trilling, Lionel, ed. The Experience of Literature: A Reader with Commentaries. New York: Holt, Rinehart and Winston, 1967. 508 pp.   432

Epith (pp. 166-177).

Tydeman, William, ed. English Poetry, 1400-1580. New York: Barnes & Noble, 1970. 283 pp.   433

October from SC, without Gloss (pp. 155-9), commentary (pp. 264-9).

Unger, Leonard, and William Van O'Connor, eds. Poems for Study. New York: Rinehart, 1959. 743 pp.   434

Repr. of 1953 ed. Short biography; FQ, V, Proem; Amor 34; discussion of Sp's sonnet style, centering on Amor 34; Amor 46, 70, 75, 79; Epith (pp. 57-75).

Untermeyer, Louis. Love Sonnets. Illus. Ben Shahn. New York: Odyssey Press, 1964. 45 pp.   435

Intro. (pp. 6-7); notes (pp. 42-5). Examples from Dante to Alice Meynell; Amor 8 (p. 15). Sp's sonnets "were inspired by Elizabeth Boyle, who became Spenser's wife and who shared his spectacular career from riches to rags" (p. 42).

Untermeyer, Louis, ed. A Treasury of Great Poems, English and American. New York: Simon and Schuster, 1955. 1288 pp. 436

Includes short biography and account of Sp's career (pp. 216-7). The Dance from FQ, VI, x, 6-11, and 7 sonnets from Amor (pp. 220-2).

Van Doren, Mark, ed. An Anthology of World Poetry. Rev. and enl. ed. New York: Harcourt, 1964. 1467pp. 437

First published 1928. Amor 70, 75, 89; Proth (pp. 1036-42).

Wallace, Robert, and James G. Taaffe, eds. Poems on Poetry: the Mirror's Garland. New York: Dutton, 1965. 328 pp. 438

October from SC (pp. 136-141).

Warburg, Sandol Stoddard, adaptor. Saint George and the Dragon, Being the Legend of the Red Cross Knight from the Faerie Queene. Illustrated by Pauline Baynes. Boston: Houghton Mifflin, 1963. 132 pp. 439

A slightly shortened version of FQ, I. Language modernized.

Ware, Sir James. Ancient Irish Histories: Works of Spenser, Campion, Hanmer, and Marlebrough. 2 vols. Port Washington, New York: Kennikat Press, 1970. 440

Repr. of 1809 ed. View in vol. 1. See 2563.

Warnock, Robert, and George K. Anderson, eds. Centuries of Transition: The Literature of the Middle Ages and of the Renaissance. Chicago: Scott, Foresman, 1950. 584pp. 441

Book two of a four-book series which also includes The Ancient Foundations, Tradition and Revolt, and Our Hundred Years. Chap. 2, Rebirth and Discovery, 1350 to 1650, includes under II. From Knight to Courtier, introduction to Sp; introduction to FQ; and FQ, I, i-ii, xii (pp. 395-414).

Weatherly, Edward H., and others, eds. The English Heritage. 2 vols. Boston: Ginn, 1945. 442

Intro. to Sp, Letter to Raleigh, FQ, I, Proem, i-ii, VI, ix, xii, Proth (I, 253-84).

Whiting, B. J., Fred B. Millett, Alexander M. Witherspoon, and others, eds. The College Survey of English Literature. 2 vols. New York: Harcourt, Brace, 1942. 443

The Sixteenth Century, I, 269-81. Introduction to Sp, I, 394-5. October from SC; Amor 1, 6, 34, 37, 67, 69; Epith; introduction to FQ, and I, i, xi-xii; II, xii, 42-75; III, vi, 29-52 (I, 395-431). Shorter rev. ed., 1952, Sp, pp. 227-55: Amor 1, 6, 34, 67, 75, 79; Epith; FQ, I, i, xi-xii; Proth.

Whitman, C. H. A Subject-Index to the Poems of Spenser. New York: Russell and Russell, 1966. 261 pp. 444

Repr. of 1918 ed.

Williams, Charles, ed. The New Book of English Verse. New York: Macmillan, 1936. 828pp. 445

Nothing included that is in Oxford Book of English Verse or The Golden Treasury (see 364). Selections from FQ: Despair (I, ix, 33-47); Garden of Adonis (III, vi, 30-42); Procession of Cupid (III, xii, 3-26); Nature (VII, vii, 1-8); Procession of Times and Seasons (VII, vii, 28-47); and October from SC (pp. 120-47).

Williams, John, ed. English Renaissance Poetry: A Collection of Shorter Poems from Skelton to Jonson. Garden City, N.Y.: Doubleday, 1963. 358 pp. 446

Intro. Epith, Proth, 6 sonnets from Amor (pp. 135-56).

Williams, Oscar, ed. Immortal Poems of the English Language: British and

American Poetry from Chaucer's Time to the Present Day. New York: Washington Square Press, 1960. 637pp.   447

    Amor 30, 75; Proth (pp. 38-43).

Williams, Oscar, ed. A Little Treasury of British Poetry. New York: Scribner's, 1951. 874 pp.   448

    Includes 5 sonnets from Amor; Epith (pp. 58-65).

Winstanley, Lilian, ed. The Faerie Queene, Book I. Cambridge: University Press, 1958. 293pp.   449

    First edition, 1915; frequently reprinted. Introduction has sections on historical allegory of Bk. I, pp. viii-xliii; and sources of Bk. I, pp. xliii-lxxx. Notes, pp. 217-93.

Wolff, Tatiana A., ed. The Faerie Queene, Book VI. Scholar's Library. London: Macmillan, 1959. 248pp.   450

    Introductory essay.

Wood, Paul Spencer, ed. Masters of English Literature. 2 vols. New York: Macmillan, 1942.   451

    Introduction to Sp, I, 167-77. Letter to Ralegh: FQ, II, Proem, i-ix, xi-xii; 10 sonnets from Amor; Epith (I, 178-299).

Zillman, Laurence J. The Art and Craft of Poetry: An Introduction. New York: Collier, 1966. 274pp.   452

    Amor 75 (p. 78).

Zitner, S. P., ed. The Mutabilitie Cantos. London: Nelson, 1968. 160 pp.   453

    Introduction deals with the structure, allegory and literary techniques of The Mutabilitie Cantos. Their status as part of Sp's Legend of Constancie casts doubt on attempts to study them in isolation.

GENERAL CRITICISM

Abrams, M.H. A Glossary of Literary Terms. 3rd ed. New York: Holt, Rinehart and Winston, 1971. 105 pp.   454

Repr. of 1961 ed. Sp cited under entries on Allegory, Alliteration, Elizabethan Age, Epic, Epithalamion, Pastoral, Platonic love, Sonnet, and Stanza.

Adams, Marjorie. The Literary Relations of Spenser and Ronsard. Doctoral diss., University of Texas, 1952. DDAAU, 1951-52, No. 19.   455

Comparison of their ideals of poetry, methods and materials in their poetry. Sp looked to Ronsard for theory, "perhaps for illustration." E. K.'s commentary on SC and Muret's on Les Amours, I, are similar in several respects. Both Ronsard and Sp wrote common variations on traditional pastoral themes. Their sonnets stem from the same general theory; "the narrative element and abrupt conclusion represent departures from tradition, whereas the Petrarchan conceits and Neo-Platonic ideas are largely conventional." Both try to localize their epithalamia, and they use many common images. Sp's letter to Ralegh suggests his knowledge of Ronsard. "His preparation of *The Faerie Queene* for publication, his choice of Arthurian matter, his marked didactic aim, all reflect Ronsard." The two poets "attempted to direct the literature of their respective countries along analogous lines."

Adams, Robert M. Reviving Spenser, NYRB, June 6, 1968, pp. 32-4.   456

Review article discussing K. Williams's Spenser's World of Glass (1741), C.S. Lewis's Spenser's Images of Life (1516), P.J. Alpers' The Poetry of The Faerie Queene (1231), R. Tuve's Allegorical Imagery (1152), and D. Cheney's Spenser's Image of Nature (1310). Chides Williams for pretending to simplify what is not simple; admires Fowler's edition of Lewis's book but feels that, as lecture notes, the material is overly schematic, without nuances; praises Alpers' skill in clearing the way for us to concentrate on Spenser's awareness of the moral and emotional duplicities surrounding certain ethical commonplaces and religious dogmas; praises Tuve for "a cogent and consecutive argument about the way allegory works" and for countering A. Fletcher's theory of allegory as a mode of compulsion (1361); and complains that Cheney's emphasis on FQ's richness and imaginative ambiguousness "leaves it wide open to charges of confusion and disorder."

Adams, Robert Martin. Milton and the Modern Critics. Ithaca: Cornell University Press, 1966. 231 pp.   457

First published 1955. Three essays appeared earlier in periodicals; see Foreword, 1955 (p. xiv). Criticism of other critics' criticism of Milton admittedly "contentious." Conclusion: Milton's ideas are dead, or no longer relevant. Sp's ideas as dead as Milton's— "the ladder of love is a Freudian joke and chivalry a long-antiquated antiquity"—but unlike Milton's they can be harmonized with "a coherent, accepted tradition of thought," and Sp's "ideas and feelings formed a more or less tractable synthesis, to which his style was truly answerable" (p. 216). For other references to Sp, see Index.

Adamson, J.H., and H.F. Folland. The Shepherd of the Ocean: An Account of Sir Walter Ralegh and his Times. Boston: Gambit, 1969. 464 pp.   458

Conditions in Ireland, Sp and Ralegh with Lord Grey at Smerwick massacre (pp. 60-7). In 1589 Ralegh when out of favor with Queen Elizabeth went to Ireland; visit with Sp at Kilcolman described in CCCHA (ll. 76-79 quoted). Publication first three books of FQ, Sp's letter to Ralegh explaining "the design of his poem," Ralegh's sonnet "Methought I saw the grave where Laura lay," Sp's dedicatory sonnet to Ralegh. Timias-Belphoebe episode (FQ, III, v, 13-50) is allegory of Ralegh's relations with Queen; Ralegh returned to favor, Sp received pension (pp. 180-8). In Timias-Amoret-Belphoebe story (IV, vii, 35-47; viii, 1-18) Sp allegorizes Ralegh's seduction of Elizabeth Throckmorton, Queen's anger and forgiveness. Timias-Serena-Blatant Beast-Hermit episode (FQ, VI, v, 11-41; vi, 1-15) reflects slander of Ralegh and wife; "Serena was Ralegh's pastoral-poetic name for his wife" (pp. 200-6; see 965, 2069, 2072). For other references to Sp, see Index.

Akrigg, G. P. V. The Renaissance Reconsidered, QQ, 52 (1945), 311-9.   459

"The Renaissance did not happen, yet there *was* the Renaissance," and while it did not happen, it did exist. The chief marks or great themes of the age were self-confidence—Ramus, Magellan, Marlowe, social mobility, exploration; awareness of environment and self—Dürer, Sp, Milton,

Aretino; individualism—Renaissance art, Montaigne; the allied cults of fame and honor; idealism—Bembo, Sp, Sidney, the Great Chain of Being.

Allen, D. C. Donne and the Ship Metaphor, MLN, 76 (1961), 308-12.   460

Donne used ship metaphor in sermon of 1627. Mentions in passing development of it from classical times, including Sp's rephrasing of Petrarch's "Passa la nave mia colma d'oblio" [Amor 34], and thinks ship of love accounts for Phaedria's boat on Idle Lake [FQ, II, vi].

Allen, Don C. The Legend of Noah: Renaissance Rationalism in Art, Science, and Letters. ISLL, 33. Urbana: University of Illinois Press, 1949; repr. 1963. 221pp.   461

Incidental references to Sp. Fidelia's lectures (FQ, I, x) express average Renaissance opinion in Protestant countries that reason was valid source of information if it did not conflict with revelation (p. 15). Uncertainty about cosmological system of Middle Ages and early Renaissance unsettled writers like Sidney, Sp, Shakespeare, and Donne and made them good poets (pp. 30-2). Idea of a plurality of worlds widespread in Sp's time and by Milton's had gained wider credence (pp. 38-9). View that earth was smooth before Noah's flood may be back of wish of Sp's communist giant to level its surface (FQ, V, ii, 38) (pp. 95-96).

Allen, Don Cameron. The Harmonious Vision: Studies in Milton's Poetry. enl. ed. Baltimore: Johns Hopkins Press, 1970. 146 pp.   462

First pub. 1954. Concealed unity of Sp's SC in confused meditations of poet seeking way: love, art, or religion? Troubadours, Sp's ancestors, found road through sophistry and compromise. Young Milton had easier choice in early poems (pp. 3-4). Why did Chaucer's Squire's Tale catch fancy of Sp and Milton? Sp charmed with theme of courtesy; Milton with its symbols of intellectual power (pp. 12-3). Above horizon in L'Allegro and Il Penseroso are towers, *topos* of man's mind as tower of body, as in Sp's House of Alma (FQ, II, ix) (pp. 17-21). Circe legend in Comus and Sp's Acrasia (FQ, II, xii) and Busyrane (FQ, III, xi-xii); two brothers composites of Guyon and Britomart, Comus brother of Acrasia; Sabrina in FQ, II, x (pp. 33-5). Lycidas and Sp's November in SC in tradition of pastoral elegy (pp. 54-7). Despair in Satan and Samson, death-wish of Adam and Red Cross in FQ, I, ix (pp. 74-85). Milton's visual imagery in Paradise Lost different from that of Donne, Shakespeare, and Sp (pp. 105-6).

Allen, Don Cameron. Image and Meaning: Metaphoric Traditions in Renaissance Poetry. Baltimore: Johns Hopkins Press, 1960; 2nd ed. enl., 1968. 175pp.   463

Essays on Sp, Shakespeare, Herbert, Lovelace, Marvell, and Vaughan. The March Eclogue of The Shepheardes Calender (pp. 1-19) is a reprint of 2197; and Muiopotmos, or the Fate of the Butterfly (pp. 20-41) is a reprint of 2324.

Allen, Don Cameron. Mysteriously Meant: The Rediscovery of Pagan Symbolism and Allegorical Interpretation in the Renaissance. Baltimore: Johns Hopkins Press, 1970. 354 pp.   464

In Chap. X, The Rationalization of Myth and The End of Allegory, mentions Sp in connection with *Tabula vitae* of Cebes, Sidney's recommendation in Apology for Poetry of Ariosto's heroes for moral virtues, Tasso's allegorization of Gerusalemme Liberata, mixture of pagan and Christian in FQ, myth of Cupid and Psyche in Milton's Comus as "a Platonized version of a pious soul's union with Christ," Milton's frugal use of allegory, and John Hughes and Richard Blackmore as Christian apologists (pp. 279-311). See Index.

Allen, Don Cameron. The Star-Crossed Renaissance: The Quarrel about Astrology and Its Influence in England. Durham, N. C.: Duke University Press, 1941. 280pp.   465

For references to astrological lore in Sp's poetry, most of them commonplaces, in Chap. IV, Some Aspects of the Dispute about Astrology among Elizabethan and Jacobean Men of Letters, see Index.

Allison, Alexander Ward. Toward an Augustan Poetic: Edmund Waller's "Reform" of English Poetry. Lexington: University of Kentucky Press, 1962. 101 pp.   466

In occasional verse Waller followed informality of Jonson and Donne rather than formality of Sp in Proth and Astro (pp. 4-5). Recreated Sp's poetic diction without his eccentricity; abundant epithets as in Milton and 17th century Spenserians; diction, syntax, verbal repetition, and balanced lines like Sp's (pp. 24-46). Spenserian "sweetness" entered prosody of Augustan couplet through Edward Fairfax's translation of Tasso's Gerusalemme Liberata (pp. 75-7, 80-1).

Alpers, Paul J., ed. Edmund Spenser: A Critical Anthology. Harmondsworth: Penguin Books, 1969. 339 pp.   467

Contemporaneous Criticism: Introduction (pp. 17-25), E. K.'s dedicatory epistle to SC, Oct. from SC, Sp-Harvey correspondence, excerpts from Sidney and Webbe, Letter to Raleigh, 3 dedicatory sonnets of FQ, Proems to FQ, II, IV, and VI (3 stanzas), excerpts from Hall, Jonson, Milton, and others. Neoclassical and Romantic Criticism: Introduction (pp. 64-72), excerpts from Dryden, Thomas Warton, Hurd, Johnson, Coleridge, Hazlitt, Ruskin, Lowell, Yeats, and others. Modern Views: Introduction (pp. 179-88), William Empson (655), C. S. Lewis (1513), Derek Traversi (1143), G. Wilson Knight (1485), Hallett Smith (1091), Yvor Winters (1212), Alastair Fowler (1917), Harry Berger (2138), Northrop Frye (1378), Frank Kermode (1827), Rosemond Tuve (1152), Martha Craig (1325A), Paul Alpers (1231), and Roger Sale (1657). Select Bibliography (pp. 373-6).

Alpers, Paul J., ed. Elizabethan Poetry: Modern Essays in Criticism. New York: Oxford University Press, 1967. 524 pp.
468

In Part II, Individual Poets and Modes of Poetry: Yvor Winters on 16th Century Lyric in England (1213); Hallett Smith on SC (1091, pp. 31-51). In Part III, *The Faerie Queene:* G. Wilson Knight (1485); A. S. P. Woodhouse (1752); Paul J. Alpers (1230); Thomas P. Roche, Jr., Nature of the Allegory (1646, pp. 3-31); Roger Sale, Sp's Undramatic Poetry, "by permission of the author" (1657); Martha Craig (1325A; see 756); Rosemond Tuve, Medieval Heritage of Sp's Allegory (1152, pp. 3-55).

Alvarez, A. The School of Donne. London: Chatto and Windus, 1961. 203 pp.
469

Contrasts Donne with Sp. Donne's conceits fit his poetry, his philosophy used pragmatically, his "intellectual tone" in keeping with his times; Sp conventional, theoretical, obscure, muddled. Donne uses ideas as pillars to support own building; Sp treats ideas as separate entities, apart from him. Rephrases Dr. Johnson's praise

of Metaphysicals: "To write on Donne's plan it was at least necessary to live and think; to write on Spenser's, to read and to write" (pp. 17-44). Herbert of Cherbury's philosophizing has little to do with Sp's (pp. 52-6). Henry King relies less on learning, as Sp does, "than on a depth and sophistication of interest" (pp. 58-60).

Alworth, E. Paul. Spenser's Concept of Nature, in His Firm Estate: Essays in Honor of Franklin James Eikenberry, ed. Donald E. Hayden, pp. 11-23. Tulsa: University of Tulsa, 1967. 78 pp.
470

To Elizabethans, order of nature and order of grace were prime "reference points." Sp usually distinguished between them; however, from SC to FQ, I, "Sp began a gradual shift from the order of nature to the order of grace, so that his primary frame of reference in the last two of the 4 Hymns culminates in a synthesis of the two orders and their values."

Anderson, Judith H. The July Eclogue and the House of Holiness: Perspective in Spenser, SEL, 10 (1970), 17-32. 471

Thomalin in July of SC represents natural point of view, Morrell supernatural one. In FQ, I, x, Redcrosse represents natural view, those at House of Holiness supernatural view. First pair of viewpoints remain separate, but second pair are reconciled. Thomalin and Morrell come to an impasse, remain static. Similarly, figures in FQ, I, x at first have no perspective, point of view one of simple "humility, simplicity, restraint." But Contemplation combines austerity of Thomalin with imagination of Morrell. Redcrosse must combine in harmonious union knowledge of world and knowledge of Other-world. Perspective in episode moves as mirror of this movement toward harmonious unity. [SpN, Vol. 1, No. 3 (1970), 7.]

Andrews, Charles M. Note on a Copy of the 1611 Folio Edition of Spenser Owned by the Yale University Library, PCSM, 28 (Transactions, 1930-1933), 357-9. Boston: Colonial Society of Massachusetts, 1935. 536pp.   472

Further discussion of quotations from Sp in Elnathan Chauncey's commonplace book; see George Lyman Kittredge, A Harvard Salutatory Oration of 1662, ibid., pp. 1-24. "There must have been in the Massachusetts Bay Colony two editions [those of 1611 and 1617] of Spenser's poems before 1654."

Anonymous. TLS, June 14, 1946, p. 288.   473

Last section of Frank Hogan's library, sold by Parke-Bernet Galleries, New York, on Apr. 23-24, 1946, included copy of first edition of FQ (1590) and copy of Proth (1596)— Gollancz copy in modern binding.

Armour, Richard. English Lit Relit: A short history of English literature from the Precursors (before swearing) to the Pre-Raphaelites and a little after.... Illus. New York: McGraw-Hill, 1969. 151 pp.   474

Sp (pp. 18-20). SC "gives the reader a good idea of the shepherd's life: sitting around all day talking in verse about women, poetry, and the classic myths, while the flock wandered at will.... The Faerie Queene is full of meaning, since everything not only means what it means but also means something else."

Armstrong, Elizabeth. Ronsard and The Age of Gold. Cambridge: University Press, 1968. 213 pp.   475

Ronsard in middle period, beginning with Les Isles Fortunées (1553), dwelt on theme of Golden Age, thought to exist in sylvan past. Discusses traditional (Lucretius, Seneca) and contemporary (Béranger de La Tour, Guillaume Postel) influences affecting Ronsard's idea of Age of Gold (pp. 121-54). Gabriel Harvey wrote to Sp, "You suppose the first age was the goulde age. It is nothing soe." He cited Jean Bodin: Golden Age is now. Sp disagreed, placed it firmly in past, as in Proem to Bk. V of FQ on "Saturne's ancient raigne." Ronsard ambivalent toward idea of progress (pp. 154-7).

Ashe, Geoffrey. Camelot and the Vision of Albion. New York: St. Martin's Press, 1971. 233 pp.   476

Arthur of legend not a Christ-figure, except in Sp's "erudite allegory" (pp. 92, 128). Sp planned FQ, probably suggested by Sidney, as elaboration of Tudor resurrection of Arthur, with Gloriana standing for Queen Elizabeth, and Tudor dynasty as restored kingdom of the Britons. "Such was the grandeur of the mystique that haloed Elizabethan England, in the eyes of its greatest narrative poet" (pp. 104-5). Sp in FQ takes up ideal of British golden age, romantic and chivalrous, implicit in Malory's Le Morte d'Arthur (pp. 141-3). For other references to Sp, see Index.

Atkins, J. W. H. English Literary Criticism: The Renascence. London: Methuen, 1947. 371pp.   477

Sp's "English Poet" (lost), and "E. K.'s" contributions to the growing interest in poetic technique (p. 140); Sp's interest in "the possibility of substituting for English rhyming verse a system based on classical metres" (pp. 143-4); Sp's denunciation of erotic verse (pp. 213-4); Jonson's criticism of Sp's diction (pp. 309-10).

Atkinson, A. D. Keats and Compound Epithets, N&Q, 197 (1952), 186-9. 478

Influence on Keats's use of compound epithets of Shakespeare, Sp, Chapman, and others.

Atkinson, Dorothy F. A Note on Spenser and Painting, MLN, 58 (1943), 57-8.

479

Two 17th-century drawing manuals, Henry Peacham the younger's The Gentlemans Exercise (1612) and Randle Holme's Academy of Armoury (1688, written ca. 1640), show the accord between Sp's poetic imagery and the painter's art.

Atteberry, James Lem, Jr. Bartholomew the Englishman and Edmund Spenser: Medieval Platonists. DA, 22 (1961), 1973A. University of Texas, 1961. 245 pp.

480

Sp's debt to medieval encyclopedic tradition largely neglected. De Proprietatibus Rerum of Bartolomaeus Anglicus in numerous editions by Sp's time, most recently in Stephen Batman's translation (1582). Bartholomew endorses numerous Platonic doctrines treated in 4 Hymns: progression that requires acceptance of theory of Ideas; and in allegories of FQ: Red Cross Knight's progress toward understanding, picture of human brain (II, ix, 27), Garden of Adonis (III, vi, 30ff.), Mutability Cantos. Medieval Platonism pervasive in Sp's thought.

Audra, E., and Aubrey Williams, eds. Alexander Pope: Pastoral Poetry and An Essay on Criticism. London: Methuen, 1961. 498 pp.

481

Introductions and notes to Pope's Pastorals, Messiah, Windsor Forest, and An Essay on Criticism contain many references to Sp's SC, CCCHA, Epith, Astro, and FQ, IV, xi. See Index.

Auld, Ina Bell. Woman in the Renaissance: A Study of the Attitude of Shakespeare and his Contemporaries. Doctoral diss., University of Iowa, 1938. UIDDAR, 2 (1938), 103-9.

482

"The conception of woman as a necessary evil was too well grounded and too popular to be greatly affected by chivalry, courtly love, the worship of the Virgin, Petrarch, or Platonism." Background of the antithesis of Sp's view of women.

Awad, Louis. Spenser and the Pléiade, in Studies in Literature, pp. 51-76. Cairo, Egypt: Anglo-Egyptian Bookshop, 1954. 254pp.

483

Aziz, Paul Douglas. The Poet's Poetry: Edmund Spenser's Uses of the Pastoral. DAI, 30 (1969), 271A-2A. Brown University, 1968. 213 pp.

484

Studies Sp's sophisticated uses of pastoral in SC, VG, Daph, CCCHA, Astro, and Pastorella episode of FQ. Uses of pastoral divided into three main categories, a chapter devoted to each: (1) pastoral for Sp was vehicle of philosophic thought; (2) he uses it to deal with contemporary affairs; (3) he found it appropriate for discussions of problems of art. Three main poems are SC, CCCHA, and Pastorella episode, in all of which persona Colin Clout appears. "Poetry becomes a way of life for Spenser, an answer in itself to his own questionings and quests."

Babb, Lawrence. The Elizabethan Malady: A Study of Melancholia in English Literature from 1580 to 1642. East Lansing: Michigan State College Press, 1951. 206pp.

485

Sp is thoroughly conversant with the physiology and psychology of the Renaissance. FQ, II, ix, 21-58, contains "an anatomy of human nature" (pp. 1-2). Although "love is merely an incidental theme" in FQ, the lover's malady is illustrated in the behavior of Timias when rebuked by Belphoebe (IV, vii-viii) (p. 158). Sp himself, like "many English intellectuals," seems to have been melancholy in disposition, in his case because of the failure of his worldly ambitions; for this cites Proth, ll. 5-10, and MHT, ll. 891-908 (pp. 180-1). See also Index.

Bacquet, Paul. Un Contemporain D'Elizabeth I: Thomas Sackville, L'Homme et L'Oeuvre. Geneva: Librairie Droz, 1966. 365 pp.   486

Praise of Sackville by George Turberville in 1574 shows him in high repute before Sp's SC. Possibly Harpalus in CCCHA is Sackville (pp. 109-10). Conventional opposition of winter and summer and mutability theme in Sackville's Induction to Complaint of Buckingham in Mirror for Magistrates, in January of SC, and FQ, VII (pp. 119-21). Portrait of Old Age in Induction and December of SC (pp. 186-7). As author of Induction and Gorboduc, Sackville best poet between Chaucer and Sp (pp. 313-4). For many other references to Sp, see Index.

Bagwell, Richard. Ireland Under the Tudors, With a Succinct Account of the Earlier History. 3 vols. London: Longmans, 1963.   487

Sp's experiences in Ireland in vol. III. Account of Smerwick massacre (pp. 65-78) cites Sp's View among other sources. Mentions Sp as Lord Grey's secretary in account of Desmond war, second stage (1580-1581). Desmond forfeitures, Sp at Kilcolman, Raleigh his neighbor, troubles with Lord Roche (pp. 198-200). Chap. 53, Elizabethan Ireland (pp. 441-58), briefly describes natural features, native customs, mentions Sp and his friends, how Ireland affected Sp's poetry, his marriage to Elizabeth Boyle. For other references to Sp, see Index.

Bahr, Howard W. Spenser and the "Painted Female Beauty of Conventional Sonneteers," SoQ, 9 (1970), 1-5.   488

Description of False Florimell (FQ, III, vii, 6-7) is "satire on the sonneteers' painted mistresses and the conventional terms used to describe them." Cites verbal parallels in Amor 15 and 81; Malecasta's lascivious eye-rolling in FQ, III, i, 41; HHOB ll. 91-97; and Shakespeare's sonnet 20.

Baker, Carlos Heard. The Influence of Spenser on Shelley's Major Poetry. DA, 12 (1952), 59. Princeton University, 1940. 295 pp.   489

Body of the study consists of five chapters: Spenser's Star Rises, on Queen Mab; Early Spenserian Gothic, on Alastor and The Revolt of Islam; Spenser and Shelley's Doctrine of Cosmic Love, on Hymn to Intellectual Beauty, Prince Athanase, Prometheus Unbound, The Mask of Anarchy, and The Sensitive Plant; Spenserian Fantasy and Fable, on The Letter to Maria Gisborne, The Witch of Atlas, and Oedipus Tyrannus; Spenserian "Platonism," on Epipsychidion and Adonais. Appendix C deals with Spenserian Archaisms in Shelley's Diction.

Baker, Herschel. The Dignity of Man: A Study of the Idea of Human Dignity in Classical Antiquity, the Middle Ages, and the Renaissance. Cambridge, Mass.: Harvard University Press, 1947. 365pp.   490

Sp prominent in Part III, The Renaissance View of Man, pp. 203-336. HOHB and FQ, V, ii quoted on order, degree, and Neoplatonic hierarchies (pp. 225-9). "Spenser's Fowre Hymnes is the most sustained essay in Neoplatonism of the English Renaissance" (pp. 246-53). Section on The Eclectic Optimism of The Faerie

Queene, and Sp's "multitudinous and rather untidy mind" (pp. 253-7). House of Temperance (FQ, II, ix) and body-soul relationship (pp. 281, 286). "An eclectic like Spenser leaped nimbly from the Neoplatonism of the *Fowre Hymnes* to the hybrid Protestantism, Platonism, and Aristotelianism of the *Faerie Queene*. . . . Spenser, thus, is a typical man of the Renaissance in his ethics"—this in connection with development of Neo-Stoicism (pp. 293-301). See Index.

Bald, R. C. *The Booke of Sir Thomas More* and Its Problems, ShS, 2 (1949), 44-63. Repr. in Evidence for Authorship: Essays on Problems of Attribution, ed. David V. Erdman and Ephim G. Fogel, pp. 146-70. Ithaca: Cornell University Press, 1966. 559 pp.   491

Sp's handwriting inconsistent (p. 162).

Baldwin, Charles S. Renaissance Literary Theory and Practice: Classicism in the Rhetoric and Poetic of Italy, France, and England, 1400-1600. Ed. by Donald Lemen Clark. New York: Columbia University Press, 1939. 251pp.   492

Comments on Sp and the style of chivalric romances (pp. 14-5), Renaissance vogue of mythology (pp. 23-5), Sp's "deliberate archaism" (pp. 36-7), influence of the classical ode (pp. 72-4), SC and the pastoral tradition (pp. 88-90), "Tasso and Spenser" (pp. 123-4), criticism of style of FQ (pp. 127-32).

Baldwin, R. G. Phineas Fletcher: His Modern Readers and His Renaissance Ideas, PQ, 40 (1961), 462-75.   493

Fletcher often justly compared to Sp but his importance is not as poet so much as historian of Renaissance ideas. Sp frequently mentioned.

Bale, John Christian. The Place of Chaucer in Sixteenth Century English Literature. DA, 13 (1953), 1181. University of Illinois, 1953. 272 pp.   494

"Though I am primarily interested in Spenser's and Shakespeare's use of Chaucer, this study has been made as a preliminary to a detailed investigation of Chaucer in the works of these two men."

Barfield, Owen. Poetic Diction: A Study in Meaning. New York: McGraw-Hill, 1964. 216 pp.   495

Repr. of 1924 ed. On meaning of *ruin* and *ruins* in material sense rather than "a falling," notes use of singular in old sense by Chaucer and Gower; 1454 date first use of plural in material sense. Sp uses singular in old sense 21 times; but also uses modern plural 13 times (pp. 115-7). Concerning archaism or conservatism in poetic diction, says poets "learn from other poets," although great poet when imitating is himself giver of meaning to language. In this sense, Milton was Sp's pupil, and Pope and Wordsworth were Milton's (pp. 172-5). Sp found use of archaism natural in FQ "to express a spirit of fantastic chivalry and devotion" from Middle Ages, recreating earlier era as seen from standpoint of a later consciousness (pp. 179-80).

Barker, Arthur E. An Apology for the Study of Renaissance Poetry, in Literary Views: Critical and Historical Essays, ed. Carroll Camden, pp. 15-43. Chicago: University of Chicago Press, 1964. 193 pp.   496

Rejects simplifications of cultural historians, emphasizes difference between Renaissance in southern and northern Europe, and urges approach to Sp, Donne, and Milton in spirit of Sidney's Defence of Poesie.

Barker, Sir Ernest. Traditions of Civility. Cambridge: Cambridge University Press, 1948. 369pp. 497

Two relevant chapters: Greek Influences in English Life and Thought, and The Education of the English Gentleman in the Sixteenth Century. Platonic doctrine of love and Platonic theory of ideas inspired 4 Hymns and some sonnets in Amor, then passed to metaphysical poets of 17th century, particularly Donne, and Cambridge Platonists (pp. 29-30). Platonic doctrine of beauty in Castiglione echoed in 4 Hymns (p. 148). Ascham more representative of English ideas concerning education of the gentleman than Sp. "Perhaps Spenser, the poet's poet, has made more poets than gentlemen; but at any rate he bequeathed to his country a good and gracious tradition of virtuous and gentle discipline" (pp. 149-53).

Barnes, T. R. English Verse: Voice and Movement from Wyatt to Yeats. Cambridge: University Press, 1967. 324 pp. 498

Fable of Oak and Briar in February of SC not one of rhythms later poets found useful, whereas "Spenser's genius for manipulation of sound" more evident in exchange between Hobbinol and Colin in June. In opening FQ, VII, vii, "the melody is broader and more sweeping." Colloquial style of couplets in MHT in keeping with Elizabethan idea of decorum (pp. 10-19). For other references to Sp, see Index.

Barnhart, Clarence L. A New Century Handbook of English Literature. New York: Appleton-Century-Crofts, 1956. 1167 pp. 499

Edmund Spenser (p. 1025). Also entries on Sp's works, e.g., Amor (p. 35) and FQ (pp. 420-1), major characters, e.g., Red Cross Knight (p. 918), and other Spenserian topics.

Baskervill, Charles Read. The Elizabethan Jig and Related Song Drama. New York: Dover, 1965. 642 pp. 500

Repr. of 1929 ed. Large number of terms used interchangeably for dance and for song; Sp in FQ, III, x, 8 extends "bransle" to cover "love song" (pp. 10-11). In early Tudor period literary men contributed to development of ballad, in some poetic miscellanies called "sonets" and "histories," but native poetry languished until publication of Sp's SC, and ballad fell into disrepute (pp. 30 ff.). Name Willie apparently applied to actor Richard Tarlton in Sp's TM (p. 100). Discusses May game customs and festivities relevant to May eclogue of SC. See Index.

Bate, Walter Jackson. John Keats. New York: Oxford University Press, 1966. 732 pp. 501

Repr. with corrections, of 2nd. ed. 1964; first pub. 1963. Keats's early introduction to Sp by Cowden Clarke; reading Epith, Keats's "ramping" through FQ, and his "acting" the image of "sea-shouldering whales" (FQ, II, xii, 23, 6); his admiration of Sp while interning at Guy's Hospital, "Imitation of Spenser," first poem, in four Spenserian stanzas (pp. 11, 33, 35-6, 49-50). Spenserian fragment "Calidore" (pp. 61-3). Use of Spenserian stanza in Eve of St. Agnes (pp. 441 ff.) Principal source of La belle dame sans merci is Sp: seduction of Red Cross Knight by Duessa (FQ, I, ii), Arthur's vision of Faerie Queene (I, ix), with details from Cymochles' allurement by Phaedria (II, vi) and story of false Florimell (III-IV) (p. 478, note). See Index.

Bateson, F. W. English Poetry: A Critical Introduction. Rev. ed. New York: Barnes and Noble, 1966. 205 pp.   502

First publ. 1950. Unlike Tudor court poets, Sp preferred to appear publicly in book form. Although this increased availability to readers, it kept him from knowing audience in advance. Made for blurred impact, "lacking intimacy and directness" (p. 106).

Bayley, P. C. Order, Grace and Courtesy in Spenser's World, in Patterns of Love and Courtesy: Essays in Memory of C. S. Lewis, ed. John Lawlor, pp. 178-202. Evanston: Northwestern University Press, 1966. 206 pp.   503

At end of Bk V Artegall attacked by Blatant Beast, quest incomplete. Corrupt world of Irena is Ireland described in View; "in a dozen places the poem reminds one of the prose work." Artegall is Lord Grey, victim of calumny on return to England from Ireland. Mission of Calidore in Bk. VI to subdue Blatant Beast; it links V and VI. It breaks loose at end of Bk. VI, asserting continued disorder in world. Pastoral world in SC and CCHA one of virtuous simplicity, but pastoral world of Bk. VI invaded (ix) and despoiled (x), showing vulnerability of virtue, as often in FQ, and in RT, TM, Muiop, and Daph. Calidore has courtesy as God's gift, a paragon. Not helped by Arthur, because his equivalent. Arthur helps Calepine, Calidore's likeness on lower level. In postscript interprets Mutability Cantos as completing whole FQ.

Bayley, Peter. Edmund Spenser: Prince of Poets. London: Hutchinson, 1971. 189 pp.   504

Introductory chap. on difficulties for readers first encountering Sp. Chaps. on SC ("Some of it is sorry stuff"), Complaints (RT brought alive

skillfully), and later minor poems. For FQ one chap. on backgrounds, one on Bks. I-IV, and one on Bks. V-VI. Last chap. "The Faerie Queene: The Poetic Achievement," evaluates specific passages and emphasizes poem's humanity. Good book on Sp in general for undergraduates and others who know little about the Renaissance. [SpN, Vol. 3, No. 1(1972), 1-2.]

Beach, D. M. The Poetry of Idea: Sir Philip Sidney and the Theory of Allegory, TSLL, 13 (1971), 365-89.   505

Sidney's poetic is a poetic of allegory, i.e., the poem is governed by a foreconceit or idea which the imagination analogically embodies in striking images; but for Sidney the striking image is essential, more powerful than the idea itself in moving the reader or hearer to virtuous action. Other theorists, like Bacon, emphasize the precept and distrust the image. Sp in his Ltr is ambivalent; he longs, like Bacon, for a philosophy unhampered by disguising fictions, but he shows some affection for the parable which leads to self-knowledge and virtue. But the Baconian attitude prevails in Sp; in the Ltr, the view of allegory is not Sidneyan, but a perfectionist, dualist view which in its enthusiasm for an ideal conception would be easily discontent with things as they are. E.K.'s defense of SC shows this same perfectionist attitude. Fortunately, these arguments do not do justice to FQ itself, "a magnificent exploration of both the grounds of viable conduct and the tension between a golden and a brazen world."

Beaty, Jerome, and William H. Matchett. Poetry: From Statement to Meaning. New York: Oxford University Press, 1965. 353 pp.   506

Introduction (pp. 3-10) on different ways of reading a poem. Section 1,

From Statement to Form (pp. 13-15); Section 2, From Form to Meaning (pp. 163-331). Simile may be brief, as in Amor 67, in which speaker compares himself to a huntsman (pp. 164-5). Allegory is continued metaphor, narrative in which characters or events "refer to individual elements of a complex A-term." When characters are personified abstractions, they allow poet to dramatize nature of man. Dryden's Absalom and Achitophel is satirical allegory; "the most famous of allegorical poems in English," Sp's FQ, is much more complex, "the allegory not a rigid one-for-one correspondence," but more fluid (pp. 233-4). Definition of Spenserian stanza, used by James Thomson in The Castle of Indolence (pp. 317-8).

Beers, Henry A. A History of English Romanticism in the Eighteenth Century. New York: Gordian Press, 1966. 455 pp.   507

Repr. 1898 ed. Sp's blend of pagan and Christian elements removed from classical tradition; many archaic aspects of his poetry had widespread influence on romantics through 18th century. Chap. on Spenserians (pp. 62-101). See Index.

Benét, William Rose, ed. The Reader's Encyclopedia. New York: Crowell, 1955. 1270pp.   508

First published 1948. Entries on Sp, Spenserian stanza, and each of the more important works.

Bengtsson, Frans G. Spenser, Edmund, in Svensk Uppslagsbok, 26, cols. 1251-2. Malmö: Förlagshuset Norden, 1953. 509

Benjamin, Adrian. "Ode to a Nightingale," TLS, 6 February, 1964, p. 12.   510

Observes that Keats's use of "ye" follows Sp's consistent usage.

Benjamin, Edwin B. Fame, Poetry, and the Order of History in the Literature of the English Renaissance, SRen, 6 (1959), 64-84.   511

Surveys uses of the term "Fame" in poetry and historiography of the English Renaissance, dealing chiefly with personal and national Fame. Cites Sp's use of Fame as a nationalistic concept in FQ and Proth.

Bennett, Alvin L. The Renaissance Personal Elegy and the Rhetorical Tradition. Doctoral diss., University of Texas, 1952. DDAAU, 1951-52, No. 19.   512

"The rhetorics were instrumental in fixing the consolatory motifs, just as they were the most readily accessible source for the pattern of praise. The rhetoricians must have been largely responsible for the form and substance of the Renaissance personal lament." Cites November in SC, and Astro.

Bennett, Josephine Waters. Renaissance Neoplatonism in the Poetry of Edmund Spenser. Doctoral diss., Ohio State University, 1936. OSUADD, 21 (1936), 21-31.   513

Discusses Platonists, Neoplatonists, allegorical tradition, practice of reasoning from analogy, and idea of a primitive Golden Age received by Renaissance. "The whole basis of Spenser's work rests upon the Platonic way of thinking." Explains at length three passages: Cantos of Mutabilitie (FQ, VII) derive from Platonic metaphysics, and Louis Le Roy's De la Vicissitude ou Varieté des Choses en l'Univers is important source: Garden of Adonis (FQ, III, vi) rests on two widely current ideas, preëxistence of forms and earthly paradise, both associated with Platonic doctrines; 4 Hymns derive immediately from Canzone dello Amor celeste & divino of Benivieni, contemporary and follower of Ficino, and commentary on it by Pico della Mirandola.

Bercovich, Sacvan. Empedocles in the English Renaissance, SP, 65 (1968), 67-80.   514

Encourages serious attention to argument of Evelyn May Albright (PMLA, 44 (1929), 715-59; Atkinson, p. 104) that Sp's "cosmic philosophy" in Mutability Cantos, CCCHA, HHOB, and HHOL was influenced by Empedocles, 5th-century Greek thinker. Her evidence has been overlooked or "blandly shrugged off" (see 1367, p. 166; 878, p. 387), but it "remains impressive." Outlines Empedocles' theories of creation and evolution, transmigration, flux, and nature of God—assimilated by Neoplatonists. "The Empedoclean cosmology was readily accessible to English poets from Spenser to Milton." Empedoclean ideas and images occur in Watson, Harvey, Nashe, Kyd, Herrick, Herbert, and Milton. Believes study of FQ, IV, from this perspective "might prove fruitful."

Berger, Harry. Biography as Interpretation, Interpretation as Biography, CE, 28 (1966), 113-25.   515

Constructs a poetic career to clarify role of biography in art and borrows E. K.'s three grouping modes (recreative, plaintive, and moral) from SC to describe progress (p. 114). Uses Clarion in Muiop to demonstrate Sp's "recreative sensibility" (p. 115). Since Sp probably created SC from original fragments, it exemplifies "recreative" phase (p. 117).

Berger, Harry, Jr. The Prospect of Imagination: Spenser and the Limits of Poetry, SEL, 1 (1961), 93-120.   516

The shift from the difficulties of contemporary life in FQ, V, to the artificial, freer world of FQ, VI, cul-

minating in the Mt. Acidale episode, marks a loss of faith in the historical process on Sp's part and a turning inward to seek the sources of moral vision and order within his mind, which must confer upon the world its own mythic forms. This movement, apparent in the Colin of SC and CCCHA, is completed in the Mutabilitie Cantos, where the Masque of Nature, a universe of symbolic forms, provides the fulfillment which Mutabilitie has been blindly seeking. MHT cited incidentally as anticipating the concern in FQ, VI, with the moral and practical functions of art.

Berger, Harry, Jr., ed. Spenser: A Collection of Critical Essays. Englewood Cliffs, N. J.: Prentice-Hall, 1968. 182 pp.   517

Editor's Introduction (pp. 1-12). Section on minor poems: criticism of Complaints vol. by William Nelson (961), SC by A. C. Hamilton (2238), Proth by M. L. Wine (2556A), and Epith by Richard Neuse (2468). Section on FQ: criticism of Bk. I by Donald Cheney (1310), Bk. II by Maurice Evans (1914), Bks. III and IV by Kathleen Williams (1742), Bk. V by William Nelson (961), Bk. VI by William Nestrick (2157), and Bk. VII by editor of collection (1266 and 518, in part). Each critical essay listed herein under appropriate heading.

Berger, Harry, Jr. The Spenserian Dynamics, SEL, 8 (1968), 1-18.   518

Sp's view of experience based on discordia concors; his thought drives toward reconciliation of opposites but not complete elimination of discord. This, in essence, is the dynamic of his poetry. Explicates FQ, IV, x, 32-35 as central in Sp's attitude toward proper equilibrium in both cosmic and human organisms. Calls this "the Spenserian World Picture." In contrast to landscape in Dante's

Divine Comedy, "Spenserian landscape . . . evolves from the projection
of inscape." Discusses Sp's dynamics
in HHOL and CCCHA, illustrates
their operation in characters and
episodes in FQ, III, IV, and V.

Bergeron, David M. The Emblematic Nature of English Civic Pageantry, RenD,
1 (1968), 167-98.   519

Emblem books profoundly influenced many English poets, particularly Sp (see 687) and Herbert. Ben
Jonson was indebted to emblem
books, especially Italian, in court
masques. Civic pageantry was "the
less sophisticated counterpart of the
masque." Discusses connection between emblems and civic pageantry in
England 1558-1640, most examples
from 17th century, showing they
drew on common iconographical tradition. Discusses "royal entry," summer progresses, and Lord Mayor's
Show. Illustrations from Geoffrey
Whitney's A Choice of Emblems
(1586; see 1197) and Henry Peacham's Minerva Brittanna (1612) of
Time and Truth, Truth, Envy, Virtue
and Fame, Ulysses, Arion, Orpheus,
and Sir Francis Drake. See 1270.

Berthelot, Joseph A. Michael Drayton.
New York: Twayne, 1967. 172 pp. 520

In Ideas Mirrour (1594) Drayton,
like Sp in Amor and other Elizabethan sonneteers, freely used Petrarchan conceits (pp. 18-27). In Idea,
the Shepheardes Garland (1593) he
followed Sp's leadership in pastoral;
Rowland "begins in I with pious repentance and ends in IX with hope-
less lovesickness"; Dowsabell best of
series (pp. 46-52). In revised Shepheardes Garland (1606) smoothed
lines by simplifying rhetoric, following Sp in CCCHA. In Endimion and
Phoebe (1595) description of Phoebe
reminds us of Belphoebe in FQ, II, iii,
26; poem ends with praise of Sp,

Daniel, and Lodge (pp. 52-7). The
Muses Elizium (1630), last pastoral,
has Bower of Bliss-like enchanted
place, but without Sp's excess (p. 64).
Poly-Olbion (1612, enlarged 1622) in
one sense has same spirit as Sp's TM;
marriage of Tame and Isis in 15th
song imitates marriage of Thames and
Medway in FQ, IV, xi (pp. 101, 105).
The Owle (1604) in same tradition of
fable as MHT (p. 121). Early poetic
theory agreed with Sidney and Sp;
receives tribute in CCCHA; popularity
continued in 18th century; poetic
ability and versatility grew with passage of time (pp. 135-50).

Bethell, S. L. Essays on Literary Criticism
and the English Tradition. London:
Dobson, 1948. 99pp.   521

Essays which first appeared in the
New English Weekly, 1945-6. Chapter
VII. "Two Streams from Helicon,"
pp. 53-87. Distinguishes two main
types of English poetry: (A) Shake-
speare-Donne stream, and (B) Sp-
Milton - Tennyson stream. These are
contrasted in language, rhythm, imagery, subject-matter, general approach,
and tone. Defends Group-B poets a-
gainst the preference of modern critics, with particular reference to F. R.
Leavis, for Group-A poets. See 864.

Beum, Robert. Some Observations on
Spenser's Verse Forms, NM, 64 (1963),
180-96.   522

Attempts to find rationale of Sp's
choice of verse forms throughout his
career, divided into three distinct periods. (1) Culminates in "vigorous and
eclectic experimentation" in SC;
forms most familiar to 16th-century
English poet—rime royal, ottava rima,
blank verse, pentameter couplet—
missing. (2) Dominated by poems in
rime royal (Daph), ottava rima
(Muiop), and FQ stanza; stanzas of 7,
8, and 9 lines "provide space for . . .
the increasing complexity and rich-

ness of maturing vision." (3) Devises unique forms for commemorative poems (Amor, Epith, Proth, CCCHA), "and the more intimately involved he is, the more unusual or exotic the verse structure." Epith most elaborate and personal of Sp's occasional poems, "his way of showing his bride how much loving trouble he has gone to."

Blake, William. Poetry and Prose. Ed. David V. Erdman. Commentary by Harold Bloom. Garden City, N. Y.: Doubleday, 1965. 906 pp.   523

Sp's Garden of Adonis (FQ, III, vi) mentioned in commentary on Plates 1 and 6 of The Book of Thel (pp. 808-9); marriage of Thames and Medway (FQ, IV, xi) in that on river of Beulah and generative Albion in Milton (p. 827); gates of Garden of Adonis (FQ, III, vi) in that on simple and not esoteric or occultist gates near end of Bk. I in Milton (p. 834); Jerusalem's structure unsolved, "yet in time it may seem no more and no less difficult in structure than *The Faerie Queene* or *The Prelude*, works curiously and wonderfully put together but each on a basis not so discursive as it may first appear" (p. 843); appearance of Sp's Talus (FQ, V) may be reflected in Spectre of Urthona in Night VI of The Four Zoas (p. 876); two poems in Poetical Sketches, To the Evening Star and To Morning, echo Sp's Epith (p. 887).

Blissett, William F. The Historical Imagination in the English Renaissance, Studied in Spenser and Milton. Doctoral diss., University of Toronto, 1950. DDAAU, 1949-50, No. 17. Abs., University of Toronto Final Oral Examinations for the Degree of Doctor of Philosophy, Session 1949-50.   524

Seeks to define relation of history to myth in Sp's imagination. "The Spenserian division of the thesis is the more extensive, largely because the context of thought and literary tradition which needs to be established there will carry over to the poet who acknowledged Spenser to be his original." Chapter 1, Letter to Raleigh: the "poet historical" and his methods, the "antique poets historical," choice of Arthur as an epic hero. Chapter 2, Sp's historical imagination in poems written before FQ. Chapter 3 examines FQ as an Allegory of History. Bk. I images life of man under Grace and historical form of Scripture; other books confined to order of nature, and colored by various historical fictions. Garden of Adonis (III, vi) and Mutability Cantos embody "in terms of myth Spenser's attitude toward time" and toward his temporal endeavor in writing FQ. Mutability Cantos are "here taken to be somewhat in the nature of a retraction." Finds Milton more rigorous than Sp in his conception of history.

Bloom, Harold. Blake's Apocalypse: A Study in Poetic Argument. Garden City, N. Y.: Doubleday, 1965. 502 pp.   525

Repr. 1963 ed. To the Evening Star and To Morning show Sp's influence on young Blake, both echoing Epith (pp. 8-9). Songs of Innocence Blake's closest approach to pastoral, centered in Sp, Milton, and Virgil; gives glimpse of heavenly city, like Red Crosse Knight's of New Jerusalem (FQ, I, x), and view of earthly paradise, as in Gardens of Adonis (FQ, III, vi) (pp. 29-31). Blake's poems use Spenserian stanza and Miltonic blank verse, but closer to Bunyan (pp. 47-8). In Hesperidean symbolism influenced by both Sp and Milton (pp. 108-9). As in Sp, political and moral allegory exist on intersecting but distinct levels; details of former not important (p. 165). As for Sp and Milton, Albion father of British people;

search for more esoteric sources un-profitable (pp. 204 ff.). Compares Abania to Sp's Sapience in HOHL (p. 241). Sp's Garden of Adonis "the most beautiful presentation in English of the state Blake called Beulah," but he reverses "the marriage of the Thames and Medway rivers as an ulti-mate image of concord in the natural world" (p. 409).

Bloom, Harold. The Visionary Company: A Reading of English Romantic Poetry. Rev. and enl. edition. Ithaca: Cornell University Press, 1971. 477 pp. 526

First pub. 1961. Best preparation for reading Romantic poetry is FQ, I, and Paradise Lost. Sp juxtaposes Puri-tan knight errant to "corrupt machin-ery of salvation" (p. xviii). William Collins' Ode on the Poetical Character in "the prophetic and Protestant line of Spenser and Milton," returns to myth-making tradition of Renaissance (pp. 7-15). Relation of Blake's con-cept of innocence or Beulah and its sexuality to Sp's Garden of Adonis and Bower of Bliss (pp. 20-31). Blake's Jerusalem recalls Sp's Thames and Medway episode (FQ, IV, xi) and his Cleopolis (pp. 109-11). Title and Spenserian stanza of Byron's Childe Harold's Pilgrimage derive from ro-mance tradition; Canto VII of Don Juan begins by parodying FQ (pp. 239, 268). Echoes of Sp in Shelley's The Two Spirits: An Allegory, The Witch of Atlas, and Adonais in line of Sp's Astro (pp. 325-28, 343). Quest theme in FQ and Keats's Endymion, bower of Acrasia and La Belle Dame Sans Merci, Mutability Cantos and Ode on Melancholy (pp. 371, 384-6, 414-5).

Blum, Irving D. The Paradox of Money Imagery in English Renaissance Poetry, SRen, 8 (1961), 144-54. 527

Standard opinion that language of commerce used for earthy, evil things.

Sp vividly describes Avarice (FQ, I, iv, 27-28) in such terms; but in Amor 15 uses same vocabulary to praise his love. Same ambivalence illustrated in Sidney, Gascoigne, Wyatt, Daniel, Shakespeare, Chapman, Donne, and Herbert.

Blunden, Edmund. Chaucer to "B.V.," With an Additional Paper on Herman Melville. Folcroft, Pa.: Folcroft Press, 1970. 265 pp. 528

Repr. of 1950 ed. Edmund Spenser: and Especially "The Faerie Queene" (pp. 17-37). Old-fashioned to call Sp "poet's poet," but contributed to ar-tistic growth of Milton, Cowley, Thomson, Collins, Wordsworth, Cole-ridge, Shelley, Keats, Tennyson, Bridges—and Shakespeare. Most poets impressed by technical brilliance of Spenserian stanza; yet Wordsworth drawn by Sp's moral powers, Lamb by his creation of fairy world. In 20th century FQ "has been losing ground": too long, artificial, some-times childish, syntax distorted, com-plex; "yet it remains among the great books." Sustained visualization in epi-sodes of Bower of Bliss, Cave of Mam-mon, Garden of Adonis, marriage of Thames and Medway, "perhaps all ex-celled in the fragment concerning Mutability." Admires 4 Hymns, "the best parts of" SC, Amor, MHT, Epith, and Proth; "he ranges from a satirical humour to an abstract beauty and honour." Special praise for Muiop, "exquisite fable."

Boegholm, N. On the Spenserian Style, Études Linguistiques 1944, Travaux du Cercle linguistique de Copenhague, 1 (1945), 5-21. 529

Relation of Sp's language to Chaucer's, vowel-changes, dialect words, coinages, linguistic liberties in phonology, spelling, rhyme, grammar. Sp compared and contrasted with Ari-osto and Tasso. Repetitions, metaphors, use of adjectives, balance and parallelism of narrative structure. Notes on Sp's mark on later English poetry: "The nearest spiritual affinity of Spenser is with Milton."

Bontoux, Germaine. La, Chanson en Angleterre au Temps d'Élisabeth. Illus. Oxford: University Press, 1936. 699 pp.
530

Not listed in Atkinson. Among influences of Pléiade poets (Ronsard, Remi Belleau) on English song are flower lists in, e.g., Shakespeare's Love's Labour's Lost, Jonson's Pan's Anniversary, Sp's April of SC and Proth (pp. 168-71). In chap. on La Chanson dans les Oeuvres Lyriques, discusses Sp's Astro, Epith, Proth, mentions Carlton's setting FQ, V, viii, 1-2, vii, 1 and VI, viii, 1, and Gibbons' setting FQ, III, i, 49-50 (pp. 214-24). In chap. on La Chanson dans la Pastorale, discusses Colin's song in April of SC, Perigot's and Willie's roundelay in August with music of Hey ho holliday from B. M. Add. MS. 4388, and elegy for Dido in November with Kirbye's setting of Up then Melpomene, stanzas 4-6, and 13 (pp. 228-36). See 844, 2242.

Boyette, Purvis E. Milton's Eve and the Neoplatonic Graces, RenQ, 20 (1967), 341-4.
531

Description of Eve as Queen of Graces in Paradise Lost, VIII, 59-61, follows Sp in linking Graces with flowers, symbol of fruition (April of SC, ll. 109-114, June, ll. 25-28, and FQ, I, i, 48, VI, x, 14-15). For Neoplatonists, Graces in triadic relationship of *pulchritudo-amor-voluptas* are inclusive symbol of love—cites 1211. Romantic love between Adam and Eve is sign of divine love; through Eve, Adam achieves transcendence.

Bradbrook, M.C. Shakespeare and Elizabethan Poetry. London: Chatto and Windus, 1961. 279 pp.
532

Repr. of 1951 ed. In Chap. II, The Artifice of Eternity: The Courtly Poetry of the Sixteenth Century (pp. 18-34)—Queen Elizabeth's various roles in FQ; kind of private code perhaps behind beast fables in February and March of SC, MHT, and Muiop; Sidney lived courtly life he celebrated, while Sp described it from outside in "great festal poems" such as Epith and Proth, Calidore's vision of Graces, April and November of SC, and 4 Hymns. In Chap. IV, The Ovidian Romance (pp. 51-83)—Lucretian Nature in Garden of Adonis (FQ, III, vi) and Mutability Cantos; tale that introduces plea of Mutability to rule world adapted from Ovid's Metamorphoses; Marlowe's Hero and Leander "a Hymn to Earthly Love and Beauty, an anti-Spenserian manifesto." In Chap. VI, The Mirror of Nature: Character in Shakespeare's Plays (pp. 84-103)—in contrast with Shakespeare's characters, "Spenser's characters are embodiments of states of mind"; Othello not possessed by passion of jealousy, but Leontes in The Winter's Tale is possessed by jealousy (FQ, III, x). For other references to Sp, see Index.

Bradbrook, Muriel C. Yeats and Elizabethan Love Poetry, DM, 4 (1965), 40-55.
533

Early influence of Sp on Yeats in edition of Sp (c. 1900) and essay on him. "A single scene may imprint itself on the poet's mind and nourish him for years." House of Busyrane (FQ, III, xi-xii) had this power for Yeats. Thought Epith best of Sp's poems and condemned Amor for lack of human feeling. Found this in SC. Rebuked Sp for anti-Irish views, but lured by Sp's pastoral landscapes, "the religion of the wilderness." Said Sp wrote better of men than of women, modeled the elegy Shepherd and Goatherd on Astro. Briefly discusses influence on Yeats of Shakespeare and Raleigh.

Bradner, Leicester. Spenser, Edmund, Collier's Encyclopedia, 21, 433-6. New York: P. F. Collier, 1971.   534

Also Robert Brittain, Spenserian stanza, ibid., 436.

Brady, William Edward. English Satire in the Sixteenth Century. DA, 19 (1959), 1751-2. Brown University, 1958. 347 pp.   535

Groups the century's satire under three headings: Medieval, Elizabethan, and Neo-classical. Sp is Medieval.

Brand, C. P. Torquato Tasso: A Study of the Poet and of His Contribution to English Literature. Cambridge: University Press, 1965. 344 pp.   536

After chaps. on "The Poet and His Work," three chaps. on "Tasso in England." Chap. 9, "The *Gerusalemme Liberata* in England," has section on Sp (pp. 228-39), "who first really brought Tasso's name before the English reader." In FQ textual debts to Tasso most obvious in Bk. II: Idle Lake (vi) and Bower of Bliss (xii). Sp "simplifies Tasso's elaborate style and imagery." Discussions of Edward Fairfax's translation (1600) and of Milton (pp. 241-6, 250-6) have references to Sp. Chap. 10, "Tasso's 'Aminta' and Lyrics in England," considers Sp's significance in developing independent English pastoral tradition that continued into 17th century, and Tasso's influence on "at least twelve sonnets" of Amor, although Sp's treatment original (pp. 277-8, 290-5).

Branscomb, Ernest Jackson. Attitudes Toward Time in Spenser, Shakespeare's *Sonnets*, and Donne. DAI, 34 (1973), 306A. University of North Carolina, 1972. 167 pp.   537

"Deals primarily with poetic presentations of individuals confronted with temporal processes, rather than with philosophies of time. . . . The Spenserian view of time is essentially medieval and optimistic. Sp is concerned with development within the limits of fixed potentials. In his treatment of cosmic and generative cycles, enduring moral qualities, and human development, he thinks in terms of human essences that persist and can be realized in the course of time." [SpN, Vol. 5, No. 2 (1974), 14.]

Brewer, Leighton. Shakespeare and the Dark Lady. Boston: Christopher Publishing House, 1966. 112pp.   538

Disputes the notion that Shakespeare's sonnets satirize conventional sonnet cycles of Sidney and Sp (pp. 22, 28).

Bridgwater, William, and Seymour Kurtz, eds. The Columbia Encyclopedia. 3rd ed. New York: Columbia University Press, 1963. 2388 pp.   539

Sp's life and works (p. 2018); mentioned in entries on pastoral (p. 1610) and sonnet (p. 1994).

Briggs, H. E. Keats' "Golden-Tongued Romance," MLN, 58 (1943), 125-8.   540

Reference in sonnet, On Sitting Down to Read King Lear, is to Endymion, not FQ. Tries to show that Keats did not reject Sp.

Brinkley, Roberta Florence, ed. Coleridge on the Seventeenth Century. New York: Greenwood Press, 1968. 704 pp.   541

Repr. of 1955 ed. Coleridge placed Sp in highest artistic order but placed his verse just below that of Shakespeare and Milton for its fragile sweetness and "melancholy grace." See Index.

Broadbent, J. B. Poetic Love. London: Chatto and Windus, 1964. 310 pp.   542

Sp's Amor disorganized, diffuse. His secular Hymns spoil quality of Platonic ideas, have form without content, "cosy narcissism . . . of Victorian tracts" (pp. 73-87). Heavenly Hymns pervert religious love, "fixated on the chaste maternal breast," in contrast to religious love poetry of Donne, Hopkins, Herbert, Eliot (pp. 88-125). In FQ unhealthy sex predominates, as with Britomart, Arthegall, and Amoret; "Spenser was a Victorian: his men can't be virile so their brides are coy"; allegory has distorting effect (pp. 159-73). Epith inferior to Donne's marriage poems; "Spenser quite lacks psychological insight" (pp. 213-20). For other unfavorable judgments of Sp, see Index.

Rev: John Carey, EIC, 15 (1965), 334: Edward Lucie-Smith, CritQ, 8 (1966), 87; Hallett Smith, MLQ, 27 (1966), 80; H. M. Richmond, RN, 19 (1966), 54.

Brooke, Tucker. Essays on Shakespeare and Other Elizabethans, ed. Leicester Bradner. New Haven: Yale University Press, 1948. 220pp.   543

On Reading Spenser (pp. 198-220) is a tribute to "the greatest of the true Elizabethans." Sp should be read today because (1) "The Fairy Queen is . . . one of the marvels of the world's fiction"; (2) "to his uncanny skill in narrative he adds a power of description quite unsurpassed in English poetry"; (3) "so long as this world remains a scene of strife . . . The Fairy Queen will remain a chief guide, incentive, and consoler"; (4) he has consistently won the admiration of the greatest English poets who came after him; (5) he is being read today more widely and with more complete understanding than ever before.

Brooke, Tucker, and Matthias A. Shaaber. The Renaissance (1500-1600). Vol. 2 of A Literary History of England, ed. Albert C. Baugh. 2nd ed. New York: Appleton-Century-Crofts, 1967. pp. 315-696.   544

Repr. of 1948 ed. Part II, The Reign of Elizabeth (1558-1603), includes chaps. on Edmund Spenser (pp. 483-95) and on The Faerie Queene: The Spenserians (pp. 496-507). Bibliographical supplement to two chaps. on Sp gives a few references to modern scholarship and criticism.

Brown, Daniel Russel. A Look at Archetypal Criticism, JAAC, 28 (1970), 465-72.   545

Demonstrates confusion among archetypal critics, argues for more rigorous methods, pleads for more understanding and acceptance of archetypal criticism. "Doubtless some authors and epochs lend themselves more readily than do others to the use of archetypes. . . . Perhaps Spenser, Blake, Coleridge, and Yeats are quite suitable because of the nature of their writing. For these writers deliberately employed the mythic. . . ."

Brown, E. K. Swinburne: A Centenary Estimate, in Victorian Literature: Modern Essays in Criticism, ed. Austin Wright, pp. 295-310. New York: Oxford University Press, 1961. 327 pp.   546

Repr. from UTQ, 6 (1937), 215-35. Swinburne copied Sp in that he tried "to protract his poems" into lulling incantations (p. 221).

Brown, J. R. Some Notes on the Native Elements in the Diction of "Paradise Lost," N&Q, 196 (1951), 424-8.   547

Milton was indebted to earlier English writers for the enrichment of his epic style, especially Sp.

Brown, Joseph Epes, comp. The Critical Opinions of Samuel Johnson. New York: Russell & Russell, 1961. 549 pp. 548

Repr. of 1926 ed. Spenserian imitations in 18th century became target for Johnson (pp. xix-xx). He disliked Spenserian stanza (pp. xxviii-xxix). Elizabethans, except for Sp and Shakespeare, "sadly neglected" in Johnson's Dictionary (p. xxxv). Johnson in surprising agreement with "the leading liberal critics of his age," Thomas and Joseph Warton (pp. xlv ff.). Johnson on Spenserian imitations (pp. 134-8), Spenserian stanza (p. 261), Sp (pp. 512-3).

Browning, D. C. Everyman's Dictionary of Literary Biography: English & American. London: Dent, 1962. 767 pp. 549

Sp, pp. 638-9.

Bryant, J. A., Jr. Hippolyta's View: Some Christian Aspects of Shakespeare's Plays. Lexington: University of Kentucky Press, 1961. 239pp. 550

Allegory and incarnation in Sp (p. 10); Una and Desdemona compared (p. 143).

Bryce, John Cameron. Spenser, Edmund, Encyclopedaedia Britannica, 21, 4-9. Chicago: Encyclopaedia Britannica, 1968, 1972. 551

Gay Wilson Allen, The Spenserian Stanza, 21, 9.

Buchan, John, ed. A Shorter History of English Literature. Rev. by Majl Ewing. New York: Nelson, 1937. 474pp. 552

Rev. ed. of larger History of English Literature, ed. John Buchan. Chapter 3, Edmund Spenser, pp. 89-96. Short biography, Sp in Ireland, variety of SC, spiritual unity of FQ.

Buchloh, Paul Gerhard. Michael Drayton: Barde und Historiker, Politiker und Prophet. Neumünster: Karl Wachholtz, 1964. 390 pp. 553

Drayton calls Sp "the very first among us, who transferred the use of the word Legend, from Prose to Verse" (Works, II, 382). Relations between Drayton's Poly-Olbion and Sp in their use of legend (pp. 22-24), allegory (pp. 38-9), and conceits (pp. 54-5); the two as poet-historians (pp. 64-6); their use of Trojan legend and other pseudo-historical materials (pp. 87-8, 97, 101-2, 119), with emphasis on FQ, II, x. For references to Sp's RT, social satire, political attitudes, and knowledge of classics—see Index.

Bullough, Geoffrey. Mirror of Minds: Changing Psychological Beliefs in English Poetry. Toronto: University of Toronto Press, 1962. 271 pp. 554

Chaucer, Sp, and Shakespeare drew on medical and ethical text-books, direct observation, folk-belief, and literary tradition (p. 5). Sp owed much to Morality tradition for allegory of mind in FQ; singles out many passions and perturbations in psychological drama of Bks. I and II (pp. 16-21). Poets in 1590's broke away from Spenserian allegory and wrote verse-expositions such as Sir John Davies' Nosce Teipsum (p. 23). Sonneteers, including Sp, frequently treated abstract mental states as separable entities (pp. 32-3). Donne's Elegies make assumptions about love very different from those of Sp and Sidney (pp. 35-6).

Burden, Dennis H. The Logical Epic: A Study of the Argument of Paradise Lost. Cambridge, Mass.: Harvard University Press, 1967. 206 pp. 555

In Chap. IV, The Satanic Poem, Part II, discusses Redcrosse's failure to distinguish the false Una (FQ, I, i) through her speech; in Chap. IX, The

Aftermath, cites Sp's November (SC), lines 153-57, in discussion of aspects of the fall and death.

Bush, Douglas. Classical Influences in Renaissance Literature. Cambridge, Mass.: Harvard University Press, 1952. 60pp.
556

Martin Classical Lectures delivered at Oberlin College in 1947. Brings Sp into the discussion of Renaissance heroic poem, Troy story as representative classical theme, pictorial elaboration and doctine of *ut pictura poesis*, convention of catalogue of beauties of female body ("*Epithalamion . . .* the finest love poem in the language"), Circe story and Bower of Bliss (pp. 35-47).

Bush, Douglas. English Literature in the Earlier Seventeenth Century, 1600-1660. 2nd rev. ed. Oxford: Clarendon Press, 1962. 680 pp.   557

Repr. of 1945 ed. First half of Chapter 3 (pp. 76-92) deals with The Successors of Spenser: Drayton, Browne, Wither, Basse, Giles and Phineas Fletcher, and others.

Bush, Douglas. English Poetry: The Main Currents from Chaucer to the Present. New York: Oxford University Press, 1952. 222pp.   558

"Spenser . . . in the unified breadth of his culture and the bulk, variety, and centrality of his accomplishment, is the most complete representative of the English Renaissance." Discussion, pp. 38-46. See also Index.

Bush, Douglas. John Keats: His Life and Writings. New York: Macmillan, 1966. 224 pp.   559

Sp "prime agent" in developing Keats's love of poetry (pp. 22-3, 27-8, 31). Eve of St. Agnes "was the natural and opulent flowering of Keats's Spenserian manner" (pp. 113-5). Main material of La Belle Dame sans

Merci conflates Duessa's seduction of Red Cross Knight (FQ, I, ii, 14, 30, and 45) and Arthur's vision of Faerie Queene (I, ix, 13-15) (pp. 124-5). Keats had begun to experiment with irregular stanzaic patterns earlier in Endymion when he wrote odes; Epith and Lycidas "had been in his mind all the way along" (pp. 126-7). Keats's "priestly and architectural role" in Ode to Psyche recalls Amor 22 (p. 130 note). For other references to Sp, see Index.

Bush, Douglas. Mythology and the Renaissance Tradition in English Poetry. New York: Norton, 1964. Rev. ed. 372 pp.   560

Repr. of 1932 ed. Sp's classical mythology integral part of FQ, yet many medieval and Renaissance influences. Contrasts Sp with Jonson, "first thoroughgoing neoclassicist." Sp's classical learning has been reduced, debt to medieval and Renaissance literature extended. Discusses artistic handling of myth in shorter poems and FQ in particular, and use of Homer, Virgil, and Ovid in latter. In FQ classical and Christian influence fuse. Troubled answer to question of change and permanence in Mutability Cantos, as in Donne's Anniversaries. Sp's treatment of myth largely colored by medievalism and continental literature of 16th century. For many other references to Sp, see Index.

Bush, Douglas. Mythology and the Romantic Tradition in English Poetry. Cambridge, Mass.: Harvard University Press, 1937. 647pp.   561

Sp referred to in many connections: conflict between poetic myth and religion in 18th century (pp. 23-6), poetry of Collins and Akenside (pp. 34-6), Coleridge (pp. 53-4), Wordsworth (pp. 58-9), Keats (pp. 85, 90, 92, 99, 101-3, 111, 120-1), Shelley (pp. 129, 133, 139-43, 147), minor poets of early 19th century (pp. 169, 172, 175-7, 181, 189-92), Tennyson (pp. 207, 225), Morris (pp. 306, 310, 313, 323-4), Swinburne (pp. 343-350, 352), Bridges (pp. 433-5, 439); and in Conclusion (pp. 526-36). See also Index.

Bush, Douglas. Pagan Myth and Christian Tradition in English Poetry. Philadelphia: American Philosophical Society, 1968. 112 pp.   562

Three lectures on Renaissance (pp. 1-31), Romantic, and Modern periods. Operative in Renaissance hospitality to pagan myths were Christian assimilation, pagan religion, Latin as conveyor of classical mythology, allegorized mythology of Boccaccio, Giraldi, Conti, and Cartari, idea pagan myths gave garbled versions of Biblical truth, and typological approach. Sp blends pagan and Christian in SC, uses mythological imagery to develop ethical themes in FQ, celebrates marriage in Epith as symbol of Christian order in terms of pagan myth. Most typical moralized myth of Renaissance was enchantress Circe's sensual temptation of man, retold in Acrasia's temptation of Guyon (FQ, II, xii). Hercules absorbed into Christian typology (FQ, I, xi). Cupid could be evil (FQ, III, xi-xii) or God (HOHL). Myth of Garden of Adonis (FQ, III, vi) reassuring on process time and change; Mutability Cantos (FQ, VII) end with "an anguished prayer for the eternal stability of heaven."

Bush, Douglas. Prefaces to Renaissance Literature. New York: Norton, 1965. 110 pp.   563

Four lectures previously published 1952 (556) and 1957 (566). New essay: The Isolation of the Renaissance Hero. Foreword contrasts homogeneity of Renaissance culture with fragmentation of modern culture (pp. ix-

xiii). Isolation of modern hero counteracted in Renaissance by veneration for classical tradition, belief in didactic purpose of literature (e.g., Sp's Letter to Raleigh), idealization of heroic figures, confidence of writer in his society, universe, and audience. Sp could rely on traditional ideas of virtues; characters inhabit world of romance while immersed in active world. Despite common Christian faith, Sp's and Milton's heroes different. Contrasts FQ, rooted in Christian humanism, with Renaissance tragedy; but in Shakespeare and heroic poets we see "isolated human goodness unconquered by evil or the traditional moral sense of mankind rallying to oppose evil" (pp. 91-106).

Bush, Douglas. The Renaissance and English Humanism. Toronto: University of Toronto Press, 1939. 139pp.   564

Four lectures given at the University of Toronto. Combats the Burckhardtian thesis of rebellious individualism as the keynote of the Renaissance. Sp's humanism represents no sharp break with medievalism. The broad aim of Tudor humanism, training in virtue and good letters, inspired the heroic romances of Sidney and Sp, who carried on the tradition of the Christian Middle Ages and supported an established order.

Bush, Douglas. Science and English Poetry: A Historical Sketch, 1590-1950. New York: Oxford University Press, 1950. 166pp.   565

The Patten Lectures delivered at Indiana University in 1949. In Chap. 1, The Elizabethans: The Medieval Heritage, pp. 3-26, takes Sp as representative, just on the eve of the new science, of the conflict between Christian humanistic belief in a world ordered by God and skeptical belief in naturalistic flux.

Bush, Douglas. Themes and Variations in English Poetry of the Renaissance. Claremont, Cal.: Claremont Graduate School, 1957. 45pp.   566

Two lectures delivered at the Arensberg Renaissance Conference. In God and Nature, describes climate of belief in 16th century England, which still saw the world, including physical nature, as rational and ordered, under control of a God who concerned himself with man's every thought. Sp in FQ, I, ix demonstrates belief in God's loving concern for weak struggling man, and in Epith position of marriage in religiously ordered world (pp. 5-23). In Time and Man, emphasizes that Renaissance poets could count on a generally Christian attitude and response in their audience. Sp illustrates idea of decline from the Golden Age (FQ, V, Proem). He shows that poetry was viewed as teaching, and that even in a Calvinist milieu man was not absolved from prime moral responsibility (pp. 24-44).

Butler, Christopher. Number Symbolism. New York: Barnes & Noble, 1970. 186 pp.   567

Provides rationale or theory for "numerological criticism." Surveys traditions which met in Renaissance number symbolism: (1) Pythagorean view of cosmos as governed by mathematical ratios, cosmology taken over by Plato especially in Timaeus; (2) Judeo-Christian exegesis of Bible in terms of number symbolism, by Philo Judaeus, Augustine, and Hugh of St. Victor, resulting in codified arithmology; (3) lore that gradually accrued to numbers in occult sciences. Examines, as representative of numerological tradition, Giorgio's De harmonia mundi, Du Bartas' Le Sepmaine, Agrippa's De occulta philosophia, and Bongo's De numerorum mysteria. In chap. on "Number Symbolism in England" gives examples of poetry by authors, including Sp, who used numerological structures.

Butler, P. R. Rivers of Milton and Spenser, QR, 291 (1953), 373-84.   568

Milton primarily concerned with foreign rivers, Sp with British. Sp uses more geographical qualifiers with his rivers than Milton; Milton has more descriptive epithets, especially for Biblical and classical streams. Sp speaks of fifty English streams in FQ alone, most readily identified today. Proth celebrates the Thames, to which all British and Irish rivers pay tribute in FQ, IV, xii. His descriptions of Irish rivers in CCCHA and Epith are fresh and intimate.

Butt, John. The Augustan Age. New York: Norton, 1966. 156pp.   569

Although Dryden would create label, Sp among earliest aware of diction theory (p. 11). Pope, Shenstone and Thomson, Sp's 18th century imitators, borrowed his diction and "childlike innocence" to produce new poetry and preserve romance aura (pp. 100-4).

Buxton, John. Elizabethan Taste. New York: St. Martin's Press, 1964. 370 pp.   570

Many allusions to Sp in Introductory (pp. 3-38), several in chaps. on Architecture, Painting, and Sculpture (pp. 41-167), many in chap. on Music (pp. 171-220). Section on SC in chap. on Literature (pp. 231-45). See Index.

Buxton, John. Sir Philip Sidney and the English Renaissance. 2nd. ed. New York: St. Martin's Press, 1964. 283 pp.   571

Repr. of 1954 ed. Sees Sidney as the Maecenas of learning "whose lively intelligence and sure taste stimulated and guided the poets of the English Renaissance" (p. 1). "The Elizabethan poets never doubted that but for Philip and Mary Sidney their work would have been negligible" (p. 3). This thesis is maintained throughout. Has much to say about Sidney's relations, personal and literary, with Sp. "This alone would be sufficient praise of Sir Philip Sidney's perspicacity as a patron of poets, that he recognized Spenser's genius so early, in spite of some dislike of his diction, and that he set him to the task of writing the greatest poem of the English Renaissance" (p. 132). Pembroke College portrait of Sp facing p. 100. See Index.

Buxton, John. A Tradition of Poetry. Illus. London: Macmillan, 1967. 190 pp. 572

Chaps. on poets from Sir Thomas Wyatt to the Countess of Winchelsea. George Gascoigne addressed Gascoigne's Woodmanship to Lord Grey, later served by Sp in Ireland; Gabriel Harvey wrote marginal notes in Certayne Notes of Instruction; E. K. praised Gascoigne in glosses on SC (pp. 42, 45, 57). Many references to Sp in chap. on Michael Drayton (pp. 59-86); Nimphidia may be first mockheroic poem in English, unless Muiop is preferred. Richard Fanshawe's sonnet A Dream, following Sp's Proth, praises Aston sisters as two swans; A Canto of the Progress of Learning in Spenserian stanzas (earliest), Mutability Cantos the model, invocations to Muse and Sp's ghost; Fanshawe's translation of Aeneid IV in Spenserian stanzas, managed "with fine assurance" (pp. 109-12, 114-7).

Cain, Thomas H. Spenser and the Renaissance Orpheus, UTQ, 41 (1971), 24-47. 573

Sp uses Orpheus as symbol of poet, not as philosopher of occult he was to Pico and Ficino. This Orpheus, epitome of humanist ideal of eloquence, in Boccaccio and Natalis Comes. Sp identifies self in SC as modern Orpheus, though Colin unable to win Rosalind as Orpheus won Eurydice with his lyre. SC "serves as an extended inability-topos before the vast encomiastic gesture" of FQ. Sp uses Orpheus archetype in FQ to define role as poet praising his queen. Scudamour and Calidore fall short of eloquent Orpheus, and Colin in Bk. VI no longer triumphant Orpheus of April in SC. In Epith, Sp plays role of Orpheus winning his bride. Disillusioned view of poet's importance to society apparent in Proth. Withdrawal from Orpheus role complete in escapist ending of Mutability Cantos. "This medieval touch of *contemptus mundi* is remote from the triumphalism and omnicompetence of the Orpheus promoted by the Renaissance humanists."

Campbell, Lily B. Divine Poetry and Drama in Sixteenth-Century England. Cambridge: Cambridge University Press, 1959. 268pp. 574

Sp's translation of the Seven Penitential Psalms is lost (p. 50); his version of the Song of Solomon is lost (p. 60); Chapter X, Du Bartas and the English Poets (pp. 84-92), is chiefly on Sp's relations with the Sidney circle and the influence of L'Uranie on RR, TM, and especially 4 Hymns (pp. 86-92).

Carpenter, S. C. The Church in England, 597-1688. London: John Murray, 1954. 516pp. 575

Elizabethan bishops were intellectually second-rate. Bishop Grindal, often criticized as weak, won Sp's praise in SC (p. 332). Sp, who was very well-read, may have known first four books of Hooker's Laws of Ecclesiastical Polity. He learned Puritanism at Cambridge, and his anti-Romanism was intensified by experiences in Ireland. Mentions ecclesiastical satire in SC and MHT. Sp's positive religious faith shines in HOHL. FQ contains religious allegory, but it is rather confused (pp. 336-7).

Carré, Meyrick H. Phases of Thought in England. Oxford: Clarendon Press, 1949. 392pp.   576

   Chap. 6, Humanism and Reforma-tion, pp. 178-223. Elizabethan exploration of human sensibility was medieval in basis. For Sp and other writers old cosmology stood. Position of man in order of things is the central interest, and their treatment rests on psychology of 13th century. Greatest systematic thinker of age Richard Hooker. Ramist logic immensely popular in England. Platonic doctrines received from Italy by Sp, Drayton, and others. This strain mingled with another and more emotional tradition, that of hermetic philosophy and the Jewish Cabbala, present in Sp and Ralegh, in Donne and Vaughan (pp. 196-210).

Carter, William Hoyt, Jr. *Ut Pictura poesis*: A Study of the Parallel between Painting and Poetry from Classical Times through the Seventeenth Century. Doctoral diss., Harvard University, 1951. HRDP, 1950-1951, p. 11; DDAAU, 1950-51, No. 18.   577

   Parallel became a critical commonplace in Renaissance and continued into 18th century. In England, pictured-wall motif used freely by Chaucer and successors. "Many Elizabethans, among them Sir Philip Sidney, Abraham Fraunce, Robert Greene, Edmund Spenser, Samuel Daniel, William Shakespeare, and Michael Drayton, were obviously practicing *ut pictura poesis* in their lavishly pictorial writing." Finds in "Painter's Scene" of The Spanish Tragedy and its parodies beginnings

of 17th-century Instructions-to-a-Painter poems. Dryden's preface to his translation of Du Fresnoy's De arte graphica was important. Long before this there were many painter-poets—Crashaw, Butler, and others. Many comparisons of painting and poetry were written. "By the end of the seventeenth century, *ut pictura poesis* was a ubiquitous and somewhat ominous phrase in the terminology of English art and literary criticism."

Cassirer, Ernst. The Platonic Renaissance in England. Trans. James P. Pettegrove, Austin, Tex.: University of Texas Press, 1953. 207pp.   578

   Die platonische Renaissance in England und die Schule von Cambridge was originally published in 1932. Sp "creates a new and original type of Platonic literature. The Platonism of the Elizabethan Age found its most complete poetic expression in Spenser's *Faerie Queene*, and in his 'Hymne of Heavenly Love' and 'Hymne of Heavenly Beautie'." Adventures of Red Cross Knight (FQ, I) are "an account of the ascent of the human soul to that source of beauty which is also the source of all wisdom and of all religious knowledge." Sp makes poetry out of Plotinus. 4 Hymns "have the same significance for England that Michelangelo's sonnets have for Italy. They are the transformation of a theory of the beautiful into an artistic act and the confirmation of this theory through the fundamental powers of artistic creation" (pp. 112-6). See also Index.

Catz, Justin Enoch. Edmund Spenser's *Amoretti* and *Epithalamion*. DA, 29 (1969), 4451A. University of Wisconsin, 1968. 314 pp.   579

   Probable that Amor and Epith, published together 1595, celebrate Sp's courtship and marriage. Amor and

Epith volume attempts to translate Sp's vision of FQ, especially parts on romantic love, into different literary form. Hence, interpretation uses FQ as illuminative background. Denies characterization of sonnet lady is inconsistent; varied aspects of womanhood in FQ focused on single figure in Amor. But presentation of lady subordinated to comic action. Cosmic passages in FQ clarify Sp's treatment of time in sonnets. Courtship viewed as heroic quest and associated with romance of Amoret and Scudamore. Style of Amor related to rhetoric of praise. Balanced style of sonnets appropriately conveys "that romantic love which is the primary expression of harmony in Spenser's imaginative world." At same time, differences between Amor and Epith in form and spirit enable Sp to represent difference between bitter and sweet love.

Cawley, Robert R. Unpathed Waters: Studies in the Influence of the Voyagers on Elizabethan Literature. New York: Octagon, 1967. 285 pp. 580

Repr. of 1940 ed. Sp reflects the heritage of the Middle Ages in the floating islands of Phaedria and Acrasia, FQ, II, vi and xii (p. 17); "gold of Opher," CCCHA, 1. 490 (p. 34); the Tree of Life, FQ, I, xi (p. 55); the magnetic Rock of Reproach, FQ, II, xii (p. 58); the unicorn, FQ, II, v, 10 (pp. 67-70); the savage man, FQ, IV, vii (p. 107). He also reflects the spirit of the voyagers (p. 124), and in many scenes shows the influence of seamen and the sea (p. 176).

Cazamian, Louis F. The Development of English Humor. Durham, N. C.: Duke University Press, 1952. 421pp. 581

Discusses Sp, pp. 358-62. Examines SC, Muiop, and MHT, and concludes that "the faculty was not lacking in him; but he was more gifted and more sincerely eager in very different

strains. The significant fact remains that the saving grace has paid him more than one visit."

Cellini, Benvenuto. Fantasie e realtà nell' opera di Edmund Spenser, in Annuario dell'Istituto Universitàrio di Venezia (1952-3 and 1956-7), pp. 12-23. 582

Chace, Jo An Elizabeth. Spenser's Celebration of Love: Its Background in English Protestant Thought. DA, 29 (1968), 226A. University of California, Berkeley, 1967. 389 pp. 583

Establishes background of Protestant thought on matrimony and illustrates the influence of this thought on Spenser's love poetry. Covers matrimony as institution for controlling sexuality, grace attending sexual union between spouses, order within household with husband as head. Allegory of Timias and Belphoebe linked to Protestant tenet of sexuality restrained by matrimony. Chapter headings: A Poet of the Delighted Senses, Spenser and the English Church, The Reformation and English Marriage Law, and the Protestant Doctrine of Matrimony.

Chadwick, Owen. The Reformation. Baltimore: Penguin Books, 1966. 463 pp. 584

First ed. 1964. Sp mentioned in connection with The Assault upon Calvinism, under The Study of the Fathers (pp. 218-20). In early 17th century fresh air in doctrine and morals of Protestantism. Discerned in "new metaphysical and mystical interests of English poets, from Spenser to Donne and Vaughan," and in consciousness of a "a sacramental universe" in Sp, Donne, Herbert, and others.

Chatman, Seymour, and Samuel R. Levin, eds. Essays on the Language of Literature. Boston: Houghton Mifflin, 1967. 450 pp. 585

Part I, Sound Texture, includes essay by Ants Oras (pp. 19-32; see 1595); in Part III, Grammar, essay by Josephine Miles (pp. 175-96, from PMLA, 70 (1955), 853-75; see 917).

Chernaik, Warren L. The Poetry of Limitation: A Study of Edmund Waller. New Haven: Yale University Press, 1968. 236 pp.   586

Waller's Cavalier lyrics draw on universal mutation of Lucretius, theme of Sp's Mutability Cantos (p. 96). Elizabethan literature abounds with praise of Queen, yet as Sp indicates poet's vision not limited to court concerns; in 17th century court world became more isolated, and panegyric became political (pp. 117-8). Waller's Battle of the Summer Islands tries to be both heroic and mock heroic; flexibility of tone indicates debt to Tasso, Ariosto, and Sp, especially FQ, III, IV and VI (pp. 183-4). Dryden in Art of Poetry associates Waller's harmony with Virgil's and Sp's; in reliance on adjectives and nouns rather than verbs resembles Sp, Milton, and Fairfax, differing from Jonson and Donne (pp. 203, 209-10). Marlowe's Hero and Leander, Drayton's England's Heroical Epistles, and Sp's MHT in closed couplets, but sense continuous, and balance and antithesis rare; heroic couplet of Waller, Dryden, and Pope uses elaborate patterns of parallel and contrast (pp. 211-2). Waller formed style on Fairfax's translation of Tasso, and in it and FQ found didactic purpose expressed in "well-sounding numbers" (pp. 219-21).

Chew, Samuel C. The Pilgrimage of Life. New Haven: Yale University Press, 1962. Illus. 449 pp.   587

Analyzes masses of information (notes pp. 299-402) on concept of man as pilgrim through life in Renaissance literature and pictorial art. Frequently refers to or quotes Sp's works on Time the Destroyer, Fortune, parallel between Seasons and Ages of Man, Deadly Sins, Faith, Hope, Charity as spiritual guardians of man, Cardinal or Stoic Virtues, guises and adventures of Cupid (Love), man's encounters with Despair, emblem books, and other literary-iconographical topics. See Index.
Rev: Harry Berger, Jr., YR, 52 (1962), 301; Maurice Valency, RN, 17 (1964), 113.

Church, R. W. Spenser. New York: AMS Press, 1969. 181 pp.   588

Repr. of 1879 ed. Chronological account of Sp's life and works, main events of former and evaluation of latter, from early years, publication of SC (1579), career in Ireland, publication of FQ (1590, 1596), to last years.

Cirillo, A. R. The Fair Hermaphrodite: Love-Union in the Poetry of Donne and Spenser, SEL, 9 (1969), 81-95.   589

Topos of hermaphrodite includes concept of spiritual union of two souls without emphasis on physical aspect. Plato's Symposium basis of tradition of virtuous spiritual union in Ficino and other Renaissance Neoplatonists. Sp compares Amoret and Scudamore at end of FQ, III (1590) to hermaphrodite and describes spiritual ecstasy. Context of transcendent harmony of this union elsewhere in FQ (IV, x, 41), CCCHA (ll. 801-802), HHOB (ll. 197-207), and conclusion of Epith. Such a concept of union in Donne's The Extasie and Valediction: Forbidding Mourning. See 2014, 2015. [SpN, Vol. 1, No. 2 (1970), 4-5.]

Clark, Earl John. Spenser's Theory of the English Poet. DA, 16, No. 13, 1956, 141. Loyola University of Chicago, 1956. 333 pp.   590

Sp's treatise on English poet, mentioned by E. K. in headpiece to October in SC, is lost; but his critical principles may be deduced from remarks in June and October of SC, TM, MHT, CCCHA, letters to Harvey, View, and FQ. These show Sp's ideas of character of poet, his training, inspiration, rewards, function, imagination, technique, and the poetic process. Concludes that Sp's theory is so consistent with Renaissance literary theory and so closely parallels Sidney's in Defence of Poesy that his lost treatise would probably not have added anything of great significance to critical theory. His most important critical dictum concerns poet's role of moral instruction, with the pleasure of poetry justified only insofar as it makes didacticism more effective.

Clear, Shelagh. Spenser the Innovator, Unisa English Studies, 2 (1967), 57-68.
591

Clements, A. L. The Mystical Poetry of Thomas Traherne. Cambridge, Mass.: Harvard University Press, 1969. 232 pp.
592

Biblical pattern of Creation-Fall-Redemption in world-view of Dante, Sp, Milton, Blake, and Wordsworth; Traherne may be understood from perspective of Christian mysticism (p. 35). Refers to Renaissance metaphors of body-soul as castle, as in Sp's Castle of Alma in FQ, II, x (p. 95). In regarding Clerist as Wisdom, Traherne follows Renaissance tradition of Sp, Donne, and Milton (pp. 111-3). Traherne's poetic theory and practice close to "metaphysical" Herbert and Vaughan, but style also points to Wyatt, Sidney, Sp, and Jonson (pp. 191-6).

Clements, Robert J. Picta Poesis: Literary and Humanistic Theory in Renaissance Emblem Books. Illus. Rome: Edizioni di Storia e Letteratura, 1960. 246 pp.
593

Several sections previously published; see 1316 and 2353. Thirteen plates following p. 246. Sp's Letter to Raleigh on symbolism in FQ of as much interest to literary historian as Raphael's letter to Castiglione on reception of Galatea to art historian. Sp translated verses for Theatre, first English emblem book. Influence of emblematists on creative literature reflected throughout Sp's poetry, and in Sidney, Jonson, Donne, Crashaw, Bunyan, and Thoreau (pp. 16-8). Sp's RT uses swan motif as it appeared in Andrea Alciati's Emblemata (1551) and Geoffrey Whitney's Choice of Emblems (1586) (pp. 36-7). Virtue emblematists taught was "the fulfillment of man's moral and intellectual potentialities, not the social and courtly vertù ... which Spenser has in mind writing the letter prefacing his Faerie Queene" (p. 105). Soldierly ideal for chivalric courtier emphasized by Castiglione, Tasso, and Sp (pp. 146-7). For other references to Sp, see Index.

Clements, Robert J. Poetry and Philosophy in the Renaissance, CLS, 8 (1971), 1-20.
594

No Greek philosopher gave Renaissance poets more exploitable themes than Plato. Principal legacy his theory of ideal form, "up in that realm described in Spenser's Hymn of Heavenly Beauty." Other Platonic themes [in Sp's poetry] include Reminiscence, Ladder of Love, Winged Soul, the Androgyne, Four Furies, Metempsychosis and Demons, and concepts of Eros and Anteros. Lucretius was accepted as great poet. "Spenser typically cribbed thirty-odd lines from De rerum natura for a hymn to Venus."

Colbrunn, Ethel B. The Simile as a Stylistic Device in Elizabethan Narrative Poetry; An Analytical and Comparative Study. DA, 14 (1954), 2064-5. University of Florida, 1954. 315 pp.
595

Examines A Mirror for Magistrates, FQ, Hero and Leander, Venus and

Adonis, The Rape of Lucrece, Endimion and Phoebe, and Mortimeriados. "The works of two Spenserians of the early seventeenth century, Giles and Phineas Fletcher, are included for contrast."

Colie, Rosalie. Castiglione's Urban Pastoral, Greyfriar: Siena Studies in Literature, 8 (1965), 5-13.   596

Achievement of pastoral is that its unreal world passes for "nature," an artificial nature in which "art" is criticized. In Castiglione's Book of the Courtier, Urbino is *locus amoenus*, in contrast to city of Machiavelli's prince. Castiglione's courtiers inhabit different world. Prince has no time for fine arts, for cultivation of self; courtier "must practice the arts, and he must be himself a work of art." Castiglione exploited notion of *sprezzatura*, "the grace of . . . seeming to do naturally what can only come from strict discipline." *Sprezzatura* works same illusion pastoral poet created. "The courtier's artifice transforms, and is transformed into, his nature." Works of art in Duke Frederick's palace include courtiers themselves. Castiglione presents himself and his work of art, his book, as examples of *sprezzatura;* says he wrote The Book of the Courtier in a few days.

Colie, Rosalie. Paradoxia Epidemica: The Renaissance Tradition of Paradox. Princeton: Princeton University Press, 1966. 553 pp.   597

Chap. II, "Being and Becoming in *The Faerie Queene*" (pp. 329-52), falls under ontological paradoxes. Sp's view of being and becoming in 4 Hymns mainly Platonic and derived from Ficino. Nature in Garden of Adonis (FQ, III, vi) different, presents problem of relation of Becoming to Being. Both paradoxically changeless and changing. In Mutabil-

ity Cantos "wicked Time" of Garden of Adonis expands into its metaphysical condition. All things, Titaness argues, change their forms as if arbitrarily. But end-product of process not important to Sp, rather "the relationships among aspects of Being." Judgment of Nature in God's favor is paradox uniting Being and Becoming. Yet Sp remains Christian, anticipating eternal rest and freedom from change with "that great Sabbaoth God" (FQ, VII, viii, 2). He united flux and form, necessary to each other because they are each other. Sp's solution illuminates method of FQ, ever moving among great variety of things (being) but stories end on metaphysical moral (becoming). Characters never get anywhere; "rather they *discover* themselves and others." Nature, external or human, is indivisible web. In Sp's world "every single thing referred finally to *one* thing . . . Becoming led to Being . . . because it *was* Being." See Index.

Collins, Joseph B. Christian Mysticism in the Elizabethan Age. Baltimore: Johns Hopkins Press, 1940. 251pp.   598

Sp, pp. 190-231. Because Sp ranks "highest in the history of Christian mysticism in the Elizabethan age . . . , the House of Holiness and the *Fowre Hymnes* deserve a crowning place in this study." Spiritual allegory of Bk. I places it in tradition of the Pilgrimage of Life type of Christian mystical treatise. House of Holiness (FQ, I, x) exemplifies the full methodology of Christian mysticism. Defends the unity of 4 Hymns. Discusses the nature of Sapience in HOHB and the theology of the poems. The last two Hymns "embody respectively the Christocentric and the Theocentric types of contemplation."

Collins, Robert Arnold. The Christian Significance of the Astrological Tradition:

A Study in the Literary Use of Astral Symbolism in English Literature from Chaucer to Spenser. DAI, 31 (1970), 353A. University of Kentucky, 1968. 261 pp. 599

Middle Ages and Renaissance did not view astrology as a deterministic science opposed to Christian tradition, but found imagery of divine providence in astrological symbolism. Studies the use of astral symbols by Chaucer, Lydgate, Henryson; by Lyly in The Woman in the Moone; by Greene in Planetomachia. Sp reflects a conservative tradition in Mutabilitie Cantos: God's providence in mechanism of the cosmos, wheel of the Zodiac, and cycle of creation. Cycle of zodiacal year is a microcosm of the grand pattern of Christian history as reflected in allegory of FQ, I, "for the spiritual journey of Red Crosse is analogous to the stages of the sun's journey through the twelve signs of the zodiac."

Colwell, C. Carter. The Tradition of British Literature. New York: Putnam's, 1971. 384 pp. 600

Sketch of Elizabethan sonnet writers, including Sp (pp. 62-7). Brief mention of Epith and FQ, greater strength of Middle Ages in England than in Italy (pp. 130-4). Mention of SC, "essentially the first pastoral in English," in discussion of Lycidas (pp. 149-56). For incidental references to Sp, see Index.

Comito, Terry Allen. Renaissance Gardens and Elizabethan Romance. Doctoral dissertation, Harvard University, 1968. 738 pp. 601

Part I studies gardens of religious and secular literature of Middle Ages and Renaissance (pp. 3-376). Chap. VI of Part II, Exile, concerned with Cymbeline (pp. 382-526). Chap VII of Part II, Return, mentions CCCHA (pp. 563-75) and SC (pp. 613-25) in connection with general discussion of Sidney's Arcadia (pp. 527-689).

Connolly, Francis X. Poetry, Its Power and Wisdom: An Introductory Study. New York: Scribner's, 1960. 370 pp. 602

Brief mention of Sp in connection with sonnet, romance, Spenserian stanza—first used in narrative but later associated with descriptive or meditative verse, obscurity in modern poetry in contrast to Chaucer, Sp, Milton. See Index.

Cory, Herbert E. The Critics of Edmund Spenser. New York: Haskell, 1964. 108 pp. 603

Repr. of 1911 ed. As noted by Carpenter (26), "Treats the criticism of Sp historically, to the nineteenth century... A substantial contribution, marred by faults of taste and style" (p. 224). Listed in Atkinson, p. 164.

Cory, Herbert Ellsworth. Edmund Spenser: A Critical Study. New York: Russell and Russell, 1965. 478 pp. 604

Repr. of 1917 ed. in University of California Publications in Modern Philology, 5. Contains separate chaps. on SC; FQ, I-III; Complaints, Elegies (Daph and Astro), CCCHA; Amor and Epith; FQ, IV-VI; Sp's Swan Songs (4 Hymns, Proth, and Mutability Cantos); Conclusion (imitations of Sp). "I agree with John Dewey that with Galileo and Descartes," and later Darwin, "there arose an attitude which ... was to play havoc with the Greek and Scholastic teleology" ... but "far more emancipating to real religion than many timorous ecclesiasts have believed. But while our philosophy cannot be entirely like Spenser's, our lives still find perennial inspiration in his life and poetry." As a whole, not very useful and dated criticism written in florid style.

Courthope, W. J. A History of English Poetry. Vol. II, The Renaissance and the Reformation: Influence of the Court and the Universities. London: Macmillan, 1962. 429 pp.   605

First ed. 1897. Chap. IX, Court Allegory: Edmund Spenser (pp. 234-87). Sp's life and works, with emphasis on SC and FQ. Quotes Letter to Raleigh in full. Relation of FQ to Ariosto's Orlando Furioso. Sp's "ideas dwell in a kind of Limbo between the mediaeval and the modern world, invested with a mild, harmonious atmosphere, which imparts a certain effect of unity to the most incongruous objects."

Craig, Hardin. The Enchanted Glass: The Elizabethan Mind in Literature. New York: Oxford University Press, 1936. 293pp.   606

Listed in Atkinson, p. 216. Sp used throughout for purposes of illustration, in connection with transfusion of soul in its bearing on love and friendship (p. 45); Calvinism (p. 56); values (p. 82); faculty psychology (p. 115); Ramism (p. 149); formalized ethics (p. 186); current theories of the state (p. 190); Aristotle (p. 200); "lightness of touch" (p. 207); Platonism (p. 221); didacticism (p. 228).

Craig, Hardin, gen. ed. A History of English Literature. New York: Oxford University Press, 1950. 697pp.   607

Book II, The Literature of the English Renaissance, Hardin Craig, pp. 175-342. Sp and SC (pp. 206-7); Elizabethan sonnet (pp. 240-5); FQ (pp. 248-50). Sp bibliography, p. 641. See also Index.

Craig, Hardin. New Lamps for Old: A Sequel to The Enchanted Glass. Oxford: Basil Blackwell, 1960. 244pp. 608

Sp's psychology in House of Alma, FQ, II, ix, 44-60 (pp. 53-5); Renaissance individualism, freedom of crea-

tivity in art and literature (pp. 119-39); Sidney's greatness as critic in estimate of Sp (p. 175); literature of politics, political significance of FQ and Shakespeare's history plays (pp. 194-8); Sp in connection with Elizabethan psychology (pp. 199-202); "there is encouragement ... in the high degree of development to be seen in the scholarship of Chaucer and Spenser. ... The vast field of Shakespeare ... has had the attention of many great scholars, but is still strangely disordered by conjecture, avoidance and dogmatism" (p. 223).

Craigie, Sir William A. The Critique of Pure English from Caxton to Smollett. SPET, 65. Oxford: Clarendon Press, 1946. 171pp.   609

Reprints E. K.'s epistle to Gabriel Harvey, prefixed to SC (pp. 133-4); Sidney's criticism in An Apology for Poetrie of "old rustick language" in SC (p. 134); reference to Sidney's criticism by Heylin in Extraneus Vapulans, 1656 (p. 154); contrast between Sp's antiquated diction and currency of Waller's in Preface to the Second Part of Waller's Poems, 1690 (p. 160); reference to Chaucer, Sp, and Shakespeare as still intelligible to Scots, in Smollett's Humphrey Clinker, 1767 (p. 164); mention of Sp in Vindex Anglicus; or The Perfections of the English Language Defended and Asserted, 1644 (p. 168).

Craik, George Lillie. Spenser and His Poetry. New York: AMS Press, 1971. 252 pp.   610

Repr. of 1845 ed.

Cruttwell, Patrick. The Shakespearean Moment and Its Place in the Poetry of the 17th Century. New York: Random House, 1960. 262pp.   611

Repr. of 1954 ed. Change in sensibility in 1590s brought change in climate from that of Arcadia and FQ to that of Hamlet and Donne. Sp used as whipping boy to illustrate thesis. Amor monotonous, abstract; Shakespeare's sonnets crackle, Donne's The Sunne Rising concrete. Sp supreme representative of Elizabethan worship in April of SC, Shakespeare of radical doubt in history plays and problem comedies (pp. 1-17, 27-32). New discoveries inspired exhilaration in Sp (FQ, II, Proem), "painful but more fruitful" dismay in Donne's First Anniversarie, and Shakespeare's King Lear. FQ true contemporary of Drayton's "mausoleum of applied patriotism" in Polyolbion (1612, 1622), not Donne's Anniversaries and Webster's plays (pp. 41-3, 53-6, 62-8, 71). "Lady and saint worship" of Sp unconvincing: Donne's "ingenious fence-sitting was pure gain." Coming from poetry of Sidney, Sp, or Marlowe to that of Donne and mature Shakespeare, reader feels "an increased thickness of texture" (pp. 80-93, 105-6). When comes to later 17th century, lays off Sp. See 2429.

Cummings, L. Spenser's *Amoretti VIII:* New Manuscript Versions. SEL, 4, (1964), 125-35.   612

Identifies as authorial the changes in the various MS forms of Amor VIII, "all but one of which can be tentatively dated as prior to or contemporaneous with the 1595 printing of the sequence by Ponsonby." A note from Ponsonby suggests that the poem be dated prior to 1580. This would help explain the close resemblance of two of the MS versions to a poem by Fulke Greville. It would also connect Sp more closely to the Sidney circle than is generally done, and would add a new dimension to the Sp-Harvey correspondence.

Cummings, R. M., ed. Spenser: The Critical Heritage. New York: Barnes & Noble, 1971. 355 pp.   613

Includes 179 critical comments, mostly very short, ending with John Hughes in 1715. Material chronologically arranged except for sections on Language and Style, Gabriel Harvey to Alexander Pope (pp. 277-314); and Biographical Notices, William Camden to John Hughes (pp. 315-41). Introduction deals with general critical trends in each period represented (pp. 1-33). From E. K. to William Warner, 1579-1600; from William Camden to Sir Aston Cockayne, 1600-1660; from John Worthington to John Hughes (27 pp., with quotations deleted, from 1715 ed. of Sp's Works), 1600-1715.

Daiches, David. A Critical History of English Literature. 2 vols. New York: Ronald Press, 1960.   614

Vol. 1, Chapter 7, Spenser and His Time (pp. 165-207). Gives a concise critical survey of Sp's poetical works (pp. 165-94).

Daiches, David. Literature and Society. London: Victor Gollancz, 1938. 287pp.   615

Chapter II (pp. 76-118) on Renaissance and Restoration. Sp, pp. 86-95. Sp is representative of the courtly tradition. His work "illustrates a fusion of different traditions to an extent that no other single work of the time does: the Middle Ages, the Renaissance and the Reformation all meet in the *Faerie Queene.*"

Danby, John F. The Poets on Fortune's Hill: Literature and Society, 1580-1610, CamJ, 2 (1949), 195-211.   616

Discusses Elizabethan-Jacobean statecraft as presented in Fulke Greville's Life of Sidney, which is "a shrewd analytic statement of the mechanics of sixteenth-century rule." Social position of representative poets explains something of literary output of the time. Sidney was free, above patronage. "For Sidney poetry is the private devotion to truth." In contrast, "Spenser's poetry must win him preferment." Donne represents a third type: "the gentleman-poet who is also . . . a mis-fit." "Unlike Donne's, Ben Jonson's career is a success story." Best example of fifth class of Elizabethan-Jacobean poet, one who makes livelihood in the theater, is of course Shakespeare.

Danby, John F. Poets on Fortune's Hill: Studies in Sidney, Shakespeare, Beaumont and Fletcher. London: Faber and Faber, 1952. 212pp.   617

Sp treated briefly, pp. 33-6. His poetry is learned, professional, and adulatory of the Queen because, unlike Sidney, Sp had to make his fortune. "For Sidney . . . poetry was truth, whereas for Spenser poetry was prestige." See also Index.

Daniells, Roy. The Baroque Form in English Literature, UTQ, 14 (1945), 393-408.   618

Defends the validity of baroque as a usable concept in literary classification, applying methods used by Heinrich Wölfflin in Principles of Art History (English translation, 1932) to differentiate the forms of baroque from those of the high Renaissance. Contrasts the poetry of Sp and Milton to illustrate the essential and distinctive features of high Renaissance and baroque poetry.

Darnell, Donald Gene. Hawthorne's Emblematic Method. DA, 25 (1965), 5903. University of Texas, 1964. 141 pp. 619

Striking similarity between works of Renaissance emblem makers and "the fictional technique of America's foremost allegorist." Link between emblematists and Hawthorne in works of Sp and Bunyan, favorites of Hawthorne. His method emblematic

for three reasons: (1) moral viewpoint throughout, (2) externalized qualities of characters through costume, physical appearance, etc., and (3) emblematic structure of significant passages, with emblem's formal divisions of motto, picture, and explanatory poem. Emblems an integral part of The Scarlet Letter, The Blithedale Romance, and The Marble Faun. Analyzes characteristic scenes to show use of emblematic technique.

Davie, Donald. Purity of Diction in English Verse. London: Routledge & Kegan Paul, 1967. 217 pp.   620

Repr. of 1952 ed. Old distinctions of genres and appropriate diction for each no longer hold. Just as well, for doubtful modern poet could write with conscious art of Sp. Diction varies according to different cultures; Sp's diction "courtly-humanist," Samuel Johnson's diction "bourgeois-pious" (pp. 6-10). Generalizing epithets characteristic of 18th century; "corruption usually took a Miltonic or a Spenserian form," as in "plashy brink" (pp. 47 ff.). Wordsworth's The White Doe of Rylstone "is a thoroughly Spenserian poem" (pp. 117-9). Analyzing Coleridge's To a Friend, Who Had Declared His Intention of Writing No More Poetry, speaks of "the embarrassed Spenserian diction of the opening," which "should be even more grotesque than it is" (pp. 126-8). In terms of Elizabethan decorum, Shelley's Letter to Maria Gisborne in base style of SC, his Julian and Maddalo in mean style of CCCHA, his The Cloud in high style of 4 Hymns (pp. 137 ff.).

Davies, Hugh Sykes, ed. The Poets and Their Critics. Rev. ed. 2 vols. London: Hutchinson Educational, 1960. 240, 351 pp.   621

First pub. 1943. Sp in Vol. 1, Chaucer to Collins. Spenser in decline at present. "The history of Spenserian criticism gives reason for believing that a revaluation of his work is both possible and probable in the near future" (p. 36). Excerpts from E. K., Letter to Raleigh, Kenelm Digby, Dryden, T. Warton, Hurd, Coleridge, Gilfillan, C. S. Lewis, Tillyard, and a few others (pp. 36-69).

Davis, B. E. C. Edmund Spenser: A Critical Study. New York: Russell & Russell, 1962. 267 pp.   622

Repr. of 1933 ed. Two chaps. on Life and Works are introductory, claiming no new biographical material (pp. 1-57). Chaps. III-V on Humanism, Romance, and Allegory regard Sp as New Poet of English Renaissance who combined traditions of classical and medieval culture (pp. 58-128); chaps. VI-VIII on Diction, Imagery, and Verbal Music, Verse regard Sp as Poet's Poet who set example for successors that has endured (pp. 129-209). Final chap. on Philosophical Ideas recognizes Sp more than painter in words or creator of fantasies, regards him as eclectic interpreter of Renaissance humanism (pp. 210-43).

Dédéyan, Charles. Dante en Angleterre: Moyen-Age—Renaissance. Paris: Didier, 1961. 225 pp.   623

Sketches Gabriel Harvey's relations with Sp, finds tenuous affiliations between Harvey and Dante (pp. 172-7). Briefly reviews Sp's career; discussing FQ tries to relate moral allegory, allegorical characters, monsters, episodes such as Cave of Despair, Red Cross and Dragon, Guyon in cave of Mammon, Britomart's love, meeting of Serena and Timias with Mirabella, and Calidore among shepherds to various features and techniques of Dante, no matter how remote resemblances may be (pp. 180-216).

De Ford, Sara, and Clorinda H. Lott. Forms of Verse: British and American. New York: Appleton-Century-Crofts, 1971. 392 pp.   624

A college text, with exercises. Sp discussed and quoted for examples of pentameter couplet, SC, May, ll. 27-38, and MHT, ll. 45-64; ornamental alliteration in FQ, I, i, 20, 41, contrasted with that in Swinburne's Chorus from Atalanta in Calydon; Amor 34 as example Sp's special type of sonnet; Sp used ottava rima in VG, but only important long poem in English in this stanza is Byron's Don Juan; Spenserian stanza for narrative (FQ, I, i, 4 quoted) used by Thomson in The Castle of Indolence, Burns in The Cotter's Saturday Night, Byron in Childe Harold's Pilgrimage, Keats in The Eve of St. Agnes, Shelley in Adonais, Tennyson in The Lotus-Eaters—samples from each quoted. For references to Sp in text and Glossary (pp. 307-82), see Index.

Delattre, Floris, and Camille Chemin. Les Chansons Élizabéthaines. Bibliothèque des Langues Modernes, 2. Paris: Didier, 1948. 459pp.   625

Introduction of 8 chapters of literary history followed by texts of songs with French translations on facing pages. Chapter 1, La poésie lyrique élizabéthaine, pp. 12-33. SC established vogue of pastoral lyric in last two decades of 16th century; pastoral convention seen as escapism; brief mention of Amor, Epith, Proth, 4 Hymns, and FQ; general qualities of Sp as a lyric poet (pp. 17-28).

DeMoss, William Fenn. The Influence of Aristotle's "Politics" and "Ethics" on Spenser. New York: AMS Press, 1970. 70 pp.   626

Repr. of 1920 ed. Part on Aristotle's influence on FQ in MP, 3 (1918). Deals briefly with Aristotle's influence on View, SC, 4 Hymns, and MHT (pp. 65-70).

De Mourgues, O. M. A Comparative Study of the French and English Poets of the Late Sixteenth and Earlier Seventeenth Centuries. Doctoral diss., Cambridge University, 1950.   627

    Noted (unseen) by Isadore Silver, Ronsard in European Literature: A Synoptic View of Scholarly Publications, BHR, 16 (1954), 242, note 5.

Dimter, Margarete. Der Adjektivgebrauch bei Spenser. Doctoral diss., University of Vienna, 1946. 128pp. Anglia, 71 (1953), 509.   628

    In three parts: 1. Grammar, 2. Stylistic, 3. Summary. "From the standpoint of stylistic, the added characterizing word is not a slovenly means of arousing attention and ornamenting language. The value of the characterizing word lies above all in its indirect association with nouns and other adjectives, not logically belonging to the chief word, to which it is syntactically related. So artful a use is naturally foreign to popular speech, but it nevertheless played an important role in Elizabethan poetry. To Spenser the adjective is a cherished means of style which he employed with great range and rich variety." In Part 2 studies Sp's adjectives in this light, demonstrating in abundance truth of last quoted sentence.

Dixon, Michael Faraday. "Words Equall Vnto My Thought": A Study of Religious Rhetoric in the Poetry of Edmund Spenser." Doctoral dissertation, Harvard University, 1970. 255 pp.   629

    Aims to show relation between Sp's religious thought and his rhetoric, and difference between rhetorical methods in religious and secular works. In moral eclogues of SC, *paroemia* and *epitheta* most prevalent. Analyzes "Rhetoric of Debate" in May, July, and September. "Rhetoric of Fear" in plaintive eclogues (January, June, and December) uses *antithesis* between youth and age for conventional *allegoria*. Most prevalent scheme in House of Holiness (FQ, I, x) is *prosopographia*, called "Rhetoric of Place." Rhetorical figures in Redcrosse's encounters with Error and Archimago prepare for encounter with Orgoglio (FQ, I, vii), in which hyperbolic elements of *prosopographia* represent "the knight's distorted vision of spiritual reality." World of FQ, VI, is secular; Sp uses "Rhetoric of Incident" in delineating Calidore's failure. "Rhetoric of Abstraction" in 4 Hymns distinguishes between earthly and heavenly, climbs the Platonic ladder. Five Appendices on rhetorical figures (pp. 222-51).

Dollarhide, Louis E. The Paradox of Ruskin's Admiration of Renaissance English Writers, UMSE, 8 (1967), 7-12.   630

    John Ruskin exalted art of Middle Ages, denigrated art of Renaissance. Shakespeare was an exception, and so was Sp. "The reading of Spenser was a religious duty in the Ruskin household, and Ruskin never lost his love for the deep moral earnestness of Spenser's work." Chief interest in Sp's allegory, description of vices and virtues in FQ, true to medieval ideas. Thought SC "bears close comparison with the . . . vitality of Gothic sculpture." Had little admiration for Milton. "Because the spreading [Renaissance] evil moved more slowly in painting, sculpture, and poetry [than in architecture], Ruskin can still admire Michelangelo, Tintoretto, Leonardo, Shakespeare, and Spenser."

Doran, Madeleine. " 'Yet am I inland bred'," Shakespeare 400, ed. J. G. McManaway, pp. 99-114. New York: Holt, Rinehart & Winston, 1964. 323 pp.   631

Claim of Orlando in As You Like It (II, vii, 91-97). This leads to discussion of Golden Age theme presented by Shakespeare sometimes in terms of nature and art, or nature and nurture, or order and disorder, or the court and the "green world." Pastoralism of As You Like It not pure, but mixed. One reference to Sp's Pastorella and his "salvage man" in FQ, VI (p. 105, note 11), but relevant to Sp's pastoralism in general.

Doughtie, Edward, ed. Lyrics from English Airs. Cambridge, Mass.: Harvard University Press, 1970. 657 pp.   632

Sp mentioned in connection with development in 1570's and 80's of conformity between language stress and stresses in metrical pattern, so that effects could be achieved by varying from pattern. "Quantitative meters and music were always linked in theoretical discussions," sometimes in practice. Cites 2315. Continental influences becoming more important, but "certain native qualities persisted in both music and poetry," witness varied verse forms of Sp's SC (1579). Cites Jane K. Fenyo, "The Rhythmic Basis for the Songs of 'August' 'April' and 'November' of The Shepheardes Calender" (unpub. M. A. thesis, Queens College, CUNY, 1964), who "makes a good case for the probability of Spenser having tunes in mind while writing these poems." See 530, 844, 2242. Musica Transalpina first anthology of Italian music with English words. Canzone stanza with free rhyme scheme and varied line lengths was welcome novelty; "it has long been recognized as an element in the success" of Sp's Epith and Proth (pp. 21-3). For references to Amor and FQ, see Glossarial Index.

Dreyfus, Norman J. Eighteenth Century Criticism of Spenser. Doctoral diss.,

Johns Hopkins University, 1938. DDAAU, 1937-38, No. 5.   633

Sp's language never won approval. Objection to his prosody and stanza lessened. Except for SC, minor poetry was neglected. After mid-century Thomas Warton and Richard Hurd "unearthed the concept of the Faerie Queene as a 'Gothic' poem." Sp shared in new attention given Chaucer, the Elizabethans, Ariosto and Tasso, Shakespeare- and Milton-worship, interest in a past blended of history and sentimentalism. "No eighteenth-century critic achieved a really comprehensive appreciation of the Faerie Queene as a romantic epic." Gradually the formula for "following nature" was liberalized to include Sp's "irregular" artistry, but this "derived far more from the general complex of pre-romanticisms than from any direct appeal of the poet himself." In fact, first quarter of 19th century had to pass "before criticism could rejoice openly and unashamed in poetry that is thick, rich and ripe to the taste like a sweet wine."

Duncan-Jones, Katherine. A Note on Tennyson's "Claribel," VP, 9 (1971), 348-50.   634

In Claribel: A Melody, "Claribel's name and situation come from . . . Spenser's Faerie Queene" (II, iv). Mentions Sp's other Claribel, "who secretly marries Bellamour and becomes the mother of Pastorella" (VI, xii), but she is not tragic like Tennyson's; and Alonso's daughter Claribel in Shakespeare's The Tempest, but she is remote.

Dundas, Judith. Allegory as a Form of Wit, SRen, 11 (1964), 223-33.   635

In Sp's and Donne's time, "wit" normally indicated reason, judgment, the controlling intellect which imposes order on the materials of the fancy or imagination. Allegory implied such control of imagination by wit. The 20th century does not like this kind of wit because it implies that life has suprasensible order. Allegory is too daring for doubtful moderns, who prefer Donne's wit of irony which, asserting likeness in opposites, is uncommitted and reflects a break-up of order.

Dunlap, Rhodes. The Allegorical Interpretation of Renaissance Literature, PMLA, 82 (1967), 39-43.   636

Sp composed explanatory letter for FQ, because he knew how doubtfully all allegories may be construed. Shakespeare's poetic method and use of allegory are "wholly different" from those of Sp and other allegorists. Coleridge says of Sp, "The dullest and most defective parts of Spenser are those in which we are compelled to think of his agents as allegories." Discussion of FQ, I, v.

Dunn, Esther Cloudman. The Literature of Shakespeare's England. New York: Scribner's, 1936. 326pp.   637

Chapter IV, Edmund Spenser, pp. 97-139. "The key to his poetry lies, I believe, in a right understanding of the man." Emphasizes education under Mulcaster, association with Harvey begun at Cambridge (pp. 97-101). Eclecticism and traditionalism of SC, liberal point of view in it; Sp closer to English Middle Ages, as shown by attitude on question of language, than to Greece and Rome (pp. 101-7). Compares FQ with Ralegh's History of the World and Donne's Sermons for spacious design and eloquent style. Effect of Sp's Irish experiences on the epic. Can be read with or without detailed attention to allegory, as Elizabethans read it. Sp's confusion in facing new problems of science and philosophy (pp. 108-22). Succinct analysis of minor poems (pp. 123-39).

Durling, Dwight L. Georgic Tradition in English Poetry. Port Washington, N. Y.: Kennikat Press, 1964. 259 pp.   638

Repr. of 1935 ed. Echoes of Virgil's Georgics in Googe, Sp, Daniel, and others in 16th century. But first georgic in English showing definite Virgilian influence is Thomas Moufat, *The Silkwormes*, 1599 (p. 33). In 18th century Bacon, Milton, Sp, and Pope were "legislators in arts of landscape" (p. 93). James Thomson's The Seasons observed natural divisions of year, as did many other 18th-century poems, following example of SC and Phineas Fletcher's Piscatorie Eclogs (1633), imitations of Sp (pp. 122-3). Thomas Pennant in British Zoology (1766) in descriptions of birds and animals often quotes Virgil, Ovid, Sp, Milton, and Thomson (p. 144). "Catching the contagion of rural verse," David Carey wrote The Pleasures of Nature (1803), long episodic poem of seasons in Spenserian stanzas (p. 173).

Dyson, A. E., ed. English Poetry: Select Bibliographical Guides. London: Oxford University Press, 1971. 375 pp.
                639

Peter Bayley, Spenser, pp. 15-39. Critical and discursive commentary on Texts, Critical Studies and Commentary from beginnings to books of 1960's written from British as distinct from American point of view; Bibliographies, Background Reading, and References divided into same sections as body of article.

Eagle, R. L. The Arcadia (1593)—Spenser (1611) Title Page, Baconiana, 29, No. 116 (1945), 97-100.   640

Follows up exchange of correspondence, ibid., 28, No. 111 (1944), 75-7 (see 643). Gives facsimile of title-page of 1611 Sp, points out same block was used for title-page of 1593

Arcadia, and interprets it in relation to Sidney's work.

Eaker, J. Gordon. The Quest for the Historical Renaissance, BuR, 9 (1961), 291-302.   641

Nature of Renaissance from perspectives of various historians: religious, cultural, economic, ideological. Consensus is that characteristics of Middle Ages extended forward into Renaissance, supported by examining sources of such writers as Sp, Shakespeare, and Milton. One reason for decline of humanism was "pedantry and artificiality" in use of classical languages, which prompted experiments of Gascoigne, Sp, and Harvey in the use of their own language.

Eccles, Mark. A Survey of Elizabethan Readers, HLQ, 5 (1942), 180-2.   642

Short Title Catalogue entries show Sp was one of the best-known authors of the period, among those who had twenty books or reissues published during the reign of Elizabeth.

Editor and others. Correspondence, Baconiana, 28, No. 111 (1944), 75-7. 643

Exchange concerning SC and title-page of 1611 edition of Sp. See 640.

Editors of ELH, eds. Critical Essays on Spenser from *ELH.* Baltimore: Johns Hopkins Press, 1970. 257 pp.   644

Thirteen essays published between 1937 and 1969, each listed herein: William Stanford Webb (1732), A.S.P. Woodhouse (1752), Kathleen Williams (1744), A.C. Hamilton (1415), James E. Phillips (996), Isabel G. MacCaffrey (2259), Millar MacLure (1535), D. Douglas Waters (1882), Maurice Evans (1914), B. Nellist (1967), Lewis H. Miller, Jr. (1959), Richard Neuse (2158), Joanne Field Holland (2180).

Edwards, Calvin Roger. Spenser and the Ovidian Tradition. DAI, 30 (1969),

1155A. Yale University, 1958. 385 pp.
645

Evaluates the two principal types of Ovidian influence in Sp's poetry, mythological and philosophical. Sp uses Ovidian mythology in allusions and similes, in tapestry descriptions, and in traditional mythological scenes. He uses Ovidian philosophy in his concepts of change and love, which are related to Metamorphoses. Discusses influence of Metamorphoses on Sp's poetry in general and FQ in particular.

Eichholz, Jeffrey Paul. Play in the Poetry of Edmund Spenser. DAI, 31 (1970), 2873A. Yale University, 1970. 327 pp.
646

Sp a playful poet whose levity inseparable from serious moral purpose. Only God worthy of wholly serious regard, so Sp regards man with gentle irony. Man redeemed by God's love and dedication to moral and intellectual discipline. FQ disciplinary exercise or cultural play. SC extremely playful. MHT shows Sp's ability to adapt several satirical purposes. Muiop masterpiece of playful narration; Sp plays with his hero, the butterfly. Levity in FQ surveyed as "synthetic" and "analytic" wit. House of Alma typifies first kind. Braggadochio chief comic figure in FQ, defective hero presented satirically. Malbecco episode witty and destructive. Mutability's rebellion falsely justifies dignity of human life; Cantos clarify Sp's playful attitude toward man.

Elioseff, Lee Andrew. Pastorals, Politics and the Idea of Nature in the Reign of Queen Anne, JAAC, 21 (1963), 445-56.
647

Discusses difference between simplicity and rusticity; expression of simple thought should be plain but not clownish and should not imitate manners, thoughts, and archaic lan-

guage of Sp. "This English pastoral-
ist's language and characters betray a
want of innocent simplicity which is
essential to the thought and pure diction of ideal pastoral life." Eclogue
should appear to be shepherd's own
poem, but the poem of a shepherd
who finds his pastoral existence his
recreation, not his business.

Elliot, G.R. Humanism and Imagination.
Chapel Hill, N. C.: University of North
Carolina Press, 1938. 253pp.   648

   Chapter 1, The Divergence of Humanism and the Spirit of Poetry, pp.
3-22. Sp, more than any other English
poet, has a keen personal sense for
divinely human realities. Too much
has been made of his Platonism and
too little of his Christianity. "The
peculiar greatness of this poet is due
to his strong and constant perception
of the substantiality of transcendent
forms, together with his rich endow-
ment in the faculty that embodies
them in poetry, namely the mythological imagination." Modern criticism has emphasized Sp's shortcomings. This is due to a fading of belief
in the eternal meaning of poetry, of
religious faith in poetry. "Spenser
pre-eminently had that faith." Yet his
view of life is inclusive, truly realistic.
His range of poetic vision "exceeds
Shakespeare's vertically and Milton's
horizontally."

Elliott, John R., Jr., ed. The Prince of
Poets: Essays on Edmund Spenser. New
York: New York University Press,
1968. 332 pp.   649

   Intro. (pp. ix-xv). Part I: The Poets'
Poet gives short estimates of Sp from
Gabriel Harvey to Virginia Woolf
(1757). Part II: The Critics' Poet gives
evaluations of Sp by William Hazlitt
and James Russell Lowell. Part III:
The Scholars' Poet has essays by Edward Dowden on Sp as poet and

teacher and by W. L. Renwick on Sp's
philosophy. Part IV: The Minor
Poems has essays by William Nelson
(961), Louis Martz (2451), Robert
Kellogg (2427), Thomas M. Greene
(2382), and Robert Ellrodt (650).
Part V: The Faerie Queene includes
modern essays by Graham Hough
(1449), A. C. Hamilton (1416), Frank
Kermode (1945), Thomas P. Roche,
Jr. (1646), and Sherman Hawkins
(2179). Selected Bibliography (pp.
319-21).

Ellrodt, Robert. Neoplatonism in the Poetry of Spenser. Geneva: Droz, 1960.
246 pp. See 649 and 2460.   650

   Reevaluation of Platonic and Neoplatonic influences on Sp's thought.
Until 4 Hymns, Sp is influenced little,
or not at all, by Ficinian Neoplatonism in any technical sense. Sp's Neoplatonism in FQ is the diffused Neoplatonism characteristic of medieval
times. Sp's romantic love fundamentally opposed to Ficinian amor ra-
zionale, which is unconcerned with
romantic fulfillment in marriage of
male-female relationship. 4 Hymns
show knowledge of, but not adoption
of, the Ficinian ladder of love.
   Rev: C.S. Lewis, EA, 14 (1961), 107
(see 879); William Nelson, RN, 14
(1961), 277; J. A. Notopoulos, MLR,
57 (1962), 85; B. E. C. Davis, RES, 13
(1962), 178; G. Boklund, SN, 35
(1963), 168.

Elmen, Paul. Shakespeare's Gentle Hours,
SQ, 4 (1953), 301-9.   651

   Interprets   Shakespeare's   word
"howers" in sonnet 5 as referring to
the Horae, goddesses of the seasons,
and cites Sp's references to the goddesses in Epith, ll. 98-102, and in
FQ, VII, vii, 45, 1.

Elton, Oliver. Michael Drayton: A Critical
Study. New York: Russell & Russell,
1966. 216 pp.   652

Repr. of 1905 ed. Sp influenced Drayton most in pastoral and sonnet; praise of Sp in Drayton's verse at intervals for thirty-five years (pp. 26-34). "It is likely" that Sp praised Drayton, "his chief lieutenant in pastoral," as Aetion in CCCHA (pp. 37-9). For references to most of Sp's works in connection with Drayton, see Index.

Elton, William R. *King Lear* and the Gods. San Marino, Cal.: Huntington Library, 1966. 369 pp.   653

In connection with motifs in King Lear, makes many scattered references to Sp in text and notes. Cites each book of FQ at least once, Astro, Muiop, TM, HHOB, and SC. See Index.

Emley, Edward. Dr. Johnson and the Writers of Tudor England. DA, 23 (1962), 224. New York University, 1958. 245 pp.   654

In preparation for his Dictionary, Johnson systematically read Tudor writers: More, Camden, Stowe, Sp, Shakespeare, and Jonson. Knew half of FQ, nearly all Sp's minor poems, and View. He read Sp in preparation for Dictionary, then discussed the poetry in Rambler, finally applied conclusions in Lives of the Poets. Unfortunately neglected practically all Tudor drama, but acquired broad knowledge of Elizabethan authors and their background.

Empson, William. Seven Types of Ambiguity. 2nd rev. ed. London: Chatto and Windus, 1947; 3rd ed., 1953. 258pp.
655

First published 1930. Incidental references to Sp. Structure, movement, and rhythm of Spenserian stanza (pp. 33-4). Allegory as one way to sublety in language, as in SC and FQ (pp.

123-4). Examples from Sp of trouble with negatives, flatness of meaning (pp. 207-9).

Endicott, Annabel M. Renaissance Theories of Poetic Decorum, and their relation to late Sixteenth Century poetic practice. Doctoral dissertation, University of London, 1966. 264 pp.   656

A study of relation between form and content in English poetry of late 16th century, applying concepts of decorum of Italian and English critics to examples of poetic technique. Under decorum of style gives examples from RR, CCCHA, FQ, 4 Hymns, and Amor. Under decorum of measure (line length) gives examples from several eclogues of SC. Under decorum of staffe (stanza, or verse form) gives examples from SC, Epith, RT, Astro, Muiop, and VG. Under decorum of ornament gives examples from FQ and Amor.

Entwistle, William J., and Eric Gillet. The Literature of England, A.D. 500-1942. London: Longmans, 1943. 292pp. 657

Part 2, The English Classics, Chap. IV, Spenser and Sidney, pp. 35-42. "There is more mastery of life to be found in Spenser's friend and patron, Sir Philip Sidney" (p. 39).

Erdman, David V. and Ephim G. Fogel, eds. Evidence For Authorship: Essays on Problems of Attribution. Ithaca: Cornell University Press, 1966. 559 pp.
658

Sp mentioned throughout in reprinted essays. See Index. Intro. to annotated bibliography section on Sp points to attribution problem concerning lines 217 ff. of Astro (p. 423) but focuses on articles dealing with Sp's questionable authorship of Axiochus (pp. 423-427). See 417, 2605, 2608.

Evans, B. Ifor. A Short History of English Literature. London: Penguin Books, 1940. 215pp.   659

Sp, pp. 23-6.

Evans, B. Ifor. Tradition and Romanticism: Studies in English Poetry from Chaucer to W. B. Yeats. New York: Longmans, 1940. 213pp.   660

Attempts to lessen clash between "romantic" and "classical" by examining conception of poetry held by poets in different periods. Chap. 2, On the Terms "Romantic" and "Classical." Chap. 3, Chaucer to Shakespeare, pp. 23-43, considers Sp's place in the tradition. Sp knew Langland but followed Chaucer. He wanted to produce a classical poetry, yet the effect and influence of his work have been romantic. FQ "reveals no design." Sp looks out at the world from the court. "The decorative, multicoloured vision removed from reality remains dominant," not his moral and social purposes.

Evans, Ifor. English Literature: Values and Traditions. New York: Barnes and Noble, 1962. 96pp.   661

Dedication of FQ to Elizabeth (p. 12); Sp as one of many Renaissance men to use language effectively (p. 34); Sp's power of language for imaginative comparison (p. 57); narrative structure of FQ (p. 62).

Evans, Maurice. English Poetry in the Sixteenth Century. 2nd rev. ed. New York: Norton, 1967. 184 pp.   662

First published 1955. In Chapter III, Poetic Theory and Practice (pp. 31-46), Sp cited passim. SC (pp. 89-93). Amor (pp. 101-3). FQ a great integrative force in late 16th century literature. Its allegory is fluid, must not be interpreted too rigidly. Method "demands a sustained intellectual effort and an unflagging sense of moral values." Love and justice receive fullest analysis. Sp tries to reconcile conflicting philosophies of his age. Greatest enemy of virtuous love is lust. Justifies style: "Spenser, like Yeats, uses simple language to express very complex symbols." Fusion of many materials gives unrivalled richness to texture of poem. "The fusion of allegory and romance is so complete and the verse moves in so many dimensions that the complexity of the Metaphysicals is thin in comparison" (pp. 132-60). Contrast of attitude toward love of Sp and Donne, the old and the new (pp. 173-5). See also Index.

Evans, Maurice. Metaphor and Symbol in the Sixteenth Century, EIC, 3 (1953), 267-84.   663

In showing parallels between the tradition of allegorical interpretation of the Bible in medieval and Renaissance homilies and the rhetorical use of metaphor by 16th-century poets, cites Sp's use of the besieged fort metaphor in attack on Alma's castle (FQ, II, ix) and in Amor 14, and his use of the storm-tossed ship metaphor in Amor 63.

Evans, Robert O. Spenser's Role in the Controversy over Quantitative Verse, NM, 57 (1956), 246-56.   664

Contends that the controversy was an intellectual game and not a real issue.

Evans, Robert O. The Theory and Practice of Poetic Elision from Chaucer to Milton with Special Attention to Milton. Doctoral diss., University of Florida, 1954. DDAAU, 1953-54, No. 21.   665

Evett, David Hal. Nineteenth-Century Criticism of Spenser. Doctoral dissertation, Harvard University, 1965. 341 pp.   666

Says in Introduction, "Spenser has never, since sometime before 1650, been a popular national favorite like Shakespeare, Milton, Bunyan, or Dickens." Unable to explain this, calls it "a displacement of interest." Concentrates in each chapter on "the more substantial critiques, selected for their intrinsic interest and historical importance." Chap. I, Gothic Invention in the Eighteenth Century: Thomas Warton. Chap. II, The Poet of Our Waking Dreams: the Romantics. Chap. III, Spenserian Scholarship 1800-1900, discusses John Wilson, George Craik, James Russell Lowell, R.W. Church, Edward Dowden, and others. Chap. IV, The Development of the Romantic View. Chap. V, The Romantic Flight: James Russell Lowell and Others. Chap. VI, Esthetics and Practical Morality: Some *Partis Pris*. Chap. VII, The Triumph of History: Church, Moulton, Percival.

Evett, David. "Paradice's Only Map": The *Topos* of the *Locus Amoenus* and the Structure of Marvell's *Upon Appleton House*, PMLA, 85 (1970), 504-13.
667

In tracing Renaissance developments of basically simple *topos* of *locus amoenus* into complexity and variety, mentions perversions of idea in Isle of Phaedria (FQ, II, vi), *locus* of sloth, or in Acrasia's Bower (II, xii), *locus* of lust, in contrast with Garden of Adonis (III, vi), *locus* of peace, or of genius. And Red Cross dallies with Duessa in a *locus amoenus* setting (I, vii). Also identifies "a familiar kind of *antitopos*," e.g., opening of January in SC.

Fairchild, Hoxie Neale. The Romantic Quest. New York: Russell and Russell, 1965. 444 pp.
668

Repr. of 1931 ed. Sp influenced Romantics in different ways: Wordsworth reflects ethics; Coleridge and Byron borrow freely, superficially; Keats absorbs dreamy richness and glories in Sp even through other Romantic imitators. See Index.

Feinstein, Blossom Grayer. Creation and Theories of Creativity in English Poetry of the Renaissance. DA, 28 (1967), 1394A. City University of New York, 1967. 383 pp.
669

One view of Creation orthodox Christian view of Creation *ex nihilo*, accepted in Middle Ages and found in writers from Hawes to Jonson. Other view of Creation *ex chaos* indebted to Near-Eastern cosmogonies and mysticism, found in writers from Wyatt to Chapman. Implications of *ex chaos* affirmed in Shakespeare's The Tempest, Sp's FQ, CCCHA, and first two of 4 Hymns, and Milton's Paradise Lost. But orthodox view of *ex nihilo* returns when Prospero's art is overthrown and only prayer remains, in Sp's last two of 4 Hymns, and in Milton's Paradise Regained and Samson Agonistes. With rejection of Chaos three great writers reach state in which all passion is spent, a state that signals end of Renaissance creativity.

Ferguson, Wallace K. The Renaissance. Berkshire Studies in European History. New York: Holt, 1940. 148pp.
670

General introduction to the period. Mixed character of English Renaissance. "Edmund Spenser (1552-99) wove both classical and Italian elements into the entirely English poetry of the *Faerie Queene*, at the same time using the machinery of Arthurian romance and medieval allegory with a detached sophistication that demonstrates the vast gap between the literary taste of his age and that of the later Middle Ages." Drama was most vigorous literary genre in Elizabethan England. Superiority of

French and English vernacular literature to that of other countries (pp. 127-8). Bibliographical note, pp. 137-43.

Finkenstaedt, Thomas, Ernst Leisi, and Dieter Wolff. A Chronological English Dictionary Listing 80,000 Words in Order of their Earliest Known Occurrence. Heidelberg: Carl Winter, 1970. 1395 pp.   671

Based on main entries in Shorter Oxford English Dictionary. Undoubtedly some of 298 words of 1579 were introduced by Sp; and also some of 344 words of 1590. Which ones would require reading of Shorter Oxford English Dictionary.

Finn, Sister Dorothy Mercedes. Love and Marriage in Renaissance Literature. DA, 15 (1955), 2188-9. Columbia University, 1955. 299 pp.   672

Two diverse cultures, classical and medieval, with opposed ideas of love and marriage were inherited by Renaissance writers. Studies attitudes toward marriage, romantic love, friendship, extra-marital love. "These two strains, the classical and the medieval, merged in later Renaissance literature. Marriage and love were then brought together in a new relation. Ariosto popularized the idea of making marriage depend on love. Tasso, and finally Spenser, followed the same plan."

Finney, Claude Lee. The Evolution of Keats's Poetry. 2 vols. Cambridge, Mass.: Harvard University Press, 1936. I, 3-405; II, 407-804.   673

Keats's first poem, Imitation of Spenser, "expressed his imaginative reactions to Spenser's Bower of Bliss" (I, 26-33). Sp's place among the Neoplatonic sources of Endymion (I, 291-9). Keats's Sonnet to Spenser (I, 362-5). Sp's influence on the form, imagery, and style of The Eve of St.

Agnes (II, 546-60), and on the form of Keats's odes (II, 610-2). See also Index.

Fisch, Harold. Jerusalem and Albion: The Hebraic Factor in Seventeenth-Century Literature. New York: Schocken Books, 1964. 301 pp.   674

Sp claimed eloquence to be inseparable blend of sweet "expression, noble birth, and virtuous life!" FQ contributes guide for attainment (pp. 21-22). Examines C. S. Lewis's argument (A Preface to Paradise Lost, Oxford, 1942, pp. 5, 78) that Milton in Paradise Lost, like Sp in FQ, created harmonious balance of Greek and Hebrew themes. Proposes Sp's Christian humanism reflected only partially in Milton and thinks imbalance and tension a result of Counter-Renaissance (pp. 128-133).

Fletcher, Angus. Two Treatments of Spenser, YR, 56 (1967), 453-8.   675

Review article on Rosemond Tuve's Allegorical Imagery (1152) and Kathleen Williams's Spenser's World of Glass (1741). Complains about Tuve's "proselytizing zeal" for her subject. Commends her argument for a two-level theory of allegory, moral and spiritual; her argument for a free polysemous reading; her care in remaining within the limits of source study; her theory of "extended ironical context" as applied to Jean de Meung; and especially her exploration of "the problematics of romance." Finally, he excuses her difficult style because "it is a style, and that is worth much." Says that Kathleen Williams has "managed better than any of her predecessors to write a clear, unpedantic, yet critically informed introduction to Spenser's masterwork."

Fletcher, Jefferson B. The Puritan Argument in Spenser, PMLA, 58 (1943), 634-48.   676

Sp in SC and other early poems was explicitly Puritan and critical of the Anglican Church. This attitude is consistent with that in FQ.

Fluchère, Henri. Shakespeare and the Elizabethans. Trans. Guy Hamilton. Foreword T. S. Eliot. New York: Hill and Wang, 3rd printing, 1960. 254pp. 677

First published as Shakespeare: dramaturge élisabéthain, 1947. Passing remarks on Sp in Part One, The Spirit of the Age, pp. 13-79. Sp erected a vast structure without life, "like a world of darkened mirrors," and unlike Shakespeare wrote a poetry not of the people (pp. 24-5). Marlowe freed himself from Sp's music "because he had . . . a spiritual ambition that could not be satisfied by smooth language" (p. 65). Fletcher's Faithful Shepherdess has "all the seductive style of Spenser stripped of its archaic affectations" (pp. 68-9). For other references to Sp, see Index.

Fogel, Ephim G. Salmons in Both, or Some Caveats for Canonical Scholars, BNYPL, 63 (1959), 223-36, 292-308. Repr. in Evidence for Authorship: Essays on Problems of Attribution, ed. David V. Erdman and Ephim G. Fogel, pp. 69-101. Ithaca: Cornell University Press, 1966. 559 pp. 678

R. W. Bond in "Lyly's 'Doubtful Poems' " (The Athenaeum, May 9, 1903) attributed work by several Elizabethan poets, Sp and Shakespeare among them, to Lyly, but later forced to rescind (p. 85). "Last Instructions," possibly written by Marvell, alludes to Sp and borrows from allegorical tradition (pp. 93-4).

Ford, Boris, ed. The Age of Shakespeare. A Guide to English Literature, 2. London: Penguin Books, 1955. 480pp. 679

References to Sp passim in connection with the social setting of Eliza-

bethan literature, background of popular taste, humanism and popular taste, satire, rhetoric and poetry, Daniel and Ralegh, and Shakespeare. See Index.

Foster, Joan M. The Influence of Spenser on Milton. M. A. thesis, University of London, 1945. ULSD, 1945, p. [7]. 680

Introduction examines Milton's acknowledgment of his debt to Sp. Separate chapters on Platonic and Neoplatonic influences in their work, their religious beliefs, their cosmic philosophy, their interest in language and orthography. An appendix gives a list of verbal parallels.

Fowler, Alastair, ed. Silent Poetry: Essays in Numerological Analysis. London: Routledge and Kegan Paul, 1970. 260 pp. 681

In Preface ed. says numerological structure was a significant literary device used by writers as late as 18th century; numerological structure was considered as important as metrical patterns and other literary structures. Includes essays by Christopher Butler introducing subject and summarizing much of his 567, by Michael Baybak, Paul Delany, and A. Kent Hieatt (1254), and Alexander Dunlop (2366, 2367).

Fowler, Alastair. Triumphal Forms: Structural Patterns in Elizabethan Poetry. Illus. Cambridge: University Press, 1970. 243 pp. 682

Wide-ranging study. Discusses Petrarch's Trionfi, Andrea Mantegna's Triumph of Caesar, and progressive internalization of form in Francesco Colonna's Hypnerotomachia Poliphili before close analysis of Sp's "triumph of Love" in FQ, III, xi-xii, which "represents a high point of the triumph in one art as Jonson's masques do in another" (pp. 37-58). Number symbolism in Mutability Cantos justifies Jupiter's sovereignty (pp. 58-61). FQ as example of literary mannerism has analogy in façade of Raphael's Palazzo dell' Aquila (Plate 11), both horizontal and vertical design. Six books of FQ form complementary pairs. Alternative grouping, most like Palazzo dell' Aquila façade, is "simultaneous coexistence" of 6- and 5-book division (pp. 108-12). Gives classical precedents for temporal numbers in epithalamia as background for analysis of Sp's Epith, modifying Hieatt's demonstration of spatial-temporal organization (2398), and explicates temporal and astronomical symbolism (pp. 180-2). For numerological references to SC, RR, RT, and Proth, see Index.

Fowler, Earle B. Spenser and the System of Courtly Love. New York: Phaeton Press, 1968. 91 pp.   683

Repr. of 1934 ed. Sketches medieval system of courtly love. Knights in FQ follow "the recognized customs, usages, and laws of the courtly system." Paridell (FQ, III, ix-x) is "a typically Ovidian lover." However, Sp "utterly rejects the ethical and moral implications of the traditional code and upholds an ideal love philosophy" in FQ, 4 Hymns, Amor, and CCCHA. He "personally embraced" a Platonic philosophy of love . . . "and adhered to it to the end of his career."

Fraser, Russell. The War Against Poetry. Princeton: Princeton University Press, 1970. 215 pp.   684

"The war against poetry recapitulates, like a metonymic figure, the passing of the old-fashioned or medieval psychology and the beginnings of the modern world." This thesis supported by citations of ancient and modern writers on economics, poli-

tics, religion—and of literature. Draws on Sp for attitudes toward change and transitoriness, and toward patronage. Contrast emerges between the new man, seeker after single truth; and allegorical poet, for whom complex nature of truth enhances its value. [SpN, Vol. 2, No. 3 (1971), 2.]

Frauwallner, E., H. Giebisch and E. Heinzel. Die Weltliteratur. 3 vols. Vienna: Brüder Hollinek, 1954.   685

Sp, III, 1684.

Freeman, Rosemary. Edmund Spenser. Lincoln: University of Nebraska Press, 1965. 39 pp.   686

Repr. of 1957 ed. Brief assessment of the works against the background of Sp's times. Selected bibliography, pp. 35-9.

Freeman, Rosemary. English Emblem Books. New York: Octagon Books, 1966. 256 pp.   687

Repr. of 1948 ed. Sp's early work in emblem tradition in Theatre, 1569 (pp. 51-2). "An interest in the methods of the emblem writers is reflected throughout Spenser's poetry." His imagery is emblematic, preferring simile to metaphor and being largely visual. "The most remarkable example of emblematic imagery in Spenser's poetry . . . is his use of the two swans in Prothalamion, for the whole poem is built round them." In general, his description has a "patterned outline," and his "movement is framed and formalised." His methods of allegory are influenced by the emblem method (pp. 101-13). Contrasts FQ and The Pilgrim's Progress, which stands at the end of the emblem tradition (pp. 207-8, 223-7).

Fridén, Georg. Studies on the Tenses of the English Verb from Chaucer to Shakespeare. EIUES, 2. Upsala: English Institute in the University of Upsala, 1948. 222pp.   688

Sp's works are among the sources used. Especially useful for late 16th century.

Friederich, W. P. Dante Through the Centuries, CL, 1 (1949), 44-54.   689

Dante's fame in France and England declined after 1500 because men of the Renaissance chose to see in the Dante of the Commedia only the poet of the past. This, plus the fact that Vita Nuova was not printed until 1576, prevented Sp and his French and English contemporaries from being significantly influenced by Dante. See 101.

Friederich, Werner Paul. Dante's Fame Abroad, 1350-1850: The Influence of Dante Alighieri on the Poets and Scholars of Spain, France, England, Germany, Switzerland and the United States. A Survey of the Present State of Scholarship. Chapel Hill: University of North Carolina Press, 1950. 582 pp. 690

In the time of Sp, Sidney, and Shakespeare there was a dearth of definite knowledge about Dante. Commedia and Vita Nuova had no significant influence on Sp or other English poets of 16th century. See 101.

Friederich, Werner P., with the collaboration of David Henry Malone. Outline of Comparative Literature: from Dante Alighieri to Eugene O'Neill. UNCSCL, 11. Chapel Hill, N. C.: University of North Carolina Press, 1954. 451pp. 691

Virgil's influence on Renaissance epic (pp. 6-7); Renaissance Neo-Platonism (pp. 12-4); Epicureanism produced conflict in FQ (pp. 14-5); continuity of Ovid's influence (pp. 20-2); Theocritus and the Renaissance pastoral (pp. 28-9); Sp was one of 16th century "readers, emulators, or translators" of Boethius (p. 31); Petrachism (pp. 56-60); Boccaccio's De Genealogia Deorum "served as a fre-

quent source both for Chaucer and Spenser" (p. 68); Boccaccio as founder of "the romanesque epic," which led to FQ (p. 72); Ariosto (pp. 74-5); Amadis de Gaula may have contributed to atmosphere of FQ (pp. 88-9); the Pléiade (pp. 90-1); baroque epic (p. 129); Tasso (pp. 139-41); Thomas Warton (p. 225); through G. B. Martelli's translation of 1831, Sp became known in Italy (p. 307); comparatist interested in Celtic revival "might wish to study also the impact of the ever-present Irish problem upon English mentality" from Sp to present. See Index.

Friedland, Louis S. Spenser as a Fabulist, SAB, 12 (1937), 85-108, 133-54, 197-207.   692

Examination of Sp's fables in SC and other minor poems. The fable appealed to Sp because it offered opportunities for a mild kind of satire, and because of its aptness for allegory. Many references to the Aesopic literature of the Renaissance.

Friedman, Donald M. Marvell's Pastoral Art. Berkeley: University of California Press, 1970. 300 pp.   693

Renaissance idea of pastoral as literary genre; Sp's use of Colin Clout as his pastoral persona in SC, CCCHA, and FQ, VI, x; Marvell learned much from Sp "especially in the matter of shaping an expressive emblem whose surface was as smooth and engaging as its meaning was complex," but did not follow him "to the extent of speaking through the pastoral mask for himself or about the art of poetry"; myth of Golden Age, prelapsarian garden, views of nature (pp. 4-14). Marvell's "Clorinda and Damon" uses convention of pastoral debate, as in Mutability Cantos, and "blazon," as in song of Eliza in April of SC (pp. 48-51). In discussion of Marvell's Mower poems mentions SC, traditional opposition between nature and conscious art epitomized in Garden of Adonis and Bower of Bliss in FQ (III, vi; II, xii), dance of Graces around Colin Clout in FQ, VI, x (pp. 119 ff.). For many other references to Sp, see Index.

Fromm, Harold. Spenserian Jazz and the Aphrodisiac of Virtue, EM, 17 (1966), 49-68.   694

Four subdivisions: 1. Spenser's Reputation: although we have inherited from the Renaissance the notion of Sp's greatness, by today's standards he is not a great poet, only a recorder of Elizabethan conventions. 2. Jazz: Sp's faulty verse categorizes him as a secondary poet. 3. Virtue: because of his Puritanism he cannot decide what is sinful and what is virtuous, as in Bower of Bliss, Garden of Adonis, and Epith, where shamefulness or sacredness of sexual delight is difficult to determine. 4. Spenser's Puritanism: causes a dichotomy between an expressed morality and a delight in the sensual. Thus Sp was a "healthy neurotic."

Frye, Northrop. Anatomy of Criticism: Four Essays. Princeton, N.J.: Princeton University Press, 1957. 383pp.   695

In Ethical Criticism: Theory of Symbols, says allegory is "a contrapuntal technique." In Dante, Sp, Tasso, and Bunyan it is systematic and continuous (pp. 90-1). Pastoral as example of convention (pp. 99-100). Dante and Sp are explicitly mythopoeic writers (p. 117). In Archetypal Criticism: Theory of Myths, mentions Florimell's disappearance under the sea (p. 138), Red Cross Knight's emblem (p. 144), "Spenser's last major allegorical vision . . . of Serena stripped and prepared for a cannibal feast," Blatant Beast as symbol of mob (pp. 148-9), other details in FQ (pp. 151-4), FQ, I, as following Bib-

lical quest-romance theme, various illustrations in FQ of "four poles of characterization," Pisgah vision theme in Mutability Cantos (pp. 194-205). In Rhetorical Criticism: Theory of Genres, refers to several features of Sp's use of rhythm and sound (pp. 258-61). For other references to Sp, see Index.

Frye, Northrop. Fables of Identity: Studies of Poetic Mythology. New York: Harcourt, Brace & World, 1963. 264 pp.   696

A collection of essays on "studies in poetic mythology." Sees literature "as a unified imaginative system that can be studied as a whole by criticism." Thus, "literature as a whole provides a framework or context for every work of literature, just as a fully developed mythology provides a framework or context for each of its myths." Critical essay, The Structure of Imagery in the *Faerie Queene*, (1378) based on literary theories established in the prefatory material and preceding essays.

Frye, Northrop. Fearful Symmetry: A Study of William Blake. Princeton: Princeton University Press, 1947. 462 pp.   697

Blake uses same symbols from Bible that Sp uses in FQ, I, and in much the same way (pp. 142-3). In Blake, as in Sp's 4 Hymns, ladder of Neoplatonic love disappears as temporal perspective is replaced by eternal (pp. 154-5). Line of liberal visionaries in Anglican culture runs through Sp, Henry Vaughan, and Traherne to Christopher Smart, Blake's contemporary. Regrettable that Blake left no commentary on Sp paralleling essay on Chaucer (pp. 157-8). Blake's Beulah, garden of Paradise, in which Orc is Adonis, related to Sp's Gardens of Adonis in FQ, III, vi, though Sp does not link his garden with Biblical Eden

(p. 228). Traditions of national (Hellenic) and religious (Hebraic) mythologies in English epic only partially synthesized by Sp in vision of purified English Church (moral allegory) and of English history in Arthurian symbolism (historical allegory). Compares FQ and Paradise Lost in these terms (pp. 318-9). For many other allusions to Sp, see Index.

Frye, Northrop. How True a Twain, in The Riddle of Shakespeare's Sonnets, pp. 25-53. New York: Basic Books, 1962. 346 pp.   698

Interprets Shakespeare's sonnets in light of courtly love tradition. Amor 22 exemplifies "mock-religious language" common in Middle Ages and Renaissance (p. 32). Sp wrote HOHB and HOHL to balance his hymns to Eros and Venus. "Mistress as potential wife," as in Amor, is nearly midpoint between heavenly and earthly love (p. 34). Brief look at love in SC and FQ (pp. 36-7).

Frye, Northrop. Nature and Homer, TQ, 1 (1958), 192-204.   699

Last stanza of Mutabilitie Cantos exemplifies Christian symbolizing of supernatural heaven (p. 193). Process of reshaping convention common throughout literary history. E. K. implies Sp "revitalized Tudor poetry" with SC (p. 201).

Frye, Northrop. Yeats and the Language of Symbolism, UTQ, 17 (1947), 1-17.   700

Attacks Yeats' early essay on Sp as preoccupied with "historical legend" (p. 5). Yeats admits Sp's strong influence on his work (p. 12). Compares Paradise and rebirth symbolism of Blake, Sp, and Yeats (pp. 13-14).

Fujii, Haruhiko. Spenser's *Astrophel* and Renaissance Ways of Idealization, SELit, Eng. No. (1968), 1-15.   701

Sp idealized Sidney according to Renaissance patterns of thought. Astro and Lay are two parts of unified whole. Shepherd-knight is conventional pastoral figure synthesizing vita contemplativa and vita activa, as seen in May, July, and September of SC and in FQ, I, x (Redcrosse), and VI, ix-xi (Calidore). Astrophel's early life accords with educational ideal of Renaissance humanists, as in Elyot's Governor. Astrophel's death while hunting and transformation into flower present version of Adonis myth. Stella of poem an idealized lady. "The final consolation is formed in the Lay, of Clorinda by means of Christian and Platonic symbols," with Astrophel in heaven described in HOHB.

Fujii, Haruhiko. Spenser no Shinko, EigoS, 115 (1969), 697-99.   702

Sp's religious faith.

Funke, Otto. Epochen der Neueren Englischen Literatur: Eine Überschau von der Renaissance bis zum Beginn des 20. Jahrhunderts. 2 vols. Bern: A. Francke, 1945.   703

Vol. I, 16. und 17. Jahrhundert: Das Zeitalter Shakespeares, Miltons and Drydens. SC, p. 50; other minor poems, pp. 53-5; FQ, pp. 62-7.

Fussell, Paul, Jr. Poetic Meter and Poetic Form. New York: Random House, 1965. 208 pp.   704

In Chap. 4, The Historical Dimension, under Modern English (c. 1500—), mentions abortive experiments of theorists and poets like Ascham, Sidney, Sp, and Campion with quantitative measures (pp. 81-2). Describes Spenserian form of sonnet in Amor, "but few poets have taken to it"; finds "structural schizophrenia" in Amor 75 because of "the internal warfare taking place between its abstract rhyme structure and its organization of thought" (pp. 128-31). Principal nine-line stanza in English is Spenserian, vehicle of FQ; found primarily in narrative poetry; 18th-century imitations, as in Shenstone's The Schoolmistress and Thomson's The Castle of Indolence, are not successful, and Burns's use of it in Cotter's Saturday Night is unfortunate; Keats in The Eve of St. Agnes succeeded so well with it that, "in effect, no one has dared to write in it since" (pp. 158-60). For other references to Sp. see Index.

Gaines, Lily. The Heroic Ideal in Sidney and Spenser. M. A. thesis, University College of Wales, 1958. ITGBI, 9 (1958-1959), Item 155.   705

Sidney's knights in Arcadia and Sp's in FQ retain the best in their medieval predecessors but also embody Renaissance and humanistic values. Sidney and Sp were influenced by Renaissance ideal of complete man—soldier, scholar, courtier. They uphold authority but remind king "that it is his moral duty to rule in the best interests of the people with the aid of an educated and responsible aristocracy." Gentleman's moral code gave him spiritual and moral strength. Heroes are distinguished from common man by idea of honor. "The ideal of the Elizabethan was the life of strenuous action. Sidney, like many of his contemporaries, confuses the contemplative life with pastoralism and hedonism. But for Spenser contemplation is an arduous way of life, to be enjoyed only by those who have worked and fought in the world."

Galimberti, Alice. Edmondo Spenser, "L'Ariosto Inglese." Turin: Giuseppe Gambino, 1938. 237pp.   706

Sp's life, Chapter I. Minor poems, Chapters II-III. In discussion of FQ, Chapters IV-VIII, calls attention to resemblances between Sp and

Ariosto, Tasso, Poliziano, and other Italian poets. Chapters IX-XI deal with Amor, Epith, and Proth in relation to Petrarch, Italian Neoplatonism, and Tasso. Chapter XII, Cantos of Mutability. Chapter XIII, Sp's place in English literature compared with Ariosto's place in Italian literature, Sp's special quality as "l'anima dell'armonia," Sp and Keats. Eight appendices on such topics as Sp's friendship with Sidney, political and ecclesiastical allegory of Book I of FQ, MHT, the Areopagus, and Sp's letter to Ralegh.

Galinsky, Hans. Naturae Cursus: Der Weg einer antiken kosmologischen Metaphor von der Alten in die Neue Welt, Ein Beitrag zu einer historischen Metaphorik der Weltliteratur, Arcadia, 1 (1966), 277-311; 2 (1967), 11-78, 139-72.   707

Traces meaning in Preamble of American Declaration of Independence of phrase "the course of human events" through interlocking ramifications in classical, medieval, Renaissance, and modern thought. On meaning of "nature" and "kind" in English Renaissance cites Sp's SC, Daph, FQ, HHOB, and Amor, showing relation of Sp's usage to that of other Tudor writers (pp. 19-42).

Garner, Barbara Carman. Francis Bacon, Natalis Comes and the Mythological Tradition, JWCI, 33 (1970), 264-91. 708

Bacon agreed with Comes concerning origin and purpose of myth. Summarizes Comes's theories, pp. 265-7. [SpN, Vol. 2, No. 2 (1971), 10.]

Garvin, Katharine, ed. The Great Tudors. 2nd ed. London: Eyre and Spottiswoode, 1956. 296pp.   709

First edition, published 1935, contained 40 essays. This has 19. W. L. Renwick, Edmund Spenser, pp. 257-

70. Sketch of the life and brief survey of the works.

Garvin, Katharine. Snakes in the Grass, REL (Leeds), 2 (1961), 11-27.   710

Sp and Milton are the chief sources for Keats's and Coleridge's knowledge and use of the tradition of "serpent literature."

Gesner, Carol. Shakespeare and the Greek Romance: A Study of Origins. Lexington: University Press of Kentucky, 1970. 216 pp.   711

Renaissance pastoral writers probably drew mainly on Vergil, but Edwin Greenlaw has shown (Shakespeare's Pastorals, SP, 13 (1916), 122-54) that Longus's Daphnis and Chloe supplied major elements in stock pastoral plot used by Sidney in Arcadia, Sp (FQ, VI), and Shakespeare (p. 18). FQ, VI, ix-xii is "Arcadian," using besides stock pastoral conventions such motifs from Greek romance as separation of lovers and mistaken death of heroine (p. 49). Motif of slandered bride in story of Phedon and Claribell (FQ, II, iv), Chariton's Chaereas and Callirhoe, Ariosto's Orlando Furioso (Canto V), Hero-Claudio plot of Much Ado About Nothing, and other works (pp. 64-8). Sp mentioned in connection with As You Like It (p. 75) and Cymbeline (p. 90).

Giamatti, A. Bartlett. Spenser: From Magic to Miracle, in Four Essays on Romance, ed. Herschel Baker, pp. 15-31, notes 76-80. Cambridge, Mass.: Harvard University Press, 1971. 87pp.   712

Concerned with vision one sees on "enchanted ground" of Romance, with revelations when a visor or helmet is raised. Cites images in Pulci, Boiardo, and Ariosto of masculine might and feminine beauty reconciled, promise of paradise in "a woman who embodies bliss beyond the reach of change." Moments of revelation frequent in FQ. Italian poets concentrate on effect of vision on beholder, Sp on quality of vision itself. Compares Red Cross's false visions of beloved woman (I, i, 47-50) with Arthur's dream of Faery Queene (I, ix, 13-50). Britomart with visor raised at Malbecco's (III, ix, 24) embodies Renaissance version of perfection. When Artegall shears Britomart's visor and sees her face (IV, vi, 19-22), magic becomes miracle in apprehension of divinity. "From the primary level of visors raised and veils laid aside," we rise to grand visions in I, x; IV, x; V, vii; and VI, x. With Britomart as guiding light (III, i, 42-43), compare fixed stars of Epith (ll. 285-91, 409-12). With Britomart's combination of "amiable grace, and manly terrour" (III, i, 46), compare Amor 13, 22, and 26.

Gilbert, Allan H. Spenserian Comedy, TSL, 2 (1957), 95-104.   713

Discusses humorous incidents in SC, and demostrates influence of Ariosto and other comic poets in incidents of FQ. Provides an annotated list of comic passages in FQ.

Gilbert, Allan H. Were Spenser's Nine Comedies Lost? MLN, 73 (1958), 241-3.   714

Harvey's reference to the comedies, in the second of Three Proper, and Wittie, Familiar Letters, may mean that they were only planned rather than written.

Gilbert, C. D. Blind Cupid, JWCI, 33 (1970), 304-5.   715

Blind love rare in classical literature, unknown in classical art, revived in 13th century by analogy with blind personifications: Night, Fortune, Death. Implied that blindness (bandaged eyes) meant irrationality of sensualtiy. Ficino and Pico developed from Proclus and Plotinus idea that ideal Love is blind because above reason. [SpN, Vol. 2, No. 2 (1971), 5.]

Gillie, Christopher, ed. Spenser, Edmund (1552?-99), in Longmans Companion to English Literature, pp. 798-9. London: Longmans, 1972. 881 pp.   716

Brief account of life, works, and influence. Short bibliography. Definition and brief account of use of Spenserian stanza in 17th, 18th, and 19th centuries. FQ, III, xii, 54 quoted as example.

Globe, Alexander Victor. Apocalyptic Themes in the *Sibylline Oracles*, the Revelation, Langland, Spenser and Marvell. DAI, 32 (1971), 918A-19A. University of Toronto, 1970.   717

FQ is an apocalyptic work revealing God's plan to transform the imperfect world into a perfect creation. "The first book of Spenser's *Faerie Queene* (1590) presents both Tudor political apocalyptism and Reformation exegesis of the Revelation as found in Van der Noodt's *Theatre for Voluptuous Worldlings*. Almost as important is Spenser's debt to the mediaeval apocalyptic characters of *Piers Plowman*."

Godshalk, William L. Prior's Copy of Spenser's "Works" (1679), PBSA, 61 (1967), 52-5.   718

Matthew Prior owned FQ (1596) and volume here discussed. Marginalia in Prior's youthful and mature hands suggest use of volume in youth and maturity. A few underlinings and marginal notes pertain to SC, VP, Astro, and CCCHA; many to FQ: I—43, II—13, III—16, IV—40, V—28, and VI—38. Other poems in volume unmarked.

Godshalk, William Leigh. Art and Nature: Herrick and History, EIC, 17 (1967), 121-4.   719

Disagrees with Richard Ross's analysis of Herrick's concepts of Art and Nature (1044). Sidney, Sp, Breton, and Shakespeare did not regard Art as norm and Nature as corruption, nor did 17th century after Donne and Bacon see Nature as "raw external reality," nor did Herrick try to achieve in new synthesis harmony of Nature and Art. As E.W. Tayler shows (2160), Renaissance considered both Nature and Art necessary to complete view of world. Thus, "Herrick might better be seen as a traditionalist than an innovator in this matter."

Gordon, R. K. Notes on Keats's "Eve of St. Agnes," MLR, 41 (1946), 413-9.   720

Verbal borrowings from FQ and Epith.

Gottfried, Rudolf. Autobiography and Art: An Elizabethan Borderland, in Literary Criticism and Historical Understanding, ed. Philip Damon, pp. 109-34. Selected Papers from the English Institute, 1966. New York: Columbia University Press, 1967. 190 pp.   721

Discusses account of his own life by Thomas Wynthorne (ca. 1576), "probably the earliest English autobiography in the modern sense of the term," Gascoigne's Adventures of Master F. J., autobiographical elements beneath formal conventions in sonnet sequences of Sidney, Daniel, and Shakespeare, Ralegh's love poems to Queen Elizabeth in The Ocean to Cynthia. Special attention to Sp's artistic and original use of autobiography, implicit or explicit, in Amor, Epith, SC, and CCCHA, in which Sp "has grafted the pastoral world of SC on the realities of his subsequent life," indeed, in Elizabethan period, "autobiographical poetry may be said to have reached its fullest development" in CCCHA.

Gottfried, Rudolf. The Pictorial Element in Spenser's Poetry, ELH, 19 (1952), 203-13.   722

Questions the traditional idea that Sp saw the world with a painter's eye, producing mainly visual images; sets out to show that most of them appeal to the ear rather than the eye. At the center of Sp's poetry is an intellectual and reflected content. See 1095.

Gottfried, Rudolf. Spenser and the Italian Myth of Locality, SP, 34 (1937), 107-25.   723

The "myth of locality" uses local geographical forms as characters. Of classical origin, it was revived by Boccaccio in the Ninfale Fiesolano and was popular for two centuries. Sp's tales of the Mulla (CCCHA, ll. 92-154) and the Molanna (FQ, VII, vi, 40-55) were written in this tradition.

Grace, William J. Ideas in Milton. South Bend, Ind.: University of Notre Dame Press, 1968. 205 pp.   724

Milton does not observe close distinction between orders of reason and grace. Sp tried to observe distinction in FQ but Holiness, Chastity, and Courtesy had Christian connotations not anticipated by Aristotle. Sp compromised with secular humanism of Renaissance by making Magnificence and Glory unitive virtues, rather than Holiness (pp. 7-8). Milton in direct line with Christian humanists such as Thomas More and Sp, agreed with E. K. in SC that poetic vocation "no art, but a divine gift and heavenly instinct" (pp. 57-9). Comus, superficially masque, more medieval debate. Achieves synthesis Sp attempted with extreme sensitivity "to the pagan combination of beauty and grace with sensuality," but Sp compromised self and reader, who feels destruction of Bower of Bliss (FQ, II, xii) rather brutal. Sp also attempted

to synthesize Christian traditions of marriage and virginity in Garden of Adonis (FQ, III, vi) by placing on equal level. In printed version of Comus (1637) Milton modified narrow doctrine of virginity to include marriage (pp. 133, 136-8). For other references to Sp, see Index.

Granville-Baker, Harley, and G. B. Harrison, eds. A Companion to Shakespeare Studies. Garden City, New York: Doubleday, 1960. 390 pp.   725

Repr. of 1934 ed. Some significant allusions to Sp in chap. by George Rylands, Shakespeare the Poet (pp. 88-115). Romeo's suicide speech owes little to "Tyrian dye" of Marlowe and Sp. In tragi-comedies "a resurrection of the imagery and mythological allusion of Spenser, Marlowe and Lyly." Imagery in Shakespeare's first period conventionally emblematic like that of Marlowe, Sp, and Lyly, e.g., two swans in Proth. In Sonnets analogies from seasons more realistic than in poetry of Sp and his school. For other references to Sp, see Index.

Graziani, R. I. C. Allegory in English Literature from Spenser to Bunyan. Doctoral dissertation, University of Manchester, 1962. 965 pp.   726

Chap. II on Sp (pp. 34-149). In second instalment of FQ, Sp moves from medieval structure and patterns of earlier books toward freer allegorical style able to contain romance of types, exempla, and "personification constructs." Discusses this development in poem, book by book. Allegorical genres of Sp's shorter poems make his work a summa of allegorical modes. Notes general direction of Sp's influence on later allegorists. In Chap. XV (pp. 890-965) compares FQ, Bk. V with Dryden's Absalom and Achitophel. With Sp "ideal patterns are more real than the historical actualities ... Spenser reads history as a symbolist." Sketches development of animal fable, background for MHT. Butterfly in Muiop may be "an image of the poet himself." Footnotes pp. i-clxvi. Pages of 41-page Selective Bibliography unnumbered.

Green, A. Wigfall. Platonism in the Works of Edmund Spenser, UMSE, 6 (1965), 23-38.   727

Sp received Platonism (1) directly from knowledge of Plato in Greek; (2) indirectly through Cicero and others; (3) indirectly through Christianity, and though his Puritanism was opposed, Platonism blended with it in FQ; (4) through Renaissance Neo-Platonists of Italy and France—Dante, Petrarch, Ficino, Castiglione, and Du Bellay. Illustrates affinity between cosmology of Plato and Sp, idea of God, nature of man as body and soul, previous existence of soul, doctrine of love, and way mortal things partake of immortality by copious quotations from 4 Hymns and Cantos of Mutability. Admits virtues forming subjects of six completed books of FQ have prototypes in twelve private virtues of Aristotle, but allies Sp's virtues to those discussed in Philebus, Gorgias, Laws, Lysis, Republic, Symposium, and Phaedrus. See 650, 2460.

Greene, Thomas. The Descent from Heaven: A Study in Epic Continuity. New Haven: Yale University Press, 1963. 434 pp.   728

Study in Renaissance epic of descent of god or angel from heaven bearing message to earth, as in Bk. IV of Aeneid or models in Iliad and Odyssey. Examples of motif in Ariosto, Tasso, Sannazaro, Camões, D'Aubigné, Sp, and Milton. Analyzes descent of Mercury in MHT, its metaphysical and mythological implications (pp. 294-311). Another epiph-

any in Mutability Cantos in rebellion of Titaness against Jove. FQ straddles epic and romance, treats theme of process, Mutability triumphs in terrestrial world but Jove in celestial, Cantos epitomize preceding six books, Spenserian stanza blurs language, characters have Protean changefulness, poem "superbly untrammeled" by convention (pp. 311-35).

Greenlaw, Edwin. Studies in Spenser's Historical Allegory. Ed. Ray Heffner. New York: Octagon Books, 1967. 220 pp.   729

Repr. of 1932 ed. Four essays. I, The Battle of the Books (pp. 1-58), on Elizabethan controversy concerning Trojan legend and historicity of King Arthur. II, Elizabethan Fact and Modern Fancy (pp. 59-103), on fallacy of interpreting FQ or Shakespeare's plays as "continued" historical allegories, e.g., by Lilian Winstanley (449), "theory and practice of historical allegory" in various 16th-century works, Edward Hall's Chronicle (1548) as "the clue to the interpretation both of Shakespeare's chronicle plays and of Spenser's *Faerie Queene*," pageants, and masques, concluding that historical allegory is simple, sporadic, and never structural in FQ. III, Satire and Contemporary Allusion (pp. 104-32), repr. of Spenser and the Earl of Leicester, PMLA, 25 (1910), 535-61. IV, Spenser and the 'Party and Progress' (pp. 133-66), repr. of Spenser and British Imperialism, MP, 9 (1912), 347-70. Commentary and notes on four essays (pp. 167-220).

Greenough, Chester Noyes. A Bibliography of the Theophrastan Character in English with Several Portrait Characters. Cambridge, Mass.: Harvard University Press, 1947. HSCL, 18. 347pp. 730

Sir Thomas Pope Blount, De Re Poetica; Or, Remarks Upon Poetry

(London, 1694), "Spenser," p. 213 (p. 138). Anonymous, The Biographical Magazine, 2 vols. (London, 1819), "Edmund Spenser," I, no. 83 (pp. 240-1).

Greg, Walter W. Pastoral Poetry and Pastoral Drama: A Literary Inquiry, with Special Reference to the Pre-Restoration Stage in England. New York: Russell and Russell, 1959. 464 pp.   731

Repr. of 1906 ed. In main discussion of SC (pp. 82-98) emphasizes historical importance, circumstances of publication, pastoral tradition relied on but originality in calendar scheme as organizing principle, brief description of each of twelve eclogues, Colin-Rosalind drama as central motive, language. Mentions CCCHA, Astro, Daph, pastoral interlude of Calidore in FQ, VI (pp. 98-101). Sp's followers: Michael Drayton, Richard Barnfield, Thomas Lodge, William Basse, George Wither, John Milton, and others (pp. 101-40). For other references to Sp, see Index.

Gregory, E. R., Jr. Du Bartas, Sidney, and Spenser, CLS, 7 (1970), 437-49.   732

Considers the three poets in context of English humanism, shows Du Bartas's theory of explicitly Christian poetry in agreement with that of Sidney, and English religious poetry in 17th century enriched by interaction of Du Bartas and Sp. Du Bartas linked with Du Bellay in RR; Urania in TM a Christian Muse; notes resemblances to Du Bartas's program in 4 Hymns. In FQ, Sp used fictional rather than explicitly Christian method to portray truth through allegory. Herbert, Cowley, and Milton influenced by both Du Bartas and Sp.

Gregory, Elmer Richard, Jr. Du Bartas and the Modes of Christian Poetry in England. DAI, 26 (1966), 5434-5. University of Oregon, 1965. 275 pp.   733

Du Bartas very popular in England not as versified storehouse of encyclopedic knowledge but as Christian humanist. Has affinities in thought and technique with Gabriel Harvey, Philip Sidney, Sp, Michael Drayton, Abraham Cowley, and John Milton. Du Bartas's theory of Christian poetry required renunciation and contemplation, subordination of all knowledge to faith, more akin to English humanism than its Continental counterpart. With Milton, last major English writer working within Christian system, his influence as shaping force in English literature ends.

Grierson, Herbert J. C., and J. C. Smith. A Critical History of English Poetry. London: Chatto and Windus, 1944. 537pp.   734

Chief emphasis on the literature after Milton. Main discussion of Sp in Chapter 7, Spenser, Sidney, and Their Circle (pp. 74-84); SC and Elizabethan pastoral (pp. 95-6); 17th-century Spenserians, Wither, Browne, Phineas and Giles Fletcher, Drummond (pp. 100-4).

Grimes, Margaret Whitehurst. Metamorphosis as a Literary Device. DAI, 31 (1970), 1229-A. Michigan State University, 1969. 231 pp.   735

Considers works by Ovid, Apuleius, Dante, Ariosto, Sp, Milton, and Kafka. Concept of metamorphosis has roots in animistic worship by primitive man. Also conceived as divine reward or punishment. Closely allied in Platonic doctrine that soul imposes its form on body. However Ovid intended Metamorphoses to be taken, interpreted allegorically throughout Middle Ages and into 17th century. In Apuleius's Golden Ass, Isis changes hero's outward form to fit his inner asinine qualities. Later writers using same concept include Dante, Ariosto, Sp, and Milton. After 17th century, metamorphosis disappears in western European literature, but has reappeared in 20th century. Explains this in terms of failure of rationalism and flexibility of modern scientific thought.

Groom, Bernard. The Diction of Poetry from Spenser to Bridges. Toronto: University of Toronto Press, 1955. 284pp.
736

Emphasizes the influence of Sp on the diction of later English poets. Chapters: (1) Spenser and the Early Spenserians; (2) Shakespeare; (3) The Spenserian Tradition and its Rivals up to 1660; (4) Milton; (5) Dryden; (6) Pope; (7) Prior, Thomson, and Young; (8) The New Spenserianism; (9) Wordsworth; (10) Coleridge, Shelley, and Keats; (11) Scott, Byron, Campbell, Crabbe; (12) Tennyson, Browning, and Arnold; (13) Rossetti, Morris, and Swinburne; (14) Thompson and Bridges. See Index.

Groom, Bernard. The Formation and Use of Compound Epithets in English Poetry from 1579, SPET, No. 49, pp. 295-322. Oxford: Clarendon Press, 1937.
737

The date of SC is a convenient starting point, for Sp's compound epithets are not indebted to earlier English writers, but of his own invention or suggested by his reading of foreign poets. His practice in the formation and use of the compound epithet has been a model for many later writers. Rarer in SC than in FQ. Never as lavishly used as in many later poems. His methods of forming compound epithets are less modern than Shakespeare's, and much less modern than Milton's. "He pointed a way; he formed a traditon; yet he remains something of a primitive."

Grundy, Joan. Keats and the Elizabethans, in John Keats: A Reassess-

ment, ed. Kenneth Muir, pp. 1-19. Liverpool: University of Liverpool Press, 1958. 182 pp.
738

Careful discrimination of the senses in which Keats may accurately be described as "an Elizabethan," with chief emphasis on resemblances to and differences from Sp.

Grundy, Joan. The Spenserian Poets: A Study in Elizabethan and Jacobean Poetry. London: Arnold, 1969. 224 pp.
739

Intro. (pp. 1-18) takes to task critics who denigrate Sp or his followers, gives some facts about latter. Packed chaps. on Sp's poetry, attitudes of 17th-century Spenserians to poetry, pastoral poetry, Michael Drayton's Poly-Olbion and other works, early poetry of George Wither, William Browne, Giles and Phineas Fletcher, and Milton. Concludes that greatest lack of Spenserian poets is "creative power," yet they are worth study. "Derivative, conventional, imitative as they are, the Spenserians paradoxically have a freshness of appeal that comes from their readiness to explore and experiment" (p. 217).
Rev: Katherine Duncan-Jones, RES, 22 (1971), 248; Stanley Friedman, RQ, 24 (1971), 94.

Gundersheimer, Werner L. The Life and Works of Louis Le Roy. Genève: Librarie Droz, 1966. 163 pp.
740

Le Roy's annotated translation of Plato's Symposium possible source of Sp's neo-Platonism in 4 Hymns, as proposed by Ellrodt (p. 39). (See 650). Gabriel Harvey wrote to Sp in 1579 that Cambridge scholars were avidly reading Le Roy's exposition of Aristotle's Politics (p. 47). His most important work was De la Vicissitude ou varieté des choses en l'univers (1575), translated into English by Robert Ashley, 1594. Appendix I, Le

Roy's Works in England (pp. 133-5), refers to possible influence on Sp, and cites 2184 and 2115, besides 650.

Gunn, Alan M. F. The Mirror of Love: A Reinterpretation of "The Romance of the Rose." Lubbock, Texas: Texas Tech Press, 1952. 592pp.   741

Sp cited on episodic structure, movement, and tempo of allegory (pp. 71-3); use of rhetorical figures for constructive purposes (pp. 81 note 8, 84 note 17, 85 note 18); see also Index.

Guss, Donald L. John Donne, Petrarchist. Detroit: Wayne State University Press, 1966. 230 pp.   742

Donne's manner is completely different from Sp's (pp. 16, 17-8), yet both belong to Petrarchan tradition, which has many aspects: Bemboist imitation (linguistic, intellectual, and psychological); innovators within tradition in 16th century introduced new sensationalism, predominance of madrigal, new Ovidianism (pp. 28-33). Donne did not repudiate Petrarchism of Wyatt or Gascoigne (pp. 34 ff.). "In a Renaissance context, the difference between Spenser and Donne is not that the first, blinded by custom, writes what he has been told, and that the second, clear-eyed and undaunted, writes what he feels. It is that the one writes as a careful, learned artist, and the other as a careless, accomplished wit." Both respect custom, strive for culture. "But Spenser's culture is that of the academy, and Donne's that of the court . . ." (p. 46). For other references to Sp, see Index.

Gwynn, Stephen. The Masters of English Literature. 2nd ed. London: Macmillan, 1938. 493pp.   743

First published 1904. Chapter 2, Spenser, pp. 21-32. See also Index.

Haase, Gladys D. Spenser's Orthography: An Examination of a Poet's Use of the Variant Pronunciations of Elizabethan English. Doctoral diss., Columbia University, 1952. 168 pp., 67 pp. Appendix III. CUDD, 1952-1953, p. 27; DDAAU, 1951-52, No. 19.   744

Haggard, Elias Martin. Syllable Stress in French Words as Used by Chaucer and Spenser. Doctoral diss., George Peabody College for Teachers, 1944. 72. Abs., Peabody Abstracts of Dissertations 1944, pp. 55-66.   745

Purpose to discover changes in position of syllable-stress between 1400 and 1600 in French words then current in English language. Position of syllable-stress determined by scansion; only words of two syllables retained for study. Field further limited to 596 two-syllable French words common to Chaucer and Sp. Findings: "(1) 17.61 per cent of the words had become Anglicized with respect to the position of the syllable-stress by the end of the fourteenth century; (2) 36.07 per cent became completely Anglicized in that respect in the period between 1400 and 1600, and 6.89 per cent became partly Anglicized in that period; (3) 2.01 per cent had become wholly or partly Anglicized prior to 1400, but by the end of the sixteenth century again received the French stress; and (4) 37.42 per cent retained the French stress as late as 1600." Concludes there was a general trend in English usage from French stress to English accent in words of French origin between 1400 and 1600.

Hagstrum, Jean H. The Sister Arts: The Tradition of Literary Pictorialism and English Poetry from Dryden to Gray. Chicago: University of Chicago Press, 1958. 337pp. 32 plates.   746

Studies relations of poetry and painting, and history of doctrine of *ut pictura poesis* in criticism, in order to define pictorial image in Dryden, Pope, Thomson, Collins, and Gray. Chief references to Sp in Chapter 3, The Renaissance, in discussions of "Ut pictura poesis": Italian and English Criticism (pp. 62-4); The "Paragone": Painter versus Poet (pp. 66, 69); Iconic Poetry: Painter and Poet (p. 75), asserting that Sp strikes us as a more "painterly poet" than Donne or Milton, Chaucer or Shakespeare (pp. 76-7), and citing passages of iconic poetry (pp. 80-1); Nature versus Art, using Bower of Bliss (FQ, II, xii) to illustrate the conflict and relationship between the two (pp. 82-5); The Masque (p. 92). For other references to Sp, see Index.

Halewood, William Harrison. The Uses of the Term "Baroque" in Modern English Literary Criticism. DA, 20 (1959), 2290. University of Minnesota, 1959. 236 pp.   747

Attempts to show that baroque, whether it refers to style or "content," has only the most limited usefulness in literary studies. So with "Mannerism," a term recently borrowed from art history. English literature in the 16th and 17th centuries has a variety that eludes the application of both terms. "A single poem may display both Mannerist and baroque features and require besides to be called 'metaphysical,' or 'Spenserian,' or 'neoclassical'." The literary historian and literary critic need all these terms.

Halio, Jay L. The Metaphor of Conception and Elizabethan Theories of the Imagination, Neophil, 50 (1966), 454-61.   748

Metaphor of conception in Plato's Symposium combined with Aristotelian view of imagination in medieval faculty psychology as one of three

major powers of intellect: imagination, reason, and memory. Sp represents these faculties pictorially in House of Alma episode (FQ, II, ix). In Daph (ll. 29-35) Sp uses metaphor of conception to describe development of an idea. Same metaphor combined with dangers inherent in shaping power of imagination in Troilus and Cressida, Measure for Measure, and especially Othello.

Hall, Vernon. Renaissance Literary Criticism: A Study of its Social Content. New York: Columbia University Press, 1946. 260pp. Reprint, Peter Smith, 1959.   749

Arranged in three parts, with parallel sections and chapters on Italy, France, and England. Sp discussed under each chapter heading: the fight for the vernacular, theories of the drama, theories of the epic (pp. 190-6), scorn for the people, opposition to the medieval romances, decorum and the minor genres, the poet and his purpose (pp. 215-28). See also Index.

Hall, Vernon, Jr. A Short History of Literary Criticism. New York: New York University Press, 1963. 184 pp.   750

From Plato to the New Criticism. In chap. on Renaissance critics mentions aristocratic bias in Sp's TM (pp. 35-6), choice of Arthur as historical hero of FQ, desire to elevate poetry in October of SC, patriotic and didactic purpose of FQ (pp. 41-6). Mentions Sp in connection with Milton, Davenant, and Samuel Johnson's dislike of Spenserian stanza (pp. 53, 56-7, 74).

Haller, William. The Rise of Puritanism ... from Thomas Cartwright to John Lilburne and John Milton, 1570-1643. New York: Columbia University Press, 1938. 464pp.   751

Milton disciple of Sp in attitude toward love and marriage (p. 122), life-view (pp. 306-10); Comus and FQ (pp. 317-8). Puritan political leaders in Parliament were moved by influence of Renaissance humanism, and by "the literary expression given to their ideals by Spenser in *The Faerie Queene*" (p. 330).

Hallett, Charles A. The Satanic Nature of Volpone, PQ, 49 (1970), 41-55.   752

As tempter of those who succumb to his temptations, Volpone resembles Sp's fox-devil in fable of May eclogue in SC. He also bears striking resemblance to traditional "god" of material world, Sp's Mammon as drawn in FQ, II, vii, Celia resisting temptation like Guyon. Mammon, as god of gold and riches, is familiar figure for the devil; "Spenser's Mammon definitely functions as a devil." Neither Sp nor Jonson believed that all men will yield to Satan; representatives of good triumph over evil in both poem and play.

Halliday, F. E. Shakespeare in His Age. New York: Thomas Yoseloff, 1964. 362 pp.   753

Repr. of 1956 ed. Lively account of Elizabethan England. Sp under Mulcaster at Merchant Taylors'; with Lord Grey and Raleigh at Smerwick, "eager for the spoils of Ireland"; at Pembroke, his resistance to "Harveian hexameters," not "carried away by exalted society" of Sidney's circle, his SC (1579) "not a great poem"; Sidney's death at Zutphen and Sp's "belated and wretchedly inadequate" Astro; plague of 1593-1594, hard times for players, death of Lord Strange, Sp's lines on "Amyntas" added to CCCHA; publication of 1590 FQ "preceded by a cloud of sonnets to the most influential men in the country," Amor and Epith in 1595; FQ, IV-VI "dragged its slow and lovely length along another 16,000 lines

of bewildering allegory"; Sp's death in London, Shakespeare perhaps among coffin-bearers, and burial in Westminster Abbey. See Index.

Halliday, F. E. Spenser, Edmund, A Shakespeare Companion, 1550-1950, pp. 617-8. New York: Funk and Wagnalls, 1952.   754

Brief life; notes Sp's influence on Shakespeare's early verse and imagery; mentions the identification of Willy in TM and Aetion in CCCHA with Shakespeare: rejects the first, and considers the second doubtful.

Hamilton, A. C. The Early Shakespeare. San Marino, Cal.: Huntington Library, 1967. 237 pp.   755

Joan of Arc in 1 Henry VI like Sp's Duessa; Shakespeare is "poet historical" in Sidney's sense. In 2 Henry VI Shakespeare has more freedom with historical matter, as allowed by Sp; proud Eleanor becomes emblematic character like Sp's Lucifera. Titus Andronicus is vision of fallen human nature represented by wrath, lust, and grief comparable to first half of FQ, II. Linguistic exuberance of Love's Labor's Lost recalls E. K.'s praise of SC for "glorious words"; early Shakespeare best revealed in description of Berowne (II, i, 69-76), as Sp appears as Colin Clout in SC. Protagonists of Venus and Adonis somewhere between Acrasia and unwilling Guyon in FQ, II, xii, and Venus and Adonis in FQ, III, vi. For these references, see Index.

Hamilton, A. C., ed. Essential Articles for the Study of Edmund Spenser. Hamden, Conn.: Archon Books, 1972. 656 pp.   756

Includes studies of FQ by C.S. Lewis (1513), N.S. Brooke (1899), Ruth Nevo (1585), John E. Hankins (1814), A.S.P. Woodhouse (1952),

Robert Hoopes (1935), A. S. P. Woodhouse (1753), Virgil K. Whitaker (1888), Robert M. Durling (1912), S.K. Heninger, Jr. (1820), Alastair Fowler (1922), Northrop Frye (1378), Millar MacLure (1535), Thomas P. Roche, Jr. (2049), A. Kent Hieatt (2075), Kathleen Williams (1742), R. F. Hill (2148), B. Nellist (1967), William Blissett (2170), Frank Kermode (1480), Richard N. Ringler (2188), Lewis H. Miller, Jr. (1959), Martha Craig (1325A), Paul Alpers (1232), James Carscallen (1905), Richard Neuse (2158), Michael Baybak, Paul Delany, and A. Kent Hieatt (1254), Harry Berger, Jr. (2005), Carol V. Kaske (1824), Judith H. Anderson (2092), James E. Phillips (2127), and A.C. Hamilton (Theatre for Sp'ians, 1973); and studies of Sp's other poems by Harry Berger, Jr. (2333), Waldo McNeir (2445), Richard Neuse (2468), Isabel G. MacCaffrey (2259), and Wolfgang Clemen (2352). Listed herein, except for Hamilton's own study, too late.

Hamilton, A. C. The Modern Study of Renaissance English Literature: A Critical Survey, MLQ, 26 (1965), 150-83.
757

Surveys developing and continuing trends in criticism of Renaissance poets of 1580's and 1590's, stressing new knowledge or awareness of conventions, technique, decorum (as truth to nature and as truth to art), historical perspective, inconography, mythography, and science. Calls for critical introduction to Renaissance English literature to supplement Hallett Smith's generic study (see 1091), illustrating how it might be written with remarks on Marlowe's Hero and Leander and Sidney's Astrophel and Stella. Believes "our response to Sidney's works measures our critical understanding of Elizabethan literature." New Arcadia "as heroic romance is the prose equivalent to Spenser's *Faerie Queene*."

Hamilton, G. Rostrevor. The Tell-Tale Article: A Critical Approach to Modern Poetry. London: Heinemann, 1949. 114pp.
758

In title essay (pp. 3-59) finds that the definite article occurs with abnormal and unhealthy frequency in modern poetry—9 or 10 per cent of total words in Eliot and Auden. Only 4 or 5 per cent in Elizabethan poets, including Sp. Attributes the difference to the preference of modern poets for the particular image rather than the general. Also, the frequency is symptomatic of a degeneration of syntax, a loss of the cadenced structure characteristic of Sp, Shakespeare, Milton, Keats.

Hanford, James Holly, and James G. Taaffe. A Milton Handbook. 5th ed. New York: Appleton-Century-Crofts, 1954. 465 pp.
759

First ed. 1926. In Animadversions ... against Smectymnuus cites passages against hireling ministers from Sp's SC, revealing one source of youthful reading (p. 83). At a Vacation Exercise and nativity ode show influence of Sp and William Browne (pp. 141-3). Among literary influences on Comus, Sp's Bower of Bliss (FQ, II, xii), House of Busyrane (III, xii), Garden of Adonis (III, vi), British history (II, x) (pp. 161-5). Lycidas in tradition of pastoral elegy, as is November in SC (pp. 166-7). Several indications first considered King Arthur as epic subject (p. 179). Spenserian element in Paradise Lost (pp. 260-4), Paradise Regained (pp. 271-2), versification (pp. 296, 304). References to Sp in Appendix B, Milton's "Biographia Literaria" (pp. 370-2).

Hardison, O. B., Jr. Criticism and the Search for Pattern, Thought, 36 (1961), 215-230.
760

FQ mentioned with Everyman and Pilgrim's Progress as "great allegory" (p. 222). Sp "relied heavily on discursive thought" rather than "nondiscursive perception" in his creative process (p. 230).

Hardison, O. B., Jr. The Enduring Monument: A Study of the Idea of Praise in Renaissance Literary Theory and Practice. Chapel Hill: University of North Carolina Press, 1962. 240 pp. 761

Theory of praise, after inception in Plato's Republic, based on Aristotle's Poetics and his explanation in his Rhetoric of epideictic or demonstrative rhetoric, and on idea in medieval formulations and Renaissance versions that praise and blame should be didactic to serve social purpose by inspiring emulation or avoidance. Sidney, Sp, and Milton influenced by theory of praise (pp. 26-41). To develop concept of justice philosophically, in accord with didactic criticism, Sp in FQ, V, gives examples of Artegal's virtuous deeds to produce moral allegory (pp. 60-3). Xenophon's techniques in Cyropaedia, "The Education of Cyrus," make it forerunner of FQ, I and II (pp. 71-6). Exposition of Virgil's Aeneid by Fulgentius and Sp's letter to Raleigh take epic to be kind of praise. Consequence of Sp's theory in FQ, I (pp. 77-84). Platonic ladder in 4 Hymns reconverts love lyric into hymn of praise (pp. 95-101). Epith, Proth, and "Lay of Fair Eliza" in April eclogue of SC as occasional poems of praise (pp. 108-12). For other references to Sp, see Index.

Harper, Carrie Anna. The Sources of the British Chronicle History in Spenser's *Faerie Queene*. New York: Haskell House, 1964. 190 pp. 762

First published 1910. Chronicle of British kings in two parts: Brutus to Uther read by Arthur in Briton Moni-

ments, II, x; Conan to Cadwallader in Merlin's prophecy to Britomart, III, iii (p. 1). Ultimate source Geoffrey of Monmouth's Historia Regum Britanniae, ca. 1136 (p. 3), intermediate sources Harding, Holinshed, and others (pp. 6-9). In IV, xi used Holinshed (1577 and 1587); in View used Holinshed and perhaps Camden's Britannia, classical authorities such as Caesar, Strabo, Tacitus, and Pliny, and Irish chronicles. In method, Sp was comprehensive and eclectic (pp. 10-23). See Conclusion (pp. 172-85).

Harper, George Mills. The Neoplatonism of William Blake. Chapel Hill: University of North Carolina Press, 1961. 324 pp. 763

Incidental references to Sp in connection with Blake's epistemology, his dislike of allegory for its "obviousness," Ficino as Renaissance transmitter of Platonism, Blake's rejection of Plato's Theory of Forms (earth as model of heaven) in contrast with "the conception of his illustrious Renaissance predecessors." See Index.

Harper, George Mills. Yeats's Quest for Eden, in No. IX of the Dolmen Press Yeats Centenary Papers, pp. 291-331. Dublin: Dolmen Press, 1966. 331 pp. 764

Like Blake, Yeats considered his work attempt to restore Golden Age. Saw pastoral as appropriate vehicle blending Christian and pagan or spiritual and physical, antidote to materialism permitting return to innocence. Sought Renaissance models, hating "that dry eighteenth-century rhetoric." At early age, under influence FQ and Jonson's The Sad Shepherd, had written pastoral play. Never ceased to appreciate Sp's delight in pastoral places, but soon concluded Colin Clout and Calidore were gone, so search for Eden had to take new direction. Gave up pastoral drama for pastoral lyric. Overcame "effete and inorganic" pastoralism of early poetry, achieved "an Eden of the mind."

Harris, Bernard. Dissent and Satire, ShS, 17 (1964), 120-137.   765

A look at dissenters and satirists of Elizabethan England. Mentions Joseph Hall's Virgidemiae (1597), in which he "rejected all poetry save satire, all poets save Spenser . . . "

Harrison, John S. Types of English Poetry: A Study of Literary Organisms. Indianapolis: Butler University Press, 1941. 229pp.   766

FQ under Epic Variations in Chap. 2, Narrative Patterns: it deviates from normal epic pattern of simplicity (pp. 58-60); HOHB under Philosophical Lyric in Chap. 4, Lyrical Patterns: Sp here uses "extra-rational methods of emotionalizing thought," relying on Plato's Ideas (pp. 142-4); Proth under Personal Lyric in same chapter: here the personal factor (Sp's musing on his unhappy lot) is out of harmony with emotional tone of marriage theme, but it is not permitted to disturb joys befitting the bridal day (p. 155).

Harrison, Thomas P. They Tell of Birds: Chaucer, Spenser, Milton, Drayton. Westport, Conn.: Greenwood Press, 1969. 159 pp.   767

Repr. of 1956 ed. Chap. III: Spenser, pp. 53-84. Science merges with folklore; Sp's similes from nature often reflect Bartholomew. In similes showing knowledge of falconry Sp is "uniquely at home," relying on experience rather than books.

Harrison, Thomas P., Jr. Jonson's The Sad Shepherd and Spenser, MLN, 58 (1943), 257-62.   768

Evidence to show that Jonson took

suggestions from the Florimell story in FQ, the fable of the Oak and the Briar in the February eclogue of SC, and elsewhere.

Harrison, Thomas P., Jr. Two of Spenser's Birds: Nightraven and Tedula, MLR, 44 (1949), 232-5.   769

Amplifies the account of the nightraven in NED by showing the name has been applied to the owl, nightjar, nightheron, and possibly cormorant. Identifies the unique coinage of Sp, tedula, with the jackdaw.

Hartley, Jesse D., Jr. Two Areas of Imagery Revealing Spenser, the Man and the Poet, SCB, 28 (1968), 138-41.   770

Sp's images were "that little bit of sugar that helped the medicine go down and which, unknown perhaps to Spenser, helped reveal something of himself." Fifty-eight percent of Sp's 13,817 images are from the imaginative or the literary areas, the former mainly personifications and "allegories," the latter drawn from classical myths and legends, the Bible, geography and history. The images show that Sp was interested in morals and ethics, and in the writings of the past, and that he was contemplative and possibly sedentary, extremely sensitive and courageous, and a strict disciplinarian who sympathized and loved while he reprimanded. Acknowledges that method comes from Caroline F. E. Spurgeon.

Hartman, Geoffrey H. "The Nymph Complaining for the Death of Her Fawn": A Brief Allegory, EIC, 18 (1968), 113-35.   771

Suggests Marvell's poem belongs in tradition of pastoral elegy, cognate with topos of "much in little" from Anacreon and Greek Anthology. "It is a little picture of the spirit of the genre—an apotheosis of the diminutive powers of poetry. What Sp does in pastoral elegy done here again. Mistake to try to decode Marvell's poem as "continued allegory" like Sp's in FQ; Marvell unique in short-form use of "dark conceit." Stylized action suggests Christian progress of the soul. "Poetry's mediating virtue is still, for Marvell, the great and necessary virtue, but no longer a sufficient one. . . . In 'The Nymph' Spenserian allegory laments itself in the pagan form of the brief elegy."

Hartmann, Maurice M. Spenser's Conceits. Doctoral diss., University of Virginia, 1937. DDAAU, 1936-37, No. 4.
772

Begins with a six-part definition of the conceit as a poetic figure. Use of conceits was at high tide with Tottel's Miscellany; thus, "there was a strong English tradition in the use of conceits behind Spenser." Bulk of study is a classification of Sp's conceits. "The two largest groups are those based on figures of fire and wounds. Martial and maritime terms are frequently involved. . . . Almost ninety-five percent of Spenser's conceits are neither verbal nor logical, and almost none of his conceits is of the logical-metaphysical type. He uses elaboration and expansion to the exclusion of compactness and brevity. . . . They lack the condensation, the surprise, power, ingenuity, the subtlety of the conceits of the Metaphysical Poets." Elizabethan critics saw nothing abnormal in their use. "To the Elizabethan the conceit was a means of enriching the poetic diction, taken largely for granted."

Harvey, Sir Paul, ed. The Oxford Companion to English Literature. 4th ed. rev. by Dorothy Eagle. Oxford: Clarendon Press, 1967. 961 pp.   773

Spenser, Edmund, pp. 774-5. En-

tries on Sir Philip Sidney, Gabriel Harvey, FQ, SC, Astro. CCCHA, Proth, Spenserian stanza, and other Spenserian topics.

Hathaway, Baxter. Marvels and Commonplaces: Renaissance Literary Criticism. New York: Randon House, 1968. 209 pp.   774

Preceding Sidney and Puttenham, Gascoigne in Certayne Notes of Instruction (1575) and Sp in SC of 1579 "(or E.K. in his gloss) worked in the direction of this stress on invention, the feigned marvelous, and a shadowy relationship to history." Sp's Letter to Raleigh of greater importance; FQ full of "all sorts of miraculous engines and invented devices," but stresses allegory far more than "Spenser's masters, Ariosto and Tasso. . . . Like Tasso, Spenser has colored his intent with a historical fiction—or rather, where Tasso colors history with fiction, Spenser colors fiction with history" (pp. 100-1).

Haydn, Hiram. The Counter-Renaissance. New York: Scribner's, 1950. 705pp.
775

"Between 1341 and 1626 a world died and a new world was born." Discerns three distinct intellectual movements in this period: the classical renaissance or humanistic revival; the Counter-Renaissance, "which originated as a protest against the basic principles of the classical renaissance, as well as against those of medieval Scholasticism"; the Scientific Reformation (p. xi). Counter-Renaissance is "anti-intellectualistic, anti-moralistic, anti-synthetic, anti-authoritarian." It was a great ideological revolution. Studies ramifications of such attitudes in cross-currents of English and Continental literature, finding widespread conflicts with orthodoxy. Sp cited at many points; e.g., conflicts between Elizabethan fascination with earthly love and beauty and vertical aspirations of Neoplatonism are well illustrated in Sp, who is one of the "pronounced romanticists" (pp. 325-73). See Index.

Heath-Stubbs, John. The Pastoral. London: Oxford University Press, 1969. 86 pp.   776

Brief survey of the form from ancients to moderns. Discussion of SC, with passages quoted from several eclogues, and mention of CCCHA, Daph, Astro, and FQ, VI (pp. 19-27).

Heffner, Ray Lorenzo, Jr. Michael Drayton as Pastoral Poet. DAI, 31 (1970), 389A. Yale University, 1953. 307 pp.
777

Traces Drayton's beginning in pastoral poetry as imitator of Sp's SC to achievement of new kind of pastoral in The Muses Elizium (1630), with imaginary landscape representing special world of poet's vision and general ideal of retreat from ugly reality. Influence of Sp strong throughout, but last poems closer to 18th-century pastoral of card games and china vases.

Heninger, S. K., Jr. A Handbook of Renaissance Meteorology, with Particular Reference to Elizabethan and Jacobean Literature. Durham, N. C.: Duke University Press, 1960. 269pp.   778

Describes Renaissance notions of atmospheric phenomena in order to shed light on intellectual background and stylistic techniques of major English writers of period by examining their use of meteorological ideas in their imagery. Chapter on Sp (pp. 153-71) concludes that Sp's meteorological imagery is largely perfunctory, stereotyped, and artificial, being based on mythology rather than technical knowledge or personal observation; such imagery therefore plays lit-

tle part in the greatness of Sp's poetry. Gives list of passages cited from Sp (pp. 249-52). See also Index.

Heninger, S. K., Jr. Metaphor as Cosmic Correspondence, in Medieval and Renaissance Studies: Proceedings of the Southeastern Institute of Medieval and Renaissance Studies Summer, 1967, ed. John M. Headley, pp. 3-22. Chapel Hill: University of North Carolina Press, 1968. 238 pp.   779

Illustrates physical and conceptual cosmos accepted by every major poet through Milton with Figures from Sebastian Munster's Cosmographia (1568), Oronce Finé's De sphaera mundi (1542), Aristotle's De caelo (1519), Franchinus Gafurious's De harmonia musicorum (1518), and Robert Fludd's Utriusque cosmi... historia (1617). In Figure from Isidore of Seville's De natura rerum (1472) four elements, four seasons, and four humours are interrelated. Sp used all these concepts as metaphor in December eclogue of SC. Description of Lucifera's House of Pride (FQ, I, iv, 4) is metaphor which assimilates both physical and conceptual reality, without doubt an allegory of human body, like House of Alma (FQ, II, ix). Other illustrations of cosmic metaphor in Marlowe's Hero and Leander (ll. 31-36), Raleigh's reply (ll. 1-6), and Shakespeare's Troilus and Cressida (I, iii).

Heninger, S. K., Jr. The Renaissance Perversion of Pastoral, JHI, 22 (1961), 254-61.   780

In pure form pastoral emphasizes optimistic simplicity in contrast to complexity of real life. This view dominant in Pastorella episode in Bk. VI of FQ. From inception pastoral described "a nostalgic reminiscence of an idealized childscape, an Eden-like state of innocence." Yet frontiers between actual and ideal are contiguous, as in As You Like It. "The signal perversion of pastoral was its adaptation for the purpose of satire," first used by Petrarch and exploited by Mantuan. Moral allegory in guise of pastoral central in SC. Opposite tendency in use of pastoral for decorous sentiment, already present in Longus' Daphnis and Chloe, first used in Renaissance by Sannazaro in Arcadia (1504). Renaissance also "revamped the method of pastoral," as in pastoral dramas such as Sidney's Arcadia, and in pastoral elegies such as Milton's Lycidas. Renaissance "most frequently expressed the enigma of perfection's finitude in terms of mutability"—hence, Sp's Cantos of Mutability. "Pastoral failed to achieve greatness in the Renaissance . . . it assumed modish, superficial forms. Unlike tragedy, pastoral never realized its potentiality."

Heninger, S. K., Jr. Some Renaissance Versions of the Pythagorean Tetrad, SRen, 8 (1961), 7-35.   781

Sir Thomas Elyot's entry on Pythagoras in his Dictionary (1538) refers to two facets of Pythagorean philosophy that appealed to Renaissance: the "mystycalle sentences" in Carmina Aurea and Symbola, and the "Scyence of noumbers" in Pythagoras' postulate that all things have innate numerical relationships. Heavily documented article illustrated with 17 black and white figures demonstrates ubiquity of tetrad in Renaissance cosmology, theology, psychology, meteorology, astrology, alchemy, "and so on literally *ad infinitum.*" Relevant to numerological criticism of Sp.

Henkel, Arthur, and Albrecht Schöne, eds. Emblemata: Handbuch zur Sinnbildkunst des XVI und XVII. Jahrhunderts. Stuttgart: J.B. Metzlersche Verlagsbuchhandlung, 1967. 2196 cols.
782

Preface discusses various problems of Renaissance emblem (pp. IX-XXVII). Bibliography of 6 sections listing bibliographical works on emblem books, 16th- and 17th-century works dealing with history and theory of emblem, modern works of same kind, works by art historians and cultural historians on emblems, by literary historians, and iconographic reference works on emblematic problems. Anthology proper contains 4000 emblems culled from 47 emblem books. Indexes of mottos, pictures, and subjects. Important for Sp studies in several ways.

Rev: William S. Heckscher and Cameran F. Bunker, RenQ, 23 (1970), 59-80.

Henn, T.R. The Apple and the Spectroscope: Lectures on Poetry designed (in the main) for Science Students. New York: Norton, 1966. 166 pp.   783

Repr. 1951 ed. Discusses Eliot's use of Proth refrain in The Fire Sermon (pp. 43-45). Sp molded Elizabethan excitement into FQ even though writing in Ireland (p. 109). "Victorian landed gentry" in Tennyson's Morte D'Arthur steeped in Sp's Twelve Moral Virtues (p. 130).

Henze, Richard Harold. Shakespeare and the Golden World of the Pastoral. DA, 26 (1965), 2752-3. University of Nebraska, 1965. 206 pp.   784

Shakespeare's changing use of pastoral in As You Like It, The Winter's Tale, and The Tempest parallels that of Sp in SC, CCCHA, and Calidore-Pastorella episode in FQ. One view of shepherds of pastoral is that they teach more cultured men how to live because they have descended least from man's first days in paradise. Another view of shepherds, implied in Shakespeare's last plays and FQ, is that they are, like other men, subject to vexation and therefore unable to teach cultured men how to live. But even when shepherds presented "realistically," pastoral ideal can remain a beautiful and noble thing, as embodied in Pastorella or in Shakespeare's fanciful vision.

Heydorn, Marianne. Spenser und der Calvinismus. Doctoral diss., University of Hamburg, 1939. 81pp. JdH 1941, p. 203.   785

Surveys criticism concerning Sp's attitude toward Calvinism. Distinguishes English from Italian humanism by development of Puritanism with Calvinism its dominant theology. Believes Sp's knowledge of Calvin's writings confined to Institutes, catechism, and Geneva Bible with commentary. Ethics of SC are Puritan. Sp intended to serve Puritan movement with MHT. Longest chapter (pp. 33-68) explores FQ, especially Bk. I, for Puritan thought, finds it in expressions of Calvinistic doctrine of predestination, idea of powerlessness of man without God's mercy, consciousness of sin and fear of punishment, fight against pride and over-confidence. Sees no conflict between English Neoplatonism and Puritanism. In House of Holiness sees junction of Calvinism and Platonism. Finds fewer direct parallels with Calvinism in Sp's later writings. Summary (pp. 77-81) attributes this lack to his absorption with foreign policy and isolation in Ireland.

Hibbard, G.R. Thomas Nashe: A Critical Introduction. Cambridge, Mass.: Harvard University Press, 1962. 262 pp.
                                             786

In Preface to Robert Greene's Menaphon (1592), Nashe holds up "Divine Master *Spencer*" against "Spaine, Fraunce, Italy, and all the world" (pp. 31-2). Discusses allusions to Sp in Act III of First Part of the Return from Parnassus; Sp's influence on Nashe's sonnet at end of Pierce Penilesse, and in The Choice of Valentines; Pierce Penilesse in figure of Greediness shows had read FQ (1590), and "had been deeply impressed by such figures as Errour and Despair in Book I, Mammon in Book II and Malbecco in Book III, as well as by the Pageant of the Seven Deadly Sins" (FQ, I, iv), learning from these how to translate "human activities ... into concrete images that cohere to form a whole that is monstrous and fantastic yet at the same time significant and convincing" (pp. 52-3, 56-9, 71-3). Dedication of Christ's Tears over Jerusalem to Lady Elizabeth Carey suggests "that the patroness of Spenser may have had something to do with Nashe's retraction of his attack on Spenser's friend, Gabriel Harvey" (p. 126). Mentions Sp in connection with Nashe-Harvey feud (pp. 188-9).

Highet, Gilbert. The Classical Tradition: Greek and Roman Influences on Western Literature. New York: Oxford University Press, 1949. 763pp.   787

The Renaissance: Epic, pp. 144-61. Four types of epics of the period: (1) direct imitations of classical epic, e.g., Ronsard's The Franciade; (2) epics on contemporary heroic adventures, e.g., The Sons of Lusus; (3) romantic epics of medieval chivalry, e.g., The Madness of Roland, The Faerie Queene, and The Liberation of Jerusalem; (4) Christian religious epics, e.g., Paradise Lost and Paradise Regained. Points out the classical elements in these poems. Notes on Sp's classical knowledge and schematism of FQ, pp. 603-4. SC brought into discussion of Renaissance pastoral, p. 171.

Hill, Christopher. The Many-Headed Monster in Late Tudor and Early Stuart Political Thinking, in From the Renaissance to the Counter-Reformation: Essays in Honor of Garrett Mattingly, ed.

Charles H. Carter, pp. 296-324. New York: Random House, 1965. 437 pp.
788

Disdain of common people seen in FQ, II, ix, 13; V, ii, 32-56; IV, i, 28; V, ii, 57-59. Underlying this disdain was fear; and some church sects, such as anabaptists, moved toward a form of communism. MHT rejects communism as a form of laziness, but also rejects wage-labor. Such over-conservative thinking paved the way to civil war.

Hillyer, Robert. In Pursuit of Poetry. New York: McGraw-Hill, 1960. 229 pp.
789

Sp among early poets who used rime royal. Spenserian stanza is Chaucer's Monk's Tale stanza with a six-foot line added. Four major Romantic poems in Spenserian stanza: Burns's Cotter's Saturday Night, Byron's Childe Harold's Pilgrimage, Keats's Eve of St. Agnes, and Shelley's Adonais. Sidney, Sp, and Daniel wrote fine sonnet sequences; Shakespeare and Drayton wrote great ones (pp. 68, 70-2, 88-106). For other Sp references, see Index.

Hinman, Robert B. Abraham Cowley's World of Order. Cambridge, Mass.: Harvard University Press, 1960. 373 pp.
790

Cowley's early stimulation by reading Sp meant commitment to poetry of high ideals glimpsed by Platonic light of 4 Hymns (pp. 15-7). Cowley accepted certainty of devastating change, yet like Sp in Mutability Cantos saw "progress in all things toward the condition first conceived and created by God" (pp. 69, 81-2). Cowley's hopes for "the divine science" kindled by poets like Sp and thinkers like Lipsius, Bacon, and Hobbes (pp. 178 ff.). David and Jonathan in Cowley's Davideis "realize the Re-naissance ideal of friendship, the earthly duplication of divine love," as in "the sixth [sic] book of The Faerie Queene" (pp. 265-6).

Hippisley, J. H. Chapters on Early English Literature. Port Washington, New York: Kennikat Press, 1969. 344 pp.
791

Repr. of 1837 ed. A serious Victorian effort. Problem of Ireland discussed by Eudoxus and Irenaeus in Sp's View not solved even in present day. Importance of Mirror for Magistrates in allegorical tradition. Sp's allegorical descriptions carried to perfection in FQ, but "except as exhibiting a peculiar stanza," not innovative. Sp chiefly imitates Ariosto but "preserves a more severe and dignified tone." FQ not concerned with real life, and in SC, which is, we are occasionally "not a little disturbed by the clownish sentiments and uncouth diction of Hobbinol or Diggon Davie." In FQ if anything is incongruous it is Sp's "occasional allusion to Christianity." Otherwise, "a pure Gothic structure, undisturbed by the introduction of classic or Christian ornaments." In MHT Sp laments "his own ill-fortune," and "in one of the eclogues" of SC bespeaks low esteem of poetry. "A general taste for English literature" revived by influence of the drama.

Hobsbaum, Philip. Elizabethan Poetry, PoetryR, 41 (1965), 80-97.
792

Modern evaluation of Elizabethan poetry shackled by wrong-headed respect for "mock-simplicity, Petrarchan convention, and prosaic philosophising." Best verse of period not by Sidney, Sp—minor poems "boring and repetitious," Faerie Queen [sic] plotless and its poetry soporific, Sp's influence pernicious—Daniel, and Drayton; key figures who "belong to our time" are Chapman, Jonson,

Marston, Donne, Raleigh, and Greville, together with great translators Stanyhurst, Golding, and Harington. "At their best, the Elizabethans were very close to the Middle Ages of *Piers Plowman* and *Sir Gawaine*, as well as to the metaphysical poetry of the seventeenth century."

Holland, Joan Nina Field. The Language of The Faerie Queene. Doctoral diss., Harvard University, 1965. 137 pp.   793

Ideas of Sp's contemporaries and predecessors concerning the English language and poetic expression in English, drawn from rhetoric books, letters, treatises on verse composition, defenses of poetry, prefaces to translations, etc., furnish background for Sp's own treatment of language. Analyzes style of SC with attention to principle of decorum as it affects language of pastoral poetry. Examines various components of FQ diction: words current, obsolete and obsolescent, Romance, and Latin, and words that Sp introduced or revived in new senses. Observes such features of syntax in FQ as inversion and continuative relative pronoun. Relates Sp's style to content and purpose of FQ.

Hollander, John. The Untuning of the Sky: Ideas of Music in English Poetry, 1500-1700. Princeton: Princeton University Press, 1961. 467 pp.   794

Sp used few musical images and references. Specific points in FQ, Epith, SC, Amor, and TM are discussed. See Index.

Hook, J. N. Three Imitations of Spenser, MLN, 55 (1940), 431-2.   795

In The Shamrock (1772), a collection of anonymous poetry edited by Samuel Whyte: a Spenserian sonnet by Whyte, and two poems in regular Spenserian stanzas.

Hook, Julius Nicholas. Eighteenth-Century Imitations of Spenser. Doctoral

diss., University of Illinois, 1941. DDAAU, 1940-41, No. 8. Abs. published. Urbana, Ill., 1941. 13pp.   796

Proposes to assemble a complete list of Spenserian imitations in the 18th century (total of 225 works), find out why imitations of Sp were written and how these were received, discuss general subject of imitation in the century, state as precisely as possible prevalent attitude toward Sp, and estimate influence of Sp and his imitators on growth of romanticism in 18th century. Deals fully with these topics.

Hopkins, Kenneth. English Poetry: A Short History. Philadelphia: Lippincott, 1962. 568 pp.   797

FQ "a great work, but not a successful poem" (pp. 63-75). For other references to Sp, see Index.

Hotson, Leslie. Mr. W. H. New York: Knopf, 1964. 328 pp.   798

William Hatcliffe may have been W. H. of Shakespeare's sonnets. Sp frequently mentioned. See Index. Explication of Sp's praise of Shakespeare in TM and CCCHA (pp. 195-200).

Houtchens, Lawrence H., and Carolyn W. Houtchens, eds. Leigh Hunt's Literary Criticism. New York: Columbia University Press, 1956. 732pp.   799

A New Gallery of Pictures: Spenser, pp. 420-45. This appeared in New Monthly Magazine, 38 (June, 1833), 161-77. Emphasizes pictorialism of FQ, and prescribes it as study for painters. Associates various Old Masters—Rembrandt, Cuyp, Poussin, Correggio, Giulio Romano, Titian, Rubens, Raphael—with scenes in the poem. See notes, pp. 678-9. The Wishing-Cap, No. VI, pp. 446-56. This appeared in Tait's Edinburgh Magazine, 3 (Sept., 1833), 695-701. Recommends Sp to all readers. He is a favorite with poets. Remarks on supposed obsoleteness of his language, Spenserian stanza, his capricious spelling. FQ supremely valuable as escapist literature. See notes, pp. 679-80. See also Index for other references to Sp.

Howarth, Herbert. The Tiger's Heart: Eight Essays on Shakespeare. New York: Oxford University Press, 1970. 210 pp.   800

First published 1961. Sp and the profuseness of the Elizabethan age (p. 24). Sp's FQ and Arthurian tales (pp. 28-30). Sp and the Chain of Being (p. 39). Idealizations of Sp contrast with realism of Shakespeare (p. 42).

Howarth, Herbert. Wyatt, Spenser, and the Canzone, Italica, 41 (1964), 79-90.
                                                801

Contrasts Petrarch's use of canzone form for transcendence with Wyatt's reduction of it to earthly reality in rhyme royal. To Sp transcendence was highest good; shared Petrarch's neo-Platonic convictions. Loved Italian pictorialism that Wyatt shunned. In 1570's aimed to overgo Ariosto, but avoided Orlando Furioso stanza and evolved own FQ stanza, "a little longer, more intricate and voluptuous." Knew how to use intermittent short lines, as in April and November of SC. Willing to use conservative rhyme royal in 4 Hymns for most ardent concepts. At last, in Epith and Proth "he takes the breath away" by constructing English equivalent of canzone, modeled on Petrarch's 18-lined stanza of "I'vo pensando." Sp's effect of "exultation and exaltation" arises from "the short lines amid the long, the garlands of rhyme." Pioneering mastery not emulated, until Milton in Lycidas wrote an Anglicised canzone "with the cerebrations of the controversialist reinforcing it." Then long hiatus till Wordsworth's Intimations of Immortality, resonant with echoes of Epith and Proth.

Howell, Roger. Sir Philip Sidney, The Shepherd Knight. London: Hutchinson, 1968. 308 pp.   802

A study of Sidney as courtier-diplomat, man of letters, and man of action. In Sidney's Arcadia at annual tournament appeared knight Philisides. Sp used this name to refer to Sidney in RT. Character of Philisides the Shepherd Knight conformed to Sidney's aspiration to play role of Protestant activist hero. Sp dedicated SC to him and "used extensively the shepherd formula to convey a distinctly Protestant theological moral" (pp. 7-8, 68). Sidney's patronage of poets, including Sp, showed interests of both courtier and scholar (pp. 114-6). Relations between Sidney, Sp, Daniel Rogers, Edward Dyer, and Fulke Greville, question of Areopagus group (pp. 156-62). For other incidental references to Sp, see Index.

Howell, Wilbur Samuel. Logic and Rhetoric in England, 1500-1700. Princeton, N. J.: Princeton University Press, 1956. 411pp.   803

Tudor logicians and rhetoricians knew Sp's work and drew from it for illustrations and examples: Abraham Fraunce in The Shepheardes Logike (early 1580's) and The Lawiers Logike (1588), William Webbe in Discourse of English Poetrie (1586), and Charles Butler in Rhetoricae Libri Dvo (1598). See Index.

Hoyles, John. The Waning of the Renaissance, 1640-1740: Studies in the Thought and Poetry of Henry More, John Norris and Isaac Watts. The Hague: Martinus Nijhoff, 1971. 265 pp.
                                                804

General Introduction announces history of ideas approach to cultural revolution of 17th century, placing great dividing line in English literature in 1700. Henry More called "source" of "the transit to the modern mind" with his Cartesianism, Renaissance Platonism, and philosophical poetry; Norris is "verge" with watered down Platonism and belated Metaphysical poetry; Watts is "result" with revolutionary poetry and typical mood of Enlightenment. In all three signs of waning Renaissance and "also intimations of the rise of Romanticism" (pp. xi-xvii). Sp's chief relevance here in connection with More, whose poetic theory is that of Sidney, Sp, and Milton, but whose practice is pietistic and Platonic, without poetic vision (p. 47). His diction, Platonic allegory, and stanzaic form Spenserian, but poetry "derivative, obscure, and unreadable" with its fuzzy groping after the "spirit of the world." Yet at times he is "transitional between the landscape of Spenserian allegory and the 18th-century prospect poem" (pp. 53-6).

Hubbell, Jay B., and John O. Beaty. An Introduction to Poetry. New York: Macmillan, 1949. 524 pp.   805

In Chap. V, Iambic Pentameter, discussion of Spenserian stanza, "the most stately and impressive stanzaic form in English poetry," illustrated by quotation of FQ, I, i, 39-42, "no finer example of onomatopoeia"; James Thomson used Spenserian stanza in Castle of Indolence, Keats in Eve of St. Agnes, and Byron in Childe Harold's Pilgrimage (pp. 217-22). In Chap. VII, The Sonnet, discussion and illustration of Italian, Shakespearian, and Spenserian forms, quoting Amor 37 (pp. 269 ff.). Milton first stimulated to write poetry by reading Sp, "the poet's poet," as was Keats (pp. 453-4).

Hudson, Hoyt H. The Transition in Poetry, HLQ, 5 (1942), 188-90.   806

FQ, I-III, and Sidney's Astrophel and Stella represent poetry thoroughly Elizabethan; CCCHA, with Astro and other elegies on Sidney, represents the new poetry with the characteristic rationalism, skepticism, and cynicism.

Hudson, Hoyt Hopewell. The Epigram in the English Renaissance. Princeton, N. J.: Princeton University Press, 1947. 178pp.   807

Thomas More's emblems on division of man's life into periods, with each figure conquering its predecessor, suggest VB with their emphasis on transience (pp. 34-5). Examples of poem called *carmen correlativum* from Fraunce, Sidney, Ralegh, and FQ, II, iv, 35 (pp. 161-5).

Hudson, William Henry. An Outline History of English Literature. New and rev. ed. London: G. Bell, 1955. 319pp.   808

Published 1912; previous ed. 1930. Chapter 6, The Age of Shakespeare (1558-1625): Non-Dramatic Verse, pp. 45-54. Sp, pp. 47-52. See also Index.

Hughes, Merritt Y. Spenser, 1552-1952, TWA, 42 (1953), 5-24.   809

Recent attacks on Sp's art and ideas stem from a poetic theory which sees Spenserian allegory as a symptom of "dissociation of sensibility," from hostility to Sp's disciples, Milton and Tennyson, and from distaste for Sp's authoritarian politics. His ideas of hierarchy and justice are based ultimately on the concept of courtesy in FQ, VI, an ideal which should not repel modern liberal democrats. Sp's ethics have continuing validity.

Hughes, Merritt Y. Virgil and Spenser. Port Washington, N. Y.: Kennikat Press, 1969. pp. 265-418.   810

First pub. 1929. In SC French and Italian influences overshadow classical precedents. Presence of personal allegory in SC contrasts with Virgil's practice in his pastorals. E. K., "with less discretion than zeal," intent on establishing Sp's "bond with the great names in the pastoral tradition, among which Virgil was—in sixteenth-century eyes—the greatest." VG, translation of Culex, has foreshadowings of FQ, and shows influence of Bembo's translation (1530). Discusses difference between epic and romance; Ariosto's influence on FQ much greater than Virgil's. Points out scattered reminiscences of Aeneid in Sp's poem. Greatest debt to Virgil in story of Glauce and Britomart in Bk. III, ii. Three imitations of Virgil's hell: I, v, 32-36; II, vii, 3, 21-23; and IV, i, 20, 22. Other chaps. on Language and Image, and The Admiration of a Profound Philosopher. Bibliography (pp. 407-13).

Hunter, G. K. Drab and Golden Lyrics of the Renaissance, in Forms of Lyric, ed. Reuben A. Brower, pp. 1-18. New York: Columbia University Press, 1970. 187 pp.   811

Ivor Winters (1212), in his objections to C. S. Lewis (878), has merely proposed a "system which preserves the polarities [Lewis's 'Drab' and 'Golden'] while it reverses the value-judgments attached to them" (p. 5). Attempts complex analysis of rhetoric, subject matter, relation to audience, and other factors in order to formulate a more careful distinction between mid-century poets and poets of 1580's and 1590's than the categories of either Lewis or Winters seem to offer. "I exclude Spenser from this distinction; in relation to it his position is highly ambiguous."

Hunter, G. K. John Lyly: The Humanist as Courtier. London: Routledge & Kegan Paul, 1962. 376 pp.   812

As court of Elizabeth was highly artificial, writers of Elizabethan court, Sidney, Sp, and Lyly, were seriously artful (pp. 6-9). Probable Lyly and Sp knew one another in London 1579-1580; Lyly imitated SC in Euphues (p. 47). Lyly hoped to be Master of the Revels, suffered common lot of Elizabethan courtier described by Sp in CCCHA (pp. 77-8). Peele's Arraignment of Paris openly depended on Sp's SC; Lyly's Campaspe, Sapho and Phao, and Gallathea used pastoralism more skilfully (pp. 134-5). On limits of allegories of Queen's relations with favorites: "Lyly is obviously less sage and serious than Spenser," but contemporary references in works show outlook on allegory not unlike that of Sp or Sidney (pp. 149-52). As in FQ "the general reference may carry a particular reference inside it," so it may in Lyly's Sapho and Phao; but "secret history" of play not necessary to understand it (p. 177). MHT, Peele's Old Wives' Tale, and Lyly's Mother Bombie (p. 224). For other references to Sp, see Index.

Hunter, Robert Grams. Shakespeare and the Comedy of Forgiveness. New York: Columbia University Press, 1965.   813

Theory of universe in Shakespeare's four romantic comedies (Much Ado About Nothing, All's Well That Ends Well, Cymbeline, and The Winter's Tale) is Empedoclean-Spenserian (pp. 89-93). For other references to Sp, see Index.

Hutcheson, W. J. Fraser. Shakespeare's Other Anne: A Short Account of the Life and Works of Anne Whateley or Beck, a Sister of the Order of St. Clare, who Nearly Married William Shakespeare in November 1582 A. D. Glasgow: Maclellan, 1950. 128pp.   814

Clifford Leech says of this in ShS, 5 (1952), 139, note 7: "Asserts that 'Anne Whateley', a nun, was Drayton's Idea, Spenser's Rosalind, Daniel's Delia, and author or part-author of *Amoretti, The Faerie Queene, Love's Labour's Lost, The*

Arte of English Poesie, and Shakespeare's *Sonnets*, and is to be traced wherever a poem was printed over the signature 'Ignoto': the book is not so entertaining as it sounds."

Ing, Catherine. Elizabethan Lyrics. London: Chatto and Windus, 1951. 252pp.

815

Many Elizabethan poets were critics: Lodge, Sp, Sidney, and others. All were interested in details of style in writing; "they see no shame in the divinely inspired poet's being a workman" (pp. 10-3). Sp-Harvey correspondence shows the period was "one of enthusiastic discussion among friends and acquaintances about literary questions" (pp. 25-6). "Harvey shows more common sense than Spenser" about meter in their exchanges (pp. 29-31). Sp's Iambicum Trimetrum illustrates interest in classical forms; its scansion is difficult (pp. 96-9). Analysis of Sp's lyrics shows that the music is in the words. "Spenser was a poet whose lyrical work was antagonistic to the addition of music." His finest lyric achievements are Epith and Proth (pp. 208-19, 231).

Ingham, Patricia. Spenser's Use of Dialect, ELN, 8 (1971), 164-8.   816

Sp used Northern forms and rhymes depending on Northern pronunciation in SC and FQ for two different and logically irreconcilable reasons. In May, July, and September of SC used Northern forms not for effect of rusticity but barbarousness and roughness. In FQ dialectal words appear along with larger number of archaisms, poeticisms, and new words for effect of strangeness and richness. Although Northern form of English was sometimes thought of as barbarous, also sometimes thought of as traditional literary medium available to make poetic language more striking.

Both views found in Alexander Gill's Logonomia Anglica (1619, 1621). [SpN, Vol. 2, No. 2 (1971), 9-10.]

Inglis, Fred. The Elizabethan Poets: The Making of English Poetry from Wyatt to Ben Jonson. London: Evans Bros., 1969. 168 pp.   817

Main discussion of Sp in Chap. 4: Courtesy and Meditation: Edmund Spenser, Sir Philip Sidney and his circle, and Robert Southwell. Sets aside FQ, "largest product of Petrarchan attitudes in English literature," because epic; it poses "ruinous" problems to poet. Epith, attached to Amor, and Proth deserve comparison with The Tempest and The Winter's Tale "which rejoice at a particular marriage, and by implication rejoice also at the human potentialities which marriage creates" (pp. 65-70). For other references to Sp, see Index.

Iser, Wolfgang. Spensers Arkadien: Fiktion und Geschichte in der Englischen Renaissance. Krefeld: Scherpe, 1970. 49 pp.   818

"Arcadia appears to us today to be an already lost world in the glimmering of history. The shepherds . . . have degenerated into a cliché of trivialized longing." Where have the shepherds gone? Sketches pastoral tradition from beginnings to Renaissance to explain disappearance of "Hirtendichtung" from literature and society. Feels significance and "message" of Sp's poetry are in verse itself, not in ideas. Sp's medium is his message.

Iyengar, K. R. Srinivasa. Shakespeare: His World and His Art. New York: Asia Publishing House, 1964. 711 pp.   819

Dismisses the 50-60 claimants, Sp included, to Shakespeare's work and points to possible Sp influences in Shakespeare. See Index.

Jack, Ian. English Literature 1815-1832. Vol. 10 of The Oxford History of English Literature, ed. F.P. Wilson and Bonamy Dobrée. London: Oxford University Press, 1963. 643 pp.   820

Many references to Sp's influence. Shelley accelerated Spenserian stanza (p. 91); FQ provided poetic escape for Keats and constantly influenced his poetics; Sp a favorite of Hazlitt and Leigh Hunt. See Index.

James, Wilfred P. The Life and Work of Richard Barnfield. Doctoral diss., Northwestern University, 1952. NUSDD, 20 (1952), 14-8.   821

"He persistently wrote as a disciple of Spenser, donning the shepherd's cloak in the role of poet, lover, and moralist." His charming prettiness and verbal dexterity are those of "a true-born Elizabethan pastoral poet and encomiast."

Januszewski, Zenon. Spenser, Edmund, Wielka Encyklopedia Powszechna Pwn, 10, 698. Warszawa: Państwowe Wydawnictwo Naukowe, 1967.   822

Jenkins, Elizabeth. Elizabeth and Leicester. New York: Coward-McCann, 1962. 384 pp.   823

Sp presented to Queen when she came to Cambridge on summer progress of 1578; Gabriel Harvey's Gratulationum Valdinensium, dedicated to Elizabeth, Leicester ("peculiarly mistimed"), Burleigh, and others. For Sp this visit exciting; by 1579 living at Leicester House as member of Sidney's circle (pp. 230-1). Sp's happiness in London, hopes and disappointments expressed in VG, allegory of MHT, and of SC; "sent away" to Ireland with Lord Grey de Wilton, "fairy vision" of FQ reflects rich and strange sights Sp had seen at Elizabeth's court, and its allegorical themes "cover the main currents of topical affairs"; Proth refers to Dudley family and RT commemorates members of Dudley family (pp. 252-62).

Jennings, Elizabeth. Christian Poetry. New York: Hawthorn Books, 1965. 121 pp.   824

Sp first English poet to see whole problem of allegory, wrote complex kind. With Sidney at heart of humanism; Sp's sense of form in creating "grand Design" of FQ makes him "a kind of moral Romantic" (pp. 40-4).

Jennings, Sister Vivien. The Continental Backgrounds of Spenser's Marriage Poetry. DAI, 33 (1972), 3586A-87A. Fordham University, 1972. 230 pp.   825

Studies Sp's marriage poetry in light of classical and Renaissance wedding customs, topoi prescribed by rhetoricians for epithalamia, and attitudes toward marriage in marriage treatises. Analyzes Carmina 66 and 68 of Catullus, epithalamia, love lyrics, and lullabies of Giovanni Pontano, and Amor, Epith, and scenes from FQ of Sp—emphasizing adaptation of conventional topoi. Catullus sees social implications of marriage, Pontano adds personal tone, and Sp makes wedding a religious occasion. He describes spiritual beauty of each heroine—Una, Britomart, and own bride Elizabeth, on sacramental occasion that begins new life on earth and will extend into eternity. Reality of human experience blends with scripture "to produce a concept of marriage that is both anthropologically realistic and eminently Christian."

Jessee, Jack Willard. Spenser and the Emblem Books. DA, 20 (1960), 3729. University of Kentucky, 1955. 204 pp.   826

Illustrates Sp's adaptations of emblematic techniques for framework of SC, teleological design of Amor, and pageants and allegorical characters of FQ. His originality stems from an eclectic combination of the emblem with other standard and approved forms.

Jewkes, W. T. The Literature of Travel and the Mode of Romance in the Renaissance, in Literature as a Mode of Travel: Five Essays and a Postscript, Intro. by Warner G. Rice, pp. 13-30. New York: New York Public Library, 1963. 119 pp.   827

Travel books of Elizabethan period reflect aims, methods, and attitudes of romance. Sp in FQ, II, Proem 1-3, on marvels: Why then should witlesse man so much misweene,/That nothing is but that which he hath seene? Ralegh in account of voyage to Guiana defends Mandeville's anthropophagi. Pages of Hakluyt and Purchas informed with same spirit as Arcadia, Euphues, FQ, Menaphon, and Rosalynde. No coincidence FQ dedicated to Sir Walter Ralegh, "that indefatigable traveler and voyage raconteur." Ideals of heroic conduct at heart of FQ and Arcadia appear in accounts of Burroughs, Grenville, Gilbert, and Cavendish. Paradox of gentle savages (FQ, I, vi) and brutish savages (VI, viii) developed by Sp also occurs in travel narratives. Blend of idealistic and pragmatic in Sp's purpose in FQ combined in voyages.

Jobson, Sister Florence M., S.C.N. Dialogue in the Major Poetry of Edmund Spenser. DA, 28 (1968), 3144A-45A. St. Louis University, 1967. 358 pp. 828

Analyzes the bulk of Sp's poetic dialogue with emphasis on FQ. Dialogue in Bk. I is varied in the colloquialisms, irony and levels of diction used by the four major characters. In Bk. II Guyon's language " . . . reflects his tremulous balance between rational stoicism and misguided passion." The dialogue of Bks. III, IV, and V " . . . reflects a thematic relation tween character and plot." Bk. VI manifests Sp's development in pastor-

al dialogue, refined through experiments in SC and CCCHA. The dialogue of Arthur is unique in that it characterizes the unity and multiplicity of FQ.

Johnson, Francis R. Astronomical Thought in Renaissance England. Baltimore: Johns Hopkins Press, 1937. 357pp.   829

Sp, pp. 193-5. As Harvey complained, Sp had no more than a minimal knowledge of astronomy.

Johnson, Paula. Form and Transformation in Music and Poetry of the English Renaissance. New Haven: Yale University Press, 1972. 170 pp.   830

Chap. 1, Serial Art: Problems and Assumptions (pp. 1-20). Points out limited amount of work relating poetry and music; posits break in musical and poetic form between 16th and 17th centuries. Chap. 2, Recurrence (pp. 21-54). Poetic structures with exact repetition undemanding, e.g., "the sestina [August of SC] in which Colin Clout took such pride." Irregularly repeated musical or poetic units can be basis of serial form, e.g., refrain in Sp's Epith. Paired analogues may balance each other; "subtotal analogues are likewise effective," e.g., opposition of FQ, I, iv and FQ, I, x, "and so on." Sp's sonnet form atypical; therefore, Amor is "an instance of consecutive analogy and a collection of analogues to a communal implied norm or formal model." Refers to Sp's poetry in Chaps. on Form as Process; Form as Product, Segmental Forms and Associative Progression, Coherence and Contrast (extended analysis of 4 Hymns), and The Emergence of Climactic Progression. See Index. [Diss., Yale University, 1969.]

Johnson, Ronald C. George Cascoigne. New York: Twayne, 1972. 167 pp. 831

Relation between Gascoigne's theory of poetry, especially diction, and Sp (pp. 74-86).

Johnston, Arthur. Enchanted Ground: The Study of Medieval Romance in the Eighteenth Century. London: Athlone Press, 1964. 249 pp. 832

Thomas Percy's Reliques of Ancient English Poetry (1765) started interest in earlier literature and birth of modern scholarship. Knowing romantic epics of Ariosto, Tasso, and Sp, reader in 1700 thought Middle Ages a time of knight-errantry and chivalry. Phrase "enchanted ground" used most frequently in describing FQ, as by James Thomson in Summer (1744); Sp's world regarded as essence of romance. Revival of interest in romances an attempt to find sources that inspired Sp, Shakespeare, and Milton (pp. 1-59). For interest in Sp and medieval literature of Richard Hurd, Thomas Percy, Thomas Warton, Joseph Ritson, and George Ellis, see Index.

Johnston, Stanley, and A. K. H. Collections of Spenser Essays in Book Form: A Review, SpN, 4, No. 1 (1973), 11-17. 833

Lists contents of 12 collections: 1. W. R. Mueller and D. C. Allen (948); 2. William R. Mueller (947); 3. William Nelson (960); 4. Harry Berger, Jr. (517); John R. Elliott, Jr. (649); 6. Hugh Maclean (349); 7. Paul J. Alpers, Jr. (467); 8. Editors of ELH (644); 9. R. M. Cummings (613); 10. Kenneth John Atchity (1244); 11. A. C. Hamilton (756); 12. Judith Kennedy and James A. Reither (A Theatre for Spenserians, Toronto, 1973). Table of essays appearing in more than one of surveyed collections.

Jones, Buford. Spenser and Shakespeare in The Encantadas, Sketch VI, ESQ, No. 35 (1964), 68-73. 834

Sketch VI, Barington Isle and the Buccaneers, central in design of ten sketches: first five describe desolate landscape of enchanted isles, last five deal with men and women associated with them. Sixth sketch emphasizes redemptive, Edenic qualities of islands and inhabitants, stands apart from other sketches. Could not use two major literary sources, Bower of Bliss (FQ, II, xii) and Red Cross Knight in Cave of Despair (FQ, I, ix), so turned to story of rascally Fox and Ape in MHT, "a singularly inappropriate source in terms of his own announced theme," altering it to suit own purpose. Similarly adopted and changed pastoral elements in As You Like It and The Tempest.

Jones, H. S. V. A Spenser Handbook. London: George Bell, 1947. 419 pp. 835

Reprint of an important reference work published in 1930. Chapters on The Age of Sp, The Life of Sp, SC, each of other minor poems, FQ (pp. 126-49), individual books of FQ, View, Letters, Language and Versification.

Jorgensen, Paul A. Elizabethan Literature Today: A Review of Recent Scholarship, TSLL, 1 (1960), 562-78. 836

Valuable survey. Mentions several works included in this bibliography: C.S. Lewis's The Allegory of Love (1513), Starnes and Talbert's Classical Myth and Legend in Renaissance Dictionaries (1109), Bullough's Narrative and Dramatic Sources of Shakespeare (1295), Ribner's The English History Play in the Age of Shakespeare (1034), Campbell's Divine Poetry and Drama in Sixteenth-Century England (574), Potts's Shakespeare and The Faerie Queene (1627), Watkins's Shakespeare and Spenser (1180). Conclusion: "I would stress above all the excellence and vitality of the thought that has gone into recent

Elizabethan scholarship. . . . What is lacking mainly is vitality of style . . . " (p. 577).

Jortin, John. Remarks on Spenser's Poems. New York: Garland, 1970. 186 pp.   837

    Facsimile of original 1734 edition in Yale University Library.

Joseph, Sister Miriam, C.S.C. Rhetoric in Shakespeare's Time: Literary Theory of Renaissance Europe. New York: Harcourt, Brace & World, 1962. 421 pp.   838

    Abbreviated repr. of Shakespeare's Use of the Arts of Language, 1947. Renaissance schoolboys trained in rhetoric and logic (pp. 8-13). Figures of speech and vices of language listed under Figures in Index (pp. 411-5). Sp mentioned in General Theory of Composition. Quoted for examples of Graecismus, definition, adjuncts, dissimilitude, cause and effect, and other topics of invention. See Index.

Juel-Jensen, Bent. Contemporary Collectors XLIII, BC, 15 (1966), 152-74. 839

    In discursive account of his personal library, describes (not bibliographically) his early editions of Sp: "The *Faerie Queen* 1590-96"; Charles Wesley's copy of FQ, Vol. I, 1596, with extensive contemporary notes; the 1609 and 1610 folios; the 1595 CCCHA; and "30-odd sonnets of the *Amoretti*, 1595."

Kalstone, David. Sidney's Poetry: Contexts and Interpretations. Cambridge, Mass: Harvard University Press, 1965. 195 pp.   840

    Sidney's heroes in Arcadia fall away from their ideal when exposed to the temptations of love, unlike Calidore in FQ, VI, who can innocently experience love in the shepherds' world while taking respite from the demands of the heroic life (pp. 53-9).

Sp's Amor (79 quoted), unlike Astrophel and Stella, is static and lacks (except for 88) the perturbations of desire (pp. 155-6).

Kauffman, Corinne Elizabeth. Spenser and Tennyson: A Comparative Study. DA, 24 (1963), 729. University of Texas, 1963. 393 pp.   841

    Finds seven important links. (1) Both Sp and Tennyson, confronted with new scientific theories, harmonized old view with new. (2) Their literary theories analogous: true poet is prophet and seer. (3) Adaptations pastoral express Virgilian attitude towards love, but Sp's composite landscape contrasts with Tennyson's accurate description of nature. (4) Both poets honor Virgil. (5) Epic theories underlying FQ and Idylls hold epic poetry has enlightening power. (6) Both chose Arthur as epic hero because ideal man. (7) Two Arthurs different, yet each embodies social ideals of age. Sp and Tennyson universal poets with mandate to preserve truth and morality.

Keats, John. A Portrait—After Spenser, Encore, 7 (1945), 280.   842

    Three Spenserian stanzas, reprinted from Caroline Wells's A Parody Anthology (1904). Keats's Spenserian Stanzas on Charles Armitage Brown, written Apr. 15, 1819.

Kennedy, Judith M. A Critical Edition of Yong's Translation of George Montemayor's *Diana* and Gil Polo's *Enamoured Diana*. Oxford: Clarendon Press, 1968. 468 pp.   843

    In Intro., Section IV, "*Diana* in England," finds echoes of Diana in Calidore-Pastorella episode of FQ (VI, ix-xi), in Epith, and, through influence of Barnabe Googe, in SC.

Kerman, Joseph. The Elizabethan Madrigal: A Comparative Study. New

York: American Musicological Society, 1962. 318 pp.   844

In Chap. 1, English Madrigal Verse (pp. 1-37), mentions relation of Sidney's and Sp's poetry, like music of Elizabethan composers, to Italian models. Richard Carlton in 1601 published "so-called madrigals," most solemn of English secular settings, including four stanzas from FQ [V, viii, 1-2, vii, 1, and VI, viii, 1] (pp. 119-20). Orlando Gibbons' only secular set, Madrigals and Motets of 1612, includes stanzas from FQ [III, i, 49-50] (pp. 122-3). George Kirbye, first serious English madrigalist, published a set in 1597 which includes "Up then, Melpomene" from November of SC [stanzas 4-6, 13]; the style is conservative and completely Italianate (pp. 221-2). See 530, 632, 2242.

Kettle, Arnold, ed. Shakespeare in a Changing World. New York: International Publishers, 1964. 269 pp.   845

Essays for Shakespeare's 400th anniversary. Robert Weimann, The Soul of the Age: Towards a Historical Approach to Shakespeare: the Tudor monarchy was of great prestige, shown by "the homage paid to it by men such as Ascham, Spenser, Hooker and Bacon," which was not "empty eulogium" (p. 21); Elizabethan religious settlement, reconciling humanism with protestantism, deteriorated under James I, when "the foundations of the national compromise—so essential to Gascoigne, Sidney or Spenser—were crumbling away, and neither side proved really acceptable to the humanist imagination" (pp. 22-5). Raymond Southal, Troilus and Cressida and the Spirit of Capitalism: maintains that bourgeois concern with money brought changes in social behavior, including relations between lovers, so that "Love, in Spenser and Shakespeare as well as

Sidney, frequently finds its apparently natural expression in mercenary terms" (pp. 218-20).

Kimbrough, Robert. Sir Philip Sidney. New York: Twayne, 1971. 162 pp. 846

Sidney as center of circle of literary friends, most important Sp, experiments of group with "Latin quantity in English poetry," Sidney's criticism of SC, "the publishing sensation of late 1579," knowledge of short-lived quantitative experiments "well publicized, thanks to Harvey and Spenser, and well documented, positively and negatively" (pp. 29, 39, 57-8, 94-5, 100-1). The "catalytic moment in Sidney's literary career was also Spenser's"—1578-1580. In these years both wrote an essay on poetry, worked with Continental forms, tried hand at quantitative verse. As poetry, their early work amounted to little: Sp's SC "is extraordinary but, if I be not deceived, hath but little poetry in it," yet in these years Sp already at work on FQ (pp. 105-6). Sp did not think Stella was Penelope Rich, but Frances Sidney [in Astro] (pp. 122-3).

Kindermann, Heinz, and Margarete Dietrich, eds. Lexikon der Weltliteratur. Vienna: Humboldt-Verlag, 1950.   847

Sp, col. 769.

Kistner, Arthur Leroy. Despair in Some Elizabethan Tragedy. DA, 24 (1963), 284. University of Illinois, 1963. 181 pp.   848

Renaissance sermons "reveal the four inherent qualities of despair: isolation, frustration, helplessness, and intolerableness." Elizabethan scientific treatises distinguish between despair and melancholy. Surveys place of despair in works of medieval and Renaissance authors. Greene, Ralegh, Sp, and Kyd were influential. Based on historical background, offers readings of Hamlet, Othello, and Doctor Faustus.

Klein, Joan Larsen. Some Spenserian Influences on Milton's *Comus*, AnM, 5 (1964), 27-47.   849

Milton's Comus influenced by Sp's poetic theories, images, philosophy, and allegory. Milton does not portray individual man as allegorical representation of specific virtues, as does Sp. Milton's figures embody mankind generally; total structure and meaning of Comus are intellectual and abstract.

Konkol, Evelyn. Die Konversion im Frühneuenglischen in der Zeit von etwa 1580 bis 1600. Ein Beitrag zur Erforschung der sprachlichen Neuprägungen bei Kyd, Marlowe, Peele, Greene, Spenser und Nashe. Doc. diss., University of Cologne, 1960.   850

Studies word coinages based on conversion, e. g., noun-verb and verb-noun, in drama, prose, and poetry by writers named in title. First part deals with rhetorical theory of conversion, second part with conversion as individual stylistic device. Sp (pp. 178-210): often corrects chronology of NED entries; most of Sp's coinages, found mainly in FQ, I-III, were short-lived, e. g., delve, dismay, flush, shriek, throb, to crest, to embosom, to entrance, to perplex, to plot, to unbosom; Sp had greater sense of rhetorical effect than his contemporaries.

Kostić, Veselin. Spenser and the Bembian Linguistic Theory, EM, 10 (1959), 43-60.   851

Sp's poetic diction considered distinctly archaic in his time. Chaucer was his linguistic model. His ideas of poetic diction resemble doctrine of Bembian school in Italy. "The theory advanced by Bembo and his followers recommends the use of a special literary diction different from the contemporary speech and based on the vocabulary of the old Italian writers Petrarch and Boccaccio." Possibly Sp knew Bembo's Prose della volgare lingua; he certainly knew Castiglione's Courtier, in which ideas of the Bembian school are set forth in Book I. E. K.'s introductory letter for SC shows Castiglione's influence. "The parallels between E. K.'s letter and Castiglione's book are of special importance because they indicate that the roots of Spenser's theory of poetic diction lie in Italian Renaissance criticism rather than in the theoretic outlook of the poets of the *Pléiade*, as has been commonly held by modern scholars."

Kostić, Veselin. Spenser's Sources in Italian Poetry. Belgrade: Novi, 1969. 394 pp.   852

Discusses elements Sp has in common with Italian pastoralists, use of dialect and the polymetric eclogue; modifications in Amor of borrowings from Petrarch and Tasso; indebtedness to Castiglione in MHT and CCCHA. Developments in Italian criticism between Ariosto and Sp: principle of imitation, theory of epic, allegory in epic poetry, establishment of Ariosto as epic model; Ariosto and Sp; Tasso and Sp; Sp and other Italian poets: Dante, Boiardo, Lodovici, Trissino, B. Tasso, Castiglione. Sp's ideas of poetic diction and their relation to Bembian linguistic theory (851), and "the Italian element in Spenser's versification." [Diss., University of Nottingham, 1958.]

Kremer, Charles F., Jr. Studies in Verse Form in Non-dramatic English Poetry from Wyatt to Sidney. Doctoral diss., Northwestern University, 1942. NUSDD, 10 (1942), 30-2.   853

Poets from Wyatt to Sidney used variety of verse forms which they found in native or foreign literature or invented. Wyatt and Sidney show greater foreign influence than any other poets of period, and also more use of native patterns and original rhyme schemes. Statistical tables at ends of sections show line totals for various forms in descending order of frequency: short meter, common meter, rime royal, 6-line stanzas ababcc, various 4-line stanzas, poulter's measure, and sonnets. About half the verse of the period is in poems of mixed line length, more than one-third pentameter. Iambic verse prevails so largely that any other foot is exceptional. Background for Sp's verse forms.

Kuhn, Bertha Mehitable. Spenser's *Faerie Queene* and *Fowre Hymnes* in the Light of Some Medieval and Renaissance Evaluations of Plato's Doctrine of Ideas. Doctoral diss., University of Washington, 1941. DDAAU, 1940-41, No. 8. UWAT, 6 (1942), 269-72.   854

Traces history of two interpretations of Plato's doctrine of Ideas that developed during Middle Ages. Argues that "Spenser's use of Neo-Platonic literary material reveals Renaissance concepts of Neo-Platonism together with some lapses into Augustinian extreme realism." Disagrees with Fletcher, Greenlaw, Bennett, and Collins (see 598) as to nature of Sp's Platonism. Sees 4 Hymns as "neither a Platonic nor a mystic unit," but mixed; similarly with Garden of Adonis episode (FQ, III, vi).

L., G. G. Queries from Spenser, N&Q, 176 (1939), 190.   855

Seven questions and suggestions on FQ, I, iii, 31; VI, vii, 36; and VI, x, 22. Also on TM, 1. 15; Epith, 1. 330 and last 7 lines; and HHOL, 1. 169.

L., G. G. Queries from Spenser, N&Q, 178 (1940), 445-6.   856

Quotes comments of Sir Edward Marsh and W.L. Renwick on questions asked, ibid., 176 (1939), 190 (see 855).

Lacava, Frederick William. The Circle of Love in the Poetry of Edmund Spenser. DAI, 32 (1971), 921A-2A. University of North Carolina at Chapel Hill, 1971. 218 pp.   857

Circle of Love metaphor used since earliest Western civilization to describe life of man. Whenever heaven is posited as beginning and end, circle image describes journey of soul. Certain conventions developed to describe stages in journey. Bk. I of FQ describes Redcrosse's journey in terms of places in Circle, e.g., Wandering Wood, Orgoglio's dungeon, Cave of Despair, House of Holiness. Britomart's career uses Circle to structure and unify it: Merlin's Mirror, fight with Artegall, vision in Isis Church. Conventions of Circle function in Garden of Adonis and 4 Hymns, Circle of Love combines with circles of day and year in SC and Mutability Cantos. Bk. VI of FQ is *expolitio*. Career of Pastorella is exemplum of whole journey of Circle of Love. See 1211, 1251, 1353, 1725.

Lalou, René. La Littérature Anglaise. Paris: Presses Universitaires de France, 1964. 128 pp.   858

Sackville's Induction to tragedy of Buckingham in Mirror for Magistrates links Chaucer and Sp (p. 13); brief account of SC as forerunner of FQ, which "offrait la plus somptueuse procession d'images de toute la litterature anglaise," Amor, Epith, 4 Hymns, letter to Raleigh (pp. 15-8); Platonic idealism of Henry Vaughan, "selon l'exemple de Spenser" (p. 35); James Thomson's Castle of Indolence an imitation of Sp (p. 44).

Lambert, Ellen Zetzel. The Pastoral Elegy from Theocritus to Milton: A Critical

Study. DAI, 31 (1970), 1233-A. Yale
University, 1969. 331 pp.   859

Study of pastoral elegy as it informs
Lycidas. English tradition considered
in detail in relation to classical genre.
Elegist's strategies analyzed in Renaissance poems, with changes observed
in moving from Italy to France to
England.

Langdale, Abram Barnett. Phineas Fletcher: Man of Letters, Science and Divinity. New York: Columbia University
Press, 1937. CUSECL, 125. 230pp. 860

Connection between Du Bartas' Divine Weeks in Sylvester's translation,
FQ, and Fletcher's The Purple Island
(pp. 114-7). Chapter IX, The Master
and the Apprentice, pp. 131-52, details Fletcher's debt to Sp in Brittain's
Idea, the Piscatorie Eclogs, The Ap-
pollyonists, and The Purple Island.
See also Appendix B, pp. 216-20, for
a tabulation of the sources of 202
passages in Fletcher's works, of which
103 are found in Sp.

Langdon, Ida. Milton's Theory of Poetry
and Fine Art: An Essay with a Collection of Illustrative Passages from His
Works. New York: Russell and Russell,
1965. 342 pp.   861

Repr. of 1924 ed. In connection
with leading principles in Milton's
theory of fine art, quotes Sp's HHOB
several times. On fine arts other than
poetry, cites CCCHA, FQ, V, ix,
27-28, IV, iv, 15, and II, xii, 42, 50,
58-59. On general aspects of poetry,
quotes October eclogue of SC and
View, cites RT, Amor 69, and Epith.
In connection with Milton and epic
poetry, quotes FQ, VI, Proem 2, and
V, iii, 3.

Larson, Edwin. Spenser and the Tradition
of Italian Style. DA, 13 (1953), 95.
Vanderbilt University, 1951. 414 pp.
                                  862

Studies elements of style developed
in seven major phases of the tradition,
from the troubadours to the Italian
tradition in 16th-century France. Last
chapter on FQ, which "reflects many
elements of Italian style, as well as
French and Chaucerian versions of
this tradition. The love theme and its
ethical and spiritual allegory are predominant." Sp was conscious of the
tradition, and more creative borrower
than imitator.

Latham, Agnes M. C. Sir Walter Ralegh.
London: Longmans, Green, 1964. 43
pp.   863

Ralegh's poetry known only to select circle that included Sp. Ralegh
visited him in 1589 in Ireland, lis-
tened to some of Sp's unpublished
verse and in exchange read some of
his own which Sp refers to in CCCHA
as "all a lamentable lay." Timias' love
of Belphoebe in FQ, III, is Sp's idealized picture of Ralegh and Queen
Elizabeth. Story has happy ending;
apparently Ralegh soothed the
Queen's vexation, but marriage to
Elizabeth Throckmorton in 1592 led
to permanent breach. Among Cecil
Papers at Hatfield House is manuscript fragment of 500 lines in Ralegh's hand entitled The Eleventh and
Twelfth Books of the Ocean to Cynthia, perhaps continuation of "lamentable lay" known to Sp. Only quality
common to all of Raleigh's verses is
their disillusionment. "Contemporaries stress their sweetness. To Spenser Ralegh's verse was 'honied' and
'with nector sprinkled' " (pp. 10-17).

Leavis, F. R. Revaluation: Tradition and
Development in English Poetry. New
York: George W. Stewart, 1947; repr.
New York: Norton, 1963. 275 pp. 864

First published 1936. In the course
of a denigrating chap. on Milton's
Verse (pp. 42-67) groups Sp, Milton,
Thomson, and Tennyson together in

contrast with Shakespeare and Donne. "Lycidas ... exhibits a use of language in the spirit of Spenser—incantatory, remote from speech." See 532.

Lecocq, Louis. La Satire en Angleterre de 1598 à 1603. Paris: Didier, 1969. 546 pp.   865

In Chap. II, Satire and Society, in section on The Court, discusses opposition between ancient purity and modern corruption, a theme "inherent in all the pastorals of the Renaissance, nowhere presented with more coherence and conviction than in the work of Spenser." Analyzes MHT and CCCHA as forerunners of social outlook of Guilpin, Hall, Donne, and Marston. Sp's "simple Suter" in MHT represents corruption of court (pp. 63-70). Section on Spenser in "La Satire Hors du Genre Satirique" (pp. 212-9) discusses satiric themes in SC, Complaints, and FQ. MHT has important relation to satires at end of century. Finds Spenserian influence in language and style of Joseph Hall's Virgidemiae (pp. 414-9). For other references to Sp, see Index.

Leech, Geoffrey N. A Linguistic Guide to English Poetry. London: Longmans, 1969. 240 pp.   866

Example of routine poetic license in FQ, II, xii, 9, 89. Of all major English poets, Sp probably claimed this kind of freedom most. In justification is "Spenser's achievement of sustaining an exacting verse form through the longest good poem in the English language" (p. 19). Lexical deviations in Sp's prefixing *a-* and *en-* to words needing extra syllable for metrical scheme; his fondness for adjectives in *-y*, *-less*, and *-full*; his propensity for compounds like *shaggy-bearded* (goats), *firie-mouthed* (steeds). Dialectal deviations in use of homely provincial words in SC for rustic naivete: *heydeguyes* (type of dance), *rontes* (young bullocks), and *wimble* (nimble) (pp. 42-9). Onomatopoeia, purely mimetic power of language, in sibilants in opening lines of Proth (pp. 97 ff.). Allegory kind of "multiple symbol," with underlying sense peeping through in proper names: House of Holiness, Bower of Bliss in FQ, I, x and II, xii (p. 163).

Lefranc, Pierre. Sir Walter Raleigh, Écrivain: l'oeuvre et les idees. Paris. Armand Colin, 1968. 738 pp.   867

Raleigh's sojourn in Ireland 1580-81, when he met Sp at Smerwick, marks end of obscure period in life (pp. 28-9). Later acquaintance with Sp in summer 1589 recounted in CCCHA (pp. 32-3). Raleigh and Sp-Colin in CCCHA, written 1591, published 1595. Raleigh's relation to FQ (pp. 113-6). Raleigh in CCCHA and in FQ (pp. 126-30). Similarities between Raleigh's and Sp's poetic treatment of Queen Elizabeth (pp. 519-22). Appendix F: Cynthia in the literature and iconography of the English Renaissance (pp. 604-13). For other references to Sp, see Index.

Legouis, Émile. Edmond Spenser. Rev. ed. by Pierre Legouis. Paris: Didier, 1956. 383pp.   868

Substantially the same as the first ed. of 1923 and the 2nd ed. of 1930. Eleven chapters on the life in relation to the poetry, 4 chapters on FQ. Emphasizes that Sp's court satire is a result of disappointment in his courtly ambitions, and stresses the basic conflict between the voluptuousness of Sp's nature and the virtuousness of his pretensions.

Legouis, Émile. A Short History of English Literature. Trans. V. F. Boyson and J. Coulson. Oxford: University Press, 1941. 420pp.   869

First published 1934. Sp, with Lyly and Sidney, in chapter on leaders of Renaissance, pp. 84-94. Patriotic ideal of SC; conflict between idealism and sensuality in 4 Hymns; Epith is "the lyrical triumph of the English Renaissance"; FQ is essentially a gallery of pictures, and Sp a great painter.

Leguois, Émile, and Louis Cazamian; Raymond Las Vergnas, Bk. VIII, The Twentieth Century (1914-1963). A History of English Literature. Part I, The Middle Ages and the Renascence (650-1660), trans. Helen Douglas Irvine. New York: Macmillan, 1964. 1469 pp.   870

First ed. 1926-1927. Bk. IV, The Flowering of the Renascence (1578-1625), Chap. II, The Pioneers: Lyly, Sidney, and Spenser (pp. 258-88). Sections on Sp, SC, 4 Hymns and MHT, Complaints, Astro and CCCHA, Amor and Epith, and FQ (pp. 268-88).

Leishman, J. B. The Art of Marvell's Poetry. 2nd ed. New York: Minerva Press, 1968. 328 pp.   871

In early part of chap. on Pastoral and Semi-Pastoral (pp. 101-92) shows relatively large number of Marvell's poems in Elizabethan pastoral tradition, not banished by Jonson and Donne; Jonson's masques have "Spenserian and pastoral elements"; pastoral dialogues by Jonson, Carew, Herrick (at least seven), Marvell, and many others approximate form of SC. "Pictorialism" in Appleton House poems different from Sp's in SC and FQ, or Keats's in Autumn (pp. 271-3). Marvell and Waller describing eternal spring of the Bermudas recall Tasso and Sp (FQ, III, vi) as well as Sylvester (pp. 277-82). Image of soul as bird in The Garden comes from Castiglione through Sp's HOHB. Marvell, "like Milton and unlike Donne, did not disdain the poetry" of Sp (pp. 317-8).

Leishman, J. B. Milton's Minor Poems. Ed. Geoffrey Tillotson. London: Hutchinson, 1969. 360 pp.   872

Carefully defines sense in which Milton was disciple of Sp (pp. 33-7). Milton's Nativity Ode in main Spenserian, only preceding poem in English comparable is Sp's Epith (pp. 51-6). Milton's Song. On May Morning in tradition of Sp (pp. 73-9). Comus contains echoes of FQ, Daph, and HHOL (pp. 233-8). In discussion of Lycidas refers to November of SC, Astro, and Daph (pp. 263-7); Sp's views about corrupt clergy and Popish peril in SC and MHT (pp. 274-5); flowers in April of SC, VG, and Muiop (pp. 301-3). For other references to Sp, see Index.

Lerner, Laurence. The Uses of Nostalgia: Studies in Pastoral Poetry. London: Chatto and Windus, 1972. 248 pp.   873

Rejects definition of pastoral as a work about shepherds. Holds theme of longing to escape to simpler time or place—Arcadia, Eden, Golden Age, Good Old Days—essential to pastoral. Comments on Dylan Thomas, Nathaniel West, J. D. Salinger, Virgil, Shakespeare, and others. Discusses pastoral satire in September of SC and CCCHA, has chapter on "Sir Calidore's Holiday" (FQ, VI). Aristocratic birth of Pastorella, condescension of Calidore, and cowardice of Coridon are anti-pastoral. This tension enriches poem in x, 1-4, but too explicit; image of ship, xii, 1, more appropriate; episode on Mt. Acidale is paradox of "simplicity temporarily exalted above culture, of rusticity above learning." [SpN, Vol. 4, No. 1 (1973), 1-2.]

Lever, J. W. Venus and the Second Chance, ShS, 15 (1962), 81-8.   874

Venus in many forms has charmed poets from Bion to Ronsard, from Ovid and Lucretius to Chaucer and

Sp. Only Shakespeare in Venus and Adonis has viewed her as absurd, ridiculous. Both Venus and Adonis are mythical beings. She is also Venus Genetrix. Breeding jennet and trampling courser enact drama of courtship at her bidding; this is theme of Lucretius's invocation beginning De Rerum Natura, of Sp's hymn in Temple of Venus (FQ, IV, x, 46). Shakespeare's boar not agent of Mars, as in Ronsard, or of "Stygian gods," as Sp implied (FQ, III, vi, 46). But Adonis does not die. In Sp's Astro and Lay his body is killed but his spirit immortal. So the Friend of Shakespeare's sonnets, though "stained by the world and wrinkled by time," is redeemed from Time and the Boar by "the creative love of the imagination. . . . And Venus and Adonis, fallen and risen as Cleopatra and her Antony, live to triumph in the kingdom of the second chance."

Levin, Harry. English Literature of the Renaissance, in The Renaissance: A Reconsideration of the Theories and Interpretations of the Age, ed. Tinsley Helton, pp. 125-51. Madison: University of Wisconsin Press, 1961. 160 pp.   875

Preceded by essays on political history, intellectual history, art history, science, and Continental literature. Says Renaissance in English literature fact, not fiction (see 1707). Gives various kinds of evidence (pp. 125-40, 146-51). Objects to C. S. Lewis's division of 16th-century literature into "Drab" and "Golden" (878), especially his praise of Sp as neo-medieval savior of England "from the catastrophe of too thorough a renaissance." Considers Sp an escapist longing for return of Golden Age (pp. 140-5).

Levin, Harry. The Golden Age and the Renaissance, in Literary Views: Critical and Historical Essays, ed. Carroll Camden, pp. 1-14. Chicago: University of Chicago Press, 1964. 193 pp.   876

Traces idea of "the good life far away and long ago" from antiquity to Tasso, Montaigne, Sp, Shakespeare, and beyond. (See 1511).

Levin, Harry. Refractions: Essays in Comparative Literature. New York: Oxford University Press, 1966. 359 pp.   877

English Literature and the Renaissance (pp. 82-106) repr. from (875). Pleasantries about FQ (pp. 92, 101-3).

Lewis, C. S. English Literature in the Sixteenth Century Excluding Drama. Oxford History of English Literature, ed. F.P. Wilson and Bonamy Dobrée. Oxford: Clarendon Press, 1954. 696pp.

878

Book III. " 'Golden'," Chapter 1, Sidney and Spenser, pp. 318-93. Sp, pp. 347-93. Insights concerning Richard Mulcaster, Sp's teacher; Gabriel Harvey, Sp's friend; E. K., who is not Sp; the poet's reading; the effect on him of long years in Ireland; chronology of his literary career; SC; correspondence with Harvey; minor poetry, with emphasis on 4 Hymns. Insists on originality of structure of FQ, Sp's "Platonized Protestantism," "depth . . . which is one of the excellences of the *Faerie Queene*," success of poem as narrative, virtues of style outweighing faults. Final judgment: "Among those who shared, or still share, the culture for which he wrote, and which he helped to create, there is no dispute about his greatness." See 811, 1212.

Lewis, C. S. Neoplatonism in the Poetry of Spenser, EA, 14 (1961), 107-16. 879

Review article on Ellrodt's book (650). Generally accepts and praises Ellrodt's refusal to allow strict or technical Neoplatonic interpretation of Sp's poetry. Rejects Ellrodt's implication that FQ does not admit of rather extensive Neoplatonic interpretation, and adopts instead view of Wind (1211) that FQ parallels work of Italian mythological painters, loaded with great weight of learning and inviting Neoplatonic association.

Lindsay, Jean Stirling. A Survey of the Town-Country and Court-Country Themes in Non-Dramatic Elizabethan Literature. Doctoral diss., Cornell University, 1943. CUAT, 1943, pp. 37-40.
880

A study of literature in relation to social and economic conditions in the second half of the 16th century. "Both themes originated in sixteenth-century England in the eclogues of Alexander Barclay." Tries to discriminate between spontaneous and conventional writings and finds the former, where these two themes are present, rare.

Lombardo, Agostino. Ritratto di Enabardo: Saggi sulla letteratura inglese. Pisa: Nistri-Lischi, 1971. 365 pp.   881

In previously published The Early Poetry of John Keats (pp. 155-98) shows Sp's influence dominant. After reading Epith with Cowden Clarkes, "ecstatic" Keats immersed self in reading FQ, responding to chivalric world and exotic atmosphere of poem. At Leigh Hunt's resolved to become "high" and "noble" Poet like Sp. In Ode to Apollo (1815) seeking own manner. Sonnet to Chatterton and Specimen of an Induction to a Poem try Spenserian cadences and "poetic" quality of Sp's world; latter ends with eulogy of Sp's "nobility" as "poets' poet" who recaptures medieval chivalry. Imitates Sp again in fragment Calidore, about youthful and virtuous knight; in description of nature identifies beauty of nature with beauty of poetry. In previously published Keats, Endymion and the Romantic Artist (pp. 199-248) mentions numerous influences on composite poem, including Sp's Epith. In this period influence of Sp remained, but overshadowed by that of Dante, Shakespeare, and others. For other references to Sp, see Index.

Lotspeich, Henry Gibbons. Classical Mythology in the Poetry of Edmund Spenser. Princeton: Princeton University Press, 1965. 126 pp.   882

Repr. of 1932 ed. A basic work. In Sp's mind "myth and poetry were ... one and the same.... Classic myth, as it came to Spenser, was 'polyseme,' rich in the meanings and associations given it by generations of poets and commentators. Much of it was ready-made for his purposes; all of it was plastic and adaptable. In many ways he made it serve his intentions: as poetic ornament for the high style; as a means of expressing a poetic response to nature; as a way of pointing out through analogies and formal similes, the links of kinship between the people and actions of his created world and those of the world of classical antiquity" (pp. 3-28). Lists Sp's allusions alphabetically, from Acheron to Zodiac.

Lund, Mary Graham. Backward-Forward in Forbidden Lands, Western World Review, 3 (1968), 21-7.   883

Refers, among other things, to Sp's influence upon the symbolism of Nathaniel West [AES, 17 (1973), Item 253].

McAlindon, T. The Idea of Byzantium in William Morris and W. B. Yeats, MP, 64 (1967), 307-19.   884

Morris believed Renaissance ushered in fragmenting, antipopular tendencies and ended popular art of Middle Ages. He influenced Yeats in finding Shakespeare and Sp more artificial and intellectual than "the old simple writers," Malory and minstrels. Sp preferred Ariosto and Tasso, was hostile to Irish people. He became representative of middle-class morality. "Morris, contrasting Byzantine popular art with that of the Renaissance, had written of Shakespeare in identical terms." Yeats found norm in Lady Gregory's translations of Irish sagas, "the creation of a perfectly unified culture." Morris admired especially forms taken by Gothic art in Byzantium, considered St. Sophia most beautiful building in Europe. In Yeats's Byzantine myth, St. Sophia holds same central importance. "Morris anticipated Yeats's conviction that the harmonizing of pagan and Christian religious thought was a fundamental part of Byzantine unity." Yeats learned from Morris that Byzantium was archetypal pattern of unified culture, chose it as symbol of perfect beauty.

McAlindon, T. Yeats and the English Renaissance, PMLA, 82 (1967), 157-69.
885

Yeats's transformation into an aristocratic poet in the first decade of the 20th century was strongly influenced by his reading of Shakespeare, Sp, and Jonson. Sp's influence is registered in the essay prefixed to Yeats's edition of Poems of Spenser (1906). Yeats concludes that everything regrettable in Sp's life and art derives from "his capitulation to the middleclass, Anglo-Saxon, modern forces gathering about him." His greatness as man and poet stems from his relationship to "stately houses and the court." Sp's allegory and moralizing, both middle-class phenomena, damaged his art; his policy of extermination in View reflects emerging Saxon, middle-class policy ultimately enforced by Cromwell. Yeats praises Sp's courtly and conservative inclinations, especially his emphasis on courtesy, as reflected in SC, RT, TM, MHT, and FQ, VI. Sees the loss of his

patron, Leicester, "to be the chief cause of his tragic disassociation from aristocratic roots."

Mack, Maynard. The Garden and the City: Retirement and Politics in the Later Poetry of Pope 1731-1743. 55 Plates. Toronto: University of Toronto Press, 1969. 341 pp.   886

Pope's identification with tradition caused him to keep in library at Twickenham busts of Homer, Sp, Shakespeare, Milton, and Dryden (p. 36), left in his will to George Lyttleton (pp. 251, 264). In connection with Pope's high conception of poet's calling, quotes ll. 61-68, 79-82 from October of SC (p. 213). In later poetry Pope realized he had to put away "oaten reeds" and take up "trumpets sterne" in order to "moralize [his] song," as Sp says he is doing in FQ, I, i, Proem (pp. 222-3). Plate 47, titlepage of William Mason's Musaeus: A Monody to the Memory of Mr. Pope, In Imitation of Milton's Lycidas (1747), shows Chaucer, Sp, and Milton welcoming Pope into immortality (pp. xviii, 214, 310).

Mackail, J. W. The Springs of Helicon: A Study of the Progress of English Poetry from Chaucer to Milton. Lincoln: University of Nebraska Press, 1962. 207pp.
887

Repr. of 1909 ed. Foreword by J. W. Robinson. Chaps. on Chaucer, Sp (pp. 73-133), Milton. In SC we see revival of native English lyric tradition combined with classicism. Sp in FQ is redundant, profuse, as "English Livy" humorless, nostalgic for Golden Age, Platonic as in HOHB and HOHL, more moral than Ariosto, disillusioned in TM, superb in Epith. Separate section on FQ: as romantic epic it is sterile hybrid, allegory is "essence of the poem," poetry sometimes fresh and sometimes mechanical, whole like a pageant or masque, invented stanza too slow moving for narrative poetry, in pastoral "Pastorella-Perdita" episode pulls back from "the opening doorway into daylight and the new world" and returns to allegorical romance; Mutability Cantos "renew the earlier splendours of the poem, but with a deeper and graver music."

McKillop, Alan Dugald, ed. James Thomson: The Castle of Indolence and Other Poems. Lawrence: University of Kansas Press, 1961. 222 pp.   888

Introduction to The Castle of Indolence (pp. 1-67) details debt to Sp: moral allegory, Spenserian stanzas, Thomson's special affinities with Sp, archaic diction used cautiously, stanza units loosely put together, setting "lightly sketched in the Spenserian manner," personification is "evanescent and shadowy," paintings and tapestries as in Sp but sentimentalized, "insidious evil in Castle explored with greater philosophical range by Spenser," overthrow of Castle is triumph of virtue. Quotations from many parts of FQ; see also Explanatory Notes (pp. 185-205).

MacLure, Millar. Spenser, in English Poetry and Prose, 1540-1674, ed. Christopher Ricks, pp. 60-79. London: Sphere Books, 1970. 442 pp.   889

Discussion in three sections of Sp's life; his career in relation to his works, especially minor poems; and FQ. Bibliography (pp. 80-1).

MacLure, Millar. Spenser's Allegories, UTQ, 32 (1962), 83-92.   890

Review article treating A. C. Hamilton's Structure of Allegory in The Faerie Queene (1416) and Paul E. McLane's Spenser's Shepheardes Calender: A Study in Elizabethan Allegory (2273). Hamilton's approach to FQ essentially admirable but he tends to present "a simpler and more consistent poem than we have," and his

own reading emerges as "an austere patterning poised upon an archetypal image structure," dominated especially by scriptural archetype. McLane's theory of allegory is too limited, and as a result he reduces SC to a topical puzzle for which he provides the key.

MacLure, Millar, and F. W. Watt, eds. Essays in English Literature from the Renaissance to the Victorian Age, Presented to A. S. P. Woodhouse. Toronto: University of Toronto Press, 1964. 339 pp.   891

Contains two essays on Sp: Rosemond Tuve, Spenserus (pp. 3-25; see 218); and William Blissett, Spenser's Mutabilitie (pp. 26-42; see 2170). Listed individually herein.

McNamee, Lawrence. Ninety-Nine Years of English Dissertations. Commerce, Texas: East Texas State University, 1969. 123 pp.   892

Breakdown and analysis of data assembled in (69). Except for Shakespeare, Sp most popular dissertation subject in Renaissance from 1865-1964, with 126 studies: 96 American, 24 German, and 6 British. Most dissertations on FQ, 43. In U.S. most work on Sp at Yale (11), Princeton (9), and Harvard (9) (pp. 30-1). Tables of Renaissance dissertations at ten leading American, German, and British universities (pp. 97-8).

McNeir, Waldo F. The Sacrifice of Serena: The Faerie Queene, VI. viii. 31-51, in Festschrift für Edgar Mertner, ed. Bernhard Fabian and Ulrich Suerbaum, pp. 117-56. Munich: Wilhelm Fink, 1969. 356 pp.   893

Climax of adventures of Calepine and Serena is her capture by cannibalistic brigands from whom Calepine saves her. Earlier examples of anthropophagy in FQ (III, vii, 22-29; IV, vii, 4-32) foreshadow these man-eaters. Discounts proposed sources of episode in Heliodorus, Achilles Tatius, or Italian epics and pastorals. Reviews reports of human sacrifice and cannibalism among western Celts, particularly Irish, by classical writers. Sp's savages reflect imperfect memory of these, familiarity with Elizabethan historians' view of sanguinary Irish history, participation in Irish affairs, and opinion of Irish outlaws in View. All these transformed by poetic imagination into sacrifice of Serena.

MacQueen, John. Allegory. London: Methuen, 1970. 82 pp.   894

Finds vital religious root of allegory in myth regarded very early as allegorical explanation of process. Starts with Dis, Persephone, and Demeter, explains levels of meaning with classical and modern examples. First chapter on Orpheus and Eurydice; journey to underworld as new tradition in epic poetry; Plato's myth of Er; Somnium Scipionis, Golden Ass, allegorization of myth under Julian the Apostate. Chapters on Biblical Allegory, Allegory and the Course of Time, Medieval Theories of Allegory. Allegory and the Individual considers relation of allegory to psychic interiorization: Psychomachia—Battle, Quest, Pilgrimage, Journey—ending with Sp's Letter to Raleigh. Allegory and Satire deals with relation of allegory of Morality plays to later satire. [SpN, Vol. 4, No. 3 (1973), 1-2.]

Magill, Andrew James. Spenser and Ireland: A Synthesis and Revaluation of Twentieth Century Scholarship. DA, 27 (1967), 4257A-8A. University of Texas, 1967. 277 pp.   895

Reviews political and social history of Ireland since Anglo-Norman invasion. Examines proposals in View, particularly widely misunderstood famine proposal. Bk. V of FQ draws fully on Sp's Irish experiences, but only canto xii allegorizes story of Sp's

patron, Lord Grey de Wilton. Minimizes allusions to Irish mythology in FQ, preferring analogues in classical literature and Italian romances. Use of Irish imagery shows intimate knowledge of Irish scene. Early books of FQ emphasize unfavorable aspects of Irish life; later books and several minor poems show growing delight in countryside around Kilcolman, though tempered by apprehension of native uprising against Munster undertakers.

Mahood, M. M. Poetry and Humanism. New Haven: Yale University Press, 1950. 335 pp.   896

Rejecting anti-humanist theory of Renaissance of Nicolas Berdyaev and Jacques Maritain as split between God-centered humanism (true) and man-centered (false), re-evaluates English 17th-century devotional poets and finds viable integration of worldly and spiritual, as in "centric happiness" of Thomas Traherne (passim). Transition from Middle Ages slow; Shakespeare and Sp not trampling on medieval past. Self-destructive dialectic of false humanism in Marlowe's plays; new learning reconciled with old faith in Ficino and Pico, Erasmus and More, Sidney and Sp (pp. 17-20, 54-86). Donne as poet and preacher became many-sided man of Renaissance ideal (pp. 87-168). Milton accepted Sp's humanistic ethics, impressed by Giles Fletcher's Spenserian Christ's Victory and Triumph (pp. 169-76), Sp's Bower of Bliss (FQ, II, xii). Points in Vaughan: The Symphony of Nature (pp. 252-95) suggests back-glances at Sp.

Malof, Joseph. A Manual of English Meters. Bloomington: Indiana University Press, 1970. 236 pp.   897

Defines Spenserian stanza: eight lines of iambic pentameter with final line alexandrine or iambic hexameter. Notes Epithalamion stanza as "long, loose stanza of eighteen or nineteen lines, has the quality of the ode." Some variation in rhythm and meter (pp. 189-90).

Manzalaoui, M. A. "Derring-Do," N&Q, 8 (1962), 369-70.   898

Sp's use of the term "derring-do" (SC, October, 65; FQ, II, iv, 42), previously interpreted as "daring to do" with courage, can be reinterpreted according to a precedent for the transitive use of "do" in Lydgate's *Troy Book.*

Marenco, Franco. Arcadia Puritana: L'uso della tradizione nella prima *Arcadia* di Sir Philip Sidney. Bari: Adriatica Editrice, 1968. 239 pp.   899

Interprets Sidney's Old Arcadia as attack on conventional pastoral and epic from extreme Protestant position. Refers frequently to SC and FQ in last chap., Pastori o Cannibali? (pp. 171-228).

Margoliouth, H. M., ed. The Poems and Letters of Andrew Marvell. 3rd ed., rev. by Pierre Legouis. 2 vols. Oxford: Clarendon Press, 1971. 454, 415 pp.   900

First ed. 1927. Vol. I, Poems. Marvell refers to Sp in Tom May's Death (l. 85) and in Britannia and Rawleigh (ll. 42 ff.). Ed. refers to Sp in commentary on Clorinda and Damon, The Garden, The Last Instructions to a Painter, and The Loyall Scot.

Marinelli, Peter V. Pastoral. London: Methuen, 1971. 90 pp.   901

Focuses primarily on pastoral genre, incidentally on Sp. Summarizes tradition, classical and later representatives. Argues that "every private Arcadia . . . really looks back to the original." Sp appears in three chapters. First on the Golden Age. Since only in mythic, prelapsarian past can

sexuality and innocence coexist, Sp's gardens are parodic. Guyon can only dream of innocent "pastoral of happiness"—cannot experience it. SC, however, belongs to category of Arcadian poetry, and "Spenser is the first English poet to reinvigorate the Arcadian tradition." Vulnerability of pastoral world in FQ, VI, shows truth that Sparta is always near Arcadia. Final chapter on retreat to childhood, and epilogue on possibilities latent in this "age of plastic." [SpN, 4, No. 2 (1973), 1.]

Marks, Emerson R. Relativist and Absolutist: The Early Neo-classical Debate in England. New Brunswick, N. J.: Rutgers University Press, 1955. 171 pp.   902

John Hughes's defense of Sp's art in Remarks on the Faërie Queene in 1715 ed. of Sp is based on historical relativism (pp. 66-7).

Marples, Morris. Romantics At School. New York: Barnes & Noble, 1967. 206 pp.   903

Traces schooling of Wordsworth, Coleridge, Southey, Byron, Shelley, and Keats. Southey read FQ and other "massive poems" before age 12 (pp. 85, 90) and worked on his own sequels (p. 101). Keats delighted in Sp's poetics and his first poems were imitations (pp. 192-3).

Maxwell, J. C. Milton in Wordsworth's Praise of Spenser, N&Q, 15 (1968), 22-3.   904

Points out strong Miltonic flavor of Wordsworth's praise of Sp in The Prelude, II, 281-2.

Mayhall, Jane. Shakespeare and Spenser: A Commentary on Differences, MLQ, 10 (1949), 356-63.   905

The differences between them as men and poets may be seen in their poetic styles. Emphasizes what she calls Shakespeare's "interverbal meanings" and Sp's lack of them.

Mayhead, Robin. The Poetry of Tennyson, in From Dickens to Hardy, pp. 227-244. Ed. Boris Ford. A Guide to English Literature, 6. New and rev. ed. London: Cassell, 1963. 516 pp. 906

Influence of Sp and Milton seen in Tennyson. "The slow, majestic progress of the verse . . . comes from Milton; and the calculated exploitation of melodious vowel-sounds derives from Spenser" (pp. 230-1). Spenserian atmosphere unmistakable in Tennyson's "Lotus-Eaters" (pp. 232-3).

Mazzaro, Jerome. Transformations in the Renaissance English Lyric. Ithaca: Cornell University Press, 1970. 214 pp. 907

Deals with way songs become modes of vision and thought. Discusses "changes from medieval to Renaissance *res-verba* sensibilities, from Italianate to English modes of love behavior, from anonymity to self-consciousness, from symbolic to symptomatic views of music, from sixteenth- to twentieth-century concepts of the poet" (pp. vii-ix). St. Paul's tripartite view of man in Sp's FQ and Amor (p. 15). Sidney notable in Apology for Poetry for originality, but "dismissal" of SC shows not altogether abandoning authority (pp. 104-6). Possible that Areopagus of Sidney and Sp took over views of French academicians on relationship of music and poetry; lyric personae of Sidney and Sp of higher social rank than those of Donne and Shakespeare; Sp in Amor may have mathematical (magical) substructure in mind, since sonnets make little sense as narratives or lyrical meditations (pp. 120-1, 137-9, 141-4).

Meadows, A. J. The High Firmament: A Survey of Astronomy in English Literature. Leicester: Leicester University Press, 1969. 207 pp. 908

Aspects of medieval universe in Sp's HHOL and FQ, III, i, 16 (pp. 17, 26-7). Fixing date by Sun's position in Chaucer's Canterbury Tales and in Sp's MHT, ll. 1-6 (pp. 31-2); decay of universe, associated with previous existence of Golden Age, in FQ, V, Proem (pp. 41-2). Astrology and influence of stars on human life in FQ, II, ix, 52, and III, vi, 2 (p. 47). Awareness of Copernican revolution in FQ, V, Proem, and VII, vii, 51 (pp. 70-1); possibility of life on other worlds, fascinating to later writers, mentioned in FQ, II, Proem (pp. 83-4).

Meagher, John C. Method and Meaning in Jonson's Masques. South Bend, Ind.: University of Notre Dame Press, 1966. 214 pp. 909

Many Elizabethan masques were frivolous but some serious, like Sp's Masque of Cupid in FQ, III, xii. Jonson's of this type (p. 5). Neoplatonic ideas, widely diffused in Platonizing poetry such as Sp's 4 Hymns, materialized in Jonson's Masque of Beauty, Hymenaei, Masque of Queens, and Love Freed, in which "highest human beauty is more than physical, which is one of the more obvious points behind the two Florimells in the *Faerie Queene.*" Many of Jonson's masques infused with Platonic concepts of beauty and love (pp. 125-43). Many purveyed humanist ideas of virtue and fame, as in FQ (pp. 146 ff.). Jonson upheld ideas of cosmic harmony, the state, and ethics in common with Sidney, Sp, and most serious writers of English Renaissance (pp. 170 ff.).

Meissner, Paul. England im Zeitalter von Humanismus, Renaissance und Reformation. Heidelberg: F. H. Kerle, 1952. 656pp. 910

A work of Kulturgeschichte in three parts: Die Welt des Wissens, Die Welt des Handelns, and Die Welt des Glaubens. Sp prominently mentioned as representative of many aspects of the culture of the period, e.g., in part one, the influence of classical rhetoric, allegory as an order of truth, the ethical mission of poetry, the ideal of concord and order in the universe; in part two, the new time-concept, mutability and pessimism, the influence of Bruno, individualism, expansionism; in part three, Calvinism, Italian influences, French influences. Extensive notes (pp. 547-615) and bibliography (pp. 617-42). See Index.

Meissner, Paul. England und die Europäischer Renaissance, in Grundformen der Englischen Geistesgeschichte, ed. Paul Meissner, pp. 191-273. Stuttgart: W. Kohlhammer, 1941. 424pp.   911

Sp in connection with Petrarchism (p. 213), Ariosto's influence (pp. 214-5), Christian humanism and Platonism (pp. 227-9), the Pléiade (pp. 241-4).

Mendilow, A. A., and Alice Shalvi. The World and Art of Shakespeare. New York: Daniel Davey, 1967. 285 pp. 912

Sp's father's trade (pp. 5-6). Sp wrote plays, none extant (p. 22). Sp, Sidney, and Shakespeare employ pastoral romance genre for a moral, didactic purpose (pp. 152, 254). Mutability of life becomes consolation for Sp and Shakespeare (p. 258).

Meres, Francis. Palladis Tamia. Ed. Don Cameron Allen. New York: SF&R, 1938.   913

Published 1598. Sp mentioned among those by whom "the English tongue is mightily enriched" (p. 280); FQ referred to as an "excellent or exquisite Poem," and author of SC as "honoured for fine Poeticall inuention, and most equisit wit" (p. 280v);

Sp praised generally and called one of "our chiefe heroicall Makers" (p. 282v); Sp "excelleth in all kinds" (p. 283r); Sp one of "the most passionate among vs to bewaile and bemoane the perplexities of Loue," and among "the best for pastorall" (p. 284r).

Meyer, Arnold Oskar. England and the Catholic Church Under Queen Elizabeth. Trans. by Rev. J. R. McKee. London: Routledge and Kegan Paul, 1967. 555 pp.   914

English ed. pub. 1915. Background of Sp's religious views.

Meyer-Baer, Kathi. Music of the Spheres and the Dance of Death: Studies in Musical Iconology. Illus. Princeton: Princeton University Press, 1970. 376 pp.   915

Quotes Sp's translation of Axiochus (see 417, 2608), once ascribed to Plato, on "heavenly Musicke . . . in the Elysian fields" (pp. 20-1). Sp's forms of invocation of Muses (p. 194). In Chap. XVI, Survivals of Earlier Images: Survivals of Ancient Figures in Fairy Tales (pp. 327-33), cites Sp's nymphs and fairies dancing with Muses.

Meyers Grosses Personenlexikon. Spenser, Edmund, 1253. Mannheim: Bibliographisches Institut, 1968.   916

Miles, Josephine. Eras and Modes in English Poetry. 2nd ed. rev. and enl. Berkeley: University of California Press, 1964. 291pp.   917

First ed. 1957. Studies the sentence structure of major poets from the Middle Ages to the present. Gives a list of the 50 words Sp used most frequently (p. 266), and the proportion of nouns, verbs, and adjectives in a representative sample of his verse (table on p. 253).

Miles, Josephine. Major Adjectives in English Poetry from Wyatt to Auden.

Berkeley: University of California Press, 1946. UCPE, 12, No. 3, 305–426. 918

Section III, Four Poets of Description: Spenser, Milton, Collins, Keats (pp. 360-88). "These were the great architects of the adjective." Analysis of Sp's adjectival usage and practice, especially pp. 360-5, but throughout this section. See also Section V, Conclusion: Good to Bright (pp. 408-21).

Miles, Josephine. The Primary Langauge of Poetry in the 1640's. Berkeley: University of California Press, 1948. UCPE, 19, No. 1, 1-160. 919

Chap. 1, The Poetry of the 1540's and the 1640's. In the earlier period "Heywood and Sackville . . . work toward the richer substantival vocabulary of the later Shakespeare and Spenser, the newer masters." Sp included in adjective-noun-verb tables, pp. 16-27.

Miles, Josephine. Renaissance, Eighteenth Century, and Modern Language in English Poetry: A Tabular View. Berkeley: University of California Press, 1960. 73pp. 920

Tabulates the recurrence of certain adjectives, nouns, and verbs in selected passages drawn from English and American poets from Laurence Minot, born ca. 1310, to Anthony Hecht, born 1923. The samples from Spenser are the first 500 lines each of FQ and Amor. Spenser appears in each of the five analytical tables of which the book is composed.

Mill, Adair. Tottel's Miscellany and England's Helicon, Ingiliz Filolojisi Dergisi (Studies by Members of the English Department, University of Istanbul), 3 (1952), 42-60. 921

Tottel's Miscellany represents the unbroken tradition of the native lyric from the 15th to the last quarter of the 16th century, when Sp and Sidney revolutionized English poetry. England's Helicon reflects a wholly new conception of poetic technique.

Miller, Audrey Berryman. Themes and Techniques in Mid-Tudor Lyric Poetry: An Analytical Study of the Short Poem from Wyatt to Sidney. Doctoral diss., Northwestern University, 1949. NUSDD, 17 (1950), 35-41. 922

Themes studied: love (more than half poems examined), friendship, man's life, death, beauty, fortune, the golden mean, marriage, mutability, and women. Techniques studied: rhetorical, Petrarchan, classical, ornamental. Background for Sp's lyric themes and techniques.

Miller, Edwin Haviland. The Professional Writer in Elizabethan England. Cambridge, Mass.: Harvard University Press, 1959. 282pp. 923

Many references to Sp in connection with the milieu of authors, the Elizabethan audience and their tastes, patronage, writers and stationers, and censorship. See Index.

Miller, G.M. The Historical Point of View in English Literary Criticism from 1570-1770. New York: Phaeton Press, 1968. 160 pp. 924

Growth from attempts to change national verse forms in 16th century to ancients vs. moderns in 17th century to reconciliation and wider appreciation of native forms in 18th century. Although not serious reformer, Sp supported Ascham and classical verse over national tradition (pp. 40-1). He represented important influence in development of discipline, and concerned critics such as Harvey (pp. 47-8), Nashe (p. 52), Phillips (p. 82), Rymer (p. 85), Johnson (p. 118), Warton (pp. 127-8), Hurd (pp. 135-6), and Pope (p. 148).

Miller, James E., Jr. Melville's Search for Form, BuR, 8 (1961), 260-76.   925

Melville's work examined in relation to tradition exemplified by FQ. Constituent part of form of Moby Dick is multi-level meaning of allegory. In his works Melville made eighteen allusions to Sp's poetry.

Millican, Charles Bowie. Spenser and the Table Round: A Study of the Contemporaneous Background for Spenser's Use of the Arthurian Legend. New York: Octagon Books, 1967. 237 pp.   926

Repr. of 1932 ed. Traces growth of Arthurian myth from nationalistic policy of Henry VII: Welsh historians, Edward Hall, John Leland's "first chauvinistic defence of the authenticity of Arthur as portrayed by Geoffrey of Monmouth" against Polydore Vergil, Arthur Kelton, and John Bale in early Tudor period. During Elizabeth's reign "the tide of Arthurian enthusiasm in England reached its flood," and Sp's use in FQ of Arthurian right of Tudor sovereigns inevitable. Richard Mulcaster's early influence on Sp; Humphrey Lhuyd, William Lambard, and Richard Harvey. Sp not so partisan in RT, SC, or FQ; but pro-Arthurians squelched antis.

Milward, Peter. Christian Themes in English Literature. Folcroft, Pa.: Folcroft Press, 1970. 297 pp.   927

Repr. of 1967 ed. Sp, Milton exerted Protestant influence on literary Renaissance (p. 9). Sp's "romantic idealism" manifest in his "medieval chivalry" (p. 10). "Personal immortality" became poetic tradition with neo-Platonism of 4 Hymns (p. 89). Garden of Adonis represents perfection and happiness but Sp points to escapism (pp. 119-20). Amor 48 one of few English poems with resurrection theme (p. 162). Sp demonstrates little Marian devotion but focuses on virgin queen (p. 176). Wisdom personified as woman in HOHB rooted in Old Testament and Greek philosophy (p. 178). Female chastity in Milton's Comus reflects 4 Hymns (p. 181). Sp uses idea of Immaculate Conception with Belphoebe's birth in FQ, III, vi (p. 189).

Mims, Edwin. The Christ of the Poets. Nashville: Abington-Cokesbury Press, 1948. 256pp.   928

The Shaffer lectures delivered at Northwestern University in 1944. Chapter II, "Edmund Spenser: Platonist and Christian," pp. 43-7. Sp is the first of 13 individual poets treated, after an introductory chapter entitled "Doubt and Faith: A General Survey." Red Cross Knight's vision of the New Jerusalem, FQ, I, x; Amor 68 on Easter; and 4 Hymns, with "the blending of the idealism of Plato in the fourth hymn and the high religion of the Gospel of John in the third."

Mincoff, Marco. The Structural Pattern of Shakespeare's Tragedies, ShS, 3 (1950), 58-65.   929

Their symmetry is not the result of classical influence. "It would seem more correct to ascribe this effect to that completeness of structure . . . which we find exemplified in so much sixteenth century art, in the closed, symmetrical composition of the Renaissance painters and—a much nearer parallel—in so many of the more complex lyrics of the sixteenth century such as . . . Spenser's *Prothalamion*, *Epithalamion*, and his *Ditty in Praise of Eliza*, which work up to the height of lyrical emotion in the exact middle and then fall slowly to the end. . . . In the simpler form of the lyric this balance and stress on the centre was more easily attainable, in the more complex forms of the drama and especially the epic it was rare."

Miner, Earl. The Metaphysical Mode from Donne to Cowley. Princeton: Princeton University Press, 1969. 291 pp.   930

Chap. I, The Private Mode (pp. 1-47), distinguished in use by metaphysical poets from public mode of Sp's FQ, and "poetry of a middle esthetic distance" that uses first person singular autobiographically as in Epith or fictionally as in SC. Satire of the court not original with Donne: Skelton and Wyatt early in 16th century, still earlier in Piers Plowman, closer to hand in MHT and CCCHA; yet Sp's protests from "one within the system," while Donne's satires more immediate. Since Donne "set the terms" of private poetry in last decade of Elizabeth that produced satire by writers as different as Hall, Marston, and Sp, "the notion of bright Elizabethan and dark Jacobean England is of course absurd." "Both [Sp and Donne] felt that they had slid on the slopes of patronage, and both reacted in very human fashion." More references to Sp in analysis of Donne's elegy, The Perfume; Herbert's longer poem, The Flower; and Marvell's narrative, The Nymph complaining for the death of her Faun (pp. 214-71). See Index.

Mizener, Arthur. Some Notes on the Nature of English Poetry, SR, 51 (1943), 27-51.   931

"Nature" in the title means the universe in which man lives. Sp's conviction of the fundamental similarity between the life of man, nature, and the supernatural enabled him to allegorize and harmonize them. The later Elizabethans and the Metaphysicals admitted uncertainties. "Pope is perhaps the last great poet" to depend "on the old explanation of the natural and supernatural contexts of man's life to justify serious comparisons among the three." Except for Wordsworth, nineteenth-century poets tended to separ-

ate man from both nature and the supernatural.

Mohinīmohana   Bhattāchārya   (Bhattacherje, Mohinimohan). Platonic Ideas in Spenser. London: Longmans, Green, 1935; repr. Westport, Conn.: Greenwood Press, 1970. 200 pp.   932

Listed in Atkinson, p. 81.

Mohl, Ruth. John Milton and His Commonplace Book. New York: Ungar, 1969. 334 pp.   933

An entry in Political Index from Sp's View on assigning land to veteran soldiers.(p. 257). In same index entry on Political Adroitness, in derogatory sense, concerning wicked policy of English governors in Ireland to prolong strife instead of crushing rebels quickly. Milton's views on unrest in Ireland set forth in several of his prose works. In Eikonoklastes wishes for iron man like Sp's Talus (FQ, V) to end tumults in both England and Ireland (pp. 283, 286-8).

Montgomery, Robert L., Jr. Symmetry and Sense: The Poetry of Sir Philip Sidney. Austin: University of Texas Press, 1961. 134 pp.   934

Sp's style is ornate, not plain (see 1213); Sp exploits "the audible patterns of language"; his ornamental style furthers symbolism and allegory; his style never seems restrained, "whether he is writing sonnet, epic, pastoral, or satire"; Amor shows Sp's religious Platonism; Sidney commonly linked with Sp in modern criticism, but "Spenser's artistic tendency is always more or less towards allegory," and Sidney lacks "the other's deliberate artificiality"; Sp's imagery in Amor "frequently transforms lyric into something like epic simile"; Sp "binds his Amoretti to the four seasons and through them traces the course of his emotions"; sexual desire only a discreet hint in Amor, "in Sidney it is frankly avowed." See Index.

Moody, William Vaughn, and Robert Morss Lovett. A History of English Literature. 8th. ed. Ed. by Fred B. Millett. New York: Scribner's, 1964. 602 pp.
935

Describes Sp's career at Cambridge, in London, and in Ireland; basic structure of FQ; Ariosto's influence; Sp's sensual poetics and moral intent (pp. 82-6). Reconciliation of Renaissance and Reformation created in Sp "spiritualized humanism" (p. 139).

Moore, John Warner, Jr. Responses to Mutability in Spenser's Early Poetry, 1569-1590. DAI, 32 (1972), 5746A-7A. Stanford University, 1971. 397 pp.
936

In early poetry Sp worries about responses to mutability, particularly among the aristocracy, on whom so much depends. Their responses of despair, sloth, and hedonism are wrong, result of failure to understand nature and implications of mutability and, even more importantly, what is immutable. Sp becomes increasingly aware that it is poetry's task to enlighten the nobility and recall them to their sense of duty. What emerges is the answer of heroism, particularly the heroism of sanctity, which will provide for the state and win heaven for the heroes. Mutability should fulfill life by separating men from transient goals and directing them to eternal ones. "Thus, by focusing on responses to mutability in Spenser's early poetry, we see how *The Faerie Queene* with its main ethic of the pursuit of glory in terms of Christian heroic holiness grows directly out of Spenser's initial concerns."

Morgan, Michael N. Paradise and Lover in the Poetry of Spenser. DAI, 29 (1969), 3105A. University of Florida, 1968. 281 pp.
937

Studies Sp's metaphors of paradise and love against Christian background of glory, ruin, and restoration (Chap. I). Adaptation of pastoral genre to paradisiacal motif his major concern (Chap. II). Sp emphasizes the Fall (Chap. III), is often interested in erring lovers who seek unattainable heaven on fallen earth. Goal of man is restoration to former righteousness, and love is the way (Chaps. IV, V, and VI). Sp views Britain as nucleus of restored paradise (Chap. VII). Emphasis throughout on literary traditions as guide to meaning.

Morris, Christopher. The Tudors. New York: Macmillan, 1957. 202pp.
938

"An essay on the personalities of the Tudor monarchs and on their impact upon English history" (p. 7). First chapter an overview of Tudor culture and politics. Sp was among those poets who "openly sought place and power for themselves" (p. 15). Mulcaster's and Ascham's educational views (pp. 21-2). Analogy between florid taste and labyrinthine Arcadia and FQ (p. 23). Civic purpose of FQ of softening manners and educating the "new men" (pp. 94-5). All-importance of time in any consideration of Elizabeth's reign (pp. 154-6). Mary Stuart was Duessa, and Alençon marriage project was satirized in MHT (pp. 172-3). Sidney and Sp, not surprisingly, in ranks of Puritans (pp. 174-9).

Morris, Harry. Richard Barnfield, Colin's Child. Tallahassee: Florida State University, 1963. 203 pp.
939

Barnfield imitated Sp in The Affectionate Shepherd, Cynthia, and Lady Pecunia. He made much use of SC, and even more of FQ. Many references to Sp; see Index.

Morris, Harry. Some Uses of Angel Iconography in English Literature, CL, 10 (1958), 36-44.
940

Gives examples from Bartolomaeus Anglicus, Sp, Heywood, and Milton.

Morris, Helen. Elizabethan Literature. London: Oxford University Press, 1958. Home University Library of Modern Knowledge, No. 233. 239pp. 941

Chapter IV, Spenser and Sidney, pp. 39-66. See also Index.

Moulton, Charles Wells, ed. The Library of Literary Criticism of English and American Authors. Gloucester, Mass.: Peter Smith, 1959. 8 vols. 942

Reprint of 1901 ed. Sp, I, 368-400. Excerpts from criticism, mostly 19th century.

Mounts, Charles E. Spenser and the Countess of Leicester, ELH, 19 (1952), 191-202. 943

Suggests that Sp fell from Leicester's favor because of an allusion in March of SC, intentional or not, to his relationship with Lettice Knollys. Rejects Greenlaw's interpretation of the historical allegory of VG, which "was intended in some way to furnish an analogy for the situation existing between Spenser and his former patron" (p. 197).

Mounts, Charles E. Spenser and the Earl of Essex, in RenP 1958, 1959, 1960, ed. George Walton Williams and Peter G. Phialas, pp. 12-19. Southeastern Renaissance Conference, 1961. 110pp. 944

A paper presented in 1958. Reasons advanced why Essex, far from being Sp's patron, had cause to be annoyed with the poet, withheld his patronage, and reluctantly but with relief paid Sp's funeral expenses. Interpretations of FQ, VI, March eclogue of SC, VG, RT, MHT, and Astro brought into the argument. A recommendation of Sp's in View may have got Essex sent on his ill-fated Irish campaign.

Mounts, Charles Eugene. The Influence of Spenser on Wordsworth and Coleridge. Doctoral diss., Duke University, 1941. 363pp. DDAAU, 1940-41, No. 8. 945

Makes use of letters of William and Dorothy Wordsworth, literary criticism and correspondence of Coleridge. Preface: "My purpose indeed has been to accomplish somewhat more in this thesis than the study of an influence usually includes. Thus I have attempted not only to exhibit Spenserian echoes and allusions wherever they may be found, but also the place the reading of Spenser held in the lives of the two later poets, their critical views on Spenser's poetry and prose, and the ideas which they shared in common with him."

Mueller, William R. Edmund Spenser and Recent Scholarship, TSLL, 3 (1961), 409-20. 946

Review of seven books on Spenser published between 1955 and 1960 with interspersed remarks on the state of Spenserian scholarship: H. C. Chang, Allegory and Courtesy in Spenser: A Chinese View (1306); John Arthos, On the Poetry of Spenser and the Form of Romances (1240); Harry Berger Jr., The Allegorical Temper: Vision and Reality in Book II of Spenser's Faerie Queene (1895); Abbie Findlay Potts, Shakespeare and The Faerie Queene (1627), William R. Mueller, ed., Spenser's Critics: Changing Currents in Literary Taste (947); Robert Ellrodt, Neoplatonism in the Poetry of Spenser (650), M. Pauline Parker, The Allegory of The Faerie Queene (1614).

Mueller, William R., ed. Spenser's Critics: Changing Currents in Literary Taste. Syracuse, N. Y.: Syracuse University Press, 1959. 256pp. 947

Introductory essay by the editor, A Brief History of Spenser Criticism, pp. 1-17, points out that most Sp criticism has to do with FQ, and nearly all of it deals with four main topics: Sp's poetic technique, the structure of the epic, the allegory, and the total effect of FQ. Book consists of essays and excerpts by John Hughes, Joseph Spence, John Upton, Thomas Warton, Richard Hurd (18th century), William Hazlitt, James Russell Lowell, Edward Dowden (19th century), Edwin A. Greenlaw, W. L. Renwick, Charles G. Osgood, B. E. C. Davis, C. S. Lewis, and W. B. C. Watkins (20th century).

Mueller, William R., and Don Cameron Allen, eds. That Soueraine Light. Essays in Honor of Edmund Spenser, 1552-1952. New York: Russell & Russell, 1967. 133 pp.   948

Repr. of 1952 ed. Collection of essays printed in ELH during 1952. Contents: 1. J. W. Saunders, The Façade of Morality (1064); 2. Kathleen Williams, Eterne in Mutabilitie (1744); 3. Raymond Jenkins, Spenser and Ireland (1460); 4. J. C. Maxwell, The Truancy of Calidore (2154); 5. Virgil K. Whitaker, The Theological Structure of The Faerie Queene, Book I (1888); 6. W. J. B. Owen, In These XII Books Severally Handled and Discoursed (1598); 7. Kerby Neill, The Degradation of the Red Cross Knight (1839); 8. Charles E. Mounts, Spenser and the Countess of Leicester (943); 9. Rudolf Gottfried, The Pictorial Element in Spenser's Poetry (722). Listed individually herein.

Muir, Kenneth. Introduction to Elizabethan Literature. New York: Random House, 1967. 207 pp.   949

Chap. on Spenser (pp. 12-33) gives brief account of Sp's poetic career and description of principal works.

Muir, Kenneth. Sir Philip Sidney. London: Longmans, 1960. 40 pp.   950

Sp mentioned passim. Defense of Poesie criticizes "rustic language" of SC. Arcadia avoids allegorical method of Sidney's friend Sp in FQ, although his "teaching in *Arcadia* covers the whole range of private and public morality." Sidney and Sp "wasted a great deal of time experimenting in classical meters," more fruitful experiments in other kinds of verse scattered through Arcadia. Astrophel and Stella is Sidney's masterpiece; no other Elizabethan sonnets have such variety, or "such a coherent dramatic structure."

Muir, Kenneth, and S. Schoenbaum, eds. A New Companion to Shakespeare Studies. Cambridge: University Press, 1971. 298 pp.   951

Community of creative interests and lack of interest in originality was European phenomenon illustrated by widespread Hero/Claudio plot in Much Ado About Nothing, which appears in Ariosto's Orlando Furioso, Sp's FQ, and several prose collections of "good stories" (pp. 58-9). Versions of Lear story in Holinshed, Mirror for Magistrates, and FQ (p. 64). "The Platonic assumptions of a great festive poem like Spenser's *Epithalamion* were challenged by a scepticism and pessimism which found its most powerful expression... in the world of *King Lear*" (pp. 151-2). For other references, see Index.

Mullik, B. R. Spenser. Rev. and enl. ed. Delhi: S. Chand, 1962. 72 pp.   952

First ed. 1955. Handbook for use of students in Indian universities. General discussion of Sp and his poetry.

Mulryan, John James. Natalis Comes' *Mythologiae:* Its Place in the Renaissance Mythological Tradition and Its Impact Upon English Renaissance Literature. DAI, 31 (1970), 2350A-51A. University of Minnesota, 1969. 270 pp.   953

Most influential of post-classical studies of myth was Mythologia of Natalis Comes (1568), more popular than mythographies of Boccaccio, Giraldi, or Cartari. Examples given of Comes' influence on English Renaissance literature, including works of Sp, Bacon, and Chapman. This influence largely beneficial.

Mulryan, John. Recent Trends in Spenser Studies: 1967-1971, A Review Article, Cithara, 11 (1971), 90-102.   954

Evaluates four books of historical criticism by D. Douglas Waters (1881), Patrick Cullen (2218), Charles G. Smith (1088), and Virginia Tufte (1149); critical commentaries by Sam Meyer (2454) and Maurice Evans (1354); and three books offering "a genuinely original approach to the Spenserian canon . . . complementary works united by the common theme of Spenser as a prophetic poet who presents an allegorical message in a rhetorical style," by Paul J. Alpers (1231), Michael Murrin (1578), and Angus Fletcher (1361). Fletcher surpasses Alpers and Murrin in "a fresh interpretation of Spenser as a profound thinker, a supreme artist in words, a renaissance reincarnation of the pagan poet-priest communicating the Christian message through the veil of allegory and the inspiration of prophecy."

Murphy, Francis, ed. Discussions of Poetry: Form and Structure. Boston: Heath, 1964. 207 pp.   955

Repr. Catherine Ing, The Lyrics of Spenser, Shakespeare, and Donne (pp. 179-200), section on Sp's SC, Epith, Amor, and Proth (pp. 179-87) emphasizes form, sound, and versification. (See 815).

Myrick, Kenneth. Sir Philip Sidney as a Literary Craftsman. Lincoln: University of Nebraska Press, 1965. 362 pp.   956

Repr. of 1935 ed. Must discount Sidney's slighting allusions to his poetry; Sp conscious in describing Bower of Bliss of principle that highest art conceals art (pp. 22-3). In Arcadia, Sidney dispenses with Christian supernatural machinery, ignoring Minturno, but Sp and Tasso do not (pp. 119-23). Renaissance love of ornament, contrary to classic ideal of beauty, in FQ, Tamburlaine, and New Arcadia; oddly enough, Sp expresses classical view of art in HHOB and would have style inseparable from form (pp. 151-2, 183). Question whether Sidney conceived poetry as mimetic or allegorical involves much consideration of Sp and old critical debate (pp. 197 ff.). In discussion of personal and moral allegory in Arcadia disputes Greenlaw's view that it is "a prose counterpart of the Faerie Queene" (pp. 233-43). Aims of Arcadia and FQ same, but Arcadia not allegory (pp. 293-5). Defence of Poesie does not represent joint critical opinions of Sidney and Sp (pp. 298-300). For other references to Sp, see Index. Bibliography Sidney studies 1935-1965 (pp. 352-8). See 113.

Neale, J. E. Essays in Elizabethan History. New York: St. Martin's Press, 1958. 255pp.   957

Quotes FQ, II, Proem, 2-3 as expression of exuberant Elizabethan spirit (pp. 40-1); MHT, ll. 895 ff. on pains of suitors at court (pp. 61-2); and RT, ll. 449 ff. on Burghley's pushing his son, Robert Cecil, as his successor (p. 80).

Neilson, William Allan, and Ashley Horace Thorndike. The Facts About Shakespeare. Rev. ed. New York: Macmillan, 1961. 263 pp.   958

Sp alluded to Shakespeare in CCCHA, possibly in TM, and Shakespeare alluded to Sp in A Midsummer Night's Dream. Shakespeare borrowed spelling of Cordelia in King Lear from FQ (p. 61). Shakespeare had greater inspiration for literary innovation than Sp or Milton (pp. 178-9).

Nelan, Thomas P. Catholic Doctrines in Spenser's Poetry. Doctoral diss., New York University, 1943. 456pp. Abridgment published. New York: New York University Press, 1946. 21pp.   959

Primarily a study of religious teachings underlying the Legend of Holiness, which is found to be in many vital instances in agreement with Catholicism, not with Calvinism or "Puritan-patterned Anglicanism." Sp was of the central tradition. Final chapter on religious allusions in Book II of FQ, SC, MHT, and 4 Hymns. See 1177, 1194, 1549, 1800, 2243.

Nelson, William, ed. Form and Convention in the Poetry of Edmund Spenser: Selected Papers from the English Institute. New York: Columbia University Press, 1961. 188 pp.   960

Foreword by ed., pp. v-x, points out that all of the contributors belong to that school of Spenserians who agree with John Upton that Spenser was a poet who planned and organized his work to achieve unity. The essays, except those by A. C. Hamilton and Harry Berger, Jr., were delivered before the meetings of the English institute in 1959 and 1960. Essays by A. C. Hamilton, The Visions of Piers Plowman and The Faerie Queene, a revision of (1813); Harry Berger, Jr., A Secret Discipline: The Faerie Queene, Book VI (2138); Sherman Hawkins, Mutabilitie and the Cycle of the Months (2192), A. Kent Hieatt, The Daughters of Horus: Order in the Stanzas of Epithalamion (2397); Hallett Smith, The Use of Conventions in Spenser's Minor Poems (2523); and Louis L. Martz, The

Amoretti: Most Goodly Temperature (2451). Individually listed herein.

Nelson, William. The Poetry of Edmund Spenser: A Study. New York: Columbia University Press, 1963; 1966. 350 pp.   961

Surveys Sp's works, their milieu, influences on them (pp. 1-30). Chaps. following analyze plan and structure of SC, its relation to later pastoral CCCHA (see 649); describe and ana= lyze pieces in Complaints volume, their defects explained by Sp's consistent disregard of "consistency and verisimilitude" to portray real world declined from ideal state; examine Amor, Epith, and 4 Hymns, explain Sp's philosophy of love in light of tradition. Introduction to FQ, and individual chapters discussing each book (pp. 116-314). Full notes, especially on FQ (pp. 315-36); Index (pp. 337-50).
Rev: Michel Poirier, EA, 17 (1964), 71; Joan Grundy, MLR, 59 (1964), 260; Virgil K. Whitaker, RN, 17 (1964), 135; Millar MacLure, UTQ, 33 (1963), 311; Michael Murrin, MP, 63 (1965), 152. See 1267.

Newdigate, Bernard H. Michael Drayton and His Circle. Oxford: Basil Blackwell, 1941. 239pp.   962

Companion volume to Works of Michael Drayton, ed. J. William Hebel, Kathleen Tillotson, and Bernard H. Newdigate, 5 vols., 1932-1941. Sp's Rosalind in The Shepheards Garland (pp. 48-9); Drayton in poetical tradition of Sidney and Sp (pp. 67-8), debt to Sp and possibility that Drayton is Aetion in CCCHA (pp. 87-8); Poly-Olbion, despite certain relations to FQ, shows much less indebtedness to Sp than Drayton's early work (pp. 171-2); Fuller and Aubrey said Drayton's tomb in Westminster Abbey was near Sp's (pp. 219-21). See also Index.

Norton, Dan S., and Peters Rushton. Classical Myths in English Literature. New York: Rinehart, 1952. 444pp.   963

A dictionary of myths and their use in English literature. Numerous references to Sp. See Index.

Oakeshott, Walter. Carew Ralegh's Copy of Spenser, Library, 5th Series, 26 (1971), 1-21.   964

Copy of 1617 folio edition of Sp's collected works, title-page of which bears signature of Carew Ralegh, son of Sir Walter, was annotated for her son by Lady Ralegh. Identifies "gentle mayd" mentioned in CCCHA as "E. Throkemorton his mistris," that is, herself. Note on MHT identifies Fox as "Burly," and Ape as "RS or Sal," that is, Robert Cecil or Salisbury. Many jottings on text of FQ, notably on Belphoebe-Timias episode in Bk. IV (see 2072, 2169). Identification of Calidore with "Sr. W. R.' plausible despite usual identification with Sidney. [SpN, Vol. 3, No. 2 (1972), 8-9.]

Oakeshott, Walter. The Queen and the Poet. London: Faber and Faber, 1960. 232pp.   965

Part I devoted to Ralegh's relationship with Queen Elizabeth; Part II an edition of Ralegh's poems associated with the Queen. Section 2 of Part I, Ralegh and Spenser (pp. 81-99), discusses evidence drawn from Sp's poems bearing on relations of Ralegh with Queen: CCCHA, FQ dedicatory sonnet, Proem to Bk. III of FQ, letter explaining FQ, and Timias as character in FQ (III, v, IV, vii-viii, and VI, v), taken to represent Ralegh throughout (see 458, 2069, 2072). Numerous other references to Sp; see Index.

O'Connell, Michael William. A Study of the Historical Dimension of Spenser's Major Poetry. DAI, 32 (1972), 6995-A. Yale University, 1971. 349 pp.   966

Sp's method of handling an historical dimension in SC and first part of FQ is not "historical allegory" but historical allusion. His model is Vergil. April eclogue of SC idealizes the ruler, moral eclogues satirize failings in ecclesiastical affairs. Material surrounding publication of Bks. I-III of FQ, shows Sp wished to tantalize reader with hint that fiction had hidden connections with contemporary world. Protestant interpretation of Book of Revelation is vehicle for historical dimension in Bk. I. Chronicles in Bks. II and III and river pageant in Bk. IV show difference between historical actuality and poetic idealization. Belphoebe is mirror of Queen Elizabeth, Timias is Raleigh. Conclusion of Timias-Belphoebe story allegorizes Raleigh's five-year loss of royal favor caused by his marriage. What may properly be called historical allegory reappears in Bk. V, first half shadowing several major events of Elizabeth's reign, at the expense of poem's moral dimension. Bk. VI is implicit reaction to attempt to confront history. Sp's vision becomes more personal, and Colin's lass in dance of Graces replaced Eliza, "fourth grace" in April eclogue of SC.

Orange, Linwood E. "All Bent To Mirth": Spenser's Humorous Wordplay, SAQ, 71 (1972), 539-47.   967

Although a serious allegorist and a better teacher than Aquinas, Sp's penchant for humorous wordplay similar to Shakespeare's in early plays. Especially apparent in singing match between Perigot and Willye in August of SC and in MHT, which use whimsically such figures as paronomasia, antanaclasis, and polyptoton. In catalogue of rivers in FQ, IV, xi, Sp employs mock etymologies. Gives other examples from FQ, I, vii; II, vi; III, x; and V, vi. [SpN, Vol. 4, No. 3 (1973), 9.]

Orange, Linwood E. Spenser's Word-Play, N&Q, N. S. 5 (1958), 387-9.		968

Examples showing Sp's use, throughout his poetic career, of rhetorical figures involving play on words. The predominant figures are antanaclasis, ploce, distinction, paranomasia, and polyptoton.

Orange, Linwood E. Wordplay in Spenser. Doctoral diss., Duke University, 1955. 191pp. DDDAAU, 1954-55, No. 22.
969

Preface says study will be divided into three parts. (1) "the recognition of Spenser's wordplay," definition of punning in Elizabethan terms, "the importance of aural reception and of a knowledge of Spenser's pronunciation"; (2) discussion of Sp's wordplay in his poetry; (3) catalogue of Sp's puns. "An analysis of rhetorical figures of wordplay and a list of words played on by sixteenth-century writers other than Spenser will be provided in appendixes."

Oras, Ants. Notes on Some Miltonic Usages, Their Background and Later Development. Acta et Commentationes Universitatis Tartuensis (Dorpatensis), B Humaniora, 43. Tartu, Estonia, 1939. 133pp.		970

Sp cited in connection with "to breathe," "horrid," "drear" and "dreary," "gloom." Compares Milton's use of adjectives in -ic and -ical with that of earlier writers, including Sp; see lists, pp. 112-4, and discussion following.

Oras, Ants. Pause Patterns in Elizabethan and Jacobean Drama: An Experiment in Prosody. Gainesville: University of Florida Press, 1960. 90 pp.		971

Feature of verse examined is incidence of pauses in nine positions possible in iambic pentameter line. Uses punctuation of original editions. Three levels of pausal emphasis distinguished: A, all pauses indicated by internal punctuation; B, "strong pauses," shown by punctuation marks other than commas; C, "line splits," breaks within pentameter line dividing speeches by different characters, rare before 1600. Includes Chaucer and foreign models, 16th century French and Italian verse (pp. 1-6). Sp made two innovations: (1) two peaks, after 6th as well as 4th syllable; (2) fifth-position depression markedly raised in A patterns, so that in FQ, II, xii, IV, xi, V, xii, and VI, x it entirely disappears, and "the jagged, spiky, ultra-iambic stiffness is gone." Average pattern of Sp prevails in 1590's (pp. 10-12). Graphs prosody of Sp's works (pp. 35-40) and tabulates it (pp. 62-5, 73).

Orgel, Stephen. The Jonsonian Masque. Cambridge, Mass.: Harvard University Press, 1965. 216 pp.		972

In Part One, The Metamorphoses of Proteus, contrasts Francis Davison's The Mask of Proteus and the Adamantine Rock, performed at court 1595, and William Hunnis's The Ladie of the Lake, one of entertainments for Queen Elizabeth at Kenilworth 1575. "Hunnis knew Proteus only as a minion of Neptune who could be commendably straightforward about the quality of his talents. But by 1595 he had characteristically changed his nature. Davison might have known him as the betrayer of Shakespeare's Valentine and the would-be seducer of Spenser's Florimel," FQ, III, viii (pp. 8-43). In Part Three, The Transformation Scene, says in The Masque of Blacknesse (1605) "color was not essential but merely accidental"; cites HHOB, ll. 132-3. In The Masque of Queenes (1609) characters in antimasque represent "disorder, misrule, Mutability," as in FQ, VII; main masque is Platonic, and Jonson may have recalled what Sp said in Letter to Raleigh about precept and example (pp. 129-46).

Momerod, David. Faith and Fashion in *Much Ado About Nothing*, ShS, 25 (1972), 93-105.   973

Interprets play as Spenserian allegory based on antithesis between faith (clear-sighted love, Benedick) and fashion (blind love, Claudio), reality and appearance. Claudio must be initiated into Platonic thought, "most accessibly described in Castiglione's *The Courtier* or Spenser's *Platonic Hymns.*" Dwells on motifs of Hercules and Blind Cupid. "The faith-fashion antithesis may be seen as one aspect of the age's preoccupation with the conflict between eternity and mutability, and with the right resolution of this conflict, a resolution which Spenser has mapped in detail in *Epithalamion*, the 'Garden of Adonis,' and the 'Mutability Cantos.' " This solution argues that, by loving chastely and wisely, man can conquer time, flux and mutability, and attain a state wherein he will be, like Spenser's Adonis, 'eterne in mutabilitie'."

Orsini, Napoleone. "Policy" or the Language of Elizabethan Machiavellianism, JWCI, 9 (1946), 122-34.   974

Cites Sp's uses of "policy" as one of many examples showing how widespread in popular literature were "the technical terms of Machiavellianism in England."

Oruch, Jack B. Spenser, Camden, and the Poetic Marriages of Rivers, SP, 64 (1967), 606-24.   975

The worthy poets that William Vallans (1590) hoped to arouse when he published Tale of Two Swannes must have been Sp and Camden. In subject and genre *De Connubio* is related to Sp's hypothetical Epithalamion Thamesis. "This relationship extends also to the marriage pageant of the Thames and the Medway in the FQ, IV, xi, 11-53 and the river-marriage hymns in CCCHA and the Mutabilitie Cantos. All of these river myths constitute an interesting but neglected subgenre in Elizabethan poetry, a subgenre which found several imitators in the following two centuries" (pp. 606-7). Sp's hypothetical river-marriage poem might have been to show his conception of the genre and therefore his artistic expression in it developed and matured in CCCHA and FQ.

Oruch, Jack Bernard. Topography in the Prose and Poetry of the English Renaissance, 1540-1640. DA, 25 (1964), 2966. Indiana University, 1964. 303 pp.   976

John Leland first important figure in development of topographical prose. Leland's patriotism and antiquarian enthusiasm influenced William Harrison, William Camden, John Stow, and other writers in the form. When poets joined patriotic effort to describe England, best models were Harrison's Description of Britain and Camden's Britannia. But when antiquarianism prevailed, poetry suffered. By using personification imaginatively, Drayton almost succeeded in Poly-Olbion. For Sp accurate description less important than artistic goal. Topography assumed various supporting functions in RT, Epith, Proth, FQ (IV, xi), CCCHA. Others followed Sp in subordinating topography to larger purpose: Daniel in Musophilus, Jonson in To Penshurst, and preeminently Milton in early poems.

Osgood, Charles G. Spenser, Edmund, Collier's Encyclopedia, 17, 591-2. New York: P. F. Collier, 1960.   977

Also Robert Brittain, Spenserian Stanza, ibid., 592-3; Charles G. Osgood, The Shepherd's Calendar, ibid., 232; Charles G. Osgood, The Faerie Queene, ibid., 7, 290-1.

Osgood, Charles G. The Voice of England. 2nd ed. New York: Harper, 1952. 671pp.   978

First published 1935. Part 3, Courtier and Burgher, Chap. 10, Spenser, pp. 163-70. Idealism and worldliness at war in Sp. SC is a studio piece; MHT got Sp sent to Ireland and frontier life. Brief comments on motive, verse, allegory, and content of each book of FQ.

Osgood, Charles Grosvenor. Creed of a Humanist. Seattle: University of Washington Press, 1963. 143 pp.   979

Eleven essays, 5 previously printed in periodicals (p. viii). Sp's debut in SC and significance to Elizabethans of appearance of "new poet," Sp's pursuit of poetry despite personal disappointments, his "tensions of the heart" and susceptibility to women's charms, his inborn Platonism, variety of FQ, Bk. I derived "from the depths of the author's hard life . . . a pilgrim's progress inspired by autobiographical recollection." Refers in passing to most of Sp's poetry (pp. 72-92). Sp and Shakespeare shared imported "merchandise": stock themes of sonneteers, Platonic doctrine of love, dream of pastoral content, world's mutability and degeneration, corruption of court. Sp a Platonist and allegorist, Shakespeare a phenomenalist. Most important bond between them the figure of their Queen. Both created idealized yet realistic heroines: Britomart, Una, and Florimel; Isabella, Rosalind, Viola, Beatrice,

Cordelia, and Portia (pp. 93-104). For other references to Sp, see Index.

Osgood, Charles Grosvenor. Poetry as a Means of Grace. Princeton: Princeton University Press, 1941; repr. New York: Gordian Press, 1965. 131 pp.   980

First delivered as the Levi P. Stone Lectures in Princeton Theological Seminary, 1940. Chapters on Dante, Spenser (pp. 53-79), Milton, and Johnson, who are recommended for "life-long companionship." Sp qualifies as a "sovran" poet because he is focal, encyclopedic, inexhaustible, humanistic, "of English poets, preeminently the singer," a breeder of poetry, and an expert craftsman.

Ostriker, Alicia. Thomas Wyatt and Henry Surrey: Dissonance and Harmony in Lyric Form, NLH, 1 (1970), 387-405.   981

The contrast between the balance and fluency of Surrey and the rugged rhythms of Wyatt is echoed in analogous dichotomy between harmonious and dissonant poets in later periods: Spenser and Donne, Tennyson and Browning, Longfellow and Whitman. [YWES, 51 (1970), 141.]

Otis, William Bradley, and Morriss H. Needleman. An Outline-History of English Literature. 2 vols. New York: Barnes & Noble, 1936. 3rd ed., 1939.   982

Vol. 1: To Dryden. Chapter IX, The Beginnings of the Renaissance: Edmund Spenser (pp. 124-36); The School of Spenser (pp. 251-4).

Ower, John. The Epic Mythologies of Shelley and Keats, WascanaR, 4 (1969), 61-72.   983

Blake's longer prophecies, Wordsworth's Prelude, Shelley's Prometheus Unbound, and Keats's Hyperion are attempts to rival epic stature of FQ and Paradise Lost. Difficult in Romantic period when medieval and Renaissance world picture had broken up, necessitating syncretic use of Bible and classical mythology. FQ and Paradise Lost "provide examples of an epic structure in which there is a fusion of Christian and Classical materials. This is perhaps most striking in the case of Spenser, whose powers of synthesis in his epic and the *Hymnes* make him the myth-builder *par-excellence* of English poetry." Shows Prometheus Unbound and Hyperion are epic syntheses in tradition of English spiritual and cultural history which also attest "the long shadows cast by the colossal figures of Spenser and Milton."

Padelford, Frederick M. Aspects of Spenser's Vocabulary, in Renaissance Studies in Honor of Hardin Craig, pp. 87-91. Stanford: Stanford University Press, 1941. 339pp.   984

On Sp's contribution to the language of words of outright foreign derivation, and of words devised by adding classical and romance prefixes and suffixes to existing words. Also deals with the relative range of Sp's vocabulary in his earlier and later work.

Padelford, Frederick M. Spenser's Use of "Stour," MLQ, 2 (1941), 465-73.   985

A favorite word, in FQ 41 times and in the minor poems 13 times.

Panofsky, Erwin. Studies in Iconology: Humanistic Themes in the Art of the Renaissance. New York: Oxford. University Press, 1939. 262pp. 6 il., 92 pl.
986

Introductory, pp. 3-30, defines iconography as the branch of art history concerned with subject matter or meaning of works of art, as opposed to their form: discusses problems of iconography in general and of Renaissance iconography in particular, with special reference to rebirth of classical antiquity. Chapters on The Early History of Man, Father Time, Blind Cupid, The Neoplatonic Movement in Florence and North Italy, and The Neoplatonic Movement and Michelangelo. Discussion of Florentine Neoplatonism (pp. 129-69, with accompanying pl. 58-68) throws light on Sp. See Index. See 1078, 1211.

Parsons, Roger Loren. Renaissance and Baroque: Multiple Unity and Unified Unity in the Treatment of Verse, Ornament, and Structure. DA, 19 (1959), 2958. University of Wisconsin, 1959. 516 pp.   987

Hypothesizes a distinction between 16th and 17th century English poetry on the basis of two kinds of unity named in title. Contrasts Sp's sonnet verse with Donne's and Milton's; Sp's couplets with those of Jonson, Marvell, and others; Sp's and Sidney's images with Donne's; Sp's epic similes with Milton's; November eclogue in SC with Lycidas; FQ with Paradise Lost.

Partridge, A. C. The Language of Renaissance Poetry: Spenser, Shakespeare, Donne, Milton. London: Andre Deutsch, 1971. 348 pp.   988

Study of English poetry 1575-1675. Concerned with exegesis and elucidation of texts by tripartite analysis: rhetorical, literary, and linguistic. Sp cited in Notes on Method, Chaucer and His Successors, and Poetry from Wyatt to Sidney. Chap. IV, Spenser (pp. 61-101), analyzes in detail November of SC; archaic diction, metrical and rhythmical movement, original stanza form of elegy and its metrical characteristics, grammatical structure, meaning as blend of paganism, Platonism, and Christian belief in immortality of soul, and identification of rhetorical figures. Same kind of analysis applied in less detail to

MHT (ll. 1033-63), Epith (ll. 59-91), FQ (II, vi, 12-15 and VII, vi, 48-50). Conclusions from linguistic analysis point to nine elements in Sp's style. Evidence of language supports literary estimates of Sp's style by Renwick (1030), Watkins (1180), and Lewis (878). Further attention to Sp's language in chapters on Non-Dramatic Poetry: Marlowe and Shakespeare, Shakespeare's Declamatory and Lyrical Dramas (to 1600), Donne, and Milton. See Index.

Patrides, C. A. Renaissance Thought on the Celestial Hierarchy: The Decline of a Tradition, JHI, 20 (1959), 155-66.
989

Although F. M. Padelford (MP, 12 (1914), 4) holds that Spenser's description of the angels in their "trinal triplicities" (HOHL, 64-74) is "substantially a poetical version" of a statement by Calvin (Institutes, I, xiv, 5), still Sp's "disagreement with Calvin is far more striking than his agreement with him." Traces the tradition of angelic hierarchies from Dionysius the Areopagite to its rejection, in Protestant thought, at the hands of Calvin, who set the dominant Protestant attitude of subsequent times. Sp, in upholding the concept of the nine orders, "looks back on a glorious past and a conception hallowed by time"; Milton, not accepting a dogmatic arrangement but still conceiving distinctions and ordering among the angels, "was able to look before and after," and, as in his ambiguous cosmology, has things both ways. Also mentions reference to "trinal triplicites" in FQ, I, xii, 39, 5.

Patterson, Annabel M. Hermogenes and the Renaissance: Seven Ideas of Style. Princeton: Princeton University Press, 1970. 240 pp.
990

Treatise Concerning Ideas of Hermogenes influenced Renaissance concepts and practice of style. His rhetorical system based on seven principles of style, or "Ideas": Clarity, Grandeur, Beauty, Speed, Ethos, Verity, and Gravity. Describes each concept as understood by critics such as Minturno and Scaliger. Sp probably knew Concerning Ideas through Harvey. November in SC and Epith described to show effect of Hermogenes' categories on form and content of ode: consolation through Nature in eclogue, movement from mutability to permanence in Epith (pp. 83-7). Discusses FQ, V as an "epic within an epic," with Artegal epic hero suited to Idea of Gravity (pp. 201-11). [SpN, Vol. 2, No. 3 (1971), 2.]

Pattison, Bruce. Music and Poetry of the English Renaissance. London: Methuen, 1948. 220pp.
991

Sp a significant figure in the relationships between music and poetry in 16th century. No formal academies of music and poetry were founded in England, but the Areopagus reflected Italian and French examples (pp. 61-2). Sp's poetry shows that he was not indifferent to music (pp. 65-7). Madrigal composers frequently used single stanzas of Ariosto and Sp (pp. 95-7). The classicist Campion, whose Observations in the Arte of English Poesie (1602) came out after "Sidney and Spenser had made the whole question [of quantitative meters] academic by their defense of English tradition," considered the air a better ally of poetry than the madrigal (pp. 128-37). Renaissance poets worked within the limitations of contemporary musical technique (pp. 141-59). Discussion of the roundelay in August eclogue of SC (pp. 173-4).

Pellegrini, Angelo Mario. Bruno and the Elizabethans. Doctoral diss., University of Washington, 1942. UWAT, 7 (1943), 211-6.
992

Giordano Bruno of Nola lived in England 1583-1585. His name is frequently associated with Sp, Sidney, Greville, and Ralegh, Bacon, Harriot, and Dee. What was his influence on either group? "The Elizabethans, both humanists and scientists, remained singularly untouched by the philosophy of the Nolan." Reasons for this found in Bruno's intellectual arrogance, the anti-philosophical spirit of the Renaissance, and his identification with a philosophical tradition, that of Dominican scholasticism divorced from theological presuppositions, which was opposed to the English experimental traditon stemming from Robert Grosseteste and Roger Bacon.

Pellegrini, G. Symbols and Significances, ShS, 17 (1964), 180-7.   993

The allegory in many passages of Spenser can be "clarified and deepened by observing his use of methods and procedures closely related to the technique established by the authors of emblem books." Much work remains to be done in this area.

Peter, John. Complaint and Satire in Early English Literature. Oxford: Clarendon Press, 1956. 323pp.   994

Contents: Satire and Complaint, Complaint Emerges, Complaint in Medieval England, Renaissance Satire, Marston and the Metamorphosis in Satire, Satire and Drama, Marston's Plays, Tourneur's Tragedies, The Legacy of Satire. Sp's allegorical method in MHT is medieval (pp. 132-3). Amor are "maudlin and tedious," lacking the salt that satire added to love poetry (p. 297).

Pettet, E. C. Shakespeare and the Romance Tradition. London: Staples, 1949. 208pp.   995

Romance tradition flowed into Elizabethan literature through medieval romance, Italian romantic epics, Petrarchan poetry, and certain early Spanish and Italian *novelle*. Sp's poetry and Sidney's Arcadia epitomize these four streams. Romance literature was above all a literature of love; its originality "was the bringing of sexual love into a more harmonious and explicit relation with religion." Illustrates this attitude in Sp's poetry, drawing most on the minor poems, "since these provide the most concentrated expressions of the romantic attitude to love" (pp. 11-23).

Phillips, James E. Spenser's Syncretistic Religious Imagery, ELH, 36 (1969), 110-30; repr. in 644.   996

Neoplatonic imagery probably came to Sp through French academies and Areopagus, Phillippe De Mornay (through Philip Sidney) and Daniel Rogers providing Sp's links with continental syncretistic thought. Recurring motifs in passages fusing different religious traditions: visions on mounts of revelation, references to Eden and the Fall, sacramental cleansing and sanctification through concord. These correspond to chapter headings in De Mornay's "The Trewenesse of the Christian Religion," which Sidney was translating shortly before his death. [SpN, Vol. 1, No. 1 (1970), 10.]

Pinto, V. De Sola. The English Renaissance: 1510-1688. New York: Robert M. McBride, 1938. Introductions to English and American Literature, 2. 381pp.   997

Sp in chapter on The Elizabethans, pp. 68-71; and in chapter on Later Elizabethan Poetry, pp. 208-11.

Plasberg, Elaine. William Hazlitt: The Structure and Application of his Critical Standards. DA, 22 (1961), 1162. Boston University, 1961. 305 pp.   998

"Chapter VI, 'The Real, the Fanciful, the Essential, and the Exalted: Fiction in Four Kinds,' shows Hazlitt's standards applied directly to Chaucer, Spenser, Shakespeare, and Milton. The Chapter examines the four poets not so much according to the genres in which they write but according to the distinct world each portrays, the manner in which each goes about his task, and, subsequently, the distinct psychological and/or moral effect each mode of art may have upon its audience."

Poggioli, Renato. The Oaten Flute, HLB, 11 (1957), 147-84.   999

Psychological root of pastoralism is double longing for innocence and happiness; pastoral implies new ethos primarily negative; shepherd practices enlightened hedonism; Erminia's stay among shepherds in Tasso's Gerusalemme Liberata (VII) mirrors pastoral of innocence, Tasso's Aminta pastoral of happiness; Virgil's Fourth Eclogue, idea of Golden Age, and start of allegorical pastoral with Mantuan's Latin eclogues; Milton's Lycidas and funeral elegy; Marvell in The Garden widened gap between pastoral of love and pastoral of self; neoclassical garden not product of nature but of convention and artifice; politics of pastoral; modern world destroyed traditional pastoral except in ironic and ambiguous versions; poetic of pastoral in The Winter's Tale and As You Like It; pastoral embodies both longing and wish-fulfillment.

Pongs, Hermann. Das Kleine Lexikon der Weltliteratur. Stuttgart: Union deutsche Verlagsgesellschaft, 1954.   1000

Sp, col. 1269.

Potts, Abbie Findlay. The Elegiac Mode: Poetic Form in Wordsworth and Other Elegists. Ithaca: Cornell University Press, 1967. 460 pp.   1001

Anagnorisis—recognition, revela-

tion, discovery—familiar in dramatic criticism, but "it is the very goal of elegiac poetry" (pp. 36-7). In Sp's Daph "the grief of Alcyon for his Daphne remains unillumined," and Astro another "doleful plaint". Times between Chaucer and Milton did not encourage elegiac speculation. Work of Sp, Shakespeare, and Milton most comparable when touched by elegiac, meditative strain (pp. 86-9). Main devices in Wordsworth's Ode 1814 not from Psalms but from ceremonies in FQ, I, xii (pp. 188-9). Elizabeth Barrett Browning's elegy for Byron in Spenserian stanzas (p. 291).

Praz, Mario. The Flaming Heart: Essays on Crashaw, Machiavelli, and Other Studies in the Relations between Italian and English Literature from Chaucer to T.S. Eliot. Garden City, N. Y.: Doubleday, 1958; repr. Gloucester, Mass.: Peter Smith, 1966. 390pp.   1002

In Petrarch in England (published here for the first time), finds Sp in Amor closer to Serafino than Petrarch (pp. 277-8). In Ariosto in England (first published in Il Veltro, June-July, 1957), emphasizes contrast between "the vague, musical dreamland" of Sp's FQ and "the neat, Mantegna-like world" of Ariosto (pp. 292-301). In Tasso in England (first published in Torquato Tasso, Celebrazioni Ferraresi, Milan, 1957), says it is only through Sp's imitation in FQ that Tasso entered English literature "with an accent which was to be found typical of him in following centuries, the accent of voluptuous enchantment and elegiac peace" (pp. 309-11). See also Index.

Praz, Mario. Mnemosyne: The Parallel Between Literature and the Visual Arts. Princeton: Princeton University Press, 1970. 261 pp.   1003

Ranges widely, bringing together works far apart in time and different in medium. Shows how all works of art in given period (even forgeries of earlier works) have general likeness. Mentions bizarre parallels Romantics drew between Sp and various painters. Speaks of crowded details in FQ, as in dominant branch of painting in Elizabethan England: the miniature. Chap. on Renaissance art, Harmony and the Serpentine Line, has remarks on parallels between architecture and poetry.

Praz, Mario. Storia della Letteratura Inglese. Rev. and enl. Florence: G. C. Sansoni, 1964. 763 pp.   1004

First pub. 1937. Preface and general bibliography (pp. 1-4). Brief account of Sp's works, with outdated bibliography (pp. 73-8, 82-3).

Prescott, Anne Lake. The Reception of Du Bartas in England, SRen, 15 (1968), 144-73.   1005

Guillaume Salluste, Sieur du Bartas most admired of contemporary European writers in England from 1580s to 1660s. Great poet to Sp, Sidney, Daniel, Drayton, Walton, and Milton. His reputation inseparable from that of best-known translator, Joshua Sylvester (pp. 144-5, 147, 171). Fullest comment on Du Bartas, epitome of reception in England, by Gabriel Harvey in Pierce's Supererogation, 1593 (p. 162), who also says Sp admired fourth "day" of Première Sepmaine. Sp praised Du Bartas in RR (p. 164).

Prescott, Anne Lake. The Reputation of Clément Marot in Renaissance England, SRen, 18 (1971), 173-202.   1006

Marot, chief poet at court of Francis I, had two self-contradictory images in England: first, father of French language; second, court jester not to be taken seriously. Neither his urbanity nor wit was comprehended. Wyatt borrowed from him occasionally for love poetry. Sp's dirge for Dido in November of SC based on Marot's elegy for death of Francis I's mother, Louise de Savoie; Sp more universal and less precious. December eclogue of SC follows Marot's Eglogue de Marot au Roy, soulz les noms de Pan et Robin in recapitulating Colin Clout's wasted life in seasonal terms; Sp's poem darker. Use of Marot by Arthur Gorges, Michael Drayton, Philip and Mary Sidney in psalms; references to Marot by Thomas Churchyard, Gabriel Harvey, John Eliot, few others. His Protestantism won no sympathy among English, who thought it clownish. Poetically old-fashioned before became known. His pastorals, epigrams, and lyrics had some admirers, not his satires and epistles.

Prettyman, V. V. Shenstone's Reading of Spenser, in The Age of Johnson: Essays Presented to Chauncey Brewster Tinker, pp. 227-37. New Haven: Yale University Press, 1949. 426pp.   1007

Traces, in three surviving versions of The Schoolmistress (imitated from Pope's Spenserian imitation, The Alley), the growth of Shenstone's knowledge of Sp.

Price, George R. Thomas Dekker. New York: Twayne, 1969. 189 pp.   1008

Dekker's belated morality play, The Whore of Babylon (1606), uses Spenserian theme of England's destiny, salvation of Queen Elizabeth and her kingdom from Spain and Catholicism. Address to readers calls play "Drammatical Poem" setting forth in "shadowed collours the Greatnes, Magnanimity, Constancy, Clemency, and the other incomparable Heroical vertues of our late Queene." Play is pageant-like series of events in England imagined as Fairyland, gathering of knights at Titania's court, Falsehood masquerading as truth, characters such as Paridel, Satyrane, and

Florimell. Dekker tries "to make his drama and Spenser's epic twin triumphs of English poetry and patriotism" (pp. 69-74). Dekker more Anglican than Puritan; he "was as orthodox a member of the Church of England as Edmund Spenser or John Donne" (pp. 134-5).

Prouty, C. T. George Gascoigne: Elizabethan Courtier, Soldier, and Poet. New York: Columbia University Press, 1942. 351pp.   1009

For suggestions as to Sp's general literary relation to the most important writer of Elizabeth's early reign, see Index.

Prouty, Charles Tyler. Some Observations on Shakespeare's Sources, SJ, 96 (1960), 64-77.   1010

Suggests we expand study of Shakespeare's sources beyond factual information amassed in Kenneth Muir's Shakespeare's Sources and Geoffrey Bullough's Narrative and Dramatic Sources of Shakespeare. Renaissance imitation meant expansion and embellishment, so obscure analogue may be important. Need to understand what story meant to Elizabethans. Cites relation of Whetstone's Promos and Cassandra to Measure for Measure, of Robert Armin and Ben Jonson's Every Man in His Humor and Every Man Out of His Humor to language of Countess and Lafeu in All's Well That Ends Well, of Rosalynde to As You Like It (pp. 64-71). Although no question direct influence, FQ "is perhaps the most important work that should be read by any student of Shakespeare or Elizabethan Literature. The point is that Spenser is writing about the same world, the same people, and the same ideas as is Shakespeare." Compares Archimago and Iago: "the Elizabethan concept of Fair-Seeming Evil" (pp. 74-7).

Psychologist. Lamb, Dante, Spenser, and Hazlitt, N&Q, 185 (1943), 317-8. 1011

Two lines from "a translation of Dante" that Lamb once quoted and Hazlitt admired in reality probably echoed Lamb's memory of several passages in Sp.

Quinones, Ricardo J. The Renaissance Discovery of Time. Cambridge, Mass.: Harvard University Press, 1972. 549 pp.   1012

"I treat time as a theme, that is, a fairly recognizable constellation of ideas, in relation to which I discuss some of the major literary figures of the Renaissance" (p. xi). Chaps. on The Setting, Dante, Petrarch, Backgrounds of History and Tragedy in 16th-century Thought, Rabelais, Montaigne, Spenser (pp. 243-89), Shakespeare's histories, tragedies, comedies and last plays, and Milton. "Spenser's great concern is to transcend time. It is the end and justification of his heroic conception of life. . . . Poetry, history, the continuity of civilization, the ideals of excellence and distinction in an aristocratic society—all of these turn on success or failure in rising above the present moment. Love and progeny too are exalted in their capacities to surmount time." Discusses Sp's complex treatment of these themes with sections on Monuments of Time, The Bower of Bliss and the Garden of Adonis, "Trial," and Mutability, and many suggestive comparisons of Sp to other writers. See 1617.

Quitslund, Jon A. Studies in Spenser and the Platonic Tradition. DA, 28 (1968), 3681-A. Princeton University, 1967. 526 pp.   1013

Establishes accessibility of Renaissance Platonism to Sp, particularly Ficinian variety. Focuses on Garden of Adonis (FQ, III, vi), parts of 4

Hymns, Temple of Venus (FQ, IV, x), CCCHA, and Mutability Cantos. Central theme in this poetry is creativity and ordering power of love, spiritual force within natural order. Argues concepts and symbols Sp used in vision of natural world not explicitly Christian, except in dealing with heavenly matters in second pair of 4 Hymns.

Qvarnström, Gunnar. The Enchanted Palace: Some Structural Aspects of Paradise Lost. Stockholm: Almqvist & Wiksell, 1967. 189 pp.   1014

In chaps. on Epic Chronology, Christocentric Structure, Structure of Epic Speeches, and Epic Modulation of Time deals with interest in symmetrical structure of Sp's Epith, FQ, Daph, and RT shown by Kent Hieatt (2398), Alastair Fowler (1367), and Maren-Sofie Røstvig (1047). See references to Sp and Symmetrical Structure in Index.

Qvarnström, Gunnar. Poetry and Numbers: On the Structural Use of Symbolic Numbers. Lund: Gleerup, 1966. 102 pp.   1015

Before analyzing Edward Benlowes' Theophila (1652) as example of composition by allegorical numbers, preparatory to study of Paradise Lost by same method, reviews Ernst Curtius on numerical composition with Sp's TM as English example (1331); A. Kent Hieatt on Epith (2398); Maren-Sofie Røstvig's conclusions about Daph and RT (1047); and Alastair Fowler's work on the numbers of time in FQ (1367) (pp. 35-6, 43-50).

Rabkin, Norman. Shakespeare and the Common Understanding. New York: Free Press, 1967. 267pp.   1016

Like Shakespeare in Venus and Adonis, Sp in HHOL undercuts "the simple glorification of physical love" (p. 161). Apothecary in Romeo and Juliet "is as powerful an allegorization of death as Spenser ever achieved" (p. 176). Rabkin's principle of "complementarity" in Shakespeare has implications for FQ.

Raine, Kathleen. Defending Ancient Springs. London: Oxford University Press, 1967. 198 pp.   1017

Many incidental but significant references to Sp in essays on Vernon Watkins and the Bardic Tradition, Yeats's Debt to William Blake, Traditional Symbolism in "Kubla Khan," On the Symbol, On the Mythological, A Defense of Shelley's Poetry, The Use of the Beautiful, and St. John Perse, Póet of the Marvellous. See Index.

Raith, Josef. Geschichte der Englischen Literatur. Munich: Max Hueber, 1961. 183 pp.   1018

One-page description of Sp's works (p. 72).

Ramsey, John Stevens. Magic and Festivity in English Renaissance Poetry. DAI, 32 (1971), 3265A-6A. University of Maryland, 1971. 435 pp.   1019

Use of magic and festive materials begins with Wyatt, Surrey, and Tudor miscellanies; becomes substantial in Sp, Jonson, and Herrick; diminishes in major poems of Milton. Magic and festive elements in poetry associated with contemporary beliefs, thus derive from social and literary context in which poet lived and wrote. In a number of major English Renaissance poems, elements of magic and festivity "form a dialectical structure ... that opposes magical threat and tyranny to festive release and emancipation. ... Especially in the poetry of Spenser, Herrick and Milton and the masques of Ben Jonson, the opposition of magical threat to festive liberation forms a basic paradigm of the work which reinforces its theme and disciplines its structure."

Randall, Alice E. (Sawtelle). The Sources of Spenser's Classical Mythology. New York: AMS Press, 1970. 128 pp.   1020

Repr. of 1896 ed. Alphabetically arranged handbook. Index of Abbreviations (pp. 11-12). Sources from Acheron (FQ, I, v, 33) to Zephyrus (FQ, II, v, 29; Proth 1. 2). Index of Authorities, "intended to assist students in discovering Spenser's indebtedness to individual authors," from Aeschylus to Virgil (pp. 125-8).

Ransom, John Crowe. The World's Body. Port Washington, N.Y.: Kennikat Press, 1964. 350 pp.   1021

Repr. of 1938 ed. The subtly irregular stanzas of Epith and Proth prepare the way for Milton's daring irregularities in Lycidas (pp. 7-9). Considers Sp's sonnets superior in "architectural design" to those of any other writer of the English or four-part sonnet (pp. 273-5). See 2442.

Rashbrook, R. F. Keats and Others, N&Q, 192 (1947), 161-4.   1022

Similarities between Shakespeare and Sp, and Keats and Sp.

Read, Herbert. The Art of Collaboration, in Of Books and Human-kind: Essays and Poems Presented to Bonamy Dobrée, ed. John Butt, pp. 209-16. New York: Hillary House, 1964. 232 pp.   1023

Recalls collaboration with Dobrée on London Book of English Verse (372). Correspondence from Dobrée to Read appears with portion discussing which Sp material to include. Would print all of Sp if space allowed (p. 214).

Reaney, James. The Influence of Spenser on Yeats. Doctoral diss., University of Toronto, 1958. DA, 18, No. 7, 1958, 102.   1024

"The early influence of Spenser on Yeats is . . . related to Yeats' failure to understand Spenser. As Yeats developed, certain things he says about Spenser after 1906 imply that he no longer regards the Elizabethan poet as having an imperfect, divided genius, but as a poet who successfully fused the two worlds of aesthetics and morality into an imaginative synthesis. This thesis explores both these early and late attitudes to Spenser as well as the area between them."

Rebora, Pietro. Aspetti dell'Umanismo in Inghilterra, LRin, 2 (1939), 366-414.   1025

Sp, pp. 405-9. In Sidney and Sp the Italian Renaissance in England began to speak with the voice of imperialism. Finds in FQ, V and View "a mystical ethics founded principally on patriotism."

Rebora, Pietro. Spenser, Edmund, Enciclopedia Italiana, 32, 332-4. Rome: Istituto della Enciclopedia Italiana, 1936-1940.   1026

Rees, Joan. Samuel Daniel: A Critical and Biographical Study. Liverpool: Liverpool University Press, 1964. 184 pp.   1027

John Florio married Daniel's sister, whose name may have been Rose and she may have been Rosalind of Sp's SC (p. 5). Between 1592 and 1594 Daniel came under influence of Pembroke circle and "our Spenser," as he calls him in dedication of Cleopatra; CCCHA praises Daniel and urges him to raise poetic sights (p. 11). Delia 31 renders Tasso's Jerusalem Delivered XVI, 14-15, but Sp's version (FQ, II, xii) much closer to original; only five examples of Spenserian sonnet form in Delia, Daniel preferring Shakesperean pattern; 46 indicates he read part of FQ by 1592, and may have seen some of Amor in manuscript (pp. 29-30). "Classical Cleopatra written, under influence of Countess of Pembroke, to carry on Sidney's ideals in drama, as Sp counted on to champion high ideal in non-dramatic verse (pp. 43-5). Daniel began Civil Wars (first 4 books, 1595) to establish self as epic poet. His Henry V exhorts some poet to write national epic celebrating his deeds, and Tillyard suggests Shakespeare's trilogy on Henry V is epic competing with Civil Wars, Arcadia, and FQ (pp. 135-8).

Rees, John O., Jr. Spenserian Analogues in *Moby-Dick*, ESQ, 18 (1972), 174-8.
                                                    1028

Guyon's voyage to Acrasia's Bower of Bliss (FQ, II, xii) well known as source of Melville's Mardi and The Encantadas. Paralleled and echoed also in Moby-Dick: Pequod meets terrors as portentous as those met by Guyon's boat; splendor of Acrasia's island suggested in lyrical imagery of first day of whale chase; menacing weather clears for both Guyon and Ahab; perfume and music haunt Bower, and attend end of search for whale. Ishmael's description of Moby-Dick at close range evokes Jove-Leda simile in Proth. [SpN, 4, No. 1 (1973), 8.]

Reeves, James. A Short History of English Poetry, 1340-1940. London: Heinemann, 1961. 228 pp.   1029

Sp is admired for smoothness. Earlier, Skelton "escaped from the soporific regularity of established practice. . . . Later, Donne was to stand in the same relation with the Spenserian school" (pp. 41-2). Sketches Sp's career. SC "was a dead end." Most of minor poetry "would perhaps have been altogether forgotten were it not for *The Fairy Queene*." Most deserving of rescue is 4 Hymns. No one who reads FQ now "cares much about its meaning in the larger sense"; modern reader is "beguiled by the narrative, and above all by the vivid and exuberant verse." Quotes Hazlitt. Views

poem "as a masterpiece of uncertain status" (pp. 53-60). For other references to Sp, see Index.

Renwick, W. L. Edmund Spenser. London: Cambridge University Press, 1952. 21pp.   1030

R. A. Neil Lecture for 1952. Attributes current neglect of Sp to his unavailability to the limited critical techniques presently popular; his failure to arouse love, hatred, or pity as a man; Hazlitt's and Arnold's inadequate critical responses; Sp's antiquated politics; his being pigeonholed as philosophically a Platonist. Refutes charge that Sp fails to distinguish between the beauty of vice and virtue. Explains the "overloaded" and occasionally unresolved and contradictory nature of FQ by the fullness and vicissitudes of Sp's life.

Renwick, W. L. Edmund Spenser: An Essay on Renaissance Poetry. London: Edward Arnold, 1961; Methuen, 1965. 198 pp.   1031

Reprints of 1925 ed. Traces emergence of new poetry in Italy and France under influence of Latin humanism and critical theory concerning vernacular, Sp's academic equipment (pp. 9-33). Renaissance theory of genres, brief mention of SC, Sp's attempt in FQ to reconcile claims of both romance and epic derived from critical theory, minor poems in Complaints (pp. 34-64). Classical bases of Sp's style and language, "masterful at times," necessarily "bold" (pp. 97-116). Imitation, variety of matter, debts to foreign and English writers, eclectic allegory (pp. 117-50). Inclusive philosophy, idealism (pp. 151-76). Poetry Sp's calling (pp. 177-88).

Renwick, William Lindsay. Spenser, Edmund, Chambers's Encyclopaedia, 13, 85-6. Oxford: Pergamon Press, 1967.
                                                    1032

Sp also mentioned in entries on Arthurian legend, Cambuscan legend, satire, Raleigh, Fletcher, and stanza.

Renwick, William Lindsay. Spenser, Edmund, Encyclopedia Americana, 25, 483-7. New York: Americana Corp., 1970.   1033

Also William Nelson, Epith, ibid., 10, 523; William Nelson, FQ, ibid., 830; Stark Young, SC, ibid., 24, 700; and Douglas Bush, pastoral, ibid., 21, 376.

Ribner, Irving. The English History Play in the Age of Shakespeare. Princeton, N. J.: Princeton University Press, 1957. 354pp.   1034

References to Sp in connection with literature most likely to have influenced Shakespeare in his formative years (p. 106); Locrine (pp. 236-41); Lear (p. 248); Vortigern (p. 259); Whore of Babylon (pp. 271, 285-8).

Richmond, H.M. Ronsard and the English Renaissance, CLS, 7 (1970), 141-60.
                                            1035

Although Sp, Sidney, Drayton, and Milton have been studied in relation to Ronsard, debts of Donne, Shakespeare, and Marvell to Ronsard have been recognized less frequently. [SpN, Vol. 2, No. 1 (1971), 9.]

Ringler, William. Spenser and Thomas Watson, MLN, 69 (1954), 484-7.   1036

In referring to "Amaranthus, made a flower of late," and to "Amintas" (FQ, III, vi, 45) Sp clearly had in mind Thomas Watson's Latin poem Amyntas (1585). Watson returned the compliment in his Latin poem Meliboeus (1590), which thus contains the earliest reference to FQ after its publication. A year later Sp praised Watson again in RT, ll. 435-7. Watson died in 1592, having published ten books, 6 in Latin and 4 in Eng-lish, in eleven years. Sp showed independent judgment in admiring him before his reputation was fully established. It is unlikely that he ever knew Watson personally.

ENTRY CANCELLED   1037

Rix, Herbert D. Rhetoric in Spenser's Poetry. University Park: Pennsylvania State College Press, 1940. PSCS, 7.1038

The principles of rhetorical adornment were indispensable to Sp in planning the architecture and choosing the details of his poems; his use of these principles shows a sound systematic craftsmanship. [Doc. diss., Princeton University, 1938.]

Robinson, Forrest G. The Shape of Things Known: Sidney's Apology in Its Philosophical Tradition. Cambridge, Mass.: Harvard University Press, 1972. 230 pp.   1039

Deals with visual epistemology of Sidney's esthetics. Chap. 2, The Renaissance Spectrum, discusses "a kind of media explosion" under headings of The Gutenberg Revolution, The Theory of Love, Mathematics, Pictures and Emblems (Sp's SC shows access to Continental emblem books before Geoffrey Whitney's A Choice of Emblems (1586)—see 1197—Method (i. e., Ramus). Abraham Fraunce's Sheapheardes Logike emphasized "natural" logic (Ramistic) as found in Sp's SC. Chap. 5, Reflections in Seventeenth-Century Literature, in discussion of Character writers, quotes FQ, V, vi, 2, 6-9 on way Britomart's image is fixed in Artegall's mind. See Index.

Robson, W. W. Pre-Raphaelite Poetry, in From Dickens to Hardy, ed. Boris Ford, pp. 352-370. A Guide to English Literature, 6. New and rev. ed. London: Cassell, 1963. 516 pp.   1040

"Italianate" lack of energy in mid-

Victorian verse had beginnings with Sp and Milton (p. 359).

Roche, Thomas P., Jr. The Spenser Collection of Charles Grosvenor Osgood, PULC, 29 (1967), 91-101. 1041

Describes Osgood's collection, which he gave to the Princeton University Library. Among other Sp items, includes early editions of SC, FQ, CCCHA, 4 Hymns, and Complaints.

Rosenheim, Edward W. What Happens in Literature: A Student's Guide to Poetry, Drama, and Fiction. Chicago: University of Chicago Press, 1960. 163 pp. 1042

Defines Spenserian stanza and sonnet (pp. 27-8).

Ross, Malcolm Mackenzie. History and Poetry, Thought, 26 (1951), 426-42. 1043

In 17th century, Christian poetry lost awareness of "the movement and pattern of events as a kind of incarnation, or true analogue, of the eternal engagement of God and man." Contrasts pessimism of Godfrey Goodman's The Fall of Man (1616) and "the analogical dynamism of Shakespearean tragedy." Milton repudiates Eucharistic theology and the analogical sense of history. Withdrawals of Vaughan and Traherne are symptomatic. "The golden childhood garden of these poets does not, like Spenser's Garden of Adonis, carry the future in its womb." Double sense of decay in nature and history is most extensive in Jacobean literature, "just as the myth of Gloriana and the world of Faerie passes from men's eyes." Young Milton for a while shared Sp's confidence in natural order, but "the return of Charles finally cancels out the return of Arthur."

Ross, Richard J. Herrick's Julia in Silks, EIC, 15 (1965), 171-80. 1044

Herrick tried to achieve new synthesis of Art and Nature, departing from earlier Renaissance view of opposition between them, and following more scientific view of nature of Donne and Bacon. Broke with view of Art and Nature in Shakespeare and Sp. See 719.

Rossky, William. Imagination in the English Renaissance: Psychology and Poetic, SRen, 5 (1958), 49-73. 1045

Concerned with the way Elizabethan poetic theory labored "to free the poetic imagination from the current disrepute of the faculty." Dense with references to the psychological and creative literature of the period. Cites passage on Phantastes (FQ, II, ix, 49-52) several times.

Røstvig, Maren-Sofie. Ars Aeterna: Renaissance Poetics and Theories of Divine Creation, Mosaic, 2(1970), 40-61. 1046

An apologia for the numerological criticism of Renaissance literature. Traces traditon of such criticism in Augustine, commentaries on Mosaic account of creation, Platonic and Pythagorean number-lore, Bonaventura, Cusanus, Ficino, and Pico. Treats several numerical notions at some length. [SpN, Vol. 2, No. 1 (1971), 9.]

Røstvig, Maren-Sofie. The Hidden Sense: Milton and the Neoplatonic Method of Numerical Composition, in The Hidden Sense and Other Essays, pp. 3-112. Oslo: Universitetsforlaget, 1963. 226 pp. 1047

Outlines interest during Renaissance in mystical symbolism of numbers expounded chiefly by Florentine Neoplatonists Pico della Mirandola and disciple, Francesco Giorgio, esoteric subject derived from Plato, Plotinus, Pythagoras, Hermes, the Cabbala, and other sources (pp. 3-36). Remainder of monograph analyzes numerical composition particularly in Milton (pp. 37-70) and Henry More (pp. 93-109). Goerge Chapman's use of numerical compositon exceeded by Sp's because of latter's allegorical bent. Cites study of numerical structure of Epith (see 2398), gives examples from FQ (I, x, 37-43; II, ix; II, xi-xii; IV, ii, 41-43), also from TM, RT, especially Daph, 4 Hymns, and SC. Sp "was completely aware of the technique of numerical compositon, and . . . he took a particular delight in so fashioning his poetry that its chief structural elements embodied a numerical formula for the ideas expressed in the contents" (pp. 71-92).

Røstvig, Maren-Sofie. Images of Perfection, in Seventeenth-Century Imagery: Essays on Uses of Figurative Language from Donne to Farquhar, ed. Earl Miner, pp. 1-24. Berkeley: University of California Press, 1971. 202 pp.   1048

Sp's 4 Hymns on Neoplatonic theme of ascent from lower to higher levels of being; also Neoplatonic is conception of creation as "wondrous Paterne" of perfect beauty imperceptible except to "inward ey" of mind. Difficult to separate "orthodox" Platonism of Ficino and Pico from many syncretistic accounts of creation from Sp to Milton. Syncretists declared poets must imitate God's pattern through mathematical ratios reflecting eternal, immutable beauty. Half-Platonic, half-Hermetic concept of bisexual or androgynous character of man as first created in Marvell's The Definition of Love, Browne's Religio Medici, and Sp's FQ (IV, x), which describes concord or love as union of opposites. Demonstrates syncretic number symbolism in Paradise Lost. Complex mathematical images in structure of Epith (2398), FQ (1367), and SC (1047). Geometrical images as familiar in Renaissance iconography as abstract images of perfection used by Renaissance poets.

Røstvig, Maren-Sofie. Renaissance Numerology: Acrostics or Criticism? EIC, 16 (1966), 6-21.   1049

A defense of numerological criticism as valid method of studying Renaissance literature. Mistakenly associated with mysticism or occult lore. Numerical symbolism part of Renaissance idea of ordered universe, hence numerical composition not esoteric but natural practice. Science of numbers, of great interest to Marsilio Ficino, Pico della Mirandola, Giordano Bruno, Robert Fludd, and Henry More, led nowhere in history of science but vital to Renaissance poetic. Numerological criticism in Sp studies pioneered by A. Kent Hieatt in analysis of Epith (2398), followed by this writer in work on early poetry (1047), applied by Alastair Fowler to FQ (1367). Need "a new Gibbon—or a new Lovejoy—to trace the rise and fall of the concept of world order or harmony as expressed by means of numbers. The field is wide open."

Rowse, A. L. The England of Elizabeth: The Structure of Society. New York: Macmillan, 1951. 547 pp.   1050

Evokes spirit of Elizabethan period as a living age, part of English heritage: "Spenser shaken to the core by his terrible experiences in Ireland, sick and needy, dying at the age of forty-six in an inn in King Street" (p. 13); Sp's tributes to Elizabeth, glittering queen (p. 15); Elizabethan drama a vital part of inheritance, especially Shakespeare, who "was not an academic, bred in the universities, like Marlowe and Spenser" (p. 19). The Elizabethans discovered England, were fascinated by their own past, as Sp's interest in legendary British history shows (pp. 63-4). Burghley greatest statesman of the age, but bitterly criticized by Sp in MHT (pp. 155-6). Metropolis of London was crowded with newcomers; Sp, London-born, was an exception (pp. 197-8). Mulcaster and Merchant Taylors' School (pp. 506-9). Attractions of Ramist logic and classical measures to Harvey, Sp, and others (pp. 517-8). Sp was the poet of the Elizabethan Age (p. 533).

Rowse, A. L. The Expansion of Elizabethan England. New York: St. Martin's Press, 1955. 450pp.   1051

Quotes CCCHA on landing in Mounts Bay in Cornwall (p. 33). Looks at Elizabethan Ireland, called "A Celtic Society in Decline," through Sp's eyes in View (pp. 103-9). "The Elizabethans sent many of their ablest and most gifted men to Ireland, both administrators and soldiers." Sp's experiences woven into account (pp. 126-57). Sp was "first of the poets to respond to the new impulses" given by American colonization (pp. 234-7).

Rubel, Veré L. Poetic Diction in the Renaissance from Skelton through Spenser. New York: Modern Language Association of America, 1941. Revolving Fund Series, No. 12. 312pp.   1052

Poetic diction of Sp's SC discussed in chapter on Pastoral Poetry (pp. 143-52); final chapter (pp. 221-72) on Sp's poetic diction in Complaints, FQ, and later poems. Throughout his career, Sp was active "in extending the medium of expression by every possible device: revival of old words, use of dialect, introduction of borrowings, enallage, neologizing, orthography, rhetorical figures in simple, compound, mutated forms."

Ruthven, K. K. The Conceit. London: Methuen, 1969. 70 pp.   1053

Common way of organizing descriptions of sonnet lady was by means of a *blazon*, or catalogue, formula established in 13th century by Geoffrey of Vinsauf and widely used after Clément Marot wrote, admired "Blason du Beau Tétin" in 1536. Sp's description of his bride in Epith (ll. 171-178) typical (pp. 22-3). In emblematic conceits poet aimed at "the vividness and stylized symbolism which in emblem books proper tend to be the engraver's responsibility." Sp's description of Seven Deadly Sins (FQ, I, iv, 18-36) "reads less like a description of an actual procession than a description of an emblematic engraving of such a procession." FQ became sourcebook for later emblem makers like Henry Peacham (pp. 33-4). In tradition of etymological conceits all names are usable "speaking names" (*sprechende Namen*); e.g., Sp's compliment in Proth (ll. 152-154) to Earl of Essex, Robert Devereux, based on discovery of *heureux* in *Devereux* (pp. 38-9).

Ruutz-Rees, C. Flower Garlands of the Poets: Milton, Shakespeare, Spenser, Marot, Sannazaro, in Mélanges offerts à M. Abel Lefranc, pp. 75-90. Paris: E. Droz, 1936. 506pp.   1054

Flower passages in Lycidas; A Midsummer Night's Dream and The Winter's Tale; April (ll. 55-63, 136-44) and May (ll. 11-14) of SC, Amor 64, and Proth (ll. 30-4); Complaincte de ma Dame Loyse de Savoye; Prose X of Sannazaro's Arcadia, De Partu Virginis, and first Eclogue of Phyllis. Another floral catalogue in Culex of pseudo-Virgil, translanted by Sp as VG. Flower garlands, not uncommon in the classics, dropped out of fashion until revived by Sannazaro and Marot.

Ryan, Lawrence V. Spenser, Edmund, Encyclopedia International, 17, 193-4. New York: Grolier, 1964.   1055

Portrait, p. 193. The Faerie Queene, 7, 20; The Shepheardes Calender, 16, 426.

Saillens, Emile. John Milton: Man, Poet, Polemist. New York: Barnes and Noble, 1964. 371 pp.   1056

Milton's first schooling at St. Paul's under Dr. Gill, who put Sp above Homer. At end Milton told Dryden Sp was his master, above all the moralist; Sir Guyon his childhood hero (pp. 8-9, 15). During Cambridge vacation 1630 probably saw Sp's disciple, William Browne, influenced by Britannia's Pastorals; composed Latin epigraph for second Shakespeare folio (1632) accepted by Ben Jonson; admired Sp but not Spenserian stanza, soon rejected poetry of both Browne and Jonson (pp. 33-6). Grandchildren of Countess of Derby, Sp's Amaryllis, performed Milton's little masque Arcades in 1633; in On Time, poem following Arcades in Cambridge notebook, have first examples of Miltonic verse-paragraph, perhaps suggested by Sp's Epith. Sp was Milton's model in writing Comus, same texture as FQ (pp. 46-54). In 1646 publisher Moseley allowed to present Milton as Sp's disciple (p. 137). Stages in gestation of Paradise Lost: attracted by Du Bartas and Sp, Genesis and chivalry; Tasso, tragic drama; return to Genesis and drama of the Fall, supreme theme adopted after long delay (pp. 216-8).

Salman, Phillips Cranston. Spenser's Representation of Queen Elizabeth I. DAI, 30 (1969), 2498A-9A. Columbia University, 1968. 143 pp.   1057

Chap. III shows that Sp's portraits of Queen—Mercilla and Gloriana in FQ, Cynthia and Eliza in pastorals, relate Elizabeth's temporal reign to God's eternal reign. Chap. IV treats Sp's portrait of Elizabeth as public and private person. Suggests shortcomings of studies by Elkin C. Wilson (1204) and Frances A. Yates (1762).

Salmon, Vivian. Some Functions of Shakespearian Word-Formation, ShS, 23 (1970), 13-26.   1058

Shakespeare's compound epithets describing natural world imitate diction "most notably exploited by Spenser," but also derived from earlier English poets, the Pléiade, and Hellenistic influences on English culture. Epithets based on physical or mental attributes mark Shakespeare's language as " 'poetic' in the tradition of which Spenser is usually regarded as the founder" (pp. 21-3).

Sampson, George. The Concise Cambridge History of English Literature. New York: Macmillan, 1941. 1094 pp.   1059

Sp possibly influenced by Stephen Hawes (p. 88). Short biography, possible influences on Sp (pp. 147-150). Sp's early career as sonneteer (p. 150), relation to the masque (p. 338), View as way of "bringing Ireland into line with the English ideal of a well-ordered society" (pp. 217, 380). Sp's influence on Samuel Butler's Hudibras (p. 410). See Index.

Samuel, Irene. Plato and Milton. Ithaca: Cornell University Press, 1965. 182 pp.   1060

Repr. of 1st ed., 1947. In light of Milton's study of Plato, explains poetic and ethical theories underlying Paradise Lost, Paradise Regained, and Samson Agonistes (p. viii). Comus most Platonic of Milton's works; Sp his guide (pp. 10-11). Milton put Plato higher than any writer except authors of Bible, higher than Sp, his favorite English poet (p. 20). May not have read much Florentine Platonism, but inevitably met it in Sidney, Sp, and other English Poets. Strongest tie with Sp: FQ model for Paradise Lost, so Sp links him with Christian mystics who drew Platonism from Ficino. But used from Plato what is reasoned and analytic, less mythical and exuberant (pp. 40-3). Comus Milton's first hedonist work; image of men turned into beasts from Homer and Sp, but Milton is Platonic in linking transformation with sensual enjoyments (pp. 73 ff.). Milton's concept of love related to Sp's 4 Hymns, influenced by Neoplatonists most interested in Phaedrus and Symposium. (pp. 150 ff.).

Sandison, Helen, ed. The Poems of Sir Arthur Gorges. Oxford: Oxford University Press, 1953. 254pp.   1061

Sp, to whom Gorges was Alcyon in CCCHA, is frequently mentioned in the introduction and notes. See Index.

Sandstroem, Yvonne Luttropp. Spenserian Influences in the Poetry of Andrew Marvell. DAI, 32, (1971), 398-A. Brown University, 1970. 152 pp.   1062

Direct borrowing can be demonstrated in A Picture of Little T. C. and To His Coy Mistress. More interesting borrowing occurs when Marvell takes a Spenserian theme and puts it to a different use, as in Bermudas and The Garden. The Nymph complaining for the Death of her Fawn modeled on allegory of White Lioness in Sp's Daph. Sp and Marvell both concerned with mutability, both used metaphors from music and architecture to order flux of fallen world. Most important impulse Marvell received from Sp was pastoral. "The greatest value Spenser had for Marvell, however, was that he provided a pattern, not to follow but to depart from."

Satterthwaite, Alfred W. Spenser, Ronsard, and Du Bellay: A Renaissance Comparison. Princeton: Princeton University Press, 1960. 282 pp.   1063

Two main theses are presented and sustained: (1) Ronsard is a pure humanist, Sp a Christian humanist, and Du Bellay somewhere in between; (2) Ronsard and Sp illustrate the ambivalence of Renaissance culture toward its dual heritage, the classical and the Christian. Sp maintained in himself

and in his work "the Christian humanist balance between his religion and his classical learning," a balance preserved after him only by Milton. [Diss., Harvard University, 1955.]

Rev. Robert Ellrodt, EA, 14 (1961), 237; Patricia Thomson, MLR, 57 (1962), 84; Waldo F. McNeir, MP, 60 (1962), 58; B.E.C. Davis, RES, 14 (1963), 74.

Saunders, J. W. The Façade of Morality, ELH, 19 (1952), 81-114.   1064

Tudor professional poets erected a façade of morality to protect their work from stigma of folly and worthlessness.. Sp's career was shaped by dualistic determination to please both court and middle-class. SC, contrived to appeal to both camps, was break in pretenses of nonprofessionalism which lasted until 1591; from this time on he published extensively and wrote for court and bourgeoisie simultaneously. FQ fails in essential unity because Sp's purposes were thus irrevocably split. Fatal crux is irreconcilability of imaginative experience and didactic truths. Conflict between dulce and utile went deep, blurring outline of allegories, causing him, e.g., to linger over Pastorella while he forgets the Blatant Beast. Nothing "could have saved the poem from the dualism of an unquenched ambition that sought to serve two masters at once." See 1744.

Saurat, Denis. Gods of the People. London: John Westhouse, 1947. 190pp.
                                        1065

Chiefly concerned with the occult in Milton, Blake, Hugo, and 20th-century thought. Cites FQ, II, viii, 1-2 on angels (pp. 20-6); says Milton knows less about angels than Sp does (p. 27); quotes HOHB on "the doctrine of the Central Sun, which is God, which is Christ, physically" (pp. 109-11), and on sexual implications of Sapience (pp. 138-9); Chap. II of

Part VI, Literary Values (pp. 158-61), is a reprint of section on Sp in Spiritual Attitudes in Spenser, Milton, Blake, and Hugo, CLS, 13 (1944), 8-12 (see 1660).

Schauer, Ruth Abbott. Pastoral Satire in the Poetry of Edmund Spenser. DA, 25 (1964), 2499. University of Wisconsin, 1964. 412 pp.   1066

Studies one strand of Sp's pastoralism: otium of shepherds as antithesis of evils of real world, and use of Christian pastoral imagery to reprove ecclesiastical abuses. Traces theory of satiric pastoral and history of satiric eclogue, sub-species of pastoral. In SC satiric eclogues serve as counterpoint of idyllic eclogues. CCCHA combines Ronsardian tradition of pastoral compliment with satiric tradition which opposes innocence of shepherds to corruption of court. Final chapter compares Christian pastoral assumptions of SC with Arcadian pastoral world where Calidore (FQ, VI) is educated in otium, opposed to courtliness.

Scherer, Margaret R. The Legends of Troy in Art and Literature. 185 Plates. New York: Phaidon Press, 1964. 304 pp.   1067

Appendix A, Works of Literature and Music dealing with the Trojan War, 9th-8th century B. C. to 20th century; Appendix B, Works of Art Dealing with Trojan Themes, 900-700 B. C. to 19th-20th century; Notes (pp. 255-77); List of Plates (pp. 279-86); Index of Mythological Personages and Places (pp. 287-94); General Index (pp. 295-304). Text and illustrations in six sections: Before the Iliad, The Iliad, The Fall of Troy, The Oresteia, The Odyssey, The Aeneid. Works of literature 12th century-16th century include Geoffrey of Monmouth, Boccaccio, Chaucer, Lydgate, Caxton, Ariosto, Giraldi, Cartari,

Conti, and Sp; works of art 14th century-16th century include painting, sculpture, tapestries, manuscripts, ivories, cassoni, rock crystals, metal work, maiolica, and enamels.

Schirmer, Walter F. Geschichte der englischen Literatur von den Anfängen bis zur Gegenwart. Halle: Niemeyer, 1937. 679pp.   1068

Spenser und die elisabethanische Lyrik, pp. 213-20; Spenser und das Epos, pp. 221-6.

Schirmer, Walter F. Geschichte der Englischen und Amerikanischen Literatur. 4th ed., rev. Tübingen: Max Niemeyer, 1967. 838 pp.   1069

Bk. 3, Period of the Renaissance. Chap. 1, Non-dramatic Literature of the 16th Century, section 5: Sp and the Elizabethan lyric. Brief descriptions of SC, poems in Complaints vol., CCCHA, 4 Hymns, Amor and other sonnet sequences, Epith (pp. 222-9). Section 6: Sp and the epic. FQ briefly considered along with poems by Daniel, Drayton, Lodge, Marlowe, and others (pp. 229-35).

Schmidt, Karlernst. Vorstudien zu einer Geschichte des Komischen Epos. Halle: Max Niemeyer, 1953. 204pp.   1070

Muiop in tradition of animal epic, but lacks humor characteristic of type (pp. 56-8). Parodies of Sp and Milton (pp. 87-8, 140-6). Discusses, among others, Somervile's Hobbinol (1740), Shenstone's The Schoolmistress (1748), Cambridge's Archimage (1810).

Scott, William O. Structure and Repetition in Elizabethan Verse. DA, 20 (1960), 3752. Princeton University, 1959. 224 pp.   1071

Handbooks of rhetoric and poetics from classical times through the Renaissance established rules for the use of various kinds of verbal repetition.

Two purposes behind repetition: transition and emphasis, each related to the development of meaning in language through syntax, the connection of poetic movement with style, and esthetic effect. Four poets studied for techniques of repetition: Wyatt, Sidney, Sp, and Donne. Sp's strategy of repetition is integrally related to his narrative pace, combination of figures, and creation of a unique style.

Scoular, Kitty W. Natural Magic: Studies in the Presentation of Nature in English Poetry from Spenser to Marvell. Oxford: Clarendon Press, 1965. 196 pp.
1072

Prints with full commentary and notes poems representing different ways of writing about natural world. Lady Nature appears in different guises; cites FQ, VII (pp. 24-5). Note on Richard Lovelace's The Falcon compares Sp's simile in FQ, VI, vii, 9 (p. 74). Discussion of small poems on small subjects refers to MHT, VG, Muiop, and CCCHA (pp. 94-7). Emblematic significance of hill and valley in July of SC and in FQ (pp. 154-61). [Diss., Oxford University, 1957.] Rev: Pierre Legouis, EA, 18 (1965), 311; S. K. Heninger, Jr., JEGP, 65 (1966), 171; H. Smith, MLQ, 27 (1966), 81.

Sells, A. Lytton. Animal Poetry in French and English Literature and the Greek Tradition. Bloomington: Indiana University Press, 1955. 329pp.
1073

Sp in Part 2, section 5, The Renaissance in England: The First Phase. November and December in SC, VG, Muiop, Una's lion in FQ, imagery of Amor 67 and 72 (pp. 78-82).

Sells, A. Lytton. The Italian Influence in English Poetry. Bloomington, Ind.: Indiana University Press, 1955. 346pp.
1074

Chapter VII, Spenser, pp. 150-87.

SC influenced by Mantuan, Castiglione, Ficino's Neoplatonism. Sp's taste thoroughly florid and Elizabethan. 4 Hymns reflect Castiglione as well as Ficino. First acquaintance with Petrarch was through Du Bellay. Complaints show little Italian influence. Sp fails as a narrative poet. Chiefly affected by Ariosto; shows this in Britomart and pastoralism of Book VI. Sees influence of Trissino in adventures of Guyon. Draws analogies between Sp's pictorialism and Italian art, particularly that of Titian and Veronese. Amor successful because Sp was for once subjected to close restraint. Imagery from Petrarch. Some sonnets straight from Tasso; their Neoplatonism largely by way of the Pléiade.

Sen, D. A Critical Study of Spenserian Imitations from 1700 to 1771. M. A. thesis, University of London, 1952. ULSD, 1951-1952, p. 6.
1075

"The writer's aim has been to present a connected and documented history of the Spenserian imitations of the eighteenth century up to 'The Minstrel' of James Beattie, who seems in some ways to foreshadow the later use of Spenser by the Romantics." Separate chapters deal with appeal of Sp to the Augustans, controversy over Sp's stanza and diction, burlesque imitations, "the attempt made by Prior to modify the Spenserian stanza," and the principal imitators—Croxall, Shenstone, Thomson, Chatterton, Beattie, and others.

Sen, Dilip Kumar. William Thompson— the Spenserian, BuDE, 4 (1968-9), 33-8.
1076

Thompson's An Epithalamium on the Royal Nuptials, The Nativity, and The Hymn to May are successful imitations of Sp.

Seronsky, Cecil. Samuel Daniel. New York: Twayne, 1967. 198 pp.
1077

Daniel's first work translation from Italian of Paulus Jovius's emblem book (1585), form in which interest shown in Sp's SC, John Donne, George Herbert, and others (pp. 15-6). Delia and Complaint of Rosamond (1592, 1594) show he tarried briefly among "loves soft lays and looser thoughts delight," Sp's phrase (pp. 18-20). Lines on Daniel in CCCHA show Sp admired sonnets, probably seen in manuscript, but expected higher achievement from him (pp. 33-5). Contemporary allusions place him alongside Sidney and Sp by 1595. Civil Wars (first 4 books, 1595) treats in epic narrative verse Wars of Roses and Tudor myth, theme of Shakespeare's English histories, touched on in FQ. Lacks imaginative power of Sp's work (pp. 58-61, 78). A Defence of Ryme (1603) fine work of literary criticism, reply to Thomas Campion, who reopened case for English quantitative verse twenty years after experiments with it in circle of Sidney and Sp. Daniel's own rhyme schemes neither varied nor intricate, in contrast with both Sidney and Sp (pp. 101-2). Tethys Festival (1610) a masque with a song that compares with music of April in SC (pp. 134-6). For other references to Sp, see Index.

Seznec, Jean. The Survival of the Pagan Gods: The Mythological Tradition and Its Place in Renaissance Humanism and Art. Translated from the French by Barbara F. Sessions. Bollingen Series, 38. New York: Pantheon Books, 1953. 376pp.   1078

Originally published as La Survivance des Dieux Antiques, Studies of the Warburg Institute, 11, London, 1940. Pagan gods in England, sources of poets' knowledge of them (pp. 312-16). See 986, 1211, 1468.

Sharp, Robert Lathrop. From Donne to Dryden: The Revolt Against Meta-physical Poetry. Chapel Hill: University of North Carolina Press, 1940. 221 pp.   1079

Donne's poetry obscure, harsh, extravagant; Sp's melodious, clear, abundant; Jonson's reasonable, simple, direct. Both Donne and Jonson reacted against Elizabethanism, but both Spenserians and Tribe of Ben had esthetic different from that of metaphysicals (pp. 3-33). Traces course of metaphysical poetry to illustrate Donne's traits (pp. 34-61). Sp's, Jonson's, and Elizabethan critical theory of decorum violated by metaphysical quiddities (pp. 65-92). Followers of Sp or Jonson never considered roughness and harshness desirable; Milton, Waller, Cowley in revolt againt metaphysicals or at crossroads (pp. 93-120). Return to nature with Davenant, Hobbes, experimental science, and religious revival (pp. 121-49). New standards prevailed in "the mundane and daylight couplets of Dryden and Pope" (pp. 150-212).

Sherburn, George, and Donald F. Bond. The Restoration and Eighteenth Century: 1660-1789. Vol. III of A Literary History of England, ed. by Albert C. Baugh. New York: Appleton-Century Crofts, 1948. 2nd ed., 1967. 1605 pp.   1080

Sp imitated by early 18th-century poets, Samuel Croxall, Thomas Purney, Matthew Prior, and James Thomson. Focus of John Hughes, critical essayist of time, was on Sp (p. 900).

Shipley, Joseph T. Dictionary of World Literature: Criticism—Forms—Technique. New York: Philosophical Library, 1943. 633pp.   1081

Useful entries on Spenserian stanza, ut pictura poesis, didacticism, English criticism (Renaissance), courtly love, Petrarchism, Arthurian legend, and other topics related to Sp.

Shipley, Joseph T., ed. Encyclopedia of Literature. 2 vols. New York: Philosophical Library, 1946. 1082

Sp, I, 217-8; II, 1168.

Shorey, Paul. Platonism Ancient and Modern. Berkeley: University of California Press, 1938. 259pp. 1083

Sp discussed in Chapter V, Platonism and the Renaissance (pp. 118-45), and in Chapter VII, Platonism and English Literature (pp. 175-236). He gave the noblest expression to the gospel of Platonic love as the yearning for great achievements in FQ, I, v, 1. Bembo's Gli Asolani is suggested as another possible source for 4 Hymns.

Shumaker, Wayne. The Occult Sciences in the Renaissance: A Study in Intellectual Patterns. Berkeley: University of California Press, 1972. Illus. 306 pp. 1084

Deals with five areas: Astrology, Witchcraft, White Magic, Alchemy, and Hermetism. Presents masses of specific details and description before offering generalizations concerning wide range of texts (Chaps. 1, 2, and 4); Chap. 3 concentrates on Ficino, Della Porta, and Cornelius Agrippa; Chap. 5 deals with Corpus Hermeticum. Combats modern acceptance of occult sciences by debunking them. Gives corrective view of Renaissance intellectual habits and some admired Renaissance scholars as illogical, naive, and gullible. Concludes that in works he describes there is "a remarkable failure to realize that the truth of poetry is rather metaphorical than factual." Few direct references to Sp; see Index. [SpN, Vol. 4, No. 1 (1973), 2-3.]

Siegel, Paul N. Spenser and the Calvinist View of Life, SP, 41 (1944), 201-22. 1085

Concludes that Sp was a Calvinist,

and his ideals were those of the new Puritan nobility.

Smith, A.J. Theory and Practice in Renaissance Poetry: Two Kinds of Imitation, BJRL, 47 (1964), 212-43. 1086

Imitation is a key Renaissance literary concept, and is understood in two ways by Elizabethan writers. Sp, as do others, satisfies and reconciles the two ways of imitation: literary imitation, as sketched by Petrarch, and the universal imitation of nature.

Smith, Barbara Herrnstein. Poetic Closure: A Study of How Poems End. Chicago: University of Chicago Press, 1968. 289 pp. 1087

Endings of Amor 15 and 47 illustrate various formal devices of closure (pp. 162, 169). Illustrates other points by reference to Epith and SC. Alexandrine at end of Spenserian stanza "will have closural force" (p. 92). See Index.

Smith, Charles G. Spenser's Proverb Lore, With Special Reference to His Use of the Sententiae of Leonard Culman and Publilius Syrus. Cambridge, Mass.: Harvard University Press, 1970. 365pp. 1088

Introduction (pp. 1-19) shows largest number of proverbs—234—in FQ, I; largest number used to "cap off, that is, to begin or end, a stanza"—104—in FQ, IV. Unlike Lyly, Sp does not use proverbs as ornament but "to enforce his ideas, to illustrate, to illuminate, and to focus, as with a lens or prism, on a particular thought." Lists 892 proverbs, many with parallels, in Sp's works. Bibliography, Distribution Index, Latin Word Index, English Word Index (pp. 303-65). Rev: James L. Shepherd, SCB, 30 (1970), 51; A. Low, SCN, 29 (1971), 36; R.F. Hill, YES, 2 (1972), 251; Burton A. Milligan, RenQ, 25 (1972), 102. See 954.

Smith, D. Nichol, ed. Eighteenth Century Essays on Shakespeare. 2nd rev. ed. Oxford: Clarendon Press, 1963. 340 pp.
1089

First ed. 1903. References by Nicholas Rowe (1709) and Lewis Theobald (1733) to Sp's praise of Shakespeare as Willy in TM (pp. 6-7, 64); by Pope (1725) to Dryden's rating of Shakespeare above Chaucer and Sp (p. 51); by William Warburton (1747) to unnamed scholar's intention to publish edition of Sp, but dissuaded "by his Friends, as beneath the dignity of a Professor of the occult Sciences" (p. 102); by Samuel Johnson (1765) to Shakespeare's discovery, with Sp, of music of English language (p. 130); by Richard Farmer (1767) to Shakespeare's—and Sp's—knowledge of classics (pp. 163ff.).

Smith, Guy E. English Literature. 2 vols. Littlefield College Outlines. Ames, Iowa: Littlefield, Adams, 1957.   1090

Sp, I, 57-63; the late followers of Sp, I, 110.

Smith, Hallett. Elizabethan Poetry. Ann Arbor: University of Michigan Press, 1968. 355 pp.   1091

Repr. of 1952 ed. Arranged by types. Treats Pastoral Poetry (SC and CCCHA, pp. 32-51, 54-7), Ovidian Poetry, The Sonnets (Amor, pp. 163-71), Satire (MHT, pp. 212-5), Poetry for Music, and Heroic Poetry (FQ, pp. 333-42). Each genre considered in relation to 16th-century ideals, values, and conventions. Deprecates over-allegorical interpretations of FQ. Sees the poem as heroic, a picture and model of Herculean effort, i.e., mighty exertion based on moral choice of which Hercules' choice of Lady Virtue over Lady Vice is the type.

Smith, Marion Bodwell. Dualities in Shakespeare. Toronto: University of Toronto Press, 1966. 252pp.   1092

Sporadic reference to Sp's reconciliation of spirit and flesh in love through "the symbolism of Christian marriage" as evidenced in Amor, Epith, 4 Hymns, and FQ excerpts. See Index.

Smith, Paul Royce. Studies in Spenser's Rimes. DA, 22 (1962), 3188. University of Florida, 1955. 277 pp.   1093

Sp "was engaged in a continuous experimentation with patterns of repeated sounds in an effort to make each poem as attractive to the ear as it is to the mind. To this end he uses the sounds in rime endings much as a composer uses the sounds in the musical scale, and in many of the extended series of rime-connected stanzas the systems of carefully designed sound echoes furnish an almost musical accompaniment to heighten the impact of the depicted actions or events." Finds in some linked passages, particularly in Bks. IV and VI of FQ, "the effect of a musical theme plus variations." Finds sound patterns "reinforced by delicately shaded assonantal or consonantal echoes." Studies "numerous other repetitional effects" to show Sp "is working with large areas of sound."

Snare, Gerald. Spenser's Fourth Grace, JWCI, 34 (1971), 350-5.   1094

Eliza in April of SC, as well as the lady of FQ, VI, x, 16, 26-7, is a fourth grace; both are intended as an encyclopedic figure who subsumes the attributes of the Three Graces in the Neoplatonic traditon of an "infolded" triad as described by Wind (see 1211). This suggests Sp's technique in characterizing both Arthur and Elizabeth in FQ; both are comprehensive figures who encompass the attributes of a number of other figures. [SpN, Vol. 3, No. 2 (1972), 7.]

Sonn, Carl Robinson. Spenser's Imagery, ELH, 26 (1959), 156-70.   1095

Takes issue with Rudolf Gottfried's view, ibid., 19 (1952), 203-13 (see 722), that Sp's imagery is largely auditory rather than visual. Though Sp does not produce images which are easily painted, the incomplete rendition of visual objects is deliberate stylization, involving distortion and patterning, so carried out that poetic truths emerge from the relation of the resulting images to the objects in nature. "The formalized particulars point to, and become, the general; the concrete merges with the abstract." Infers from this that C.S. Lewis has not completely diagnosed the evil implications of art in, e.g., the Bower of Bliss (see 1513). It is not that art imposes itself on nature, which is what Sp would expect it to do; in the Bower of Bliss, art competes with nature and fails to give it order, direction, significance.

Spence, Joseph. Observations, Anecdotes, and Characters of Books and Men. Ed. James M. Osborn. 2 vols. Oxford: Clarendon Press, 1966. 939 pp.   1096

Waller, Sp, and Dryden were Pope's favorite poets in early reading (pp. 19-20). Addison's opinion of Sp (pp. 73-4). On Sp's "picturesqueness" (p. 182). Sp a model for Drayton, Fairfax, and Milton (p. 187). Sidney and Sp (p. 341). Sp's debt to Ariosto (pp. 552-3). For other references to Sp, see Index.

Spencer, Theodore. The Poetry of Sir Philip Sidney, ELH, 12 (1945), 251-78.   1097

Conclusion compares Sidney and Sp. What Sidney accomplished in poems in Arcadia and Astrophel and Stella has been overshadowed by more ambitious and professional work of Sp in SC and FQ. But Sidney's love poetry is superior to that of Sp—except for Epith. Compared to Sidney's lines, Sp's are thin, lack weight; they are rarely pungent, and

almost never dramatic. The reader is soothed, not challenged. In qualities of depth and directness it is Sidney, not Sp, who is most central of English poets of generation before Shakespeare.

Spencer, Theodore. Selected Essays. Ed. Alan C. Purves. New Brunswick, N. J.: Rutgers University Press, 1966.   1098

See 1097 for general criticism of SC, FQ, and especially Amor. For other references to Sp, see Index.

Spencer, Theodore. Shakespeare and the Nature of Man. New York: Macmillan, 1961. 233 pp.   1099

Repr. of 1942 ed. Among those who upheld optimistic theory of cosmic order and man's place in nature was Sp. Order is Nature's sergeant (FQ, VII, vii, 4). Under influence of Neoplatonism, Sp in HOHB arranged Empyrean heaven into hierarchies of intellectual beings. Suggestion of Platonic ladder of love, as in Castiglione's Book of the Courtier, in HHOB (pp. 1-20). Religious and political situation becoming uncertain by end of 1590's. Change signaled when literature (outside of drama) turned away from romance to realism, different Zeitgeist from that which inspired Sp, in 1580's, to plan huge Christian poem. Sp's death in 1599 "can be seen by the symbolically-minded as a microcosmic reflection of what had happened to the ideals of the early Renaissance which had originally inspired him. The 1590's had begun—in spite of their professed admiration for his genius—to turn away from Spenser" (pp. 47-8).

Spender, Stephen, and Donald Hall, eds. The Concise Encyclopedia of English and American Poets and Poetry. New York: Hawthorne Books, 1963. 415 pp.   1100

Douglas Bush, Edmund Spenser, pp. 316-8. See also articles by Charles

Madge, Metaphor, pp. 198-202; by J. M. Cohen, Foreign Influences on English Poetry, pp. 130-9; and portrait painted by Benjamin Wilson, at Pembroke College, Cambridge, p. 36.

Sperry, Stuart M., Jr. Richard Woodhouse's Interleaved and Annotated Copy of Keats's *Poems* (1817), LM, 1 (1967), 101-64.   1101

Copy of Keats's first published volume owned by his friend and adviser, Richard Woodhouse, now in Henry E. Huntington Library. This monograph has sections titled Introduction, Biography and Dating, Text and Transcripts, Criticism, Prosody, Woodhouse and Keats, and Conclusion, followed by complete text of Woodhouse's annotations. For numerous references to Sp and his poetry, see Index.

Spivack, Charlotte. George Chapman. New York: Twayne, 1967. 180 pp.
1102

Chapman's Ovid's Banquet of Sense superficially erotic, but "the momentarily soft Spenserian tone" is varied with metaphysical imagery. His continuation of Marlowe's Hero and Leander includes in fourth sestiad allegorical digression and "the exquisite Epithalamion Teratos. . . . The rest of the poem is Edmund Spenser reborn" (pp. 38-40, 41-4). Chapman many-sided writer, has been compared to poets as different as Sp and Donne, Dante and Milton, Pope and Yeats (p. 152). For references to Chapman's Platonism, see Index.

Spurgeon, Patrick O'Dyer. The Poet Historical: Edmund Spenser—A Study of Renaissance Methods and Uses of History. DA, 25 (1964), 456-7. University of Tennessee, 1963. 357 pp.   1103

Sp's writing affected by disparate historical traditions: Greek and Roman, Old Testament, medieval literature, humanistic histories of Renaissance and particularly Geoffrey of Monmouth. Even more important influence on Sp "antique Poets historicall," Homer, Virgil, Ariosto, Tasso, and Ronsard. In FQ, Calliope subordinate to Clio. Historical methods in Sp's works range from chronicle to prophetic and allegorical. Most important are prophetic and allegorical. Uses history to glorify past, present, and future of English people and their rulers.

Spurgeon, Patrick O'Dyer. Spenser's Muses, in RenP 1969, ed. George Walton Williams and Dennis G. Donovan, pp. 15-23. Southeast Renaissance Conference, 1970. 78 pp.   1104

In FQ, Sp looked for inspiration both to Calliope, muse of epic poetry, who confers fame, and to Clio, muse of history, who confers wisdom. Clio is dominant. Sp concerned with heavenly wisdom in 4 Hymns; but TM, like FQ, concerned with fallen world that needs examples from history. Dedicatory sonnets for FQ of 1590 support view of Sp as "Poet historicall."

Stack, Richard Catesby. From Sweetness to Strength: A Study of the Development of Metrical Style in the English Renaissance. DA, 29 (1968), 616A. Stanford University, 1968. 223 pp.1105

Relies on system of notation developed by George Trager and Henry Smith in An Outline of English Structure (1951) for marking suprasegmental patterns. "The nexus of expression and form in poetry is the suprasegmental pattern of stress and juncture, which is both the main articulating agent for syntax and rhetoric and also the phonemic feature which satisfies the formal demands of the metre." Deals with "sweetline" in one or two poems of Wyatt, Surrey,

Gascoigne, Sidney, and Sp. These poets seek virtuosity in "the ability to manipulate conventional linguistic and rhythmic counters within a legalistically defined framework," using line as unit of composition rather than sentence, and accommodating syntax to metre rather than playing with tension arising from their conflict. Mode is hieratic rather than expressionistic. Analyzes six poems of Donne to show he is virtuoso poetic craftsman with "unparalleled ability to render lifelike imitations of speech within complex formal structures."

Stamm, Rudolf. Englische Literatur. Wissenschaftliche Forschungsberichte, 2. Bern: A. Francke, 1957. 422pp.   1106

Sp, pp. 63-7. See also Index.

Standop, Ewald, and Edgar Mertner. Englische Literaturgeschichte. Heidelberg: Quelle & Meyer, 1967. 679 pp.   1107

Standop, Old and Middle English literature; Mertner, English literature since the Renaissance. Sp mentioned in connection with Chaucer's Franklin's Tale and Hawes' Pastime of Pleasure. Precursors of Sp in pastoral in early Renaissance, Sackville in Mirror for Magistrates, poetic and rhetoric, quantitative experiments, Sidney's Apologie for Poetrie, sonneteers. Sketch of Sp's life and poetry, 17th-century followers (pp. 201-9). Sp mentioned in connection with Shakespeare and Elizabethan drama, schools of Jonson and Donne, Milton as "the last great poet of the English Renaissance," and Bunyan. Warton, Hurd, Blake, Wordsworth, Coleridge, Byron, Keats, and Tennyson in relation to Sp. See Index.

Starnes, D. T. Spenser and the Graces, PQ, 21 (1942), 268-82.   1108

Sp refers to the Graces more than a dozen times. The ultimate sources of his knowledge of them have been noted. Shows that he consulted Renaissance dictionaries, in which a synthesis of information on the subject was readily available. "In the articles on *Charites* in Cooper's *Thesaurus* and Charles Stephanus' *Dictionarium*, he would have found a unified account of the Graces, synthesizing ideas from Seneca, Servius, and probably Boccaccio" (p. 282). See 1211.

Starnes, Dewitt T., and Ernest William Talbert. Classical Myth and Legend in Renaissance Dictionaries. Chapel Hill: University of North Carolina Press, 1955. 517pp.   1109

Chapter IV, Spenser and the Dictionaries, pp. 44-110. Details Sp's reliance on Cooper's Thesaurus; Charles Stephanus's Dictionarium Historicum, Geographicum, Poeticum; Robert Stephanus's Thesaurus Linguae Latinae; Friar Ambrosius Calepine's Dictionarium; Cartari's Imagines Deorum; and other similar reference books. See also Index.

Stauffer, Donald A. The Nature of Poetry. New York: W. W. Norton, 1946. 291pp.   1110

Sp used to illustrate "economy in choosing details" in "the first glimpse of Abessa in the *Faerie Queene*," I, iii, 10 (p. 63). General method in FQ "affords an example, the best in English, of intensity gained by multiple variations upon a theme" (pp. 87-8). Sp's "conviction that the poet's function is didactic" is characteristic of the Renaissance (pp. 95-9): its overt didacticism alienates us from FQ (pp. 102, 110-1). Complexity of poetry, and allegory as one cause of complexity (pp. 166-8). Sp's verse technique (pp. 197-8): "musical form" in Sp (pp. 252, 262-3). See also Index.

Steadman, John M. Milton's *Haemony:* Etymology and Allegory, PMLA, 77 (1962), 200-7.   1111

In major epics and romances of Renaissance, including FQ, "the magical elements are rationalized through the moral allegory." Thus, Sp's magical personages, Archimago, Duessa, Acrasia, and Busyrane, symbolize hypocrisy, falsehood, incontinence, and tyrannic love (pp. 200-1). In Astro, Sp mentions "the grassie banks of Haemony" (l. 3). He may have been referring, not to Thessaly (as suggested by Sara Ruth Watson, An Interpretation of Milton's "Haemony," N&Q, 178 (1940), 260) but to the river Haemon, "possibly a symbol for the Thames" (p. 202).

Steadman, John M. Milton, Valvasone, and the Schoolmen, PQ, 37 (1958), 502-4.   1112

Valvasone in preface to Angeleida observes that "persons incapable of understanding either Scotus or St. Thomas can learn much about theology from pious poets." Similarly, in Areopagitica Milton says Sp is "a better teacher than Scotus or Aquinas."

Steinberg, Clarence. Atin, Pyrochles, and Cymochles: On Irish Emblems in "The Faerie Queene," NM, 72 (1971), 749-61.   1113

Sp's intention with Atin, Pyrochles, and Cymochles (FQ, II, iv-viii) may be discerned in Irish derivation for "Atin." Anglicized Irish *athainne*, "embers," or Irish and Old Irish *aithinne*, "firebrand," are likely etymons for the name, and by extension "violent youth" may apply. Irish identity for the trio suggested by their resemblances to characters in tale of Cuchulain, especially in fight between Cuchulain and Ferdiad at the ford. Pyrochles' slogan, "Burnt I do burne," would suit Cuchulain, who bursts into flame when provoked; and

Atin's deadly darts like those of Cuchulain's man, Laeg. Proof of Sp's familiarity with Cuchulain appears in canceled section of View, where he refers to "the olde Cullaine." His association of Irish hero with trio consistent with unfavorable attitude toward Irish material in FQ and elsewhere. [SpN, Vol. 4, No. 2 (1973), 5.]

Steinberg, S. H., ed. Cassell's Encyclopaedia of Literature. 2 vols. London: Cassell, 1953.   1114

Entries on epic, pastoral poetry, sonnet, and other topics pertinent to Sp; biographical sketch and bibliography.

Štěpaník, Karel. The Problem of Spenserian Influence in Keats's Poetry, BSE, 2 (1960), 7-54.   1115

Rev. English version of author's chap. on Sp and Keats in Básnické dílo Johna Keatse (The Poetry of John Keats), Prague, 1958. Sp's influence strongest in Keats's earlier poetry (1814-1817), though it did not cease in latest poems, such as The Cap and Bells, the Odes, and Fall of Hyperion. Sp was to Keats "an example to emulate, rather than to imitate." Followed Sp when own natural bent coincided, as in love of beauty of nature, or "exquisite craftsmanship," but remained hostile to Sp's "reactionary political or obscurantist religious ideology." Summaries in Czech and Russian (pp. 52-4).

Stevens, David M. Emerson on the Saxon Race: A Manuscript Fragment, ESQ, 47 (1967), 103-5.   1116

Emerson's manuscript fragment on the achievements of the Saxon race mentions Sp.

Stevenson, David Lloyd. The Love-Game Comedy. New York: Columbia University Press, 1946. 259 pp.   1117

Three medieval views of sex foundation of Shakespeare's romantic comedies: (1) ritual of courtly love, idealizing woman; (2) ascetic Pauline tradition, condemning woman; (3) realistic view accepting sensual pleasure as normal. Wyatt, Sidney, Sp, and Donne represent vain search for consistency concerning complexity of love. Only Sp attempted to formulate composite ideal, Britomart in FQ uniting passion and chastity under sanction of marriage (pp. 8-10). Sp's Platonic adaptation of courtly love in 4 Hymns, Epith, and Bk. II of FQ, and his marital adaptation of it in Amor, Epith, and Britomart's pursuit of Artegall in Bk. III of FQ isolated from actual behavior of men and women, not useful to Shakespeare for final pairing of uncongenial couples (pp. 89-101). Amorous conflict lacking in Sp but "the nature of passion in real life" present in Wyatt, Sidney, Donne, and Greville, as in Castiglione's Courtier (pp. 123-36), and in love-duel in Lyly's and Shakespeare's comedies. For other references to Sp, see Index.

Stewart, Stanley. The Enclosed Garden: The Tradition and the Image in Seventeenth-Century Poetry. Madison: University of Wisconsin Press, 1966. 226 pp.   1118

Chapters on The Song of Songs, The Enclosed Garden, Shade, Time, and Marvell and "The Garden Enclosed." Joseph Beaumont's Psyche (1648) is long Spenserian poem analyzing allegorical function of burning sun in human events. Not popular, but works of Spenserians serve as gloss on more popular contemporaries (pp. 68-71). Time important factor in meditative poem; December in SC is Colin's spiritual autobiography, as in Herbert's Temple "man's confrontation with Time is virtually an epitome of the Christian life" (pp. 103-7). Use

of garden image presupposes choice. Not all gardens represent regeneration. Roman de la Rose, William Nevill's Castell of Pleasure, and Sp's FQ deal with unwarranted love in defiance of God as first sower and husbandman (pp. 123-8). For other references to Sp, see Index. See 1483.

Stock, A. G. Yeats on Spenser, in In Excited Reverie: A Centenary Tribute to William Butler Yeats, 1865-1939, ed. A. Norman Jeffares and K.G.W. Cross, pp. 93-101. New York: Macmillan, 1965. 353 pp.   1119

As young man Yeats influenced by four poets in particular: Sp, Shelley, William Morris, Blake. Learned from Sp certain formality and courtly irony. Later commissioned to write essay on Sp. Delight in Sp's art overcame hatred of "that horrifying government report" Sp's View. Saw Sp as poet writing most of his life in Ireland, where he had no roots. What he admired was not allegory, but "glorification of life," or moments when Sp's allegory "melts into vision," as in Garden of Adonis (FQ, III, vi) and Vision of Scudamore (IV, x).

Stöger, H. Ovids Einfluss auf die poetischen Werke Spensers. Doctoral diss., University of Vienna, 1938. Listed in bibliography of Adolf Münster; see 2283.   1120

Stoll, Elmer E. Criticisms Criticized: Spenser and Milton, JEGP, 41 (1942), 451-77.   1121

Defends the astronomical inaccuracy of VG, ll. 313 f.; Epith, l. 285; and FQ, III, iv, 51. Takes issue with Osgood's note on Satyrane (Variorum, I, 245) calling him unromantic, unidealistic, coarse. Objects to Padelford's "rigidity" in notes on Marinell and Florimell (Variorum, III, 324-5). Sides with Lewis (Allegory of Love, pp. 341-4) in taking Amoret to be pure and blameless, against Padelford (SP, 21 (1924), 376). Ruskin, who found Maleger (FQ, II, xi) greater than anything in Dante, overdid it, but he was righter than Osgood (Variorum, II, 343). "Leaving the wildest interpretations of Spenser untouched, we return to Milton" (p. 462).

Stoll, Elmer Edgar. Poets and Playwrights: Shakespeare, Jonson, Spenser, Milton. New York: Russell & Russell, 1965; Minneapolis: University of Minnesota Press, 1968. 304 pp.   1122

Repr. of 1930 ed. Essay on Sp (pp. 167-202) given "in part" as lecture at Vassar, 1927; certain *argumenta ad feminam* not removed. Half-serious comments on Sp as "high priest of English romanticism": he looked back to Middle Ages, although greatest debt to classics and Renaissance Italians; delight in beauty of women, who should keep their place, "and those who don't keep to it he puts in hell"; he is sentimental and tender in portrayal of Una, bolder with Britomart; not lacking in humor or dramatic power, but chiefly picturesque and lyrical. Compares and contrasts Sp and Milton, makes many allusions to English Romantics.

Stoll, Elmer Edgar. Shakespeare Studies, Historical and Comparative in Method. New York: Ungar, 1960. 502 pp.   1123

Based on 2nd ed. of 1942. Many miscellaneous references to Sp. Contrasts Shakespeare's carelessness about printing sonnets with carefulness of Sp. Refers to Sp's possible but dubious reference to Shakespeare as Aetion in CCCHA (see 210, 798). Shakespeare's heroines follow their lovers as pages, as women in medieval romances, Ariosto, and Sp disguise selves in armor in pursuit of their mates. Shakespearean comedy is Latin, though seems home-grown,

whereas Sp's epic amplitude directly from Ariosto and Tasso. On dead Duke Humphrey's hair and hair of dying Cardinal described in Henry VI, Part 2 as standing up, refers to FQ, II, xi, 20. Shakespeare knew about ghosts from living superstitions, not like Sp from books. Among precedents for Shylock as Jack-in-the-box when learns of double loss is Malbecco's behavior in FQ, III, x, 13-15. Falstaff in Henry IV, Part 1 claiming he killed Hotspur like Braggadochio in FQ, V, iii; and Falstaff capturing Colville in Henry V like comic combat of Braggadochio and Trompart in FQ, II, iii, 4-10. See Index.

Stowell, H. E. An Introduction to English Literature. London: Longmans, 1966. 192 pp.   1124

Primarily capsule sketches of writers and work. Sp (pp. 28-9); influence on Keats (pp. 26, 122), and Lamb (p. 150), and deliberate use of archaic language (pp. 26, 162). See Index.

Stürzl, Erwin. Der Zeitbegriff in der elisabethanischen Literatur: The Lackey of Eternity, Weimar Beiträge zur englischen Philologie, 69 (1965). 524 pp.   1125

Numerous references to Sp's poetry under such headings or subheadings as the Nature of Time, The Appearance of Change, Tempus omnia terminat, Linear and Cyclical Time, The Danger of Delay, The Brevity of Life, the Ubi-sunt?-Theme, The Mirror of the Past, Present Time, the Favorable Occasion, Wasted Youth, the Golden Age, and Aere perennius. Bibliography (pp. 482-97). See Index.

Sutherland, James. A Preface to Eighteenth Century Poetry. Oxford: Oxford University Press, 1963. 175 pp.   1126

Repr. of 1948 ed. The 18th century relied too much on literary allusion, which always requires familiarity of "common reader" with original. Dr. Johnson criticized Gilbert West's imitations of Sp for this reason, and Pope's imitations of Horace (p. 57). Popular taste demanded immediate intelligibility. "The popularity of Spenser in the eighteenth century is almost certainly due in some measure to his perfect lucidity, his unfailing harmony of thought and expression: the popularity of Shakespeare was achieved in spite of the obscurity of his language" (pp. 103-4). Imitations of Sp and Milton flourished. Need not be taken very seriously. In this spirit William Shenstone wrote The Schoolmistress. Spenserian stanza sort of fancy dress (p. 151).

Sypher, Wylie. Four Stages of Renaissance Style: Transformations in Art and Literature, 1400-1700. Garden City, N. Y.: Doubleday, 1955. 312pp.   1127

A study of analogies between shifts in technique in fine arts and literature which produced successively the styles called Renaissance, Mannerism, Baroque, and Late-Baroque. Sp's art typifies Renaissance style: fragile and decorative (p. 3), singing a formal humanist system in 4 Hymns (p. 64), showing logic and symmetrical design in Amor 26 (p. 92), celebrating a comely pattern framed by God (p. 117). It is an illustrative art (p. 175). Milton typifies the more powerful Baroque style. In painting, Botticelli is Renaissance and Rubens is Baroque. See Index.

Tate, Allen. On the Limits of Poetry. Selected Essays: 1928-1948. New York: Swallow Press and William Morrow, 1948. 379pp.   1128

In John Peale Bishop (1935), contrasts situation of poetry in Elizabethan and modern times, calling SC, only Elizabethan experiment with language as such, a failure (pp.

239-40). In A Note on Elizabethan Satire (1932), says it has been unfairly neglected by anthologists and critics because, "In singling out the leading impulse of the Elizabethan age one is constantly guided by the genius and magnitude of Spenser" (pp. 333-40).

Tate, Gary Lee. Gabriel Harvey: Catalyst of the English Renaissance. Doc. diss., University of New Mexico, 1957. DA, 18, No. 7 (1958), 96.   1129

Attempts to raise Harvey in general estimation. Anti-Harvey were Lyly, Greene, Nashe, Peele, and author of Pedantius; pro-Harvey were Sir Thomas Smith, Dr. John Young, Lord Burghley, the Earl of Leicester, Sp, and Sir Walter Mildmay. "Spenser's friendship was the highest tribute Harvey ever received." The more he tried to match the wits, the more ridiculous he became. "Thus Harvey is seen as the victim of a new breed of writer, the college professor versus the Bohemians of the sixteenth century." Divided opinions of him still prevail; these are surveyed. But Harvey made worthwhile contributions to English Renaissance culture, "a noted scholar, a dedicated teacher, a tireless reformer, and a far-sighted patriot."

Tayler, Edward W., ed. Literary Criticism of Seventeenth-Century England. New York: Knopf, 1967. 427 pp.   1130

Comments on Sp by Ben Jonson, Edmund Bolton, Michael Drayton, Sir Kenelm Digby in Observations on FQ, II, ix, 22 (pp. 203-13), Henry Reynolds, Sir William Soames in Art of Poetry (pp. 364-76). See Index.

Taylor, Henry Osborn. Thought and Expression in the Sixteenth Century. 2 vols. 2nd rev. ed. New York: Ungar, 1959.   1131

First published 1920. Sp in vol. 2. Ralegh, Sidney, Sp, pp. 207-37; section 3, pp. 230-7, on Sp. FQ is a world of the imagination shaped by Sp's Platonism out of the materials provided by antique mythology and medieval romance and allegory. See also final chapter, Forms of Self-Expression: The Sixteenth Century Achievement.

Thompson, Francis. Collected Works. 3 vols. in 1. Ed. Wilfrid Meynell. Westminster, Md.: Newman Press, 1947.

1132

Reissue of 3 vols. ed. published 1913. The Poet's Poet (originally published in Academy, Sept., 1903), pp. 140-6. Sp's real power not in narrative but in lyric passages of FQ, in 4 Hymns, Proth, and Epith.

Thomson, J. A. K. The Classical Background of English Literature. London: Allen & Unwin, 1948. 272pp.   1133

Sp, pp. 179-81. "It is evident that he was a good classical scholar for an Englishman of his time."

Thomson, P. The Patronage of Letters under Elizabeth and James I, English, 7 (1949), 278-82.   1134

Both writers and patrons were in difficulties before the public could take over the work of patronage. October eclogue of SC and MHT show Sp's dissatisfaction with system of patronage. Mentions Donne, Jonson, Daniel, Drayton, and other writers. Old system was decaying in 16th century. "Nashe, struggling to survive as a full-time author, has rightly been called the first professional author."

Thornton, Frances Clabaugh. The French Element in Spenser's Poetical Works. Thèse pour le Doctorat de l'Université de Toulouse. Toulouse: Lion et fils, 1938. 379pp.   1135

Preface: "The title of this study may be somewhat misleading. By *The French Element in Spenser's Poetical Works*, is meant a study of the words in Spenser's vocabulary that have entered the English language through the French, most of which have their origin in Latin" (p. 9). The French element in English; Sp's education, orthography, vocabulary; statistical comparison of Sp's vocabulary with that of other English writers; etymology of 1004 adjectives of French origin in Sp (pp. 89-295); 16th century contributions. Two Appendices: list of 4023 French derivatives in Sp's vocabulary (pp. 323-56), and etymology of 457 nouns and verbs of French origin used by Sp (pp. 357-67).

Tillotson, Geoffrey. Essays in Criticism and Research. Cambridge: University Press, 1942. 215pp.   1136

In Chapter II, Elizabethan Decoration (pp. 5-16, reprinted from TLS, July 3, 1937), distinguishes two kinds: "the kind that is formal, numerical, geometrical, and . . . the kind that is rich, profuse, sometimes luxuriously meandering. The formal is the more common and the rich is seldom without a stiffening of it." Sp illustrates "decoration by enrichment." In Chapter XIX, Epithets in English Poetry (pp. 167-70, reprinted from Bookman, 1932), calls "Spenserian" those epithets which have a "sensuous or immediately perceptible abstract content." See also Index.

Tillyard, E. M. W. The Elizabethan World Picture. London: Chatto and Windus, 1943; repr. New York: Randon House, 1963. 116pp.   1137

Sp's poetry cited in illustration of ideas of cosmic order, the scheme of salvation, the chain of being, various links in the chain of being, and the correspondence between body politic and microcosm; see Index.

Tillyard, E. M. W. The Miltonic Setting Past and Present. London: Chatto and Windus, 1938. 208pp.   1138

Sp cited and quoted in connection with Milton's visual imagination (p. 95), and with Tillyard's definition of epic (pp. 142-4, 154-60). "The growth of Milton's epic plans," pp. 168-204, is a slightly revised version of 1708. For other references to Sp, see Index.

Tillyard, E. M. W. Myth and the English Mind: From Piers Plowman to Edward Gibbon. New York: Collier Books, 1962. 126 pp.   1139

Clark Lectures 1959-60. Tudor "myth of pedigree," that House of Tudor would "re-enact the glory Britain enjoyed in Arthurian days" and that Henry VII was descended from Cadwallader, inspired Sp's FQ. Topic fully treated by Edwin Greenlaw (729). Myth's vogue illustrated in William Warner's Albion's England and Michael Drayton's England's Heroical Epistles (pp. 43-8). Discusses "myth of aggression" and "myth of retirement." Wyatt's satires and Sp's CCCHA "are sour-grapes poems and not retirement poems at all" (pp. 60-8). See also 926.

Tillyard, E. M. W. Shakespeare's History Plays. London: Chatto & Windus, 1944; 5th printing, 1959. 336pp.   1140

Significant references to Sp in Part I, The Background: Elizabethan knowledge of Machiavelli (pp. 21-3); the Tudor myth (pp. 30-2); A Mirror for Magistrates as "essential prelude" to FQ, Sidney's Arcadia, and Shakespeare's histories (pp. 71-91). In Part II, Shakespeare: idea of education or "nurture" (pp. 144-5); resemblance of Richard III as symbol to Malbecco

(FQ, III, ix and x; p. 211); Shakespeare's Lancastrian tetralogy as epic (p. 263); resemblance of Henry IV, Parts 1 and 2, to FQ, Bk. II (pp. 265-6); Shakespeare's combination of abstract psychology and realistic observation of life, as in Sp's Britomart (pp. 280-1); by mingling politics with the personal and cosmic in Macbeth, Shakespeare was doing what Sp and Sidney had already done (pp. 317-18).

Tillyard, E. M. W. Some Mythical Elements in English Literature. London: Chatto & Windus, 1961. 143 pp.   1141

As Greenlaw has shown (729), FQ based on myth that Arthur was reincarnated in House of Tudor. This myth a "communal possession" (p. 49). CCCHA regarded as product of "sour grapes retirement" (p. 74).

Toliver, Harold E. Pastoral Forms and Attitudes. Berkeley: University of California Press, 1971. 391 pp.   1142

Chap. 3 on Sidney's pastoralism (pp. 45-62). Chap. 4, "Spenser: The Queen and the Court Singer" (pp. 63-81). Sp never at ease in social position. In SC poet-shepherd suffers from unrequited love of Rosalind and unfulfilled ambition. Accepts identification of Rosalind with Queen Elizabeth (see 2273). All eclogues "except the sportive exercises deal with . . . the ambition-humility complex and its mixed style." Calidore's pastoral interlude (FQ, VI, ix-xi) has analogies with SC, VG, and MHT, also with knights' encounters in earlier books with crudity, goodness, corruption, and perversity. Calidore's intrusion on dance of Graces irritates Colin. Art results in circular dance; social order requires pursuit of Blatant Beast. Destruction of "shepherdom" argues against pastoral retirement. Sp in FQ remains in dilemma represented by nature and grace, never resolves it. Chap. 5, "Shakespeare's Inner Plays and the Social Contract," Chap. 6 on Herbert and Marvell, Chap. 7 on Milton. For other references to Sp, see Index.

Traversi, D. A. Revaluations (X): The Vision of Piers Plowman, Scrutiny, 5 (1936), 276-91.   1143

Compares Langland and Sp to disadvantage of latter. Sp speaks with "the voice of a new sophistication." He is "remote from the real soil . . . his words become little more than pleasant decorative trimmings." Sp "is the first great Puritan poet," the second Milton. "No two men have done more, by their very genius, to crush the true poetic tradition of England." Sp tries to escape the body and live by the spirit (Neoplatonism), resulting in a caricature of Christian sanctity. "The bitter Fifth Book of the *Faerie Queene* only emphasizes what is characteristic of the whole work." It "represents a view of Justice coloured by the bitter Puritan melancholy so typical of Spenser." No difference between Red Cross Knight and Guyon; "both live only in the intellect." "This suggests that Puritanism, as embodied in Spenser, is nothing else than the disembodied and destructive intellect preying on the body to kill the soul."

Travis, Mildred K. Spenserian Analogues in *Mardi* and *The Confidence Man*, ESQ, 50 (1968), 55-8.   1144

Compares three scenes in Melville's Mardi with similar scenes in episodes of Bower of Bliss (FQ, II, xii), Garden of Adonis (FQ, III, vi), and Temple of Venus (FQ, IV, x). The Confidence Man was influenced by MHT.

Trousson, R. Ronsard et la Légende d'Hercule, BHR, 24 (1962), 77-87. 1145

Surveys complex myth of Hercules,

given symbolic and allegorical interpretation very early. Ronsard gives the myth more diverse meanings in more varied contexts than any other poet, in his Hercule Chrestien completely synthesizing mythological and Biblical themes to merge pagan hero Hercules and Christian hero Christ. Relevant to Sp's use of Hercules.

Truesdale, Calvin William. English Pastoral Verse from Spenser to Marvell: A Critical Revaluation. DA, 17 (1957), 1087. University of Washington, 1956. 342 pp.   1146

Rejects approaches to pastoral of Dr. Johnson and William Empson. "The purpose of this study is to display the significant variety possible within the convention." Sp discussed in connection with pastoral encomium, satire, and the "sad shepherd" theme. "The final chapter deals with the recovery of innocence as a dominant theme in the sixth book of *The Faerie Queene*, in *The Winter's Tale*, and finally in its ironic representation in Marvell's *Garden*." Emphasizes throughout "the relationship between natural simplicity and social sophistication . . . in its dramatic and lyrical implications."

Tucker, Martin, gen. ed. The Critical Temper: A Survey of Modern Criticism on English and American Literature from the Beginnings to the Twentieth Century. 3 vols. New York: Ungar, 1969.   1147

Irving Ribner, ed., Elizabethan and Jacobean Literature, I, 251-515; Sp, 458-70. Criticism of FQ from Watkins (1180), Berger (1895), Hough (1449), and Nelson (961); general criticism from Renwick (1031) and Hamilton (1416).

Tucker, Martin, ed. Moulton's Library of Literary Criticism of English and American Authors. 4 vols. New York: Ungar, 1966.   1148

Vol. I, The Beginnings to the Seventeenth Century, contains criticism of Sp under Personal, SC, FQ, individual minor poems, View, and General (pp. 144-62).

Tufte, Virginia. The Poetry of Marriage: The Epithalamium in Europe and Its Development in England. Los Angeles: Tinnon-Brown, 1970. 341 pp.   1149

In Part I deals with tradition of nuptial poetry in Greek, Latin, medieval, Neo-Latin, and Continental vernacular literature (pp. 9-138). In Part II discusses development of genre in England (pp. 141-258). Sp's Epith is "the masterpiece in the genre . . . the first such poem for the poet's own marriage." Sp uses more motifs from preceding centuries than any other poet, at same time introducing more innovations. Proth a betrothal poem; wedding of Thames and Medway (FQ, IV, xi) a topographical epithalamium; April eclogue in SC is epithalamium to Virgin Queen, Elizabeth I; Mutability Cantos reflect aspect of genre called "anti-epithalamium" (pp. 159-93). Ben Jonson, John Donne, and George Chapman each wrote three epithalamia, Robert Herrick wrote five. Epithalamia appear in four of Shakespeare's plays, and in Paradise Lost. [DA, 25 (1965), 5265).] See 954.

Turnage, Maxine. Samuel Johnson's Criticism of the Works of Edmund Spenser, SEL, 10 (1970), 557-67.   1150

Has counted 2,878 illustrations from Sp's works in Johnson's Dictionary, only 2.9% of total number of illustrations. Most from Bks. I and II of FQ; large number from View; SC and MHT significantly represented; 4 Hymns, Amor, Epith, and Proth seldom used. Johnson neglected some of Sp's best poetry. Comments on Sp become more unfavorable as Dictionary progresses. Johnson found Sp's works useful source for obsolete and archaic words. While working on Dictionary, Johnson criticized Sp's use of pastoral, Spenserian stanza, and imitators of Sp in Rambler essays 37 and 121. No life of Sp in The Lives of the Poets. Yet "Johnson graciously recognized Spenser as an important Elizabethan poet."

Turner, W. J., ed. Romance of English Literature. New York: Hastings House, 1944. Britain in Pictures. 324pp.   1151

Lord David Cecil, The English Poets, pp. 61-100. Sp as chief nondramatic poet of the Elizabethan period. FQ "is a long symphonic poem" (pp. 64-5, 68).

Tuve, Rosemond. Allegorical Imagery: Some Mediaeval Books and Their Posterity. Illus. Princeton: Princeton University Press, 1966. 461 pp.   1152

Elizabethan writers, e. g., Thomas Lodge, unhampered by modern theories of allegory. Sp transforms one kind of image into another without explaining in scene at Malbecco's house (FQ, III, ix). FQ double courtesy-book, major figures in its quests simultaneously religious and secular. Magnificence as virtue containing all the rest from Aristotle, as Sp says, but also from Seneca, Cicero, and Macrobius. Other "Aristotelian" virtues have mediaeval sources in literature and iconography. Likewise, the vices. Frequent citations from Somme le roi, translated by Caxton, to illustrate episodes and characters in FQ. When Sp alternates between universals and particulars, allegory is multiple. Imaginative allegorist like Sp combines ancient images in various ways, "seeming to evoke rather than impose." Unless proposed reading is "in" the poem, warns against imposing Christian doctrine, myth, or cosmology on FQ. Discusses Roman de la Rose, Christine de Pisan's Othéa, and Ovide moralisé. Compared to these, Sp's moral plain. Useless to look for motifs in FQ in mediaeval romances, yet they give poem its character as narrative. Discusses other-worldly places, ordinary mediaeval world of chivalry, topicality of Arthurian materials, structure, use of Malory, multiple action with multiple characters, interlacing technique (see 1654), Ariostan plot, clearly marked allegorical meanings that vitiate modern notion of levels, and much more. For references to Letter to Ralegh, MHT, SC, and CCCHA, see Index.

Rev: J. A. W. Bennett, ELN, 5 (1967), 52; U. T. Holmes, Manuscripta, 11 (1967), 55; O. B. Hardison, CLS, 4 (1967), 327; D. C. Allen, JEGP, 66 (1967), 118; R. E. Kaske, Speculum, 42 (1967), 196; William Matthews, RenQ, 20 (1967), 83; J. Norton-Smith, RES, 18 (1967), 305; J. M. Steadman, MLQ, 29 (1968), 99. See 675.

Tuve, Rosemond. Baroque and Mannerist Milton?, JEGP, 60 (1961), 817-33. 1153

Challenges validity of literary categories, particularly for Milton, due to vagueness of criteria. Attacks Sypher's "linear" and "painterly" labels to differentiate Sp and Milton (1127, p. 19) as too subjective. Also refutes Sypher's use of metaphor as categorizing agent in Proth and FQ. Uses Daph and SC to demonstrate difficulty of accurate interpretation of author's intent. Sp's flower list in Proth similar to Milton's in Lycidas, but they create dissimilar paradise of abundance. Points to inadequacy of absolute categories.

Tuve, Rosemond. Elizabethan and Metaphysical Imagery. Chicago: University of Chicago Press, 1947. 442pp.   1154

Sp used copiously for illustrative purposes, in connection with "imitation" (pp. 36-7, 46-7); doctrine of ut

pictura poesis (pp. 53-5, 58-60); style and functional sensuous imagery (pp. 63-5, 67-8); sensuous vividness (pp. 102-4, 107-9); significancy (pp. 153-4); decorum (pp. 220-1, 240-1); Renaissance logic (pp. 296-7, 305-7, 322-6, 328); Ramist logic (pp. 332, 347-9); effects of logical functions on images (pp. 357-8, 360); didactic theory of poetry (pp. 382-3). See also longer notes E (p. 415), L (p. 420), and Q (p. 422).

Tuve, Rosemond. Essays by Rosemond Tuve: Spenser, Herbert and Milton, ed. Thomas P. Roche, Jr. Princeton: Princeton University Press, 1970. 294 pp.   1155

Reprints selected essays on these poets and educational topics. Sp essays: The Red Cross Knight and Mediaeval Demon Stories (Atkinson, p. 123); A Mediaeval Commonplace in Spenser's Cosmology (Atkinson, p. 108); Spenser and the Zodiake of Life (Atkinson, p. 137); Spenser's Reading: The De Claris Mulieribus (Atkinson, p. 77); Spenser and Mediaeval Mazars: With a Note on Jason in Ivory (1156); Spenser and Some Pictorial Conventions: With Particular Reference to Illuminated Manuscripts (1714); and Spenserus (218).

Tuve, Rosemond. Spenser and Mediaeval Mazars; with a Note on Jason in Ivory, SP, 34 (1937), 138-47.   1156

Denies that the mazar in SC (August, l. 26) is a pastoral convention drawn from Theocritus and Virgil. Numerous artfully carved mazars were popular in Sp's day as drinking bowls. Thus Sp made imaginative use of suggestions from other than literary sources. Similarly, for the story of Jason and Medea carved in ivory on the gate of the Bower of Bliss (FQ, II, xii, 44-45), not in Tasso, it is probable that Sp was utilizing another visual source. The story was a fairly common subject for carvings in ivory at this time.

Upham, Alfred Horatio. The French Influence in English Literature from the Accession of Elizabeth to the Restoration. New York: Octagon Books, 1965. 560 pp.   1157

Repr. of the 1908 ed. Areopagus group, Sp's early work, literary associations, Pléiade's influence in England (pp. 25-90); Sp's sonnets and others' (pp. 120 ff.); Du Bartas and Sp (pp. 167-70). Appendix B, Du Bartas and FQ, II, ix (pp. 506-19). For incidental references to Sp, see Index.

Ure, Peter. The Poetry of Sir Walter Ralegh, REL, 1 (1960), 19-29.   1158

Sp gave idealized account in CCCHA of Ralegh's visit to Kilcolman in autumn 1589. Ralegh aware he was living in Age of Sp, but not a Spenserian. Sp in FQ writes as outsider, addresses Queen humbly. Court is Ralegh's own ground, rejects it savagely in The Lie. Poem of disappointment, 500 lines of Cynthia, is Ralegh's counterpart to FQ. "Spenser plays the role of the vassal-bard, Ralegh that of the rejected lover." Ralegh's sonnet printed in 1590 edition of FQ, I-III, celebrates appearance of great work of art, but has "a tragic rather than a joyous air." Same sombre tone in Nature that washed her hands in milk, in which horror of ravaging Time in contrast with Sp's final attitude that "Time itself was only an aspect of revolving change." Another contrast in Sp's Astro and Ralegh's poem on death of Sidney. "Ralegh is more affected by post-medieval melancholy than by Jacobean disillusion." His greatest poem, The Passionate Man's Pilgrimage, is least characteristic, in it "a Spenserian Ralegh, which turns upside down the usual contrast between the two poets." Ra-

legh's vision of a "florid and baroque" heaven draws near Red Cross Knight's vision of New Jerusalem (FQ, I, x).

Valency, Maurice. In Praise of Love: An Introduction to the Love-Poetry of the Renaissance. New York: Macmillan, 1958. 319 pp.   1159

Deals with formative stages of lyric tradition which culminates with troubadours, in Italy with *stilnovisti*, stops with Dante's Vita Nuova. Refers to Sp in connection with view that only those of noble ancestry are capable of virtue; *prodom* of *chansons de geste* is, from sexual point of view, ancestor of Sp's Guyon and Tasso's Rinaldo; troubadour tradition passes to great Renaissance lyricists—line of Petrarch, Tasso, Ronsard, Sp, Shakespeare, and Donne; three centuries after troubadours, Sp considered *losengier* chief enemy of courtier, talebearer who causes lovers in Amor to part, and Blatant Beast (FQ, VI) is "the enemy of true lovers in allegorical shape"; hyperbolic grief of troubadours more restrained in Marot's dirge for Louise de Savoie and Sp's lament for Dido in SC. See Index.

Vallese, Tarquinio. Spenser: Studio critico della poesia di E. Spenser seguito dalla versione a fronte del I Canto del I Libro della *Faerie Queene*. Naples: Raffaele Pironti, 1946. 128pp.   1160

Intended as an introductory guide for students. Introduction has sections on Sp's allegory, his art, sources of FQ, and Spenserian stanza (pp. 9-20). Summarizes each book of FQ and comments on characters, literary resemblances, and allegory (pp. 23-56). Comments on minor poems (pp. 59-79). Text of FQ, I, Proem and i, with Italian translation in Spenserian stanzas on facing pages (pp. 82-

119). Notes and bibliography (pp. 123-8).

Van Dorsten, J.A. Poets, Patrons, and Professors: Sir Philip Sidney, Daniel Rogers, and the Leiden Humanists. Leiden: University Press, 1962. 227 pp.
1161

A study of relations between England and University of Leiden, founded 1575, with emphasis on Sidney and his associates. Discusses Anglo-French literary contacts and SC, English and Dutch antiquarian interests and Sp's View, Dutch literary reform movement similar to earlier efforts of Pléiade in France and later efforts of Sidney, Sp, and their group in England as reflected in Sp-Harvey correspondence, reference to SC in Apologie for Poetrie as "the only contemporary English poem mentioned" by Sidney in it, Sp's Astro on Sidney in Low Countries, and Astro in connection with building "a Sidney-myth . . . representing him as the ideal Christian Knight." For these and other references pertaining to Sp, see Index.

Van Gelder, H.A. Enno. The Two Reformations in the 16th Century: A Study of the Religious Aspects and Consequences of Renaissance and Humanism. The Hague: Martinus Nijhoff, 1961. 406 pp.   1162

In Chap. X, Christian Humanism in England, argues Sp not Puritan because classical mythology of Humanism permeates his thought, but neither was he systematically Christian because he wanted to enjoy earthly life and love, little incorporation of Christian doctrine in works, e.g., "The 'Mutabilitie' of everything on earth is chanted without one Christian thought or image," education of gentleman in FQ emphasizes Aristotelian rather than religious ideals, and elevated view of human dignity long

way from Christian idea of fallen man. More closely allied with Plato, Lucretius, Cicero, Italian poets, and Erasmus than with Established Church of England and Book of Common Prayer (pp. 338-47). Compares and contrasts Sp's religious position with Sidney's and Shakespeare's.

Van Heyningen, Christina. Poet's Poet, Theoria, A Journal of Studies of the Arts Faculty, University of Natal (1950), pp. 93-100.   1163

Sp can be read successfully only by those who have the varied responsiveness and comprehensive perceptiveness of a poet.

Van Tieghem, Paul. Histoire Littéraire de l'Europe et de l'Amérique de la Renaissance à nos Jours. Paris: Colin, 1946. 426pp.   1164

Book I, L'Age de la Renaissance, pp. 1-57. Sp's SC and other minor poems (p. 16). Medieval allegory flowered anew in FQ. Sp is the English Ariosto. Characters have little individuality. One reads Sp for his sumptuous and colorful tableaux, the charm and melody of his stanzas (pp. 24-5).

Van Tieghem, Philippe, ed. Dictionnaire des Littératures. Vol. 3, O-Z. Paris: Presses Universitaires de France, 1968.
1165

Spenser (Edmund), Spensérienne (Strophe), 3696-7; Sp listed under Poète Lauréat, 3082-3.

Vickers, Brian. Classical Rhetoric and English Poetry. London: Macmillan, 1970. 180 pp.   1166

Figures of rhetoric in English poetry between Chaucer and Wordsworth related to emotional effects. Chaps. I and II on history of rhetoric since classical times. Chap. III defines rhetorical figures as "channels of emotional expression," and outlines principles of rhetorical analysis. List of selected figures with illustrations from English poets, including Sp. In last chapter analyzes passages from Sidney, Sp, Shakespeare, and Herbert. Rhetoric of Sp's early poetry stiff, but in FQ it is "a marvellously flexible device." [SpN, Vol. 2, No. 2 (1971), 4.]

Viglione, Francesco. L'Italia nel Pensiero degli Scrittori Inglesi. Milan: Fratelli Bocca, 1946. Piccola Biblioteca di Scienze Moderne, No. 489. 545pp. 1167

Chapter V, La Letteratura dalle Origini alla Restaurazione, pp. 215-301. Sp (pp. 254-8): his British imperialism and anti-Romanism.

Viglione, Francesco. La Poesia Lirica di Edmondo Spenser. Genoa: Emiliano degli Orfini, 1937. 375pp. 1168

Persons of court, church, politics, and literature with whom Sp is associated. Poems in Theatre, RT, and TM discussed in relation to Petrarch, Du Bellay, and others. SC indebted to Sannazaro and Chaucer, but distinctly national and autobiographical elements emphasize Sp's originality. Tradition of satire and VG, MHT, Muiop, CCCHA. Amor in three parts, first two inspired by Elizabeth Boyle and third by Rosalind; spiritual and sensual love, Italian and French sources. Epith and Proth recall Petrarch. 4 Hymns and multiple Neoplatonic sources. Conclusion: Sp's lyric poetry is the product of an eclectic culture which seeks to harmonize, not always happily, antique, medieval, and Renaissance strains; yet it has a distinctly English character. Sp was more comfortable in the epic than the lyric mode.

Vyvyan, John. Shakespeare and Platonic Beauty. London: Chatto & Windus, 1961. 224pp. 1169

Shakespeare's admiration of Sp (p. 12). Sp indebted to Plato, Ficino, and Benivieni (pp. 26, 34). Sp's possible influence on Shakespeare (pp. 59-60, 83-4). Selected stanzas from Sp showing Platonic ideas (pp. 208-12).

Walker, Ralph S. Literary Criticism in Jonson's Conversations with Drummond, English, 8 (1951), 222-7. 1170

Jonson's condemnation of Sp's style, language, and stanza expresses his conviction that style is an index of personal integrity. An artificial language invites hypocrisy, and the demands of a complicated stanza may tempt a poet to change his meaning to meet demands of form. Jonson's conviction that perspicuity is the chief virtue of style gives rise to his objection to Sp's allegory, as requiring exposition instead of carrying its full meaning itself.

Walker, Roy. The Golden Feast: A Perennial Theme in Poetry. New York: Macmillan, 1952. 272 pp. 1171

Theme of Golden Age—Earthly Paradise in contrast to Land of Cockaigne, or Fools' Paradise—from antiquity to English Romantics and American Edens. Much on anthropology and ancient rites; emphasizes vegetarianism as integral in theme. Chaps. 4-5 on English Renaissance (pp. 111-56). In Cave of Mammon and Bower of Bliss (FQ, II, vii, xii) Sp's symbolic technique faulty; his attempt in Garden of Adonis and Temple of Venus (FQ, III, vi; V, vii— [sic] for IV, x) to reconcile spirit and flesh fails. Sp presents "a false antithesis of promiscuity and austerity." Synthesis more successful in Epith. Hospitality of Salvage Man (FQ, VI, iv) "is a sort of refrigerated survival of the Golden Age." Nature's "primal glory" in Mutability Cantos (pp. 116-20). Other references to Sp in connection with Tasso, Shakespeare, and Jonson. No Index.

Wallerstein, Ruth. Studies in Seventeenth-Century Poetic. Madison: University of Wisconsin Press, 1950. 421 pp.   1172

Describes influence of Sp and aureate poetry in poems on death of Prince Henry by James Maxwell, Sir William Alexander, Richard Niccols, Giles Fletcher, and others (pp. 59-67). Dissonant influences of Sp's Christian Platonism and Donne's dialectic in poems on death of Edward King (pp. 96-102); resemblances of Lycidas to Sp's pastoral art and humanist attitudes, and differences (pp. 107-12). Rifts in Sp's neo-Platonism in contrast between Garden of Adonis (FQ, III, vi) and Acrasia's Bower (II, xii) hardly reconcilable (pp. 220-25). Sp and paradox of nature and nurture in relation to Marvell's garden poetry (pp. 272-6).

Ward, A. C. English Literature: Chaucer to Bernard Shaw. London: Longmans, Green, 1958. 781pp.   1173

One-volume ed. without plates of Illustrated History of English Literature, 3 vols., 1953-1955. Survey of Sp's work, pp. 115-27. See 1174.

Ward, A. C. Illustrated History of English Literature. 3 vols. London: Longmans, Green, 1953-1955.   1174

Vol. 1: Chaucer to Shakespeare. Sp, pp. 115-27. See also Index.

Warton, Thomas. History of English Poetry. 4 vols. in 3. New York: Johnson Reprint Corp., 1968.   1175

A facsimile reproduction of the 1774-1781 ed.

Warton, Thomas. A History of English Poetry: an Unpublished Continuation. Ed. Rodney M. Baine. Los Angeles: Augustan Reprint Society, 1953; repr. New York: Kraus, 1967. 24 pp.   1176

Among papers of Thomas and Joseph Warton at Winchester College. This continuation of Thomas's History of English Poetry, touched up by Joseph, completes analysis of Elizabethan satire and discusses Elizabethan sonnet. Treatment of sonnet very brief; no mention of sequences of Sidney, Barnes, Lodge, and Percy (pp. i-iii). Sp's Amor too abstract and philosophical, sonnets show more of scholar than lover. Quotes 15 and 43 (pp. 6-8). Appended is long note on Gabriel Harvey and his relations with Sp (pp. 16-9).

Waters, Daniel Douglas, Jr. Edmund Spenser's Theology. DA, 20 (1960), 4393. Vanderbilt University, 1960. 369 pp.   1177

"Spenser's theology is neither Catholic nor Calvinistic but Anglican with its basis in the Neo-Platonic Protestant scholasticism developed by the humanistic wing of the Huguenot movement in sixteenth century France. His entire emphasis is exactly like that of De Mornay and other Huguenot humanists." See 959, 1194, 1549, 1800, 2243.

Watkins, W. B. C. Johnson and English Poetry before 1660. Princeton: Princeton University Press, 1936. 120pp. 1178

Dr. Johnson knew Elizabethan prose and non-dramatic poetry better than he knew the drama, except Shakespeare. Bacon, Sidney, and Sp were his favorites, frequently quoted in the Dictionary. He thought Sp the peer at least of the great French and Italian poets of the Renaissance.

Watkins, W.B.C. The Kingdom of our Language, HudR, 2 (1949), 343-76.   1179

Reprinted as Chapter 8 of Shakespeare and Spenser, pp. 259-92 (see 1180). Protests against O'Connor's strictures on Sp, Tension and Structure of Poetry, SR, 51 (1943), 555-73 (see 2475). More profitable to consider Sp's poetic craftsmanship in relation to Shakespeare. Technical mastery of Elizabethan age and richness of its poetic language can best be demonstrated by Shakespeare in combination with Sp. Discusses analytically diction of SC, Sp's poetry of direct statement, syntax and narrative style, dramatic couplets of MHT, Sp the satirist as "the Elizabethan Dryden," opening stanzas of Muiop as mockheroic, structure of later style in Mutability Cantos and Proth. Contrasts Sp's comparison of a tree in winter and approaching age in January eclogue of SC with first quatrain of Shakespeare's sonnet 73. In general, Sp a poet of simile and Shakespeare of metaphor. "No poet can fail to profit by a study of Spenser's prosody in all its range."

Watkins, W. B. C. Shakespeare and Spenser. Princeton: Princeton University Press, 1950, 1966; repr. Cambridge, Mass.: Walker-de Berry, 1961. 339 pp.
                                         1180

Essays on Shakespeare's time concept and Mutability Cantos; techniques of allegory and characterization in FQ and Shakespeare; "elaborate maze of the first two interlocked books" of FQ; the marriage theme in FQ and Shakespeare; the pictorial in Sp; Sp's poetic craftsmanship in relation to Shakespeare's (1179). Two other essays concern Shakespeare alone. Notes on high comedy of FQ, II, iii; colors in Sp and Ariosto.

Watson, Elizabeth A. F. Spenser. London: Evans Brothers, 1967. 176 pp.
                                         1181

Wants to remove difficulties in way of enjoying Sp's work (pp. 9-22). Sp's life: family, Richard Mulcaster and Merchant Taylors' School, Cambridge and Sp's Puritanism, Harvey and Sidney, career in relation to literary output (pp. 23-57). Sp as a poet: use of allegory, literary models, influence of

Aristotle, Plato and neo-Platonism, conception of world order and change (pp. 58-85). Chap. on FQ discusses general characteristics of each book (pp. 86-150). Chap. on Sp's other poems emphasizes significance of SC; MHT, "the most direct and powerful of Spenser's satirical works"; CCCHA, sequel to SC; seasonal structure of Amor, brilliance and inventiveness of Epith; 4 Hymns, "by far the most difficult of Spenser's poems" (pp. 151-73). Brief bibliography (pp. 174-5).

Watson, George. The Literary Critics: A Study of English Descriptive Criticism. Baltimore: Penguin Books, 1962. 249 pp.   1182

Three kinds of criticism: legislative; theoretical, or literary aesthetics; descriptive, analysis of literary works (pp. 9-31). Dryden a precursor of descriptive criticism in remarks on Sp's SC, "passing intuition" that "Milton was the poetical son of Spencer" (pp. 33, 59). Johnson thought Sp went wrong in SC, though Thomas Warton's Observations on the Fairy Queene (1754) showed him, on Johnson's admission, importance of Sp's background and sources (pp. 87-8, 105). Warton's work explains how 19th century came to see Sp as romantic visionary, before C. S. Lewis's Allegory of Love (1513) "restored to us a poet of rugged Protestantism and almost muscular Christianity"; Warton's invention of "sensibility" to justify Sp's lack of structure in FQ "is nonsense" (pp. 107-8). C. S. Lewis's Allegory of Love and volume on 16th century (878) show "unexpected vigour" in their respect for "such defunct forms as the Christian epics of Spenser and Milton" (p. 224).

Watson, Sarah Ruth. A Note on Spenser's Uses of the Word "Lee," N&Q, 195 (1950), 448-9.   1183

"Lea" means a piece of ground, or a shelter. "Lee" means either the Irish or the English river.

Wedgwood, C. V. Seventeenth-Century English Literature. London: Oxford University Press, 1950; repr. 1963. 186pp.   1184

Sp's influence on Michael Drayton, Giles and Phineas Fletcher, William Browne, and William Drummond (pp. 48-58).

Weisinger, Herbert. Yet Another Theory of the Renaissance, BuR, 12 (1964), 1-16.   1185

The Renaissance world view is essentially the medieval world view. But pressure of knowledge warps the symmetry of medieval order out of shape. For example, medieval clarity of the symbols of Dante is replaced by the fuzzy allegories of Spenser.

Weiss, Robert H. Primitivism and the Satiric Mode in English Renaissance Verse and Prose (To Spenser's *Prosopopoia*): The Shaping of a Tradition. DAI, 30 (1969), 2504A. Temple University, 1969. 661 pp.   1186

Images of vice and folly in satiric mode require counter-images, almost inevitably, of primitivistic virtue in reaction against civilization and progress. Golden Age or Earthly Paradise subject of ridicule from Aristophanes to Sp, but mockery of primitivistic ideas "requires their emotional and moral appeal." Nostalgia for good old days persists in complaints of Dunbar "and in the more biting ironies of Skelton and Spenser."

Weiss, Wolfgang. Der Refrain in der elizabethansichen Lyrik. Munich: University of Munich, 1964. 109 pp.   1187

Studies use of refrain in ballads and carols, Wyatt's songs, Sidney, Sp, Shakespeare, and Donne. In chapter on Sp (pp. 50-62) discusses refrain in roundelay of August and in dirge of November in SC; artistic function of refrain in Epith, in which it becomes structurally integral.

Wellek, René. The Concept of Baroque in Literary Scholarship, JAAC, 5 (1946), 77-109.   1188

Many-sided study. "Baroque is now used in general cultural history for practically all manifestations of seventeenth century civilization," in contrast to Renaissance. First application of term to 17th-century English literature by German scholars. "To England and America the term . . . came late, much later than the revival of interest in Donne and the Metaphysicals." But it seems likely to spread fast and far. Issues warnings about imprecision of term, overextension by some literary scholars, difficulty of valid definition. Yet "baroque . . . is still the one convenient term which refers to the style which came after the Renaissance but preceded actual Neo-Classicism." Especially important for a history of English literature. Extensive bibliography and documentation. Helps to make intelligible much modern literary criticism concerned with Renaissance writers, including Sp.

Wells, Henry W. New Poets from Old: A Study in Literary Genetics. New York: Russell and Russell, 1964. 356 pp. 1189

Repr. of 1940 ed. A study of "the character, quantity, and worth of our poetical heritage in terms of its active use by our contemporaries." Many references to Sp in chapters on Our Poetic Tradition (pp. 3-29), The Heritage of Technique (pp. 34, 74, 79 ff.), Hereditary Rhythms (pp. 131, 139, 151-2), The Heritage of Form (pp. 175-7, 181 ff., 186-7, 189-95, 200-2), and The Heritage of Spirit (pp. 230 ff.).

Wells, William, ed. Spenser Allusions in the Sixteenth and Seventeenth Centuries. Part I: 1580-1625. SP, 68 (1971), No. 5, pp. 3-172.   1190

In 1931 Sp Group of Modern Language Assn. began preparation of Sp allusion book. Twelve hundred (1200) entries in collection, passages relating to Sp the writer and his works. Usually secondary reference to a modern edition provided, "to indicate the specific passage by Spenser wherever borrowing or imitation is recognized, and to provide necessary explanatory notes." Original spelling and punctuation retained (pp. v-viii). Fifty-nine contributors listed (pp. ix-x). First allusion by Abraham Fraunce, The Sheapheardes Logike (1580-5); last by Sir John Davies prefacing translation of Charles Sovel's The Extravagant Shepherd (Davies writing before 1626). See 1191.

Wells, William, ed. Spenser Allusions in the Sixteenth and Seventeenth Centuries. Part II: 1626-1700. SP, 69 (1972), No. 5, pp. 175-351.   1191

Lists allusions from Peter Heylyn ? (1626) to undated quotation from SC in B. M. MS Sloane 1489 (pp. 175-312). Indexes of Authors and Titles, Allusions to Characters and Passages, and Allusions to Persons Other Than Spenser (pp. 315-51). See 1190.

Wheeler, Harold P. Studies in Sixteenth Century English Literature of Rustic Life. Doctoral diss., University of Illinois, 1939. DDAAU, 1938-39, No. 6.   1192

Relevant for comparison and contrast with Sp's SC, CCCHA, and FQ, VI.

Whitaker, Virgil K. The Mirror Up to Nature: The Technique of Shakespeare's Tragedies. San Marino, Cal.: Huntington Library, 1965. 332 pp.   1193

Idea in Sidney's Apologie for Poetry that literature should teach virtue to youth a common one; compares ll. 19-24 of October in SC (pp. 58-9). Quotes Melpomene in TM on medieval view of tragedy (pp. 71-2). Contrast between painter and poet in Timon of Athens, poet's masterpiece praised as "the kind of word painting that Spenser so often employed for his great allegorical set pieces such as the Bower of Acrasia" in FQ, II, xii (pp. 86-9). Refers to Sp's allegorical presentation of internal conflict in FQ in connection with Romeo's unawareness of imprudence despite Friar Lawrence's reproach (pp. 115-8). Mentions FQ three times in discussion of King Lear (pp. 211, 216, 220).

Whitaker, Virgil K. The Religious Basis of Spenser's Thought. Stanford: Stanford University Press, 1950; repr. Brooklyn, N. Y.: Gordian Press, 1966. 70 pp.   1194

Takes the position that Sp was consistently a conservative Anglican, and that any deviations were Catholic rather than Calvinistic. See 959, 1177, 1549, 1800, 2243.

White, Harold Ogden. Plagiarism and Imitation during the English Renaissance: A Study in Critical Distinctions. New York: Octagon Books, 1965. 209 pp.   1195

Repr. of 1935 ed. See Atkinson, p. 165.

Whitlock, Baird W. The Counter-Renaissance, BHR, 20 (1958), 434-49.   1196

Period lying between High Renaissance of 14th-15th centuries and Baroque of 17th century needs a new label. Proposes term "Counter-Renaissance" for 16th Century (about 1520-1620) and all its developments in art, religion, literature, music, philosophy, government, and science.

Contrasts Castiglione's courtier and Sp's knight as typical of Renaissance and "Counter-Renaissance." "There is little of the spiritual motivation [in Castiglione's courtier] that we find in his Counter-Renaissance counter-part, the 'image of the brave Knight' of Spenser's *Faerie Queene*, which obviously returns to the chivalric ideal. The two heroes are separated by an entire ideological world, the world of the Reformation. Spenser is often described as the ideal union of the Renaissance and the Reformation. Inasmuch as this is so, he fullfills one of the major characteristics of Counter-Renaissance art" (p. 444).

Whitney, Geffrey. A Choice of Emblems. New York: Benjamin Blom, 1967. 434 pp.   1197

Repr. of ed. of Henry Green (1866), with Intro. by Frank B. Fieler (pp. ix-xvii). First pub. Leiden, 1586. Intro. points out "quickening of interest in emblem literature" as "one of the most representative and widespread manifestations of Renaissance sensibility." For Green's references to Sp's use of emblems in SC, VB, and other points, see Index.

Wilkinson, L. P. Ovid Surveyed. Cambridge: University Press, 1962. 484 pp.   1198

Repr. of 1955 ed. titled Ovid Recalled. Description of Cave of Sleep in Metamorphoses XI "is the ancestor of one of the most famous passages in the *Faerie Queene*" (I, i, 39-41): translates Ovid's lines 592-614 into Spenserian stanzas (pp. 184-6). Idea for division of SC into months may have come from Fasti, but its pastoral poetry owes nothing to Ovid (p. 408). Notes Sp's debt to Ovid in Muiop and in FQ (I, i, 7-9; III, vi, and ix-x); but Sp owed more to Virgil in FQ (p. 410). Tapestries in House of Busirane

(FQ, III, xi, 29-49) depict scenes "from the *Metamorphoses* or works derived from it" (pp. 415-16). Whole conception of Milton's Comus in allegorizing tradition of "*Ovide Moralisé*, which comes down to Milton through his admired forerunner, Spenser." But in maturity Milton "too sophisticated, to follow Spenser in carefree blending . . . of pagan and Christian elements" (pp. 430-31).

Williams, Arnold. The Common Expositor: An Account of the Commentaries on Genesis, 1527-1633. Chapel Hill: University of North Carolina Press, 1948. 297pp.   1199

Sp's account of creation in CCCHA, ll. 846-62, mixes Genesis with the Empedoclean concept of Love, or Concord (pp. 49-50, 59). The commentators and the Platonic doctrine of ideas, as reflected in HHOB, ll. 29-32 (pp. 43-5). Theory that angels were created before visible universe adopted in HOHL, ll. 50-6 (p. 62). Sp on the reason for the creation of man and the nature of the soul (House of Alma and Garden of Adonis, FQ, II, ix, and III, vi) in relation to the commentators and Renaissance literature (pp. 71, 76-7).

Williams, Kathleen. Spenser: Some Uses of the Sea and the Storm-tossed Ship, RORD, 13-14 (1970-1971), 135-42.   1200

Iconographic tradition presents the sea as emblem for flux, danger, and death, but with suggestion of fecundity, providential order, and control. Reviews Sp's use of traditional meanings in FQ, especially in stories of Guyon and Britomart (II-V), story of Florimell and Marinell completed in Bk. IV, and story of Amidas and Bracidas in Bk. V. Gives other examples of sea imagery in VP, Amor, MHT, and CCCHA.

Williams, T. G. English Literature: A Critical Survey. London: Pitman, 1951. 316pp.   1201

For the general reader. Pastoral convention and SC (pp. 32-4); quantitative principle of meter (pp. 44-6); Spenserian stanza (p. 54); SC and classical antiquity (pp. 79-80); moral and religious aspects of Renaissance humanism (pp. 85-6); Sp as "the first full expression of Renaissance poetry in England" (pp. 89-91); Elizabethan songs and sonnets (pp. 91-2); Keats's Eve of St. Agnes and Sp (p. 136).

Williamson, George. Mutability, Decay, and Jacobean Melancholy, in Seventeenth Century Contexts. London: Faber and Faber, 1960. 291 pp.   1202

First published 1935. Main cause of 17th-century melancholy, mood of writers from Sp to Milton, concept of decay of nature in late 16th-century astronomical studies. As Burton says in Anatomy of Melancholy, Aristotelian and Ptolemaic notions of universe being exploded by Tycho, Kepler, and Galileo. Case for decay of world stated by Godfrey Goodman, The Fall of Man (1616), answered by George Hakewill, Apologie of the Power and Providence of God (1627); his answer anticipated in Nature's reply to Mutability in Sp's FQ, VII. Sp and Hakewill mingled Lucretian theory of mortality with Ovid's Pythagorean philosophy of change. Decay of world, using astronomical reasons, most explicit in FQ, V, Proem. In Mutability Cantos, Nature declares constancy final victor over mutability; but Sp still disturbed, in two stanzas of Canto viii falls back, in prayerful mood, on "pillours of Eternity." Raleigh's History of the World draws melancholy eloquence from belief in decay of world. Same view expressed by John Donne,

William Drummond, Henry Reynolds, and Thomas Browne.

Wilpert, Gero Von. Lexikon der Weltliteratur. Vol. II, Hauptwerke der Weltliteratur in Charakteristiken und Kurzinterpretationen. Stuttgart: Alfred Kröner, 1968. 1254 pp.   1203

Entries on Sp's SC, FQ, and Epith, with brief bibliographies (pp. 912-3, 293, 255).

Wilson, Elkin Calhoun. England's Eliza. Cambridge, Mass.: Harvard University Press, 1939; repr. New York: Octagon Books, 1966. 479 pp.   1204

A study of the idealization of Queen Elizabeth in the literature of her age. Sp figures prominently in the book (see Index), particularly in Chapter IV, Fayre Elisa, Queene of Shepheardes All, and in Chapter VIII, Gloriana and Belphoebe. The shadows of Elizabeth in FQ "show the inclusiveness of Spenser's idealization—the fullest and richest of all. Gloriana, Una, Mercilla, Belphoebe, and Britomart incorporate all the types of praise which have been studied."

Wilson, F. P. Elizabethan and Jacobean. Oxford: Clarendon Press, 1945. 144pp.   1205

The Alexander Lectures in English delivered at the University of Toronto in 1943. Many references to Sp. "Donne's poetry has a better claim to be called baroque than Spenser's" (p. 26). Injustice has been done both Sidney's Arcadia and FQ because their manner keeps us from appreciating their matter (pp. 51-4). Michael Drayton, "who was both Elizabethan and Jacobean," as the heir of Sidney and Sp (pp. 76-82). See also Index.

Wilson, F. P. The English Drama, 1485-1585. Ed. G. K. Hunter. New York:

Oxford University Press, 1969. 244 pp.
                                    1206

Misleading to call characters in Tudor morality plays abstractions. For example, seven deadly sins real to Elizabethans. When morality play almost dead, Sp described sins in FQ (I, iv) "with a wealth of pictorial detail," and Marlowe introduced them in Doctor Faustus (pp. 74-5). See 1777. Stephen Gosson in Plays Confuted in Five Actions (1582) says many sources ransacked for dramatic material, including medieval chivalric romances. In letter to Sp, Gabriel Harvey fears he may be asked "for sum newe devised interlude, or . . . comedye." Sidney in Apology for Poetry (ca. 1582) ridicules contemporary drama's improbabilities. Arcadia and FQ have improbable incidents, but with "poetical sinnewes" lacking in few surviving plays for professional players. That so few survive no great loss (pp. 118-25).

Wilson, F. P. Marlowe and the Early Shakespeare. Oxford: Clarendon Press, 1953. 144 pp.   1207

Incidental references to Sp. By 1580 nothing in drama comparable to SC (p. 4). True poetry first enters drama with Peele's The Arraignment of Paris (1584), influenced by virtuosity of verse in SC (pp. 9-11). Borrowing in Marlowe's Tamburlaine from FQ, not yet in print (pp. 25-6, and note, p. 133). Marlowe, unlike Shakespeare, used few figures of speech: "We can imagine an E. K. exclaiming at many a passage in Titus Andronicus and Richard III 'a pretty parison and withal a paronomasia': he would have had fewer opportunities in Marlowe" (p. 121).

Wilson, Robert Rawdon. The Problem of Time in the Poetry of Edmund Spenser. DAI, 31 (1971), 5434-A. University of Oregon, 1970. 134pp.   1208

Three independent essays. In "Spenser's Time-sense" discusses fusion in Sp's poetry of differing views of time from Aristotelian, Platonic, Judaic, and Christian traditions. Dominant is "Aristotelian-Christian concept of the fulfillment of human potential in time according to the invariable standards of a timeless eternity." In "Images of Time in the Poetry of Spenser" distinguishes three kinds of imagery: (1) configurational (recurrent patterns related to conceptual substructure); (2) eidetic (solitary images with one or more time concepts, vividly visual); (3) allegoremic (compound images that function as allegorical units). In "The Deformation of Narrative-time in The Faerie Queene" shows that when two characters are separated and reunited, much time has elapsed for one and only a short span for other. Rejects view that time in FQ is "vague" or "dream-like." Distortions function as bonds, or touching surfaces between narrative and allegorical dimensions. See 1745.

Wimsatt, W. K., Jr., and Monroe C. Beardsley. The Concept of Meter: An Exercise in Abstraction, PMLA, 74 (1959), 585-98.   1209

In attempt to clarify "traditional English syllable-accent meter," Seymour Chatman's interpretation of FQ, I, ii, 13, 4-5 (Linguistics, Poetics, and Interpretation: The Phonemic Dimension, OJS, 43 (1957), 254) is cited as evidence that correct understanding and intonation are interdependent. Sp's meter is quickly discernible. February in SC exemplifies "strong-stress" meter. See 1826.

Winbolt, S. E. Spenser and His Poetry. New York: AMS Press, 1971. 157 pp.
                                    1210

Repr. of 1912 ed. For beginning students.

Wind, Edgar. Pagan Mysteries in the Renaissance. New and enl. ed. London: Faber and Faber, 1968. 345 pp.   1211

First pub. 1958. Posture of Sp's Graces (April gloss in SC; FQ, VI, x, 24) explained by Seneca and Servius, the two views "not quite easy to reconcile" (pp. 28-30). Mottos for July in SC express Neoplatonic "union of balance and transcendence" (pp. 47-8). Combination of Thenot's and Hobbinol's emblems in April of SC suggests question "whether the worship of Queen Elizabeth as Diana was not also a cult of Venus in disguise" (pp. 77-8). Quotes FQ, IV, Proem, 3, on antistoical bias of Renaissance Neoplatonism (p. 141). Heroic proportions of Michelangelo's Leda would "dispel the lyricism of a myth which was so beautifully rendered by Spenser," in FQ, III, xi, 32 (pp. 164-5). "Unfolding" of Agape into her three sons (FQ, IV, ii, 41-43) "is no more than a didactic exercise"; but Sp is "quite fearless in tracing the reverse," the "infolding" of Love and Hate in Concord, and Venus, "in whom these contraries are united," is described as Hermaphrodite (FQ, IV, x, 31-36, 41) (pp. 209 ff.). All references to Sp should be studied in Wind's broad context. See Index. See 986, 1078.

Winters, Yvor. The Function of Criticism: Problems and Exercises. Denver: Alan Swallow, 1957. 200pp.   1212

Includes Problems for the Modern Critic of Literature (see 1748), pp. 11-78; and English Literature in the Sixteenth Century, pp. 191-200, ostensibly a review of C. S. Lewis's English Literature in the Sixteenth Century Excluding Drama (see 878).

Winters, Yvor. The 16th Century Lyric in England, Poetry, 53 (Feb., 1939), 258-72; (Mar., 1939), 320-35; 54 (Apr., 1939), 35-51.   1213

A reinterpretation of literary history. The "Petrarchists"—Sidney, Sp, Daniel, Drayton, Greville, and Shakespeare, with Green, Peele, Lodge, Lyly and other lesser figures showing the same influence—are seen as a transitional school linking two periods of mastery. Gascoigne and Ralegh in their "great poems" are the masters of the first period. Greville, Jonson, Donne, and Shakespeare in their poems most closely resembling the work of these two are the best poets of the second period. Taken together, these represent "the major traditon of the century." Of secondary significance are "Sidney, Spenser and the songbooks."

Wion, Phillip Kennedy. The Poetic Styles of Edmund Spenser. DA, 29 (1968), 919A. Yale University, 1968. 184 pp.   1214

Sp's poetic style a mixture of seemingly opposed elements, e.g., artifice and simplicity. Emphasizes ways Sp adapts style to needs of each particular poem. Chapter on diction and word origins. Explores effects of deviations from normal word order, variations in sentence length, rhetorical schemes. Considers Sp's metaphors, abstract and concrete terms. Detailed analysis of passages from Sp's three poetic styles—low, middle, and high.

Wittreich, Joseph Anthony, Jr., ed. The Romantics on Milton: Formal Essays and Critical Asides. Cleveland: Case Western Reserve University, 1970. 594 pp.   1215

Observations drawn from editions, letters, marginalia, lectures, poetry, and prose of Blake, Wordsworth, Coleridge, Lamb, Landor, Hazlitt, Hunt, De Quincey, Byron, Shelley, and Keats. Sp frequently mentioned in general way in association with Milton, most often by Wordsworth,

Coleridge, and Hazlitt. See Index; cf. 1225.

Wolff, Emil. England und die Antike, in Grundformen der Englischen Geistesge-schichte, ed. Paul Meissner, pp. 1-94. Stuttgart: W. Kohlhammer, 1941. 424pp.   1216

In section 3, Humanismus und Puritanismus (pp. 64-80), on Sp and Milton, discusses union of classical and Christian symbols in SC and FQ. Guyon's destruction of Bower of Bliss (FQ, II, xii) reveals "the latent con-flict between the humanistic revival of antiquity and the reforming earn-estness of Christian conviction," a conflict deepened in Milton.

Woodhouse, A.S.P. The Poet and His Faith: Religion and Poetry in England from Spenser to Eliot and Auden. Chi-cago: University of Chicago Press, 1965. 304 pp.   1217

Chap. II, Elizabethan Religion and Poetry: Spenser and Southwell (pp. 11-41). Sp an Anglican poet with Protestant emphasis. Expounds FQ with reference to distinction between nature and grace (see 1752), which would have had to be synthesized if Sp had completed poem; 4 Hymns, Platonically progressive; mentions religious motive coupled with theme of love in Amor. "Protestant religion and national patriotism join forces in his poetry, as they did in Elizabethan England" (pp. 20-36).
Rev: E. D. Mackerness, MLR, 61 (1966), 666; Millar MacLure, UTQ, 36 (1966), 390; R. W. Battenhouse, SAQ, 66 (1967), 126.

Wrenn, C. L. Word and Symbol: Studies in English Language. London: Long-mans, Green, 1967. 197 pp.   1218

Includes On Re-Reading Spenser's *Shepheardes Calender* (2322). The Language of Milton (pp. 114-28). Mil-ton "extremely language conscious"

like Chaucer, Shakespeare, Sp, and Wordsworth. Like Sp especially, Mil-ton determined early to exploit re-sources of native English. As with Sp, three periods in use of poetic lan-guage: youthful experiment, maturi-ty, and finally "deployment of a special diction developed expressly to suit the theme of *Paradise Lost* in his case, as of *The Faerie Queene* in Spenser's." On the Morning of Christ's Nativity, like SC, represents experimentation. Lycidas shows "lin-guistic maturity," as does Epith. Mil-ton finds exact medium he needed in Paradise Lost, "as Spenser in the most poetical passages of *The Faerie Queene* exhibits ... a deliberately sought language of *Faerie* with all its romantic connotations and associa-tions." Illustrates precision of Mil-ton's word choices, such as "rathe" in flower-passage of Lycidas, which fol-lows April of SC and pastoral episode in Shakespeare's The Winter's Tale.

Wright, John. Keats's Endymion as Spen-serian Allegory, AULLA, Proceedings of 9th Congress (1964), 63-4.   1219

Difficulties in interpreting Endy-mion arise from failure to realize Keats using allegorical method of Sp, sometimes general, sometimes partic-ular. Image of main figures constant, though meaning changes. Endymion appears as in love with nature, poetry, and an Indian maid; "he represents the poet on his way to immortality." His Cynthia is nature, muse, mistress; "she offers the complete ecstatic vi-sion."

Wyatt, A. J. History of English Litera-ture. 6th ed. rev. C. W. R. D. Moseley. London: University Tutorial Press, 1965. 315 pp.   1220

Publication in 1579 of North's Plutarch, Lyly's Euphues, and Sp's SC "marks the upward limit of the Eliza-bethan period." General survey of

Sp's works, with emphasis on FQ, for which Sp chose wrong model in Ariosto (pp. 71-82).

Yates, Frances A. Elizabethan Chivalry: The Romance of the Accession Day Tilts, JWCI, 20 (1957), 4-25.   1221

On the custom of the annual tilt held Nov. 17, when Elizabeth's loyal knights jousted before her, and the chivalrous, patriotic, and religious implications of these pageants. Sir Henry Lee was their chief promoter. Sidney describes such a tilt in the Arcadia (Bk. II, chap. 21). Makes several suggestive comments on SC and FQ as further reflections of "the peculiar passion and intensity of Elizabethan chivalry."

Yuasa, Nobuyuki. Spenser's Catalogue of Trees and Flowers and What They Tell Us About His Poetry, Hiroshima Studies in English Language and Literature, 18, No. 2 (1972), 1-18.   1222

Zanco, Aurelio. Storia della Letteratura Inglese: dalle Origini alla Restaurazione, 650-1660. 2nd ed. Torino: Loescher, 1958. 642pp.   1223

Chap. 6, L'Età di Shakespeare (1579-1625), pp. 164-201; Sp, pp. 173-92. Sketch of Sp's life; SC ushers in modern English lyric and shows English language perfect instrument for artistic expression; MHT, RT, TM, View, CCCHA, Amor, Epith, and Proth discussed in literary and biographical context; FQ as romantic

epic, letter to Ralegh, moral and historical allegory, relation to native and foreign literature, poetic technique, imitators.

Zesmer, David Mordecai. Love and Marriage in The Anatomy of Melancholy. DA, 25 (1964), 490. Columbia University, 1961. 408 pp.   1224

Burton, "like Spenser and Milton ... distinguishes chastity, a spiritual condition attainable by the married as well as the unmarried, from virginity, or celibacy. He opposes enforced celibacy because it violates the principle of Christian liberty identified with Milton and Puritan theologians...."

Zimmerman, Dorothy Wynne. Romantic Criticism of Edmund Spenser. DA, 17 (1957), 2602-3. University of Illinois, 1957. 226 pp.   1225

A study of the attitudes toward Sp of Coleridge, Wordsworth, Hazlitt, Lamb, and Hunt. See 1215.

Zitner, S. P. Spenser's Diction and Classical Precedent, PQ, 45 (1966), 360-71.   1226

Criticism of Sp's archaic diction shows lack of critical perspective and failure to consider linguistic context of the poems. Precedents in Homer, Virgil, Ariosto, and Tasso. A mythic-epic poet must use words that are part of the history of the race or culture. Modern readers familiar with lyric tradition wrongly object to Sp's archaisms, part of epic tradition.

The Faerie Queene: General Criticism

Abercrombie, Lascelles. The Idea of Great Poetry. Freeport, N.Y.: Books for Libraries Press, 1961. 232 pp. 1227

Repr. of 1925 ed. Remarks on Sp in Chap. II, Greatness of Form, Refuge and Interpretation (pp. 59-99). FQ "is a serious world, but there is a spell on it . . . that . . . leaves us free to enjoy, simply and equably. Yes, in *The Faery Queene* we can even enjoy moral values!" (pp. 79-82).

Aguzzi, Danilo L. Allegory in the Heroic Poetry of the Renaissance. DA, 20 (1960), 3736-7. Columbia University, 1959. 599 pp. 1228

Traces the tradition in the Renaissance of allegorizing classical heroic poetry, and the importance of Aristotle's Ethics to both poets and critics. "This double tradition of allegorizing as a means and moralizing as an end forms the background of Spenser's *Faerie Queene*." Moral allegory similar to Sp's was common in Italian epic poetry in the 16th century. Counter-Reformation epic poets were trying to outline the new ideal hero: the gentleman. Sp uses allegorical methods in a more consistent and orderly way than did the Italian poets. FQ is a cosmopolitan poem, the culmination of cultural strains found throughout Renaissance Europe.

Allen, Don Cameron. The Degeneration of Man and Renaissance Pessimism, SP, 35 (1938), 202-27. 1229

One of the basic causes of pessimism was the body of conflicting philosophies uncovered by the new learning. Perturbation over the degeneration of man and the universe and the resulting pessimism found its primary poetic expression in FQ: Despair passage (I, ix); decline since the Golden Age (IV, viii, 29-33, and V, Proem); and Mutability Cantos.

Alpers, Paul J. Narrative and Rhetoric in *The Faerie Queene*, SEL, 2 (1962), 27-46. 1230

The rhetorical mode of FQ is continually directed toward eliciting a response from its readers, and therefore simplistic readings of the work create inconsistencies through attempts to mold the allegorical structure into an ordered whole.

Alpers, Paul J. The Poetry of *The Faerie Queene*. Princeton: Princeton University Press, 1967. 415 pp. 1231

Aims "to bring *The Faerie Queene* into focus—to enable the ordinary reader and student to trust Spenser's verse, and scholars and critics to agree on what the realities of the poem are and on the ways in which it is profitable to discuss them." Part I analyzes verse and narrative, emphasizing poet's manipulation of reader's response and discontinuity of various parts of the poem outside limits of single cantos; Part II considers historical and iconographical materials as aids to reading. Part III applies assertions of Part I and II to a reading of Bks. I and III. [Diss., Harvard University, 1958.]

Rev: William Nelson, RenQ, 21 (1968), 486; R. L. Montgomery, CLS, 5 (1968), 494; Harry Berger, Jr., MLQ, 30 (1969), 135; M. Evans, RES, 20 (1969), 333; K. Williams, JEGP, 68 (1969), 171. See 954, 1302, 1412.

Alpers, Paul J. Review Article: How to Read *The Faerie Queene*, EIC, 18 (1968), 429-43; repr. in 756.   1232

On Donald Cheney's Spenser's Image of Nature (1310). Praises Cheney for accepting the ambiguity and shifting perspectives of FQ, and for close analysis; but condemns the book for rigid interpretations and "distortion of details in the interest of a previously determined point of view or argument."

Alvarez, A. The Savage God: A Study of Suicide. London: Weidenfeld & Nicolson, 1971. 249 pp.   1233

Traces ways in which attitudes to suicide have changed through the ages. Section devoted to literary bearings of suicide deals with power exerted by idea of suicide on Dante, Sp, Donne, Shakespeare, Burton, Cowper, English Romantic poets, and others.

Alves, Robert. Sketches of a History of Literature (1794). Introduction by Patrick O'Flaherty. Gainesville, Fla.: Scholars' Facsimiles and Reprints, 1967.   1234

FQ, pp. 112-3.

Anonymous. MS Notes to Spenser's Faerie Queen, N&Q, N.S. 4 (1957), 509-15.   1235

Discussion of marginal notes in a copy of Ponsonby's FQ, Books IV-VI, 1596, in the Cambridge University Library. Notes were apparently made within a generation or two after publication. Many of them have to do with political allegory of Book V.

Archer, Susan Mary. Hawthorne's Use of Spenser. DA, 28 (1967), 1424A. University of Pennsylvania, 1967. 326 pp.   1236

Studies Hawthorne's "use" of Sp rather than any influence he may have received. Examines Hawthorne's literary technique in (1) use of allegory, (2) treatment of Puritanism, and (3) concept of romance, and compares these with Sp's technique in FQ. Concludes that Hawthorne uses many allegorical devices used in FQ: emblems, iconographical "speaking picture," personification, and ambivalence. Both writers avoid theological disputes. Hawthorne's concept of romance was not derived from 19th century romanticism or the Gothic tradition, but from the concept of medieval romance used by Sp.

Arestad, Sverre. Spenser's *Faery* and *Fairy*, MLQ, 8 (1947), 37-42.   1237

Clarification of the two senses in which Sp uses the term in FQ. It means both "human" and "fairy," that is, of supernatural origin. Emphasis on the latter meaning has led to misunderstanding. Sp's "Faery Land" is clearly Elizabethan England, presented in a context of moral allegory.

Armens, Sven. Archetypes of the Family in Literature. Seattle: University of Washington Press, 1966. 264 pp.   1238

Treats the Oresteia, Theban plays of Sophocles, Hamlet and King Lear. "Obviously my commentary is Jungian in orientation" (p. vii). Duessa (FQ, I) is Archetypal Temptress of Red Cross, the Youthful Hero, but Una, the Good Mother, brings him to "a certain ancient manor . . . an elaborate allegorical version of the Physical Hearth" (x), where "a transformation mystery occurs" (pp. 29-31). The Good Mother is the Faerie

Queene, Una, Britomart, "and the hope of marital love . . . as one of the ultimates of the Hero's quest" (pp. 44-5). The Statesman-Hero also a form of the Savior Hero, "patriarchy's last hope against the onslaught of Spenser's proud *Titanesse*, MUTABILITIE, who seeks absolute sovereignty over men and their gods. . . . [This] echoes the doom of a damning Original Sin" (pp. 91-2, 241). Cordelia, among other things, represents "as in Spenser, the frequent identification of love with divine virtue" (p. 185).

Armstrong, John. The Paradise Myth. London: Oxford University Press, 1969. Illus. 153 pp.   1239

Suggestive for mythic and iconographic approaches to FQ. Tries to unify imaginatively tree and snake in Sumerian and Greek myth and sculpture, Botticelli's Primavera (especially concerned with figure of Mercury), Shakespeare's Antony and Cleopatra (the snake), The Winter's Tale (the tree), and The Tempest ("the final return of power to its elemental origin"), Giorgione's La Tempestà and The Finding of Paris, Bellini's Sacred Allegory, Milton's Paradise Lost, and Coleridge's The Ancient Mariner and Kubla Khan. In tradition of "imaginatively supine poetic and visual treatments of the ideal enclave . . . even though they may take on the semblance of energy and depth from allegorical and Neoplatonic trappings," are Cologne Paradise-Garden and Sp's Garden of Adonis in FQ, III, vi (pp. 102-3).

Arthos, John. On the Poetry of Spenser and the Form of Romances. London: Allen and Unwin, 1956; repr. New York: Books for Libraries, 1970. 207 pp.   1240

Relying extensively on medieval literature and Italian Renaissance poets and critics, surveys the tradition of romance to show that FQ in its general scheme exemplifies the pattern of the knightly quest. This gives the poem unity; it is not a mixture of two or more classical or nonclassical forms.

Ashley, Leonard R. N. Spenser and the Ideal of the Gentleman, BHR, 27 (1965), 108-32.   1241

Sp's ideal gentleman in FQ combines ideal of Elyot and Castiglione with that of neo-medieval knight. Must be of gentle birth, choosing his ancestors carefully, but self-help also helps; educated in Renaissance curriculum, not scholarly, however, but soldierly; grounded in basic truths of his religion, reconciling Aristotle and Christ (what Cornelius Agrippa and Erasmus said was impossible); practioner of friendship and love on cosmic scale, just, clement, civil, courteous, Magnanimous. Sp's knights "are too dedicated to be nonchalant. . . . They are more likely to commit a good deed than to toss off a *beau geste*." Sp's ideal composite: one-fourth Castiglione's courtier, more than half warring Christian knight, whole "not quite in line with the contemporary English ideal."

Ashton, John W. Folklore in the Literature of Elizabethan England, JAF, 70 (1957), 10-15.   1242

Part of Folklore in Literature: A Symposium, ibid., pp. 1-24. Elizabethan literature blends "the literary impulse and the native and derived folk material." Folk expression in literature may be casual, "or it may be . . . the very core of a substantial and extended masterpiece like the *Fairy Queen*." Sp's poem is "one of the greatest repositories of folk materials." Much of it "stems ultimately from popular story: St. George and the dragon, transformations, black and white magic, spells and ointments of magical powers, numberless figures and monsters out of classical mythology, a whole nightmarish zoo of creatures." Sp makes his folk materials an integral part of the whole work.

Atabay, Ercüment. Büyük Ingiliz Destanlari [The Great English Epics], Yenitürk, 10 (1942), 6-9.   1243

On FQ.

Atchity, Kenneth John, ed. Eterne in Mutabilitie: The Unity of *The Faerie Queene*. Essays Published in Memory of Davis Philoon Harding 1914-1970. Hamden, Conn.: Shoe String Press, 1972. 209 pp.   1244

Ten student essays, not listed individually herein, using different approaches find FQ unified. (1) Judith Cramer, Motif and Vicissitude in FQ, compares quest motif to Beethoven's last piano sonata, Opus 111. (2) Susan C. Fox, Eterne in Mutabilitie: Spenser's Darkening Vision, finds books related by progressive disillusionment. (3) Janet Gezari, Born to Live and Die, sees creative love at center of epic. (4) Gerald Grow, Form or Process? says process of experiencing FQ is its essence. (5) Jean McMahon Humez, "This Richly Patterned Page," emphasizes sense of poem's final resolution. (6) Paula Johnson, Literary Perception in FQ, applies criteria for satisfying form—closure, balance, coherence, resolution—and maintains poem is complete. (7) Susanne Murphy, Love and War in Spenser's FQ, uses duality of values in Petrarch's Secretum Meum to make perpetual openendedness chief significance of Sp's poem. (8) John E. O'Conner, Prince Arthur: The Cohesive Tempering Grace, finds Arthur link between virtues and basis of unity. (9) Richard Pindell, The

Mutable Image: Man-in-Creation, says mutability itself, forever creating new out of old without loss, is unifying principle. (10) Sherry L. Reames, Prince Arthur and Spenser's Changing Design, says six books of FQ fall into various patterns, finds unity in relationships between books.

Baker, Carlos. Literary Sources of Shelley's *The Witch of Atlas*. I. Spenser and *The Witch of Atlas*, PMLA, 56 (1941), 472-9.   1245

Parallels from FQ and other poems.

Baker, Carlos. Spenser, the Eighteenth Century, and *Queen Mab*, MLQ, 2 (1941), 81-98.   1246

Earliest indication of Shelley's knowledge of FQ. The poem owes most to the eighteenth century, particularly the Spenserian allegory of neoclassical poetry.

Baldwin, T. W. The Genesis of Some Passages which Spenser Borrowed from Marlowe, ELH, 9 (1942), 157-87. 1247

Examines in detail seven parallels, already known, between Tamburlaine and FQ. Shows how Marlowe may have put together creatively words and images from a variety of commonly accessible Elizabethan reference books. Sp does not use the same images creatively but takes them from Marlowe as bits of unassimilated ornament. Sp need not have seen a manuscript of the unpublished play; he could have seen a commonplace book of quotations gathered from the manuscript. Because these borrowings occur early in FQ, suggests late 1587 or early 1588 for the compositon of Books I and II. See 1248, 1467, 1730.

Baldwin, T. W. The Genesis of Some Passages which Spenser Borrowed from Marlowe, ELH, 12 (1945), 165.   1248

A reply to W. B. C. Watkins, ibid., 11 (1944), 249-65 (see 1730); reiterates his original view, ibid., 9 (1942), 157-87 (see 1247, 1467).

Baldwin, T. W. On the Literary Genetics of Shakespeare's Plays, 1592-1594. Urbana: University of Illinois Press, 1959. 562 pp.   1249

Examines the plays written between 1592 and 1594 in relation to contemporary literature, dramatic and non-dramatic. Among sources of anonymous Selimus were Sidney's Arcadia and Sp's FQ (pp. 223-4). See Index.

Barber, Richard. Arthur of Albion: An Introduction to the Arthurian Literature and Legends of England. London: Barrie and Rockliff, 1961. 218 pp. 1250

Surveys historical background, growth of the myth, and literary treatments in England to modern times. Sp's Arthur (pp. 137-8) a mixture of Lord Berners's lover (Arthur of Little Britain), seeking a fairy mistress met in a dream, with the Arthur imagined by patriotic antiquarians; an idealized hero rather than a specific character.

Barkan, Leonard. Elementated Man: Studies in the Metaphor of the Human Body. DAI, 32 (1972), 6365A. Yale University, 1971. 441 pp.   1251

Reviews analogies between the universe and the human body in selected works from Plato's Timaeus to Donne's Devotions. Sp's House of Alma (FQ, II, ix) cited as example of tension between man's harmonious place in cosmos and his internal multiplicity. FQ is in endless flux between the One and the Many. Red Cross must recognize the multiple body of evil before he can grasp his own oneness. Bk. III subjects love to corporeal multiplication. Bk. IV reinfolds these diversities by a unifying

but physical act of love. "The whole poem points outward toward a physical reunification via a larger, external human body."

Barnum, Priscilla H. Elizabethan "Psychology" and Books I and II of Spenser's Faerie Queene, Thoth, 3 (1962), 55-68.   1252

Establishment of correspondences between Redcrosse and the Vegetative soul, Guyon and the Sensible soul, and Arthur and free will, an aspect of the Intellective soul, provides the structure of Bks. I and II of FQ. This tripartite division of the soul, a common tenet of Elizabethan psychology, mirrors the triadic nature of man: the division of body, soul, and mind or spirit.

Bartlett, Ruth. Life is an Allegory: A Study of the Spenserian Elements in "Eve of St. Agnes," by Keats, Studies (Kobe College), 6 (1959), 1-7.   1253

Baybak, Michael, Paul Delany, and A. Kent Hieatt. Placement 'In the Middest' in The Faerie Queene," PLL, 5 (1969), 227-34; repr. in 756.   1254

Authors identify a series of symbolically central passages which fall within the range of certain numerically "middle" stanzas in the 1590 FQ. These materials can be useful in indicating the direction of the narrative. These arithmetical locations were somewhat offset by variations in the 1596 edition.

Beer, Gillian. The Romance. London: Methuen, 1970. 88 pp.   1255

Romance is European form, e.g., Chrétien and Ariosto. Element of enromancier in achievement of Malory and even Sp. Until after Sp romance was still dominant form of fiction, in verse as often as in prose (pp. 5-7). Powerful impulse toward passivity felt in romances: Sp "showed how such enclosed and quietist images of bliss ... can also become the cave of despair" (FQ, I, viii); Bower of Bliss (FQ, II, xii) very seductive, but delusory. Chivalric romance survived in Elizabethan pageants and shows; ceremonial allegory in FQ drew upon this fashion. Playfulness in midst of splendor penetrates work of Sp, which draws on strong native romance tradition sophisticated by familiarity with Italian romance epic. In both Sidney and Sp idealization encourages heroic activity. In FQ, III, xii, "the false ideal of Cupid is expressed through mask and show"; true ideal is noble reciprocity in love—only in 1590 FQ. Spenserian stanza "formally expresses the controlled intricacy of romance" (pp. 29-37).

Belson, Joel Jay. Escaped Faults in the Spenser Concordance, AN&Q, 8 (1970), 69-72.   1256

All references pertain to FQ. "The most serious errors are errors of omission, and the most serious of these is the omission of the entire four line argument at the beginning of V. ix."

Belson, Joel Jay. The Names in *The Faerie Queene*. DA, 25 (1965), 7239-40. Columbia University, 1964. 424 pp.
1257

Contains over 200 separate articles, each devoted to one name. These articles " 'expound' a name in terms of words or names to which it seems similar in order to show the appropriateness of the name to its bearer." Assumes "that names which identify characters playing several allegorical roles have themselves several significances," and that meanings irrelevant to the apparent meaning of the text should be held in abeyance until further understanding of the text reveals their relevance. Primary functions of

names discussed are to identify (1) their bearers' major characteristics and (2) the themes especially relevant at the point where the names occur. Secondary functions: to stress links between characters (the Sans brothers), to relate similar ideas (Sans Joy and Despair), and to add to sense of mystery of the "dark conceit." See 1277.

Bender, John B. Spenser and Literary Pictorialism. Princeton: Princeton University Press, 1972. 218 pp.   1258

Examines Sp's poetry as imitation of cognitive process of visualization, i.e., it transmits "the author's active encounter with visual phenomena as they are puzzled out, interpreted and ordered by the mind." Argument developed in terms of three techniques: focusing (dwelling on a single image or detail), framing (excluding elements outside the area of concern), and scanning (shattering our impressions of Faerie Land, reorganizing them, and juxtaposing them). [Doctoral diss., Cornell University, 1967.] [SpN, Vol. 3, No. 3 (1972), 1-3.]

Benjamin, Edwin B. A Borrowing from the *Faerie Queene* in *Old Mortality*, N&Q, N. S. 4 (1957), 515.   1259

Scott's description of Habbakuk Mucklwrath in Old Mortality (Chapter 22) seems to borrow from Despair (I, ix) and Mammon (II, vii).

Bennett, J. A. W. The Parlement of Foules: An Interpretation. Oxford: Clarendon Press, 1957. 217pp.   1260

Chapter III, Nature and Venus (pp. 107-33), discusses in detail Nature and Venus in Chaucer and Sp, "Chaucer's ... greatest disciple," citing Mutability Cantos (FQ, VII), Bower of Bliss (FQ, II, xii), and Garden of Adonis (FQ, III, vi) (pp. 112-21). FQ, VII, vii, 5 and 9 quoted as epigraph at beginning of chapter. See also Index.

Bennett, Josephine W. Britain Among the Fortunate Isles, SP, 53 (1956), 114-40.   1261

On the locale and implications of Sp's fairyland. "His concept of fairyland is easy enough to understand if we place it in perspective with the Platonic doctrine of Ideas as that doctrine was understood in his day and with the tradition that England was one of the Fortunate Isles, or Islands of the Blest." Fused with these notions was the serious belief among English Protestants that the English reformed church fulfilled the prophecies of the New Jerusalem. Thus fairyland is England itself, the Fortunate Isle and New Jerusalem, seen by the timeless light of eternity.

Bennett, Josephine W. Genre, Milieu, and the "Epic-Romance," EIE, 1951, pp. 95-125. New York: Columbia University Press, 1952.   1262

Suggests that in assessing Sp's purpose in writing FQ, more insight can be attained by regarding the poet as a Protestant Dante than by trying to fit the poem into "the non-existent genre of the 'epic-romance'."

Bennett, Josephine Waters. The Evolution of The Faerie Queene. Chicago: University of Chicago Press, 1942; repr. New York: Burt Franklin, 1960. 299pp. 1263

Deals with problem of structure of FQ from point of view of actual process of composition, which was not seriatim, surveying in 16 chapters structure of whole work and of each book in relation to Sp's use of his sources and his conduct of the narrative. Chapters 17, 18, and 19 recapitulate. Throws searching light on each narrative segment, theme, and character. Three appendices analyze poem by episodes, discuss importance

of enjambment test, and comment on Sp's use of compound words.

Bennett, Josephine Waters. The Rediscovery of Sir John Mandeville. New York: Modern Language Association, 1954. 436pp.   1264

Mandeville, rather than Tasso, is suggested by the artificial vines and birds in Acrasia's garden (FQ, II, xii); and by the physical features of the giant who seizes Amoret (FQ, IV, vii) (pp. 248-9).

Berek, Peter. The Transformation of Allegory from Spenser to Hawthorne. Amherst: Amherst College Press, 1962. 48 pp.   1265

Part I, The Allegory of Certainty: Spenser and Bunyan. II, The Allegory of Doubt: Samuel Johnson and Hawthorne. Sp's ideas "public quantities," truths available to private reader. In FQ two worlds coexist: that of Romance, narrative fact, and that of dialectic, abstract "meaning." World of Romance illustrated through disrobing of Duessa (I, vii, 47) and Glauce's consolation of Britomart (III, ii, 34); world of dialectic through procession in House of Busirane (III, xii, 14) and healing of Redcrosse (I, x, 24). Paridell-Hellenore-Malbecco story links romance and dialectic. Allegory of Pilgrim's Progress, like Sp's, "objective," its doctrine public property; Rasselas presents Johnson's personal attitudes. Hawthorne's allegory visionary; presents not corporate beliefs as in FQ and Pilgrim's Progress, which he grew up with, or own personal beliefs (Rasselas), but "the psyche of the author," making interpretation much more difficult.

Berger, Harry, Jr. Archaism, Immortality, and the Muse in Spenser's Poetry, YR, 58 (1969), 214-31.   1266

Sp writes a poetry of process which exemplifies evolution in human life and society. The three sages in Alma's castle (FQ, II, ix) represent faculties corresponding to this process. Reference also to TM (p. 230).

Berger, Harry, Jr. At Home and Abroad with Spenser, MLQ, 25 (1964), 102-9.
                                                1267

A review article on Hough's Preface to The Faerie Queene (1449) and Nelson's Poetry of Edmund Spenser (961). Praises Nelson for skill in showing how FQ and the minor poems illuminate one another; disparages Hough for lack of knowledge of recent developments in Sp criticism, which have made needless Hough's efforts to rehabilitate the poem for modern reader.

Berger, Harry, Jr. The Renaissance Imagination: Second World and Green World, CentR, 9 (1965), 36-78.   1268

Discusses complex relation between Neoplatonic idealism and poetry (fiction), often confused with each other; Northrop Frye's green world as second world created by poet, and Meyer Abrams' *heterocosm* (second nature or second world) created by poet; Alberti's idea in On Painting of emulating and replacing *natura naturans*; this technique in More's Utopia. "Plato treats Critias and his Atlantis very much as More treats Hythloday and his Utopia, as Spenser treats Faerie, Sidney poetry and Shakespeare the green world. All are useful only if they proclaim their hypothetical status . . . literal existence not in space or time but solely, as Spenser put it, 'deepe within the mynd'."

Berger, Harry, Jr. Spenser's Gardens of Adonis: Force and Form in the Renaissance Imagination, UTQ, 30 (1961), 128-49.   1269

Movement from Bk. V to Bk. VI reflects transformation from objective

to reflective view of the world in which the poet himself replaces myth. Movement is from chaos to ordered thought; from reality of contemporary life to artificiality of symbolic forms in Mt. Acidale episode and Mutabilitie Cantos.

Bergeron, David S. C. M. English Civic Pageantry, 1558-1642. Columbia, S.C.: University of South Carolina, 1971. 325 pp.   1270

Metaphor, symbol, and didactic purpose united in royal progresses, royal entries, and Lord Mayor's shows of Elizabethan, Jacobean, and Caroline periods. In such an atmosphere Sp's FQ was a natural growth. Civic pageants employed several of Sp's themes. For specific references, see Index. See 519.

Bernheimer, Richard. Wild Men in the Middle Ages: A Study in Art, Sentiment, and Demonology. Cambridge, Mass.: Harvard University Press, 1952. 224pp.   1271

Satyrane (FQ, I, vi) and "the salvage man" (FQ, VI, iv-vii) belong to the tradition of the wild man. "Medieval literature and art are shot through with the mythology of the wild man: we find him in the clipped verses of French Arthurian romance, in the epics of German minstrel singers, and in the writings of Cervantes and Spenser" (p. 2). Inquires into the psychology and sociology of the figure, combining the methods of folklore, mythology, and the history of art and literature. With 50 illustrations. See Index for Sp references. See 1363, 1392.

Beutner, Sister Mary Louise. Spenser and the Emblem Writers. Doctoral diss., St. Louis University, 1941. MA, 4 (1943), 115-6.   1272

A study of relationships between FQ and Emblem-books. Defines emblems and Emblem-books, shows "Spenser's knowledge of this genre . . . in his interest in and close association with writers and works in the genre." Surveys iconologies, vision literature, and works of better known Emblematists, and cites analogous passages in FQ to establish that "Spenser wrote in what is termed the 'Emblem-book frame of mind'."

Bezanker, Abraham. An Introduction to the Problem of Allegory in Literary Criticism. DA, 15 (1955), 815-6. University of Michigan, 1955. 231 pp.
                                    1273

Alternative to defective approaches to allegory of Benedetto Croce, C. S. Lewis, and H. F. Dunbar is Geistesgeschichte method of analysis used by Ernst Cassirer in Das mythische Denken. Expounds this method and finds it applicable to four medieval allegories: The Castle of Love, Anti-Claudianus, The Battle of the Seven Arts, and The Quest of the Holy Grail. Applies same method to some Renaissance views of Biblical allegory, showing increased "freedom to allegorize." Suggests correlation between literary allegory and Biblical allegory in Renaissance period along with changed standard of valid interpretation as possible solution of one of the special problems of literary criticism. Background for Sp's method in FQ.

Black, J. B. The Reign of Elizabeth, 1558-1603. Oxford: Clarendon Press, 1936. 448pp. 2nd ed., 1959.   1274

Chapter 8, Literature, Art and Thought (pp. 239-84). Sp, pp. 240, 246-8. FQ is "the most remarkable poem of the age."

Bland, D. S. Shakespeare and the "Ordinary" Word, ShS, 4 (1951), 49-55. 1275

Contrasts two verbally similar passages in Sp and Shakespeare: FQ, I, v, 2, 1-5 and 3 Henry VI, II, i, 21-4.

Shakespeare's word "younker" is his distinguishing mark. Together with "prancing," it gives a liveliness to his lines that Sp's lack. Goes on to illustrate Shakespeare's fondness for the "ordinary" word that sets him apart from his contemporaries.

Blissett, William. Florimell and Marinell, SEL, 5 (1965), 87-104.   1276

Although Sp's account of Florimell and Marinell in FQ, III and IV, parallels myths of Adonis and Proserpine, departures from these myths make Sp a "myth-maker" in his own right.

Blitch, Alice. Etymon and Image in The Faerie Queene. DA, 26 (1966), 4652A. Michigan State University, 1965. 274 pp.   1277

Etymology of primary importance in Sp's writing of FQ. Etymons suggested myths or led to creation of myth. Etymology and imagery are causally related. Etymology influenced conception of Guyon, Amoret and Scudamore, Timias and Belphoebe, Artegall, and Calidore. Sp derived images from multiple etymologies for most characters in each book. See 1257.

Blitch, Alice F. The Mutability Cantos "In Meet Order Ranged," ELN, 7 (1970), 179-86.   1278

Debates the intended location of Cantos within FQ. Reviews diverse methodology used by scholars in seeking a solution: prosodic analysis, external evidence, and thematic evidence. Employing an "etymological clue," concludes that Mutability Cantos may be placed "with their present numbering, into an early version of the third book: 'The Legend of Sir Peridure, or of Constancy'."

Bloom, Edward A. The Allegorical Principle, ELH, 18 (1951), 163-90.   1279

Allegory presents at least two meanings: primary or surface, and secondary or abstract. Discusses critical attitudes toward it as literary mode in classical, medieval, Renaissance, and recent times. Sir John Harington's views in Brief Apology for Poetry (1591) prefacing his translation of Orlando Furioso are representative. "Allegory . . . was a valuable tool for those Renaissance and Elizabethan critics and authors who insisted upon the moral utility of poetry and who regarded the imaginative elements as mere adjuncts for the purpose of making more palatable the didactic elements" (pp. 166-7). Hence the position of Sidney and the practice of Sp. Reviews perennial objections to allegory, e.g., Samuel Johnson's. Concludes by placing Dante, Bunyan, Hawthorne, Melville, and Kafka as allegorists above Sp, Swift, George Orwell, and Norman Mailer. The latter writers have been concerned with essentially topical and less universal matters than have the first group (p. 190).

Bloom, Harold. The Daemonic Allegorist. VQR, 47 (1971), 477-80.   1280

Review article on Fletcher's The Prophetic Moment (1362). Rhapsodical appreciation of Fletcher's learning, fecundity of ideas, and sympathy with Sp's poetic creation. Fletcher's special contribution is to show why FQ was so influential on later English poets: he was a true prophet, a seer of the highest order.

Bonadeo, Alfredo. The Function and Purpose of the Courtier in The Book of the Courtier by Castiglione, PQ, 50 (1971), 36-46.   1281

Proposes a compromise between views that art of Courtier leads to civil values through spiritual virtue and that aim of the Courtier is self-centered: ideal of Castiglione is achieved through reputation Courtier

acquires by display of his qualities, and through mystical state of grace which compensates for lack of moral and political wisdom. Castiglione's career is ironic footnote to his treatise. [SpN, Vol. 2, No. 2 (1971), 10.]

Boss, Judith E. The Golden Age, Cockaigne, and Utopia in The Faerie Queene and The Tempest, GaR, 26 (1972), 145-55.   1282

Three Utopian traditions in Renaissance correspond to three parts of human psyche: bestial, normal, and rational. Sp uses concept of Golden Age as recurrent contrast to struggles against evil in FQ, e.g., shepherds' community in Bk. VI; antithetical idea of Cockaigne or sensual paradise has analogues in House of Pride (FQ, I, iv), Phaedria's Isle (I, vi), Cave of Mammon (II, vii), and Bower of Bliss (II, xii); philosopher's Utopia represented by Gloriana's city of Cleopolis, earthly counterpart of New Jerusalem. In The Tempest, Cockaigne embodied in villains, Golden Age in Gonzalo's ideal commonwealth, and Utopia in regenerated society governed by Prospero, who must acknowledge, like Sp's shepherds (FQ, VI, x), evil in fallen world and rational man's duty to control his own and others' passions. [SpN, Vol. 3, No. 3 (1972), 10.]

Both, Willy Hans. Aristotelisches Gedankengut in Spensers Faerie Queene. Doctoral diss., University of Hamburg, 1940. 84pp. JdH 1941, p. 203.   1283

Illustrates virtues and their opposites in FQ in accordance with Aristotle's idea of virtue as a mean between two extremes of excess and deficiency, and in same order in which they appear in Nichomachean Ethics. Some representative examples given: courage in Arthur, cowardice in Terwin, temperance in Guyon and Medina, passion in Amavia, self-indulgence in Acrasia's victims, liberality in Guyon, prodigality in Mammon, avarice in Malbecco, good temper in Calidore, irascibility in Turpine, truthfulness in Calidore, boastfulness in Crudor, shame in Amoret, justice in Artegal, wisdom in Canace, incontinence in Pyrochles, friendship in Arthur-Timias and Calidore-Tristram and Cambell-Triamond.

Bowra, C. M. From Virgil to Milton. London: Macmillan, 1967. 248 pp.   1284

Repr. of 1st ed. 1945. Incidental references to Sp, mostly in contrast to Virgil, Camões, Tasso, and Milton. See Index.

Bradner, Leicester. Edmund Spenser and *The Faerie Queene*. Chicago: University of Chicago Press, 1948. 190pp.   1285

An effort to rehabilitate FQ for the educated general reader, but especially useful to students. After chapters on Sp's world-view, his life, and his poetic technique in SC, there follow chapters of running summary and commentary on The Narrative Poet (FQ, III-V), The Allegorist (FQ, I-II), Pastoralism Glorified (FQ, VI), and Mutability, with a final chapter on The Poet of Love pointing out that "To Spenser love was the central force of the universe," and a Conclusion stating Sp's relevance for the modern world.

Braude, Nan. Tolkien and Spenser, Mythlore, 1 (1969), 8-13.   1286

The Lord of the Rings frequently compared, with some justification, to Ariosto, Malory, and Wagner; with less justification, to Sp. (Writer's dissertation director, Paul Alpers, refuses to read Tolkien despite her efforts to persuade.) Tolkien's epic and Sp's have in common (1) motif of the quest, although in Tolkien "it is a quest-in-reverse, to lose rather than to find something," and in Sp "it is a quest-within-a-quest"; (2) "the narrative pattern of *entrelacement*, or interlacing"; and (3) "the admixture of the marvelous with ordinary daily reality." Differences: (1) The Lord of the Rings is prose epic, easy to read, while FQ is a poetic epic, "complex, indirect, elaborate, ornate," and to read it requires "a specialized skill, like riding a bicycle," which can be acquired by reading The Poetry of *The Faerie Queene*, by Paul Alpers; (2) the intention—"Tolkien is telling you a story; Spenser is showing you how to live."

Briggs, K. M. The Anatomy of Puck: An Examination of Fairy Beliefs Among Shakespeare's Contemporaries and Successors. London: Routledge and Kegan Paul, 1959. 284 pp.   1287

Sp used the fays of romance for his allegory, but they were already a little bookish and enervated. They are not kin to the still vital country fairies of Elizabethan England (p. 6). The fairylands of his followers Drayton and Browne belong to rural tradition, and are truer to folklore (pp. 56-65). Sp's unicorn, FQ, II, v, 10 (pp. 159-60).

Bronson, Bertrand H. Personification Reconsidered, ELH, 14 (1947), 163-77.   1288

An apologia for the use of personification in 18th-century poetry, but broad in its implications. Because of a great "shift of sensibility," we are preoccupied with individual experience and prefer the concrete in poetry, unable to reach compelling generalizations. The explanation for this has its roots in growth of science. "An artist sure of what he wishes to say about the nature of the ordered, ideal world will . . . like Spenser . . . invent his own personifications, give them appropriate and transparent names, and set them in motion to express his doctrine." Allegory the most direct method of conveying ethical message. Ventures opinion that "allegory is a more advanced form of intellectual-artistic expression than its opposite, naturalism." Neoclassicism, in its use of personification, "was at one with the medieval and renaissance impulse toward allegorizing."

Brooke, Nicholas. Shakespeare's Early Tragedies. London: Methuen, 1968. 214 pp.   1289

Shakespeare's use in Titus Andronicus (pp. 13-47) of emblematic imagery, adaptation of non-dramatic verse to the stage, radical variations of style and tone (cf. two halves of FQ, VII, vi), achievement of unity in each Act by dominant verse tone—Act I heroic, Act II pastoral, "the transformation of Tamora from dramatic character into emblem of the play" (cf. FQ, III, x, 60), emphasis on poetic stylization—all with reference to Sp's technique in FQ. See Index.

Brophy, Brigid, Michael Levy, and Charles Osborne. Edmund Spenser: *The Faerie Queene*, in Fifty Works of English Literature We Could Do Without, pp. 5-7. New York: Stein and Day, 1968. 150 pp.   1290

Sp's fear, expressed in the Letter to Raleigh, that the FQ might seem tedious and confused, "turns out to be the truest and shrewdest" judgment ever made on the poem. Other works the authors feel we can do without: Hamlet (p. 11), Wuthering Heights (p. 71), Poems of A. E. Housman (p. 101).

Brumble, Herbert David, III. Genius and Other Related Allegorical Figures in the *De Planctu Naturae*, the *Roman de la Rose*, the *Confessio Amantis*, and the *Faerie Queene*. DAI, 31 (1971), 4113A. University of Nebraska, 1970. 139 pp.
                                                    1291

It is the Genius formulated by Alanus, in his *De Planctu Naturae*, which is "the real source of the allegorical tradition in which the Genii of De Meun, Gower, and Spenser rejoice." Treats Amoret (FQ, III-IV), Garden of Adonis (III, vi), Bower of Bliss (II, xii), and Epith.

Bruser, Fredelle. Concepts of Chastity in Literature, Chiefly Non-dramatic, of the English Renaissance. Doctoral diss., Radcliffe College, 1948. HRDP, 1947-1948, p. 23; DDAAU, 1947-48, No. 15.
                                                    1292

Deals with coy mistress of Petrarchan tradition, and reactions glorifying unchastity by Donne and Cavalier poets; subtler and more effective answer is Sp's treatment of Mirabella (FQ, VI, vii). Surveys libertine tradition. "The debate on custom and nature is vital to the problem of the ultimate sanction of chastity," as in Sidney's Arcadia. Sp, Chapman, and others tried to introduce "rational and religious controls on the hedonistic paradise of the libertines." Chapter on FQ discusses Sp's "superbly imaginative realization of the Protestant ideal of marital chastity." Britomart's chastity is active and ideal; minor figures in Bks. III and IV are found wanting. Treats aristocratic and bourgeois standards; prudential chastity of latter is starting point for double standard of morality. Sp in FQ and Milton in Comus "make decisive reply" to arguments for unchastity "based on 'nature' and a sophisticated reason."

Buchanan, Edith. Milton's True Knight, SAQ, 71 (1972), 480-7.   1293

One pattern in Samson Agonistes is the chivalric. Every division of poem "uses either the ghost of chivalry, the romance, or its heir, the code of honor." Cites references in Samson Agonistes to arms, knighly combat, trophies, and nature of the chivalric hero, with parallels wherever possible from "Milton's revered Spenser" to show what was customary in romance. Refers to Arthur's shield, Arthur's "baffling" of Turpin (FQ, VI, vii, 27), Braggadocchio's "bare head" [sic; "shaving" of Braggadocchio, V, iii, 37], swoons of Redcrosse and Arthur (I, ix, 48; V, x, 36), Artegall's and Arthur's rescues of Irena and Belge, and Sp's use of words "blaz'd" (proclaimed aloud) "adventure" (quest), and "champion."

Buchwald, Emilie. The Earthly Paradise and the Ideal Landscape: Studies in a Changing Tradition, Through 1750. DAI, 32 (1971), 1465A-6A. University of Minnesota, 1971. 250 pp.   1294

Christian cartographic tradition tried to locate earthly paradise, until Luther and Calvin said historical Eden was destroyed by Flood. Stylization of classical landscape as *locus amoenus* became linked with Biblical Eden. Writers of Renaissance epic, especially Tasso and Sp, implicitly compared Christian earthly paradise with hedonistic bowers of Venus. In 17th-century love poetry image of earthly paradise was increasingly secularized. Arcadia, Elysian Fields, and gardens of Venus are combined in image of a love paradise. Discusses rejection of free love and "argument from nature" in Milton's Comus. Final chapter deals with fusion of pastoral and classical paradise in poetry, painting, and gardening in early 18th century.

Bullough, Geoffrey, ed. Narrative and Dramatic Sources of Shakespeare. Vol. 2, The Comedies, 1597-1603. New York: Columbia University Press, 1958. 543pp.   1295

Sp's story of Claribell and Phedon (FQ, II, iv) is among the sources of Much Ado About Nothing (pp. 63-4, 73); Beatrice in Shakespeare's play has been compared with Mirabella (FQ, VI, vii), a disdainful lady (p. 80). Prints FQ, II, iv, 16-38 (pp. 106-12) as probable source. For other references to Sp, see Index.

Burgholzer, Sister Carolyn. Edmund Spenser's *The Faerie Queene:* A History of Criticism, 1948-68. DAI, 31 (1970), 2334A-5A. Duquesne University, 1970. 359 pp.   1296

Examines major trends since Bradner's Edmund Spenser and The Faerie Queene (1285), to update surveys of Sp criticism by Cory (603), Wurtsbaugh (116), and Mueller (947). Categories used by Mueller for earlier criticism are no longer appropriate. Major studies of FQ, 1948-68, fall into three categories: (1) those that draw on medieval and Renaissance traditions to explore the meaning of the poem; (2) those that study structure of individual books and poem as a whole; and (3) stylistic studies that suggest different ways of arriving at allegorical meaning. See 1719.

Burke, Charles B. The "Sage and Serious" Spenser, N&Q, 175 (1938), 457-8. 1297

Humor in Duessa, Britomart, and Britomart's nurse, Glauce.

Bush, Douglas. Marlowe and Spenser, TLS, Jan. 1, 1938, p. 12.   1298

Marlowe's works, especially Tamburlaine, contain many echoes of FQ, I-III.

Bush, Sargent, Jr. Bosom Serpents before Hawthorne: The Origins of a Symbol, AL, 43 (1971), 181-99. 1299

Various traditional material influenced Hawthorne's Egotism, or The Bosom Serpent, but greatest influence was Sp's FQ. The image of the bosom serpent echoes FQ, I, iv, 31, and III, xi, 1.

Campbell, Lily B. Shakespeare's "Histories": Mirrors of Elizabethan Policy. San Marino, Cal.: Huntington Library, 1947. 346pp.   1300

The division of philosophy into ethics (concerned with private moral virtues) and politics (concerned with public virtues) is illustrated by reference to Sp's letter to Raleigh. The old division of morals into private and public is "most clearly explained among the poets by Spenser in his letter to Raleigh" (pp. 16, 307). See also Index.

Cantelupe, Eugene Benjamin. Representations of Venus in Italian Renaissance Painting and English Renaissance Poetry. DA, 20 (1960), 3724-5. Washington University, 1959. 439 pp.   1301

Uses the method of iconography to explicate the meaning of one major mythological figure in painting and poetry. Vindicates Shakespeare's Venus and Adonis, which is not full of discordant elements. Establishes many pertinent relations between the two media. "For example, Botticelli's much-disputed *La Primavera* is an allegory of the medieval doctrine of *Naturae plenitudo*, which Chaucer employs in the *Parliament of Fowls* and Spenser in two notable episodes of the *Faerie Queene*."

Carruth, Hayden. Spenser and his Modern Critics, HudR, 22 (1969), 139-47. 1302

Review article on Alpers' The Poetry of The Faerie Queene (1231), Dunseath's Spenser's Allegory of Justice in Book Five of The Faerie Queene (2099), and Sale's Reading Spenser (1657). Commends Alpers for showing that the poem is an accessible, modern one whose full meaning "escapes the allegory" and is engendered in the "shifting pattern of rhetoric," and for providing a weapon against the "allegorists, numerologists, iconographers, and others who insist on the poem's mystifications." Praises Dunseath for supporting Carruth's own awareness of the poem's continuing power in Bk. V; for establishing Artegall as Art-egal, Arthur's equal; and for pointing out that Bk. V finishes up the hitherto unfinished business of the poem, providing a culmination which leaves Bk. VI as a kind of epilogue. Considers Sale's book to be "in effect a reduction of much material in Alpers' book ... satisfactory as far as it goes," but no substitute for reading the poem.

Caspari, Fritz. Humanism and the Social Order in Tudor England. Chicago: University of Chicago Press, 1954. 293pp.   1303

Sp, pp. 176-205. Book deals with the attempt of English humanists to improve existing order of society, evolving on a foundation of Greek and Roman ideas a doctrine which they hoped would make the ruling elements the best men. Considers Erasmus, More, Elyot, Starkey, Sidney, and Sp as representative humanists. Finds Sp's ideals electric, like those of other humanists. Specifically Christian heritage of humanism more strongly expressed in Sp than Sidney. Sp follows Sidney and Elyot in emphasizing friendship. He is equivocal on the relation of "good" blood and character, reflecting the social mobility of the times. His use of chivalric crusading has contemporary validity in reflecting the spirit of the Elizabethans. His concept of justice is perilously close to being merely whatever was the policy of the Queen. The virtues of temperance, friendship, and courtesy are restatements of humanistic doctrines.

Castelli, Alberto. La *Gerusalemme Liberata* nella Inghilterra di Spenser. Milan: Società Editrice "Vita e Pensiero," 1936. Pubblicazioni della Università

Cattolica del Sacro Cuore, Serie Quarta, 20. 130pp. 1304

Chapter 2, pp. 14-40, deals with "La *Gerusalemme Liberata* e la *Faerie Queene.*" Discusses the extent of Sp's knowledge of Italian culture, parallels between Tasso and Sp, the way in which Sp uses and differs from Tasso. Influence was strongest in FQ, I and II. This influence was transmitted to Sp's followers: Daniel, Drayton, Giles and Phineas Fletcher.

Chambrun, C. Longworth. Ten Days in the Life of Keats, TLS, 28 March, 1952, p. 221. 1305

Disputes suggestion (1388) that Keats was influenced by Sp's FQ in La Belle Dame sans Merci, suggests instead Thomas of Ercildoun's visit to England in Walter Scott's Border Minstrelsy.

Chang, H.C. Allegory and Courtesy in Spenser: A Chinese View. EUPLL, No. 8. Edinburgh: University Press, 1955. 227pp. New York: Humanities Press, 1957. 1306

In three parts. Part I consists of an introduction and translation of an episode, The Storming of the Passes of the Four Vices, from the romance of Ching Hua Yüan, Romance of the Flowers in the Mirror. Part II explains that this Chinese allegory is offered as a parallel to FQ, II; one difference is the kind of allegory: incidents in the story which illustrate the moral conflict in the Chinese work, conflicting virtues and vices personified in Sp. Short chapter on the knight-errant as a type in Sp and chivalric romances. Comparison of FQ, VI with Sidney's Arcadia and the romances. Discussion of Timias in Books III and IV as Sir Walter Ralegh. Part III, Spenser's Ideal of Courtesy: A Chinese View, compares Western courtesy and Chinese manners, concluding that they have much in common.

Charles, Amy Marie. The Poetry of Ralph Knevet (1601-c. 1671). DA, 12 (1952), 184-5. University of Pennsylvania, 1951. 199 pp. 1307

In 1635 Knevet completed A Supplement of the Faery Queene in Three Books, which remains in a 576-page manuscript "long ascribed to Robert Jegon because a commendatory verse by him is included. Examination of the handling of the Spenserian stanza, handwriting, and spelling, however, affirms that Knevet wrote this work, from which all traces of authorship have been removed, probably for political reasons. Both the dedications and the allegory reflect Knevet's Royalist sympathies." His third elegy on the death of Lady Katherine Paston is in Spenserian stanzas, showing his handling of the form and providing a link with the Supplement of the Faery Queene. "Knevet's poetry reflects an interest in the classics, public weal, science, and his two chief poetical masters, Spenser and Herbert."

Charles, Amy M., ed. The Shorter Poems of Ralph Knevet. Columbus: Ohio State University Press, 1966. 426 pp. 1308

Knevet best known for A Supplement of the Faery Queene, left in manuscript (see 1307, 1507). Critical ed., with full introductions and notes, of Stratitikon (1628), Rhodan and Iris (1631), Funerall Elegies (1637), and A Gallery to the Temple (British Museum Addit. MS. 27447). "When the full body of Knevet's writing is considered, we see him in proper perspective as a minor poet whose work reflects not only the influence of Elizabethan verse in the seventeenth century, but a microcosm of Caroline verse as well" (p. 5). For references to Sp, see Index.

Chauviré, Roger. L'homme élisabéthain, BAGB, 3 (1957), 53-80. 1309

An attempt to define the species. He believed in a divine order, but was attracted by pseudo-science. "Inconsistance, voilà sans doute le mot-clef." Lack of clarity in thought and allegory in FQ shows difficulty 16th century Englishman had forming any coherent view of life. Discusses simple and sufficient religious faith of the Elizabethan, his self-interest, national pride, scorn of Spain, contempt for Irish, personal courage, economic imperialism, ostentation, sophisticated vices, latent violence and drive of his society, self-confidence, individualism, adaptability, creative greatness.

Cheney, Donald. Spenser's Image of Nature: Wild Man and Shepherd in "The Faerie Queen." New Haven: Yale University Press, 1966. 262 pp.   1310

FQ reflects and exploits the tensions between "hard" and "soft" pastoralism (i.e., between savage and shepherd) and also between epic and pastoral, public and private, courtly and primitive, ideal and real, grace and nature; poem demands that reader participate in creating meaning by perceiving ironies and ambiguities of poem's predications. By analyzing Bk. I, infers Sp's conception of Nature, i.e., sense of reality. Traces Sp's ironic treatment of chivalric and Petrarchan tradition to Italian romantic epics, proceeds to a reading of parts of FQ, especially Garden of Adonis and Bks. V, VI, and VII. Useful index of episodes, pp. 249-54. [Diss., Yale University, 1961.]
Rev: S. K. Heninger, Jr., JEGP, 66 (1967), 257; E.W. Tayler, MLQ, 28 (1967), 105; R.M. Cummings, RES, 18 (1967), 318; A. K. Hieatt, MP, 65 (1967), 158; M. MacLure, RenQ, 20 (1967), 55. See 1232, 1414.

Chew, Samuel C. Time and Fortune, ELH, 6 (1939), 83-113.   1311

Primarily concerned with the symbolism of Time and Fortune in Tudor and Stuart dramatic literature. Refers to the encounter of Mercury and Mutability (FQ, VII, vi, 16-18) and to Occasion (FQ, II, iv, 4ff.).

Chew, Samuel C. The Virtues Reconciled: An Iconographic Study. Toronto: University of Toronto Press, 1947. 163pp., 18 plates.   1312

Analogies and parallels between verbal images in literature and visual images in the graphic arts in representations of the Parliament of Heaven and the four virtues: Truth, Justice, Mercy, and Peace. In connection with Sp, see discussions of Peter Pett's Times Journey (pp. 72-7); John Day's Peregrinatio Scholastica (pp. 82-4); allegorical figures of Justice (pp. 96-8); the Seven Works of Mercy (pp. 104-6); Despair (pp. 110-5); Mercy (pp. 118-9). See also Index for other Spenserian references.

Cirillo, Albert Richard. Spenser's Myth of Love: A Study of *The Faerie Queene*, Books III and IV. Doc. diss., Johns Hopkins University, 1964. 380 pp.   1313

Renaissance idea that love is a motion toward the object underlies FQ, III and IV, and provides context of central quest, motion that follows lines established in Renaissance love treatises. Principal pattern illustrated in Florimell story, only one in these books that illustrates transcendent concept of love. Essence of Florimell's story is motion of her continuous flight through fairyland. Begins with her mythical origin and education among Venus' Graces, moves to object, Marinell, in sea, her constancy in movement establishing concord necessary for virtuous love, ends with her union with Marinell on highest spiritual level. In this story lie seeds of all love stories in Bks. III and IV, and of meaning of love in FQ.

Clark, Earl John. Spenser's "To the Right Honourable the Earle of Cumberland," 2, Expl, 27 (1968), Item 10.   1314

In Sp's dedicatory sonnet to George Clifford, third Earl of Cumberland, appended to first edition of FQ, the naval hero is extolled as the "flowre of cheualry now bloosming faire." Sp's poetic virtuosity exemplified by his interlinking of this imagery with flowery designs of Cumberland's coat of arms.

Clark, Judith P. His Earnest unto Game: Spenser's Humor in *The Faerie Queene*, ESRS, 15 (1967), 13-27.   1315

Examples of discordant harmony in FQ reveal Sp's sense of the compatability of serious purpose and humor. Three aspects of poem reveal examples of discordant harmony: *sententiae*, coinage and meaningful names, and frequent acknowledgment of sources.

Clements, Robert J. Pen and Sword in Renaissance Emblem Literature, MLQ, 5 (1944), 131-41.   1316

Emblem book writers compared pursuits of poet and soldier, leaned toward literature as more glorious of two. Longest discussion of topic in Emblemata Politica of Juan de Solorzano. In Renaissance ideal of complete gentleman, man of letters and man of arms coexisted in same individual. Reawakened interest in chivalry provided 16th century with some of its favorite reading: Italy's Jerusalem Delivered, France's Life of Bayard, Spain's Amadis of Gaul, Portugal's Palmerin of England, England's FQ. Many Renaissance figures skilled in letters and war. Renaissance writer, believing in classical doctrine that poet is "monarch of all sciences," had to share glory with another profession on which Renaissance placed high value.

Coogan, Mary Jane. The Concept of Honor in *The Faerie Queene*, Books I and II. Doctoral dissertation, Loyola University of Chicago, 1964. 337 pp.   1317

Chaps. treat development of concept of honor in classical and medieval writers, chivalric code, Continental courtesy books, English courtesy books, and Fixation of the Shifting Concept of Honor. Chaps. VII and VIII analyze religious, chivalric, political, and moral aspects of honor in character and career of Red Cross. Chaps. IX and X analyze temperance as a source of honor in character and career of Guyon. Conclusion discusses Sp's concept of honor in terms of personal integrity and service to the state, finds chief influences on his concept of honor in chivalric and Scholastic thought.

Cook, Albert. The Classic Line: A Study in Epic Poetry. Bloomington, Ind.: Indiana University Press, 1966. 314pp.   1318

Five-line stanza of Chanson d'Alexis, in contrast to longer *laisses* of Chanson de Roland, makes impossible simplicity of epic fullness, as also in "lyrically limited" stanzas of Tasso, Ariosto, and Sp (pp. 31-2). Would expect Homer's poetic effects of limpidity only in the mass, as with Sp, "notably limpid" (p. 74). Normally pattern like *terza rima*, "to judge by the comparable stanzas of Tasso and Ariosto, of Spenser," would be limiting; but not so to Dante (p. 232). When Milton finally chose subject for epic poem, ruled out Dante's and Sp's kind of allegory, and Sp's Arthur as not "unitary enough" (pp. 246-8). Did not write "the syllabic poetry" of Sp; Sp's "equality of accent" has "Italian and French limpidity, and nothing like the Miltonic grandeur" (pp. 267-8, 272-3). See Index.

Corder, Jim. Colin Against Art Again, N&Q, 8 (1961), 301-2.   1319

George Mason uses Sp's poetry in An Essay in Design in Gardening (1795) to support an informal style in laying out gardens. Influence of Sp's descriptions continued into 19th century, to some extent affecting plantation design.

Corder, Jim. Spencer [sic] and the Eighteenth Century Informal Garden. N&Q, N.S. 6 (1959), 19-21.   1320

Bower of Bliss (FQ, II, xii), Garden of Adonis (FQ, III, vi), and Mount Acidale (FQ, VI, x) show that Sp puts naturalness above artificiality. This influenced the informal garden of the 18th century.

Corns, Albert R., and Archibald Sparke. A Bibliography of Unfinished Books in the English Language. Detroit: Gale, 1968. 225 pp.   1321

Reprint of 1915 ed. Atkinson, p. 58.

Corse, Larry Bailey. "A Straunge Kinde of Harmony": The Influence of Lyric Poetry and Music on Prosodic Techniques in the Spenserian Stanza. DAI, 33 (1973), 4404A-5A. North Texas State University, 1972. 217 pp.   1322

Two formal prosodic orders function simultaneously in stanzas of FQ: (1) visible structure; (2) order apparent in oral reading "which involves speech stresses, syntactical groupings, caesura placements, and enjambments." Sp controls both visible and audible patterns. Music and poetry written for music furnished techniques and precedents used. In madrigals and other contrapuntal forms rhythmic or melodic motifs unify a passage of music. Studies union of poetry and music in English lyric poetry written for existing melodies, French experiments with quantitative verse, and especially relation of Orlando Furioso to tradition of singing narrative poetry to folk melodies. Support for thesis in Sp's use of Tudor masque, combination of art forms, in structure of FQ. Sees processional masque as unifying foundation of whole epic. Musical techniques in prosody unify individual stanzas and also integrate prosody with larger plan of FQ.

Cosman, Madeleine Pelner. Spenser's Ark of Animals: Animal Imagery in the Faery Queen, SEL, 3 (1963), 85-107.   1323

Animal imagery in FQ, primarily mammalian, establishes contrasts between moral allegorical elements, produces movement as well as aural and visual impressions, interlinks episodes, provides secondary connotations and humor, and especially prevents characters from being insipid allegorical personifications.

Craig, Joanne. The Image of Mortality: Myth and History in The Faerie Queene, ELH, 39 (1972), 520-44. 1324

FQ reflects Sp's growing distrust of the secular order. Although first 3 books, published 1590, regard the past through rosy medium of the "Tudor myth," they also adumbrate moral and artistic dilemmas of FQ, IV-VI. These books, published 1596, reflect poet's inability to integrate the myth with contemporary fact; in these books the Tudor myth and then the FQ itself are eclipsed. [SpN, Vol. 4, No. 1 (1973), 5.]

Craig, Martha Alden. Language and Concept in the Faerie Queene. DA, 19, No. 13, (1959), 108. Yale University, 1958.   1325

Explains certain features of Sp's style—archaism, coinage, alliteration and rhyme—in light of view of language expounded in Plato's Cratylus as understood by Renaissance Neoplatonists. Words show the nature of the thing named through their etymological elements of meaning. Sp's new words "do suggest meaning through apt etymologies. The archaic words and forms he revived are frequently etymologically significant as well. And sound . . . often suggests important connections in sense which are not explicitly stated." Plato's Seventh Epistle, translated into Latin by Peter Ramus, completes a "hypothetical poetic" and explains "a final quality of the style which has been disparaged, redundancy," which "is important in the poem to draw apart the etymological elements of the word." This view of language provides an explanation and justification for the style of FQ. See 1325A.

Craig, Martha Alden. The Secret Wit of Spenser's Language, in Elizabethan Poetry: Modern Essays in Criticism, ed. Paul J. Alpers, pp. 447-72. New York: Oxford University Press, 1967. 524 pp.
1325A

Condensed version of 1325.

Crampton, Georgia Ronan. The Protagonist as Sufferer: A Critical Inquiry into a Topos in Chaucer and Spenser. DA, 28 (1967), 2205A. University of Oregon, 1967. 461 pp.   1326

The *topos* of action and suffering came to Chaucer and Sp from many sources, classical and medieval. Passion of Christ offered model of suffering hero. In Knight's Tale images of man as sufferer predominate; in Troilus and Criseyde suffering and action internalized. Suffering and action alternate in careers of Red Cross Knight and Una in FQ, I. In Bk. II idea that passion makes man a sufferer is dramatized. In Bks. III and IV *topos* appears in love of Britomart

and role of Scudamour; III, iv through series of lyric complaints emphasizes man's perception of self as sufferers. Both Chaucer and Sp treat paradox that acceptance transforms suffering into action. "Spenser's ethical and thematic emphasis tends to be on the value of acceptant suffering."

Culp, Dorothy W. Courtesy and Moral Virtue, SEL, 11 (1971), 37-51.   1327

Courtesy books offer little help in defining Sp's courtesy, vaguely relate it to general moral duty. Sp carefully distinguishes between justice and courtesy in Pollente-Munera episode of Bk. V, ii, and Briana-Crudor episode of Bk. VI, ii; similarly, development of episodes in V, ii and VI, ii is quite different. Courtesy governs relationships outside one's political, economic, or personal interests. Above all, "it is a graciousness of manner, a comeliness of demeanor and appearance, that reflects inward virtue." See 2141.

Cummings, R. M. Two Sixteenth-Century Notices of Numerical Composition in Virgil's *Aeneid*, N&Q, 16 (1969), 26-7.
1328

Precedent, hitherto lacking, for numerical pattern in Sp's FQ (see 1367), found in claims of Sebastianus Regulus and Jacobus Pontanus that Aeneid attained perfection because numerologically based. [SpN, vol. 1, No. 2 (1970), 6.]

Curry, Stephen J. The Use of History in Bishop Hurd's Literary Criticism, TWA, 54 (1965), 79-91.   1329

Richard Hurd falsely labeled "preromantic" in mid-18th century. His Letters on Chivalry and Romance (1762) "does not espouse any kind of preromanticism." He uses history in describing nature of Gothic romance and defending unity of FQ; but his view of art is same as that of Dryden and Pope. Despite love of Shakespeare, Sp, and Chaucer, holds they could have been greater by observing Neoclassic unity. Hurd's difference from other English Augustans is "his full discovery of how to use history as an important adjunct to criticism." See 1330.

Curry, Stephen Jefferis. The Literary Criticism of Richard Hurd. DA, 23 (1962), 2133-4. University of Wisconsin, 1962. 242 pp.   1330

Analyzes Hurd's critical and philosophical principles; his affinity is with Augustan age rather than with age of Wordsworth and Coleridge. Clearest example of his critical method and most cogent piece of writing is the Letters on Chivalry and Romance. Shows classical desire for purity of genre, concentration on single aim in each work of art, and "an enlightened attempt by the critic and reader to understand and sympathize with the intent of the artist." See 1329, 1551.

Curtius, Ernst Robert. European Literature and the Latin Middle Ages. Trans. Willard R. Trask. Bollingen Series, 36. New York: Pantheon Books, 1953. 662pp.   1331

Originally published as Europäische Literatur und lateinisches Mittelalter, 1948. Sp mentioned in connection with Alan of Lille and Genius (pp. 117-22); nautical metaphors—quotes FQ, VI, xii, 1 (pp. 128-30); the topos sapientia et fortitudo—cites FQ, II, iii, 40 (p. 178); the epic grove—cites FQ, I, i, 8 (pp. 194-5); practice of allegorizing (pp. 203-7); the Muses—tradition of Sp's invocations (pp. 228-46).

Dallett, Joseph B. Ideas of Sight in The Faerie Queene, ELH, 27 (1960), 87-121.   1332

Divided into four parts: (1) Narrative and Observers, (2) Aesthetics and Optics, (3) Dialectics, (4) Enlightenment. Shows relation between ideas of sight in FQ, and how unity depends in part on visual perceptions. Suggests Bk. I is most unified because of logical sight imagery. Explains the kind of "seeing" done by the main characters, quoting many passages from the poem. Finds three levels of sight: physical, spiritual, and metaphorical.

Davis, C. Pruitt, Jr. "From This Darke World": The Active and the Contemplative Ways of Life in Spenser. DAI, 33 (1972), 3579-A. Texas Christian University, 1972. 172 pp.   1333

Could Sp advocate man's fulfillment through contemplation of God as best way in process of his temporal life? Surveys medieval background in Augustine, Dionysius, Richard of St. Victor, Bernard of Clairvaux, and Dante. Triumph of reason in Summa of Thomas Aquinas a process resolved for Sp in via media of Richard Hooker. Throughout FQ, Sp puts premium on active life in pursuit of honor, but does not neglect contemplative way. Contemplation for Sp, however, more rational than suprarational. Justification of process and contemplation as basis for proper action subject of 4 Hymns, but contemplation only a foretaste of eternal life and ultimate rationale for active obedience to God. Tension between active and contemplative ways of life justifies process itself. Contemplation without action is idleness; action without vision is futile.

Davison, Mary Carol. The Metamorphoses of Odysseus: A Study of Romance Iconography from the Odyssey to The Tempest. DAI, 32 (1971), 1467A. Stanford University, 1971. 474 pp.   1334

Aims to clarify Shakespeare's late plays through an understanding of the "romance form as it originated in

Homeric epic and developed from antiquity through the Renaissance." Iconographic scenes of FQ considered as exemplifying Renaissance aesthetic theories.

Dees, Jerome S. The Narrator of *The Faerie Queene:* Patterns of Response, TSLL, 12 (1971), 537-68.   1335

In FQ Sp's narrator changes flexibly in response to the poem. His comments and explications may be oversimplified, contradictory, or misleading; they require the reader to become fully engaged in order to achieve the revelation. In addition, the reader gains "a sense of struggle on the part of the narrator to reconcile opposing forces within himself and in his age." See 1336, 1337, 1349.

Dees, Jerome Steele. The Narrator's Voice in *The Faerie Queene, Christs Victorie, and Triumph,* and *The Locusts, or Apollyonists.* DAI, 29 (1968), 564-A. University of Illinois, 1968. 335 pp.   1336

Renaissance heroic narrator is voice created by poet to guide reader's response. Narrator of FQ is, at need, orator, homilist, and sophist in manipulating audience. Dominant attitude homiletic, reinforced by sophistic irony. Interaction of rhetorical attitudes produces two kinds of narrator in poem: one who increasingly wearies of poetic burden and seeks release in rest; and one whose understanding of virtues deepens as he progresses. Classical and Christian frames of reference held in balance by full involvement of individual in experience, epitomized by Arthur's magnanimity. This fullness of human response symbolized by heroic quest. In contrast, narrator of Christ's Victorie is visionary for whom human concerns are subordinate. Narrator of The Locusts lets historical preoccupations dominate and conflict with poetic vision. See 1335, 1337, 1349.

Delasanta, Rodney. The Epic Voice. The Hague: Mouton, 1967. 140 pp.   1337

Connects in medias res structure and corollary use of restricted narrator in Odyssey, New Arcadia, FQ, and Paradise Lost. FQ (pp. 110-30). Of the English epic writers, only Sp fails to utilize the many "narrative strategies resulting from a commitment" to in medias res structure. This happens because "the demands of his allegory and the necessary delegation of the narrative to a restricted narrator pulled his attention in opposite directions." See 1335, 1336, 1349. [DA, 23 (1962), 2524.]

Dent, R. W. Marlowe, Spenser, Donne, Shakespeare—and Joseph Wybarne, RenQ, 22 (1969), 360-2.   1338

Wybarne's 1609 work The New Age of Old Names refers frequently to FQ: Errour's Den, the disrobing of Duessa, the story of Phaedria, and to Archimago and "Argoglio." Derives the name of the "blattant" beast from βλαπτω, "to hurt."

Dhesi, Nirmal Singh. The Paynims and Saracens of Spenser's *The Faerie Queene.* DAI, 30 (1969), 317A. Michigan State University, 1968. 252 pp.   1339

The nature and function of the seven paynims or Saracens of FQ, namely the Sans brothers, Pyrochles and Cymochles, Pollente, and the Souldan, must be understood in order to understand the protagonists of Bks. I, II, and V, and the structure of the allegory in these books. Chapters: I, the uniqueness of the paynims among the antagonists of FQ; II, the paynims of Bk. I; III, the paynims of Bk. III; IV, the paynims of Bk. V, who do not measure up to those of I and II.

Dickey, Franklin M. Not Wisely But Too Well: Shakespeare's Love Tragedies. San Marino, Cal.: Huntington Library, 1966. 205 pp.   1340

Repr. of 1957 ed. Sp's aim in Bower of Bliss (FQ, II, xii) to make sensuousness look fair but point out viciousness; so with Elizabethan dramatists (pp. 11-18). Sp praises love as ladder to God, but love melancholy makes lovers antic (FQ, I, ix), and excessive love weakens (V, v-vii); carnal overindulgence brings death (II, i), and lust and bloodshed are linked (II, iv-v) (pp. 35-41). Interprets Venus and Adonis as allegory of love and Rape of Lucrece as exemplum, compares with attack by senses on Castle of Alma (FQ, II, xi) (pp. 46-60). Sp condemns Antony and Cleopatra to Lucifera's dungeon (FQ, I, v), compares Artegall in Radigund's bondage to Antony (V, viii, 1-2) (pp. 157-8). Imagery in Antony and Cleopatra associates lust with gluttony, as throughout FQ (pp. 184-7).

Dickson, Arthur, ed. Valentine and Orson. EETS, OS, 204 (1937). 375 pp.   1341

French prose romance written 1475-1489, English translations printed by Wynkyn de Worde and William Copland, popular as "an epitome of chivalric character and adventure" (pp. ix-xiv). Section 9 of Intro., "*Valentine and Orson in The Faerie Queene*" (pp. li-lix), lists many parallels between the romance and Bks. I-II, IV-VI. A "possible source" of FQ.

Dorn, Alfred. The Mutability Theme in the Poetry of Edmund Spenser and John Donne. DAI, 30 (1970), 4407-A. New York University, 1966. 361 pp.   1342

Preoccupation of Sp and Donne with mutability caused in part by failure of their political ambitions. FQ full of historical allegory; Donne emphasized subjective reality. Donne's morbidity partly projection of chaos within himself. Accepted doctrine of universal degeneration, used it in prose and poetry. Sp's cosmic symbol a garden, Donne's a graveyard. For Sp, principle of chaos personified by Titanesse. Subscribed to prevailing doctrine of decay, but this counter-balanced by idea of cosmic and historical cycles, awareness of natural fertility, and New-Platonic conception of nature. Sp, sensuous and idealistic, harmonized worldly and spiritual values. Donne's dissonant art reflects malaise of men who no longer trusted nature or believed in man.

Dressler, Graham McFarland. A Study of Aphorisms in the Poetry of Edmund Spenser. Doctoral diss., University of Washington, 1937. DDAAU, 1936-37, No. 4. UWAT, 2 (1937), 559-60.   1343

Classifies aphoristic passages under various headings: Love and Womankind, Courtesy, Fame, Justice, Fate, Mutability, etc. Many express "meditative and somber thoughts," indicating "the general moral purpose underlying his poetry." Collects analogous sayings from contemporary, traditional, and classical sources. Analyzes sententious material in FQ in relation to character portrayal.

Duncan, Joseph E. Milton's Earthly Paradise. Minneapolis: University of Minnesota Press, 1972. 329 pp.   1344

Renaissance writers distinguished between golden age sites (classical), earthly paradises (Christian), and enchanted gardens (false paradises like Sp's Bower of Bliss (FQ, II, xii), perverted mixtures of first two). Jean Bodin's attack on idea of golden age in remote past probably known to Sp, endorsed by Gabriel Harvey. Among several descriptions of golden age sites, Sp's "luxuriant description" of Garden of Adonis (FQ, III, vi) was best known (pp. 26, 29, 36). In Paradise Lost, "Raphael, like Spenser a better teacher than Aquinas, has told Adam of Abdiel who knew that 'God and Nature bid the same' " (p. 128). More on Sp's relation to Milton's ideas of paradise in Paradise Lost and Comus (pp. 216-9, 228-31).

Dundas, Judith. Elizabethan Architecture and *The Faerie Queene:* Some Structural Analogies, DR, 45 (1966), 470-8.
1345

In Elizabethan times there was no settled sense of style. But in both FQ and architecture, "the old Gothic meets the new Renaissance, and from this meeting comes a new exuberance not matched again" in English literature or architecture. Both Sp and the architects employ "symmetry, lucidity, ornament" to "match the expansiveness of the new age."

Dundas, Judith. The Rhetorical Basis of Spenser's Imagery, SEL, 8 (1968), 59-75.
1346

Sp wrote in the pictorial tradition. The concept of *ut pictura poesis* and the practice of developing images according to rhetorical schemes provide keys to Sp's artistic procedure. "By assembling details according to the schemes for time, place, person, and action, Spenser could give reality to his romance concepts. For it is these, not the epic similes or the inset allegories, that carry his narrative burden and that therefore demand an art analogous to the painter's." See 722, 1095, 1332, 1389.

Dundas, Judith Oenone. The Imagery of Spenser's *Faerie Queene.* DA, 17 (1957), 2008. University of Wisconsin, 1957. 220 pp.
1347

Examines the content and form of the descriptive, or non-metaphorical, imagery in FQ. Sp is "the painter of poets" because he followed the doctrine of *ut pictura poesis*. He is a "dream poet" in that his contemplation expressed itself in the ordered and dreamlike calm of his imagery.

Dunn, Millard Charles, Jr. Rhythm and Allegory: The Development of Narrative Structure in *The Faerie Queene.* DA, 27 (1967), 3424A. Indiana University, 1966. 274 pp.
1348

Analyzes structure of FQ with particular attention to (a) the formal resemblance of narrative units of different sizes to one another, and (b) the growing fusion of narrative and allegory. Beginning with an analysis of SC and the Mutabilitie Cantos, demonstrates (1) that Sp's structural instincts were similar at the beginning and end of his career, and (2) that these instincts developed as his skill as a poet increased. The analysis of structure proceeds with Bks. III and IV, I and II, and V and VI in this order, "because it is most probably the sequence in which the books were written." The analysis of narrative structure considers problem of revision as larger form of poem took shape.

Durling, Robert M. The Figure of the Poet in Renaissance Epic. Cambridge, Mass.: Harvard University Press, 1965. 280 pp.
1349

Central theme is significance of Narrator's changeability or instability. In Part I studies four writers of older tradition of self-contradiction and deprecation: Horace, Ovid, Chaucer, and Petrarch. In Part II singles out passages where Poet-Narrator refers to "himself": Boiardo in Orlando Innamorato, Ariosto in Orlando Furioso, Tasso in Gerusalemme Liberata, and Sp in FQ. Sp did not follow Tasso's adaptation of Homeric and

Virgilian epic Poet. "He elected to adapt the intrusive, discursive Poet developed by Boiardo and Ariosto." Analyzes references to himself by Sp's Narrator-Poet in moralizing comments on action of preceding canto (Ariosto's usual practice), or of present canto, and in comments and exclamations of various kinds interspersed through the narration. "Spenser imitates and echoes Ariosto's canto openings and endings, interjections, and, less frequently, transitional topoi. The changes he makes are characteristic and important." See 1335, 1336, 1337.

Estrin, Barbara. The Lost Child in Spenser's *Faerie Queene*, Sidney's *Old Arcadia*, and Shakespeare's *The Winter's Tale*. DAI, 33 (1973), 4340-A. Brown University, 1972. 271 pp. 1350

Sees foundling theme as alternative to other Renaissance answers to mutability: art's eternal stasis and nature's recurring cycles. Child provides another possible refutation of time and age. Outlines typical lost child plot. Conclusive recognition arranged by gods in romance, by characters in comedy without divine interference. Argues from different uses of theme that FQ is romance, Old Arcadia between romance and comedy, and The Winter's Tale purely comic. Chap. I discusses foundling formula in Bible, Greek myth, and Greek romance; Chap. II discusses its prominence in English Renaissance.

Evans, Frank B. On the 1596 Printing of the *Faerie Queene*, in RenP 1957, pp. 4-8. A Selection of Papers Presented at the Renaissance Meeting in the Southeastern States, Duke University, April 12-13, 1957. Southeastern Renaissance Conference, 1957. 1351

Copy of 1596 edition of FQ in library of College of William and Mary reveals three more corrected forms than are indicated in Variorum apparatus. Compares this copy with errata sheet of 1590 edition.

Evans, Frank B. The Printing of Spenser's *Faerie Queene* in 1596, SB, 18 (1965), 49-67. 1352

Textual proofs (type ornaments, spelling, capitalization, type cases, italics and roman fonts) suggest that at least three compositors were involved in the 1596 printing of two volumes of FQ.

Evans, Maurice. Platonic Allegory in *The Faerie Queene*, RES, 12 (1961), 132-43. 1353

Renaissance painters, particularly Botticelli, provided Sp with a model for his treatment of Christian Platonists' concept of circle of love, movement of love from carnal to spiritual to divine and harmony created through this process. This model most clearly evidenced in pictorial elements of FQ, III and IV, which together embody Ficino's Circle of Love. See 1211, 1724.

Evans, Maurice. Spenser's Anatomy of Heroism: A Commentary on *The Faerie Queene*. Cambridge: University Press, 1970. 244 pp. 1354

Argues that FQ "embodies a double perspective throughout which replaces the simple distinction between virtue and vice by something altogether more complex" (p. viii). Four chaps. as introduction to poem (pp. 3-85): Arthur is central, measure of other heroes, Artegall "most explicitly heroic"; FQ "takes its whole being from Spenser's profound sense of the Fall," Arthur becomes "increasingly the symbol of the Christ within"; criticizes Hamilton (1416), K. Williams (1741), Alpers (1231), and Tuve (1152) on Sp's allegory, gives own theory of it as changing from book to book; all-embracing quality of the poem. Commentaries on individual books (pp. 89-239) offer many novel ideas.

Rev: K. Williams, JEGP, 70 (1971), 656; J. Mazzaro, Criticism, 13 (1971), 312; B.E.C. Davis, RES, 22 (1971), 476. See 1541.

Evans, Robert O. Spenserian Humor: *Faerie Queene* III and IV, NM, 60 (1959), 288-99.   1355

Says humor is important aspect of Sp's technique, with Books III and IV of FQ "the most favorable hunting ground." There is "little room for humor" in Books I and II. But Britomart is less an allegorical figure, like Red Cross Knight and Guyon, than a woman. Discovers little verbal humor, as in Shakespeare's early comedies. Discusses Florimell at witch's cottage (III, vii), quest of Squire of Dames (III, vii), Florimell and fisherman (III, viii), Malbecco fabliau (III, x), various combats, Braggadochio, contest of ladies for Florimell's magic girdle (IV, v). Sp's humor is situational and depends on visualization.

Feinstein, Blossom. On the Hymns of John Milton and Gian Francesco Pico, CL, 20 (1968), 245-53.   1356

Shows that long before major poems Milton in Nativity Ode rejected pagan deities and rituals attending pagan worship in ancient Near East. In this he resembles extreme orthodoxy of Gian Francesco Pico della Mirandola, who in Latin Hymns denounces all pagan themes; gives detailed comparison of Milton's Nativity Ode and Pico's Hymns. In contrast, "Spenser equates Near-Eastern splendor with beauty and love": FQ, III, iii, 22-24; IV, iii, 38; and V, vii, 16.

Feinstein, Blossom. *The Faerie Queene* and Cosmogonies of the Near East, JHI, 29 (1968), 531-50.   1357

Some of Sp's ideas, images, and emblems derive not from classical and Hebrew traditions but from Egyptian, Babylonian, Phoenecian, and Persian traditions.

Felperin, Howard. Shakespearean Romance. Princeton: Princeton University Press, 1972. 319 pp.   1358

Chap. I, Golden-Tongued Romance (pp. 3-54), discusses Cymbeline, The Winter's Tale, The Tempest, with (sometimes) Pericles and (sometimes) Henry VIII as related group of Shakespeare's plays, their relation to preceding tragedies, their relation to "the other great romances and romantic epics of the English Renaissance, the *Arcadia*, *The Faerie Queene*, and even *Paradise Lost*," and romance as literary genre. Believes religious drama of later Middle Ages more important influence on Shakespeare than Greek romance or chivalric romance. For specific references to Sp and FQ, see Index.

Ferguson, Arthur B. The Indian Summer of English Chivalry. Durham, N. C.: Duke University Press, 1960. 242pp.
                    1359

Chivalric practices and pageantry at court continued throughout 16th century. Hard to tell when they ceased to represent realities in life of the nation and became, like romances of Ariosto and Sp, expressions of conscious romanticism (pp. 23-6). Stephen Hawes's The Pastime of Pleasure (1509) is "thoroughly medieval in its components, yet in its totality foreshadowing, if only dimly, the kind of thing Spenser brought to mature perfection in *The Faerie Queene*." Dangerous to assume conscious archaism on part of Hawes, such as we find in Sp's choice of setting for FQ (pp. 58-68). With Surrey "we are well on the way toward the romantic, humanistically oriented chivalry of Spenser and Sidney" (pp. 93-4). Not till loyalty to national church was identified with loyalty to the Queen "could a Spenser once more find in chivalric tradition, despite its ingrained Catholicism and its implied universality, a vehicle for moral instruction in a protestant and Erastian England" (pp. 94-103).

Fitz, Irmgard. Maximilians *Theuerdank*—Spensers *Feenkönigin*. Doctoral diss., University of Vienna, 1950. 138pp. OeB, 12 (June 30, 1951), 8.   1360

Begins with four-page section on The General Political and Intellectual Situation of Europe in the 15th and 16th Centuries, in effort to establish common background for the two works. Sketches the Burgundian Renaissance. Discusses sources, questions of authorship, editions, artistry, and literary relationships of Maximilian's Theuerdank, a chivalric romance containing political and personal allegory published 1517 (pp. 14-85). Discusses Elizabethan England and life of Sp (pp. 86-95), and FQ itself with most attention to Bk. I (pp. 95-113). Conclusion compares and contrasts two works in very general terms (pp. 114-32). Only seventy-two years separated Theuerdank and FQ: "Zweiundsiebzig Jahre—und welch ein Unterschied!" (p. 85).

Fletcher, Angus. Allegory: The Theory of a Symbolic Mode. Ithaca, New York: Cornell University Press, 1964. 418 pp.   1361

In Intro. says allegory is protean device employed in many literary genres, especially traditional romances such as FQ and Pilgrim's Progress; all literary commentary more or less allegorical; psychological part of critical theory has become more sophisticated under influence of Carl Jung, collapsing literary distinctions; Coleridge's identification of symbol with synechdoche made possible

double approach to allegory; suggests allegory is closely related to religious ritual and symbolism (pp. 1-23). Many illustrative examples from Sp: Redcrosse as conceptual hero who generates subcharacters (pp. 35 ff.); Malbecco possessed by daemon, jealousy (pp. 49 ff.); archetypal rhythm in symbolic procession of Seven Deadly Sins, FQ, II, iv (pp. 168-9); thematic effects of FQ as sublime poem and its ambivalence (pp. 268-73); Sp's knights and ladies as compulsive neurotics (pp. 288-9); pastoral is syncretic art halfway between attack and defense of *status quo* (pp. 331-4); visionary rituals in Sp's symbolic centers—House of Holiness, House of Alma, Gardens of Adonis (pp. 346-51). For other references to Sp, see Index.

Rev: Barbara Shapiro, L&P, 15 (1965), 48; D.C. Allen, ShS, 1 (1965), 303; A.C. Hamilton, QQ, 28 (1971), 480. See 954.

Fletcher, Angus. The Prophetic Moment: An Essay on Spenser. Chicago: University of Chicago Press, 1971. 326 pp.   1362

In temporal terms "the prophetic moment" occurs when time and eternity are aligned; in spatial terms it occurs where "temple" meets "labyrinth." These concepts frame multifarious generalizations, "temple" and "labyrinth" giving rise to further oppositions that tend not to eliminate one or the other, but to merge. Identifies five "typological matrices" in FQ: Biblical, Virgilian, Ovidian, Galfridian, and Hermetic. Part Two focuses on FQ, V and VII for Sp's prophetic role in Elizabethan literature and history. Heavily footnoted with references to traditional and modern sources. Four Indexes (pp. 305-26). Rev: Jane Aptekar, RenQ, 24 (1971), 560; A. C. Hamilton, QQ, 78 (1971), 480; B.E.C. Davis, RES, 23 (1972),

333; Hugh Maclean, JEGP, 71 (1972), 243. See 1280.

Foltinek, Herbert. Die Wilden Männer in Edmund Spensers *Faerie Queene*, NS, 11 (1961), 493-512.   **1363**

Discusses interest taken in wild men in Middle Ages and Renaissance, and their place in folklore, graphic arts, pageantry, drama, and entertainments of Elizabethan England. Sp's motifs in this area are built on those of his age; gives examples in Bks. I, III, IV, and VI. Wild men, though not central figures, are a characteristic element in Sp's epic. See 1271, 1392.

Ford, George H. Keats and the Victorians. New Haven: Yale University Press, 1945; repr. Hamden, Conn.: Anchor Books, 1962. 197 pp.   **1364**

Most references to Sp are in Chap. III, Tennyson's Debt to Keats (pp. 22-48). Tennyson's genius was imitative; his debt to Sp has been traced (Carpenter, p. 277). Picture of Lancelot in The Lady of Shalott recalls Sp's Prince Arthur (FQ, I, vii, 29-30), as well as Keats's Endymion. Keats's use of Sp is important factor in bringing Tennyson into same tradition of poets who paint word pictures. For other references to Sp, see Index.

Fosso, Doyle Richard. Epic Simile in Edmund Spenser's *The Faerie Queene*. Doctoral dissertation, Harvard University, 1965. 299 pp.   **1365**

Chap. 1, Modern Critical Response. "An epic simile is one that is more than two lines in length." FQ has 165 such similes. Most critics have condemned Sp's epic similes as decorative rather than functional, unaware "that ornamental beauty and thematic functioning are not only compatible with each other but also that they often are inseparable." Chap. 2 shows that English 16th-century books of rhetoric advocated use of ornamental language, and also recognized that "exornation" could serve functional purposes. Chap. 3 discusses recurrent patterns of eagle, lion, and nautical similes, shows "how they carry within themselves interrelated themes that transcend their particular contexts." Chap. 4 relates similes of Bk. I to Red Cross Knight's developing character, Chap. 5 those of Bk. II to theme of temperate actions, Chap. 6 those of Bk. III to nature of Britomart's chastity. Chap. 7 studies similes of whole poem in contexts of battle and of characterization. Chap. 8 classifies similes of whole poem according to kind. Chap. 9 examines relationship of similes in Bk. I to stanzaic form.

Fowler, Alastair. Numerical Composition in *The Faerie Queene*, JWCI, 25 (1962), 199-239.   **1366**

Anticipates Fowler's Spenser and the Numbers of Time (1367) by describing components in numerological pattern of FQ. Structural arrangements of various books correspond, in order, to their own numbers in the Pythagorean series; and finds numerological basis to the placement of analogous material in similar canto positions in various books.

Fowler, Alastair. Spenser and the Numbers of Time. London: Routledge and Kegan Paul, 1964. Illus. 314 pp. **1367**

Study of numerical symbolism in FQ which argues that every complete book is permeated with reference to and suggestive application of its own number in the Pythagorean series (Bk. I is the book of the Monad, II of the Diad, III of the Triad, etc.), with associated references to the planets in the order of the planetary week. 25 iconographical plates between pp. 148 and 149. Appendices on The Arithomological Stanza, FQ, II, ix, 22—see 1254, 1908, 1920, 1936,

1962; and The Horoscope of Phantastes, FQ, II, ix, 52.

Rev: Joan Grundy, MLR, 60 (1965), 92; Patricia Thomson, RES, 16 (1965), 414; William Nelson, RN, 18 (1965), 52; David Kalstone, EIC, 15 (1965), 446.

Fowler, Alastair D. S. Oxford and London Marginalia to *The Faerie Queen*, N&Q, 8 (1961), 416-9.   1368

Examination of marginal notes in ten Oxford and London copies of FQ tends to justify reading of Sp as "emblematic," for such a reading has sound historical precedent.

Fowler, Earl B. Spenser and the System of Courtly Love. Louisville, Ky.: Standard Printing Co., 1935; repr. New York: Phaeton, 1968. 91 pp.   1369

Atkinson, p. 112.

Fox, Robert C. The Allegory of Sin and Death in *Paradise Lost*, MLQ, 24 (1963), 354-64.   1370

Thesis: "Sin and Death represent the respective sins of lust and gluttony in addition to their nominal concepts." Shows this allegory relevant to theme and structure of Paradise Lost in appearances of Sin and Death in Bks. II and X. Sp adapts from Hesiod genealogy of Sin and Death in meeting of Squire of Dames and Sir Satyrane with incestuous siblings Argante and Ollyphant (FQ, III, vii, 47-51; xi, 3-4). Ties of blood and sex that unite Sin and Death emphasized by Church Fathers. Relationship between drunkenness and lust axiomatic in Middle Ages, occurs in Bower of Bliss (FQ, II, xii), at Castle Joyous (III, i, 31-67), and at Castle of Malbecco (ix, 27-31). Discusses other fusions of carnal sins in imaginative embodiments by Milton.

Fox, Robert C. The Character of Mammon in *Paradise Lost*, RES, 13 (1962), 30-9.   1371

Three phases to avarice of Milton's Mammon: miserliness, industrialism, and prodigality. This division corresponds to pattern used by Sp in Cave of Mammon episode in FQ (II, vii). Evil of Mammon's soul expands to include more comprehensive vice of injustice, examples of which Artegall puts down in Bk. V of FQ. Sp was decisive influence in characterization of Milton's Mammon.

Frantz, David Oswin. Concepts of Concupiscence in English Renaissance Literature. DAI, 30 (1969), 1133A. University of Pennsylvania, 1968. 345 pp.   1372

Passion termed "concupiscence" in Renaissance means excessive sexual appetite, physical and psychological lust, generally condemned as a sin. Different from physical love glorified in Ovidian works. Shows treatment of concupiscence ranges from theology to pornography. Chapters on theological discussions of lust, problems of definition, traditional views of subject, treatments in artistic and salacious non-dramatic works. Chapter on Sp's story of Malbecco in FQ, III, ix-x, showing how Sp transformed varied and pedestrian materials into artistic unity. Discusses Thomas Dekker's The Roaring Girl and John Marston's The Dutch Courtesan. Ends with chapter on Shakespeare's Antony and Cleopatra.

Freeman, Rosemary. "The Faerie Queene": A Companion for Readers. Berkeley: University of California Press, 1970. 350 pp.   1373

Part One: Chap. I, versatility of poetry, relation between landscape and characters in it, continuous variety; Chap. II, construction and narrative design; Chap. III, "multiple allegory." Part Two recounts in detail narrative of each book under suggestive heading: (I) "illusion"; (II) "distortion"; (III) "solitude and separation"; (IV) "unity and reconciliation"; (V) "justice and politics"; (VI) "humanity and courtesy"; (VII) "truth." Topical and name Index (pp. 339-50).

Rev: A. Kent Hieatt, RenQ, 24 (1971), 557; Carol V. Kaske, JEGP, 71 (1972), 121.

Friedmann, Anthony E. The Diana-Acteon Episode in Ovid's *Metamorphoses* and *The Faerie Queene*, CL, 18 (1966), 289-99. 1374

Sp, employing grammar-school technique of imitating classical authors, used the Ovidian episode in descriptive details of Bower of Bliss, Belphoebe's bower, Diana's fountain, Garden of Adonis, Faunus-Diana episode, meeting of Una and the lion, Arthur's dream of Gloriana, and tapestry in House of Busirane.

Friedmann, Anthony Edward. The Description of Landscape in Spenser's *Faerie Queene:* A Study of Rhetorical Tradition. DA, 26 (1966), 6039A. Columbia University, 1965. 303 pp. 1375

Concerns FQ passages which portray settings of major allegorical episodes: FQ, I, sacred hill; II, Bower of Bliss; III, Garden of Adonis; IV, Temple of Venus; VI, Mt. Acidale; VII, Dame Nature's pavilion. Distinguishes on basis of rhetorical tradition between what is conventional and what original in Sp's descriptions. Chap. I: defines problem, showing that romantic critical conceptions of landscape have obscured Sp's intent. Chap. II: outlines concepts in traditional rhetorical theory which illuminate Sp's description. Chap. III: illustrates from classical authors traditional elements in Sp's descriptions. Chaps. IV and V cite Virgil and Ovid as models for Sp's descriptions. Chaps. VI and VII: the medieval contribution, especially symbol, emblem, allegory. Chap. VIII: landscape in Sannazaro, Ariosto, and Tasso. Chap IX: influence of Elizabethan gardens and landscapes.

Chap. X concludes that "the importance of landscape descriptions in the poem results both from the resonance of tradition and from Spenser's imaginative innovations and adaptations."

Frost, David L. The School of Shakespeare: The Influence of Shakespeare on English Drama 1600-42. Cambridge: University Press, 1968. 304 pp. 1376

Discussion in Chap. 6, "Beaumont and Fletcher": "Crows and Daws," The return to Romance (pp. 209-26), discounts any influence of younger dramatists on Shakespeare in last plays, detailing implausibility of such influence. By 1600 romance was most honored form of fiction, Sidney's Arcadia and Sp's FQ dominant examples. Shakespeare in dramatic romances of last phase employed their mixed techniques, e.g., last Act of Pericles resembles symbolic episodes in FQ, Hermione's statue in The Winter's Tale raises question of Art and Nature, Prospero in The Tempest an image of controlling Providence. Shakespeare's audience trained in allegorical interpretation. See 1477.

Frye, Northrop. Levels of Meaning in Literature, KR, 12 (1950), 246-62. 1377

A modern restatement of the medieval theory of four levels of meaning: (1) literal, (2) allegorical, (3) tropological or moral, and (4) anagogical. (1) requires total comprehension of a verbal structure and precedes criticism. (2) occurs explicitly when the writer indicates a continuous relationship of his central structure to a set of external facts. "This continuous counterpoint between the saying and the centrifugal meaning is called allegory only when the relation is direct. If the relation is one of contrast, we call it irony." (3) is the archetypal or mythical level, also the social level. (4) is an intuition of total form in a totally intelligible universe, in historical fact given a religious bent because of the inescapability of Christian theology. Sp's method in FQ in a context of modern criticism.

Frye, Northrop. The Structure of Imagery in *The Faerie Queene*, UTQ, 30 (1961), 109-27; see 696; repr. in 756.
1378

Assumes as working hypothesis, and concludes at end of essay, that six complete books of FQ form a unified structure. FQ is a romance; its imagery is organized (1) by the natural cycle of days and seasons and (2) by the "moral dialectic," in which symbols of virtue are parodied by their vicious or demonic counterparts, fact which allows Sp to use any image ambivalently. Central themes of FQ are private and public education; Bks. I-III, the books of private education, are tied together by the virtue of fidelity, Bks. IV-VI, books of public education, by the virtue of concord. Four levels of imagery: two extremes, heavenly imagery and its demonic parodies; and two levels of natural imagery, that of Faerie or unfallen, ideal nature, of Eden and the Golden Age, and that of ordinary nature of man since the fall.

Fujii, Haruhiko. Spenser no Graces, Eigo Seinen [The Rising Generation] (Tokyo), 114 (1968), 442-3.　　1379

The Graces in FQ.

Gang, Theodor M. Nature and Grace in *The Faerie Queene:* The Problem Reviewed, ELH, 26 (1959), 1-22.　　1380

Reassesses the problems raised by Woodhouse, ibid., 16 (1949), 194-228 (see 1752), whose dichotomy between the order of Nature and the order of Grace in FQ, I and II is an unwarranted oversimplification of Renaissance Protestantism. Reviews Luther's and Calvin's expositions of the two orders, and the Catholic teaching concerning natural and supernatural virtues; Woodhouse's concept of the two orders is closer to the Catholic concept but not identical with it, and in fact looks like a fusion of incompatible Catholic and Protestant views. This leads him to misinterpret Una's lion and the satyrs, Satyrane, Red Cross's falling victim to Orgoglio after escaping Lucifera, the relation of practical good conduct to Christian virtue, the significance of Maleger, and various other points in the two books. Concludes that "Spenser is not usually interested in the contrast between nature and supernature." The poem is not affected in any significant way by the distinction. See 1753.

Gang, Theodor M. Spenser and the Death of Socrates, TLS, Aug. 3, 1956, p. 463.
1381

Gives reason for Sp's confusion of Critias and "the 'dearest Belamy' of Socrates" in FQ, IV, Proem, 3 and II, vii, 52.

Geller, Lila Green. The Three Graces in Spenser's *Faerie Queene:* Image and Structure in Books III and VI. DAI, 30 (1970), 4985A. University of California, Los Angeles, 1969. 237 pp. 1382

Neoplatonic image of the graces, who unfold from Venus, is a paradigm for the structure of FQ, III, wherein Florimel, Belphoebe, and Amoret unfold from Britomart (related to the loving Venus of Garden of Adonis), and the anti-grace figures False Florimel, Malecasta, and Hellenore relate to the lusting Venus of Castle Joyous. FQ, VI emphasizes the graces not in relation to Venus, but as symbols of liberality, and in relation to Apollo, the god of poetry. The fourth grace illustrates special providence of God, who can lift a man from base to noble position, and also shows order of art comparable to order of social relationships and to order of the heavens. See 1211.

Giamatti, A. Bartlett. The Earthly Paradise and the Renaissance Epic. Princeton: Princeton University Press, 1966. 374 pp.   1383

Examines word *paradise*, traces concept of Golden Age, surveys lovely gardens in classical and medieval poetry and development of Christian earthly paradise. Shows garden in Dante's Purgatorio XXVIII is pivotal in Divine Comedy. Briefly considers garden in Petrarch's Trionfo d'Amore, Poliziano's Le Stanze, Mantuan's Parthenica Secunda, then concentrates on Alcina's garden in Ariosto's Orlando Furioso. Compares gardens in Trissino's Italia Liberata da' Goti, Tasso's Gerusalemme Liberata, and Camões' Os Lusiadas. Chap. 5 on Sp (pp. 232-94) gives general commentary on FQ, detailed comparison and contrast of Bower of Bliss (II, xii) with Italian gardens, brief remarks on Garden of Adonis (III, vi, 29-54), and discursive bibliography. Chap. 6 on Milton. See 1331. [Diss., Yale University, 1964.]
Rev: J. L. Lievsay, CLS, 4 (1967), 331; A. Bullock, RenQ, 20 (1967), 31; L. M. Ferrarri, Italica, 44 (1967), 368; Michael N. Nagler, CL, 21 (1969), 377.

Giamatti, A. Bartlett. Proteus Unbound: Some Versions of the Sea God in the Renaissance, in The Disciplines of Criticism: Essays in Literary Theory, Interpretation, and History, ed. Peter Demetz, and others, pp. 437-75. New Haven: Yale University Press, 1968.
                                            1384

Cites 1646 on tradition of Proteus as King of Egypt, and for commentary on story in FQ, III, viii, 29 ff., of Proteus's rescue and attempted rape of Florimell, Proteus the lawbreaker (pp. 437 n., 470 n.). Archimago ex-

plicitly identified with Proteus in FQ, I, ii, 10, passage that "looks back to the whole tradition of the *magus* and Proteus's associations with him," and Sp applies imagery of Proteus again to Archimago in I, xii, 35, and II, i, 1. Demonic forces in FQ can never be entirely defeated: Duessa, the Dragon, Archimago, Despair, the Blatant Beast (pp. 458-9).

Gilbert, Allan H. The Qualities of the Renaissance Epic, SAQ, 53 (1954), 372-8.   1385

Defines the Renaissance epic as a narrative poem involving warfare and adventure. Orlando Furioso is representative of the type and exerted extensive influence, particularly through its multiple actions, on later European works, e.g., FQ, and even Bartholomew Fair and King Lear. Paradise Lost derives its parallel earthly and heavenly actions from Orlando Furioso, making it primarily a Renaissance creation and only secondarily "classical."

Gilbert, Allan H. Spenserian Armor, PMLA, 57 (1942). 981-7.   1386

In his descriptions of armor Sp was not concerned with realism or military exactness, but was governed by the formulae of earlier romances and literary ideas.

Gilde, Helen Cheney. "The Sweet Lodge of Love and Deare Delight": The Problem of Amoret, PQ, 50 (1971), 63-74.
                                            1387

Amoret is unable to reconcile her inbred conception of love as "chaste affection" with her experience of sexual passion in the real world. Withdraws from Scudamour and becomes victim of Busyrane (FQ, III, xi-xii). Rescued by Britomart, who unites love and passion; her hermaphroditic reunion with Scudamour (1590 ending) indicates acceptance of sexuality.

Separated from husband and protectress, falls victim to Lust (FQ, IV, vii), rescued by Belphoebe, "mere chastity." [SpN, Vol. 2, No. 2 (1971), 6.]

Gittings, Robert. Ten Days in the Life of Keats, TLS, 14 March, 1952, p. 196.

1388

A ten-day fictional diary of Keats leading up to composition of La Belle Dame sans Merci, influenced by Sp's FQ. See 1305.

Glazier, Lyle. The Nature of Spenser's Imagery, MLQ, 16 (1955), 300-10.

1389

Sp's imagery is different from that of the painter, the lyric poet, or the non-allegorical poet. "Where in Shakespeare imagery is a by-product of drama, in Spenser drama or narrative is a by-product of imagery, for the characters in the poem are themselves images of moral values, and the resolution of conflicts between these images is the true subject of the poem." FQ is much simpler than is sometimes supposed. Most important is "the general and simple contrast between images of Good and images of Evil which permeates the whole poem."

Glazier, Lyle Edward. Spenser's Imagery: Imagery of Good and Evil in the Faerie Queene. Doctoral diss., Harvard University, 1950. HRDP, 1949-1950, p. 20; DDAAU, 1949-50, No. 17.   1390

Imagery of FQ has reiterative antitheses—Life-Death, Light-Dark, Health-Disease, Naturalness-Artificiality, Courtesy-Discourtesy, Truth-Falsehood, Love-Lust—which result in "a complex tissue of interlocking imagistic motifs." Characters often become symbols on one side or the other of these imagistic and moral antitheses. Similarly with descriptions of places, through favorable or pejora-

tive connotations. Study of imagery helps explain ambiguous characters like Radigund (Bk. V), Talus (Bk. V), and Mutability (Bk. VII). Defends Sp against charge of thin imagistic texture. Introductory chapter on nature of Sp's imagery, chapters on imagery of each book of FQ, two others of general criticism. See 1807.

Gohlke, Madelon Sprengnether. Narrative Structure in the New Arcadia, The Faerie Queene I, and The Unfortunate Traveller. DAI, 33 (1972), 723A. Yale University, 1972. 356 pp.   1391

Each work has been criticized for lack of coherent narrative structure. Charge of "formlessness" derives from narrow conception of literary structure, which for us involves spatial rather than temporal orientation. In these three works "structure" is temporal, not spatial. In them "structure emerges in conjunction with the progressive revelation of the thematic organization of the work." Narrative structure "not rigid or uniform, but rather flexible and even metamorphic." It derives from these authors' attitude toward external world, belief in "the fundamental darkness of perception and the difficulty of discerning human purpose and design.... The form of the fiction" reflects their sense of reality.

Goldsmith, Robert N. The Wild Man on the English Stage, MLR, 53 (1958), 481-91.   1392

Sp well acquainted with mythology of the wild man. Uses two conflicting themes in repulsive cannibal who captures Amoret (FQ, IV, vii), kin to medieval wodewoses, in whom "the carnal and the carnivorous appetites are symbolically joined"; and in gentle savage who is courteous to Serena (FQ, VI, iv), "but he is a reformed wild man." Relates first figure to "the fantastic tales of the far voyagers . . . from Eden to Ralegh" (pp. 488-90). See 1271, 1363.

Gottfried, Rudolf, ed. Ariosto's *Orlando Furioso:* Selections from the Translation of Sir John Harington. Bloomington: Indiana University Press, 1963. 351 pp.   1393

Based on Harington's revised text of 1607; modernized punctuation and spelling. "The passages selected are primarily intended to show the quality and character of Ariosto's poem, but it is hoped that they may also serve as background reading for students of Spenser's *Faerie Queene*" (p. 23).

Gottfried, Rudolf B. Edmund Spenser and the NCTE; and Ohmann, Carol. Reply to Rudolf B. Gottfried, CE, 33 (1971), 76-83.   1394

Exchange arising from Gottfried's attack on archetypal approach to Sp (1395) and Ohmann's reply to it (1590). Gottfried reaffirms his point that Northrop Frye's "archetypal approach has distorted criticism" of FQ, and concludes: "knowledge of the poet and his work . . . is primary for literary scholarship. . . . My first allegiance is not to Northrop Frye but to Edmund Spenser." Ohmann denies that Frye's approach is purely archetypal, and questions whether his treatment of the Mutability Cantos is "even archetypal at all." She concludes: "As Frye habitually reminds us, both poetry and criticism are acts of communication; they take rise from a social context and they speak, always, to our social, even political, concerns." [SpN, Vol. 2, No. 3 (1971), 8.]

Gottfried, Rudolf B. Our New Poet: Archetypal Criticism and *The Faerie Queen*, PMLA, 83 (1968), 1362-77.   1395

Rejects Northrop Frye's systems of archetypal criticism (695) as dogmatic and simplistic, tending to distort structure and meaning of FQ. Frye's refusal to consider artist's intention leads to view that artist is both irresponsible and unconscious, and opens the door to the archetypal hunt for universal patterns. In analyzing FQ (1378) Frye is ambiguous about completeness of work in six books and is so unclear about defining allegory and image that reader is understandably lost. A. C. Hamilton (1416) follows Frye in assuming that FQ is structured on images, that autonomous archetypal patterns govern these images, and that FQ is a complete whole. Hamilton's program of concentrating on the surface of the poem is not new; he does not write clearly; he misreads the text; he ignores Bennett's conclusions (1263) about structure of FQ; and he cannot make up his own mind about FQ's structure. See 1394, 1590.

Gransden, K. W. Allegory and Personality in Spenser's Heroes, EIC, 20 (1970), 298-310.   1396

Examines Sp's epic heroes, especially Artegall and Guyon. Concludes they are "more instruments than agents" of their particular virtues of justice and temperance.

Gransden, K. W. A Critical Commentary on Spenser's *The Faerie Queene.* London: Macmillan, 1969. 98 pp.   1397

A companion to the reading of the poem. Chapters on Plan and Purpose of FQ, The Style of the Poem, Influence and Ideas. Reviews allegory, epic tradition, Virgil's Aeneid, the idea of "Metamorphosis," medieval legend and romance, Italian Renaissance epic, the moral virtues, significance of Arthur. Bk. I, The Allegory of Holiness; The Middle Books, II and III; Bk. VI, Sp and Pastoral. Deals only briefly with Bk. IV, hardly mentions Bk. V.

Gransden, K. W. The Pastoral Alternative, Arethusa, 3 (Spring 1970), 103-21; (Fall 1970), 177-96.   1398

Discusses interplay of values in classical pastoral (poetry of content) and epic (poetry of discontent). Cites visits of Aeneas to Evander (Aeneid, 8), "regal authority in a simple pastoral context," and to Dido (Aeneid, 4), "regal authority in a sophisticated 'courtly' context." Contrast between "nature" and "art" reappears in Ariosto's Isle of Alcina, Tasso's bower of Armida, Sp's Garden of Adonis and Bower of Bliss (FQ, III, vi and II, xii), and Milton's Eden. Discusses pastoral courtesy as idealized courtly virtue in FQ, VI; contrasts time-scale of pastoral and heroic poetry; retirement to harsh surroundings when hurt, e.g., Timias's expression of failure by becoming a hermit, paradoxically similar to withdrawal from Didonian Bower of Bliss. [SpN, Vol. 1, No. 3 (1970), 12.]

Grant, Douglas. Barker Fairley on Charles Doughty, UTQ, 36 (1967), 220-28.
        1399

John Hayward's recent anthology of 19th-century English verse includes nothing of Charles Doughty's The Dawn in Britain, first published in six volumes 1906-1907. Barker Fairley's critical study of Doughty published 1927, and his selection of passages from poem published 1935, tried to introduce Doughty as poet to wider public but failed. The Dawn in Britain written in tradition of Chaucer and his disciple Sp on "a great national theme, the evolution of the English people and the planting of Christianity among them . . . the narrative is in the spirit of Spenser's mythology." Poem lacks "the quality that wins complete acceptance for the

prose of [Doughty's] Arabia Deserta"—irony. Therefore Doughty's poem, like his master Sp, remains unread.

Gray, Jack Cooper. Major Patterns of Imagery in The Faerie Queene. DA, 25 (1965), 5904. Syracuse University, 1964. 424 pp.   1400

Examines imagery of vision (in descriptions of persons, places, and times of day) and imagery of action (including journeys, bondage, wounding, serpents) in FQ, and concludes that this imagery "reinforces Spenser's twin themes of love and war by evoking twin moral imperatives—first see the ideal, then act properly in response to it."

Greaves, Margaret. The Blazon of Honour: A Study in Renaissance Magnanimity. London: Methuen, 1964. 142 pp.   1401

Studies use of term "magnanimity," Aristotle's "megalopsychia," in medieval and Renaissance English writers, including Chaucer, Malory, Elyot, Marlowe, Sidney, Sp, Jonson, Traherne, and Milton. Chap. 5, "The Eternal Brood of Glorie" (pp. 75-93), deals with FQ. Discusses each book in succession, concludes that in FQ the magnanimous man is neither medieval man seeking heaven and heedless of worldly honor nor Renaissance man seeking worldly honor consistent with his Christian ethic, but "the Christian soul in quest of glory." He looks forward to vaster conception of "the divine magnanimity of the unfallen Adam."

Greco, Francis Gabriel. Torquato Tasso's Theory of the Epic and its Influence on Edmund Spenser's The Faerie Queene. DAI, 30 (1970), 2967A-8A. Duquesne University, 1969. 188 pp.   1402

Tasso is a literary theorist as well as poet. His principles of the epic poem are set forth in Discorsi dell'arte poetica and later in Discorsi del poema eroico. Presents evidence establishing feasibility of Sp-Tasso relationship in literary theory. Detailed analysis of parallels between principles in earlier Discorsi and their embodiment in FQ deals with poetic selection and illustration of single virtues in individual characters, use of obscure allegory, attempt to achieve unity out of diversity, and use of lexical and syntactic innovation to enhance epic effect. Sp's use of Tasso's Discorsi in composing FQ is strongly suggested.

Green, Zaidee E. Swooning in the *Faerie Queene*, SP, 34 (1937), 126-33.   1403

Sp's use of the swoon as a narrative device.

Greene, Thomas. The Norms of Epic, CL, 13 (1961), 193-207.   1404

Distinguishes four major characteristics of epic: (1) expansiveness of its imagery; (2) limitation placed on the hero, who is not a god but a political figure subject to society; (3) predominance and alternation of "pathetic" episodes, involving activity, and "ethical" episodes stressing character, manners, politics; (4) overwhelming energy which charges character and action. FQ mentioned under (2): to degree that landscape of Faerieland is merely the hero's soul, FQ is not epic; to degree that Sp evokes a world exterior to the hero, FQ participates in epic.

Guth, Hans P. Allegorical Implications of Artifice in Spenser's *Faerie Queene*, PMLA, 76 (1961), 474-9.   1405

Disputes C. S. Lewis's position that Sp's attitude toward deliberate artifice is solely negative (1513). Both nature and art in FQ are employed beyond the literal, pictorial level and

are essential to the poem as allegory. Being allegorical rather than symbolic, they need not assume exclusive connotations as either "good" or "evil." See 1535.

Guth, Hans P. Unity and Multiplicity in Spenser's *Faerie Queene*, Anglia, 74 (1956), 1-15.   1406

The poet's moral purpose is to define the chivalric ideal, especially as this ideal affects the relation between the sexes and the relation between the individual and society. Finds in this two-fold theme the artistic unity of the poem.

Haeffner, Paul. Keats and the Faery Myth of Seduction, REL (Leeds), 3 (1962), 20-31.   1407

Endymion shows Keats's fondness for Spenserian romanticism and Celtic mythology, also bears on own psychological crisis. Knew several versions of myth of faery seduction, including A Midsummer Night's Dream—"not wholly in satirical vein, despite the ass's head in lieu of immortality." In FQ, "connection between faery and seduction is prominent and ubiquitous": Red Cross (by Duessa), knights at Castle Joyous (by Malecasta), Artegal (by Radigund), Timias (by Amoret), Calidore (by Pastorella).

Hageman, Elizabeth Harrison. Spenser and the Rhetoricians: A Study of Rhetorical Forms and Figures in *The Faerie Queene*. DAI, 32 (1972), 6929A. University of North Carolina at Chapel Hill, 1971. 259 pp.   1408

The patterns of rhetoric in FQ often follow Homer, Virgil, Cicero, Quintilian, Ariosto, and Tasso. Sp openly utilized classical orations in Bk. III (Britomart's threnos, Arthur's complaint to Night, and Scudamour's lament), as well as effictio, acquired from Chaucer, picturae, chronographia, apostrophe, and topographiae. Thus "Spenser's meaning is determined by his choice of structures and by his use of figures of sound and sense which reinforce and even create those structures."

Hallowell, Robert E. Ronsard and the Gallic Hercules Myth, SRen, 9 (1962), 242-55.   1409

Greek sophist Lucian in his Heracles claimed to have seen curious picture of Hercules in Gaul symbolically identifying god with Eloquence—origin of Gallic Hercules. Renaissance mythographers embellished this myth, chroniclers spread exploits of Hercules in Spain and traced origin of French nation to Gallic Hercules. Most important popularizer in picture and word Alciati's Emblemata, translated into French 1536. Most famous allusion to myth du Bellay's exhortation at end of Deffence et illustration de la langue françoyse (1549). For Ronsard in several poems Hercules Gallicus was symbol of eloquence, "of the 'golden word' dear to the Neoplatonists." Relevant to Sp's use of Hercules. See 1468, 2093, 2099.

Hamilton, A. C. The Faerie Queene, in Critical Approaches to Six Major English Works, ed. Robert M. Lumiansky and Herschel Baker, pp. 132-66. Philadelphia: University of Pennsylvania Press, 1968. 266 pp.   1410

Criticism of FQ lacks restraint and needs to be controlled, allowing more inclusive and central interpretation of the poem. Gives particular attention to allegory and Wandering Wood of Bk. I, canto i. The poem's complexity derives from its simultaneous operation as epic, allegory, and romance. Concerning allegory, argues "that Spenser controls his meanings through the structure of images within each book, the relationships between the books and groups of them,

and the unity of the whole poem." FQ needs less commentary and interference with the reader's responses; criticism should help him to approach the work as a whole.

Hamilton, A. C. "Like Race to Runne": The Parallel Structure of The Faerie Queene, Books I and II, PMLA, 73 (1958), 327-34.   1411

A refinement and sharpening of Woodhouse's explanation (see 1752) that the two orders of grace and nature, respectively, provide a frame of reference for the action of Books I and II. Studies in detail "the pattern of inner meaning realized by the parallel structure of the first two books." Red Cross Knight exemplifies "man's fall from grace into sin," while Guyon "shows how temperance may prevent that fall." Sp's method is one of full parallel with contrast. The two orders of grace and nature, and the different levels, religious and secular, are not exclusive; "Book I transcends the natural level explored in Book II by including it."

Hamilton, A.C. Spenser and the Common Reader, ELH, 35 (1968), 618-33. 1412

Review article on Alpers' The Poetry of The Faerie Queene (1231). Praises his examination of the reader's response to individual stanzas as an original and major contribution. Condemns Alpers for "limiting our response to the initial impact of an episode or canto as though it existed in isolation," and for adopting a thesis which applies, if at all, only to the first three books of the poem.

Hamilton, A. C. Spenser's Letter to Ralegh, MLN, 73 (1958), 481-5.   1413

Purpose of letter is to defend fictional method of FQ, and therefore to underline its didacticism. Sp does not say poem is rigorously formal; the adventures are to be "severally handled and discoursed." Letter accomplishes its purpose. Rightly read, it is in harmony with the scheme of the poem. See 1604, 2561.

Hamilton, A. C. Spenser's Pastoral, ELH, 33 (1966), 518-31.   1414

Review article on Donald Cheney's Spenser's Image of Nature (1310). Cites central theme of "man's quest for his identity," and emphasizes attention to psychological probing in the poem and attention to ambiguities which, for Cheney, invite reader's active participation in bringing meaning to the poem. Criticizes book for excluding from serious consideration much of the heroic aspect of FQ and much of the moral, religious, and historical background which this aspect implies. Suggests that Cheney's emphasis on ambiguities may well tend to undercut, negate, or confuse plain meaning of many crucial passages. Praises interest and sensitivity of treatment of Bk. VI, sustained quality of central argument, and energy and sophistication which Cheney's response to the poem shows.

Hamilton, A. C. Spenser's Treatment of Myth, ELH, 26 (1959), 335-54; repr. in 644.   1415

Sp's treatment of classical mythology throws light on the allegory and method of FQ. His recreation of classical mythology is so thorough that it belongs to the invention of his poem. In Book I, "his treatment is episodic, and provides a point-counterpoint analogy between classical and Christian elements of man's fall and restoration." In Book II, his treatment is organic, containing the myths within his own poetic pattern. In Books III and IV, his treatment is thematic: the classical myths of Venus and Adonis and Cupid and Psyche "provide the contrapuntal framework for his alle-

gory." In Book VI, his treatment is romantic.

Hamilton, A. C. The Structure of Allegory in The Faerie Queene. Oxford: Clarendon Press, 1961. 227 pp. See 649.   1416

We must read the poem simultaneously on the literal and allegorical levels, and receive its language as an attempt to create the literal impression of Biblical fiction in which Truth equals the word (in this case Arthur becomes the Word). In Bk. I especially, we must see the poem as an allegorical epic in the ancient tradition, actually a rejection of pastoralism for the business of life. In Bks. I and II especially, we must understand that the architectonics of the poem derive from apocalyptic doctrine. In Bks. III and IV especially, we must read the poem as fiction—an imaginative argument. In Bk. V we must allow for the succumbing of fiction to didacticism. Red Cross's struggle with Error (I, i) prefigures the whole of Bk. I, and the pattern of fall, redemption, regeneration and restoration in Bk. I prefigures the remaining books. [Diss., University of Cambridge, 1953.]

Rev: Michel Poirier, EA, 15 (1962), 73; Joan Grundy, MLR, 57 (1962), 241; Hugh Maclean, DR, 42 (1962), 131; Hallett Smith, RN, 15 (1962), 41; Millar MacLure, UTQ, 32 (1962), 83; Waldo F. McNeir, CL, 15 (1963), 67; Maurice Evans, RES, 14 (1963), 192.

Hamilton, A. C. The Visions of Piers Plowman and The Faerie Queene, in Form and Convention in the Poetry of Edmund Spenser, ed. William Nelson, pp. 1-34. New York: Columbia University Press, 1961. 188 pp.   1417

Develops the ideas in 1813. Langland the Homer of English tradition, Sp his son. FQ, I and Piers Plowman relate as analogues (detailed, parallel analysis). One chief difference is structural: structure of Piers Plowman is cumulative, growing as if shaped while being written; structure of FQ is rhetorical (analysis of Bk. II shows that it follows the form of classical oration). Allegory of both poems requires we read literal level not by translating it but by retaining it as metaphor (demonstrated from the Dreamer's vision of Piers-Christ harrowing hell and Redcrosse's battle with the dragon).

Hammerle, Karl. Das Laubenmotif bei Shakespeare und Spenser und die Frage: wer waren Bottom und die Little Western Flower? Anglia, 71 (1953), 310-30.   1418

Carries further A. G. van Kranendonk's Spenserian Echoes in A Midsummer Night's Dream, ES, 14 (1932), 209-17 (listed in Atkinson, p. 81). Sees in the fairy drama of Shakespeare a burlesque of Sp's fairy epic. Relies on the common "foliage theme." Stresses verbal parallels. Bottom is Sp. The "kleine westliche Blume" is Elizabeth Carey, who appears in CCCHA, ll. 434-43.

Hammerle, Karl. Ein Muttermal des deutschen Pyramus und die Spenserechos in A Midsummer Night's Dream, WBEP, 66 (1958), 52-66.   1419

Tries to show, by quoting pertinent passages, that much of the humor in the interlude of Pyramus and Thisbe derives from a parody of Sp's style and diction, especially in FQ. Attributes weaknesses in German translations of the Pyramus passage to the translators' failure to understand the point of the parody.

Hankins, John E. Spenser's Lucifera and Philotime, MLN, 59 (1944), 413-5. 1420

The name "Lucifera" (FQ, I, iv) seems to be derived from Natalis Comes, and "Philotime" (FQ, II, vii) from Thomas Aquinas.

Hankins, John Erskine. Source and Meaning in Spenser's Allegory: A Study of The Faerie Queen. Oxford: Clarendon Press, 1971. 337pp.   1421

Argues that Sp's use of the virtues follows that of Francesco Piccolomini in Universa Philosophia de Moribus (1583). Develops this argument in four chapters applicable to FQ as whole: The Basis of Allegory, The Method of the Allegory, The Allegorical Quest, and The Allegorical Landscape. Emphasizes internal allegory, in which "the interior of the soul is the battleground on which the action is fought," as in Prudentius's Psychomachia. Allegorical quest proceeds through place of testing, place of perfecting, and final test to glory and honor. Allegorical landscape contains castles, forests, caves, and waters (pp. 1-98). Five chapters discuss moral allegory of holiness (see 1814 and 756); temperance; friendship, chastity and love; justice; and courtesy (pp. 99-199). Chap. on historical allegory deals mainly with Bk. I (pp. 200-27). Chap. on physical allegory discusses Florimell, Marinell, and Proteus; various aspects of Garden of Adonis; and Mutability Cantos (pp. 228-97).

Hanson-Smith, Elizabeth Ann. Be Fruitful and Multiply: The Medieval Allegory of Nature. DAI, 33 (1972), 2892A. Stanford University, 1972. 416 pp.   1422

Main influences in development of allegory were Augustine, Macrobius, and Boethius. Universe is personified in figure of Nature. Shows allegory of Nature taking form from various traditions, gathering force in Middle Ages, expressing itself in Roman de la Rose, Parlement of Foules, and Piers the Plowman. FQ is revival of combined romance-allegory mode. Bunyan treated as last allegorist of importance and first novelist.

Hard, Frederick. Two Spenserian Imitations, by "T. W.," ELH, 5 (1938), 113-26. 1423

The Lamentation of Melpomene, for the death of Belphaebe our late Queen ... By T. W. Gentleman (1603) shows Sp's influence. "T. W." is probably Thomas Walkington, who is generally credited with authorship of The Optick Glasse of Humors (1607), which closes with another poem in Spenserian manner.

Harnet, Arthur. Dante en Angleterre. Doctoral diss., Univ. of Paris, Sorbonne, 1956. 1424

FQ is the Divine Comedy of Christian experience (pp. 144, 158). Compares Dante's and Sp's conception of allegory and concludes that poems like FQ and the Commedia "are radically different in sum from anything that can be embraced by a definition of allegory of whatever kind, theological or poetic" (pp. 177-81).

Harris, William O. Skelton's *Magnyfycence* and the Cardinal Virtue Tradition. Chapel Hill: University of North Carolina Press, 1965. 177 pp. 1425

Interprets Skelton's morality play, and others, in the light of St. Thomas Aquinas' partial fusion of Aristotle's magnanimity with cardinal virtue of magnificence, and tradition stemming therefrom. Discussion touches Sp's virtue of magnificence in FQ at many points, relates poem to morality play tradition, shows Aristotelian magnanimity synonymous with magnificence in context of non-Aristotelian cardinal virtues. See Index for references to Sp's FQ.

Harrison, Thomas P., Jr. Aspects of Primitivism in Shakespeare and Spenser, TxSE, 20 (1940), 39-71. 1426

Shakespeare's expressions of primitivism occur mainly in The Winter's Tale, The Tempest, and Cymbeline, romances which have a general kin-

ship with Sp's epic romance. Discusses pastoral scene in The Winter's Tale in relation to April eclogue of SC, Garden of Adonis (FQ, III, vi), and Phaedria's island (FQ, II, vi); ignoble savage Caliban in The Tempest in relation to unnamed noble savage who helps Calepine and Serena (FQ, VI, iv-v); idea of the importance of noble birth and discipline in Cymbeline in relation to this idea in Sp. Brings Timon of Athens and King Lear into the discussion also, but not with particular relevance to Sp.

Hartley, Jesse Dyson. A Study of the Imagery in Edmund Spenser's *The Faerie Queene*. DA, 24 (1963), 1160. University of Minnesota, 1963. 327 pp. 1427

Using Caroline F. E. Spurgeon's method of tabulation and pattern of classification, classifies Sp's imagery and draws conclusions about Sp's interests and ways of thinking. The images come from two areas, Sp's imagination and his everyday life. The imaginative images occur in personifications, allegory, myths, and legends; images from everyday life come from experience in law, warfare, the arts, rural life, and travels, and knowledge of England and its history. Reaches a wide variety of conclusions about Sp's interests and ways of thinking.

Heninger, S. K., Jr. The Tudor Myth of Troy-novant, SAQ, 61 (1962), 378-87. 1428

Treats amusingly unprecedented interest in England's past promoted by Tudor monarchs who linked themselves to Arthur and Cadwallader. Retells story of how Geoffrey of Monmouth added Brutus to European cults of folk heroes, discusses his descendants known in literature (Locrine, Leir, Gorbogudo and sons Ferrex and Porrex, Kymbelinus), and English place-names derived from Geoffrey. Sp's "orgy of adulation" in

FQ includes "chronicle of Briton kings" (II, x) and Merlin's prophecy to Britomart (III, iii). In Sp's time "the British chronicle was legendary history."

Hennessy, Helen. The Uniting of Romance and Allegory in *La Queste del Saint Graal*, BUSE, 4 (1960), 189-201.
1429

La Queste (ca. 1220), of Vulgate Cycle, attempts to reconcile castle (courtly romance) and cathedral (contemplative allegory). Christ becomes knight-errant on mission; after Piers Plowman, FQ, and Pilgrim's Progress, we hardly realize quest implicit in Bible is explicit for first time in French romances. Writer glosses allegorical incidents, whereas later allegorists (Sp, for instance) make meaning arise from incident. Compares groping of La Queste author with Malory's more successful union of romance narrative and allegory of human life, and complete integration of two in Sp; "the line of demarcation between romance and allegory is no longer visible. Courtly life has become contemplative."

Henry, Nathaniel H. The Mystery of Milton's Muse, in RenP 1967, ed. George Walton Williams, pp. 69-83. Southeastern Renaissance Conference, 1968. 103 pp.
1430

Thesis: Milton's muse primarily a literary conceit which reflects prayers to abstractions of Father, Son, *and* Holy Ghost; in this multiple appeal Milton follows practice of Homer, Lucretius, Virgil, Dante, Tasso, Du Bartas, and Sp. Cites Sp's multiple invocations in Proems to Bks. I and VI of FQ, and invocation of Clio by name in FQ, III, iii, 4.

Herron, Dale. The Focus of Allegory in the Renaissance Epic, Genre, 3 (1970), 176-86.
1431

Although Sp's FQ is "one of the first successful Renaissance epics," it is "often denied the status of epic entirely." Sp's poem product of several traditions: allegorical interpretation of Vergil's Aeneid and of scripture, Neo-Aristotelian studies, long poems of Boiardo and Ariosto, Tasso's allegorized version of his Jerusalem Delivered in Jerusalem Reconquered, Sidney's defense of poets as creators of golden worlds who "provide a bridge between ... the world of the ideal and the lapsarian world we know." In FQ many levels of allegory, also much literal truth. "As Spenser himself says in the letter to Raleigh, he will encompass the scope of all epics, romances, and allegories within his poem." We should accept his idea of what he thought he was doing.

Hieatt, Constance B. The Realism of Dream Visions: The Poetic Exploitation of the Dream Experience in Chaucer and his Contemporaries. The Hague: Mouton, 1967. 117 pp.
1432

FQ and "interesting allegory" of the Renaissance are as much from 14th-century "kaleidoscopic visions" as from 15th-century "systematic" allegory such as Everyman (p. 110).

Higashinaka, Itsuyo. Spenser's Use of the Idea of Love Melancholy in *The Faerie Queene*, SELit, English No. (1972), 129-50.
1433

Influence of contemporary ideas on Sp's treatment of causes, symptoms, prognostics, and cures of love melancholy in Bks. III and IV of FQ.

Hill, John M. Braggadocchio and Spenser's Golden World Concept: The Function of Unregenerative Comedy, ELH, 37 (1970), 315-24.
1434

Braggadocchio belongs outside Golden World toward which most narratives from FQ, II, iii-V, iii are directed. His figure defines Guyon's: braggart is temperate in non-virtuous way; his eviction by Artegall helps define one aspect of Justice. "Absurdity" of Braggadocchio enhances by contrast "sanity" of Golden World. [SpN, Vol. 1, No. 3 (1970), 9.]

Hill, R. F. Spenser's Allegorical "Houses," MLR, 65 (1970), 721-33.
                                                        1435

Evaluates allegorical "Houses" in terms of how well narrative dynamism and static allegory mesh or seem at cross purposes. Finds Cave of Despair (I, ix), Garden of Adonis (III, vi), and House of Care (IV, v) successful; Cave of Mammon (II, vii) and Bower of Bliss (II, xii) are not successful. Discusses other "Houses." [SpN, Vol. 2, No. 1 (1971), 5.]

Hoffman, Arthur W. An Apprenticeship in Praise, in Dryden's Mind and Art, ed. Bruce King, pp. 45-64. Edinburgh: Oliver and Boyd, 1969. 213 pp.   1436

Repr. from John Dryden's Imagery (Gainesville: University of Florida Press, 1962), pp. 1-19. In Astrea Redux faced problem of creating hero accommodating classical and Christian images, problem of Sp in FQ and Milton in Paradise Lost. Much later in career Dryden in translation of Virgil acknowledged "Spencer in English" as master, meaning in versification. Claimed Sp's example for concluding couplet with Alexandrine (pp. 62-4).

Hogan, Patrick Galvin, Jr. Sir Philip Sidney's Arcadia and Edmund Spenser's Faerie Queene: An Analysis of the Personal, Philosophic, and Iconographic Relationships. DA, 26 (1965), 1021-2. Vanderbilt University, 1965. 534 pp.   1437

First, evaluates in detail tradition of personal friendship. Second, studies assimilation by Sidney and Sp of Christian Neo-Platonism. They treated common philosophical themes such as moral virtues of Magnanimity, Justice, Courtesy, Temperance, and Constancy. Third, demonstrates possibility of link based on graphic arts, analyzes relation of pictorial influence to their imagery. Debt of Sidney and Sp to Renaissance iconography is climax of study.

Holleran, James V. Spenser's Braggadocchio, in Studies in English Renaissance Literature, ed. Waldo F. McNeir, pp. 20-40. Baton Rouge: Louisiana State University Press, 1962. 240 pp.   1438

Braggadocchio's career is anti-chivalric, a mock-heroic parallel to Guyon's adventures in FQ, II, a source of humor in III, x; and his fakery at Satyrane's tournament in IV, iv-v is exposed at "the spousals of faire Florimell" in V, iii.

Holleran, James V. A View of Comedy in The Faerie Queene, in Essays in Honor of Esmond Linworth Marilla, ed. Thomas Austin Kirby and William John Olive, pp. 101-14. Baton Rouge: Louisiana State University Press, 1970. 387 pp.   1439

FQ is full of "mockery, ridicule, adornment, pure joy," though Sp's humor is usually deadpan. Especially important to Sp's humor is the visualization of his episodes. Points out comic aspects of Squire of Dames (III, vii), Britomart and Glauce (III, ii-iii), and gives special attention to Malecasta episode (III, i) and comic adventures of Redcrosse (I).

Holleran, James Vincent. The Minor Characters in Spenser's Faerie Queene. DA, 22 (1962), 3664. Louisiana State University, 1961, 325 pp.   1440

Attempts to establish the importance of the minor figures in FQ, to "arrange them into groups on the basis of their functions, and to evaluate them as dramatic figures." Two principal groups are the antagonists and the protagonists. Among antagonists, outstanding figures Radigund and Braggadocchio reveal Sp's deftness in creating tragic and comic characters. Protagonists fall into three outstanding groups, lovers (Timias), squires (Glauce), and savages (Satyrane). Minor characters not only enhance dramatic dimensions of major characters, but deserve special attention in their own right.

Honig, Edwin. Dark Conceit: The Making of Allegory. New York: Oxford University Press, 1966. 210 pp.   1441

Repr. of 1959 ed. Challenges view in most literary histories that allegory is dead—from FQ on or earlier. Sp figures prominently in sections headed The Ideal of Love: Natural Woman Redeemed, Polarities: The Metamorphosis of Opposites, Dream Artifice: The Familiar Unknown; Chapter 4, Authority (see 1443); sections headed The Expanding Analogy, and Irony: The Meaning of Incongruity; Chapter 6, The Ideal. Sp, Bunyan, and Swift are viewed as earlier counterparts of Melville, Hawthorne, Lawrence, Kafka, and Joyce (see 1442). Literary allegory is a still vital form. See Index for references to Sp.

Honig, Edwin. Hobgoblin or Apollo, KR, 10 (1948), 664-81.   1442

Compares the "epiphanies" of the Red Cross Knight and Stephen Dedalus. Compares Sp and Joyce as creators of symbolic characters, innovators in the use of language, and mythmakers. Conclusion: Gabriel Harvey censured Sp for putting Hobgoblin, i.e., bogy medieval figures of moral allegory, ahead of Apollo, i.e., pure beauty and poetry, in FQ. If Sp had followed Harvey's advice, we would not have in FQ a spiritual literary precedent for the myth of Joyce. "As it is, we now have evi-

dence of the fact, in both Spenser and Joyce, that a universal fiction may be created in epic terms on the subject of *l'homme moyen sensuel* and *l'homme moyen spirituel*. Excepting Cervantes, perhaps, there are no writers between Spenser and Joyce who have so consciously demonstrated in a work of great imaginative scope that Hobgoblin is indeed Apollo." See 1441.

Honig, Edwin. Recreating Authority in Allegory, JAAC, 16 (1957), 180-93.
1443

Defends the allegorical method against critical opprobrium. "What the allegorical writer seeks is not just a new form or a new poetic, but rather a new or recoverable authority for the creative imagination, an authority transcending and often incorporating all past formulations." Discusses FQ. When Sp wrote it, the epic was an anachronism. "Spenser succeeds by rediscovering a serious use for the epic form after it had been exploited comically by Tasso and Ariosto." See 1441, Chapter 4.

Hoopes, Robert. Right Reason in the English Renaissance. Cambridge, Mass.: Harvard University Press, 1962. 248 pp.
1444

Both Richard Hooker and Neo-Stoics, such as Guillaume du Vair and Justus Lipsius, reject antinomy of God's will versus man's pretentions, providing basis for balance of nature (right reason) and grace (Providence) seen everywhere in FQ (pp. 141-5). See 1935, 756. Chap. VIII, Reason's "Due Regalitie": Spenser (pp. 146-59). Easy alliance between nature and grace basic in Sp's religious thought. Milton in Paradise Lost emphasizes right reason and free will, rather than grace preceding and making possible exercise of free will. Conflict and tension essence of Milton's epic, Sp's epic more assured. Bks. I and II of FQ dramatize indispensability of faith and continence in man's life. Discusses significance of right reason in relation to nature and grace in other episodes in Bk. II. Analogue of intellectual pattern of Bk. II in scale of values in Milton's Comus; another analogue in Paradise Regained, with "the Aristotelian magnanimous man transmuted and raised to a Christian level." Sp in FQ, Bk. II, shows what gives reason its "due regalitie" (II, i, 57): grace of God. See 1495, 1752.

Hornstein, Lillian Herlands. Analysis of Imagery: A Critique of Literary Method, PMLA, 57 (1942), 638-53.   1445

Shows that Caroline Spurgeon in Shakespeare's Imagery (1936) uses inconsistent methods in tabulating Shakespeare's images and draws unwarranted inferences from them about his personal experiences, habits, and tastes. Gives numerous references to Sp's FQ to show that Shakespeare's allegedly distinctive and highly individual images were common in poetic usage, inevitable, natural, proverbial, or part of "a literary residuum from secondary sources."

Horton, Ronald Arthur. The Unity of The Faerie Queene: An Essay in Macroscopic Structures. DAI, 34 (1973), 275A. University of North Carolina at Chapel Hill, 1972. 351 pp.   1446

"The unity of the existing fragment of The Faerie Queene appears on a consideration of the poem in relation to the structural principals revealed in the Letter to Raleigh. Arthur exemplifies what the reader is intended to become and the process of fashioning (delineating) Arthur is the process of fashioning (forming the character of) the reader. The private-public dichotomy proposed for the twenty-four book scheme obtains in the lesser structural dichotomies of the poem. Multiple embodiments... provide a structure of association supplementary to the framework of the virtues. ... The aesthetic and didactic intentions of The Faerie Queene are mutually supporting and inseparable." [SpN, Vol. 5, No. 2 (1974), 15.]

Hotson, Leslie. Literary Serendipity, ELH, 9 (1942), 79-94; repr. in The Practice of Modern Literary Scholarship, ed. Sheldon P. Zitner, pp. 46-57. Glenview, Ill.: Scott-Foresman, 1966. 392 pp. 1447

Compares, pp. 83-4, the Public Record Office to Eumnestes' Chamber of Memory (FQ, II, x, 53-8). The page Anamnestes, who fetches rolls and books, "does very well for an acolyte to the poet's fancy; but the Record Office in fact contains thousands of rolls which would stagger half a dozen of him." Pp. 85-6, compares the jungle of records to the Wandering Wood and Error's Den (quotes from I, i, 13).

Hough, Graham. First Commentary on The Faerie Queene: Annotations in Lord Bessborough's Copy of the First Edition of The Faerie Queene, TLS, April 9, 1964, p. 294.   1448

Identifies the annotator as John Dixon; dates the notes in 1597. Dixon is "indifferent to the courtly and romantic aspects" of FQ; "it is the Protestant divinity, the ascetic morality, and the national history that concern him." Dixon perceives clearly the dependence of FQ, I on Revelations; glosses minutely the chronicle histories in II, x and III, iii; and "has a field day with Guyon's attack on the Bower of Bliss, on which he comments with some fullness and evident relish."

Hough, Graham. The First Commentary on "The Faerie Queene": Being an Analysis of the Annotations in Lord

Bessborough's Copy of the First Edition of "The Faerie Queene." Privately published, 1964.   1448A

See 1448.

Hough, Graham. A Preface to *The Faerie Queene*. London: Duckworth, 1962. 239 pp. See 649.   1449

Part I: Background. FQ is a romantic epic, genre peculiar to Renaissance. Chaps. on Ariosto, epic theory, and Tasso. Part II: Form. Arthur ineffective as unifying device. Sp's mode of presentation pictorial, not dramatic. Organization like that of a dream; cf. Freud (pp. 95-8). Poem is image of "man's inner experience, political, military, social, erotic, moral and religious." Uses clock diagram (p. 107) derived from Northrop Frye (see 695) to discuss allegory in FQ, mostly multivalent. Part III: Commentary. Discusses each book (pp. 138-222). Poem not complete but gives impression of completeness (pp. 223-36).

Rev: K. W. Scoular, CritQ, 5 (1963), 177; R. W. Zandvoort, ES, 44 (1963), 455; Kathrine Koller, SCN, 22 (1964), 11; Millar MacLure, UTQ, 33 (1964), 311; Michael Murrin, MP, 63 (1966), 152. See 1267.

Hough, Graham. Spenser and Renaissance Iconography, EIC, 11 (1961), 233-5.
1450

Strict correspondences between Renaissance iconography and images of Sp's allegory should not be sought; Sp used them for his private purposes and sometimes inaccurately. Disagrees with Alastair Fowler's opinion in his review of 1895 in EIC, 10 (1960), 334-41. See 1918, 1937.

Howarth, Enid. Venus Looking Glass: A Study of Books III and IV of *The Faerie Queene*. DA, 28 (1968), 3640A. University of New Mexico, 1967. 214 pp.   1451

Study of moral sententiae which underlie imagery in FQ, III and IV as manifested in the medieval heritage, especially in pageants, emblem books, and other symbolic arts widely available and popular in Sp's day.

Hughes, Merritt Y. The Arthurs of *The Faerie Queene*, EA, 6 (1953), 193-213.
1452

Arthur appears in three lights, as the Imperial Arthur, as the Minister of Grace, and as the Rival of Hercules.

Hughes, Merritt Y. The Christ of *Paradise Regained* and the Renaissance Heroic Tradition, SP, 35 (1938), 254-77. 1453

Christ's contemptus mundi may not be, as usually regarded, product of Calvinism, Machiavellism, and stoicism. Argues that Christ is ideal figure resulting from effort during preceding centuries to Christianize the Aristotelian ideal of magnanimous man—"the effort which came to a head in the Arthur of *The Faerie Queene*." This influence on Milton "played a decisive part in the *contemptus mundi* of the hero of *Paradise Regained*." Traces issue of active and contemplative life in Renaissance poetic, with attention to Tasso's doctrine of heroic virtue, of which Hercules was supreme example to Neo-Platonists. This combines with vision of Redeemer, the Word of St. John's Gospel, in Milton's Christ.

Huston, J. Dennis. The Function of the Mock Hero in Spenser's *Faerie Queene*, MP, 66 (1969), 212-7.   1454

Braggadocchio, like Red Cross, seeks knightly status, but instead of performing noble deeds he seeks it through general notoriety. Standing in opposition to Arthur's magnificence, Braggadocchio lends mock-heroic comic relief to the narrative.

He also parodies militant chastity in Bk. III and justice and courtesy in Bk. V. After Justice banishes him for threatening the public weal, he nevertheless reappears as the Blatant Beast.

Huston, J. Dennis. "Some Stain of Soldier": Six Braggart Warriors and their Functions. DA, 27 (1967), 2498-9. Yale University, 1966. 314 pp.   1455

A study of Lamachos, Pistol, Braggadocchio, Parolles, Bessus, and Falstaff. Braggadocchio's presence in FQ "first provides a definite contrast to Guyon's aristocratic self-discipline and later suggests the limitations of a life in which all action is the ceaseless alternation between warfare and love affairs."

Huttar, Charles A. The Christian Basis of Shakespeare's Sonnet 146, SQ, 19 (1968), 355-65.   1456

Rebuts recent readings which deny "the shape of Christian doctrine" in the sonnet and traditional interpretation. Places image of rebellion and Platonic soul-body dichotomy in Christian context by quoting Sp's FQ, II, xi, 1-2; cf. II, iv, 34, 7-8. On rewards of virtue, which contradict Stoic idea that virtue is its own reward, cites FQ, III, xii, 39, and other Christian sources.

Isler, Alan D. The Allegory of the Hero and Sidney's Two Arcadias, SP, 65 (1968), 171-91.   1457

Sp adopted the sapientia-fortitudo topos in forming his conception of ideal hero, and assigned wisdom as virtue par excellence of the private man, courage as virtue par excellence of the public man.

Jacobs, Karen Langpap. A Continuing Metaphor: A Study of Seven Images of Virtue in The Faerie Queene. DAI, 31 (1971), 4166A. Auburn University, 1970. 223 pp.   1458

Examines style of the allegory in FQ, assuming that "the prime characteristic of Spenserian allegory is a statement of belief which in turn dictates a code of action." Seven images of virtue considered: House of Holiness (I, x), Castle of Alma (II, x), Garden of Adonis (III, vi), Temple of Venus (IV, x), Church of Isis (V, vii), Mt. Acidale (VI, x), and Mutabilitie fragment. Investigates Sp's belief that Divine Will manifests itself in human time and concludes that these images of FQ "have a literal level in which Divine Will may manifest itself."

Javitch, Daniel. Poetry and Court Conduct: Puttenham's *Arte of English Poesie* in the Light of Castiglione's *Cortegiano*, MLN, 87 (1972), 865-82.   1459

Castiglione's Il Cortegiano widely known among educated Elizabethans, including Puttenham, who advocates same training and accomplishments for poet as those required of perfect courtier. Puttenham's analogies between poetry and courtly conduct not ironical, not placed in context of flattery; regarded as truly mutual.

Jenkins, Raymond. Spenser and Ireland, ELH, 19 (1952), 131-42.   1460

The constant state of war in Elizabethan Ireland "drove into Spenser's consciousness the Calvinistic conviction that the righteous live involved in a bitter warfare with gigantic forces of evil. And that warfare in *The Faerie Queene* bodies forth the constant clash between the poet's idealized vision of noble human beings and his disheartening perception of the gross flaws of the actual men among whom he lived."

Johnson, Ralph Glassgow. A Critical 3rd Edition of Edmund Tilney's *The Flower of Friendshippe*, Published in 1577, Edited, with Introduction, Notes, and

Glossary. DA, 22 (1961), 247-8. University of Pittsburgh, 1961. 279 pp.
1461

Tilney, later Master of the Revels (1579-ca. 1610), dedicated The Flower of Friendshippe, 1st ed. 1568, to Queen Elizabeth. Modelled upon the *conversazione* form of Castiglione's Courtier, it presents typical Elizabethan views of marriage. Dedication of FQ to Elizabeth echoes Tilney's Epistle Dedicatorie.

Jones, Buford. The "Faery Land" of Hawthorne's Romances, ESQ, 48 (1967), 106-24.
1462

Hawthorne's concept of romance theoretically a neutral ground between real world and fairyland. This idea manifest in many of his works and some influences on it may be traced to FQ. See 1464.

Jones, Frederick L. Shelley and Spenser, SP, 39 (1942), 662-9.
1463

Gives three instances of Sp's influence, and presents in chronological order everything relating to Sp—especially the reading of FQ—to be found in Mary's and Shelley's journals and in Shelley's letters.

Jones, William Buford. Nathaniel Hawthorne and English Renaissance Allegory. Doctoral dissertation, Harvard University, 1962. 307 pp.
1464

Herman Melville understood Hawthorne's use of Spenserian allegorical structures, although his own use of FQ, II, xii in The Encantadas differed from Hawthorne's in Rappaccini's Daughter. Chap. II, An American Arcadia, deals with Hawthorne's use in The Blithedale Romance of Sidney's Arcadia, Sp's FQ—especially Calidore-Pastorella episode in VI, ix-xii, and Mutability Cantos—Shakespeare's As You Like It, and Milton's Comus to undercut pastoral idealism.

Chap. III, The Moral Picturesque, shows how Hawthorne in The Man of Adamant "borrowed several details from [Walter Scott's] *Old Mortality*," and then "proceeds to develop them by means of Spenserian allegory." See 1462.

Jorgensen, Paul A. Lear's Self-Discovery. Berkeley: University of California Press, 1967. 154 pp.
1465

In Chap. II, Some Renaissance Contexts (pp. 12-43), examines treatises on self-knowledge, their interest in the human body, "topics" for self-discovery found in many treatises such as study of one's passions. Renaissance humanists did not separate philosophy and literature; cites Sidney's view in Apologie for Poetrie on relation between them, and Sp's in Letter to Raleigh. Sp "more sorely torn" than Shakespeare between demands of teaching and delighting purposes of poetry. Sp's knights in FQ offer parallel to King Lear in that they are in quest of virtue (self-knowledge). Best parallel to King Lear is Legend of Temperance. Argues for "the dynamics of self-discovery" in FQ. Sp, like Shakespeare, transmutes lessons of the *nosce teipsum* treatises into poetry.

Judson, Alexander C. Samuel Woodford and Edmund Spenser, N&Q, 189 (1945), 191-2.
1466

Woodford, who is cited by John Aubrey as authority for Sp's residence in Hampshire, was a late 17th-century admirer and imitator of Sp. The Epilogue to his paraphrase of the Psalms (1679) consists of 189 Spenserian stanzas, in three cantos, entitled The Legend of Love.

Jump, John D. Spenser and Marlowe, N&Q, 11 (1964), 261-2.
1467

Marlowe is known to have echoed FQ, I, vii, 32 in 1 Tamburlaine IV, iii,

119-24. Other parallels between Sp and Marlowe (1 Tamburlaine, V, ii, 60 and FQ, I, vii, 43; V, ii, 196 and FQ, I, vii, 22), may be accidental but worth recording. Possible echo of FQ, III, x, 46 in invocation scene of Faustus (1604 quarto). See 1247, 1248, 1730.

Jung, Marc-René. Hercule dans la Littérature Française du XVIᵉ Siècle: de l'Hercule Courtois à l'Hercule Baroque. Geneva: Droz, 1966. 220 pp.   1468

Intro. points out faulty methodology of Seznec (see 1078), lists works of 16th-century mythographers, mentions four 15th-century works on Hercules, "one of the most complex figures of Greco-Roman mythology," by Salutati, Bassi, Villena, and Le Fèvre (pp. 3-11). Chaps. on courtly Hercules, nationalized Gallic Hercules, Christian Hercules, labors of Hercules (twelve canonical labors and others), many amorous adventures of Hercules, historical persons compared to Hercules (e.g., Francis I, Henry II, and Charles IX), apotheosis of Hercules at Avignon in 1600 in the triumph for Henry IV and Marie de Médicis, and Conclusion. Background for use of Hercules in literature of English Renaissance. See 1409, 2093, 2099.

Kano, Hideo. Spenser to Hopkins— Sozoryoko no Seitshitsu ni tsuite, Eigo Seinen [The Rising Generation] (Tokyo), 116 (1970), 520-1.   1469

Sp and Hopkins, the nature of their imagination.

Kaska, Thomas N. The Matter of Just Memory: Temporal Perspectives in Books I and II of The Faerie Queene. DAI, 32 (1972), 5187A. Duquesne University, 1971. 213 pp.   1470

Decisive influence on FQ is apocalyptic pattern of history which assumes design in movement of time from Creation to Judgment. Narratives of FQ imitate this design. The reader is drawn into the poem to share its moral predicates, and comes to share shaping imagination of poet, so that poem exists as a "matter of just memory." FQ concretizes the past, making it a means to "purge the infected will" (Sidney) and determine action. Fairyland is symbolic spatiotemporal construct related to real space and time through Cleopolis, a perfected city within grasp of man, moved by "torment of inquiry" (Ficino) to transcend fallen nature. The "poetic idea" of Bk. I is Pauline commitment to a new order of history, the order of grace and mercy. Redcrosse's legend defines pattern of fall and regeneration that is typical pattern of history. Bk. II is sustained by a conception of history as memory. Acrasia makes man forget his divine origins; temperance preserves those origins and insures apocalyptic glory.

Kaula, David. The Low Style in Nashe's The Unfortunate Traveler, SEL, 6 (1966), 43-57.   1471

The Unfortunate Traveler is poorly organized, relies on "low style," parodies rhetorical modes, and has a "serial or paratactic" quality. Does not approach complex harmonies found in Arcadia, FQ, or Shakespeare's plays. See 1808.

Kendrick, T. D. British Antiquity. London: Methuen, 1950. 171pp.   1472

Chapter 3, The Tudor Cult of the British History (pp. 34-44), useful in connection with chronicle history in FQ, II, x and III, iii. Chapter 7, The Eclipse of the British History (pp. 99-133), deals with "an ever-growing contempt for the British History." Sp was a serious antiquary, as View shows. Neither he nor his intelligent friends believed in the British History. Passages in FQ cited to show liberties

Sp took with it. "Yet Spenser had two institutionalist uses" for fabulous account of early Britain: as an invitation to study the past, and "the idea that the past is evolutionary, a preparation for the future that in this case is a striving forward to reach Elizabethan England. . . . The splendour of Elizabeth was in itself both an entire justification of the English past and also its fruition. In the extraordinary complexity and ingenuity of his attitude to the British History, Spenser is without a peer" (pp. 126-32).

Kennedy, William John. Modes of Allegory in Ariosto, Tasso and Spenser. DAI, 30 (1970), 3431A-2A. Yale University, 1969. 386 pp.   1473

Chap. I compares medieval and Renaissance concepts of allegory with modern concepts. Chap. II: the medieval and Renaissance allegorizing of Virgil, Ovid, and Dante provided Ariosto, Tasso and Sp with materials which had clear and distinct meaning. Chap. III: Orlando Furioso inverts and deflates these materials for comic effect. Chap. IV: Gerusalemme Liberata dissolves oblique meaning into mimetic drama; allegory evaporates completely. Chap. V: Sp's more continuous allegory in FQ "transposes and modulates episodes with clear and distinct meanings into episodes with oblique and problematic meanings." Image of the "bleeding and speaking bush," which occurs in Virgil, Ovid, Dante, Ariosto, Tasso, and Sp, used throughout as a device for focus and control.

Kermode, Frank. The Faerie Queene, I and V, in The Practice of Modern Literary Scholarship, ed. Sheldon P. Zitner, pp. 315-34. Glenview, Ill.: Scott-Foresman, 1966. 392 pp.   1474

Reprint of 1480.

Kermode, Frank. The Mature Comedies, in Early Shakespeare, Stratford-upon-Avon Studies, 3, pp. 211-27. London: Edward Arnold, 1961. 232 pp.   1475

All Shakespeare's comedies are "problem" comedies. The Two Gentlemen of Verona is a legend of Friendship (FQ, IV, ix, 2-3, could be a prologue to Shakespeare's play); A Midsummer Night's Dream is a legend of Love; As You Like It is a legend of Courtesy; and The Merchant of Venice is a legend of Justice. In reply to Shylock's story of Jacob (Genesis xxxi. 37 ff.), Antonio says Jacob was making a venture, "A thing not in his power to bring to pass, / But sway'd and fashion'd by the hand of heaven" (I, iii, 66 ff.); compare FQ, V, iv. Arguments for justice are strongly in Shylock's favor (IV, i), and in Christian doctrine it is satisfied before mercy operates. Mercilla has her blunted sword, but also a sharp one for punishment (FQ, V, ix, 30). When appeal to Shylock for mercy fails, he gets justice he demanded (pp. 220-3).

Kermode, Frank. The Sense of an Ending: Studies in the Theory of Fiction. New York: Oxford University Press, 1967. 187 pp.   1476

Sp's thoughts on problems of time and eternity, in Garden of Adonis canto (FQ, III, vi) and Cantos of Mutability (FQ, VII), are based on concept of aevum, "a kind of time between time and eternity." Sp "is concerned with the time-defeating aevum, and uses it as a concord-fiction" (pp. 74-81).

Kermode, Frank. Shakespeare: The Final Plays. London: Longmans, 1963. 60 pp.   1477

Why did Shakespeare, after the tragedies, write romantic tragicomedies? "I believe the most profitable explanation is that which postulates a revival of theatrical interest in romance, and seeks the reason for it not so much in the older drama as in the great heroic romances of the period, Sidney's *Arcadia* and Spenser's *Faerie Queene.*" Mood of these plays is that of Mutability Cantos (FQ, VII, vii, 58) (pp. 7-12). See 1376.

Kermode, Frank. Shakespeare, Spenser, Donne. New York: Viking, 1971. 308 pp.   1478

Introduction (pp. 1-11) mainly answers critics of author's Spenser and the Allegorists (1827, reprinted here, pp. 12-32); *The Faerie Queene,* I and V (1474, reprinted here, pp. 33-59); and The Cave of Mammon (1945, reprinted here, pp. 60-83).

Kermode, Frank. World Without End or Beginning, MHRev, 1 (1967), 113-29.
                                             1479

"Fictive orders in literature reflect man's efforts in philosophy to describe a form of continuity in life which is not eternal yet transcends time and mutability. *Aevum,* Aquinas's explanation of angels as forms less than God but more than man, was humanized during the Middle Ages to explain the perpetual aspects of human life, such as the cycle of generation which Spenser uses as a fictive order in *The Faerie Queen.*" [AES, 11 (1968), 231.]

Kermode, J. F. The Faerie Queene, I and V, BJRL, 47 (1965), 123-50; repr. in 756.   1480

Objects to simplifications of Sp, as by Greenlaw in subordinating historical to ethical allegory (see 729), and more sophisticated modes of simplification, as practiced by Hamilton (1416) and Hough (1449). Gives a recondite reading of Bk. I as apocalyptic "Anglican version of church history" in which historical allegory is paramount, then considers a different aspect of Spenser's allegory, the episodes of Mercilla [canto ix] and the Church of Isis [canto vii] in Book V,

in which "the allegory is both juristic and imperialist," and proceeds to interpret them as "a most elaborate juristic-imperialist allegory." Concludes: "I believe in a Spenser more rather than less historical in his allegory, a Spenser more susceptible than it has lately been fashionable to believe, to historical analysis."

Kesterton, David Bert. Nature in the Life and Works of Nathaniel Hawthorne. DA, 26 (1965), 1023A. University of Arkansas, 1965. 494 pp.   1481

Throughout his life Hawthorne enjoyed nature and had associations with it. In reading Sp, James Thomson, and Walter Scott, Gothic novelists came to see how nature could be used effectively in literature. Hawthorne preferred cultivated nature as man's link with natural world. Rejected Rousseau's idea of return to nature because it is an amoral realm in contrast to moral human life. Hawthorne's major symbolic use of nature in connection with isolation and withdrawal-return themes. Found Sp's symbolic use of nature in FQ highly suggestive.

Kirk, Ruby Brindley. An Inquiry into Elements of Time and Space in Spenser's *The Faerie Queene*, ESRS, 17 (1968), 5-13.   1482

Time and space in the poem are irrational. "Having come from one point and now going toward another, they [Redcrosse and Una] are occupying in time and space a midpoint that moves when they move along their plane of existence."

Kleinberg, Seymour. A Study of the Image of the Garden in English Literature in the Sixteenth and Seventeenth Centuries. DA, 24 (1963), 746. University of Michigan, 1963. 206 pp.   1483

Classifies image according to various themes: love, art, paradise, order, retreat, and innocence. Deals with largest number of poems in Chap. 2, The Garden of Love; Chap. 3, The Garden of Art; Chap. 4, The Eternal Garden; Chap. 7, The Garden of Eden, particularly Milton's. See 1118.

Kleinstück, Johannes. Mythos und Symbol in Englischer Dichtung. Stuttgart: W. Kohlhammer, 1964. 172 pp.   1484

Chap. II, Quest and Earthly Paradise in Spenser's Faerie Queene. Discusses Sp's debt to Chaucer, general plan of FQ, Oriental and other versions of quest motif, mainly emphasizes Guyon's journey to Bower of Bliss and its mythic nature (FQ, II, xi-xii), and Garden of Adonis (FQ, III, vi).

Knight, G. Wilson. The Burning Oracle. New York: Oxford University Press, 1939; repr. Folcroft, Pa.: Folcroft Press, 1969. 292 pp.   1485

Chapter I, The Spenserian Fluidity, pp. 1-18. A commentary on Sp's poetic technique, principally in FQ. Fluidity is the poem's greatest fault. The significances shift too often. Nor is there dramatic suspense or an organic heart. It tends to dissolve into books, books into cantos, cantos into events. The poem fails to blend medieval allegory with realism effectively. See 1486.

Knight, George Wilson. Poets of Action; Incorporating Essays from The Burning Oracle. London: Methuen, 1967. 302 pp.   1486

First essay is reprint of The Spenserian Fluidity. See 1485.

Knight, W. N. "To Enter Lists with God": Transformation of Spenserian Chivalric Tradition in Paradise Regained, Costerus, 2 (1972), 83-108. 1487

Milton's minor epic owes much to FQ and Arthurian tradition. Milton makes Christ's virtues courtly as well

as saintly, and describes his encounters with Satan in terms of knightly combat. Christ, like Sp's heroes, is like a wandering knight on a spiritual quest in the wilderness. Parallels between Belial's proposal to tempt Christ and sensual delights of Bower of Bliss (FQ, II, xii), between Christ's viewing Jerusalem and Redcrosse's view of New Jerusalem (I, x, 53-57); and between storm scene and Redcrosse in the Wood of Error (I, i, 6-10). [SpN, Vol. 3, No. 3 (1972), 11.]

Kocher, Paul H. Science and Religion in Elizabethan England. San Marino, Cal.: Huntington Library, 1953. 340pp. 1488

Sp in Castle of Alma (FQ, II, ix) "used the sciences of anatomy and psychology for religious and moral edification" (p. 21). He used the doctrine of decay "for a moral purpose resembling that of the clergy" in Proem to FQ, V. Symptoms of universal decay are basis of Sp's moral pessimism, a mood that became obsessive in Donne. Stanza 3 of Proem to FQ, II refers to possibility of a world in the moon (pp. 84-6). Suggests Sp intended in FQ, VII to describe conquest of created universe by Mutability "in terms of the new scientific developments" (p. 174).

Kogan, Pauline. Class Struggle in the Superstructure in Spenser's Faerie Queene, L&I, 5 (1970), 19-40.   1489

Sp was bourgeois with imperialist tendencies. FQ is great work in itself because it embodies struggle against reactionary feudalism; but in context of struggles against U.S. imperialism it ought to be condemned, because its recent revival is a self-defensive device of capitalists working through pro-imperialist scholar despots. Redcross a bourgeois hero, learning that service to the earthly city is basis of human reward. In battle with Dragon ("all that is feudal and sinful in life"), Redcross's recovery not supernatural (FQ, I, xi, 36 cited as proof), for Sp's anti-feudal attitude would not let Red-crosse become helplessly dependent on a power outside himself.

Kohler, Sandra Iger. "But yet the end is not . . .": Spenser's *Faerie Queene* as a Vision of History. DAI, 32 (1972), 5795A. Bryn Mawr College, 1971. 193 pp.   1490

FQ creates a model of the world of history in many ways, all centering on the present, and explores various Renaissance theories of history. Chapters: I, genre and conventions of FQ; II, historicity of man and the world, and its relation to faith and freedom, in context of providential history of FQ, I; III, secular history as myth and mutability in FQ, II; IV, Britomart as a heroine of secular apocalyptic history; V, Mutabilitie Cantos as a vision of the historicity of entire natural universe, with implications for genre of FQ.

Kok, John. The Manipulations of the Narrative Lines in Spenser's *Faerie Queene*. DAI, 32 (1971), 1516-A. Michigan State University, 1971. 170 pp.   1491

"Narrative line" means story line. Aims to show how many narrative lines are orchestrated to carry forward the story. Three major narrative-line manipulations are presented: shift, when focus of the narrative cuts away to an entirely different line; separation, when confluent lines diverge; and junction, when two or more lines join or cross each other. The poem's narrative lines, "like the threads of a vast medieval tapestry, are begun, interrupted, resumed, crossed, intertwined, separated, and ended"—all giving narrative of FQ its special texture.

Kostić, Veselin. Ariosto and Spenser, EM, 17 (1966), 69-174.   1492

Doctrine of imitation, theory of the epic, function of poetry, allegory, and Ariosto as epic model in Elizabethan context, illustrate changes which occurred in principles of poetic composition in fifty years between Ariosto and Sp. Ariosto's Orlando Furioso served as model for FQ since it was only contemporary epic worthy of imitation. Not a perfect model. Sp lacked "precision and clarity of imaginative vision . . ." to incorporate successfully best of Ariosto into poem. Best parts of FQ still Sp's.

Kuhl, E. P. Hercules in Spenser and Shakespeare, TLS, Dec. 31, 1954, p. 860.   1493

FQ, V, i, 2; end of Proth. Interprets references to Hercules in the two poets as signifying the Earl of Essex. "For Spenser, by the middle nineties, Essex had superseded Raleigh as the hope of imperial Britain." Mostly about Shakespeare's Hercules-Essex allusions.

Kurth, Burton O. Milton and Christian Heroism: Biblical Epic Themes and Forms in Seventeenth-Century England. Berkeley: University of California Press, 1959. 152 pp.   1494

Earlier attempts to reconcile Christian doctrine and moral teaching with classical epic form are relevant to Milton's epic designs in Paradise Lost and Paradise Regained. Mentions Sp's FQ; Giles Fletcher's Christ's Victorie was first English work to center on Christ as hero. See Index.

Lacey, William Robert III. Right Reason in Edmund Spenser's *Faerie Queene*. DA, 28 (1967), 1789A. Louisiana State University, 1967. 372 pp.   1495

"The concept of right reason, as modified by centuries of Christian Humanism, served Edmund Spenser as a unifying theme for his didactic epic." Redcrosse must learn to add worldly wisdom and theological sophistication to naive faith. Guyon must learn the opposite, that knowledge without faith is unavailing. Bks. III and IV concern the regulation of personal relationships by right reason. Bk. V expands into social justice, where Christian humanism requires that mercy temper justice. Calidore learns that courtesy must originate in and lead to Christian virtues. VII explores the validity of right reason— "whether there exists an Infinite in which the finite mind of man can participate," and concludes in the affirmative. See 1444.

Laguardia, Eric. Nature Redeemed: The Imitation of Order in Three Renaissance Poems. The Hague: Mouton, 1966. 180 pp.   1496

FQ, III and IV, Comus, and All's Well That Ends Well aim to establish integrated and ordered natural world (pp. 1-12). Chap. I, Nature and Spirit, on Renaissance double aspect of nature, demonic and divine (pp. 13-51). Chap. II, The Imitation of Nature, on figural and secular representation of reality in the Renaissance (pp. 52-81). Metaphor of love as agent of order more complex in Sp than in Milton or Shakespeare, for Sp can create cosmic concord as in 4 Hymns or discord as in FQ, IV, viii, 30-34. SC shows disintegration caused by human passion; Epith is lyric expression of harmony in marriage. World redeemed in FQ, III and IV, by reconciliation of doubleness of love. Lowest region of fairy land in House of Busirane (FQ, III, xi-xii), highest in Temple of Venus (IV, x). Conflict between demonic nature (wanton sexuality) and divine nature (chastity) in love quests of Britomart for Artegall, Scudamour for Amoret, and Florimell for Marinell. Gives running account of three love quests (pp. 82-125). [DA, 22 (1962), 2786.]

Landrum, Grace W. Imagery in The Faerie Queene Based on Domestic and Occupational Life, SAB, 17 (1942), 190-9.   1497

Shows that Sp's imagination was stirred to expression in figurative language by the daily round of normal living.

Landrum, Grace W. Imagery of Fire in The Faerie Queene, SAB, 18 (1943), 22-9.   1498

Sp's images of fire are based on similarities between this element and the sheen of metals, animal physique, and human behavior in both beneficent and devastating aspects.

Landrum, Grace W. Imagery of Water in The Faerie Queene, ELH, 8 (1941), 198-213.   1499

Concerned not so much with enumeration as with aesthetic effects. Finds imagery of water of great variety, and it is derived from multiple literary sources as well as from personal contact with the Irish environment.

Landrum, Grace W. Images in The Faerie Queene Drawn from Flora and Fauna, SAB, 16 (1941), 89-101, 131-9.   1500

Sp made use of first-hand observation in drawing imagery from the vegetable and animal life of England and Ireland.

Landrum, Grace W. Spenser's "Clouded Heaven," SAB, 11 (1936), 142-8.   1501

Use of sky-imagery in FQ. Concludes that Sp was capable of delicate and truthful observation and should be admitted to the group of English landscape poets.

Langendorf, Sister M. Loretta. The Attitude Toward History in English Renaissance Courtesy Literature. Doctoral diss., St. Louis University, 1948. 350pp. DDAAU, 1947-48, No. 15. 1502

A study of twenty courtesy books between 1500 and 1660. Ten of these before Sp, those of Erasmus, Castiglione, Guevara, Elyot, Della Casa, Guazzo, Cinthio, anonymous Institution of a Gentleman, Ascham, and Lyly. Shows "the importance of history in the formation of the gentleman was universally recognized in the Renaissance." Relates to Sp's general purpose in FQ, and specifically to II, x and III, iii.

Langenfelt, Gosta. Shakespeare's Danskers (*Hamlet* II, i, 7), ZAA, 12 (1964), 266-77.   1503

Conjectures, in the process of identifying Shakespeare's Danskers as citizens of Danzig, that Sp's "Danisk" (FQ, IV, x, 31) and "Daniske" (III, iii, 47) may refer to Danzig rather than Denmark.

Lanham, Richard A. The Literal Britomart, MLQ, 28 (1967), 426-45.   1504

Sp, in giving Britomart her contradictory male-female characteristics, makes her "a literal embodiment of the violence of the man-woman relationship" while also a compliment to the Queen and an exemplar of chastity. Further, her bisexual nature "may suggest a hermaphroditic vision of static union to which the best of human love is only an uneasy, sometimes violent approximation."

Larsen, Joan Elizabeth. The Use of Natural Imagery and the Concept of Nature in Spenser's *Faerie Queene*. DA, 18, No. 7 (1958), 101. Radicliff College, 1958. 242 pp.   1505

Chapters on Nature as Metaphor: Fairyland, The Forest, The Sea, Natural Description; Nature as Allegory and Symbol: The Beasts, The Garden, The Forest, The Earth; Nature as Myth: Classical Allusions, The Underworld, The Creation of Myth; Man and Nature: The Natural State, Man

and the Process of Nature. Finds Sp's attitude toward his universe consistent throughout FQ; religious emphasis that governs first book also governs rest. Sp an orthodox, not original, thinker. "Although he uses natural imagery to describe both good and evil, Spenser sees the natural world as good, created to serve man and glorify God." His great achievement is in range of FQ; it is "a history of the world, an interpretation of the universe, and an ethical treatise on man." He has a simple conception of man and nature, viewing them from every side "through the accumulation of examples."

Lasher, William Everett. A Grammar of the Auxiliary Component in the *Faerie Queene*. DAI, 32 (1971), 949A-50A. University of North Carolina at Chapel Hill, 1971. 93 pp.   1506

"This study describes the syntax of one component of the sentence in the language of Spenser's *Faerie Queene*. It is intended to add to the present body of knowledge about Early Modern English syntax by the use of transformational methods of analysis, with the entire set of Spenser's sentences in the *Faerie Queene* used as corpus."

Lavender, Andrew. An Edition of Ralph Knevett's *Supplement of the Faery Queene* (1635). Vol. 1: Introduction and Text. Vol. 2: Notes and Textual Corrections. DA, 18 (1958), 2144-5. New York University, 1955. 1270 pp.
                                              1507

Copious notes and glosses explain Knevett's "continuous allegory." These are intended to "encourage and facilitate further study" of Knevett's 7th, 8th, and 9th books of FQ. See 1307.

Leibowitz, Herbert A. Hawthorne and Spenser: Two Sources, AL, 30 (1959), 459-66.   1508

(1) Finds a general parallel between the quest, characterization, symbolism, and situations of FQ, I and Young Goodman Brown. (2) Sees influence of the Bower of Bliss (FQ, II, xii) on the moral and spiritual atmosphere of the garden in Rappacini's Daughter.

Lerch, Christie Ann. Spenser's Ideal of Civil Life: Justice and Charity in Books V and VI of *The Faerie Queene*. DA, 28 (1968), 4134A-5A. Byrn Mawr College, 1967. 251 pp.   1509

Medieval and Renaissance theory concerning virtues of justice and charity shows FQ, V and VI have a special relationship to one another. Bk. V is unified around the Temple of Isis; Sp's equity is a natural law, traditional concept of ideal justice. Limitation of justice is that it cannot reform man's inner nature; it must be supplemented by charity, as suggested by transitional episodes linking V and VI. Sp's courtesy springs from charitable love of one's fellow man, as strongly suggested by romance plot and pastoral interlude. "Calidore's vision of the Graces represents the completion of the quest for the just society in which both he and Artegall are engaged, and redeems Artegall's failure, since justice and charity together can, ideally, establish social harmony."

Lesage, Debrah Dillon. The Renaissance Heritage of Apocalyptic Tradition and Its Bearing upon Edmund Spenser's *Faerie Queene*. DA, 22 (1962), 4016-17. Pennsylvania State University, 1961. 196 pp.   1510

In the Letter to Raleigh, Sp "cryptically identifies himself as a vatic poet consciously writing illegal prophecy under censorship." His poem is to be "Millenial, with England the New Israel. The figurae of the poem, the polarity of Spenser's rhetoric, and

much of the dramatic tension of the poem" stem from the "Apocalyptic *pietas* of nation and faith" wherein man, caught between the Powers of Light and Darkness, "fights his way from Jerusalem *perplexae* to the grace of New Jerusalem," championed by charismatic Wisdom in various female representations and opposed by the Whore of Babylon. Proposes apocalyptic readings for Bk. I, Proem (Elizabeth identified with Wisdom), Bk. I itself (concentrating on Una), Bk. V (concentrating on Isis Church), and last lines of Mutabilitie Cantos.

Levin, Harry. The Myth of the Golden Age in the Renaissance. Bloomington: Indiana University Press, 1969. 231 pp.   1511

Main section on Sp in Chap. IV, Fictions. Off-stage Gloriana unifies FQ; her viceroy Arthur, her surrogates various Amazonian heroines. Proem to Bk. V identifies her with Astraea, Artegall her protégé, and contrasts present Iron Age with Golden Age. Artegall conservative (V, ii). Sp clings to obsolete, "holds up an ideal Middle Ages as an object-lesson for a decadent Renaissance." Arthur's and Guyon's reading (II, viii) plays tricks with time and space. "The pictorial allegory zigzags between contrasting extremes of loveliness and loathsomeness." Welcome relaxation of tension in Pastorella episode (VI, ix-xi), but brigands carry off shepherds. "Fascinated with the state of nature, Spenser is continually approaching and backing away from it." Naturalness of prelapsarian Garden of Adonis (III, vi) contrasts artificiality of Bower of Bliss (II, xii). Art and nature opposed. Compares attitudes of Sp, Bacon, and Sidney toward imaginative literature (pp. 99-107). For other references to Sp, see Index.

Levin, Harry. Paradises, Heavenly and Earthly, HLQ, 29 (1966), 305-24. 1512

"Fabulous terrain" of Sp's Fairy-land "is fertile soil for earthly para-dises, such as the Garden of Adonis glimpsed in Book III, where Bel-phoebe . . . has been nurtured amid the haunts of pagan voluptuousness." Contrasts this with Bower of Bliss: "Paradise, traditionally associated with carnal temptation, thus presents a demoralizing ambush of forbidden delights to the virtuous knights of Spenser . . . Ariosto and Tasso."

Lewis, C. S. The Allegory of Love. Ox-ford: Clarendon Press, 1936. 378pp.
                                                1513

FQ, pp. 297-360; pp. 321-33 repr. in 756. Finds in Bks. III and IV "the final defeat of courtly love by the romantic conception of marriage." Sketches the development of "Spen-ser's immediate model—the Italian epic." Sp allegorizes the genre, giving it a mythic quality; "he is endlessly preoccupied with such ultimate anti-theses as Light and Darkness or Life and Death." Defends Sp against "the charge of actual sensuality and theo-retical austerity" by contrasting the Bower of Bliss (II, xii) and the Gar-den of Adonis (III, vi); "the one is artifice, sterility, death: the other, na-ture, fecundity, life." Interprets the moral allegory, finding that "it is Spenser's method to have in each book, an allegorical core, surrounded by a margin of what is called 'ro-mance of types', and relieved by epi-sodes of pure fantasy." Sp emerges as "the great mediator between the Mid-dle Ages and the modern poets," and as "the greatest among the founders of that romantic conception of mar-riage which is the basis of all our love literature from Shakespeare to Mere-dith." Appendices on "Genius and Genius" and "Danger" (pp. 361-6) treat Sp's use of these words.

Lewis, C. S. The Discarded Image: An Introduction to Medieval and Renais-sance Literature. Cambridge: University Press, 1967. 232 pp.   1514

Sp frequently cited for illustrations of medieval Model of Universe (also Donne and Milton) "because, at many points, the old Model still underlies their work," an image not discarded till end of 17th century. Military met-aphor in Despair's temptation of Red-crosse to suicide (FQ, I, ix) from Cicero's Somnium Scipionis and Plato's Phaedo. Demogorgon, new deity in Sp, Milton, and Shelley, was result of "a scribal blunder." On for-tune cites FQ, VI, ix, 30; on four elements VII, vi, 7-8; on fairies (longaevi, i.e., longlivers) into Graces VI, x; on Platonic doctrine of pre-existence III, vi, 33; on localization of wits in parts of brain II, ix, 44 ff. "The Salone, (Palazzo della Ragione) at Padua (see 1078, p. 73) is, in a different art, a close parallel to Spenser's Mutabilitie cantos." For these and other references to Sp, see Index.

Lewis, C. S. An Experiment in Criticism. Cambridge: University Press, 1961. 143pp.   1515

Proposes criticism of fiction based on reading styles produced. Quality and lure of Sp's fantasy men-tioned (pp. 38, 70, 137).

Lewis, C. S. Spenser's Images of Life. Ed. Alastair Fowler. Cambridge: Cambridge University Press, 1967. 144 pp.   1516

An expansion of Lewis's Cambridge lecture notes. Views FQ as a series of pageants, masques, and emblems har-monized and sophisticated by a poly-phonic technique. Essays on The False Cupid; Antitypes to the False Cupid; Belphoebe, Amoret, and the Garden of Adonis; The Image of Evil; Mutability; The Image of Good; Britomart's Dream; Faceless Knights; The Misery of Florimell; and The Story of Arthur.

Rev: Paul E. McLane, SCN, 26 (1968), 35; Patrick Cruttwell, HudR, 21 (1968), 197; R. L. Raymond, DR, 48 (1968), 268; Michel Poirier, EA, 21 (1968), 189; L. Cataldi, EIC, 19 (1969), 70; S. K. Heninger, Jr., RenQ, 23 (1970), 89.

Lewis, C. S. Studies in Medieval and Renaissance Literature. Cambridge: University Press, 1966. 196 pp.   1517

Preface by Walter Hooper, Lewis's private secretary, explains origins of five essays on Sp (pp. vii-x). Edmund Spenser, 1552-99 originally appeared in 311. On Reading The Faerie Queene originally titled Edmund Spenser and comes from 297. Neoplatonism in the Poetry of Spenser (see 879) is review-article from EA, 14 (1961) on 650. Spenser's Cruel Cupid, study of FQ, III, xi, 48, comes from 1516. Genius and Genius reprinted from RES, 46 (1936), reminiscent of Appendix I, Genius and Genius, in 1513, which draws same conclusion that Sp was probably confused.
Rev: Douglas Bush, CE, 28 (1966), 254; John X. Burrow, EIC, 17 (1967), 89; Jean-Pierre Barricelli, IQ, 10 (1967), 102.

Lichtenegger, Wilhelm. Antike Mythologie in Spensers Faerie Queene. Doctoral diss., University of Graz, 1941. Anglia, 71 (1953), 250.   1518

Concerned with the relation between Sp's use of mythology and his allegory. Divided into four parts: 1. The Gods and Goddesses of the Heavens and the Earth (most important Jupiter, Venus, and Apollo); 2. The Gods of the Sea (most important Neptune and Proteus); 3. The Underworld (most important Atè); 4. The Heroes (most important the Trojans).

Lievsay, John L. Braggadocchio: Spenser's Legacy to the Character-Writers, MLQ, 2 (1941), 475-85.   1519

Braggadocchio (FQ, II, iii; III, viii and x; IV, iv-v; V, iii) derives from the type-character of the boaster in Theophrastus, Aesop, Plautus, and Terence. Sp's character was often imitated by later writers.

Lievsay, John L. "D. T., Gent.," Spenser, and the Defense of Women, JEGP, 47 (1948), 382-6.   1520

"D. T." is Daniel Tuvill, who used excerpts from FQ in his defense of women in Asylum Veneris (1616).

Lievsay, John L. Trends in Tudor and Stuart Courtesy Literature, HLQ, 5 (1942), 184-8.   1521

Sp's FQ was one of the courtesy books read by the English aristocracy during the Tudor-Stuart period.

Lievsay, John Leon. Spenser and Guazzo: A Comparative Study of Renaissance Attitudes. Doctoral diss., University of Washington, 1936. DDAAU, 1937-38. No. 5 UWAT, 3 (1938), 323-9.   1522

Listed in Atkinson, p. 215. Reviews life and writings of Stefano Guazzo (1530-1593), especially his Civil Conversation (1574), a "courtesy" book translated into English by George Pettie and Bartholomew Young, 1581-1586. It enjoyed European popularity. Views in it much like Sp's in FQ. Analyzes and compares attitudes toward morality and conduct, showing Guazzo's book offers a complete commentary on thought and purpose of FQ. See 1523.

Lievsay, John Leon. Stefano Guazzo and the English Renaissance, 1575-1675. Chapel Hill, N. C.: University of North Carolina Press, 1960. 344pp.   1523

A study of the place of Guazzo's Civil Conversation in the courtesy book tradition. Sp's friends Lodowyck Bryskett and Gabriel Harvey certainly knew the work, and Sp probably knew it (pp. 83-9). Points out extensive parallels between it and FQ (pp. 96-9). See 1522.

Lodge, Robert Aloysius. The Elements of the Baroque in the *Faerie Queene* of Edmund Spenser. Doctoral diss., St. Louis University, 1955. Abs., SLUB, 52 (1955-1956), 48.   1524

Defines baroque inductively by examining and contrasting examples of High Renaissance and baroque architecture, painting, and sculpture. "The baroque artist . . . creates a unity and suppresses it in a multiplicity of linked segmentation and detail that, coupled with contrasts in light and shade, or light and dark colors, induces a sense of motion or restlessness." Italian critics in their discourses on heroic poetry suggested a combination of single hero and variety of action for an effect analogous to that of baroque artists and by comparable techniques. Such literary criticism possibly influenced Sp's development of FQ. "Spenser creates linkages and strong contrasts in his poem by means of characters, imagery, and other poetic devices, quite like the baroque artists in other fields of art."

Louthan, Vincent Alan. Spenser's Double: The Dark Conceit of Reality in *The Faerie Queene*. DAI, 30 (1969), 688A-89A. University of Connecticut, 1969. 250 pp.   1525

Studies in Sp's use of double figures (Una-Duessa, the two Florimells, etc.) and conceptual doubling (as with Art, Nature, and Grace, all of which "designate concepts with double potentials for man," one a moral vision, the other a "servant of infected will and errant vanity"). Doubles represent moral forces in opposition and are a part of the pattern of discordia concors. This pattern extends to androgynous doubles, especially Artegall and Britomart. Sp's idea of perfection in unity derives from his awareness of

the double aspects and potentials within himself.

MacDonald, K. I. Allegorical Landscape in the *Faerie Queene* (Books I-III), DUJ, 63 (1971), 121-4.   1526

Treats an isolated, narrow aspect of the allegory, an allegorical "simple" or uncompounded idea. Chooses landscape as the "simple" to be examined, and, for brevity, concentrates on forest background. Throughout Bks. I-III forests connected with temptation: "unjustified rest to Redcrosse, excess to Temperance, and ungoverned passion to Chastity." Adds that "the forest is a moral symbol in relation to the individual virtue, a non-moral concept in general."

McGilley, Sister Mary Janet. A Study of Illusion in the *Faerie Queene*. DA, 17, No. 13 (1957), 120. Fordham University, 1957.   1527

Analyzes "the transposition of the conventional subterfuges of romance into symbols for man's illusions." This transposition is done with a sure touch in Bk. I. Discrepancy between "is" and "seems" may be comic, as in Braggadocchio, who "becomes for Spenser a kind of comic microcosm of the dilemma of appearance and reality." Black magic has much to do with disguises: Duessa, False Florimell, Até; it "adds to deceit a diabolical dimension." But disguise may be an instrument of good; "all the titular heroes of the last four books take to disguise to further their virtuous careers." This device reaches summit in Britomart's martial mask; in her double role as maiden and warrior she dispels the deceptions of courtly love from troubadours to sonneteers. Discusses the deceiver and hypocrite in earlier allegorical literature. Illusions which pervade FQ may be "symptomatic of a certain distrust of the things of this world, a distrust which

culminates in the figures of Mutability."

MacInnes, Margaret Joyce. Color Imagery
in the Landscapes of the *Faerie
Queene:* An Aspect of the Renaissance
Visual Imagination. DA, 25 (1964),
2496A. University of Minnesota, 1964.
298 pp.   1528

Analysis of types and functions of
Sp's nature imagery. Each book has
its characteristic landscape, and its
characteristic patterns of nature imagery. Discerns four descriptive techniques: (1) "the broad delineation of
Spenser's cosmos"; (2) "a 'micro-
scopic' view of nature as embodied in
epic simile"; (3) "thematic nature imagery, consisting of allusions to . . .
fire, air, earth, water"; (4) set pieces
of landscape derived from literary
sources. Analyzes landscapes and allusions to nature in relation to "the
great, pervasive themes of the poem:
the nature of holiness, the nature of
love, the oppositions of nature and
art, permanence and change, appearance and reality." Concludes that Sp's
nature imagery is more closely related
to pageantry and literary description
than to painting; and is notable for its
moral, cosmic, and philosophical significance.

MacIntyre, Jean. Artegall's Sword and
the Mutabilitie Cantos, ELH, 33
(1966), 405-14.   1529

That Mutabilitie Cantos are part of
FQ is evidenced by their language,
mythology, and imagery. Artegall's
sword offers key to this correspondence.

MacIntyre, Jean Ann. Imagery, Mythology, and Romance: The Significance of
the Marinell-Florimell Story in Spenser's *Faerie Queene.* Doctoral diss., Yale
University, 1963.   1530

Story of Marinell and Florimell explains important elements in Brito-

mart-Artegall story through similarities in marine and mythological
elements. Sea is metaphorical background of Britomart's complaint before she overthrows Marinell. This
metaphor, with Proteus added, then
becomes allegorical romance in adventures of Florimell, which define true
beauty. Marinell denies love until
taught by suffering to love true beauty. Similar qualities in Britomart-
Artegall story, both stories exemplifying beauty and love abstractly defined
in 4 Hymns. Principal mythological
characters embody timeless ideas of
chastity, beauty, love, and fierceness.
Florimell and Britomart both resemble Venus and Diana; Marinell and
Artegall resemble Mars. Correspondences of imagery, mythology, and
adventure give unity to diverse stories
of Bks. III, IV, V. Meaning of allegory
widens "to suggest the immanence of
beauty and love in all regions of the
cosmos."

MacIntyre, Jean. Spenser's Herculean
Heroes, HAB, 17 (1966), 5-12.   1531

Hercules is the origin of moral characteristics of Artegall, Calidore,
Arthur, and Colin Clout in FQ, V and
VI. Connection established through
(1) adventures derived from Hercules'
adventures, (2) verbal comparison
with him, (3) allusions to mythological persons connected with him. By
this device Sp symbolizes essential
identity of justice and courtesy while
maintaining their distinctness in romance.

McKillop, Alan D. The Poet as Patriot—
Shakespeare to Wordsworth, RIP, 29
(1942), 309-35.   1532

Deals with Tudor nationalism of
16th century, with "the imperial
theme and Elizabeth as the culmination of England's glory," expressed in
Shakespeare's chronicle plays, progresses of Queen Elizabeth, poetry of

Sp, prose of Hooker. Decisive effect of legendary British history on plan of FQ. Less common in Elizabethan poetry than theme of national triumph is theme of England in danger, as in FQ, II, x, 69 (pp. 311-21).

McLennen, Joshua. Allegory and *The Faerie Queene*. Doctoral diss., Harvard University, 1940. HUST, 1940, pp. 350-3.   1533

Excludes historical allegory. Chap. 1 defines allegory as "the use of abstractions in action to tell two stories at once." Discusses critical practice of allegorizing secular literature, original allegories such as Roman de la Rose, Castle of Perseverance, and The Pastime of Pleasure, possible influence on Sp's allegory of critics of Orlando Furioso. Bk. I of FQ "contains the only complete and systematic allegory; ... it describes the successive spiritual states experienced by a man who is endeavoring to become holy." Bk. II illustrates theme of continence by examples, containing little allegory. In Bk. III "the allegory has become almost completely episodic. . . . Ethical types . . . predominate." Bk. IV much like Bk. III. In Bk. V "the main emphasis is on the historical allegory." In Bk. VI allegory "has shrunk almost to the vanishing point." It is absent from Mutability Cantos. Steady decline noted.

McLennen, Joshua. On the Meaning and Function of Allegory in the English Renaissance. Ann Arbor, Mich.: University of Michigan Press, 1947. 38pp.   1534

Discussion of Sp (pp. 7, 8-9, 20) falls under the two headings: Allegorical Poems and Passages, and Allegory as Historical or Contemporary Reference. Relies mainly on Sp's letter to Ralegh.

MacLure, Millar. Nature and Art in *The Faerie Queene*, ELH, 28 (1961), 1-20; repr. in 644 and 756.   1535

"Art" and "Nature" can be identified with good or evil or have indifferent connotations according to how they operate within Sp's major allegorical device in FQ, the emblem. Fusion of elements, as in emblematic marriage of Isis and Osiris in Bk. V, suggests anthropological as well as mythical traditions. See 1405.

McMurphy, Susannah J. Spenser's Use of Ariosto for Allegory. Folcroft, Pa.: Folcroft Press, 1969. 54 pp.   1536

Reprint of 1924 ed. See Atkinson, p. 117.

McMurtry, Josephine Scott. Spenser's Narrative Imagery: The Visual Structure of *The Faerie Queene*. DAI, 30 (1969), 1989A-90A. Rice University, 1969. 244 pp.   1537

Concentrates on functions and techniques of visual structure. Chaps.: I, the reader's and the characters' experience of seeing. II, the spatial setting of FQ and its visual characteristics. III, the visualization of FQ characters, especially the differences between those derived from romantic narrative and those derived from allegorical emblems. IV, the visual portrayal of magic. V, the visual settings of specific episodes: romance episodes differ from allegorical ones, the latter more fully visualized.

McNamee, Maurice B. Honor and the Epic Hero: A Study of the Shifting Concept of Magnanimity in Philosophy and Epic Poetry. New York: Holt, 1960. 190pp.   1538

Aims to bring into focus the Greek, Roman, and Christian ideals of human greatness as formulated by Aristotle, Cicero, Augustine, and Aquinas. We may see in Achilles, Aeneas,

Beowulf, the Red Cross Knight, Adam, and the Christ of Paradise Regained approximations of these ideals of greatness as conceived at certain moments of the Greek, Roman, and Christian societies. Chapter 8, Magnanimity in Spenser (pp. 137-59), emphasizes Sp's reliance on the view of Aquinas, in which earthly glory may be the concern of a Christian provided he pursues it with humility and charity. This contrasts with the more Augustinian view of Milton's epics, which look with suspicion on any concern for earthly glory.

McNeir, Waldo F. Barnfield's Borrowings from Spenser, N&Q, N. S. 2 (1955), 510-1.   1539

Parallel passages show that Barnfield in Cynthia (1595) imitates and sometimes adopts the phrasing of Books I-III of FQ.

McNeir, Waldo F. Canto Unity in *The Faerie Queene*, PQ, 19 (1940), 79-87.
                                          1540

The increasing looseness of the narrative structure of the later books is accompanied by an increasing relaxation of canto unity. Cantos having divided rather than single narrative interest increase in number as the poem progresses. In giving up the idea of making each canto a narrative unit, Sp moved closer to the practice of his avowed rival, Ariosto.

McNeir, Waldo F. Review-article on Maurice Evans, *Spenser's Anatomy of Heroism: A Commentary on "The Faerie Queene,"* SpN, 2 (1971), 1-4.
                                          1541

Commends, with some reservations, discursive Introduction to the Poem (pp. 3-85) discussing The Heroic Poem, Meaning and Myth, Spenserian Allegory, and Fashioning a Gentleman. Takes exception to many points

in commentary on individual books of FQ (pp. 89-239), e.g., Una as responsible for Red Cross's derelictions, obscure excursus on Acrasia's riddle (II, i, 55), Britomart's invasion of Busyrane's castle as "a journey within her own mind," Florimell as aged virgin marrying impotent Marinell, obsession with Sp's "profound sense of the Fall," and other interpretations. See 1354.

McNeir, Waldo F. Trial by Combat in Elizabethan Literature, NS, 15 (1966), 101-12.   1542

Ceremonial trial of Middle Ages "served as a symbol of stirring moments in England's past" in Sidney's Arcadia, in Sp's FQ (I, v; IV, ii-iii), in several popular Elizabethan plays, e.g., Robert Greene's Orlando Furioso, and in Shakespeare's Henry VI, Part 2, Richard II, and King Lear.

MacNiece, Louis. Varieties of Parable. Cambridge: University Press, 1965. 157 pp.   1543

In chapter on Sp and Bunyan (pp. 26-49), refers to Samuel Beckett, William Golding, Harold Pinter, other modern writers of parable. Can identify with Christian, but only with Red Cross and Calidore among heroes of FQ. Poem religious only incidentally. Moral and historical allegory work simultaneously; Sp "keeps changing his camera angles." Same "trick vision" notably in Proth. Scudamore at house of Care (FQ, IV, v) "effective cartoon"; can't accept Até (IV, i); Savage Man (IV, vii) "palpable monster"; Bower of Bliss (II, xii) "has the haunting quality of a dream"; another such passage Amoret in house of Busirane (III, xi-xii). Paridell-Hellenore-Malbecco (III, ix-x) like Jonsonian comedy of humours. Compares and contrasts FQ with Pilgrim's Progress.

McShane, Mother Edith E. Tudor Opinions of the Chivalric Romance: An Essay in the History of Criticism. Doctoral diss., Catholic University of America, 1950. DDAAU, 1949-50. No. 17.
1544

Marchesani, Joseph. Loosely in Disguise as Virtue: Chastity, Friendship, and the Idea of Order in *The Faerie Queene*, Era, 4, No. 2 (1968), 36-53.   1545

The whole poem is a quest for order—personal, social, cosmic. The apparently rambling inconsequence of the episodes in Bks. III and IV draws significance from Sp's technique of indirect definition, which establishes these episodes as part of "an overarching order."

Marinelli, Peter Vincent. The Dynastic Romance: A Study in the Evolution of the Romantic Epics of Boiardo, Ariosto and Spenser. DA, 25 (1965), 5931A. Princeton University, 1964. 420 pp.
1546

Begins with comparison of Boiardo's Orlando Innamorato and Ariosto's Orlando Furioso. Theme of dynastic love appears in Orlando Innamarato, purely romantic and comic poem. Orlando Furioso an allegory of temperance which transfers interest from Orlando to Ruggiero and Bradamante, forebears of Este family. Themes of lust and avarice interpenetrate Ariosto's romance. Reviews 16th-century allegorizers of Orlando Furioso, rejecting some as specious but vindicating "Simone Fornari's extended and by no means fantastic allegorization." Rest of dissertation traces dynastic theme in FQ. Sp was as much influenced by Ruggiero-Bradamante story in FQ, I, as in FQ, III, and was also influenced by it in FQ, II. Sp intended to overgo Ariosto both nationalistically and theologically.

Marotti, Arthur F. Animal Symbolism in *The Faerie Queene;* Tradition and the Poetic Context, SEL, 5 (1965), 69-86.
1547

Understanding of animal symbolism in FQ is dependent upon knowledge of "science and pseudo-science, classical, medieval, and renaissance literature, mythology, iconography, scripture, and scripture commentary" in same context these were known by Renaissance audience.

Marre, Louis Anthony. Spenser's Control of Tone as a Structuring Principle in Books Three and Four of *The Faerie Queene.* DAI, 33 (1972), 1691A. University of Notre Dame, 1972. 182 pp.
1548

These books are structured and unified by a sequence of ironic tones employed by the narrator: authorial ironic humility, comic dramatic irony, tragic dramatic irony, and verbal irony. In Bk. III and Bk. IV, i-viii, tones of satiric irony prevail; in last three cantos of Bk. IV a tone of non-irony provides the internal norm requisite to satire. Appendix A diagrams the balance of ironic and non-ironic tones.

Marshall, William H. Calvin, Spenser, and the Major Sacraments, MLN, 74 (1959), 97-101.   1549

Conclusion: "Spenser was a Calvinist to the extent that the Established Church was Calvinistic, but in the essential points of difference between the Establishment and Calvinism, Spenser seems to have been more orthodox than has sometimes been supposed" (pp. 100-1). See 959, 1177, 1194, 1800, 2243.

Marshall, William H. Spenser and General Election, N&Q, N. S. 5 (1958), 95.
1550

Three characters who represent the

generally elect—the lion and Sir Satyrane (FQ, I), and the "salvage man"
(FQ, VI)—indicate that the theology
of FQ is not Calvinistic.

Martz, Edwine Montague. Bishop Hurd as
Critic. DA 27 (1967), 4258A-9A. Yale
University, 1939. 609pp.   1551

Proposes to modify received opinion of Hurd as a typical neoclassicist
by evaluating the whole body of his
literary criticism, including the papers
in Hurd's library. Concludes that
Hurd "defies neo-classical didacticism
by exalting pleasure as the end of
poetry, and pronounces the gothic
manners and marvelous more poetical
than the classical, the gothic unity of
design equally justifiable with the
classical unity of action." Hurd's criticism is important in "the revival of
Italian poetry, the enlightened interpretation of Spenser, and the ad-
vancement of the historical point of
view." Hurd was an influential member of the circle which included Gray,
Mason and the Wartons; and, through
a redating of Letters on Chivalry from
1762 to 1768, Hurd's influence on
the second edition of Thomas Warton's Observations on the Faerie
Queene can be more definitely traced.
See 1330.

Matthiessen, F. O. The American Renaissance: Art and Expression in the Age of
Emerson and Whitman. New York: Oxford University Press, 1941. 678 pp.
                                           1552

Fundamental difference between
Hawthorne's and Melville's art is
former's taste for allegory, latter's
inclination   toward   symbolism.
Though Sp and allegory are out of
style (1941), must remember that
Milton admired Sp for the insight into
human nature to be derived from FQ
(pp. 246-8). Pearl in The Scarlet
Letter "is worth dissecting as the
purest type of Spenserian character-

ization, which starts with abstract
qualities and hunts for their proper
embodiment. . . " (pp. 277-9). For
other references to Sp, see Index.

Maynard, Theodore. The Connection between the Ballade, Chaucer's Modification of it, Rime Royal, and the Spenserian Stanza. Washington, D.C.: Catholic
University of America, 1934. 139pp.
                                           1553

Listed in Atkinson, p. 212.

Melczer, Willy. "The Winged Vessell"—
Variations on the Journey of the Epic
Hero in Late Sixteenth-Century Literature. DAI, 29 (1969), 4462A. University of Iowa, 1968. 252 pp.   1554

Portions of text in Portuguese,
Spanish, French, and Italian. Body of
dissertation concerns Camões (Os
Lusiadas), Ercilla (La Araucana) and
d'Aubigné (Les Tragiques); the last
two chapters, on Tasso's Gerusalemme Liberata and Sp's FQ, "are to
be considered as an appendage." In
FQ, the epic hero and his deeds are a
personification of and an allegory for
the moral imperative of the poet.

Mennine, Suzanne Ailman. The Theory of
World Harmony in Spenser's The Faerie
Queene. DA, 25 (1964), 3578A. University of California, Los Angeles,
1964. 300 pp.   1555

Reviews theory of world harmony
from origins in pre-Socratic thought
through definition by Plato, treatment by Neoplatonists, reconsideration by Boethius, and reinterpretation
by 16th-century English poets. "Originally the mathematical ratio of a
musical interval, the concept of harmony offers the poet a way of relating the many and different parts of
the micro-macrocosm." Harmony of
universe is musica mundana; of human soul, musica humana; of voices
and instruments, musica instrumentis.
Last of these, only heard music, espe-

cially important since it penetrates and influences the soul. Measured words and harmony are evidence "of that state of character in which constancy of purpose and action express the soul's inner state of harmony"; and poet charms hearer away from discord of evil. In FQ, I, harmony is part of soul's search for grace; II demonstrates harmony between body and soul; III and IV, harmony between man and woman; V, in body politic; VI, between heroic souls and God; VII treats world harmony.

Merchant, Paul. The Epic. London: Methuen, 1971. 103 pp.   1556

In Chap. 4, Renaissance and Later Epic, section on Sp's FQ (pp. 45-53). Sp's epic style owes something to Golding and Chapman. FQ "the first major work to combine romance and epic successfully." Use of "morall vertues" adds a third tradition: allegory. Mention of Ariosto and Tasso in Letter to Raleigh relates FQ to epic poetry of Spain and Italy. At Sp's elbow as he worked on FQ was Ariosto's Orlando Furioso, translated by Sir John Harington (1591), with a "Brief and Summary Allegory" of the Italian epic in his folio edition. "Spenser of course has his irony," but for most part serious. "The chivalry of the Arthurian legends and of the romances of Charlemagne become for him as important as the Crusaders' faith was to Tasso." Best qualities of FQ "are those of Elizabethan literature, exuberance and largeness of thought combined with an astonishing lyricism and a capacity for schematization and complex allegory." For other references to Sp, see Index.

Merriman, James Douglas. The Flower of Kings: A Study of the Arthurian Legend in England Between 1485 and 1835. DA, 23 (1963), 3354-5. Columbia University, 1962. 425 pp.   1557

No satisfactory treatment of Arthur's story between Malory and Tennyson. During the Renaissance the story became bogged down in controversy about the historicity of Arthur and dynastic considerations. Sp ignored the core story, which was not to his purpose, although he used names from the old tales.

Meyer, Helmut. Spenser's "Earthly Paradises." Contributions to the Genesis, Form, and Function of the Gardens in the *Faerie Queene*. Doc. diss., University of Cologne, 1971. EASG, 3 (1971), 58-60.   1558

"Peripheral" gardens—Garden of Proserpina (II, vii, 51-63), Garden of Venus (IV, x, 21-29), and Phaedria's Garden (II, vi, 11-18, 24-25)—spring from ancient concept of *locus amoenus*, satisfy Renaissance ideal of *delectare et prodesse*, develop common motifs: beautiful semblance of illusion and also deceit, creativity and sterility. These ambivalent motifs in "central" gardens—Bower of Bliss (II, xii, 42-87) and Garden of Adonis (III, vi, 29-51). Bower tries to imitate Eden so as to disorient hero; this presumptuous and falsifying character is punished. Garden of Adonis develops Sp's attitudes to central theme of chastity or love, procreation and death. Life is created in cyclic wanderings of "naked babes" and in sexually neutral fusion of form and substance according to law of mutability; inside garden this process repeats itself sexually in love-meetings of Venus and Adonis. "Time" and death work relentlessly, chaos in shape of "Bore" only temporally fettered. Garden of Adonis is microcosm of divine order, of creation; Bower of Bliss is poetic image of hubris. Thus Sp contrasts *natura naturans* and *natura naturata*.

Michie, Sarah. Celtic Myth and Spenserian Romance. Doctoral diss., University of

Virginia, 1935. DDAAU, 1934-35, No. 2. 1559

"The Celtic spirit constitutes the most powerful harmonizing force as well as the least understood element" in FQ. *Arthur of Little Britain*, 13th century French romance related to Irish saga and Arthurian romance, may be "the ultimate inspiration" accounting for Sp's fusion of "things Irish and things Arthurian." Analyzes and shows influence on FQ of Celtic magic, legends of the Otherworld, spell of the Faery Mistress, floral legends, vigils, Amazonian tradition. "The Blatant Beast is paralleled by the Irish Coinchend.... The dragon fight is related in detail to *Arthur of Little Britian*.... The Sangliere episode is connected with the Perceval story.... In conclusion, it is observed that the Celtic narrative and pictorial machinery reviewed certainly comprises the bulk of the *Faerie Queene* and accounts for its pervading Celtic spirit." See 1635.

Michie, Sarah. *The Faerie Queene* and *Arthur of Little Britain*, SP, 36 (1939), 105-23. 1560

Parallels in narrative sequence, incident, and descriptive detail indicate that this romance, translated from the French by John Bourchier, may have influenced Sp more than any other except Ariosto's Orlando Furioso.

Miller, Frances S. The Historic Sense of Thomas Warton, ELH, 5 (1938), 71-92 1561

Evidence that Warton used the historical point of view and its corollary, the theory of milieu, in his Observations on the Faerie Queene (1754, 1762), in his History of English Poetry (1774-1781), and indeed in all his writings.

Miller, Lewis H., Jr. The Ironic Mode in Books 1 and 2 of *The Faerie Queene*, PLL, 7 (1971), 133-49. 1562

Examines instances of disparity between narrator's evaluations and reader's judgments of Sp's allegorical characters. Sp's allegory compasses abstract world of correspondences and concrete world of men, "offers his readers the opportunity to partake imaginatively of Red Cross's pride, Una's blind devotion, Guyon's complacency, and Acrasia's euphoria." [MLA Abstracts, I (1971), 42.]

Miller, Lewis Holmes, Jr. Phaedria, Mammon, and Sir Guyon's Education by Error, JEGP, 63 (1964), 33-44. 1563

Striking similarities between Bks. I and II of FQ, and between stories of Red Crosse and Guyon. Like Red Crosse (I, vii) Guyon is not strong in virtue until he has fallen (II, vii) and, in his error, he redeems himself. Both heroes acquire virtue through the necessary, and blessed, fall.

Miller, Milton. Nature in *The Faerie Queene*, ELH, 18 (1951), 191-200. 1564

Sp's view of nature does not involve contradiction. Nature "is considered perfectible, in the sense that it returns to a fixed teleological goal. Having gone from perfection to mutability, it is ceaselessly regenerated in its decay, and it carries within itself still something of its original nature, which will at last take it back to its original perfection" (p. 200).

Millican, C. Bowie. Ralph Knevett, Author of the Supplement to Spenser's *Faerie Queen*, RES, 14 (1938), 44-52. 1565

Advances Knevett, rather than Robert Jegon, as author of the MS (c. 1635) in Cambridge University Library.

Millican, C. Bowie. Spenser's and Drant's Poetic Names for Elizabeth: Tanaquil, Gloriana, and Una, HLQ, 2 (1939), 251-63. 1566

Traces Sp's use of these names to a

Latin poem to Elizabeth by Drant, ca. 1578. Discusses the exact significance of the names.

Minichino, Patricia Josephine. Vergil in Spenser's *Faerie Queene*. DAI, 32 (1971), 3262A. Columbia University, 1971. 223 pp.   1567

Sp heralded FQ as the English Aeneid although its structure, character, and setting are vastly different from Vergil's. Sp's imitation of Vergil is of two types: "language closely echoing Vergil's in episodes which are also Vergilian," and "larger, looser imitation in such areas as the use of allegory and the choice of a hero." Similarities in language are mainly found in first three books. Sp did not select Vergilian material at random, but selected and adapted "memorable bits of the *Aeneid* with reminiscences of the Italian poems."

Mirza, Taqi Ali. The Theme of Courtesy in Spenser's *Faerie Queene*, OJES, 8, No. 1 (1971), 11-7.   1568

Calidore is "the typical Renaissance hero, possessing all the qualities laid down by Castiglione for the ideal courtier." Sp's debt to The Courtier extends throughout FQ.

Moloney, Michael F. St. Thomas and Spenser's Virtue of Magnificence, JEGP, 52 (1953), 58-62.   1569

Magnificence in the Summa Theologica includes magnanimity. Magnificence is the special virtue of the prince, and Sp's Arthur represents this sense of the word.

Moody, Joann. Britomart, Imogen, Perdita, the Duchess of Malfi: A Study of Women in English Renaissance Literature. DAI, 33 (1972), 1146A-7A. University of Minnesota, 1971. 244 pp.
1570

Sixteenth-and early seventeenth-century England produced several embodiments both actual and artistic of ideal Renaissance woman, who unites graciousness, chastity, and affection with conventionally "masculine" traits of self-assurance, adventurousness, and independence. "Britomart shows how magnanimity can be expressed in a chivalric world beset with confusions." Britomart and the others appear to be literary translations of the ideals of womanhood created by humanists and courtesy books, accomplishments of such women as Elizabeth and other feminine monarchs, and vigorous women of the time as they met the demands of daily life. Values personified by Britomart and the other figures are central to literary works in which they appear.

Moorman, Charles. The Allegorical Knights of *The Faerie Queene*, SoQ, 3 (1965), 131-50.   1571

Sp's knights do not reflect Spenserian concept of knighthood or continuance of literary tradition of knighthood; they are fashioned of "stylized qualities of . . . type" to suit their allegorical purposes.

Moorman, Charles. A Knyght There Was: The Evolution of the Knight in Literature. Lexington: University of Kentucky Press, 1967. 170 pp.   1572

Knight as hero in chansons de geste, lover in Chrétien, philosophical pilgrim in Chaucer, tragic representative of chivalry in Malory, allegorical figure in Sp, outmoded in Shakespeare and after. Tudors nationalized Arthurian legend, in which Prince Arthur has no counterpart. Graunde Amour in Stephen Hawes's Pastime of Pleasure is "the father of Spenser's allegorical questors" (p. 120), purely literary. His knights are vehicles of moral instruction. Not from 16th-century Italian romantic epics, "their allegorical nature determines their forms and actions" (pp. 123-8). Comments on patterns in several books of

FQ (pp. 129-36). "Spenser's knights, like his language, are deliberately archaic" (p. 137). For other references to Sp, see Index.

Morgan, Kenneth Scott. Formal Style in *The Faerie Queene*. DA, 27 (1967), 3846A. Princeton University, 1966. 167 pp.   1573

An "extensive analysis and exemplification of rhetorical figures that are fundamental to Spenser's style" in FQ. Emphasizes particular functions of pervasive rhetorical figures when used in conjunction with rhyme, meter, the line-unit, and the stanza. Such analysis identifies "unified expanses" in terms of which Sp's verse must be perceived, and provides a means of recognizing formal beauty of the poem.

Mounts, Charles E. Coleridge's Self-Identification with Spenserian Characters, SP, 47 (1950), 522-33.   1574

Demonstrates that Coleridge was given to self-identification with various Spenserian characters: Satyrane, representative of his child-like humility and iconoclastic tendencies; Cuddie (in October eclogue of SC), representative of his mixed consciousness of poetic gifts and inadequate inspiration to use them; Scudamore in the House of Care, representative of his inclination to worry and to have nightmares; and Britomart, some of whose experiences Coleridge associates with his own loss of hope.

Mounts, Charles E. The Place of Chaucer and Spenser in the Genesis of *Peter Bell*, PQ, 23 (1944), 108-15.   1575

Sees general reminiscence of Sp's "realm of Faery," and perhaps an allusion to FQ, I, i, 34.

Mounts, Charles E. Virtuous Duplicity in *The Faerie Queene*, MLQ, 7 (1946), 43-52.   1576

Examines cases in which virtuous characters depart from strict truth and finds that, when these departures are not intended to harm any good person, they are not condemned.

Mulryan, John. The Occult Tradition and English Renaissance Literature, BuR, 20 (1972), 53-72.   1577

Occult philosophies—Pythagorean, cabalistic, Hermetic, and Platonic —synthesized by Ficino, Pico, Agrippa, and others, who transmitted them to Platonic writers of English Renaissance. Finds occult associations in Sp's Letter to Raleigh, Proem to FQ, II, and veils of Venus in Bk. IV and Nature in Bk. VII. Shows occult magic used for good or evil purposes by Archimago, Merlin, and Coelia, and in Church of Isis (FQ, V, vii, 1-24). Sp uses occult metaphors. Unlike Bacon and Chapman, he is true occultist. [SpN, Vol. 4, No. 2 (1973), 9.]

Murrin, Michael. The Veil of Allegory: Some Notes Toward a Theory of Allegorical Rhetoric in the English Renaissance. Chicago: University of Chicago Press, 1969. 224 pp.   1578

Wishes to illuminate Sp's FQ and other allegorical poems by showing continuity of late classical tradition of allegory, and in so doing "to change our perspective on the major early critics in English: Sidney, Puttenham, and Jonson." Final chap. on romantic resurgence of allegory with Wordsworth and Shelley. In arriving at theory of allegory frequently cites Boccaccio, Pico, and Sir John Harington's preface to translation of Orlando Furioso. Renaissance identified poetry with allegory, upheld poet's divine commission to veil truth from all but elite, conceived poet's "memorial role" as selector of material from history for educational purposes. In applied criticism evaluates Sp's success in FQ.

Rev: M. C. Bradbrook, RenQ, 23 (1970), 474; Sister Miriam Joseph, ELH, 8 (1970), 53: Jerome Mazzaro, Criticism, 12 (1970), 155.

Nagle, John Daniel. From Personification to Personality: Characterization in *The Faerie Queene.* DAI, 30 (1969), 1533A-34A. Fordham University, 1969. 181 pp.   1579

Sp's characters are not personified abstractions but models of human life in a mimetic mode. Analysis of Una relates her to the distressed lady of medieval romance. Techniques used to characterize Una are repeated for a wide variety of characters, mainly through parallel and contrast. Braggadocchio is a parody of serious characters. Calidore and Calepine are complementary. Most personifications are not named abstractions but real characters with significant roles. The role of mere abstraction in personifications is restricted to allegorical set pieces.

Neill, Kerby. *The Faerie Queene* and the Mary Stuart Controversy. Baltimore: Johns Hopkins Press, 1935.   1580

Reprinted, with additions, from ELH, 2 (1935), 192-214 (listed in Atkinson, p. 97); a portion of Spenser and the Literature of the Elizabethan Succession, a Study in Historical Allegory, Johns Hopkins doctoral diss.

Nelson, Nicolas Harding. A Study of *Hudibras:* Satiric Theme and Form. DAI, 32 (1971), 393-A. University of Wisconsin, 1971. 275 pp.   1581

Chapter 2 studies relation of Hudibras to precursors in anti-Puritan satire. "In chapter three the affinity between *Hudibras* and the romantic epic is explored. Instead of the imitation of *Don Quixote* for which *Hudibras* is often taken, I suggest that

Butler wrote in the tradition of such poems as *Orlando Furioso, Jerusalem Delivered, The Faerie Queene,* and *Gondibert.*" Two principal topics of romantic epic, love and valor, are present, as well as more specific aspects of structure and style. Butler's portrait of mock knight-errant inverts ideal of romantic hero.

Neuse, Richard Thomas. Diction in *The Faerie Queene:* Some of its Principles and Patterns. DA, 19, No. 13, (1959), 108, Yale University, 1958.   1582

Neuville, H. Richmond, Jr. The Scepter and the Soul: The Nature and Education of a Prince in Renaissance Literature. DAI, 30 (1969), 692A. New York University, 1968. 297 pp.   1583

Treats two attitudes toward the ruler in Renaissance theoretical and literary writing: ideal Christian prince vs. politically astute ruler. FQ shows Sp's concern with dichotomy between tyrant and ideal ruler. Highest literary manifestations of ideal of courtier-gentleman   are   Rabelais' Abbey of Thélème and Sp's Mt. Acidale. Renaissance ideal of the individual finds political expression in the ideal prince and social-artistic expression in the ideal courtier.

Neuville, H. Richmond. Spenser's *The Faerie Queene.* New York: Barrister, 1966. 133 pp.   1584

Summary of FQ; charts to show frequency of appearance of main characters, main action and location, delineation of characters, and theme of poem in relation to structure.

Nevo, Ruth. Spenser's "Bower of Bliss" and a Key Metaphor from Renaissance Poetic, SWL, 10 (1962), 20-31; repr. in 756.   1585

Opposes C. S. Lewis's negative-positive contrast between Art and Nature in Acrasia's Bower of Bliss (FQ,

II, xii). See 1513. Finds in George Puttenham's Arte of English Poesie (1589) analogies between carpenter, painter, or sculptor, and poet or maker which carry full implications of improper alliance between Art and Nature such as exists in Bower of Bliss. "Natural" mode of Art-Nature relationship referred to by Sp in Garden of Adonis (FQ, III, vi, 34) and Temple of Venus (FQ, IV, x, 21, 24). Polixenes' application of gardening metaphor in Shakespeare's The Winter's Tale (IV, ii) is in line with Puttenham's and Sp's.

Newkirk, Glen Alton. The Public and Private Ideal of the Sixteenth Century Gentleman: A Representative Analysis. DA, 27 (1966), 1034A. University of Denver, 1966. 345 pp.   1586

Classical and medieval concept of the virtuous man contained an ideal which was both public and private. The 16th century developed a distinction between public and private ideals. In England, "a pattern of gentility, inspired by the humanists and modified by northern European Christianity, developed through the works of More, Elyot, Ascham, Sidney, Lyly, and, finally, through Edmund Spenser's fusing of the feudal and humanist world to form the perfect gentleman." Shakespeare modifies the abstract ideal, influenced by solutions of problems of statecraft by Machiavelli.

Nohrnberg, James Carson. A Study of The Faerie Queen. DAI, 32 (1972), 6939A-40A. University of Toronto, 1970. 293 pp.   1587

Commentary on genre, integrating themes, symbolism, mythography, and re-creation of tradition in FQ. First 3 books private, second 3 public treatments of epic subject. Describes sequence of each installment, following Northrop Frye (see 1378). Ex-

pounds Sp's typology and the messiah myth; balances Redcrosse's sacramental imagery against Una's revelation of the Word; explores parallels in Mammon's Cave and Alma's Castle; studies parallels in Bks. II and V, related to private and public governance; Britomart's, Florimell's, and Amavia's activity and/or suffering treated as variations of unbalanced "Oedipal" energy. [SpN, Vol. 4, No. 1 (1973), 10.]

Nuttall, A. D. Two Concepts of Allegory: A Study of Shakespeare's The Tempest and the Logic of Allegorical Expression. London: Routledge and Kegan Paul, 1967. 175 pp.   1588

In defining allegory, begins by attacking the first concept (C. S. Lewis's radical distinction between allegory and sacramental symbolism, 1513) and arguing for a second concept, which "proposes a number of intimate connections and a certain community of purpose" between allegory and sacramentalism. Concludes by defining allegory as "a set of things in narrative sequence standing for a different set of things in temporal or para-temporal sequences; in short, a complex narrative metaphor" (p. 48). In Chap. IV, which explores gradual approximation of image to precept in artistic representation, uses opening scene of FQ, I, i, to illustrate non-realistic imagery (how do Redcrosse, Una, and the dwarf stay together?). For other references to Sp, see Index.

O'Connor, John J. Amadis de Gaule and Its Influence on Elizabethan Literature. New Brunswick, N. J.: Rutgers University Press, 1970. 308 pp.   1589

Based on French translation of Nicholas de Herberay, "the principal source of English knowledge of the romance," sampling of it in The Treasury of Amadis of France (1568), used by Anthony Munday in his translation begun ca. 1589 (pp. 131 ff.). Chap. IX, *Amadis* and Spenser's *Faerie Queene* (pp. 163-81). "The probability that Spenser knew *Amadis*, at least in part, is very strong." Points out analogues in each book of FQ, stressing Amadis de Gaule as possible source of Calidore-Pastorella interlude (VI, ix-xii), Britomart at Castle Joyous (III, i), Pyrochles in burning lake (II, vi), journey of Guyon and Palmer to Bower of Bliss (II, xii), and especially Mask of Cupid (III, xii).

Ohman, Carol. Northrop Frye and the MLA, CE, 32 (1970), 291-300. **1590**

Criticism of Rudolf B. Gottfried's article which received the MLA award for 1968 (see 1395). "Gottfried's essay is . . . largely dependent on misunderstandings of Frye's texts, overemphasis of points that are minor to Frye, and irrelevant argument. . . . The ideational context in which Gottfried responds to Frye . . . is too narrow, hence conservative in an unfortunate sense." Other critics have more accurately pointed out weaknesses in Frye's theory of criticism in the *Anatomy* (695). "The conclusion of Gottfried's essay amounts to a virtual dismissal of Frye's *Anatomy*." Gottfried's article begins and ends with avian metaphors, which frame it. " . . . the Spenserian should admit other birds to his bough. . . . And they might . . . usefully sound their songs, if not in harmony, at least in the intervals left by one another's silence." See 1394.

Olson, Paul A. *A Midsummer Night's Dream* and the Meaning of Court Marriage, ELH, 24 (1957), 95-119. **1591**

With its occasion a court wedding, the play speaks throughout of Renaissance doctrines of love and marriage, using traditional symbols to present both rational and irrational love. For sophisticated audience. Context of the drama found in FQ, Sidney's Arcadia, Lyly's earlier court comedies, and Jonson's later court masques. Refers many points to Sp. Interprets mythical fairy plot in a manner "consonant with what we know of the literary use of fairies in the 1590's from the *Faerie Queene*." "The major symbols used in *A Midsummer Night's Dream* had been made the property of the court by the works of Lyly and Spenser, authors who also exercised an influence on Shakespeare at the time he wrote the play."

Ong, Walter J. From Allegory to Diagram in the Renaissance Mind: A Study in the Significance of the Allegorical Tableau, JAAC, 17 (1959), 423-40. **1592**

Follows author's earlier studies of "the aural-to-visual shift which in the West marks a transition from the ancient world through the Middle Ages to the Renaissance." Middle Ages had a manuscript culture, Renaissance a typographical culture. Discusses vogue of allegorical tableau in 16th and 17th centuries as important phenomenon attending transition from a verbal to a visual culture. Chaucer's Canterbury Tales is product of verbal culture; Sp's FQ, "which has many known connections with the allegorical tableau through the emblem tradition, exemplifies the new fascination with space even more than it exemplifies Aristotle's moral virtues" (pp. 439-40).

Oras, Ants. Darkness Visible: Notes on Milton's Descriptive Procedures in *Paradise Lost*, in All These To Teach: Essays in Honor of C.A. Robertson, ed. Robert A. Bryan, Alton C. Morris, and others, pp. 130-43. Gainesville: University of Florida Press, 1965. 148 pp. **1593**

Disagrees with T.S. Eliot's objection to oxymoron "darkness visible" in Milton's describing the indescribable, not accepted narrative technique in Renaissance England. Contrast between Milton and Sp glaring. "Spenser, almost unaware of the existence of visual perspective, tends to present his descriptions tapestry-fashion, with much detail but seldom with any three-dimensional coordination." Suspense almost entirely absent, "minimum of dramatic organization."

Oras, Ants. Intensified Rhyme Links in *The Faerie Queene:* An Aspect of Elizabethan Rhymecraft, JEGP, 54 (1955), 39-60.   1594

Sp intensified and varied his rhymes by using "phonetic correspondences preceding the last metrically stressed vowel," as in strive-drive; swound-stound; beheld-befeld.

Oras, Ants. Spenser and Milton: Some Parallels and Contrasts in the Handling of Sound, in Essays on the Language of Literature, ed. Seymour Chatman and Samuel R. Levin, pp. 19-32. Boston: Houghton Mifflin, 1967. 450 pp.   1595

Phonetic demonstration that "the contrast between the smooth fluency of *The Faerie Queene* and the sonorous power of *Paradise Lost* is . . . a very real one." Examines the two styles from the specific point of view of sound. Finds two diametrically opposed tendencies: Sp places his consonant clusters at the beginning of syllables, as in *prey*, and Milton at the end, as in *earth*. Accentuating this contrast are Sp's use of alliteration to emphasize the initial clusters, line endings, repetition of rhymes, rhyme links, stanza patterns. His phonetic motifs are more obtrusive, less subtle, more transparent than Milton's, whose "avoidance of strict symmetry, of very obvious patterning, is post-High Renaissance."

Osenburg, Frederick Charles. The Ideas of the Golden Age and the Decay of the World in the English Renaissance. Doctoral diss., University of Illinois, 1939. DDAAU, 1938-39, No. 6. Abs. published. Urbana, Ill., 1939. 18pp.   1596

Traces myth of Golden Age from Hesiod. Considers versions of Sp, Drayton, Hall, Alexander, Drummond, and Browne. Sp's was "the most elevated concept of the ideal," a Golden Age in which justice was highest virtue. Donne made it a time of free love. Satiric treatments of the myth rare. Discusses idea of decay and its numerous treatments. Minimizes its importance as indication of true or widespread pessimism. Sp's solution of phenomenon of change was "that change was merely an expression of a higher law, a fulfillment rather than a destruction." This view supported by translations of LeRoy and Lipsius, and beginning in 1603 Bacon took optimistic side. In last chapter Golden Age myth explained as criticism of contemporary economic and social conditions. Puritan attitude toward money-making. References to Golden Age unimportant after 1630.

Osgood, Charles Grosvenor. Murals Based upon Edmund Spenser's *Faerie Queene* by Lee Woodward Zeigler. Baltimore: Enoch Pratt Free Library, 1945. 20pp. 10 Plates.   1597

Descriptions of the scenes depicted in Zeigler's murals in the Enoch Pratt Free Library. There are 18 panels, one "a portrait of Spenser supported by the Spirit of Nature and the Spirit of Chivalry, and crowned by the Muse of Epic Poetry." The 10 plates show panels 1, The Red Cross Knight and Una meet the wizard, Archimago; 2, The Palace of Pride, the Seven Deadly Sins, Una, Prince Arthur, Duessa, Archimago; 3, Red Cross slays the

Dragon; 6, Britomart sees Cupid's Masque and rescues Amoret from the charms of Busirane; 11, The Tournament at Florimel's wedding with Marinel; Sir Artegal presents the Girdle of Chastity to Florimel; 12, Duessa before the Court of Mercilla; 13, Colin Clout pipes to his Lady; 15, Day, Night, and the Hours; 16, Life, Death, Time, and the Months; 17, The Seasons.

Owen, W. J. B. "In These XII Books Severally Handled and Discoursed," ELH, 19 (1952), 165-72.   1598

Draws attention to some features of the Letter to Ralegh which indicate that the version of FQ described in the letter was never actually written. Thinks Sp planned to revise Books I-III in a form that would agree with Book XII as their sequel. See 1263, 1599, 1605, 1721, 1722.

Owen, W. J. B. Narrative Logic and Imitation in The Faerie Queene, CL, 7 (1955), 324-37.   1599

Argues that Sp, in attempting to produce a heroic poem in imitation of Ariosto, simply failed to achieve a coherent structure; the flaws or lapses in narrative logic cannot be explained as the result of revisions. See 1263, 1598, 1605, 1721, 1722.

Owen, W. J. B. Orlando Furioso and Stanza-Connection in The Faerie Queene, MLN, 67 (1952), 5-8.   1600

Differs with Tucker Brooke, ibid., 37 (1922), 223-7, who proposed Virgil as source of Sp's device of linking stanzas by verbal repetition (see also 1665). Ariosto is a more likely source for this technique. Presents examples of several kinds from Orlando Furioso.

Owen, W. J. B. Spenser and Ariosto, N&Q, 194 (1949), 316-8.   1601

As addenda to those given in the

Variorum, points out several parallels between FQ and Orlando Furioso.

Owen, W. J. B. A Spenser Note, MLR, 43 (1948), 239-41.   1602

Haste, perhaps because of affairs of Ireland, prevented Sp from revising FQ during its printing so as to make it agree with his letter to Ralegh.

Owen, W. J. B. Spenser's Letter to Ralegh, MLR, 45 (1950), 511-2.   1603

A reply to Janet Spens, ibid., 44 (1949), 87-8 (see 1681). Defends his own theory about the letter prefixed to 1590 edition of FQ, ibid., 43 (1948), 239-41 (see 1602). Says Spenser's theory does not account for discrepancies between the poem as it stands and the description of the poem in the letter.

Owen, W. J. B. Spenser's Letter to Ralegh—A Reply, MLN, 75 (1960), 195-7.   1604

See 1413. Contends Sp's letter does not show he had any preconceived idea of form and structure of FQ. Takes word "severally" in phrase "severally handled and discoursed" to mean "individually," not "differently." Argues for non-repetitive rather than repetitive structure in whole poem.

Owen, W. J. B. The Structure of The Faerie Queene, PMLA, 68 (1953), 1079-1100.   1605

Argues that one cannot establish and define an earlier version of FQ on the basis of available external evidence; that it is meaningless to assume that FQ as we have it contains large-scale revisions which led to disorder and formlessness, for this "disorder" can be explained on other grounds; that the quest for such versions is probably futile because the present version seems to be a primitive version itself; that in the 1590 version Sp may have arbitrarily taken the material in Bk. III from an early Ariostan romance and added it to Bks. I and II, with the intention of bringing the whole poem into line with the letter to Ralegh at a later date, but in the 1596 version, after attempting to write Bks. V and VI on the plan of the letter, he formed Bk. IV and parts of V from what was left of the Ariostan romance. See 1263, 1598, 1599, 1721, 1722.

Padelford, F. M. E. W. His Thameseidos, SAB, 12 (1937), 69-76.   1606

Printed in 1600, the poem shows direct influence of FQ. The author was probably Edward Wilkinson.

Page, F. Keats and the Midnight Oil, DubR, 201 (1937), 87-97.   1607

April 15, 1819, Keats wrote a "little extempore," 96 lines in heroic couplets, that he pretended came from some lost book of FQ. The lines are interpreted as Spenserian allegory.

Pallikunnen, Augustine G. The Treatment of Virtues and Vices in the Courtesy Literature of the Sixteenth Century. DAI, 31 (1971), 4131A-32A. Duquesne University, 1970. 308 pp.   1608

Only indirectly related to Sp, providing background for Bks. I and VI of FQ. Examines 16th-century courtesy books written in English or translated into English and traces dominant traditions and patterns of virtues and vices. Chap. I discusses definition, classification, and origin of courtesy literature and relation between courtesy and the virtue-vice framework; explores traditions and patterns of four cardinal virtues and seven cardinal vices prior to 16th century. Chap. II examines passages on virtues and vices in 24 courtesy books. Chap. III concludes there is a tradition in 16th-century courtesy books which sets the 4 cardinal virtues against the 7 cardinal sins.

Palmer, Barbara Dallas. The Guide and Leader: Studies in a Narrative Structural Motif. DAI, 31 (1970), 1336A-7A. Michigan State University, 1969. 212 pp.   1609

Deals with examples of guide convention in Gilgamesh, classical myth, Biblical myth, Arthurian Legend, Divine Comedy, The Pearl, Piers Plowman, Canterbury Tales, FQ, and For Whom the Bell Tolls. In Bks. I and II of FQ, guide figures "effect a classical model of the quest, diverse, complex, but completely unified and understandable. The convention is adapted to the narrative's demands. In Book I, a quest for holiness, the figures reveal Spenser's themes; and in Book II, a quest for temperance, they explicate a representational narrative."

Pansegrau, Günter. "Leid" in der *Faerie Queene*: Studien zum literarischen und sprachlichen Charakter eines Wortfeldes bei Spenser. Doctoral diss., University of Mainz, 1955. 242pp. JdH 1955, p. 484.   1610

Part I, Descriptive Analysis, summarizes poem canto by canto with particular attention to manifestations of pain and suffering (pp. 4-74). "Especially abundant are occurrences of the 'Pain'-motif in Bks. I and III (within the scope of this study 21 and 17, respectively, have been noted), with fewer in comparison in Bks. VI, II, IV, and V (for the descriptive analysis 10, 9, 9, and 7, respectively, have been noted)." Part II, Systematic Analysis, discusses function of the "Pain"-motif in moral allegory; the problem of suffering in the frame of the "Fortuna"-concept; Pain, Care, and Grief as allegorical figures (pp. 75-103). Analyzes linguistically all words expressive of pain (pp. 104-231). Appendix E (pp. 234-7) tabulates 139 words for "Leid," from *afflict-affliction* to *wound-wounding*; commonest of all is *wound*, used 166 times, then *grief,* used 130 times, and *pain,* 98 times.

Paolina, M. (M. Pauline Parker). Spenser and Dante, EM, 14 (1963), 27-44. 1611

Sp could have known, and probably did know, Dante's Commedia (especially the Inferno) and Convivio. Both seem to have left their mark on FQ. See 101.

Paolucci, Anne. The Women in the *Divine Comedy* and *The Faerie Queene.* DA, 27 (1966), 1791A. Columbia University, 1963. 250 pp. 1612

Need for more thorough comparative study of Divine Comedy and FQ stressed by recent Sp critics. Concentrates on treatment of women in two poems because both poets inspired by visions of women, and both intended to glorify women. Both poems are love poems. Starts with first impressions of variety of female types in two poems, proceeds to analysis of particulars that make up full portraits, techniques of characterization, and allegorical interpretation of women's major roles as guides and teachers in moral as well as narrative structure. Concludes each poem is "a great monument to a great age."

Parker, M. Pauline. The Allegory of the *Faerie Queene.* Oxford: Clarendon Press, 1960. 326pp. 1613

Sp's prosody, diction, and thought are interdependent, have to be taken as a whole. Both characters and incidents are mixture of allegory and romance, abstract and concrete. Chapters on virtues represented in poem— Holiness and Truth; Temperance; Chastity, Love, and Concord; Justice and Equity; Courtesy; The Mutability Fragment—give detailed interpretation and commentary. Sees FQ as at once allegorical and realistic, emphasizing its truth to man's inner experience. Suggests Mutability Cantos

intended to be conclusion of whole poem (pp. 259-69). Chapter VIII, Spenser's Poetic World (pp. 270-310), deals with formative influences in London and Ireland; England as faerie land and kingdom of Elizabeth at same time; use of Irish mythology, popular romances, and folklore, all treated with same freedom as more literary or classical sources; his knowledge of earlier literature, with emphasis on his originality. Note on Sp's treatment of history (pp. 313-22) maintains it is ideal rather than real.

Parker, M. Pauline. The Image of Direction in Dante, Spenser, and Milton, EM, 19 (1968), 9-23. 1614

The story of Dante's Commedia, taking place in a soul which has seen itself against the background of eternity, continually employs the image of upward movement, even in Hell. FQ is a story of this world, located in time; Faerieland is a place of transit, wherein the image of direction is one of continual traveling which was to have terminated with Arthur's ultimate perfection. Milton in Paradise Lost depicts Satan and Adam moving downward, although Adam is able to stop. See 1611.

Parkes, H. B. Nature's Diverse Laws: The Double Vision of the Elizabethans, SR, 58 (1950), 402-18. 1615

The "disharmony between two kinds of knowledge, one which interpreted nature as the expression of divine reason while the other regarded it as the battleground between amoral and destructive forces, is the central theme of Elizabethan and Jacobean literature. The almost unbearable tension which it produced is the chief element in the greatness of that literature." As to FQ, sees in it a mixture of paganism and Christianity, sensuality and puritanism, which mirrors the whole mind of the age.

Parrotti, Phillip Elliott. The Female Warrior in the Renaissance Epic. DAI, 34
(1973), 283A. University of New
Mexico, 1972. 458 pp.   1616

The female warriors owe their
mystique to literary and intellectual
traditions related to union of Mars
and Venus. Britomart mirrors, socially, both Harmonia, the uniter, and
Venus armata; privately, she evolves
toward the embodiment of chaste
personal concord as she moves toward
Christian marriage with Artegall.
[SpN, Vol. 5, No. 2 (1974), 16.]

Patrides, C. A. The Grand Design of God:
the literary form of the Christian view
of history. London: Routledge and
Kegan Paul, 1972. 157 pp.   1617

Amplified version of The Phoenix
and the Ladder: the Rise and Decline
of the Christian View of History
(1964). Relevant for both Sp and Milton. Cycles of flux and reflux common to Greco-Roman view of history
like legendary phoenix, periodically
dying and reviving; to Christians, history like Jacob's ladder, leading pilgrim upward in straight line toward
Eternal City. Traces Christian view in
post-classical, medieval, and Renaissance historiography, with much information on Elizabethan cross-currents, e.g., Arthurian and Trojan
legends. Documented with 455 footnotes in small type. 8 pages of plates
following p. 54. See 1012.

Pearce, Roy Harvey. Primitivistic Ideas in
the Faerie Queene, JEGP, 44 (1945),
139-51.   1618

Seeks to examine such ideas in relation to Sp's intellectual milieu, including voyage literature. Deals with
both chronological and cultural primitivism. An example of the former is
Sp's idea of the Age of Chivalry as a
Golden Age, one when order prevailed. "The most striking aspect of

Spenser's use of ideas related to cultural primitivism is not his concern
with beastliness at its best [Una's
satyrs, I, vi; Serena's savage, VI, iv],
but rather with humanity at its
worst—that is, at its most beastly. . . .
Phaedria, Acrasia, the besiegers of the
House of Alma, Gryll, Malecasta,
Argante, the fisherman in whose boat
Florimell takes refuge, the rabble
roused by the Giant with the Scales,
Adicia, and Maleger—all these Spenser
associates with the beasts like which
they behave" (p. 148).

Pellegrini, G. Symbols and Significances,
ShS, 17 (1964), 180-7.   1619

Unlike France and Italy, England
had no firm emblem-book tradition.
But clear that spirit of French and
Italian authors was vital in Elizabethan and Jacobean world. "We
need turn, for example, only to
Spenser in order to realize how the
allegory in many passages [in FQ]
can be clarifed and deepened by observing his use of methods and procedures closely related to the technique established by the authors of
emblem books" (p. 183). See 687,
1197.

Perry, John Oliver, ed. Approaches to the
Poem: Modern Essays in the Analysis
and Interpretation of Poetry. San
Francisco: Chandler, 1965. 433 pp.
                                1620

Repr. of parts of Northrop Frye's
Archetypal Criticism: Theory of
Myths, from 695, with sundry
remarks on Sp's FQ.

Petit, Herbert H. The Fortuna-Vertu Conflict in Spenser's Faerie Queene. Doctoral diss., Western Reserve University,
1953. DDAAU, 1952-53, No. 20. 1621

The conflict between the two basic
concepts of human existence and human achievement, represented by
Fortuna and Vertu, is a dominant

theme in the theological, philosophical, and literary thought of the Renaissance. Sp employs this conflict throughout the six books of FQ and the Cantos of Mutability, and, in fact, makes the relationship of Fortuna and Vertu basic to the action of each of the heroes.

Phialas, Peter G. Shakespeare's Romantic Comedies: The Development of Their Form and Meaning. Chapel Hill: University of North Carolina Press, 1966. 314 pp.   1622

Among Shakespeare's sources for A Midsummer Night's Dream, mentions treatment of fairy-world by Chaucer and Sp (p. 111). In discussing sources of Hero-Claudio plot in Much Ado About Nothing, refers to story of Phedon and Claribell (FQ, II, iv) and Mirabella (FQ, VI, viii) (pp. 177-81, and notes, pp. 297-8). Shakespeare's treatment of pastoralism in As You Like It "is quite different from that of Sidney and Spenser and Lodge" (p. 218).

Piehler, Paul. The Visionary Landscape: A Study of Medieval Allegory. London: Arnold, 1971. 170 pp.   1623

Discussion of medieval allegory relevant to study of Sp. Treats Boethius, Alanus de Insulis and Bernardus Silvestris, John of Hanville, Roman de la Rose, Dante, Pearl poet, and others, finding in them continuity of tradition. Archetypal figures and situations (often Jungian or quasi-Jungian) designed for reintegration of soul in crisis. Brief discussion of symbolic landscape. Influenced by C. S. Lewis (1513), in some ways successor and corrective. Believes allegorical works have integrative value for moderns. [SpN, Vol. 2, No. 2 (1971), 2-3.]

Piloto, Albert Edward. The Theme of Friendship in Elizabethan Literature.

M. Litt. thesis, University of Cambridge, 1954, ADUC, 1954-1955, pp. 90-1.   1624

Chapter 4 shows that in certain chief Elizabethan writers, including Sp, the early Renaissance attitude to friendship was greatly modified, with the ideal human relationship rapidly becoming married love.

Potts, Abbie F. Spenserian "Courtesy" and "Temperance" in Much Ado About Nothing, SAB, 17 (1942), 103-11, 126-33.   1625

Points out parallels between Sp's characters (Serena, Braggadocchio, Phedon, Belphoebe, Britomart, Arthur, Una, Guyon, Calidore) and the characters and motives in Shakespeare's play.

Potts, Abbie Findlay. Hamlet and Gloriana's Knights, SQ, 6 (1955), 31-43.
                                    1626

Comments on the text of Q2 of Hamlet by paralleling it with passages in FQ describing the adventures of Red Cross, Guyon, Arthur, and Artegal.

Potts, Abbie Findlay. Shakespeare and The Faerie Queene. London: Greenwood Press, 1969. 269 pp.   1627

Repr. of 1958 ed. "A study of ethical action as a comparable term in the art of Spenser and Shakespeare ... the mythic and ethic substructure on which both poets have relied." Detailed analysis of symbolic and archetypal resemblances between individual books of FQ and Shakespeare's plays beginning with 2 Henry IV, together with much reliance on verbal parallels. Conclusion: Sp's narrative form and Shakespeare's dramatic form take shape in disciplinary action in connection with a revelatory ordeal.

Preminger, Alex, ed. Encyclopedia of Poetry and Poetics. Princeton: Princeton University Press, 1965. 906 pp.   1628

Frank J. Warnke, Spenserian Stanza, p. 807.

Preston, John. The Informing Soul: Creative Irony in *The Rape of the Lock*, DUJ, 27 (1966), 125-30.   1629

Points out echoes of Acrasia, the Bower of Bliss (FQ, II, xii) and the Masque of Busirane (FQ, III, xii) in the portrayal of Belinda and her world, and observes parallels between the caves of Spleen and Atè (FQ, IV, i) and between the ethic of Pope and that of Sp. But Pope has, unlike Sp, no impulse to destroy the Acrasiaworld, "for he sees clearly how it destroys itself." See 2404.

Preston, Michael J. The Folk Play: An Influence on the "Faerie Queene," AN&Q, 8 (1969), 38-9.   1630

Commentary in Variorum ignores tradition of native folk play. This tradition explains description of "iolly Iune" dressed "in greene leaues, as he a Player were," and his connection with "plough-yrons" (FQ, VII, vii, 35, 1-4); and arrival of Duessa at castle of Lucifera (FQ, I, iv, 13, 1-4), "much like the Molly of the folk plays in that she is an ugly hag treated like a beautiful woman."

Prokesh, Mary Jane. Marriage in the *Faerie Queene* as a Reflection of the Divine Order. DAI, 32 (1971), 2702-A. Texas Christian University, 1971. 152 pp.   1631

Marriage in FQ central symbol of reconciliation of opposites. Studies four betrothals and marriages and meaning of each: Red Crosse and Una (religious), Britomart and Artegall (political), Marinell and Florimell (cosmic), Calidore and Pastorella (eth-ical). Also offers iconographical interpretation of Sp's poetic technique in relation to thematic study of marriage.

Pyles, Thomas. "Dan Chaucer," MLN, 57 (1942), 437-9.   1632

FQ, IV, ii, 32, and VII, viii, 9. Through Sp's use of "Dan Chaucer" rather than "Dan Geoffrey," Dan came to be used as a title with other surnames.

Raine, Kathleen. Blake and Tradition. 2 vols. Princeton: Princeton University Press, 1968. 428, 367 pp.   1633

Discusses relation of The Book of Thel to Sp's Garden of Adonis (FQ, III, vi). "Mutability is *Thel's* theme, as it was Spenser's; but the particular resemblances are even more striking" (I, 100-14). Under drawing in Blake's Notebook of schoolboy knocking down fairies with his hat (Plate 109) Blake wrote lines from FQ, II, ii, 2 (I, 340-1). For other references to Sp, see General Index, II, 364.

Rashbrook, R. F. *The Eve of St. Agnes*, and Spenser, N&Q, 193 (1948), 29-31.   1634

Verbal parallels between Keats's poem and FQ.

Rathborne, Isabel E. The Meaning of Spenser's Fairyland. New York: Russell & Russell, 1965. 275 pp.   1635

Repr. of 1937 ed. "I have tried to show what Fairyland could mean to a learned Elizabethan poet, and to do for the setting and heroine of Spenser's 'historicall fiction' what Professor [Charles Bowie] Millican (926) has done for its hero" (pp. vii-viii). Chapters dealing with Renaissance ideas of earthly fame in relation to Gloriana, her city of Cleopolis, and its tower called Panthea, mythology, pseudo-history, and history in relation to Arthur's Briton Moniments and Guyon's Antiquitie of Faerie Lond (FQ, II, x); folklore and medieval romance in relation to Sp's fairy mythology; fairy queens of myth and romance in relation to Gloriana. See 1559.

Reed, Regina Balla. Rebellion, Prophecy and Power in Four Works of the English Renaissance. DAI, 31 (1971), 4731A. State University of New York at Buffalo, 1970. 190 pp.   1636

"A study of the power play and its limitation through use of prophetic device" in FQ, 1 and 2 Tamburlaine, and Coriolanus. Deals with paradox of power which depends on weakness and with the ambivalence which results when any struggle is resolved through the imposition of prophetic statement. Each work is allegorical, and each hero's symbolic identity is important. Each hero struggles for power, assumes arrogance, then discovers he is a servant. Discusses "Galfridic dream prophecy" in FQ, V, and the vision of Dame Nature in FQ, VII, which elucidates the balance between the powers and limitations of Mutabilitie.

Rees, Compton, Jr. The Hercules Myth in Renaissance Poetry and Prose. Doctoral diss., Rice University, 1962. 406 pp.
                                      1637

Mythopoeic approach emphasizing "the euhemeristic Hercules as a foreshadowing of Christ." Chaps. on classical and medieval approaches to Hercules myth (Dante's symbolism), 14th-century movement toward Renaissance (Petrarch, Boccaccio, euhemerism, Chaucer), 15th-century in Italy, France, and England, 16th-century England including Sp (pp. 289-343). Sp interested in Hercules myth throughout career. Hercules "associated with many of Spenser's central heroic figures: Redcrosse, Guyon, Britomart, Cambell and

Cambina, Artegall, and especially Arthur," also with Calidore. "Spenser places Hercules within his historical allegory as an euhemeristic hero who foreshadows the fulfillment of the Tudors and the Queen to bring about the downfall of Catholicism and the return of political harmony and universal empire."

Rees, John Owen, Jr. Hawthorne and the Emblem. DA, 26 (1965), 357A. University of Iowa, 1965. 256 pp.   1638

Much of Hawthorne's technique derives from emblem books published in England, on the Continent, and in America from 16th through 19th centuries. He inherited their symbolism and depicted scenes as tableaux to be "moralized." Influence of emblem book marked Hawthorne's two favorite works, Sp's FQ and Bunyan's Pilgrim's Progress. Gives evidence Hawthorne knew first hand Alciati's Emblematum Liber.

Reeve, Frederic Eugene, Jr. The Stanza of the Faerie Queene. DA, 12 (1952), 307-8. Princeton University, 1942. 296 pp.   1639

A study of Sp's prosodic structure in terms of rhythmic, metric, and harmonic features. Finds the Spenserian stanza "most appropriate to the Faerie Queene."

Reid, Margaret J. C. The Arthurian Legend: Comparison of Treatment in Modern and Mediaeval Literature. Doctoral diss., University of Aberdeen, 1937. Edinburgh: Oliver and Boyd, 1938; 2nd ed. 1960. 277pp.   1640

More concerned with modern than early treatments. Incidental references to Sp; see Index.

Reid, Robert Lanier. Spenser's "Noble Rider" and the Pattern of Redemption in The Faerie Queene. DAI, 32 (1972),

4576A. University of Virginia, 1971. 279 pp.   1641

Refutes Woodhouse's segregation of FQ, I from the rest of the poem (1752), proposes that FQ as a whole follows a "hierarchical sequence or pattern of redemption." The "noble rider," Prince Arthur, consistently demonstrates in all six books the "Christian-neoplatonic conceptions" of the "heroic image."

Renwick, W. L. *The Faerie Queene*, PBA, 33 (1947), 149-61.   1642

Warton Lecture on English Poetry, 1947. Historical study is useful to present criticism. Two ways of projecting view of world, logical and artistic; FQ freely ranges between formal philosophy, story-telling, and incantation. Sp "attempted the most comprehensive statement of the principles of . . . our Western European civilization." Difficulties in reading FQ from 18th to 20th centuries have varied. "We are out of training for *The Faerie Queene*." Real difficulty of the allegory lies in breadth of Sp's thought. Sp is fundamentally opposed to the modern mood of disillusion. He did not take refuge in escape or denial of responsibility; "Spenser was never the victim of his own enchantments." Historical study of FQ may enable us to "see philosophy and imagery in proportion and enjoy the enchantments without obsession."

Richmond, Velma E. Bourgeois. The Development of the Rhetorical Death Lament from the Late Middle Ages to Marlowe. DA, 20 (1960), 2807. University of North Carolina, 1959.   1643

Chapter IV discusses, among other things, laments in "romances like those of Sidney, Spenser, and Greene."

Ricks, Beatrice. Catholic Sacramentals and Symbolism in Spenser's *Faerie Queene*, JEGP, 52 (1953), 322-31.   1644

Deals with the use of hermits, beads, vestments, mitres, palms, ashes, crosses, etc.

Ringler, Richard N. Two Sources for Dryden's *The Indian Emperour*, PQ, 42 (1963), 423-9.   1645

First scene of The Indian Emperour recalls Donne's First Anniversary. In Act IV, scene iii, including song, Ah! fading joy, how quickly art thou past? Dryden borrows from scene in FQ, I, vii, and Phaedria's song in FQ, II, vi, 15-17. "Donne and Spenser represent the opposite poles of earlier English poetry, and their very polarity serves to suggest the eclectic quality of Dryden's imagination."

Roche, Thomas P., Jr. The Kindly Flame: A Study of the Third and Fourth Books of Spenser's *Faerie Queene*. Princeton: Princeton University Press, 1964. 220 pp.   1646

Bks. III and IV, taken individually, are carefully structured, though not in the same way as I, II, V, and VI. Taken together, III and IV form a continuous narrative "comprising four movements of six cantos each, moving from the inception of love to marriage." The allegorical meaning is tied to these four movements, namely (1) love in the individual, (2) beauty as motive for love, (3) love as social phenomenon, (4) the union, through friendship, of nature and society in marriage. The story of Britomart ties the four movements together. The Introduction, Faeryland as Fiction, develops an elaborate theory of allegory. See 2049; 2075. [DA, 20 (1960), 3306.]

Rev: K. Williams, RN, 17 (1965), 341; R. F. Hill, MLR, 60 (1965), 245; David Kalstone, EIC, 15 (1965), 446; A. C. Hamilton, JEGP, 65 (1966), 168; Michel Poirier, EA, 19 (1966), 76.

Rodgers, Catherine. Time in the Narrative of *The Faerie Queene*. DA, 28 (1967),

1407A-8A. Brown University, 1963.
192 pp.   1647

In FQ timeless narrative of Psycho-machia is placed in a particular histor-ical period and so arranged that the immediate action relates to history of the world and reflects on design of Providence. Narrative lacks resolution because total design of Providence is hidden from us, but poem makes us look forward to some resolution. Mu-tabilitie Cantos show that beauty of creation is made apparent through time, but man does not live long enough to see it unfold.

Roelofs, Gerrit H. The Law of Nature, the Tradition, and the *Faerie Queene*. Doctoral diss., Johns Hopkins Univer-sity, 1955. DDAAU, 1954-55, No. 22.
                                           1648

Central doctrine of poem is obedi-ence to law of God, nature, and rea-son. Tradition of law of nature traced in Plato, Aristotle, the Stoics, the Church Fathers, Roman law, and medieval schoolmen. Renaissance writers took over medieval tradition. Its content found in Decalogue, Christ's commandments, God's com-mand to increase and multiply; hier-archical order of macro- microcosm is insisted on; ideal of whole man, of right reason, is ethical goal. FQ in this tradition. "The Cantos of Mutabilitie allegorize explicitly the dynamic rule of nature." Discusses each book in light of law of nature, finds FQ a consistent and unified whole.

Rollin, Roger B. Beowulf to Batman: The Epic Hero and Pop Culture, CE, 31 (1970), 431-49.   1649

Compares heroes in Beowulf, FQ, and Paradise Lost with contemporary heroes of "pop" epics such as Super-man, Batman, Star Trek, Gunsmoke, etc. Pop heroes exemplify same vir-tues as Sp's heroes, Magnanimity, Justice, Chastity, Holiness, etc. "The

world of *The Faerie Queene* and frequently, of the American Western, is largely static, a version of pastoral." Villains of FQ, like the Western vil-lain, characterized by unnatural de-sires and a craving for fornication. Thus, involvement of students in pop romance no more "escapist" than in-volvement in "great" literature urged upon them by English instructors.

Rose, Mark. Heroic Love: Studies in Sid-ney and Spenser. Cambridge, Mass.: Harvard University Press, 1968. 156 pp.
                                           1650

On Sidney's New Arcadia and Sp's FQ. Both authors sought images which would inspire virtue in their readers. Both added to classical epic a new subject, love. Describes Eliza-bethan concept of love as reflected in Arcadia and FQ. Chapters: I, some-times antithetical concepts of love, sinful and irrational, desirable and laudable, meet in Elizabethan concept of married love. II, Sidney's reconcil-iation of love and reason in Arcadia. III, the love of Britomart and Artege-gall, which passes from courtly love into wedded love. Conclusion: for both Sp and Sidney "love is an educa-tion, a process of self-realization." [Diss., Harvard University, 1967.] Rev: J. A. Burrow, YR, 58 (1969), 605; C. W. Hieatt, JEGP, 69 (1970), 169; K. Duncan-Jones, RES, 21 (1970), 382.

Rose, Mark. Sidney's Womanish Man, RES, 15 (1964), 353-363.   1651

In demonstrating that Pyrocles' transvestism in Arcadia is an image for his spiritual state, i.e., that the "woman" in him is dominant, refers to the Artegall-Radigund story as a prominent example of the Eliza-bethan beliefs that (1) men should not wear women's clothes and (2) it is unjust for a woman to dominate a man. Also refers to the hermaphrodite symbol at the end of FQ, III (1590).

Rudrum, Alan. A Critical Commentary on Milton's "Comus" and Shorter Poems. London: Macmillan, 1967. 113 pp.   1652

In On the Morning of Christ's Nativity influence of Sp detected in final alexandrine and "the general mellifluousness of the verse." Leisurely development of theme one of Milton's debts to Sp. Verse technique in handling octosyllables in L'Allegro and Il Penseroso shows divergence from Sp. FQ, II, xii "is a pervasive influence throughout the temptation-scene in *Comus.*" Story of Sabrina (ll. 825 ff.) adapted from FQ, II, x, 14-19. Sp not mentioned in discussion of Lycidas.

Russell, R. W. Spenser's Use of the Bible in Books I and II of *The Faerie Queene.* Doctoral diss., University of Oklahoma, 1938. UOB (Jan., 1939), p. 116.   1653

Preface: "This study is an attempt to show Spenser's dependence on the Bible for plan, story content, and diction in the first two books of *The Faerie Queene.*" Three 16th-century Bibles—Cranmer's, the Genevan, and the Bishops'—are used. "Unless otherwise specified the 'Bible' indicates the Bishops' version." Biblical parallels noted by editors and critics "have been carefully reexamined and catalogued. Other allusions to the Scriptures, particularly from the books of St. Paul and St. Peter, have been recorded."

Ryding, William W. Structure in Medieval Narrative. The Hague: Mouton, 1971. 177 pp.   1654

Important for study of FQ. Intro. (pp. 9-37) outlines debate over narrative structure beginning with Tasso's criticism of Ariosto's interlaced actions in Orlando Furioso. Conclusion (pp. 162-68). Structural style of medieval narrative developed through three phases: (1) simple to compound, with bipartite design dominant; (2) compound to complex, with controlled multiplicity through interlacing; (3) complexity back to simplicity, theoretical formulation in Tasso's Discorsi del poema eroico (1594). Sp organized FQ in late medieval manner with familiar structural patterns: Bks. I and II single biographical line, with some interlacing, some bipartite features; transitions I-II and II-III a form of interlacing; in III Sp "begins systematically to interlace his story in the manner of Ariosto"; continues this in IV; V and VI return to biographic pattern, with good deal of interlacing in VI, and influence of thoroughly non-Aristotelian late Greek romance. See 1152.

St. George, Priscilla P. Psychomachia in Books V and VI of *Paradise Lost*, MLQ, 27 (1966), 185-96.   1655

Answers literalist critics of Milton's War in Heaven by interpreting it in light of "the Spenserian heresy," i.e., in accordance with Sp's acceptance of "a Neoplatonic oneness in all levels of the phenomenal world, the scale of abstraction" in FQ could range from Una (a quality) to Hellenore (a fallen woman), and "the genre could shift effortlessly from allegory, to romance, to pure poetical entertainment." Similarly, the War in Heaven is, almost simultaneously, epic entertainment (fictional), sacred history (true), and allegory (symbolic). Calls "fully Spenserian" incidents in Bks. II and X involving Sin and Death, compares monster Error (FQ, I, i, 14-16) and Dragon (I, xi, 9-14). In scenes in Hell and Heaven, Milton "used physical correlates for spiritual qualities as deliberately as had Spenser."

Saintsbury, George. A Last Vintage: Essays and Papers. Ed. John W. Oliver,

Arthur Melville Clark, and Augustus Muir. London: Methuen, 1950. 255pp.
                                    1656

Notes on Six Poets, pp. 239-41. Defends statement of his that FQ is the only long poem he ever wished longer.

Sale, Roger. Reading Spenser: An Introduction to *The Faerie Queene*. New York: Random House, 1968. 209 pp.
                                    1657

An informal introduction to FQ. Believes poetry of FQ is a vehicle of understanding rather than experience, to be read and understood in sequence without juxtaposition of widely separated passages. Discussion of Bk. III occupies bulk of the work. Rev: Joan Rees, MLR, 65 (1970), 869; Richard Schoeck, SEL, 10 (1970), 229. See 1302.

Salman, Phillips Cranston. Spenser's Representation of Queen Elizabeth I. DAI, 30 (1969), 2498A-9A. Columbia University, 1968. 143 pp.   1658

Uses FQ to demonstrate how Sp painted his laudatory portrait of Elizabeth.

Sammut, Alfonso. La Fortuna dell' Ariosto nell'Inghilterra elisabettiana. Milan: Vita e Pensiero, 1971. 146 pp.
                                    1659

Discusses influence of Ariosto on George Turberville, George Whetstone, George Gascoigne in Supposes and Adventures of Master F. J., Philip Sidney, Thomas Lodge in Phillis, translators Robert Tofte and John Harington, Greene in Orlando Furioso, Shakespeare in Much Ado About Nothing, and others. Chap. III, L' "Orlando Furioso" e la "Faerie Queene" (pp. 45-77). Reviews older scholarship, agrees Ariosto's influence on FQ evident in parallel characters, episodes, and narrative technique beginning with Bk. III. Reviews modern criticism, agrees two poems proceed mainly on different planes because of author's different attitudes toward chivalry and love, Ariosto's surface brilliance contrasting with Sp's allegorical seriousness, his materialism and levity with Sp's spirituality and didacticism. Gives examples of likenesses and differences by setting Orlando Furioso and FQ side by side, discussing FQ book by book.

Saurat, Denis. Spiritual Attitudes in Spenser, Milton, Blake and Hugo, CLS, 13 (1944), 8-12; 14 and 15 (1944), 23-7.
                                    1660

"I. Spenser." Sp's fundamental intuition is the sense of his own nobility. With this goes a kind of humility—feudal humility. "The noblest form of feudalism is the knight errant," with the forces of good behind him. The Spenserian stanza expresses the nobility-humility poles of feudalism. "Spenser has the complete picture." Only the feudal world made a complete picture, not absolute monarchy or democracy. "That is why, in our Christian tradition, Spenser alone gives us a complete picture of the spiritual world." Later sections compare and contrast Sp with Milton, Blake, and Hugo. See 1065.

Sayers, Dorothy L. Dante's Imagery: I. Symbolic; II. Pictorial, in Introductory Papers on Dante, pp. 1-43. New York: Harper, 1954. 225 pp.   1661

Contrasts Sp's and Dante's approach to allegory. Sp uses personified abstractions, e.g., Belphoebe; Dante uses historical personages as "*symbolic images* of the qualities they represent." If Dante had written FQ, he would have used Elizabeth herself instead of Belphoebe. Further, Dante always keeps the literal and allegorical meanings separate, whereas Sp fuses them without concern for the probability of his literal story.

Sayers, Dorothy L. The Poetry of Search and the Poetry of Statement, And Other Posthumous Essays on Literature, Religion and Language. London: Victor Gollancz, 1963. 287 pp.   1662

No. IX, The Writing and Reading of Allegory (pp. 201-25), defends allegory as a mode, defines it, briefly traces its history from classical through medieval and Renaissance eras to Tennyson and Kafka. Three chief errors to avoid when reading allegory: (1) "finicking insistence on finding a significance for every word in the text"; (2) "confusing the allegorical with the literal meaning"; (3) "widespread notion that the best way to enjoy Allegory is to read for the sake of the 'poetry,' or the literal story, and not bother about what it signifies. That is the direct opposite of the truth."

Scaglione, Aldo. Nature and Love in the Late Middle Ages. Berkeley: University of California Press, 1963. 250 pp. 1663

Sp offered "a paradigmatic conception of nature within the framework of his view on love." Sp opposes the Garden of Adonis to the Bower of Bliss, and sees courtly love as opposed to chastity in marriage (pp. 45, 172). For other references to Sp, see Index.

Schanzer, Ernest. The Problem Plays of Shakespeare. London: Routledge & Kegan Paul, 1963. 196 pp.   1664

Shakespeare solves problem of structure in Antony and Cleopatra "mainly by establishing a series of parallels and contrasts." Structural pattern "becomes a silent commentator, a means of expressing the playwright's attitudes and concerns." Much the same could be said of structural pattern of FQ, or of Paradise Lost (pp. 132-3). Antony's intense vitality both as voluptuary and as soldier is why Sp's image of knight in Acrasia's arms (FQ, II, xii, 76-80)

"fits Antony's case so little, in spite of its surface similarities" (pp. 139-40). Discusses choice of Hercules between Pleasure and Virtue in Renaissance literature as analogue of Antony's choice, and quotes FQ, V, viii, 2 (pp. 155-9).

Schoeck, R. J. Alliteration as a Means of Stanza Connection in The Faerie Queene, MLN, 64 (1949), 90-3.   1665

Classifies and illustrates linkage by various kinds of alliteration: regular or primary, subordinate or secondary, complex or double. "Spenser's use of alliteration for this purpose was frequent, studied and skillfully varied." It has been suggested that Sp got the idea of using alliteration to combine his stanzas (1) from Virgil, or (2) from Irish influence. Adds to these, possibility that practice may reflect stanza-linking in certain Middle English rimed romances. See 1600.

Scholes, Robert, and Robert Kellogg. The Nature of Narrative. London: Oxford University Press, 1966. 326 pp.   1666

Traces with many illustrative examples emergence from epic synthesis of "two antithetical types," empirical and fictional; first divided into two types, historical and mimetic; second divides into romantic and didactic. Narrative allegories of Middle Ages and Renaissance are fictional and didactic. Mostly concerned with "the new synthesis in narrative which has been the main development in post-Renaissance narrative literature"—the novel. Many illustrations from FQ, most in Chap. 4, Meaning in Narrative, Part 2, The Problem of Control: Allegory and Satire (pp. 105-59). "Spenser and Dante are among the few narrative poets really to master allegorical composition." Examples of "qualities . . . indispensable to allegorists" seen in Sp's treatment of Bower of Bliss (II, xii), illustrative imagery of FQ, political allegory in Bk. V, multiple meanings of Duessa, "constellation of symbolic meaning in House of Holiness" (II, x), and much else. Sp in relation to Dante, Langland, Chaucer, and Milton. See Index.

Schrinner, Walter. Castiglione und die Englische Renaissance. Berlin: Junker and Dünnhaupt, 1939. Neue Deutsche Forschungen, Abteilung Englische Philologie, 14. 174pp.   1667

Section on Sp (pp. 89-97) under Künstlerische Gestaltung des englischen Courtier-Ideals: Sp's conception of the ideal courtier or knight is more ethical, inner, and spiritual than that of Castiglione. Further discussion of Sp (pp. 125-8) under Der "Cortegiano" als Vermittler neuplatonischer Ideen—Liebesproblem: Sp, like Castiglione, recognizes the power of true love to free man from his baser desires.

Schulze, Ivan L. Reflections of Elizabethan Tournaments in The Faerie Queene, 4.4 and 5.3, ELH, 5 (1938), 278-84.   1668

The two episodes employ the conventions of romance, but the same conventions were observed in the chivalric practices of Elizabeth's court.

Seaman, John E. The Chivalric Cast of Milton's Epic Hero, ES, 49 (1968), 97-107.   1669

Christ fulfills the heroic role as it was approved by Tasso and Sp. [YWES, 49 (1968), 217.]

Segura, Andrew Richard. Primitivism in The Faerie Queene. DA, 22 (1962), 2800. University of New Mexico, 1961. 246 pp.   1670

Renaissance primitivism is literary interest in, and/or preference for, (1) past times as possessing sturdier virtues and the good life, and (2) a less sophisticated life of leisure and contemplation as found in the shepherd figure or the noble savage. In FQ, primitive material is part of Sp's reflection on man and his place in the universe. This material, extensive and varied, not always used in traditional ways; e.g., golden age gardens are types of true and false fulfillment for England and the English gentleman. Savages and animals also typify action that is "kind" or "unkind." Lion, satyrs, "salvage man" allegorize effect of divine truth and goodness; figures which act against "the course of kynde" fall into degradation. Sp's gentleman needs to develop side of his nature represented by Calidore in the Pastorella episode (VI, ix-xii)— yearning for a simple life, love, and creative leisure. Finally, "noble blood" in Sp is allegorical as well as literal, signifying relationship to God and moral beauty.

Sensabaugh, G. F. A Spenser Allusion, TLS, Oct. 29, 1938, p. 694.   1671

In Maria Triumphans (1635) worship of the Virgin Mary is defended by reference to Sp's calling Elizabeth "goddess heavenly bright" in FQ. Sp is called "the chiefest poet of this age."

Shaheen, Naseeb. Spenser's Use of Scripture in The Faerie Queene. DAI, 30 (1969), 1535A-6A. University of California, Los Angeles, 1969. 373 pp.   1672

Using nine English translations of the Bible printed up to end of sixteenth century, lists five hundred allusions to the Scripture. Sp's religious position was that of Low churchman. Which version of the Bible he used is not as certain. Defines four ways in which Sp recast individual texts. In Bks. I, II, and V, Sp's allusions are meaningful and coherent; in other books of the poem allusions are more decorative and less interrelated.

Shanley, James Lyndon. A Study of Spenser's Gentleman. Doctoral diss., Princeton University, 1937. Menasha, Wis.: George Banta, 1940. 55pp.   1673

Sp's conception of the ideal gentleman agrees in the main with ideas accepted in his time and expressed in the courtesy literature, differing most notably in his emphasis on the worth of military prowess.

Sharrock, Roger, ed. The Pilgrim's Progress, John Bunyan. Harmondsworth, Middlesex, England: Penguin Books, 1965. 377 pp.   1674

Intro. (pp. 7-26) emphasizes Bunyan's realism. "The allegory of The Pilgrim's Progress is not intellectual or highly organized as in the sophisticated religious allegory of Dante or Spenser."

Sheridan, Edward P. Modes of Allegory in the Faerie Queene. Doctoral diss., Yale University, 1949. DDAAU, 1948-49, No. 16.   1675

Summary: "The first chapter is a statement of the problem of allegory and The Faerie Queene, with a brief description of the three modes of allegory. The second chapter describes the medieval mode, its creation of its vehicle out of the whole cloth, its subordination of the vehicle to the demands of the tenor, and its use of personified abstractions. The third chapter describes the employment of the established vehicles of poetic mythology by the classical mode, its constant concern with divinity, and its concern with transcendental implications of human experience. The fourth chapter attempts to define the romantic mode, particularly in its relation to romance proper, and to discuss the important part it plays in The Faerie Queene in providing atmosphere and as an exploratory and discursive mode. The fifth chapter discusses the working of the three modes

together in the poem, and the part they play, by their concurrence and alteration, in establishing an appropriate manner of approach to the material of the various Books."

Shih, Chung-Wen. The Criticism of The Faerie Queene. Doctoral diss., Duke University, 1955. Modern Humanities Research Association, Annual Bibliography of English Language and Literature, 32 (1955-1956), No. 4614.   1676

Points out inadequacy of Herbert Cory's two works on critics of Sp (603, 604). Study divided into three parts, each dealing with criticism of one feature of poem: structure, allegory, poetic qualities. Notes continuity of "romantic" criticism of FQ from Dryden to Pope, Warton to Yeats. "There is what may seem disproportionate emphasis on early criticism, not so much because of its greater historical value as because later opinions are often only repetitions, though more elaborate, of earlier." Does not "venture on the intricate byways of general Spenserian scholarship."

Skarstrom, Alarik Wenning. "Fortunate Senex": The Old Man, A Study of the Figure, his Function and his Setting. DAI, 32 (1972), 6944A. Yale University, 1971. 317 pp.   1677

First 4 chapters establish contours of senex and transference of his function to "wise old man," who either achieves sudden conversion of some youth or gradually cultivates a young man's soul in a setting described as "georgic." Final chapter examines process as recapitulated in FQ.

Smith, Hallett. Shakespeare's Romances: A Study of Some Ways of the Imagination. San Marino, Cal.: Huntington Library, 1972. 244 pp.   1678

Chap. I, Romance Tradition As It Influenced Shakespeare (pp. 1-20).

Contributing to atmosphere of romance in Shakespeare's milieu was Sp's FQ. In Chap. 2, Innocence and the Pastoral World, compares Perdita in The Winter's Tale with Pastorella in FQ, VI, ix, 9-10; and Belarius's view in Cymbeline that country is morally superior to court with Meliboe's discourse to Calidore in FQ, VI, ix, 20-25 (pp. 29-30, 36). In Chap. 7, *A Midsummer Night's Dream* and *The Tempest*, quotes FQ, II, Proem 2-3 on indistinct line between fiction and geographical reporting of New World (pp. 139-40). In Appendix A, Myth, Symbol, and Poetry, takes wry look at myth-archetypal interpretation of Shakespeare's romances, and quotes with approval Rosemond Tuve's dismissal of "Christological allegory" in FQ (1152, p. 417; pp. 206-7).

Smith, Roland M. Irish Names in *The Faerie Queene*, MLN, 61 (1946), 27-38. 1679

Erivan (IV, v); Malfont (V, ix); Amavia, Mortdant, and Ruddymane (II, i); Dony (III, v); Devon and Douglas (IV, iv); Malbecco and Hellenore (III, ix); Druon (IV, ix); Dolon (V, vi).

Sonn, Carl Robinson. Some Contexts of Belief: Studies in Johnson, Arnold, Spenser, Browne, and Milton. Doctoral Dissertation, Harvard University, 1968. 163 pp., Footnotes, pp. i-xxiii.   1680

Discursive essay on Sp (pp. 90-136) interprets Guyon's experience in Cave of Mammon and his swoon on emerging from it (FQ, II, vii-viii), in opposition to all previous critics, in light of Aristotle, Plotinus, Ficino, Calvin, and Augustine. Argues, in opposition to Rudolf Gottfried (see 722), that Sp's art is pictorial. Analyzes a few images and concludes: "The reader's experience of the mental event is far more substantial than his perception of the picture is sharp; he has been

led from the concrete to the abstract, from the particular to the universal . . . . The half-images that emerge from the pageants illustrate further a striving toward generalization and abstraction; but insofar as they are declarative, they are prone to the inadequacies of flat statement."

Spens, Janet. *The Faerie Queene:* A Reply, MLR, 44 (1949), 87-8.   1681

A reply to W. J. B. Owen, ibid., 43 (1948), 239-41 (see 1602). Sp wrote the letter to Ralegh not to explain FQ, but to elaborate the connection between the poem and Queen Elizabeth. Owen's reply to this, ibid., 45 (1950), 511-2 (see 1603).

Spens, Janet. Spenser's Faerie Queene: An Interpretation. New York: Russell and Russell, 1967. 144 pp.   1682

Repr. of first ed. of 1934. Believes "that the whole plan of the poem, and in part the philosophical basis, was altered after nearly half of what we now possess was already written, and altered for more or less external reasons to a scheme alien to the poet's thought and genius." Originally FQ "was to consist of eight books of eight cantos each and Prince Arthur's quest of the Faerie Queene was its main theme." Sp's philosophy derived from Plato and Plotinus; Aristotelian element in FQ was inserted during process of reconstruction. Compares and contrasts Sp with Shakespeare, Milton, and Wordsworth. In addition to redesigning FQ, offers many other stimulating hypotheses.

Spivack, Bernard. Shakespeare and the Allegory of Evil: The History of a Metaphor in Relation to his Major Villains. New York: Columbia University Press, 1958. 508 pp.   1683

Discusses morality play as dramatized metaphor; history of central feature of morality, psychomachia;

emergence of Vice as a focusing of concept of the Seven Deadly Sins; decline of morality play; fusion, in "hybrid plays," of abstract elements of morality play with concrete elements of history and romance; emergence of "mankind" figure, who becomes the human figure of drama at end of 16th century; increasing concentration of vice-abstraction in farce and serious drama, paralleling multiplication of human figures; Shakespeare's adoption of Vice for his villain figures from Richard of Gloucester in 3 Henry VI to Iago. FQ cited, along with Phineas Fletcher's Purple Island, as instance of application of psychomachic image of siege warfare: Alma's castle, metaphor of human body and its functions, beset by enemies of temperance including 7 Deadly Sins. For other references to Sp, see Index.

Starnes, D. T. The Figure Genius in the Renaissance, SRen, 11 (1964), 234-44.
1684

Supplements E. C. Knowlton's essays on Genius, Classical Philology, 15 (1920), 380-4, MLN, 39 (1924), 89-95, and SP, 25 (1928), 439-56, by pointing out a number of concise treatments not hitherto mentioned. Draws upon Renaissance dictionaries further to elucidate FQ's two Geniuses (Bower of Bliss, II, xii, 48; Garden of Adonis, III, vi, 31) as porters, i.e., gatekeepers. Shows source of the appearance of Genius in Bower of Bliss (a woodcut in Cartari's Imagines, p. 303). Suggests significance of "glad Genius" and word "geniall" in Epith, ll. 398-9: Renaissance dictionaries provide appropriate meanings and associations, all related to happiness and marriage; Cooper's Thesaurus cites them under "gigno" and "genialis."

Starnes, D. T. Spenser and the Muses, TxSE, 22 (1942), 31-58.   1685

Sides with those who believe that Sp was writing in the tradition of heroic poetry and that his muse was Calliope.

Steadman, John M. Milton and the Renaissance Hero. Oxford: Clarendon Press, 1967. 209 pp.   1686

Studies "pattern of a Christian hero" in Renaissance theory and practice. Cites Sp's portrayal of single virtue in different heroes of FQ, in Arthur sum of moral virtues. Differing from Virgil, Tasso, Vida, and Sp, Milton stressed patient fortitude as heroic norm. Error commonly personified as evil enchanter, e.g., Archimago. Tradition of romance makes love heroic motif in Renaissance, either wedded love (Artegall-Britomart, Scudamour-Amoret, Marinell-Florimel, Redcrosse-Una) or illicit lust (Acrasia's false paradise). "Magnificence" of Sp's Arthur is heroic virtue. Like Tasso, Sp presents operation of divine grace allegorically (FQ, I, vii and ix); Milton depicts grace and regeneration literally. For numerous references to Sp, see Index.

Steadman, John M. Stanzaic Patterns in the English Wagner Book, N&Q, N. S. 4 (1957), 376-7.   1687

A poem of three 7-line stanzas, each ending in an Alexandrine (ca. 1592-1594), is perhaps an early example of Sp's influence on English poetry.

Steele, Oliver Lee, Jr. The Rhetorical Functions of the Narrator in The Faerie Queene. DA, 26 (1966), 6054A. University of Virginia, 1965. 242 pp. 1688

Investigates "the most obviously intrusive aspects" of the omniscient narrator in FQ, classifying them by form or function. The intrusions include "invocations, formal digressions, instructive intrusions, informative intrusions, long similes, maxims, and allusive and ethically weighted diction." These establish author's ethical authority, showing him as good, humble, devoted to perfections of the past, wise, sympathetic and critical of characters and events in his fiction and in real world of the reader. Author is also learned in classical and English literary traditions, in British history and geography, and in natural science. Typically the intrusions serve, as in the modern novel, to engage reader's sympathy and to relate fictional world to world of the audience. This is crucial, for if reader is not convinced that fictional world is real in same sense as his own world, both fiction and its doctrine will lose cogency.

Stein, Arnold. Stanza Continuity in *The Faerie Queene*, MLN, 59 (1944), 114-8. 1689

Among the rhetorical devices used to secure continuity and to counterbalance the architectural stability of the stanza are rhymes repeated and re-echoed from stanza to stanza, assonance, alliteration, and rhythm—metrical and narrative.

Stephens, G. Arbour. Brechfa and the Lady of the Fountain: What Spenser said about her, Swansea and West Wales Guardian, Oct. 2, 1936. 1690

Stephens, G. Arbour. Spenser's *Faerie Queene* and Wales. 1691

Paper read before the Celtic Congress at Edinburgh, reported in Western Mail and The Scotsman, July 17, 1937.

Stewart, James Tate. Elizabethan Psychology and the Poetry of Edmund Spenser. DA, 14 (1954), 1401-2. Vanderbilt University, 1954. 289 pp. 1692

Sketches the background of Elizabethan psychology. Garden of Adonis (FQ, III, vi) "is the abode of souls." "The Red Cross Knight achieves the level of the understanding and receives the beatific vision during his visit to the hermit Contemplation." The vegetable and sensible souls are treated in the House of Alma episode (FQ, II, x); the theme of Bk. II is the war between the reason and the passions. "Spenser's most significant use of psychology is in his treatment of love," of which there are many levels.

Stillman, Frances J. The Visual Arts and Spenser's *Faerie Queene*. DAI, 32 (1971), 934A. The City University of New York, 1971. 378 pp. 1693

Sp was "intimately acquainted with the materials of the graphic arts and the art of the tapestry of the fifteenth and sixteenth centuries," as shown by style of themes and motifs in FQ. Must have known Sidney's hypothesis that poetry was "a speaking picture," surely had encountered woodcuts, engravings, and etchings characteristic of his time. Examines Sp's adaptation of the graphic arts in FQ under two headings: individual prints and book illustration. Focuses on the art of tapestry adapted in FQ.

Stoll, Elmer Edgar. Shakespeare and Other Masters. New York: Russell & Russell, 1962. 430 pp. 1694

Repr. of 1940 ed. Incidental references to Sp, several in chap. on The Tempest (pp. 281-316), maintaining that play, unlike FQ, is not an allegory. See Index.

Stow, Elizabeth Glenn. "Such an Excellent Mystery"; Some Major Symbols in Spenser's *The Faerie Queene*. DAI, 31 (1971), 6570A. Emory University, 1970. 147 pp. 1695

FQ's meaning is fundamentally manifested in several major symbols, Venus, Gloriana, and Arthur, and in the sacrament of marriage. Although FQ is best described as "epic romance," its characters are stimulated by love of God, not mere romantic love. The three symbols and marriage represent "love in all its forms, including that divine love which is expressed in the essential harmony and unity of God's creation."

Strathmann, Ernest A. A Scotch Spenserian: Patrick Gordon, HLQ, 1 (1938), 427-37.   1696

The Spenserian characteristics of Gordon's Penardo and Laissa (1615) are evident in both incident and language. The first book of a romance, the poem deals with war, enchantment, and heroic rescue. The rescue of Laissa, the central episode, owes much to the adventures of Britomart in the House of Busyrane (FQ, III, xi-xii). Gordon's two other poems, Neptunus Britannicus Corydonis (1614) and The Famous Historie of Bruce (1615), do not borrow so extensively from FQ.

Stroup, Thomas B. The Cestus: Manuscript of an Anonymous Eighteenth Century Imitation of Comus, SEL, 2 (1962), 47-55.   1697

"The Cestus: A Mask," written between 1783 and 1791 by an unidentifiable author who was interested in the current Spenser-Milton revival, derives its name from the girdle of Florimell, heroine of both this work and FQ. The chastity theme, central to both the Florimell incident in FQ (Bks. III and IV) and to the poems of Milton, is also paralleled in "The Cestus."

Stroup, Thomas B., ed. The Cestus: A Mask. Gainesville: University of Florida Press, 1961. 71pp.   1698

This anonymous manuscript in the library of the Duke of Leeds, written in late 18th century, includes as dramatis personae the Duke, Sir Guyon, Cupid, Fairy Queen, Duchess, and Florimel, and links stories of

Guyon and Florimel in FQ with Milton's Comus, as does Thomas Warton in his ed. of Milton (1785).

Sugden, Herbert W. The Grammar of Spenser's Faerie Queene. Philadelphia: Linguistic Society of America, 1936. Language Dissertations Published by the Linguistic Society of America, 22. 228pp.   1699

Sp's grammar conforms in general to the standard and usage of Elizabethan writers. He is more careful of his grammar than Shakespeare. A free use of archaic forms distinguishes the language of FQ from that of other literary works. Versification has an important influence on form and syntax. Dialect is inconsiderable. Few Latin constructions. Following these introductory observations, presents a systematic study of the inflection and syntax of all the parts of speech except the interjection.

Sullivan, Edward D. S. The English Ariosto. Doctoral diss., University of California, Santa Barbara, 1966.
                                               1700

Not concerned with Sp's use of Ariosto's Orlando Furioso but with Sir John Harington's translation (1591). Holds that Harington, despite expansion of indecent passages and insensitivity to nuances, differs from most Elizabethan translators by accurately reproducing tone and spirit of original. Chapters discuss Elizabethan translations in general, romantic epic as literary phenomenon in a humanistic age, Harington's merits, English verse translations of Orlando Furioso in 18th and 19th centuries.

Swallow, Alan. Allegory as Literary Method, NMQ, 10 (1940), 147-57.   1701

Sketches progress of allegory from Dante, for whom it had a valid philosophical and psychological basis, to

Sp, for whom it had not. Sp's attempt to fuse his materials by method of allegory is unsuccessful because allegory no longer served "the vital function . . . as a literary means of expressing the inexpressible." Consequently, most of the poetry of FQ is thin and abstract, without body. Warns modern writers against attempting allegory. See 1702.

Swallow, Alan. Allegory as Literary Method, UDQ, 2 (1967), 73-81.   **1702**

Reprint of 1701.

Tasso, Torquato. Jerusalem Delivered. Trans. Edward Fairfax. Intro. John Charles Nelson. New York: Capricorn Books, n. d. 446 pp.   **1703**

Intro. mentions Rinaldo's sojourn with Armida in sensual paradise in Fortunate Isles (XIV, XV, XVI), "Tasso's most brilliant poetry," and its influence on Sp's Bower of Bliss (FQ, II, xii). Sp denies Acrasie [sic] the reconciliation Tasso permitted Armida; "to Tasso's Latin mind, her sin was not so reprehensible as for Spenser." Sp's FQ "borrows freely from Tasso's poem," and Fairfax's translation (1600) borrows words, images, and archaisms from Sp (pp. xxix-xxx, xxxii-xxxiii). See 1733.

Tate, Allen. A Reading of Keats (I), ASch, 15 (1945), 55-63.   **1704**

"The testimony of the criticism of Keats which I have read is that he was a pictorial poet in the Spenserian tradition." Would add to "this very general statement" that Keats's progress from Endymion to revised Hyperion is in direct line, at end of which "he achieved under Milton's influence a new kind of blank verse, but in it he could not control an heroic action." Thinks The Eve of St. Agnes "his masterpiece in the Spenserian tradition of *ut pictura, poesis.*"

Thomas, Sidney. "Hobgoblin Runne Away with the Garland from Apollo," MLN, 55 (1940), 418-22.   **1705**

Harvey's reference to "Hobgoblin" means Sp's use of Arthurian material in FQ, which Harvey considered irrational. Title quoted from Three Proper and Wittie Familiar Letters.

Tillyard, E. M. W. The English Epic and Its Background. New York: Oxford University Press, 1954. 548pp.   **1706**

As part of larger discussion of the epic in literary history (pp. 262-93), points out general characteristics of structure and method in FQ. Concludes: "It thus turns out that although the *Faerie Queene* cannot pretend to the close and unrelenting concatenation of the *Aeneid* and *Paradise Lost* and must forego the peculiar thrill and pleasure that such concatenation gives, it does possess more than one partial substitute. Spenser had the sheer drive of will to carry through, without deterioration of quality, a very long poem. He had a mind that commanded certain steady modes of though and feeling and imparted these consistently to his theme. And finally he organized his six books into a genuine if loose totality."

Tillyard, E. M. W. The English Renaissance: Fact or Fiction? Baltimore: Johns Hopkins Press, 1952. 118pp.   **1707**

Turnbull Memorial Lectures given at Johns Hopkins University in 1950-51. Emphasizes differences between Middle Ages and Renaissance as a warning against exaggerating their similarities. "The trend . . . was to give an enlarged scope to the human spirit as such" (p. 34). Finds measurable differences in the lyric, criticism, and the epic between medieval and Elizabethan products in each form.

The epic requires quality, abundance and amplitude, control commensurate with the quantity, and the expression of group-feeling. Piers Plowman qualifies as one, and Sp's FQ and Sidney's Arcadia "emerge as at least partial successes." Despite their medievalism, the last two are not medieval (pp. 91-110). Conclusion: the English Renaissance is a fact.

Tillyard, E. M. W. Milton and the English Epic Tradition, in Seventeenth Century Studies Presented to Sir Herbert Grierson, pp. 211-34. Oxford: Clarendon Press, 1938. 415pp.   1708

Shows that Milton was firmly grounded in contemporary epic theory and practice. He was "profoundly influenced all through his life by Spenser's version of the medieval theme of the soul's pilgrimage" in FQ, I. He could have learned little from Sp about the hero of a heroic poem, or about its form (pp. 217-22). Conjectures as to the scope, nature, and possible models of Milton's planned Arthuriad (pp. 222-6), which he abandoned in favor of the Fall of Man as the subject of his epic. See 1138.

Tillyard, E. M. W. Poetry Direct and Oblique. London: Chatto & Windus, 1934. Revised ed., 1945, 1948. 116pp.   1709

Listed in Atkinson, p. 103. In Chapter III, Obliquity, section I, The Sphere of Obliquity, subsection ii, The Great Commonplaces, discusses FQ and finds two great commonplaces emerging from the poem: Sp's idealism and his philosophical conservatism (pp. 43-6).

Traversi, Derek. Spenser's *Faerie Queene*, in The Age of Chaucer, ed. Boris Ford, pp. 203-19. London: Cassell, 1961. 490 pp.   1710

Repr. of 1954 ed. Damns the poem. Sp had lost the wholesome, vital tradition represented by Piers Plowman. FQ is last expression of great medieval allegorical tradition, which Sp did not understand. Beginning with SC, his poetry is cast in a sickly courtly mold, ornamental but moribund. FQ, "for all its superior finish and polished style," is a failure structurally, allegorically, and stylistically. Sp does not initiate anything. Spenserian tradition not in main line of English poetic achievement represented by Chaucer and Langland, Sir Gawain and the Green Knight, Shakespeare, Jonson, and Donne.

Trienens, Roger J. The Green-Eyed Monster: A Study of Sexual Jealousy in the Literature of the English Renaissance. Doctoral diss., Northwestern University, 1951 NUSDD, 19 (1952), 45-9.   1711

Surveys classical and medieval treatments of jealousy. Elizabethan psychology of it as mixture of love, hate, and fear. Color symbolism, animal and monster symbolism, and symbolic personification used in writing about it. Jealousy has prominent role in prose fiction, lyric and narrative verse (Sp in FQ has ideal lovers experience it as Ariosto does in Orlando Furioso, makes Malbecco's conjugal jealously blameworthy), didactic and satirical writings, drama. "Only Shakespeare and his followers in tragedy and tragicomedy regarded its victims with much sympathy or moral detachment."

Tuve, Rosemond. Notes on the Virtues and Vices. Part I: Two Fifteenth Century Lines of Dependence on the Thirteenth and Twelfth Centuries, JWCI, 26 (1963), 264-303.   1712

Similarities exist in the virtue traditions of the Bodleian MS. Laud misc. 570, Jehan Mansel's 1454 manuscript, and their common source, John of Wales' Breviloquium de Virtutibus.

Further examination of classical and medieval treatises concerning the interpretation and ordering of virtues and sub-virtues shows no division occurs between classical and medieval traditions. Common predominant influences are Ciceronian and Macrobian. Emphasizes sub-virtues, consequential for their iconographical and ideological derivations.

Tuve, Rosemond. Notes on the Virtues and Vices. Part II: "Hely"; Two Missing Notes in the *Somme le Roi* Illuminator; the Unicorn; "Sevens" in the Belleville Breviary and some Psalters and Horae, JWCI, 27 (1964), 42-72.   1713

A. Explains traditional fifteen pictures in manuscripts of Somme le Roi (1279), especially puzzling "Hely" (Invidia, Envy), and program followed in illustrating virtues and opposing vices. B. Adds instructions for illuminating no. 1 (Moses receiving and breaking the tables) and no. 4 (Last Judgment) in Somme le Roi, missing in B. N. MS. fr. 14939. C. On development in 14th-century iconography of unicorn over which Humility triumphs. D. On allegorical numbers in some traditional canonical observances.

Tuve, Rosemond. Spenser and Some Pictorial Conventions with Particular Reference to Illuminated Manuscripts, SP, 37 (1940), 149-76.   1714

An examination of conventional figure-motifs which may have influenced Sp's portrayal of characters in FQ; e.g., his visualization of Belphoebe was influenced by details in the pictures of Amazons in medieval manuscripts.

Vance, Eugene Augustus. Warfare as Metaphor in Spenser's *Faerie Queene*. DA, 26 (1966), 5418A-9A. Cornell University, 1964. 262 pp.   1715

Each book of FQ uses warfare as metaphor of man's life. SC introduces themes Sp will reject as he turns from pastoral to heroic, from shepherd to warrior. In pastoral world man trapped in cycle of time, in FQ conception appropriately affirmative. Shows importance of transition from SC to Bk. I of FQ. Traces Christian notions of warfare from classical and Old Testament thought. Studies variations on theme of warfare in each book in relation to hero's situation and experiences as vehicles for moral allegory. In Bk. VI way of warrior not defended for heroism, but for its necessity in preserving from lawlessness order of society as represented by courtesy.

Van Doren, Mark. Mark Van Doren on Great Poems of Western Literature. New York: Collier, 1962. 253pp. 1716

First published 1946 as The Noble Voice: A Study of Ten Great Poems. Chapter on FQ (pp. 185-202). See 1717.

Van Doren, Mark. The Noble Voice: A Study of Ten Great Poems. New York: Henry Holt, 1946. 328pp.   1717

Sp, pp. 231-56. Merits and faults of Sp in FQ. Emphasis is on the weaknesses of the poem: use of exaggeration and sensation, faults arising from use of Ariosto and Chaucer as models. Considers Sp's music his greatest merit, and the brilliant characterization of Britomart the saving force. See 1716.

Van Kranendonk, A. G. Shakespeare en Zijn Tijd. Amsterdam: Querido's Uitgeversmij N. V., 1947. 275pp. 1718

First published 1938. Venus and Adonis has something of Rubens' manner, or Sp's. Shakespeare knew Sp's work, may have parodied his style in A Midsummer Night's Dream. Brief analysis of Sp's art; compares it to that of Titian and Giorgione. Sees

FQ as based on Christian humanism, like Paradise Lost, but with unresolved conflict between Puritan morality and sensuous beauty (pp. 124-8). Portrait of Sp facing p. 124. Mentions Sp in connection with intrigue against Hero in Much Ado About Nothing (pp. 179-80).

Vondersmith, Bernard J. A History of the Criticism of *The Faerie Queene*, 1910-1947. DAI, 32 (1972), 5247A. Duquesne University, 1971. 462 pp. 1719

Chapters: I, background and rationale; II-IV, Sp's sources in ancient, medieval, and contemporary literature; V, Sp's style; VI-IX, studies of the whole poem; X, historical allegory; XI, influence of FQ on subsequent poets. See 1296.

Wade, Clyde Gregory. The Comedy of *The Faerie Queene*. DA, 28 (1968), 3651A-52A. University of Missouri, 1967. 289 pp. 1720

Comedy is abundant in FQ. Sp writes a "divine comedy in Book I and sustained, interwoven narratives of classical and romantic comedy throughout the remaining books. . . . Irony proves to be the principal mode of his divine comedy; satire, the classical; humor, the romantic." Concludes that FQ is "the most sustained and sweeping comedy in the English language." See 2165.

Walter, J. H. *The Faerie Queene:* Alterations and Structure, MLR, 36 (1941), 37-58. 1721

Inconsistencies provide evidence of alterations and revisions: (1) differences between the account of the first 3 books in the letter to Ralegh and the books themselves, and (2) internal inconsistencies of story and character. Few inconsistencies in I, most remarkable in x and xii. Bk. II shows more disagreement with letter to Ra-

legh than internal disorder. Numerous internal inconsistencies in III, IV, and V. Gives a speculative "reconstruction" of these books to account for internal inconsistencies. Ends with suggestion that general plan of FQ was based on a seasonal idea; discusses possible influence of Googe's translation of Palingenius's Zodiake of Life (1560). As second influence on whole poem, suggests Roman de la Rose. See 1263, 1598, 1599, 1605, 1722.

Walter, J. H. Further Notes on the Alterations to *The Faerie Queene*, MLR, 38 (1943), 1-10. 1722

Speculations concerning the original versions of Bks. III and IV. Amoret and Florimell were probably the original twins, not Amoret and Belphoebe; Scudamore's story was intended to end with III; Florimell's story first belonged to IV. Ends with an attempt "to reconstruct, within limits, the making of *The Faerie Queene.*" See 1263, 1598, 1599, 1605, 1721.

Walton, Charles E. *To Maske in Myrthe:* Spenser's Theatrical Practices in *The Faerie Queene.* ESRS, 9. Emporia, Kan.: Kansas State Teachers College, 1960. 47pp. 1723

Chap. I, Significant Features of the Tudor-Stuart Masque, pp. 7-18; Chap. 2, The Child Actor at Court and in the London Theatres, 1570-90, pp. 19-29—largely irrelevant to Sp. Chap. 3, The Maskes in *The Faerie Queene* and Their Significance, pp. 30-41. Sp "must have 'experimented' with the drama in his formative years." Discusses masque of Cupid (III, xii), dance of satyrs (III, x), and dance of Graces (VI, x) in relation to structure and conventions of masque. Takes up procession at House of Pride (I, iv); tapestries in Castle of Busirane (III, xi), "highly reminiscent of an entertainment held in the court of Henry VIII in 1527"; scenic features of Bower of Bliss (II, xii). These and a few other passages "point . . . to Spenser's apparent knowledge of renaissance art principles and emphasize his familiarity with some of the staging conventions of the day."

Wanamaker, Donna Sue. The Circle of Perfection: A Study of Love in *The Faerie Queene*. DAI, 32 (1971), 2656A. University of California, San Diego, 1971. 246 pp.   1724

Renaissance motif of circularity makes FQ, III and IV the imagistic core on which rest of books center like a series of concentric circles. Circularity proliferates to include Neoplatonic philosophy, medieval reverence for perfect geometric forms, cyclical nature of time, fertility myths of dying and resurrection, Cestus, the snake swallowing its tail, hermaphroditism, the dance of Graces on Mt. Acidale, and the Providential Will of God. Story of Florimell and Marinell is circular, and imposes unity on a large portion of FQ. Temple of Venus anticipates Dame Nature in Mutabilitie Cantos. Nature's defense of an ordered and abiding universe is based on God's Providence viewed as a circular process. See 1211 and 1353.

Wang, C. H. Sartorial Emblems and the Quest: a Comparative Study of the *Li Sao* and the *Faerie Queene*, Tamkang Review, 2 (1971), 309-28.   1725

Warr, Nancy Nairn. The Body-Soul Debate in Seventeenth-Century Poetry. DAI, 32 (1970), 1243A-4A. University of New Mexico, 1970. 214 pp.   1726

"Chapter II compares the ethical choice of Hercules (implicit in the epics by Tasso and Spenser) to similar choices in the poems of the seventeenth century."

Warton, Thomas. Observations on The Fairy Queen of Spenser. 2 vols. 2nd ed., corr. and enl. New York: Greenwood Press, 1968; New York: Haskell House, 1969; Farnborough: Gregg, 1969. 228, 270 pp.   1727

Reprints of the 2nd, corrected and enlarged ed. of 1762.

Wasserman, Earl R. Elizabethan Poetry in the Eighteenth Century, ISLL, 32, Nos. 2-3 (1947). 291pp.   1728

Despite the ignorance of Elizabethan literature in the 18th century, the Augustans "kept constantly before them the major artists, Spenser and Shakespeare" (p. 29). FQ was printed nine times in 18th century; Sp was the most popular and influential Elizabethan poet during the Augustan age (p. 36). Sp was admired for his rich fancy in creating pictures and for his moral allegory; Sp "improved"; imitations of FQ by Thomson, Shenstone, Beattie, and others (pp. 92-139; see also bibliography of poems influenced by FQ, pp. 260-8). The minor poems were much less influential (pp. 139-52). Development of historical method of scholarship and historical point of view toward Elizabethan literature before and after Thomas Warton in 1754 published Observations on the Faerie Queene of Spenser (pp. 202-23). See also Index.

Wasserman, Earl R. The Scholarly Origin of the Elizabethan Revival, ELH, 4 (1937), 213-43.   1729

Thomas Warton's formulation and use of the historical point of view in Observations on the Faerie Queene (1754) had been preceded by the development of this method earlier in the 18th century by Lewis Theobald, Francis Peck, Zachary Grey, and John Upton, whose expansion of the knowledge of minor Elizabethan writers led in the latter half of the century to more accurate appreciation of Jonson, Shakespeare and Sp, the major Elizabethans who had always been well known.

Watkins, W. B. C. The Plagiarist: Spenser or Marlowe? ELH, 11 (1944), 249-65.
1730

Takes issue with Baldwin, ibid., 9 (1942), 157-87 (see 1247). Detailed analysis of seven passages in Tamburlaine that Baldwin claimed Marlowe originated and Sp borrowed, and also two lines in Doctor Faustus having a remote parallel in FQ. The first part of FQ and Tamburlaine were both published in 1590, but it is known that the former circulated in manuscript while the play could hardly have been seen in manuscript by Sp in Ireland. Points out that our conception of plagiarism "would have been incomprehensible to Spenser, to Marlowe, and to their age." See 1248, 1467.

Weatherby, H. L. Atheological Symbolism in Modern Fiction: An Interpretation of Hardy's *Tess of the D'Urbervilles*, SHR, 4 (1970), 81-91. 1731

Atheological symbolism is "symbolism drawn from apostate thought." Contrasts theological elements in FQ with "atheological" ideas in Hardy's novel, "representative of the modern novel as a whole," witness Joyce, Lawrence, Hemingway, and to a lesser degree, Faulkner.

Webb, William Stanford. Vergil in Spenser's Epic Theory, ELH, 4 (1937), 62-84; repr. in 644. 1732

Concerned with the problem of "imitation," as the humanists conceived that term; the artistic or structural significance of national history in the education of the hero; and the inclusion of natural philosophy in the epic.

Weiss, Roberto. Torquato Tasso's *Jerusalem Delivered*. The Edward Fairfax Translation newly introduced by Roberto Weiss. London: Centaur Press, 1962. 545 pp. 1733

Tasso is the Italian Sp, Sp the English Tasso. Fairfax a poet in his own right who, though indebted to Sp, influenced such later poets as Waller. [YWES, 43 (1962), 154.] See 1703.

Wellek, René. The Rise of English Literary History. Chapel Hill, N. C.: University of North Carolina Press, 1941. 275pp. 1734

In the 18th century, "interest in Renaissance literature outside the drama centered necessarily in Spenser," who "became the center of much literary discussion. With him was bound up the whole problem of romance, the debate on non-classical composition, discussions on the admissibility of allegory and the 'fairy way of writing'" (pp. 102-4). Ends with a chapter on Thomas Warton (pp. 166-201), in which the importance of the earlier Observations on the Faerie Queene of Spenser (1754) in understanding Warton's method and attitude in the later History of English Poetry is clearly brought out (pp. 166-71). See also Index.

Wells, Stanley. Shakespeare and Romance, in Later Shakespeare, Stratford-upon-Avon Studies 8, pp. 49-79. London: Arnold, 1966. 264 pp. 1735

Discusses romance as enduring genre: Odyssey, Euripides, Greek New Comedy, Plautus and Terence, late Greek romances of Heliodorus, Longus, and Achilles Tatius, sub-genres of chivalric, heroic, epic, pastoral, and Arthurian romance. All of these provide complex literary context of Greene's novels, Lodge's tales, Sidney's Arcadia, Sp's FQ—and Shakespeare's final plays. "Sidney,

Spenser, and Shakespeare appeal primarily to our imaginations, not our brains; and the standard motifs and conventions of romance were invaluable raw material to them" (pp. 49-56). Remainder of article deals with Shakespeare's handling of romance motifs and conventions in comedy, particularly The Comedy of Errors and Twelfth Night; and same materials with different emphasis in final plays, particularly The Winter's Tale and The Tempest.

Whalley, George. Poetic Process. Cleveland: Meridian Books, 1967. 256 pp.
1736

Repr. of 1953 ed. Chap. IX, Symbol and Myth (pp. 164-89) appends A Note on Allegory (pp. 190-2), which says "C. S. Lewis's *Allegory of Love* (1936) . . . has clarified the nature of true allegory, but only at the expense of confusing the nature of symbol" (see 1513). Fully developed allegory is a symbolic mode, "and in its formulated state is a species of cyphering." True allegory as symbolic mode is rare, achieved only in parts of FQ. In many sections of FQ "symbolism has degenerated into cyphering."

Wheeler, Charles B. The Design of Poetry. New York: Norton, 1966. 302 pp. 1737

In chap. on uses of allegory in modern poetry (pp. 121-50) mentions FQ and Divine Comedy as "the great achievements of allegory." Discusses and illustrates Spenserian stanza as traditional form of poetry, "its reputation for being languid" derived more from James Thomson than from Sp, "in whose hands it is an instrument for vigorous narrative" (pp. 256-8).

Whiter, Walter. A Specimen of a Commentary on Shakespeare, Being the Text of the First Edition (1794) Revised by the Author and Never Pre-

viously Published. Ed. Alan Over and Mary Bell. London: Methuen, 1967. 233 pp.   1738

Introduction   (pp.   xvii-lxxxi). Whiter anticipated the modern study of Shakespeare's imagery. February of SC mentioned by eds. (p. xlv). Whiter quotes FQ, III, ii, 1-4 as illustrating Locke's association of ideas (p. 107); meaning of "boulted" in II, iv, 24, 2 (p. 115); derivation from masque and pageant of imagery in I, v, 30, 1-2, 6-9 (p. 175).

Wiley, Margaret L. Creative Sceptics. London: Allen and Unwin, 1966. 352 pp.
1739

Four   phases   of   skepticism   in Montaigne's definition in An Apologie of Raymond Sebond: nescience (man's ignorance), dualism, paradox, and knowing by doing. These phases traceable in history of skepticism (pp. 13-6). Chap. I, Edmund Spenser: Mutability, the Seed Bed of Skepticism (pp. 21-46). Mutability of all things earthly links Sp's thought with skeptic tradition. His perception of nescience in Calidore's interruption of dance of Graces (FQ, VI, x), presumption of Giant with scales (FQ, V, ii), quests of Britomart and Arthur in search of an unknown. Dualisms such as appearance and reality in machinations of Archimago and Duessa. Combination of dualisms results in paradox as Sp maintains both halves of opposites: arguments of Despair and Una (FQ, I, ix), Phaedria and Mammon (FQ, II, vi-vii), and rescue of Arthur by Timias (FQ, II, xi). Sp "saw as a real and moving answer to mutability its creative transformation into a dynamic life . . . an answer to the problem . . . out of . . . the problem itself." Salvation in oblique action prompted by love. Treats other creative skeptics from Bacon to Henry Adams.

Williams, Kathleen. Romance Tradition in *The Faerie Queene*, RSSCW, 32 (1964), 147-60.   1740

FQ is a product of creative conservatism, a reworking of materials of medieval romance and allegory from perspective of new classicism.

Williams, Kathleen. Spenser's World of Glass: A Reading of The Faerie Queene. Berkeley: University of California Press, 1966. 241 pp.   1741

Substance of 1742 included in Chaps. III and IV; of 2167 in Chap. VI. Takes view that Sp is "the maker, the creator of his own coherent universe, the serious, mature, and dedicated poet whose work is a personal vision of truth." Everything in FQ is "part of a structure which for all its effortless ease is massive in its scope and exactly functional in its detail. . . . Such an ordered richness can be achieved only through complex organization" (pp. xi, xvii). Discusses episodes in each book which best illustrate complex order in chaps. suggestively titled The Warrior Saint, The Image of Mortality, The Terms of Mortal State, Inviolable Bands, Heavenly Justice, All Gifts of Grace, and The Law of Nature. "Art of a very complex kind creates the poem's sense of spontaneous life."
Rev: Arnold Williams, ELN, 4 (1967), 288; Maurice Evans, RES, 18 (1967), 452; Carol V. Kaske, JEGP, 67 (1968), 302; R. F. Hill, MLR, 65 (1970), 137. See 675.

Williams, Kathleen. Venus and Diana: Some Uses of Myth in *The Faerie Queene*, ELH, 28 (1961), 101-20; repr. in 756.   1742

In FQ, III and IV, Venus and Diana are mythological figures who retain their identity. They are manipulated in such a way as to support Sp's theme of discord and resolution of the problem in discordia concors. Discusses parallel stories of Britomart, Amoret, and Florimell as thematically interlinked.

Williams, Kathleen. Vision and Rhetoric: The Poet's Voice in "The Faerie Queene," ELH, 36 (1969), 131-44.   1743

Passages in which Sp directly addresses the reader combine modesty appropriate to the visionary material being related, with the stance of a competent craftsman discussing his vision with his reader.

Williams, Kathleen M. "Eterne in Mutabilitie": The Unified World of *The Faerie Queene*, ELH, 19 (1952), 115-30; repr. in 644.   1744

Refutes the position of J. W. Saunders, ibid., pp. 81-114 (see 1064). Contends that FQ presents a consistent scheme of theology and ethics, developed through "a series of interlinked and expanded symbols." Mutability Cantos draw into unity the diversity of the preceding books.

Wilson, Robert Rawdon. The Deformation of Narrative Time in *The Faerie Queene*, UTQ, 41 (1971), 48-62. 1745

Discrepancies in Sp's treatment of time are not merely dreamlike; they have artistic purposes. Sp uses differing time schemes for differing narrative purposes, especially when two normally united characters are separated. Certain situations, e.g., Holiness ensnared by Pride, require extended periods of suffering to achieve proper effect; others, e.g., Truth coming to aid Holiness, call for contracted time schemes. Sp uses varying time schemes to arrange and interpret his narrative and to connect the literal and allegorical dimensions. [SpN, Vol. 2, No. 3 (1971), 4.]

Wilson, Rod. Further Spenserian Parallels in Hawthorne, NHJ, 2 (1972), 195-201.   1746

Makes three points. First, Priscilla and Hollingsworth of The Blithedale Romance show influence from Sp's Pastorella and Calidore in FQ, VI, ix-xii. Second, the scene in which sinners are punished by the puritans in "Endicott and the Red Cross" derives from the scene in front of Mercilla's palace, FQ, V, ix, 25-26, in which Malfont's tongue is nailed to a post. Third, Hawthorne for obscure reasons tried to conceal his debt to Sp.

Winkelmann, Sister Mary Anne. Spenser's Modification of the Renaissance Idea of Glory as the Motivation of The *Faerie Queene*. DA, 22 (1962), 3191-A. St. Louis University, 1961. 378 pp. 1747

Concentrates on the idea of Glory "as it came to Spenser from his predecessors and as he finally modified it to suit his own purposes and his own character." Chap. I traces "glory-fame-honor" complex, beginning with Aristotle and the Greek epic; noting, in Cicero and Virgil, Roman emphasis on service to others or performance of duty; observing Augustinian negation of earthly glory as a worthy motive and Aquinas' attempt to synthesize pagan and Christian elements of magnanimity and magnificence. Chap. II notes varying attitudes toward glory of Italian writers of Renaissance, and increasingly Augustinian suspicion of glory as a motive among Renaissance English writers. Chap. III finds in Sp's early poems, especially MHT, a similar distrust of desire for glory. Chaps. IV and V find in FQ a more balanced Christian attitude, akin to Cicero, Virgil, and Aquinas rather than either Aristotle or Augustine.

Winters, Yvor. Problems for the Modern Critic of Literature, HudR, 9 (1956), 325-86. 1748

Section V, pp. 353-60, deals with epic and allegory. Both forms are

dead. Faults of allegorical method easily seen in Sp, e.g., in encounter of Red Cross Knight with Error (FQ, I, i). "The poem has other defects: the clumsy and tyrannical stanza, the primitive and unvaried use of the iambic pentameter line, and an habitual redundancy; but at present I am concerned only with the incurable flaws in the method."

Wolk, Anthony William. Hercules and *The Faerie Queene*. DA, 26 (1966), 5420A-1A. University of Nebraska, 1965. 141 pp. 1749

Reads FQ as a Heracleid. Comparison of Arthur's killing of Orgoglio's beast with Hercules' killing of the Hydra suggests that labors of twelve heroes of FQ are like Hercules' twelve labors. Arthur's slaying of Maleger (Antaeus/libido) parallels Guyon's capture of Acrasia. Busirane, defeated by Britomart, is named for Busiris, slain by Hercules. In Bk. IV competition for Florimell's girdle may parallel Hercules' winning of Hippolyta's girdle. In Bk. V Arthur's killing of the Souldan and Geryoneo parallels Hercules' killing of tyrants Diomedes and Geryon, especially since both Geryons are Spanish. Attempt to capture Blatant Beast in Bk. VI is like Hercules' attempt to capture and control Cerberus. Hercules myth forms an organizational scheme for whole allegory of FQ.

Woodhouse, A.S.P. The Argument of Milton's *Comus*, UTQ, 11 (1941), 46-71. 1750

What Milton is saying, i.e., the argument, must be understood in terms of the two orders of nature and grace as an intellectual frame of reference found in many works of literature in 17th and earlier centuries—in Sp, for example, no less than Milton. Doctrine of chastity, which partakes of both orders, is central theme of

Comus. In temptation scene Lady meets same temptation Guyon meets in Bower of Bliss (FQ, II, xii), "an episode immensely impressive to Milton." Discusses relation of Milton's doctrines of nature and temperance to Sp's. Distinguishes between his doctrine of chastity and Sp's in FQ, III. Order of grace, or level of religion, is not reached until concluding lines of Epilogue. In allusion to Garden of Adonis, Milton does not limit roles of Venus and Adonis and Cupid and Psyche to natural level, as Sp does (FQ, III, vi), but moves to higher level of grace. Epilogue deals with experience on level of grace and is thus key to Milton's intention in poem. See 1751.

Woodhouse, A. S. P. *Comus* Once More, UTQ, 19 (1950), 218-23.   1751

Among other things, notes allusions to Sp in Comus and argues that the Sabrina episode signals the achievement of the level of grace. See 1750.

Woodhouse, A. S. P. Nature and Grace in *The Faerie Queene*, ELH, 16 (1949), 194-228; repr. in 644 and 756.   1752

Sp agreed with the assumptions of Christian humanism "that the order of grace was the superstructure whose foundations were securely laid in nature;... that grace came to perfect nature;... that well-being must be defined in terms of the two orders simultaneously" (p. 196). This frame of reference was an important part of Sp's intellectual background. Sp carefully differentiates the two orders. Thus, Bk. I moves in the order of grace on the level of religion; the other books on that of nature only. Specifically, "what touches the Redcross Knight bears primarily upon revealed religion, or belongs to the order of grace, whatever touches Guyon bears upon natural ethics, or belongs to the order of nature" (p.

204). Analyzes major characters and key incidents of FQ in this light. Somehow before the end of the work a synthesis would have been called for showing the priority of the order of grace. See 1380, 1411, 1444, 1753, 1755, 1935.

Woodhouse, A. S. P. Nature and Grace in Spenser: A Rejoinder, RES, N. S. 6 (1955), 284-8; repr. in 756.   1753

Spirited reply to Hoopes, ibid., 5 (1954), 14-24 (see 1935), insisting on a more precise distinction between nature and grace, and reiterating that FQ as we have it is short of the final synthesis of the two orders. See 1752.

Woodhouse, A. S. P. The Poetry of Collins Reconsidered, in From Sensibility to Romanticism: Essays Presented to Frederick A. Pottle, ed. Frederick W. Hilles and Harold Bloom, pp. 93-137. New York: Oxford University Press, 1965. 585 pp.   1754

William Collins lived in two literary worlds of 1740's on: one still Augustan, other Pre-romantic. In second world Collins had contacts with Joseph and Thomas Warton, and with James Thomson of The Seasons and The Castle of Indolence. Hence Spenserian flavor of his Persian Eclogues and Odes on Several Descriptive and Allegoric Subjects. Ode on Poetical Character echoes Sp in magic girdle, repudiates the Neoclassical, advances theory of "creative imagination." Odes address personifications such as Simplicity, Pity, Mercy, and Peace, develop "idea" of things pictorially. Discovery of symbol basis of Collins's best achievement in poetry. Further step in Pre-romantic world when Collins finds in Highlands of Scotland subjects for "strange lays had charm'd a Spencer's ear." For other associations with Sp in text and footnotes, see Index.

Woodhouse, A. S. P. Spenser, Nature and Grace: Mr. Gang's Mode of Argument Reviewed, ELH, 27 (1960), 1-15. 1755

Says that Gang, ibid., 26 (1959), 1-22 (see 1380) in attacking his Nature and Grace in The Faerie Queene (see 1752) has misunderstood or misrepresented his thesis, and certainly has misstated that thesis. Restates his thesis.

Woolf, Virginia S. Collected Essays, Volume 1, ed. L. Woolf. London: Hogarth Press, 1968. 361 pp.   1756

The Faerie Queene, pp. 24-30, repr. of 1757.

Woolf, Virginia Stephen. The Moment and Other Essays. New York: Harcourt Brace, 1948. 240pp.   1757

The Faerie Queene, pp. 24-30. The poem appeals to different layers of the mind, because Sp "is alive in all his parts." Personification of human passions gives the characters amplitude. Sp asks the reader to think poetically. He is easier to read than William Morris. The difficulty "lies in the fact that the poem is a meditation, not a dramatisation." The characters "lack definition." The verse is soporific. To compensate, we have Sp's mind, "the sense that we live in a great bubble blown from the poet's brain."

Wordsworth, William. From the Preface to Poems 1815, in Romantic Criticism, ed. R. A. Foakes, pp. 60-70. London: Edward Arnold, 1968. 224 pp.   1758

Wordsworth praises Sp's allegorical technique (p. 67).

Wright, Carol Von Pressentin. The Lunatic, the Lover, and the Poet: Themes of Love and Illusion in Three Renaissance Epics. DAI, 30 (1970), 3962A. University of Michigan, 1969. 301 pp.   1759

Studies themes of illusion and reality in Orlando Furioso, Gerusalemme Liberata, and FQ. FQ pursues these themes in more specifically moral terms, "working with metaphors of blindness and vision as well as with those of art and nature to create a poem whose structure depends on a neo-Platonic vision of time and timelessness, of a stable, ideal reality unfolding into a world of change, time and illusion."

Wright, Lloyd Allen. Spenser's Heroic Poem. Doctoral diss., Harvard University, 1969. 243 pp.   1760

Chap. I, Spenser and the Heroic Tradition, analyzes in detail the Letter to Raleigh under the headings Epic and Romance, Poetry and Philosophy, and Poetry and History. Chap. II, A Heroic Morality, discusses Bk. I of FQ. Chap. III, Heroic Contemplation, discusses "the most admired cantos" of Bk. II, vii and xii. Chap. IV, A Heroic Romance, discusses "the Marinell-Florimell tale." Intends to show that all of these sections "are decorous elements of Spenser's heroic poem." Conclusion: "*The Faerie Queene* is radically different from poetry of the twentieth century, and therefore may initially seem foreign to our sensibilities. But its merits become clear when we approach it as an Elizabethan heroic poem, and emphasize its didactic efficacy as the proper measure of its success."

Wurnig, Gertraud. Arthur und sein Kreis in der englischen Literatur von Spenser bis Masefield. Doctoral diss., University of Innsbruck, 1951. 137pp. OeB, 5 (Mar. 15, 1953), 7.   1761

Mentions as contributors to Arthurian materials in 16th century, historians Edward Hall, Raphael Holinshed, John Stow, and John Speed; and poets Thomas Hughes and Sp (pp. 7-14). Sp appears in discussions of Arthur's character and his place in the legend (pp. 81-97), Merlin (pp. 112-5), and Tristram (pp. 131-2).

Yates, Frances A. Elizabeth as Astraea, JWCI, 10 (1947), 27-82.   1762

Spenser and Astraea, pp. 65-70. Concept of Elizabeth as the imperial virgin reflected in Gloriana, Belphoebe, Mercilla, Una, and the dance of the Graces on Mount Acidale.

Young, John Jacob. Artegall and Equity: *The Faerie Queene*, Books III-V. DAI, 29 (1969), 4472A. Case Western Reserve University, 1968. 252 pp. 1763

Two false assumptions have obscured the moral significance of Artegall: first, that Sp, in treating justice, carelessly permitted historical considerations to intrude upon his moral design, thus distorting the moral significance; second, that the poet's treatment of justice is contained in Bk. V. Argues that Sp, in fact, structured Artegall's story in the conventional epic manner of in medias res and that the episodes are accordingly woven into FQ, III and IV as well as into V. Further, the incidents which involve Artegall follow a pattern used in the first two books. Like Red Cross and Guyon, Artegall becomes overconfident, falls, is rescued, and completes his quest.

Zacha, Richard Bane. Ariosto and Spenser: A Further Study in the Relationship Between the *Orlando Furioso* and the *Faerie Queene*. DA, 23 (1962), 1690. Catholic University of America, 1962. 168 pp.   1764

Emphasizes influence of contemporary edited texts of Orlando Furioso on Sp's conscious imitation of Ariosto. Holiness and temperance were primary virtues pointed out in Orlando Furioso by allegorizing commentators; there is "scarcely any serious aspect of the *Faerie Queene* which Italian editors and allegorists had not already demonstrated" in Orlando Furioso. "Spenser is most successful as an allegorist precisely in those matters where he had a model in the edited text of the *Furioso.*"

Zocca, Louis R. Elizabethan Narrative Poetry. New Brunswick, N. J.: Rutgers University Press, 1950. 306pp.   1765

Restricted to three classes of poems: historical, fictional, mythological (p. xi). Lear story in Mirror for Magistrates, its popularity, and Sp's use of it in FQ, II, x (pp. 31-2); Thomas Churchyard is Palemon in CCCHA (pp. 60-1); widespread practice of adding a long poem to a sonnet sequence, as Sp added Epith to Amor (pp. 69-71); popularity of Ariosto's story of Ariodantes and Ginevra, used by Sp in story of Phedon, FQ, II, iv (pp. 146-8); mythology in England, idolization of Queen Elizabeth, who "received a final coronation as a divinity at the hands of Spenser in the *Faerie Queene*" (pp. 189-91); Sp's translation of pseudo-Virgilian Culex in VG (p. 206); Muiop as a mythological poem, a genre Sp tried only once (pp. 227-9); Sp's influence on Drayton's Endimion and Phoebe (pp. 262-4). For other Sp references, see Index.

Allen, Don Cameron. Arthur's Diamond Shield in *The Faerie Queene*, JEGP, 36 (1937), 234-43.   1766

Sp borrowed the marvelous shield from Ariosto, but changed its substance from carbuncle to diamond. Finds the reason for this change in the Christian symbolism of the two stones. See I, vii, 32-35.

Allen, Don Cameron. Spenser's Sthenoboea, MLN, 53 (1938), 118-9.   1767

On the myth alluded to in FQ, I, v, 50, 5-6. Finds a possible source of Sthenoboea's suicide in Textor's Epithets.

Anderson, Judith H. Redcrosse and the Descent into Hell, ELH, 36 (1969), 470-92.   1768

Redcrosse's sojourn at House of Pride and Duessa's visit to Hades (FQ, I, iv and v) echo and elaborate Redcrosse's battle with Error and encounter with Archimago in I, i. Especially significant is Redcrosse's false dream, where the action moves from an exterior to an interior landscape. In this interior landscape of Redcrosse's mind his combat with Sans Joy and Duessa's trip to Hell to cure Sans Joy take place. Duessa's descent to cave of Aesculapius projects Redcrosse's spiritual condition, and he proceeds from Lucifera's house, his wounds only partly healed, to total defeat by Orgoglio (vii).

Arnold, Paul. Occultisme Élizabéthain, CS, 34 (1951), 88-101.   1769

Finds adventures of Red Cross Knight and Una paralleled in Les Noces Chymiques de Christian Rosenkreutz, published Strasbourg 1616, by Johann Valentin Andreae, noted Rosicrucian. The two works are two versions of the same occult tradition (pp. 90-3). Goes on to find much occult symbolism in Shakespeare.

Atkinson, Dorothy F. *The Wandering Knight*, the Red Cross Knight and "Miles Dei," HLQ, 7 (1944), 109-34.   1770

Reprinted in The Sword, 11 (1947), 3-26. William Goodyear's The Wandering Knight (1581), a translation of Jean Cartigny's Le Voyage du Chevalier Errant (1557), bears remarkable episodic and structural resemblance to FQ, I. Suggests that Sp's allegory may be a version of the prodigal son parable, this providing "another key to the 'darke conceit' of *The Faerie Queene*." Cartigny then becomes another formative influence on Sp. See 1789.

Baretti, J. M. The Story of Fradubio and Fraelissa in *The Faerie Queene:* Notes on Witchcraft, CLS, 5 (1942), 25-7.   1771

On FQ, I, ii, 28-44. Sources and analogues of characters and incidents in popular literature.

Bauer, Robert J. Pictorial Art and Spenser's Styles, SHR, 6 (1972), 73-80.   1772

2 plates. In FQ, I, i, 47-9, Sp in portraying Redcrosse's dream of the

wanton Una is appealing to the intellect in traditions of medieval allegory. In I, vi, 7 ff., portrayal of Una's encounter with satyrs is appeal to tactile and emotional faculties in manner of romantic visionaries. [SpN, Vol. 3, No. 3 (1972), 8.]

Bell, Bernard W. The Comic Realism of Una's Dwarf, MSE, 1 (1968), 111-8.

1773

Like the dwarf in the romance of Gareth and Linet, Una's dwarf is a "nameless, dutiful menial whose stature and deeds are characterized by comic overtones." Una's dwarf is more practical and pictorial than allegorical.

Bennett, Josephine W. Spenser's *The Faerie Queene*, Expl, 1 (1943), 62.

1774

Answers Q16, ibid., two questions about St. George's origin and pagan rites at the marriage of Truth and Holiness.

Berger, Harry, Jr. Spenser's *Faerie Queene*, Book I: Prelude to Interpretation, SoRA, 2 (1966), 18-49.   1775

FQ, I is an apocalypse, involving visionary promise and eschatological fulfillment. Sp works on three levels: romance, theology, and faerie. The hero goes from the selfishness of his quest through the sacramental dragon fight to the oneness of a shared life.

Blayney, Margaret S., and Glenn H. Blayney. *The Faerie Queene* and an English Version of Chartier's *Traité de l'Espérance*, SP, 55 (1958), 154-63.

1776

Striking similarities exist between FQ, I, ix and x, and Alain Chartier's Traité de l'Espérance. In the Earl of Leicester's library was a manuscript copy of an English version of this work. Sp may have been recalling the French work or its English translation in the episode of the Red Cross Knight in the Cave of Despair and the sojourn with Una in the House of Holiness.

Bloomfield, Morton W. The Seven Deadly Sins. East Lansing, Mich.: Michigan State College Press, 1952. 482pp. 1777

Traces the concept of seven or eight cardinal sins from Evagrius to Gregory the Great, and thence to Thomas Aquinas. The cardinal sins became confused with the deadly sins in the popular mind. Both kinds widespread in Continental and English literature and art from Middle Ages to Sp. The Procession of Sins, deriving from their very early association with animals (see Appendix I, pp. 245-9), received its most influential expression in the Lumen animae of Matthias Farinator, a Viennese Carmelite, ca. 1330. First elaborate English version of procession, surpassed only by Sp, is in John Gower's Mirour de l'omme (pp. 194-6). Attacks J. L. Lowes' contention (see Variorum, I, 407-13) that Sp's source for pageant of Seven Deadly Sins (FQ, I, iv) is Gower (p. 423, note 284). Scene in FQ represents breakdown of the tradition; it is treated with a freedom and humanism which reveal a new and nonmedieval approach. "It is fitting that we close with Spenser, as his is the last great treatment of the Sins in English literature." After this they no longer evolved or inspired great writing (pp. 241-3). See 587, 1206, 1778, 1791, 1887.

Blythe, Joan Heiges. Spenser and the Seven Deadly Sins: Book I, Cantos iv and v, ELH, 39 (1972), 342-52. 1778

Kirkegaardian reading of the procession episode and Duessa's subsequent visit to Cave of Night. Redcrosse is subject to unconscious despair, as figured forth in the Cave; his preoccupation with particular sins blinds him to his fundamentally prideful and erroneous stance toward God. Opposite of this general sin of despair is not virtue but faith, and Redcrosse returns to it when he and Una are ultimately united. [SpN, Vol. 4, No. 1 (1973), 5-6.]

Boase, T. S. R. The Decoration of the New Palace of Westminster, 1841-1863, JWCI, 17 (1954), 319-58.   1779

Palace of Westminster destroyed by fire in 1843. Parliamentary Commission announced competition for paintings to adorn new palace illustrating subjects from British history or from works of Sp, Shakespeare, or Milton. Exhibition of 140 cartoon drawings, not less than 10 ft. or more than 15 ft. in longest dimension, opened at Westminster Hall in summer of 1843. Milton (40), Shakespeare (12), and Sp (11) provided themes for 63 of these. Among Spenserian pieces: Frank Howard's "Una coming to seek assistance of Gloriana," E. V. Rippingille's "Una and the Red Cross Knight led by Mercy to the hospital of the Seven Virtues," and W. E. Frost's "Una and the Satyrs" (for this last, see Plate 47a).

Botting, Ronald B. Spenser's Errour, PQ, 16 (1937), 73-8.   1780

Finds a source in Hesiod's Echidna.

Bowe, Elaine Campbell. Doctrines and Images of Despair in Christopher Marlowe's *Doctor Faustus* and Edmund Spenser's *The Faerie Queene*. DAI, 29 (1969), 2206A. University of Oregon, 1968. 270 pp.   1781

Attempts to show that "religious discussions of the causes, manifestations, and remedies of the sin of despair and the images recurring in them significantly influenced the treatment of despair in two of the most highly developed narrative forms of the period, tragedy and epic." In Doctor Faustus examines despair of protagonist. In FQ, Sp "depicts two kinds of despair in his epic, the damnable despair of the Red Cross Knight in canto ix and the Knight's salutary suffering in canto x. Both authors develop images familiar from religious analyses to organize and clarify events as well as to present the spiritual travails of their tragic and epic protagonists." See 1783, 1834, 1865.

Bradner, Leicester. The Authorship of *Spenser Redivivus*, RES, 14 (1938), 323-6.   1782

Suggests Edward Howard, who made attempts at heroic poetry and whose prefaces praise Sp except for his language. In Spenser Redivivus (1687) FQ, I is rewritten in heroic couplets.

Brittain, Kilbee Cormack. The Sin of Despair in English Renaissance Literature. DA, 24 (1963), 281. University of California, Los Angeles, 1963. 421 pp.   1783

Studies Biblical, Greek, Roman, and patristic concerns with despair. Discussions of it abound in English medieval literature. Particularization of mankind in 16th century morality plays made despair and damnation dramatic possibilities. Tradition culminates in Marlowe's Doctor Faustus; FQ, I; and Shakespeare's portraits of the desperate, with Macbeth his greatest example. See 1781, 1834, 1865.

Broes, Arthur T. Journey into Moral Darkness: "My Kinsman, Major Molineux" as Allegory, NCF, 19 (1964), 171-84.   1784

Robin, "like Spenser's Redcross Knight, to whom he bears a marked and perhaps not unconscious resemblance, is too sure of his ability to comprehend and withstand the evils of the world and suffers, in the course of his encounters, the same rude awakening." Hawthorne's method is allegorical, borrowed from Dante, Sp, and Bunyan.

Bryan, Robert A. Apostasy and the Fourth Bead-Man in the *Faerie Queene*, ELN, 5 (1967), 87-91.   1785

The "faultie" Christians redeemed by the fourth Bead-man (FQ, I, x, 40) are faulty because they renounced their faith to avoid punishment by Moslems.

Bryan, Robert A. Spenser and the Death of Arius, MLN, 76 (1961), 104-6. 1786

Children of Error in FQ, I, i die the death of Arius, which was the death wished upon heretics in official church anathemas: the straining out of the bowels.

Burke, Charles B. Keats and Spenser Again, PQ, 19 (1940), 149-50.   1787

Finds one of H. Buxton Forman's notes on Hyperion (Book II, l. 61) in error. Suggests reference to Hope and her anchor is a reflection of FQ, I, x, 14.

Burke, Joseph. Archbishop Abbot's Tomb at Guildford, JWCI, 12 (1949), 179-88.   1788

Refutes Philip G. Palmer's theory (advanced in The Knight of the Red Cross, or, the Romance of Archbishop Abbot's Tomb, in the Church of the Holy and Undivided Trinity, Giuldford, Surrey, Printed and Published by Frank Lasham, 61 High Street, Guildford, 1911) that the iconographic programme of the tomb was derived from certain passages on the House of Holiness (FQ, I, x), with Archbishop Abbot as the Red Cross Knight. Relates it instead to the iconography of the Sovereign of the Seas, launched in 1637, famous for its carved decorations designed by Thomas Heywood. Four plates of the tomb.

Cartigny, Jean. The Wandering Knight. Reprinted from the copy of the First English Edition in the Henry E. Huntington Library, with an introduction and notes by Dorothy Atkinson Evans. Seattle: University of Washington Press, 1951. 161pp.   1789

Introduction has sections on Cartigny's life, texts, the English edition of 1581, later English editions, William Goodyear and Robert Norman, literary aspects, sources and analogues, and influence. "*The Wandering Knight* is a chivalric moral allegory, remarkably similar in plan and import to one of the most famous of all such allegories, Spenser's story of Una and the Red Cross Knight" (p. xi). "Three English writers have remembered . . . Cartigny. In the ascending order of their indebtedness they are Stephen Batman, John Bunyan, and Edmund Spenser" (pp. xlii-xlvii). For numerous parallels with Bk. I of FQ, see notes (pp. 133-61), passim. See 1770.

Charitina, Sister Mary. Adventures of the Redcrosse Knight. Illus. by Jeanyee Wong. London: Sheed and Ward, 1945. 109pp.   1790

A retelling from FQ, I.

Chew, Samuel C. Spenser's Pageant of the Seven Deadly Sins, in Studies in Art and Literature for Belle da Costa Greene, pp. 37-54. Princeton, N. J.: Princeton University Press, 1954. 502pp.   1791

Builds an imaginative environment and visual context for Sp's scene (FQ, I, iv) by printing and describing a number of English and Continental illustrations of it. See 587, 1777, 1778, 1887.

Cooper, Lane. The "Forest Hermit" in Coleridge and Wordsworth, MLN, 24 (1909), 33-6.   1792

Not in Carpenter or Atkinson. Description of the hermit in The Rime of the Ancient Mariner, Parts VI and VII, shows remarkable similarities to Sp's description of Archimago and his cell, FQ, I, i, 34.

Cornelius, David K. Spenser's Faerie Queene, I, xi, 46, Expl, 29 (1971), Item 51.   1793

The tree of "life," rather than tree of "knowledge," is "the crime of our first fathers fall" (FQ, I, xi, 46). It is the tree of Genesis and also a figure of the Cross of Calvary, consequence of the Fall. [MLA Abstracts, I (1971), 41.]

Crawford, John W. The Fire from Spenser's Dragon: The Faerie Queene, I, xi, SCB, 30 (1970), 176-8.   1794

The fire may represent difficulties a Christian must face in his quest for holiness. For Redcrosse the fire is a purging as well as a hazard.

Doyle, Charles Clay. Smoke and Fire: Spenser's Counter-Proverb, Proverbium, 18 (1972), 683-85.   1795

Una's warning to Redcrosse at Den of Errour, "Oft fire is without smoke," FQ, I, i, 12, 4, inverts proverbial "There is no fire without some smoke." This denial of proverbial wisdom suggests basic issue of FQ, I, i.e., need to transcend mere appearances to attain other-worldly truth. [SpN, Vol. 3, No. 2 (1972), 5.]

Dust, Philip. Another Source for Spenser's Faerie Queene I. v. 26-27, EM, 23 (1972), 15-19.   1796

Sees Duessa's genealogy ("daughter of Deceipt and Shame") as parody of Diotima's genealogy of Eros in Plato's Symposium.

Eidson, Donald Ray. The Sun as Symbol and Type of Christ in English Non-Dramatic Poetry from the Anglo-Saxon Period Through the Victorian Period.

DAI, 30 (1970), 4407A. University of Missouri, 1969. 169 pp.   1797

A survey. Treats Lucifera, FQ, I, iv, 8-17. Christ the sun of righteousness is the implicit standard with which Lucifera is contrasted when she usurps the symbols of Christ: the sun and its rays, the east, gold, dawn, Aurora, light itself.

Emry, Hazel Thornburg. Two Houses of Pride: Spenser's and Hawthorne's, PQ, 33 (1954), 91-4.   1798

Similarities between Sp's description of the House of Pride (FQ, I, iv, 4 and v, 53) and Hawthorne's description of the House of the Seven Gables.

Falls, Mother Mary Robert. Spenser's Kirkrapine and the Elizabethans, SP, 50 (1953), 457-75.   1799

A reinterpretation of FQ, I, iii. Abessa probably personifies the evils of non-residency; Kirkrapine the contemporary usurpation of benefices and spoliation of church goods; Corceca the ignorance of the resident vicars. Shows Sp's concern with church robbers, and emphasizes the need to interpret Kirkrapine in accord with events and abuses contemporary with Sp.

Falls, Mother Mary Robert. Spenser's Legend of Redcrosse in Relation to the Elizabethan Religious Milieu. Washington, D. C.: Catholic University of America Press, 1951. Printed on microcards. Listed in DDAAU, 1950-51, No. 18, as Spenser's Legend of Holinesse and its Religious Milieu: A Study of Relationships.   1800

By investigation of relationship between Bk. I of FQ and its religious milieu, aims to discover nature of Sp's allegorical method as key to structure of the poem. Chapters on theme of Christian warfare in 16th century literature, Red Cross Knight and the

Christian warfare theme, the Apocalypse in 16th century. Sp's use of the Apocalypse in Bk. I, the meaning of Kirkrapine. FQ is the epic of English Protestantism, a repudiation of the Holy See and of historical development of liturgy and dogma, but not of allegiance to the orthodox tradition of Christian asceticism and Christian mysticism. Finds no reason for identifying Sp with any of the numerous shades of religious dissent of his time. See 959, 1177, 1194, 1549, 2243.

Fitzmaurice, James Berry. Iconography and Book I of the *Faerie Queene*. DAI, 32 (1972), 5180A. University of Iowa, 1971. 195 pp.   1801

Studies iconographical backgrounds of the tree and well in canto xi, and relates them to Fradubio's "living well," the diamond box which Arthur gives Redcrosse, Fidelia's cup, and Redcrosse's shield, and by contrast to Orgoglio's tree, the well of canto vii (Slow Fountain), Duessa's cup, and Sansfoy's and Sansjoy's shields. Debates alternative readings (1) of tree and well as Eucharist and (2) of tree as Eucharist and well as baptism, and discusses the divergent implications for structure of the two alternatives. Concludes that Sp might have intended both readings and both structures.

Fleischmann, Wolfgang Bernard. A Note on Spenser and Pope, N&Q, N. S. 1 (1954), 16-7.   1802

Lines 340-41 of Pope's Epistle to Dr. Arbuthnot resemble FQ, I, Proem, 1. Both distinguish between the poet's youthful works and the gravity of the present endeavor.

Fleming, John V. The *Roman de la Rose:* A Study in Allegory and Iconography. Princeton, N. J.: Princeton University Press, 1969. 257 pp.   1802A

In Chapter 3, pp. 78-79, parallels and contrasts Sp's treatment of Duessa with Gillaume's treatment of Oiseuse. Also, pp. 79-80, emphasizes that for medieval commentators the spiritual sense was the moral sense (quid agas), not the allegorical sense (quid credas). Thus, implicitly, Fleming attacks Rosemond Tuve's position in Allegorical Imagery (1152); Tuve holds that medieval allegories characteristically move on both levels simultaneously. [DAI, 28 (1967), 627.]

Fox, Robert C. Milton's *Lycidas*, 192-193, Expl, 9 (1951), No. 54. 1803

Color of shepherd's mantle (blue) symbolizes Hope, after examples in FQ, I, x, 14 and in Phineas Fletcher's Purple Island.

French, Roberts W. Spenser and Sonnet XVIII, MiltonQ, 5 (1971), 51-2.   1804

Influence of FQ, I, viii, 36-37 on Milton's sonnet XVIII, Avenge O Lord thy slaughter'd Saints, "suggested by verbal parallels, similarity of subject, and both poets' organization of one set of rhymes around sound of 'groan,' another set around sound of 'fold.' "

Füger, Wilhelm. Ungenutzte Perspektiven der Spenser-Deutung: Dargelegt an "The Faerie Queene" I. viii. 30-34, DVLG, 45 (1971), 252-301.   1805

New orientation in Sp studies seeks synthesis of materials from rhetoric, symbolism, mythology, numerology, and iconography. Offers analysis of Ignaro episode (FQ, I, viii, 30-34) as possible model for illumination of its vast impenetrability. Discusses, among other topics, synonyms and antonyms of "ignorance," its proverbial uses, connotations of Ignorance as figure in Lord Mayor's Shows, personifications of Ignorance in Morality plays and Tudor interludes, topos of *puer senex*, tower guards and watchmen in Christian mysticism, occult rites, and Franz Kafka, Ignaro's way of walking, staff, and key in relation to Janus cults, emblems, hieroglyphs, topos of *senex doctus*, and outsider figures, and use of Ignaro episode in paraphrases of FQ for children.

Gilbert, Allan H. Dante and His Comedy. New York: New York University Press, 1963. 207 pp.   1806

Compares the ugly woman (Purgatorio 19, 7), who becomes a beautiful siren and then is revealed as foul by a "holy lady," with Duessa, whose ugliness is revealed by Una and Arthur (FQ, I, viii, 46-50).

Glazier, Lyle. The Struggle between Good and Evil in the First Book of *The Faerie Queene*, CE, 11 (1950), 382-7.   1807

Book I parallels the psychomachia, except that the struggle is not for possession of a soul but for one of the qualities of the soul—holiness. Sp aims everywhere to teach by example, using symbols whose conflict will arouse in us the same emotions that are aroused when we meet specific acts of moral heroism, guilty self-indulgence, etc. See 1390.

Gohlke, Madelon Spengnether. Narrative Structure in the *New Arcadia, The Faerie Queene I* and *The Unfortunate Traveller.* DAI, 33 (1972), 723A. Yale University, 1972. 356 pp.   1808

In these works structure emerges as thematic organization reveals itself. Reader's original impression of confusion dissolves as fundamental concerns of the work emerge. Structure "is a function of internal organization, which in turn derives from a peculiar cast of mind, expressing a particular attitude toward the world." This kind of structure corresponds to and stresses the authors' attitude toward the cosmos and toward human experience, which only painfully and reluctantly yield a sense of order. See 1471.

Gohn, Ernest S. A Note on Spenser's Use of Trope, MLN, 64 (1949), 53-5.   1809

Tree passage in FQ, I, i, 8-9 indicates Red Cross's error in permitting the sense of sight to allure him so that he is incapable of rational judgment. This conforms to the Aristotelian dictum that the "first impulse of a passion must come from the senses." The passage is, then, not merely decorative but functional imagery.

Goldstein, Melvin. Spenser and Dante: Two Pictorial Representatives of Evil, JAE, 2 (1968), 121-9.   1810

Compares two versions of fallen, sin-uglied serpents, the first the dragon which Redcrosse fights in FQ, I, xi, and the other the serpent which confronts Cianfa and Agnello in Inferno XXV, 49-78. Concludes that Sp's creation is concrete and Dante's abstract, the result of different verse techniques.

Gordon, R. K. Keats and Milton, MLR, 42 (1947), 434-46.   1811

Milton's description of Satan enthroned, Paradise Lost, II, 1-6, which influenced Neptune's palace in Endymion, derives from Sp's picture of Lucifera, FQ, I, iv, 7-8. Both Keats and Milton condense and concentrate the material they borrow from Sp.

Gray, J. M. Tennyson's Doppelgänger: *Balin and Balan.* Lincoln, England: The Tennyson Society, 1971. 61 pp.   1812

Reads last of Idylls of the King, not published until 1885, in terms of modern idyl, showing deep relationship between Tennyson and source in Malory's Book II. Vivien is one of the doubles that afflict Balin, as wholly unreal as they; if not part of his phantasmagoria, "she can be regarded as a

Victorian Duessa posturing in Tennyson's *Idylls* in much the same way as do her devious predecessors in the woods and plains of Spenserian romance" (pp. 19-20). Balin descends into "skyless woods" (ll. 285-290), symbolic of moral darkness like Sp's woods in FQ, I, i, 7 (p. 37, n. 1). Vivien as a Doppelgänger illustrates polarity often expressed by one of partners being female, sometimes doll-like, e.g., Hoffmann's Olimpia, or a magical device, e.g., Sp's Duessa, Wagner's Kundry (p. 47, n. 1). Analyzes Tennyson's technique "of making from this medieval prose legend, itself far subtler than so far descried, a complex symbolic poetic whole."

Hamilton, A. C. Spenser and Langland, SP, 55 (1958), 533-48.   1813

Sets out to show that FQ, I is significantly related to Piers Plowman. They are parallel as analogues, revealing a common Christian vision in a common language of allegory, and mutually illuminating each other, both in a general way and in specific passages. Detailed comparison of the two poems. "Spenser was Langland's son in the English heroical tradition." See 1417.

Hankins, John E. Spenser and the Revelation of St. John, PMLA, 60 (1945), 364-81.   1814

Exposition of Revelation from Protestant point of view, seeing it as presenting conflict between good and evil, Jerusalem and Babylon. Based on a study of texts of Revelation and Renaissance commentaries available to Sp. Finds evidence of Biblical influences on imagery, action, and allegory which are "pervasive and decisive" throughout Bk. I. See 1421.

Harding, F. J. W. The Legend of St. George and Literature in England. London: Royal Society of St. George, 1965. 47 pp.   1815

Traces legend to two main sources, account attributed to George's servant Pasicrates, and Acta Graece attributed to Andreas of Crete and Gregorius Cyprius. Cult reached England by 7th century. Traces legend in literature from Aelfric to Hardy and Chesterton. Sp's treatment reviewed briefly. [YWES, 46 (1965), 28.]

Harmon, Alice Irene. *Loci Communes* on Death and Suicide in the Literature of the English Renaissance. Doctoral diss., University of Minnesota, 1939. RDUM, p. 97. UMST, 3 (1949), 121-4.   1816

Stoic doctrine on subject of suicide held the "wise man" may end his own life voluntarily, and under certain circumstances ought to do so. Opposed to this view is belief, supported by Christian doctrine, that a man must not take his own life against the will of God. Background of Red Cross Knight's meeting with Despair (FQ, I, ix).

Hasker, Richard. Spenser's "Vaine Delight," MLN, 62 (1947), 334-5.   1817

The episode of the false Una and the False Squire (FQ, I, ii) is an instance of current ideas about the sexual intercourse of spirits.

Hay, Eloise Knapp. Joseph Conrad's Last Epigraph, Conradiana, 2 (1970), 9-15.   1818

Conrad's epigraph to The Rover was taken from Despair's speech in FQ: "Sleepe after toyle, port after stormie seas, / Ease after warre, death after life does greatly please" (I, ix, 40). Discusses relationship of epigraph with Peyrol's death in the novel. The same passage was also chosen to be Conrad's epitaph; this connotes a "fierce kind of poetic justice" with respect to his attempted suicide while in his twenties.

Hefferman, James A. W. Wordsworth on Imagination: The Emblemizing Power, PMLA, 81 (1966), 389-99.   1819

To Wordsworth, goal of imaginative mind is "the meditative discovery of meaning, whereby visible objects become emblems of invisible truths." In Preface of 1815 he cites Sp's freedom from bondage of definite form by aid of his allegorical spirit, enabling him to create persons out of abstractions or to give universality to his human beings, "by means of attributes and emblems that belong to the highest moral truths and the purest sensations." Process of emblemization essentially the same in Wordsworth's early and late poetry. Most extensively revealed in The White Doe of Rylstone (1815), in which heroine Emily is modelled on Una in Sp's FQ, I, a character elevated to spiritual permanence by "attributes and emblems" of highest order. Analysis of The White Doe shows how emblemizing power of Wordsworth's imagination works. See 1892.

Heninger, S. K., Jr. The Orgoglio Episode in The Faerie Queene, ELH, 26 (1959), 171-87; repr. in 756.   1820

Orgoglio is an earthquake "serving to chastise Redcross for his sinfulness, a warning to repentance, the destruction of the world heralding the Last Judgment, physical death preparing for the resurrection, the Antichrist who brings misery to mankind, the embodiment of Catholic tyranny." All this is tied together by Sp's use of the Typhon myth.

Higgins, Dennis Vincent. Intellect-Will in Poetry of the English Renaissance. DAI, 28 (1968), 4130-31A. Claremont University, 1964. 180 pp.   1821

Examines use of intellect-will framework of medieval psychology in Nicholas Breton's Wil of Wit, Davies'

Nosce Teipsum, Stephen Batman's Travayled Pylgrime, and FQ; prose works of Cudworth, Browne, Bacon, Cambridge Platonists, Donne; Phineas Fletcher's The Purple Island, Fulke Greville's A Treatise on Humane Learning, and Paradise Lost. In FQ, reads Redcrosse as will and Una as intellect, leading to joint discovery of their interdependence and their joint dependence on grace. In Paradise Lost, Adam and Eve show characteristics of intellect and will respectively, though this is subordinate to their significance as prototypes of the human sexes.

Hoffman, Daniel. Barbarous Knowledge: Myth in the Poetry of Yeats, Graves, and Muir. New York: Oxford University Press, 1967. 266 pp.   1822

In The Only Jealousy of Emer, Yeats's Ghost of Cuchulain sees a false vision of Aoife, illusion conjured by malicious Bricriu, "a brilliant adaptation of an episode from Spenser" [FQ, I, i, 45-55; ii, 3-6] (p. 109). In Graves's story The Shout appears "a belief of ancient Celtic provenience which Yeats had drawn on for his story, 'Hanrahan's Vision'," i.e., round stones of County Sligo used for cursing, "the stones of malediction," a belief known to Sp—quotes FQ, I, vii, 35, 6-9 (p. 194).

Hughes, Merritt Y. A Boethian Parallel to F. Q. I, ii, 1, 2-4, MLN, 63 (1948), 543.   1823

The "northerne wagoner" of FQ, I, ii, 1, 1 is Boötes, as Todd pointed out. The conception of the pole star and its constellation in the lines following was stated in Boethius' De Consolatione Philosophiae. Quotes Chaucer's translation of the passage.

Kaske, Carol V. The Dragon's Spark and Sting and the Structure of Red Cross's Dragon-fight: "The Faerie Queene," I.

xi-xii, SP, 66 (1969), 609-38; repr. in 756.   1824

Role of Red Cross changes from day to day. The first day he represents unregenerated man vulnerable to lust requiring baptism in the Well of Life. On second day he is the Christian man, assailed again by the dragon's sting (lust), but from which he can recover through sacraments (communion). On third day, representing the Christian who carries Christ within, Red Cross wins the victory.

Kehler, Dorothea. Anne Bradstreet and Spenser, AN&Q, 8 (1970), 135.   1825

Anne Bradstreet's debt to Sp is shown in "an arresting example of inverted but parallel imagery" in FQ, I, iii, 30 and Contemplations, stanza 31.

Kellogg, Robert L., and Oliver L. Steele. On the Punctuation of Two Lines in The Faerie Queene, PMLA, 78 (1963), 147-8.   1826

Rejects metrical and intonational analyses of FQ I, ii, 13, 4-5 by Seymour Chatman, QJS, 43 (1957), 254, and by Wimsatt and Beardsley, PMLA, 74 (1959), 586. These analyses disregard disparity between Elizabethan and modern syntax and ignore similar, more clearly constructed passages within FQ which better direct modern reader. See 1209.

Kermode, Frank. Spenser and the Allegorists, PBA, 48 (1962), 261-79.   1827

Warton Lecture on English Poetry, 7 Nov. 1962. Attacks archetypal criticism of FQ which emphasizes symbol and archetype in and for themselves and ignores determining importance of context. Illustrates his position through the Apocalyptic imagery in FQ, I and the associated Tudor myth

of Arthur returned in the person of Elizabeth as the eschatological emperor of the Last Days. Contrasts Sp's public use of Apocalyptic symbol in FQ with D. H. Lawrence's private use of it in Apocalypse and Lady Chatterley's Lover. See 1478.

Kincaid, James R. Tennyson's Mariners and Spenser's Despair: The Argument of "The Lotus-Eaters," PLL, 5 (1969), 273-81.   1828

Thematic and verbal parallels show Tennyson saw Redcrosse at Cave of Despair (FQ, I, ix) as in same plight as mariners captivated by enchantment. Poet aware of moral issues, leaves tension unresolved between Christian context and allurements of Lotusland. [SpN, Vol. 1, No. 2 (1970), 8.]

Koller, Kathrine. Art, Rhetoric, and Holy Dying in The Faerie Queene with Special Reference to the Despair Canto, SP, 61 (1964), 128-39.   1829

Subtle combination of rhetoric and art employed in Despair Canto ix in Bk. I of FQ to illustrate attitude, common in 16th century and having its roots in classical paganism, toward spiritual death.

Landrum, Grace W. St. George Redivivus, PQ, 29 (1950), 381-8.   1830

St. George, martyred ca. 303, though originally revered for holiness and only in medieval times endowed with the dragon exploit, was by Sp's day chiefly known as the dragon-killer. Sp's revival of the saint as a spiritual victor, who overcomes the sins of inobedience to the call of truth and of despair of the mercy of God, was an independent and difficult feat.

Lievsay, John L. Spenser in Low Company, SAB, 19 (1944), 186-9.   1831

Richard Venner's The Right Way to

Heaven (1601, 2nd ed., 1602) is a poor imitation of Sp recalling Una, her lamb, and the Red Cross Knight.

MacIntyre, Jean. *The Faerie Queene*, Book I: Toward Making It More Teachable, CE, 31 (1970), 473-82. 1832

Notes the difficulties of teaching FQ, I to college students and suggests treatment of large patterns instead of discrete episodes. Redcrosse's adventures fall into four groups: error, sin, regeneration, and victory.

McLane, Paul E. Was Spenser in Ireland in Early November, 1579? N&Q, N. S. 6 (1959), 99-101. 1833

Sp may have derived Red Cross's distinguishing mark from Sir William Pelham's order of Nov. 6, 1579, that the Queen's horsemen should wear a red cross on heart and back. See 1863.

Maier, John Raymond. Religious Melancholy and the Imagination in Book One of *The Faerie Queene*, DAI, 31 (1970), 2391A-2A. Duquesne University, 1970. 402 pp. 1834

Examines classical and medieval backgrounds of relationships among melancholy, acedia, imagination, and contemplation; Renaissance treatments of religious melancholy, especially Timothy Bright's Treatise of Melancholie (1586); Renaissance transformations of imagination, culminating in works of Giordano Bruno. In FQ, examines theme of true and false imagination; imagination first leads to disaster, but later to heavenly contemplation. Relates Sp's treatment of melancholy to problems of fate, justice, and election, of importance in Sp's understanding of holiness. Redcross's basic problem is religious melancholy. See 1781, 1783, 1865.

Major, John M. *Paradise Regained* and Spenser's Legend of Holiness, RenQ, 20 (1967), 465-70. 1835

Most critics agree that Milton had Bk. II of FQ in mind when he wrote Paradise Regained; evidence that Bk. I was also influential. In fall and death of Sp's dragon and fall of Milton's Satan (IV), definite rhetorical similarities. Red Cross is an image of Christ in that his quest is to conquer the dragon (sin). Like Christ, Red Cross is an untried redeemer attempting to restore a lost kingdom; both are tempted but each finally conquers on the third day.

Major, John W., Jr. The Education of a Young Knight, UKCR, 29 (1963), 269-74. 1836

Exposition of the adventures of Redcrosse through the Despair episode (ix), and a summary comment on the remainder of FQ, I.

Means, James A. A Spenserian Echo in Collins, N&Q, 15 (1968), 463. 1837

In Collins' Ode to Evening the phrase "short, shrill Shriek" (1, 1, 10) resembles FQ, I, v, 33, 5.

Mounts, Charles E. Spenser's Seven Bead-Men and the Corporal Works of Mercy, PMLA, 54 (1939), 974-80. 1838

The closest resemblance to Sp's treatment of the Seven Works of Mercy (FQ, I, x) is in Lactantius, possibly as reflected in the Decades of Henry Bullinger. The listing of the Seven Works of Mercy most familiar in Sp's time was Aquinas's.

Neill, Kerby. The Degradation of the Red Cross Knight, ELH, 19 (1952), 173-90. 1839

The structure of FQ, I arises from, or takes shape with, Red Cross's separation from Una and reliance on Duessa. Red Cross is not guiltless in making this shift. He is separated from Truth and allied with Falsehood because of "the illusion of the senses; that is, passion, working through the senses, overthrows reason and fills his mind with illusion." Neither contemporary interpretations of similar incidents in Ariosto's Orlando Furioso nor current beliefs concerning witchcraft would excuse the Knight's moral weakness. The moral lesson taught by his deception by Archimago and Duessa is thoroughly integrated with both plot and character.

Oetgen, Jerome. Spenser's Treatment of Monasticism in Book I of *The Faerie Queene*, ABR, 22 (1971), 109-20. 1840

Upholds Whitaker's view (1194) that Spenser, as a supporter of Anglican church, sometimes deviated in direction of Catholicism rather than Calvinism. With respect to monasticism, Sp adheres to "the ideal of holiness which traditionally had been identified with the monastic life." Archimago and Corceca are demeaned in FQ for their corruption of monastic principles.

Orange, Linwood E. Sensual Beauty in Book I of *The Faerie Queene*, JEGP, 61 (1962), 555-61. 1841

Separation of Red Cross from Una (Platonic beauty) and Fradubio incident (FQ, I, ii) show incompatibility of sensual infatuation with union of Knight of Holiness and Platonic beauty.

Orange, Linwood E. Spenser's Old Dragon, MLN, 74 (1959), 679-81. 1842

The dragon in FQ, I, xi represents Death rather than Sin or Satan.

Padelford, F. M. Anthony Copley's *A Fig for Fortune*: A Roman Catholic Legend of Holiness, MLQ, 3 (1942), 525-33. 1843

Parallels showing that A Fig for

Fortune (1596) was one of the earliest imitations of FQ. Copley, through allegory, tried to demonstrate that a good Catholic could be a loyal Englishman and subject of the Queen.

Padelford, F. M. The Political and Ecclesiastical Allegory of the First Book of the Faerie Queene. New York: AMS Press, 1970. 62 pp. 1844

Repr. of 1911 ed. See Carpenter, p. 160.

Patrick, John M. Milton, Phineas Fletcher, Spenser, and Ovid—Sin at Hell's Gate, N&Q, N. S. 3 (1956), 384-6. 1845

On the sources of Milton's figure of Sin in Paradise Lost, Book II. One of them is Sp's Error (FQ, I, i).

Pecheux, Mother M. Christopher. Spenser's Red Cross and Milton's Adam, ELN, 6 (1969), 246-51. 1846

Resemblances between Adam's vision of the future, Paradise Lost, XI-XII, and Redcrosse's vision of the heavenly Jerusalem, FQ, I, x. Discusses origins of names "George" and "Adam." Each learns that true heroism includes both contemplation and action.

Pyle, Fitzroy. Six Notes on "The Rape of the Lock," N&Q, 4 (1957), 252-4. 1847

Note 4, p. 253, relates Rape of the Lock, II, 132 (Ariel's threat against Sylphs who do not effectively guard Belinda) to FQ, I, viii, 41 (description of Redcrosse shrivelled in Orgoglio's dungeon).

Rashbrook, R. F. Keats' "La Belle Dame sans Merci," N&Q, 194 (1949), 210. 1848

A parallel to FQ, I, ix, 14.

Ribner, Irving. Una's Lion: A Folklore Analogue, N&Q, 196 (1951), 114-5. 1849

THE FAERIE QUEENE: BOOK I

Defense of a maiden and the faith by a lion appears in Tale No. 775 of the Alphabetum Narrationum of Estienne de Besançon.

Rockwood, Robert John Remington. Alchemical Forms of Thought in Book I of Spenser's *Faerie Queene*. DAI, 34 (1973), 3355A. University of Florida, 1972. 340pp.   1850

FQ, I is organized on the Hermetic mysteries, especially esoteric alchemy. Examines esoteric tradition within milieu of Elizabethan culture and presents alchemical interpretation, and psychological analysis, of the book. Applies alchemical theory of separation and synthesis of opposites to Redcrosse (Sol) and Una (Luna), to Redcrosse (Sol) and Duessa (Luna), and Arthur, the last of whom represents the synthesis leading to the final consolidation in House of Holiness and the betrothal to Una. Views FQ as alchemical psycho-therapeutic discipline directed toward transforming a "clownish younge man" into a perfected Saint George. [SpN, Vol. 5, No. 2 (1974), 16.]

Rosinger, Lawrence. Spenser's Una and Queen Elizabeth, ELN, 6 (1968), 12-7.   1851

Sp's decision to use the name "Una" for heroine of Bk. I of FQ was partly influenced by correlation it had with Elizabeth's motto, "Semper Eadem," "Be Always One."

Ross, Morton L. Hawthorne's Bosom Serpent and Mather's *Magnalia*, ESQ, 47, (1967), 13.   1852

Although Hawthorne was rereading FQ at about the time he wrote Egotism: or the Bosom Serpent (1842), he had used the bosom serpent as early as 1832 in Roger Malvin's Burial. Thus Mather's Magnalia may be as legitimate a source for the serpent as FQ, I. See 1857.

Rusche, Harry. Pride, Humility, and Grace in Book I of *The Faerie Queene*, SEL, 7 (1967), 29-39.   1853

Many critics believe Despair is Redcrosse's most dangerous foe. Attempts "to demonstrate that pride, both physical and spiritual, retains for Spenser its traditional primacy as the most deadly sin in Christian life and that as such he assigns to it a central role throughout Book I." Despair is, like other sins, an outcome of central sin of pride. Pride is eradicated, along with other sins, by humility and grace.

Rush, Richard Russell. Studies in the Renaissance Concepts of Pride: Spenser and Marlowe. DAI, 31 (1971), 6630A. University of California, Los Angeles, 1970. 210 pp.   1854

Classical ideal of human perfection included awareness of one's own worth. Christian ideal of self-abnegation in Augustine's definitive condemnation of pride. These ideals clashed in Tudor England, where educated writers were familiar with both humanistic and Christian concepts. Sp emphasized Christian background in FQ, I, where pride is unquestionably condemned; but Sp was more concerned with relation between personal pride and theoretical concept of pride. Marlowe in Tamburlaine, Parts I and II, portrays hero who goes beyond mean and violates both classical and Christian value systems.

Sachs, Arieh. The Religious Despair of Doctor Faustus, JEGP, 63 (1964), 625-47.   1855

Mentions Devil in the guise of "the Man of Dispaire," successfully tempting one knight to commit suicide, nearly working the trick on another, and unable to kill himself, much as he would like to (FQ, I, ix). Compares Faustus' argument ("we must sin"- and-therefore "che sera sera") in I, i,

64-75 to Man of Dispaire's argument to trap Red Cross Knight.

Sehrt, Ernst Th. Der Wald des Irrtums: zur Allegorischen Funktion von Spensers *Faerie Queene* I, 7-9, Anglia, 86 (1968), 463-91.   1856

Spenser's Wandering Wood, drawn from many sources, is a complex symbol of unhealthiness.

Shroeder, John W. Hawthorne's "Egotism; or, The Bosom Serpent" and Its Source, AL, 31 (1959), 150-62.   1857

The story is heavily indebted to FQ, I in plot, characterization, and theme. See 1852.

Shroeder, John W. Hawthorne's "The Man of Adamant": A Spenserian Source-Study, PQ, 41 (1962), 744-56.   1858

Strong influence of Sp upon Hawthorne apparent in "The Man of Adamant," which derives its characters and plot almost directly from the Wandering Wood and Cave of Error episode of FQ, I, i.

Shroeder, John W. Spenser's Erotic Drama: The Orgoglio Episode, ELH, 29 (1962), 140-59.   1859

The Orgoglio episode (FQ, I, vii) may be understood on three levels: narrative, symbolic, and allegorical. Suggests symbolic reading which blends narrative and allegory organically. Symbolic elements, chiefly giant and fountain, represent "organic portions of the drama."

Sirluck, Ernest. A Note on the Rhetoric of Spenser's "Despair," MP, 47 (1949), 8-11.   1860

Despair's specious argument, which persuades Red Cross of the necessity of suicide, is based on a careful omission of the Covenant of Grace. Una saves the knight by recalling this Covenant to his mind.

Smith, Charles W. Structural and Thematic Unity in Gascoigne's *The Adventures of Master F. J.*, PLL, 2 (1966), 99-108.   1861

Theme of Gascoigne's work is "the destruction of moral perception by untempered passion." This lack in F. J. is similar to problem facing Red Cross Knight in FQ, I.

Smith, Roland M. A Further Note on Una and Duessa, PMLA, 61 (1946), 592-6.   1862

An addition to his Una and Duessa, ibid., 50 (1935), 917-9 (listed in Atkinson, p. 122). Gives examples of the Irish use of the names.

Smith, Roland M. Origines Arthurianae: The Two Crosses of Red Cross Knight, JEGP, 54 (1955), 670-83. Also in Studies by Members of the English Department, University of Illinois, in Memory of John Jay Parry, pp. 189-202. Urbana, Ill.: University of Illinois Press, 1956.   1863

Sp's source was possibly Sir William Pelham's Proclamation from Limerick, Nov. 6, 1579, which required all members of Her Majesty's forces to wear crosses on both breast and back, for identification. See 1833. Believes Arthur's magical, Ariosto-inspired shield was an afterthought, invented to correspond to Red Cross's shield, which according to legend was rightfully Arthur's. Supports identification of Sir Sergis (FQ, V, xi) with Pelham by reference to documents attesting to Pelham's long service to Elizabeth.

Snyder, Susan. The Left Hand of God: Despair in Medieval and Renaissance Tradition, SRen, 12 (1965), 18-59.   1864

At key points quotes FQ, I, ix. Studies medieval background of encounter between Despair and Redcrosse: accusations of sinfulness; premise that fallen man is unable to fulfill God's law—"devil's syllogism" used by Luther and Marlowe's Mephistophilis; Redcrosse's over-seriousness, "concept of despair as a pathological upset of emotional balance"; Despair's double appeal to Redcrosse's tormented conscience and weariness (cf. FQ, I, vii); in FQ and Pilgrim's Progress Despair's aim to make hero commit suicide; death—physical and spiritual—behind traditional imagery of despair, "helpless imprisonment and danger, of barrenness, cold winter, sleep, and sickness."

Snyder, Susan Brooke. The Paradox of Despair: Studies of the Despair Theme in Medieval and Renaissance Literature. DA, 25 (1964), 1201A. Columbia University, 1963. 268 pp. 1865

Notes recurrent ideas, images, and associations in medieval and 16th-century religious writings, and uses these to illuminate Greban's Mystère de la passion, Wolfram's Parzival, Marlowe's Dr. Faustus, and FQ. Despair in medieval theology is both a soul-destroying sin and the peculiar temptation of God's elect. Emphasis on balance between fear and hope contrasts with "a contrary conviction that . . . the joy of salvation comes only after a dark period of self-accusation and apparent abandonment by God." Also, "desperatio" is used to describe "both an active sense of damnation and a state of spiritual insensibility," despair related to both superbia and acedia. In FQ, I, Red Cross's encounter with Sans Joy emphasizes the self-destroying tendency; the slow fountain emphasizes dependence on grace; the Orgoglio captivity "shows individual conversion"; and the spiritual crisis is finally placed in the whole pattern of Christian life. See 1781, 1783, 1834.

South, Malcolm H. A Note on Spenser and Sir Thomas Browne, MLR, 62 (1967), 14-6. 1866

Cites precedents for Gluttony's long neck (FQ, I, iv, 21). Sp possibly derived the image from Alciati. Browne's remarks in Vulgar Errors "illuminate the conceit." Popular errors slow in dying, "but Vulgar Errors reveals the diminishing role of many conceits and emblems which had once possessed great appeal." Sp's conceit is false, as Browne shows, "but it does serve to emphasize the dehumanizing effect of gluttony."

Spiegler, Marlene. Spenser's Pictorial Rhetoric: Imagines Agentes in The Faerie Queene, Book I. DAI, 31 (1971), 3566A. University of California, Los Angeles, 1970. 242 pp. 1867

Classical art of memory and its Elizabethan descendants are employed for structural and pictorial principles. Sp knew the art of memory and used it to construct Bk. I, wherein the ten dwellings visited by Redcrosse and Una are memory-places corresponding to the ten Articles of salvation, IX-XVIII of the Thirty-nine Articles. Details of the Article are enacted in each place by imagines agentes who are characters in the fiction. House of Holiness corresponds to Article XVI, "Of sinne after Baptisme." For each place, finds three episodes in the fiction.

Steadman, John M. Errour and Herpetology, N&Q, N. S. 4 (1957), 333-4. 1868

Error's vomiting of frogs and toads (FQ, I, i, 20) may have been based on first-hand observation of the behavior of snakes.

Steadman, John M. Felicity and End in Renaissance Epic and Ethics, JHI, 23 (1962), 117-32. 1869

For many Renaissance theorists, final cause of poetry was instruction as well as pleasure. Illustrates idea of beatitude or the "chief good" in work of Tasso, Gratiani, Sp, and Milton. In FQ, I, x, Redcrosse is granted vision of eternal beatitude at House of Holiness. This is orientation toward felicity through allegory. In both of Milton's epics "the idea of beatitude is the cornerstone of his argument and fable."

Steadman, John M. Sin, Echidna and the Viper's Brood, MLR, 56 (1961), 62-6.
1870

"Error" is derived from contemporary notions about vipers which are supported by classical authors, e.g., Hesiod's Echidna (serpent woman). Viper as used by Sp (FQ, I, i) is associated with sin and Satan and depicted as being destroyed by its progeny.

Steadman, John M. Spenser and Martianus Capella, MLR, 53 (1958), 545-6.
1871

Finds in Martianus Capella's De Nuptiis Philologiae et Mercurii a parallel to Error's vomiting of books and papers (FQ, I, i, 20).

Steadman, John M. Spenser's *Errour* and the Renaissance Allegorical Tradition, NM, 62 (1961), 22-38.   1872

Errour (FQ, I, i) is derived from traditional Renaissance association of serpentine hybrid with rhetorical subtlety, also from mythological "forest-labyrinth."

Steadman, John M. Una and the Clergy; the Ass Symbol in *The Faerie Queene*, JWCI, 21 (1958), 134-7.   1873

The ass accompanying Una (I, i, 4) symbolizes the ministry, the proper vehicle for orthodox doctrine. The ignorant country people who attempt to worship the ass (I, vi, 19) symbolize the superstitious reverence which illiterate Christians gave their

pastors. Quotes from biblical, patristic, Neo-Latin, and vernacular sources of the Renaissance conception of the ass as a symbol of the clergy.

Strode, Lena Virginia. A Study of Descriptive Techniques in Narrative Poetry from Chaucer to Milton. DA, 23 (1962), 226. University of Denver, 1961. 293 pp.   1874

Description in narrative poetry results from author's use of language, his view of reality, and "fabric of society." Examines 15,000 lines from five of Chaucer's Canterbury Tales, Bk. I of Sp's FQ, Marlowe's Hero and Leander, Shakespeare's Venus and Adonis, and Bks. I-IV of Milton's Paradise Lost. Statistical data given in tables end of each chapter. Discusses each author's descriptive art and method. Concludes that "Renaissance technique" is different from Chaucer's "medieval technique."

Szövérffy, Joseph. The Master of Wolves and Dragon-Killer (Some Aspects of the Popular St. George Traditions), SFQ, 19 (1955), 211-29.   1875

St. George the dragon-killer in European folk tradition (in a Roumanian folktale he is thrown in a well), and his influence on calendar customs and popular art. In England and Ireland several popular stories, ballads, and dramatized versions of the dragon-killer legend seem to originate from Richard Johnson's Seven Champions of Christendom (pp. 217-27).

Torczon, Vernon James. The Pilgrimage of the Red Cross Knight. DA, 21 (1961), 1942-3. University of Nebraska, 1960.   1876

Journey of Red Cross Knight from court of Gloriana to kingdom of Una's parents (FQ, I) is an allegory of Christian's pilgrimage to salvation. Explains events and details in light of iconography, iconology, commentaries on allegory and scripture. Finds Bk. I epic in nature; it presents "a highly organized theological pattern of sin and regeneration."

Torczon, Vernon James. Spenser's Orgoglio and Despaire, TSLL, 3 (1961), 123-8.   1877

Orgoglio and Despair in FQ, I, allegorical figures for major sins of presumption and despair, represent stages in process of spiritual conversion and regeneration; spiritual death is a necessary precurrent stage of spiritual re-birth. The figures fulfill requirements of continued allegory, since they are distinctly associated with a consistent level of meaning beyond literal ones.

Vickers, Brian. Classical Rhetoric in English Poetry. New York: St. Martin's Press, 1970. 180 pp.   1878

Last chapter is rhetorical analysis of a Sidney sonnet, Despair's speeches to Red Cross Knight (FQ, I, ix, 38-49), Shakespeare's Sonnet 129, Herbert's A Wreath.

Viswanathan, S. Spenser's "The Faerie Queene," Book I, i.v.7, Expl, 27 (1969), Item 44.   1879

"Uproar," which here means "revolt" or "military uprising" is an allusion to Satan's rebellion and therefore connects the dragon with the Devil.

Waters, D. Douglas. Duessa and Orgoglio: Red Crosse's Spiritual Fornication, RenQ, 20 (1967), 211-20.   1880

On assumption that Duessa is a symbol of Roman mass, traces Redcrosse's spiritual fornication. When he rests after fleeing from House of Pride, tree (which may represent whoring and idolatry) and fountain (symbolizing spiritual sloth or lust) combine with Duessa's wiles to bring about his spiritual fornication. That

Redcrosse escapes from Lucifera (Pride) only to be seduced by Duessa (spiritual fornication) makes him vulnerable to Orgoglio (Pride). See 1881, 1882, 1883.

Waters, D. Douglas. Duessa as Theological Satire. Columbia: University of Missouri Press, 1970. 169 pp.   1881

Duessa is conceived in terms of the Mistress-Missa tradition, which personified Roman mass as whore and witch. Goes back and forth between Protestant writers on mass such as Cranmer, Ridley, Jewel, Bullinger, and Fulke, and episodes in FQ in which Duessa has symbolic significance. Duessa as a satire on the mass helps to unify narrative of Bk. I, which is not episodic but organically structured. Bibliography, pp. 143-58. See 954, 1880, 1882, 1883.

Waters, D. Douglas. Errour's Den and Archimago's Hermitage: Symbolic Lust and Symbolic Witchcraft, ELH, 33 (1966), 279-98; repr. in 644.   1882

Theological allegory of FQ, I is Protestant vs. Roman Catholic. Symbolic lust reflects false religious doctrine; witchcraft is "spiritual seduction" of Catholic Church. See 1880, 1881, 1883.

Waters, D. Douglas. "Mistress Missa," Duessa, and the Anagogical Allegory of The Faerie Queene, Book I, PLL, 4 (1968), 258-75.   1883

Duessa has symbolic import in Sp's anagogical allegory. As Red Cross becomes debased Duessa may be linked, in certain episodes, with the Roman mass, following the Mistress-Missa tradition, which personified the mass as a whore. Separated from the Truth (Una) Red Cross is attracted to the beauty of the whore Duessa (the Mass). She leads Red Cross to spiritual degeneration until he is rescued by Arthur, who delivers him from false worship and restores him to Truth (Una). See 1880, 1881, 1882.

Waters, D. Douglas. Prince Arthur as Christian Magnanimity in Book One of *The Faerie Queene*, SEL, 9 (1969), 53-62.   1884

In Bk. I Arthur is a specifically Christian form of magnanimity, not inconsistent with humility.

Waters, D. Douglas. Spenser's "Well of Life" and "Tree of Life" Once More, MP, 67 (1969), 67-8.   1885

These items in FQ, I, xi parallel Fidelia's cup and book in the preceding canto. Each pair represents, respectively, communion and the reading of God's word. They demonstrate Sp's Protestant emphasis on the need to make diligent use of these particular means of grace. [SpN, Vol. 1, No. 2 (1970), 7.]

Weidhorn, Manfred. Dreams in Seventeenth Century English Literature. The Hague: Mouton, 1970. 167 pp.   1886

See Chap. 3, section E, pp. 60-9. Redcrosse's false dream akin to those in Homer, Virgil, and Tasso. Sp adapts his use of the dream to suit his allegory.

Wenzel, Siegfried. The Seven Deadly Sins: Some Problems of Research, Speculum, 43 (1968), 1-22.   1887

Proposes areas in which Bloomfield's study of the Sins (1777) can be extended: (1) origins, by study of Evagrius Ponticus, earliest writer to speak of a series of vices; (2) scholastic analysis of the vices, which followed three models, concatenational, psychological, and cosmological, all actually attempts to explain the vices psychologically; (3) intellectual and theoretical significance of the vices for theology and moral philosophy in medieval times; (4) pictorial representation: a catalogue of extant representations and their analyses is needed; (5) use of the vices as structural tool: to what extent are allegorical pilgrimages poetical treatments of catechetical handbooks, and to what extent do the vices structure English moralities? (6) other literary uses of the vices besides structure, e.g., characterization; (7) fate of the vices after the Middle Ages. FQ cited as a poem whose study would profit from investigation in area (2). See 587, 1206, 1791.

Whitaker, Virgil K. The Theological Structure of the *Faerie Queene*, Book I, ELH, 19 (1952), 151-64; repr. in 756.   1888

Seeks to show that the moral allegory of Book I is theological in structure and "is based upon the arrangement of points customary in Renaissance confessionals." Treats original sin, justification, the church, and the sacraments. Theological structure of the book accounts for repetitions; and the fact that this structure has been overlooked for so long indicates the poet's skill in weaving the theology into the narrative.

Williams, J. M. A Possible Source for Spenser's Labryde, MLN, 76 (1961), 481-4.   1889

Labryde, Satyrane's father (FQ, I, vi, 20), could be derived from Labraid, a Gaelic god whose name means "swift hand on the sword," a more likely source than the Greek root meaning "greedy."

Wolkenfeld, Suzanne. The Christian Hero in Arthurian Romance. DAI, 31 (1970), 1821A. Columbia University, 1970. 116 pp.   1890

Purpose twofold: "to examine the conception of the Christian hero in a series of Arthurian romances from the medieval through the Renaissance periods and to consider the various solutions that the individual writers found to the problem of adapting the romance narrative to their spiritual themes." Chap. IV deals with FQ, especially Bk. I. It is "an allegorical adaptation of Arthurian romance in which the tendency of the Christian romances to treat chivalric fiction as the symbolic vehicle of a theme reaches its full fruition. Spenser's allegorical technique is characterized by a distinctive range, which derives from his use of romance materials to create a story that is both morally and spiritually allegorical."

Woodruff, Bertram L. Keats's Wailful Choir of Small Gnats, MLN, 68 (1953), 217-20.   1891

Cites FQ, I, i, 16 as the first of a series of probable or possible sources for To Autumn, ll. 27-29.

Wordsworth, William. The White Doe of Rylstone. Ed. Alice Pattee Comparetti. CSE, 30. Ithaca, N. Y.: Cornell University Press, 1940. 311pp.   1892

"The poet of *The White Doe* was influenced by *The Faerie Queene* more than by any other poem. . . . In temper much of the First Book of *The Faerie Queene* is akin to *The White Doe*." Comparison of "Una, . . . Spenser's type of the true Church" and "Wordsworth's concept of the holy woman, Emily." Wordsworth's knowledge of Sp's general allegory of the events of Elizabeth's reign (pp. 108-13). See also Index. See 1819.

THE FAERIE QUEENE: BOOK II

Anderson, Judith H. The Knight and the Palmer in *The Faerie Queene*, Book II, MLQ, 31 (1970), 160-78.   1893

Examines symbolic import of Guyon's two separations from the Palmer in cantos i and vi, on premise that both the Palmer and Guyon's horse are psychomachic fragments of the protagonist: the Palmer is associated with his reason, his horse with his heroic passions.

Baxter, Charles. Spider Lady: Images of Domination in Book II of *The Faerie Queene*, Paunch, No. 35 (1972), 67-99.   1894

Most formidable perils to temperance in FQ, II, are "the disorienting and formless image of woman (Phaedria and Acrasia), drawing their victims in, spider-like, by seduction." Explicates circle (rational soul), triangle (vegetative soul), and quadrate (trunk of body) in II, ix, 22, from Batman's translation of Bartholomew Anglicus. Uses circle (masculine, perfect) and triangle (feminine, imperfect) to interpret II, iii: Belphoebe partial androgyne and Braggadocchio feminized buffoon in a comedy of temperance. Applies same geometric figures to Alma and Phantastes (ix), and Maleger (xi). All ramifications of imperfect feminine triangle come together within Acrasia's undefended gate (xii, 43), "a sexual metaphor [that] corresponds to Acrasia's genital freedom." Theme of seductive women puts blame on Acrasia "not just for falsely seducing Verdant or

the others, but especially for dominating them, for separating them from their armor" (including swords).

Berger, Harry, Jr. The Allegorical Temper: Vision and Reality in Book II of Spenser's *Faerie Queene*. New Haven: Yale University Press, 1957; repr. Hamden, Conn.: Archon, 1967. 248 pp.   1895

Sp writes from a double perspective, i.e., dramatically, presenting Guyon's experiences and view, while occupying an entirely separate position of his own. Guyon embodies, and is limited by, Aristotelian temperance; this insufficient *pietas* is replaced, after the hero's faint outside Mammon's cave, by Christian temperance, which Guyon at this point does not understand. Confrontation of classical and Christian temperance, of Guyon's limited view and Sp's broader one. When the two attitudes are brought together in last canto, Guyon belatedly "awakens to the consequences of Original Sin within himself." The central chapters, 3-9, develop the theory that FQ operates allegorically not only by literal plus figurative meanings but also by confronting, on the literal level, the ideal and the imperfect striving humanity which seeks the ideal: Faerie and Briton, Faerieland and England, Gloriana and Arthur. [Diss., Yale University, 1955.]

Block, Edward A. *King Lear:* A Study in Balanced and Shifting Sympathies, SQ, 10 (1959), 499-512.   1896

313

Studies conflicts in early part of play between Lear and Cordelia; Lear, Goneril, and Regan; Edmund, Gloucester, and Edgar. Shows how these conflicts in Shakespeare's sources differ from his fair and balanced presentation. Among sources considered is Lear story in FQ, II, x, 27-32.

Bowers, Fredson. The Faerie Queene, Book II: Mordant, Ruddymane, and the Nymph's Well, in English Studies in Honor of James Southall Wilson, pp. 243-51. UVS, 4. Charlottesville, Va.: University of Virginia Press, 1951. 298pp.   1897

The Mordant episode may be taken as an exemplum to introduce the House of Medina, or reason (FQ, II, i-ii). Man is to be saved not by direct contact with Godhead but by use of reason, assisted by grace. The cup of Acrasia from which Mordant drinks may signify the Roman Communion; Mordant may typify Roman Catholics who "still cling to belief in Roman formulas of salvation though cured of traitorous allegiance to Mary Stuart" (p. 250).

Briggs, H. E. Keats' "Gather the Rose," MLN, 58 (1943), 620-2.   1898

Letter to John Hamilton Reynolds, a confirmed Spenserian, shows direct influence of FQ, II, xii, 75.

Brooke, N. S. C. S. Lewis and Spenser: Nature, Art, and the Bower of Bliss, CamJ, 2 (1949), 420-34. Repr. in 756.   1899

Disagrees with Lewis (see 1513) in interpreting both the Bower (FQ, II, xii) and Sp's attitude toward nature and art. Art has the duty of perfecting things left imperfect by nature. In the Garden of Adonis (FQ, III, vi) this process is properly carried out and neither is evil. In the Bower of Bliss art fails its task and allows the hierarchy of human activities to get

out of balance: the brain has voluntarily abandoned its duty of controlling the passions.

Browning, I. Critical Forum: Spenser and Iconography, EIC, 11 (1961), 480-1.   1900

The bird described in the line "ashamed how rude Pan did her dight" (FQ, II, ix, 40) cannot be a turtle-dove, for a turtle-dove would not have a "rude" appearance. Whether or not it is an owl, as Mr. Fowler (1918) suggests, is insignificant.

Bruser, Fredelle. Comus and the Rose Song, SP, 44 (1947), 625-44.   1901

The carpe diem argument of Milton's Comus traced as a theme which "receives decisive formulation in the odes of Horace." Ausonius contributed the comparison, which left its mark on all subsequent treatments, between the brevity of life and the short flowering of the rose. Tasso's bird song became part of the English tradition; "Fairfax renders the original with Spenser in mind." Consummate expression of rose song in FQ, II, xii, 74-75. Guyon resists its temptation and destroys Acrasia's Bower of Bliss. "Here we are left with only two alternatives—sensual indulgence, or the 'rigour pittiless' of Guyon." Both Giles and Phineas Fletcher took up Sp's rose song; discusses their versions. Carries the theme further into the 17th century.

Buck, Katherine M. The Elfin Chronicle, TLS, June 19, 1948, p. 345.   1902

New sources for the ideal country, rulers, and wonders which Sp describes in FQ, II, x, 70-76 (see 1911, 1943, 1944, 1974, 1996).

Bullough, Geoffrey. Narrative and Dramatic Sources of Shakespeare. 7 vols. London: Routledge and Kegan Paul, 1957-1973.   1903

Vol. II, The Comedies, 1597-1603. Among probable sources of Much Ado About Nothing: Sp's story of Claribell and Phedon in FQ, II, iv, 16-38, notable for "the tragic climax, and the succinct allegorical treatment" (pp. 63-4, 73, 106-12). Vol. VII, Major Tragedies. Among verse accounts of King Lear that Shakespeare knew was Sp's in FQ, II, x, 27-33: Cordelia's name and manner in which she was murdered (pp. 276, 332-4).

Camden, Carroll. The Architecture of Spenser's "House of Alma," MLN, 58 (1934), 262-5.   **1904**

On the interpretation of the structure of the House of Alma (FQ, II, ix, especially 23) given by William Austin in Haec Homo (1637).

Carscallen, James. The Goodly Frame of Temperance: The Metaphor of Cosmos in *The Faerie Queene*, Book II, UTQ, 37 (1968), 136-55; repr. in 756.   **1905**

Parallels Elizabethan notion of temperance of universe with man's achievement of temperance through his reason's government of his passions. Bk. II frames evolution of Guyon's progress towards temperance. His soul is purged as he progresses through successful encounters with elements represented by Furor (fire), Cymochles (water), Mammon (earth), and Phaedria (air). Final triumph in Bower of Bliss where the "combination of the uncombinable" presents a spurious earthly paradise which chastened knight readily recognizes.

Cullen, Patrick. Guyon *Microchristus:* The Cave of Mammon Reexamined, ELH, 37 (1970), 153-74.   **1906**

Temptations of Guyon in Cave of Mammon (FQ, II, vii) not lust, pride, and curiosity (see 1945), but gluttony-lust, vainglory, avarice. Outside cave Mammon and Guyon debate these vices (9, 11, 16-17); they correspond to action inside cave, Mammon's offer of riches (31), offer of Philotime (48), and Garden of Proserpina (51-62). Guyon's subsequent faint not caused by individual fault, for in resisting temptation he has performed *imitatio Christi*; it shows fallen man consumes self in resisting vice and needs grace. Relates earlier and later episodes in Bk. II to his interpretation of Cave of Mammon. [SpN, Vol. 1, No. 3 (1970), 9.]

Cummings, R. M. An Iconographical Puzzle: Spenser's Cupid at "Faerie Queene" II, viii, JWCI, 33 (1970), 317-21.   **1907**

In comparing the angel at the head of the sleeping Guyon with Cupid, Sp is employing an emblem of spiritualized love with Neoplatonic associations. Mercury might seem more obvious choice. But association of Mercury with Cupid has precedent in all-embracing power of love as conceived by Neoplatonists.

Cummings, R. M. A Note on the Arithmological Stanza: *The Faerie Queene*, II.ix.22, JWCI, 30 (1967), 410-4.   **1908**

Discusses physical and allegorical aspects of the "frame" of the House of Alma (II, ix, 22) by correlating it with a similar structure described by Francesco Colonna. Sp is not concerned with the mathematical integrity of the description but rather "employs two different forms of the mean to harmonize two sets of incompatibles." See 1920, 1936, 1962.

Cutts, John P. Spenser's Mermaids, ELN, 5 (1968), 250-6.   **1909**

In FQ, II, xii, 31, Sp describes a singing contest between the mermaids and the "Heliconian maids" (the Muses), derived from Comes' Mythologiae. His change from three to five mermaids suggests temptation of the five senses. Some details may be from the contest in Ovid's Metamorphoses, V.

Daly, Peter M. Trends and Problems in the Study of Emblematic Literature, Mosaic, 5 (1972), 53-68.   1910

Discusses not emblem-books proper, "but rather the verbal art of literature which reveals those qualities associated with emblem-books." Opposes traditional view that emblem is arbitrary or contrived, as in 687. Gives examples of difficulties in "positivistic source-hunting" in emblem-books for images in Shakespeare's plays. More successful are critics who use emblem-books "not as sources but as parallels or keys to the understanding of literature," e.g., Fowler's discovery of "emblems of temperance threaded through Book II" of Sp's FQ to produce structural unification (see 1917). "Emblematic attitudes of thought and expression inform all the cultural and artistic activities" of Renaissance, which may be called "the Emblematic Age."

Doran, Madeleine. On Elizabethan "Credulity," with Some Questions Concerning the Use of the Marvelous in Literature, JHI, 1 (1940), 151-76.   1910A

Cites the sea monsters encountered by Guyon (FQ, II, xii, 22-25) in discussing the "unnatural natural history" of the Elizabethans, the associations with such marvels in contemporary minds, and the extent to which they were accepted by Elizabethan readers and theatrical audiences.

Duffield, Kenneth T. The Elfin Chronicle, TLS, June 26, 1948, p. 359.   1911

Sp's Elfin emperors (see 1902, 1943, 1944, 1974, and 1996) may ultimately derive their names from a number of Greek words connected with giants and the other world.

Durling, Robert M. The Bower of Bliss and Armida's Palace, CL, 6 (1954), 335-47.   1912

Though he borrows the materials in Tasso's passage, Sp uses them to his own ends in FQ, II, xii. He makes the bathing girls more wanton, and implies that their sensuality is a perversion of the right kind of love, a perversion which entraps the soul in such a way that escape requires the aid of divine grace. Sp also makes the bower in general exhibit the effects of corrupted art.

Ericson, Eston E. "Reaving the Dead" in the Age of Chivalry, MLN, 52 (1937), 353-5.   1913

On FQ, II, viii, 15. Historical basis of Pyrochles' attempted pillage of Guyon's armor.

Evans, Maurice. The Fall of Guyon, ELH, 28 (1961), 215-24; repr. in 644.   1914

Disputes Kermode's view (1945) that Fall of Guyon (FQ, II, vii) is comparable to temptations of Christ, contending that Guyon's loss of right reason mirrors the fall of Adam.

Evans, Maurice. Guyon and the Bower of Sloth, SP, 61 (1964), 140-9.   1915

Theme of FQ, II is that man's essential duty is to struggle upwards. Because Guyon's task is to labor in the cause of virtue, his basic temptation is sloth, the temptation to relax. Acrasia's garden, which is Sp's "Pallace of Art," provides an escapist substitute for "virtuous action" and is thus a subtle temptation to sloth.

Fogle, Richard H. Empathetic Imagery in Keats and Shelley, PMLA, 61 (1946), 163-91.   1916

Keats's reaction to Sp's phrase "sea-shouldering whales" (FQ, II, xii, 23) is a "familiar and unchallengeable instance of empathetic response," involving kinesthetic and organic sensation.

Fowler, A. D. S. Emblems of Temperance in *The Faerie Queene*, Book II, RES, N. S. 11 (1960), 143-9.   1917

Sp built into imagery of FQ traditional emblems of the virtues, because these made allegory intelligible and were essential to the poet's oblique method. Golden set-square was emblem of temperance, because it was used to establish mean proportion; all architectural and structural images are extensions of this emblem. Bridle is an emblem of control over Platonic horse of man's desire. Wine and water are emblematic of rebellious flesh and spirit, extremes which Guyon brings together.

Fowler, Alastair. Review of H. Berger, The Allegorical Temper: Vision and Reality in Book 2 of Spenser's *Faerie Queene*, EIC, 10 (1960), 334-40.   1918

Praises Berger for concentrating on plot, where he's at his best; castigates him for studying Bk. II in isolation. At least he has defied the New Critics "in showing Spenser to be intelligent, witty, and amenable to close reading." But Berger doesn't know anything about Renaissance iconography. See 1450, 1900, 1937.

Fowler, A. D. S. The River Guyon, MLN, 75 (1960), 289-92.   1919

Guyon is usually derived from Elizabethan chronicles, on basis of historical allegory. Proposes instead a derivation from one of Biblical rivers branching from River of Eden, and cites commentaries of Philo and Ambrose. These sources available to Sp.

Fowler, Alastair. Comment, N&Q, 14 (1967), 457-8.   1920
On J. L. Mills' Spenser's Castle of Alma and the Number 22 (1962),

which associates description of Alma's castle in stanza 22 (FQ, II, ix, 22) with moderation or temperance. Buttresses Mills' suggestion with fact "the Castle of Alma canto has a stanza-total of 60: a number held to signify the control of Reason over passion." See 1908, 1936.

Fowler, Alastair. The Critical Forum: The Owl and the Turtle-Dove, EIC, 12 (1962), 227-9.   1921

Expands I. R. Browning's interpretation (1900) of the line "ashamed how rude Pan did her dight" (FQ, II, ix, 40) to include consideration of the reasons for shamefulness in human nature and the process by which it came into existence. Disagrees with Browning's ordering of the sequence of that process and with his rejection of all iconographical evidence.

Fowler, Alastair D. S. The Image of Mortality: *The Faerie Queene*, II, i-ii, HLQ, 24 (1961), 91-110; repr. in 756.   1922

The sequence of Mordant, Amavia, and Ruddymane is not a psychological episode but one depicting the effects of original sin and baptismal regeneration.

Fox, Robert C. Temperance and the Seven Deadly Sins in *The Faerie Queene*, Book II, RES, 12 (1961), 1-6.
1923

The Seven Deadly Sins provide a basic structure for Bk. II; they have counterparts in the major episodes, e.g., Avarice becomes Mammon. All are subordinated to concept of Temperance. An expansion of article by J. Holloway (1934). Fox differs in his interpretation of Tantalus and offers an alternative interpretation for Gluttony.

Friedman, Donald M. Wyatt and the Ambiguities of Fancy, JEGP, 67 (1968), 32-48.   1924

Sp's admission of Phantastes to Alma's "mental advisory staff" (FQ, II, ix, 44 ff.), although imagination can be either unreliable or creative, follows medieval doctrine concerning its dual nature. Renaissance entertained similar notions about duality of melancholy, associated with anti-social attitudes and also with artistic powers. Imagination and Fancy not assigned to separate parts of mind, but unified faculty regarded as "capable equally of forging delusive fantasies and of shaping divine epics." Shows this contradiction left imprint on love poetry of Sir Thomas Wyatt with poignant consequences, since his mind "is the scene of his erotic psychomachias and the major resource in his struggle to achieve integrity and permanence."

Fucilla, Joseph G. A Rhetorical Pattern in Renaissance and Baroque Poetry, SRen, 3 (1956), 23-48.   1925

A study of the "disseminative-recapitulative type of correlative verse" having the formula:

$$A_1 \quad A_2 \quad A_3 \ldots\ldots\ldots A_n$$
$$A_1 \quad A_2 \quad A_3 \ldots\ldots\ldots A_n$$

from its origin in two satirical epigrams of Lucilius. Cites many Elizabethan examples in lyric, drama, and music, of which one is found in FQ, II, vi, 13.

Gilbert, Allan H. Those Two Brethren Giants (*Faerie Queene*, 2. 11. 15), MLN, 70 (1955), 93-4.   1926

The "brethren giants" who defend the walls of the Castle of Temperance are hands, continuing the allegory of the body.

Hageman, Elizabeth H. Alma, Belphoebe, Maleger, and the Number 22: Another Note on Symbolic Stanza Placement, N&Q, 18 (1971), 225-6.   1927

Two more instances of Sp's placement of the topic of moderation in a

22nd stanza: II, iii, 22 (Belphoebe), and II, xi, 22 (Maleger the intemperate). See 1908, 1920, 1962.

Hamilton, A. C. A Theological Reading of *The Faerie Queene*, Book II, ELH, 25 (1958), 155-62.   1928

Interprets the book in the light of Sp's Letter to Raleigh, where the episode of the bloody-handed babe is described as "the beginning of the second book and the whole subject thereof." Mordant-Amavia episode (i and ii) prepares way for all that follows. Bloody-handed babe stands for mankind, tainted with original sin. Arthur's slaying of Maleger (xi), original sin, represents cleansing of mankind by divine grace. Guyon, in his quest, seeks to undo the effects of the Fall, betokened by the bloody hands, by asserting the power of the temperate body over sin. His quest leads him back to Eden (Bower of Bliss) where, armed with temperance, he triumphs over Eve (Acrasia).

Harrison, Thomas P., Jr. The Whistler, Bird of Omen, MLN, 65 (1950), 539-41.   1929

The Whistler in FQ, II, xii, 36 is a clarion of death.

Hieatt, A. Kent. Milton's Comus and Spenser's False Genius, UTQ, 38 (1969), 313-8.   1930

Iconographical similarities make almost certain that false Genius (FQ, II, xii) was model for Milton's Comus. Antithesis between this false Genius and true Genius of Garden of Adonis (FQ, III, vi) may also have influenced Milton's conception. [SpN, Vol. 1, No. 2 (1970), 8.]

Hieatt, A. Kent. Spenser's Atin from "Atine"? MLN, 72 (1957), 249-51.   1931

Prefers an Old French etymology for the name of Pyrocles' squire to a Greek.

Hollander, John. Spenser and the Mingled Measure, ELR, 1 (1971), 226-38. 1932

"The mingled measure of the Bower [of Bliss, FQ, II, xii, 70-71] was designed to transcend, in the manner of its excesses, all of the indoor, outdoor, vocal, instrumental, literary, and actual typologies of music, both in the poem and in the world of Elizabethan reference." In a sense, it parodies itself. Music Cymochles and Guyon hear (v and vi) is different but premonitory of Acrasia. Sp transforms ordinarily beneficent music into signal of moral danger. Cites other instances of pastoral music in fourth sonnet of VP, April of SC, TM, and FQ, VI, x, 7. "In post-Spenserian tradition the Bower's mixture becomes morally legitimate," in Giles Fletcher, Drayton, and William Browne. See 794.

Holleran, James V. Spenser's Irony in Book II of The Faerie Queene, McNR, 15 (1964), 11-7.   1933

Analyzes Guyon's humiliations (Braggadochio steals his horse) and successes (against Phaedria), and the Palmer's incompetence (deceived by Archimago and Duessa, wrong about everything in Mordant-Amavia-bloody handed babe-defiled fountain episode) and new power in Bower of Bliss (he captures Acrasia). Concludes that Sp has reversed roles of knight and squire: Guyon has more sense than the Palmer, the Palmer accomplishes Guyon's quest.

Holloway, J. The Seven Deadly Sins in The Faerie Queene, Book II, RES, N. S. 3 (1952), 13-8.   1934

Suggests that the seven deadly sins "provide a basic pattern for Book II as a whole, underlying its structure from Canto ii onward." Sp drew from Dante's idea that all things are moved by love, and thus both virtue and vice spring from it. The seven deadly sins spring from ignoring the virtue of temperance in love; i.e., from inordinate, perverse, or sluggish love.

Hoopes, Robert. "God Guide Thee, Guyon": Nature and Grace Reconciled in The Faerie Queene, Book II, RES, N. S. 5 (1954), 14-24; repr. in 756.   1935

Agrees with Woodhouse's thesis in Nature and Grace in The Faerie Queene, ELH, 16 (1949), 194-228 (see 1752) that Sp sets up a distinction between the order of grace in Book I and the order of nature in Book II, but the contrast is not absolute. Holds that Sp shows the harmony of the two orders, especially in Book II, with God's grace nourishing and upholding Guyon's reason. Also finds analogies in the scale of values between Book II and Comus and Paradise Regained. See 1753.

Hopper, Vincent F. Spenser's "House of Temperance," PMLA, 55 (1940), 958-67.   1936

FQ, II, ix, 22 reflects the mathematical demonstration known as the mean proportion, indicating that the House of Temperance is "a combined human, geometrical, and arithmetical image of the mean proportion." Sp's immediate inspiration may have been a 1570 edition of Euclid. See 1908, 1920, 1962.

Hough, Graham, and Alastair Fowler. The Critical Forum: Spenser and Renaissance Iconography, EIC, 11 (1961), 233-8.   1937

Spirited exchange over the identity of the bird (FQ, II, ix, 40) in Fowler's critical review, EIC, 10 (1960), 334-41 (see 1918), of Berger's The Allegorical Temper (1895; see 1900, 1921).

Hughes, Merritt Y. England's Eliza and Spenser's Medina, JEGP, 43 (1944), 1-15.   1938

The portrait of Elizabeth as Medina—the Aristotelian mean—is set against a background of contemporary discussions of Temperance, especially of Temperance in women, most of these in Italian works of the sixteenth century.

Hughes, Merritt Y. Spenser's Acrasia and the Circe of the Renaissance, JHI, 4 (1943), 381-99.   1939

Sp's conception of Circe and her beasts had a broad literary background, so that his Acrasia comes from no single source. "All the Circes of the Renaissance illuminate Spenser's Acrasia." Defends the destruction of the Bower of Bliss and stripping of Acrasia as appropriate to the moral temper of the age.

Jones-Davies, M. T. Note sur la Légende de Sabrina dans le *Comus* de Milton, EA, 20 (1967), 416-9.   1940

To acknowledged sources of Sabrina story—Geoffrey of Monmouth, Sp's FQ (Bk. II), and Drayton's Polyolbion—adds Lodge's Complaint of Elstred and anonymous Locrine (ca. 1591).

Jorgensen, Paul A. Our Naked Frailties: Sensational Art and Meaning in *Macbeth*. Berkeley: University of California Press, 1971. 234 pp.   1941

On theme of futile handwashing in Macbeth (II, ii), compares theme "in Spenser, that master of the nightmarishly futile compulsion" (FQ, II, ii, 3-4), also in Seneca and symbolically in Bible (pp. 85 ff.). For "concept that labor is futile unless it is good labor, the most compelling inspiration was surely Edmund Spenser" (cites FQ, II, vi, 47; vii, 58, 61; xi, 44). "There is almost no real rest in *The Faerie Queene*" (pp. 140-41). For other references to Sp, see Index.

Kaske, Carol V. Spenser's *Faerie Queene* and Exegetical Tradition: Nature, Law

and Grace in the Episode of the Nymph's Well. Doctoral diss., Johns Hopkins University, 1964. 256 pp. 1942

Mordant's and Amavia's tragedy (FQ, II, i) dramatizes man's concupiscent rebellion against law (Romans 7) and also re-enacts the Fall, which caused concupiscence. Mordant is all that is fallen in man; Amavia is the unfallen remnant. Ruddymane is the entire offspring of Adam and Eve, tainted by original sin; Guyon and the Palmer are a chorus, first classical, then converted by Mosaic law. Three patterns unify the episode: "questionings and defenses of God's justice; a re-enactment of the historical epochs of nature, law, and grace; and contrasts between classical and Christian ethics." Episode introduces an image-pattern of three wells and other important patterns in Bk. II and FQ as a whole.

Kendrick, T. D. The Elfin Chronicle, TLS, Feb. 7, 1948, p. 79.   1943

Suggests identifications for each of the Elfin kings mentioned in FQ, II, x, 70-76. See 1902, 1911, 1944, 1974, 1996.

Kendrick, T. D. The Elfin Chronicle, TLS, May 15, 1948, p. 275.   1944

Reiterates former views (see 1943, 1974) concerning identification of the three sons (FQ, II, x, 70-76), but is mainly concerned with Sp's use of the British History in other parts of FQ.

Kermode, Frank. The Cave of Mammon, in Elizabethan Poetry, pp. 151-73. Stratford-upon-Avon Studies, 2. London: Edward Arnold, 1960. 224 pp. Repr. in 649 and 1478.   1945

In Cave of Mammon (II, vii) Guyon undergoes necessary preparation for his assault on Acrasia, paralleling the temptation of Christ in the wilderness. He passes not from Aristotelian temperance to continence, but from temperance of natural habit to heroic virtue, which contains all the natural virtues. Mammon's temptation includes all possibilities except lust of the flesh, already overcome in Phaedria: wealth, pride of life, and knowledge. Guyon becomes not a saint but a hero, prepared not for charity but for fortitude.

Kermode, Frank. A Spenser Crux: "The Faerie Queene," II, v, 12, 7-9, N&Q, 197 (1952), 161.   1946

Emends "deeme" to "mete" in l. 8 and paraphrases: "Do not measure your force by the injustice of fortune; after all, it prevailed only in defiance of fortune."

Kirkpatrick, Robin. Appearances of the Red Cross Knight in Book Two of Spenser's Faerie Queene, JWCI, 34 (1971), 338-50.   1947

Based on assumption that St. George, or Redcrosse, gradually becomes Guyon; likewise Guyon gradually becomes Britomart. Specifically, the figure who appears to the Palmer during Guyon's faint (II, viii, 5), and the unnamed figure in the second room of the mind in the House of Alma (II, ix, 54) are Redcrosse. [SpN, Vol. 4, No. 2 (1973), 5.]

Koller, Katherine. The Travayled Pylgrime by Stephen Batman and Book Two of The Faerie Queene, MLQ, 3 (1942), 535-41.   1948

Batman's work (1569) presents allegorically the same elements of Elizabethan psychology which appear in the trials of Guyon.

Lever, Walter. Phallic Fallacies in the Bower of Bliss, WCR, 7 (1972), 62-3.   1949

A parody of the parody in 1952. "Demonstrates" that Verdant (FQ, II, xii), all "swinging knights" of FQ, and John Donne are homosexual.

McGee, Arthur R. Macbeth and the Furies, ShS, 19 (1966), 55-67.   1950

Witches were associated, identified, confused with classical Furies, biblical demons, and fairies of folklore. Little wonder Sp's Celeno is a Harpy/Siren (FQ, II, vii, 23). Ben Jonson's witches in Masque of Queenes, like medieval devils, come from hell. Sp's associations similar: Duessa appears with Night and with Até (on whom Dame in Masque of Queens is modelled, in part), and hag Occasion has Furor as her son (FQ, II, iv, 10). Weird Sisters in Macbeth have multiple sources.

McKenzie, James J. Two possible Housman Sources, N&Q, N. S. 1 (1954), 539.   1951

FQ, II, vi, 26 is a possible source of "Could man be drunk forever," Housman's Last Poems, X.

McNeir, Waldo F. Spenser's Bower of Bliss Revisited, WCR, 6 (1972), 3-4.   1952

Parodic interpretation of Bower of Bliss (FQ, II, xii) in the manner of heterosexual sex-research of Masters and Johnson. "Corrects" C. S. Lewis's interpretation (1513), and other "Victorian pruderies." See 1949.

Magill, Andrew J. Spenser's Guyon and the Mediocrity of the Elizabethan Settlement, SP, 67 (1970), 167-77.   1953

"In the Medina episode of Book II the poet celebrates at once both the Idea of Temperance and the Elizabethan Church, the most illustrious example, for Spenser, of temperance in his world. The English Church under Elizabeth actively pursued and took pride in a moderate religious course between Puritanism and Romanism." Name Guyon is anagram of surname of Bishop John Young, Sp's patron and leader of moderate party in Church. [MLA Abstracts, I (1970), 29.]

Manzalaoui, M. A. The Struggle for the House of the Soul: Augustine and Spenser, N&Q, 8 (1961), 420-2.   **1954**

The *Confessions* (VIII, viii; X, viii-xvii; and elsewhere) may be a source for the House of Alma (FQ, II, x). Most evident parallel is use of architectural model for the soul, but most interesting is use of the stomach and the digestive system to portray inner condition of the mind in both works.

Maxwell, J. C. Guyon, Phaedria, and the Palmer, RES, N. S. 5 (1954), 388-90.   **1955**

Agrees in general with Sirluck's interpretation of FQ, II as a restatement of the Nicomachean Ethics, with practical wisdom added to the moral virtues (see 1977). Yet the Phaedria incident needs further clarification in these terms. Guyon embodies "true temperance in his dealings with Phaedria, while at the same time we recognize that he offends (momentarily and venially) against practical wisdom."

Maxwell, J. C. A Virgilian Echo in Spenser, N&Q, 14 (1967), 458.   **1956**

Suggests that in FQ, II, iii, 41, 5-9, Sp was alluding to account of descent to lower world in Virgil's Aeneid (VI, 127).

Miller, Lewis H., Jr. Arthur, Maleger, and History in the Allegorical Context, UTQ, 35 (1966), 176-87.   **1957**

Arthur's conflict with Maleger (FQ, II, xi) is a psychomachia reflecting Arthur's own inner-struggles with impatience and impotence in his quest of Gloriana. This parallels the Locrine-Humber struggle in the chronicle of FQ, II, x.

Miller, Lewis H., Jr. A Secular Reading of *The Faerie Queene*, Book II. DA, 25 (1965), 4691. Cornell University, 1964. 206 pp.   **1958**

Considers actions of Guyon and Arthur in isolation from the operation of grace; views Guyon and Arthur as fallible human figures working out their own destiny. Guyon's descent into Mammon's cave is an exploration of his own psyche, an extreme reaction to damaging visit with Phaedria. Arthur is excessively ambitious, unconcerned with private virtues. Both are educated at Alma's castle by confronting parts of themselves which they had not previously known. Arthur in fighting Maleger overcomes, without God's grace, "the pernicious elements of his soul. A similar movement is traced in Sir Guyon's final overthrow of Acrasia." Concludes by linking Temperance with Chastity; "Temperance must, in Spenser's scheme, precede the redeeming power of married love." See 1959.

Miller, Lewis H., Jr. A Secular Reading of *The Faerie Queene*, Book II, ELH, 33 (1966), 154-69; repr. in 644 and 756.   **1959**

The quest of Temperance in FQ, II is not rooted in theology; it is based upon the humanistic ideal that man controls his own destiny. Points up secular nature of events in Bk. II "which have hitherto been shrouded in sacramental or religious drapery" (refers to 1922 and 1928), hoping to "provide a new perspective from which to view the allegorical movement of Book II." See 1958.

Mills, Jerry Leath. Symbolic Tapestry in *The Faerie Queene*, II. ix. 33, PQ, 49 (1970), 568-9.   **1960**

Tapestries in Alma's parlor represent "the initial stages of perception," or "the initial phase in assimilation of sensory data." [MLA Abstracts, I (1971), 42.]

Mills, Jerry Leath. A Source for Spenser's Anamnestes, PQ, 47 (1968), 137-9.   **1961**

Anamnestes, the youth who assists Eumnestes (FQ, II, x), personifies a mental function within the realm of memory and recollection. Suggests that Sp's source for this concept was Thomas Blenerhasset's The Second Part of the Mirrour for Magistrates (1578).

Mills, Jerry Leath. Spenser's Castle of Alma and the Number 22: A Note on Symbolic Stanza Placement, N&Q, 14 (1967), 456-7.   1962

Suggests that Sp's description of Castle of Alma (FQ, II, ix, 22) in twenty-second stanza of canto may be explained by fact number 22 itself was associated by Isidore of Seville with moderation or temperance. See 1908, 1920, and 1936.

Mills, Jerry Leath. Spenser's Emblem of Prudence: Four Studies in *The Faerie Queene*, II. ix-x. Doctoral diss., Harvard University, 1968. 185 pp.   1963

Each of four studies deals with an aspect of Prudence in relation to theme and organization of Bk. II. Chap. I, Prudence, Wisdom, and the Parallel Structure of Books I and II, "points out and explicates the emblem of prudence, demonstrating its centrality in the overall thematic contrast between Books I and II." Chap. II, The Castle of Alma and the Mortalist Controversy, "attempts to utilize the emblem as one of several keys to the recondite numerological symbolism in II. ix. 22." Chap. III, Prudence, History, and the Prince, "traces the traditional association of prudence with history and statecraft," hence its appropriateness "in connection with Prince Arthur's experience of his national and ethnic past." Chap. IV, The Meaning of Spenser's Chronicles, proposes a rationale for Sp's manipulation of source materials in ordering his chronicle. In each chap. "the emblem of prudence directs my interpretation."

Narkin, Anthony. Spenser's *The Faerie Queene*, Book II, ii, iii, (4), Expl, 31 (1972), Item 18.   1964

Ruddymane's hands are red, "gules," not red, guilty. [SpN, Vol. 4, No. 1 (1973), 6.]

Nearing, Homer. Caesar's Sword (*Faerie Queene*, II, x, 49; *Love's Labour's Lost*, V, ii, 615), MLN, 63 (1948), 403-5.   1965

A sword that was regarded as Caesar's seems to have been preserved in the Tower of London.

Neill, Kerby. Spenser's Acrasia and Mary Queen of Scots, PMLA, 60 (1945), 682-8.   1966

Evidence that Sp's contemporaries regarded Mary Stuart as the personification of intemperance, and "characterized her as a Circean enchantress."

Nellish, B. The Allegory of Guyon's Voyage: An Interpretation, ELH, 30 (1963), 89-106; repr. in 644 and 756.   1967

Guyon's voyage, while it has much in common with Tasso's voyage of Ubaldo (Gerusalemme Liberata XV) and other traditional epic works, is extended beyond mere moral narrative by a blending of Christian and Renaissance allegorical conventions, easily recognizable to Sp's contemporaries. The voyage, a romantic motif, represents journey man makes through life along with obstacles, personal and social, which he must overcome. Several romance motifs are interlinked with allegory and impose an organizational discipline.

Nilsen, George Howard. This Faire Mirhour: Nature in the *Faerie Queene*, Book II. DAI, 33 (1972), 2337 A.

Michigan State University, 1972. 198 pp.   1968

Book contains aspects of Nature in 4 categories, ground, water, vegetation, and atmospherics. Sometimes Nature and good personages in Bk. II have a reciprocal relationship: this is happy situation of "natura naturans." But when Nature is unnatural it reflects the bad personages, as in Mammon's Cave, the Idle Lake, the Bower of Bliss. In these instances, "unnatural love and 'natura naturata' are parallel—both are perversions." Faerieland is thus an image of the mind, reflecting its tensions. In the course of Bk. II, Guyon "swings from extreme to extreme in describing a circle," but finally discovers his own nature.

Okerlund, Arlene Naylor. Literature and Its Audience: The Reader in Action in Selected Works of Spenser, Dryden, Thackeray, and T. S. Eliot. DAI, 30 (1969), 1991A. University of California, San Diego, 1969. 234 pp.   1969

Introductory chap. reviews critical approaches that recognize importance of interaction between reader and artform. Separate chaps. on narrative poetry, drama, novel, and modern poetry investigate interaction that develops between reader and selected works of authors discussed. In Bower of Bliss, Sp creates evil place more appealing than "good" counterparts in FQ, II. Seductive actions of wanton maidens "cause us, as readers, to forget the quest after temperance in an overpowering impulse to fulfill our concuspicible [sic] desires." Thus Sp shows us belief in abstract virtue offers no defense against temptation. He "forces us into an embarrassing confrontation with our own precarious morality."

Oruch, Jack B. Imitation and Invention in the Sabrina Myths of Drayton and Mil-ton, Anglia, 90 (1972), 60-70.   1970

Milton's myth of Sabrina in Comus makes more use of Drayton's in Poly-Olbion than Sp's in FQ, II, x, 17-19. Milton follows his sources, but Sp not a major influence.

Parker, Roscoe E. "Let Gryll Be Gryll," PQ, 16 (1937), 218-9.   1971

On FQ, II, xii, 87, 8. An analogue in Thomas Norton's translation of Calvin's Institutes of the Christian Religion.

Perkinson, Richard H. The Body as a Triangular Structure in Spenser and Chapman, MLN, 64 (1949), 520-2.   1972

Cites Chapman's Hymnus in Cinthiam, where Palace is triangular and symbol of intellect circular, to support view that triangle and circle in description of Castle of Alma (FQ, II, ix, 22) represent body and soul or intellect, respectively.

Purpus, Jean R. The Moral Philosophy of Book II of Spenser's *Faerie Queene.* Doctoral diss., University of California at Los Angeles, 1947. DDAAU, 1946-47, No. 14.   1973

An analysis of the book in terms of contemporary ethical theory. "Spenser, following contemporary theory, presented temperance both as seeking for a mean between two extremes and as combating excess of passion. The first aspect is dealt with in Canto ii. The other cantos delineate the victory over individual passions which is achieved by Sir Guyon and the Palmer. Elizabethan moral philosophy stressed that the man who would achieve true temperance must understand himself, must be motivated by desire for true honor, and must be blessed with God's grace; Spenser carefully equips Guyon with this necessary knowledge, gives him desire for real glory as a spur to action, and

grants him the blessing of heaven."
Book II is skilfully constructed to
create a full picture of a complex
virtue.

Rathborne, Isabel E. The Elfin Chronicle,
TLS, Apr. 24, 1948, p. 233.   1974

Disagrees with Kendrick (see 1943)
in his identifications of the Elfin
kings (FQ, II, x, 70-76), agreeing only
with his identification of Elfinan;
agrees with his identification of rulers
of Cleopolis as British (not Trojan);
and questions his interpretation of
various landmarks and wonders which
Sp describes. See 1902, 1911, 1944,
and 1996.

Shanley, James L. Spenser's Temperance
and Aristotle, MP, 43 (1946), 170-4.
                                    1975

Guyon can not be taken to represent the Aristotelian Continence, nor
can he be described by any one term
taken from Aristotle. Discusses the
difference between Temperance and
Continence.

Shepperson, Archibald Bolling. Earth's
Only   Paradise,   VQR,   33   (1957),
595-603.   1976

FQ, II, Proem, 2 is the earliest of a
series of references to Virginia by
English authors.

Sirluck, Ernest. The Faerie Queene, Book
II, and the Nicomachean Ethics, MP, 49
(1951), 73-100.   1977

Concludes with the suggestion that
Book II was meant to be a poetic
version of the Nicomachean Ethics,
adding the intellectual virtue of practical wisdom, for which an appropriate title would have been "The
Legend of Moral Virtue," but it was
retitled The Legend of Temperance to
meet the requirements of the changed
plan presented in Sp's letter to Ralegh. See 1955.

Sirluck, Ernest. "God Guide Thee, Guyon," etc. Letter, RES, N. S. 6 (1955),
401-2.   1978

Feels that he has been misquoted
by Hoopes, ibid., 5 (1954), 14-24 (see
1935) with respect to the ethical significance of Guyon and the Palmer;
this letter restates his position.

Sirluck, Ernest. Milton Revises The Faerie
Queene, MP, 48 (1950), 90-6.   1979

Milton's incorrect reference to Guyon, the Palmer, and Mammon is due
to his ethical position, which is unlike
Aristotle's and Sp's in holding that
choice is always dependent upon reason, habit being unreliable.

Snyder, Susan. Guyon the Wrestler, RN,
14 (1961), 249-52.   1980

Supports Fowler (1919), identifying Guyon with the River Gihon in
Genesis 2:13, while adding another
significance by identifying him with
three medieval etymologies of "gyon"
meaning "wrestling" in Jacobus de
Voragine's Legenda Aurea with which
Sp was familiar in Caxton's English
version.

Sonn, Carl Robinson. Sir Guyon in the
Cave of Mammon, SEL, 1 (1961),
17-30.   1981

Argues that in FQ, II, vii, Guyon's
inability to comprehend universal
reality epitomized in Cave of Mammon is necessary to demonstrate natural man's need for the infinite mercy
and love of God.

Steadman, John M. Acrasia in The Tablet
of Cebes, N&Q, N.S. 7 (1960), 48.
                                    1982

Acrasia is older than critics of FQ
have realized. She first appeared "as
an allegorical seductress" in The Tablet of Cebes, a work of the first century, A. D.

Stewart, Bain T. A Note on Spenser and Phineas Fletcher, PQ, 26 (1947), 86-7.   1983

Passage in which Guyon first sees Acrasia (FQ, II, xii, 77-78), is "adapted directly" in Daphnis' description of his beloved in the 7th of Fletcher's Piscatorie Eclogues.

Stewart, Bain T. The Psychology of Spenser's Anamnestes, MLQ, 1 (1940), 193-4.   1984

On FQ, II, ix, 58. Anamnestes is Memory's helper. Suggests Sp followed a theory of memory which came from Plato, Aristotle, and Aquinas.

Stoll, Elmer E. The Validity of the Poetic Vision: Keats and Spenser, MLR, 40 (1945), 1-7.   1985

Discusses Keats's Ode on a Grecian Urn and Ode to a Nightingale, and a stanza in the Bower of Bliss passage (FQ, II, xii, 71) as a key to the independent nature and autonomy of poetry. Notes also Wordsworth's critical admiration for Sp, and Coleridge's justification of FQ.

Strathmann, Ernest A. William Austin's "Notes" on The Faerie Queene, Huntington Library Bulletin, 11 (1937), 155-60.   1986

Devotionis Augustinianae Flamma (1635) comments on and quotes from FQ, II, viii, 1-5 (Guyon's angel). Haec Homo (1637) quotes extensively from FQ, II, ix (House of Alma). Notes differences between Digby's and Austin's interpretations of the latter passage.

Super, R. H. Spenser's Faerie Queene, II, i, 490-92, Expl 11 (1953), No. 30.   1987

Acrasia's curse (stanza 55) is a play on Mort-dant and Ama-via: "him that death does give," and "her that loves to live."

Thaler, Alwin. Mercutio and Spenser's Phantastes, PQ, 16 (1937), 405-7. 1988

Generic kinship between Shakespeare's fantastic courtier in Romeo and Juliet and the custodian of "idle thoughts and fantasies" in the House of Alma (FQ, II, ix, 49-52).

Thaler, Alwin. Spenser and Much Ado About Nothing, SP, 37 (1940), 225-35.   1989

Shakespeare's Hero-Claudio story owes more to the Phedon-Claribell story (FQ, II, iv) than has been previously recognized.

Thomson, Patricia. Phantastes and His Horoscope, N&Q, 13, (1966), 372-5.   1990

Phantastes' complexion (FQ, II, ix, 52) and his "malefic nature" are a result of Saturn's position in the twelfth house of mundane astrology at the time of his birth. Sp softens this by placing him in the House of Alma episode and by presenting him as a wise counselor.

Wall, L. N. Some Notes on Marvell's Sources, N&Q, N. S. 4 (1957), 170-3.   1991

Finds an echo of the Bower of Bliss (FQ, II, xii) in The Garden.

Walsh, Thomas F. Rappaccini's Literary Gardens, ESQ, No. 19 (1960), 9-13.   1992

Shows that Hawthorne in Rappaccini's Daughter draws on Ovid's Metamorphoses (XIV, 623 ff.) and Sp's FQ (II, xii) "in addition to the Bible in his depiction of Rappaccini's garden."

Wimsatt, W. K., Jr. The Verbal Icon. Lexington, Ky.: University of Kentucky Press, 1954. 299pp.   1993

In History and Criticism: A Problematic Relationship, pp. 253-65, raises objections to the historical side of history of ideas on ground that "the fact that in a certain age and by certain persons an idea or system of ideas was actually entertained" cannot affect our value judgments of past literature. For example, knowing that the Elizabethans disapproved of Acrasia, which has been shown (see 1939), has no bearing on how we take the destruction of the Bower of Bliss (pp. 255-6).

Woodward, Frank L. Bacon as Spenser and Shakespeare, Baconiana, 28, No. 110 (1944), 36-8.   1994

A letter to the editor. Finds Bacon's cipher in FQ, II, viii, 40-41.

Wright, Nathalia. A Note on Melville's Use of Spenser: Hautia and the Bower of Bliss, AL, 24 (1952), 83-5.   1995

Parallels between Guyon's visit to Acrasia's bower (FQ, II, xii) and the meeting between Taji and Hautia on the island of Flozello. Both heroes hear the call of a maiden as they cross the water in a boat; each has a vision of mermaids; both islands are enveloped in mist; the boats land abruptly; and, after the landing, the two stories pass through five similar scenes.

Yates, Frances A. The Elfin Chronicle, TLS, July 3, 1948, p. 373.   1996

The "Elfin" genealogy of Queen Elizabeth may be interpreted as a religious story with the ancient British imperial legends used to sanction Tudor claims. See 1902, 1911, 1943, 1944, and 1974.

Allen, Michael J. B. The Chase: The Development of a Renaissance Theme, CL, 20 (1968), 301-12.   1997

Attempts "to indicate some of the variations to which the related images of the chase, the wound, the deer, and the woman gave rise, and to indicate how the three different groupings in which they occurred were variously combined during the Renaissance." Examines FQ, III, vi, in which Diana and Venus meet, symbols of chastity and love, brought together by the wanton Cupid; discusses episode in light of traditional hart/heart pun.

Atkinson, Dorothy F. Busirane's Castle and Artidon's Cave, MLQ, 1 (1940), 185-92.   1998

Suggests The Mirrour of Knighthood as a source, and 1585 as the probable date for the completion of Book III, the year in which the second part of the Mirrour appeared. Notes three important parallels with FQ, III, xi and xii.

Bahr, Howard W. The Misery of Florimell: The Ladder of Temptation. SoQ, 4 (1965), 116-22.   1999

Florimell's misery is that her chastity undergoes a "tripartite trial" in FQ, III, iii-ix. The witch's son, subhuman; the fisherman, human; Proteus, superhuman.

Baker, William Price. *The Faerie Queene*, Book III: an Elizabethan Synthesis of Ethical Theory. Doctoral diss., Harvard University, 1949. HRDP. 1948-1949, p. 11; DDAAU, 1948-49, No. 16.   2000

Uses Hooker, Davies, and Burton as keys to "what the assumptions and the psychological system of the age were." Each of them dealt with one or another facet of the subject matter implicit in FQ, and "each of these writers arranged his subject matter in terms of the psychology of the age. . . . It is the psychological system common to the age which makes clear the organization and often the emphasis of episodes or allusions within Book III." It illustrates throughout the power of chaste love as unifying force operative at lowest and highest levels of man's existence. "Chaste love, analogous to the love of God and implying both earthly regeneration and the ultimate quest of the soul for God, was the 'philosopher's stone' which enabled Spenser to synthesize the virtues into an ethical system."

Bennett, Josephine W. Reply: On Methods of Literary Interpretation, JEGP, 41 (1942), 486-9.   2001

A reply to Brents Stirling, ibid., pp. 482-6. See 2053.

Bennett, Josephine W. Spenser's Garden of Adonis Revisited, JEGP, 41 (1942), 53-78.   2002

Opposes the interpretation of the Garden (FQ, III, vi) as reflecting commonplaces of Renaissance thought (Brents Stirling, PMLA, 49 (1934), 501-38, abstracted in Variorum ed. Bk. III, 347-52), and reaffirms her belief in Sp's use of Neoplatonic sources (see PMLA, 47 (1932), 46-78, abstracted in Variorum ed. Bk. III, 345-7).

Berger, Harry, Jr. Busirane and the War Between the Sexes: An Interpretation of *The Faerie Queene*, III.xi-xii, ELR, 1 (1971), 99-121.   2003

Britomart's experience in House of Busirane is sequence divided into phases represented by episodes in three rooms. First room depicts lust of gods in tapestry. In middle room Britomart sees obsessive false love venting itself in sadistic hatred, revenging itself on Amoret. Two episodes summarize preceding experiences in Bk. III. In inner room, where Britomart rescues Amoret, reference of whole experience changes; Sp emphasizes relation to feminine psyche, significance for both heroines. Together with rejected stanzas of 1590 edition, cantos xi and xii suggest limitations of Amoret and Scudamore as lovers, "and as personified psychic dispositions." [MLA Abstracts, I (1971), 41.]

Berger, Harry, Jr. The Discarding of Malbecco: Conspicuous Allusion and Cultural Exhaustion in *The Faerie Queene* III. ix-x, SP, 66 (1969), 135-54.   2004

As the Britomart story develops, conventional characters of erotic tales—Paridell, Hellenore, Malbecco—are discarded and replaced by figures like Marinell and Florimell, Scudamour and Amoret, Timias and Belphoebe. These "boundary" figures are in turn displaced by, or coalesced in, Artegall and Britomart, who prefigure Queen Elizabeth.

Berger, Harry Jr. *Faerie Queene* Book III: A General Description, Criticism, 11 (1969), 234-61; repr. in 756.   2005

Focuses on the rift between male and female in FQ, III, a rift precipitated by emotional drives toward sexual unity which, ironically, entail hostility. Eros in primitive psychocultural experience is confusing disjunctive force blocking normal forms of affection, a pain-giving force involving warfare or reversal of sexual roles, and a regressive force drawing creatures back to an undifferentiated matrix. Gives many examples of these forces in Bk. III. [SpN, Vol 2, No. 1 (1971), 6.]

Berger, Harry, Jr. The Structure of Merlin's Chronicle in *The Faerie Queene* III, (iii), SEL, 9 (1969), 39-51.   2006

Describes parallels between three analogous stages of (1) Merlin's prophecy for Britain and (2) his prediction of Britomart's future.

Blayney, Glenn H. Nathan Field and *The Faerie Queene*, N&Q, N. S. 2 (1955), 59-60.   2007

Similarities of the theme of romantic married love, the use of character, and the name Scudamore suggest that FQ, III was one of the influences on A Woman is a Weather-cocke.

Bowers, Fredson T. Evidences of Revision in *The Faerie Queene*, III, i, 2, MLN, 60 (1945), 114-6.   2008

Inconsistencies pointed out. Guyon was probably Britomart's original companion to Castle Joyous, not the Red Cross Knight.

Brady, Emily K. The Probable Source for Spenser's Tobacco Reference, MLN, 71 (1956), 402-4.   2009

John Frampton's Joyfull Newes Out of the New Found World, which was dedicated to Sir Edward Dyer, Sp's personal friend, includes a passage from Liébault's Praedium Rusticum dealing with the curative powers of tobacco. Since Sp describes the use of tobacco as a vulnerary in FQ, III, v, 32, and the publication dates of the two books (1567, 1577) are amenable, they are likely sources. See 2017.

Briggs, K. M. Pale Hecate's Team: An Examination of the Beliefs in Witchcraft and Magic among Shakespeare's Contemporaries and His Immediate Successors. London: Routledge and Kegan Paul, 1962. 291 pp.   2010

"The most complete witch in the regular English tradition . . . even to her loutish son, Caliban, Firestone or Lorell" is in FQ, III, vii (pp. 75-6). Merlin's marvellous birth left unexplained by Geoffrey of Monmouth, and also by Sp in FQ, III, iii, 13 (pp. 118-9).

Briggs, Katharine M. The Folds of Folklore, ShS, 17 (1964), 167-79.   2011

"Mr. Fox, the English Blue-Beard story, was certainly known to both Shakespeare and Spenser, for Benedick quotes, 'It is not so, nor 'twas not so' [Much Ado About Nothing, I, i, 18-20], and the cumulative inscription, 'Be bold, be bold,' is used in the Faerie Queene" [III, xi, 54] (p. 171). See 2027.

Brill, Lesley W. Chastity as Ideal Sexuality in the Third Book of The Faerie Queene, SEL, 11 (1971), 15-26.   2012

Chastity in Britomart is a complex and aggressive virtue deriving from the nature of human sexuality. Chastity is "a passionate desire to achieve honor, fidelity to 'kind,' and gentleness and gentility." Britomart's ardent sexuality is often intense and unruly—inner threat. External threats are Malecasta and Busyrane. Florimell, comic heroine of melodramatic subplot, demonstrates need for Britomart's martial ferocity. Busyrane misuses sexuality, Florimell flees from it, only Britomart maintains perfect balance.

Brill, Lesley W. The Legend of Britomartis or of Chastitie: A Study of the Third Book of Spenser's Faerie Queene. DAI, 32 (1972), 5220A. Rutgers University, 1971. 174 pp.   2013

Six chapters, "Concerned with (1) the function of canto i in introducing the central images and conflicts of Book III; (2) Britomart's 'career'; (3) the subplots of Hellenore, Malbecco, and Paridell, and of Florimell and Marinell; (4) the subplots involving Amoret and Belphoebe; (5) the closing movement of the poem; and (6) the wholeness and meaning of Book III."

Cheney, Donald. Spenser's Hermaphrodite and the 1590 Faerie Queene, PMLA, 87 (1972), 192-200.   2014

Hermaphrodite image in original conclusion to FQ, III draws on Ovidian Hermaphrodite-Salmacis scene, symbol of marriage in emblem books, and on androgynous figure in Roman statuary. This conflation symbolizes Britomart's ambiguous status at end of Bk. III, androgynous and self-sufficient savior of Amoret but tormented by her own visions of love. Sp's poem in its 3-book form shares the preoccupation of other Elizabethan works with the identification of love and death, "a recognition that the self can triumph over change only by accepting its own destruction in marriage." See 589, 2015. [SpN, Vol. 3, No. 2 (1972), 5-6.]

Cirillo, Albert R. Spenser's "Faire Hermaphrodite," PQ, 47 (1968), 136-7.   2015

In Bk. III, xii, 45, 2-4 (1590 ed.) of FQ, Sp compares embrace of Amoret and Scudamour with that of the "Faire Hermaphrodite" of a "rich Romane." Although impossible to determine with certainty source of this allusion, external evidence points to statue of Cardinal Farnese, who was both a rich Roman and a clergyman, indicating that Sp may have offered a critical reminder of the corruption of the Roman Church. See 589, 2014.

Coogan, Robert. Petrarch's *Trionfi* and the English Renaissance, SP, 67 (1970), 306-27.   2016

Petrarch's Trionfi celebrated in linked order Love, Chastity, Death, Fame, Time, and Eternity. Demonstrates their vogue in England by reference to Sir Thomas More's cloth hangings, and tapestries at Hampton Court and in palaces of Henry VIII. Continuing vogue evidenced in Masque of Cupid in FQ, III, xi. At end of century Trionfi gave way to Petrarch's Canzoniere as current "rage." [SpN, Vol. 1, No. 3 (1970), 13.]

Dickson, Sarah A. Panacea or Precious Bane: Tobacco in Sixteenth Century Literature, BNYPL, 57 (1953), 367-81, 419-32, 471-96, 544-66, 580-97; 58 (1954), 42-7, 55-73, 110-25, 174-85, 230-41, 274-304, 315-36.   2017

Last two installments deal with tobacco in English literature of the period. Sp was first to pay poetic tribute to tobacco (FQ, III, v, 32-33). Merchant Taylor's School portrait of Sp facing p. 315. See 2009.

Fowler, Alastair. Six Knights at Castle Joyous, SP, 56 (1959), 583-99.   2018

"Usually Spenser makes his meaning clear enough; but we may have to wait a few cantos for him to do so, or else we may have to remember that he already did so a few cantos before. For he gives his directions as often retrospectively as prospectively." Sees Malecasta's wooing of Britomart as a development of the allegory of the six knights (FQ, III, i), and the Paridell-Hellenore affairs (FQ, III, ix-x) as a parallel to the allegory of the knights.

Sp modifies the traditional "ladder of lechery" (see 2020) in such a way as to satirize both contemporary licentious love and medieval courtly love. See 2028.

French, Roberts W. Milton and Spenser, N&Q, 17 (1970), 249.   2019

References to Chaos in Paradise Lost (II, 150, 911, 916; X, 476-477) may be associated with Sp's Chaos (FQ, III, vi, 36).

Gilbert, Allan H. The Ladder of Lechery, *The Faerie Queene*, III, i, 45, MLN, 56 (1941), 594-7.   2020

The scale of desire represented by the six knights serving Malecasta may derive ultimately from Lucian, but more important than the sources is the moral instruction conveyed. See 2018 and 2028.

Gilde, Helen C. Spenser's Hellenore and Some Ovidian Associations, CL, 23 (1971), 233-9.   2021

Hellenore-Paridell episode (FQ, III, ix-x) shows influence of Ovid's Ars Amatoria and Amores. Main theme, futility of trying to enforce chastity together with necessity for sexual passion in marriage, is Ovidian in ironic and witty tone. Paridell's technique of seduction and Hellenore's "sexual athletics" with satyr are paralleled in Ovid's works. [MLA Abstracts, I (1971), 42.]

Gottfried, Rudolf. Spenser Expands his Text, RN, 16 (1963), 9-10.   2022

Stanzas 19 and 25 in FQ, III, ix were originally one stanza and later divided into two stanzas with fifty-four intervening lines to accommodate discovery of true sex of Britomart, a character whose addition late in the poem made alterations necessary.

Gottfried, Rudolf B. Spenser and *The Historie of Cambria*, MLN, 72 (1957), 9-13.   2023

As a source for the British chronicle history in FQ, III, iii, 35, 40-1, and 45, Sp apparently used Humfrey Llwyd's Historie (1584), the English translation of the Chronicle by Caradoc of Llancarfan.

Grellner, Mary Adelaide, S. C. L. Britomart's Quest for Maturity, SEL, 8 (1968), 35-43.   2024

Britomart's experiences in House of Busirane (FQ, III, xi-xii) are crucial in her quest for maturity. Cupid's Mask not only sums up her psychological development to this point, but foreshadows later emotional upsets. Also, Amoret's experience may be an aspect of Britomart's character. When, persuaded by Amoret (love), she does not slay Busirane (passion), Britomart learns that "passion must be subdued, not destroyed." Britomart thus learns self-knowledge and self-mastery, which prepare her for purification at the Temple of Isis (FQ, IV, x).

Hankins, John E. The Sources of Spenser's Britomartis, MLN, 58 (1943), 607-10.   2025

Most probable immediate source in Natalis Comes. Gives many connotations of the name.

Harrison, Thomas P., Jr. Divinity in Spenser's Garden of Adonis, TxSE, 19 (1939), 48-73.   2026

Interprets the "stately mountain metaphor" and the lower garden as divinity or faith contrasted with nature or reason. Sp harmonized the claims of reason and faith in the belief that they taught the same truths.

Hill, Iris Tillman. Britomart and *Be Bold, Be Not Too Bold*, ELH, 38 (1971), 173-87.   2027

Motto over Busirane's door (FQ, III, xi, 54) paralleled in Golding's Ovid (Metamorphoses X, 621-631). Venus tells Adonis "bee bold" in hunting easy prey—soft hunt, and "forbeare too bold to bee" with dangerous animals—hard hunt. Views soft hunt as metaphor for lover's hunt and hard hunt as metaphor for warrior's. Sp tries to reconcile distinction; Britomart is martial Venus. Both commands over door meant to mislead, for Britomart must not "be bold" in love-play, and must not "be not too bold" in dealing with Busirane, which requires full measure of true boldness. Neither command intended to be obeyed in own context; both are ironic. Outside house of Busirane, Britomart will find "hard" hunt also leads to "soft" pleasures of love. [SpN, Vol. 2, No. 2 (1971), 4-5.] See 2011.

Hutton, James. Spenser and the "Cinq Points en Amours," MLN, 57 (1942), 657-61.   2028

Suggests that the names of the six knights in FQ, III, i, 45 may be derived from moral treatises dealing with the five stages of amatory progression. Cites parallels in Marot, Ronsard, and other French writers. See 2018 and 2020.

Kendall, Lyle H., Jr. "Melt with Ruth," N&Q, 198 (1953), 145.   2029

As parallels to the phrase in Lycidas, l. 163, cites two passages in Chaucer's Troilus and FQ, III, vii, 9, 5-7.

L., G. G. Milton's Eglantine, N&Q, 176 (1939), 225.   2030

Milton's error in making eglantine honeysuckle in L'Allegro may have been caused by a somewhat confused recollection of Sp's arbor in FQ, III, vi, 44.

Lawrence, C. E. English Humour, QR, 270 (1938), 132-45.   2031

"Chaucer and Shakespeare stand out in a true succession of humour, with Edmund Spenser—of all poets!— carrying on between them." Pity Sp did not use more humor to strengthen the languid beauty of FQ. Story of Malbecco and Hellenore (III, ix-x) is main example (p. 140).

Le Comte, Edward S. Milton: Two Verbal Parallels, N&Q, 184 (1943), 17-8. 2032

"Finny drove" in FQ (III, viii, 29, 9) also occurs in Comus (l. 115). Milton was not the first to echo Sp's phrase; Drayton's Poly-Olbion (Song II, l. 439) has "finny heard." Reply by Hibernicus, ibid., p. 85.

Low, Anthony. The Image of the Tower in *Paradise Lost*, SEL, 10 (1970), 171-81.   2033

Relates the development of Milton's Tower of Babel in Paradise Lost with Renaissance images, including Sp's allusion in FQ, III, ix, 34.

McAuley, James. Edmund Spenser and George Eliot: A Critical Excursion. Hobart: University of Tasmania, 1963. 21 pp.   2034

An inaugural public lecture. Episode of Malbecco, Hellenore, and Paridell (FQ, III, ix-x) is paralleled in central story of Casaubon, Dorothea, and Will Ladislaw in George Eliot's Middlemarch. "The likenesses are found in the central concerns of each writer, while the differences are in the obvious externals."

MacIntyre, Jean. Spenser's *The Faerie Queene*, III, xi, 47-48, Expli, 24 (1966), Item 69.   2035

Idol of Cupid in House of Busirane from Alciati's emblem "Custodiendas virgines," which shows Minerva standing beside recumbent dragon. Busir-

ane's idol parodies Alciati's wise virgin, and explains why dragon is blinded by Cupid's arrows to serve as symbol for imprudence that is both cause and effect of love exalted by Busirane. But Busirane's Cupid is prisoner of victim, held by foot, detail not in Alciati: blind love and imprudence inextricable.

McNeir, Waldo F. Ariosto's Sospetto, Gascoigne's Suspicion, and Spenser's Malbecco, in Festschrift für Walther Fischer, pp. 34-48. Heidelberg: Carl Winter, 1959. 332pp.   2036

Compares Ariosto's story of Sospetto in Cinque Canti, rejected cantos of Orlando Furioso; Gascoigne's story of Suspicion, a translation of Ariosto, in The Adventures of Master F. J.; and Sp's episode of Malbecco-Hellenore-Paridell in FQ, III, ix-x. On basis of this analysis, rejects view that Sp relied on Gascoigne (see 2042), or Ariosto. Sees Malbecco as an original creation.

McPeek, James A. S. The Genesis of Caliban, PQ, 25 (1946), 378-81.   2037

Sp's Chorle (FQ, III, vii) may have suggested to Shakespeare the monster in The Tempest.

Manzalaoui, Mahmoud. English Analogues to the *Liber Scalae*, MAE, 34 (1965), 21-35.   2038

This Islamic work must be considered a possible source for parts of Chaucer's House of Fame, The Pearl, and The Land of Cockayne; it also parallels the naked babes in Sp's Garden of Adonis (FQ, III, vi, 32) and fall of Angels in Milton's Paradise Lost.

Maxwell, J. C. "Here, There, and Everywhere," N&Q, 18 (1971), 13.   2039

The phrase, cited in OED as appearing ca. 1590 in Doctor Faustus, does not appear in Marlowe's play except in the bad quarto of 1604. It does occur, however, in the 1590 FQ, III, i, 66, 5.

Meier, Hans Heinrich. Ancient Lights on Kubla's Lines, ES, 46 (1965), 15-29.
2040

Proposes that myth of Adonis forms part of literary background of Coleridge's Kubla Khan. Cites parallels in Paradise Lost and Sp's Garden of Adonis (FQ, III, vi).

Meier, Hans Heinrich. Xanaduvian Residues, ES, 48 (1967), 145-55. 2041

Examines concept of earthly paradise in Coleridge's Kubla Khan with reference to Milton, the Bible, and Sp's Garden of Adonis in FQ.

Nelson, William. A Source for Spenser's Malbecco, MLN, 68 (1953), 226-9.
2042

The story of Suspicion in Gascoigne's Adventures of Master F. J. suggested the character and experiences of Malbecco, and Hellenore in the same episode (FQ, III, ix-x) is related to Gascoigne's Elinor. See 2036.

Prezyna, Louise Ann. That Fair Hermaphrodite: Vision of Atonement in *The Faerie Queene*. Doctoral diss., State University of New York, Buffalo, 1970-71. 2043

Rajan, B. *Comus:* The Inglorious Likeness, UTQ, 37 (1968), 113-35. 2044

Must seek "a metaphorical interpretation of chastity and virginity" in Comus, and Sp's Britomart shows "that there is no conflict between chastity and married love." Milton in Epilogue refers to Garden of Adonis (FQ, III, vi) but his Cupid and Psyche differ markedly from Sp's. In Milton they are above Sp's Venus and Adonis, have Platonic connotations of higher dimension demanded by

"strict proportion in the order of things. Not to observe that proportion is to fall, as Comus does, from the divine image to the inglorious likeness."

Ramsay, Judith C. The Garden of Adonis and the Garden of Forms, UTQ, 35 (1966), 188-206. 2045

Distinguishes between the "Garden of Forms," FQ, III, vi, 29-38, and the Garden of Adonis, stanzas 39-50. The Garden of Forms equals Venus Urania's "heavenly house" (stanza 12); it is a timeless, emotionless world of innocence and immortality, directly governed by God's will. Old Genius takes the forms, clothes them in "sinfull mire," and sends them into the world where they stay until death sends them back. Sp's tirade against Time signals the shift to the Garden of Adonis, a place of natural procreation presided over by Venus Genetrix and subject to time and death. Adonis brings together the two worlds, uniting forms with matter but powerless to resist decay. The theme of the canto is the principle of organization vs. the danger of chaotic disorganization. Psyche is the self-discipline which must unite with Cupid, the force of generation, if man is to prosper. Britomart will achieve in marriage the balance between instinct and self-control which is symbolized in the two gardens of this canto.

Rathborne, Isabel E. The Political Allegory of the Florimell-Marinell Story, ELH, 12 (1945), 279-89. 2046

Florimell is Civility. Marinell is sea power. The defeat of Marinell by Britomart represents the passing of sea power to England after the Armada.

Ringler, Richard N. Dryden at the House of Busirane, ES, 49 (1968), 224-9. 2047

Dryden, in All for Love, I, i, where

Serapion describes the portents of Isis' temple, carefully echoes the situation and the language of Britomart's experience in the House of Busirane (III, xii, 3). Dryden chose not to mimic the 'passionate' Shakespeare, "but the master in English of the 'enthusiastic'—Spenser." Dryden also echoes Sp in the Examen Poeticum (1693), his translation of the Aeneid (1697), and his modernization of The Knight's Tale (1700).

Ringler, Richard N. Spenser and the *Achilleid*, SP, 60 (1963), 174-82. 2048

Publius Papinius Statius' Achilleid is primary influence on Cymoent's journey to Marinell (FQ, III, iv). Several other classical influences apparent but less prominent.

Roche, Thomas P. The Challenge to Chastity: Britomart at the House of Busyrane, PMLA, 76 (1961), 340-4; repr. in 756. 2049

Britomart's recognition of ambivalence (love/lust) of the mask at House of Busyrane is the key to her triumph over Busyrane, who represents the "abuse of marriage" and not merely lust in Bk. III of FQ. See 2075.

Saurat, Denis. Spenser and the Zohar, CLS, 1 (1941), 12-3. 2050

The Garden of Adonis (FQ, III, vi) compared with the Zoharistic Garden.

Scott, William O. Proteus in Spenser and Shakespeare: the Lover's Identity, ShakS, 1 (1965), 283-93. 2051

Shakespeare's Proteus (Two Gentlemen of Verona) and Sp's Proteus (FQ, III) are both based upon the Vertumnus myth in Ovid's Metamorphoses (XIV, 623f.), but are presented differently. Sp's Proteus tries to seduce Florimell; he never effects a stable form. Shakespeare's Proteus changes to sincerity because of Julia's

hold on him. Thus, he realizes a true identity.

Sims, Dwight Johnston. Syncretic Neoplatonism in the Imagery and Structure of Book III of *The Faerie Queene*. DAI, 32 (1972), 3965A. University of California, Los Angeles, 1971. 302 pp. 2052

Places Bk. III in tradition of syncretic Neoplatonism of Pico and Leone Ebreo. FQ uses syncretistic conceptions of cosmology, allegory, and literary organization. Sp's cosmology accommodates classical and Christian hierarchies of being; the faeries Belphoebe, Amoret, and Florimell are archetypes, respectively, of celestial, practical, and sensual natures. Triadic division of these faeries into three basic natures derives from Neoplatonic triadic Venus as explicated by Pico. Iconology of Venus unfolds in three allegorical versions: (1) in Diana, Venus of Garden of Adonis, and Venus of Malecasta's and Busirane's tapestries; (2) in the three faerie women, and (3) in Britomart. Bk. III has triadic structure, three sections of four cantos each: nature of innocent new love; three modes of love; human love rejecting sensuality and accepting "noble loves."

Stirling, Brents. Spenser's "Platonic" Garden, JEGP, 41 (1942), 482-6. 2053

A reply to Josephine W. Bennett, ibid., pp. 53-78. See 2002.

Stroup, Thomas B. *Lycidas* and the Marinell Story, in SAMLA Studies in Milton, pp. 100-13. Gainesville, Fla.: University of Florida Press, 1953. 197pp. 2054

The Marinell story is one of the sources of the extensive sea-imagery in Lycidas. Milton's reading of this story in FQ had sunk to the bottom of his unconscious mind, but it rose to the surface in the process of poetic creation. "One finds most of the suggestive materials in III. iv. but a few as Spenser returns to the story in III. viii and IV. xi-xii."

Taylor, A. B. Britomart and the Mermaids: A Note on Marlowe and Spenser, N&Q, 18.(1971), 224-5. 2055

Discusses relationship between similar mermaid episodes in Hero and Leander, II, 161-64, and FQ, III, iv. Marlowe's mermaids in their scorn of shipwrecked treasure parody Britomart's scorn of Marinell's treasure (iv, 18).

Thompson, Claud A. Spenser's "Many Faire Pourtraicts, And Many a Faire Feate," SEL, 12 (1972), 21-32. 2056

Sp's illusion of vividness and vivacity in the tapestries of FQ, III; i, 34-38 and xi, 28-46 not created through graphic detail but through rhetorical devices, especially figures of pathos: exclamation, apostrophe, interrogation, parenthesis. Reader accepts narrator's wondering response.

Tillyard, E. M. W. The Action of Comus, E&S, 28 (1942), 22-37. Reprinted in Studies in Milton (London: Chatto & Windus, 1951), pp. 82-99. 2057

The 1637 addition to the epilogue, with its reference to Sp's account of the Garden of Adonis (FQ, III, vi), changes the meaning of the poem and decides the debate between Comus and the Lady. Milton's readers, because of their familiarity with Sp, would be alert to the allegory intended. "The play concerns chastity and the Lady is the heroine. Comus advocates incontinence, Acrasia; the Lady advocates abstinence [Belphoebe]. The Attendant Spirit gives the solution, advocating the Aristotelian middle course, which for the Lady is the right one; and it is marriage [Amoret]." Phineas Fletcher's Purple Island and Jonson's Pleasure Reconciled to Virtue brought into the discussion.

Weld, J. S. The Complaint of Britomart: Wordplay and Symbolism, PMLA, 66 (1951), 548-51. 2058

Britomart's lament (FQ, III, iv, 8-10), far from being merely an elaboration of a stereotyped conceit, is a highly relevant and closely-wrought comment on her state of mind at this point.

Wells, Minnie E. "The Eve of St. Agnes" and "The Legend of Britomartis," MLN, 57 (1942), 463-5. 2059

Keats borrowed from the Britomart story certain references to musical effects, the story of the nurse, Madeline's awakening scene, and some other sentences and ideas.

THE FAERIE QUEENE: BOOK IV

Anderson, Judith H. Whatever Happened to Amoret? The Poet's Role in Book IV of *The Faerie Queene*, Criticism, 13 (1971), 180-200. 2060

Have too easily assumed that Bk. IV of FQ is disorganized. Meaning may exist despite loose ends, or include them. Disappearance of Amoret at end of canto ix reflects strains present throughout Bk. IV. Her disappearance followed by Temple of Venus (ix) and Marriage of Thames and Medway (x), "two cantos which balance between them the radically opposite techniques and values which have threatened to split Book IV apart." [MLA Abstracts, I (1971), 41.]

Berger, Harry, Jr. Two Spenserian Retrospects: The Antique Temple of Venus and the Primitive Marriage of Rivers, TSLL, 10 (1968), 5-25. 2061

Sp's concept of experience is dynamic, not a static "world picture." He intends to depict characters in development and to show how the phases are projected on the environment: his "world picture" is an evolutionary model of "discordia concors." Detailed reading of FQ, IV, x and xi.

Blair, Seabury M. The Succession of Lives in Spenser's Three Sons of Agape, MLQ, 2 (1941), 109-14. 2062

Suggests that FQ, IV, iii gives allegorical expression to the idea, possibly derived from Ficino or Cicero, that friendship outlives death.

Brink, J. R. The Masque of the Nine Muses: Sir John Davies's Unpublished

"Epithalamion" and the "Belphoebe-Ruby" Episode in *The Faerie Queene*, RES, 23 (1972), 445-7. 2063

Sp's account of the heart-shaped ruby delivered from Timias to Belphoebe by a dove (FQ, IV, viii, 6-7) may reflect an incident in which Arthur Throckmorton, Raleigh's brother-in-law, gave such a ruby to Queen Elizabeth during a masque (probably a presentation of Davies's Epithalamion) at the Stanley-Vere wedding, 26 January, 1594/5.

Buchan, A. M. The Political Allegory of Book IV of *The Faerie Queene*, ELH, 11 (1944), 237-48. 2064

The Medway is Sidney, the Thames is England, the marriage of the rivers (xi) means that the Sidney-Leicester Protestant and anti-Spanish policy is the right policy for the nation. That policy can be carried out only if Essex and Ralegh, its heirs, work together harmoniously. The conflict between Essex and Ralegh (Concord and Discord) is the subject of IV.

Cummings, Peter March. Friendship in the *Faerie Queene:* A Study of Book IV. DAI, 32 (1971), 914A. University of North Carolina at Chapel Hill, 1971. 229 pp. 2065

Friendship for Sp exists not only in the traditional concept of relationships among members of the same sex but also as "the fundamental bond that makes order out of chaos and creates harmony in all human society." Sp develops his concept with tetradic composition: the characters of each canto function in groups of four. Bk. IV is thematically balanced: "True friendship, as seen most profoundly in the relationships of Britomart and Artegall, Amoret and Scudamour, and Florimell and Marinell ... is a *discordia concors* which creates the concord of friendship out of ... discord."

Dallett, Joseph B. *The Faerie Queene*, IV, i-v: A Symposium of Discord, MLN, 75 (1960), 639-43.   2066

Ironically, passages on Até have been thought to show Sp's faulty narrative logic, forgetfulness, and inability to visualize with consistency. Actually, changes which seem to show Sp was self-contradictory are themselves allegorical expressions of the discord Até creates in herself and others.

Emerson, Francis W. The Bible in Spenser's Chaucer. N&Q, N. S. 5 (1958), 422-3.   2067

The continuation of the Squire's Tale (FQ, IV, ii-iii) contains echoes of the Bible.

Emerson, Francis W. The Spenser-Followers in Leigh Hunt's Chaucer, N&Q, N. S. 5 (1958), 284-6.   2068

Hunt's modernization of the Squire's Tale slightly indebted to Sp (FQ, IV, ii-iii), but more to Cambuscan, or the Squire's Tale of Chaucer (1741, 1785) and Spenser's Squire's Tale (1616), reprinted as Chaucer's Pillar (1630).

English, H. M., Jr. Spenser's Accommodation of Allegory to History in the Story of Timias and Belphoebe, JEGP, 59 (1960), 417-29.   2069

Story told in FQ, IV, vii, 35-47; viii, 1-18. Treats allegorical significance of twins, Belphoebe (virginity) and

Amoret (chaste sexual love), and their relation to Timias (protector of both kinds of love). Argues the relevance of the historical parallel, i.e., the triangle linking Queen Elizabeth (Belphoebe), Ralegh (Timias), and Elizabeth Throckmorton (Amoret)—one of the Queen's court ladies, later the wife of Ralegh. See 458, 965, 2072.

Fletcher, Jefferson B. "The Legend of Cambel and Triamond" in *The Faerie Queene*, SP, 35 (1938), 195-201.   2070

Disagrees with the interpretation that friendship is really championed in the legend. Views Book IV as a story without a hero.

Flint, M. K., and E. J. Dobson. Weak Masters, RES, 10 (1959), 58-60.   2071

Interprets Shakespeare's *masters* (The Tempest, V, i, 41) and Sp's *maysters* (FQ, II, vii, 1) as a form of the obsolete *mister*, from Latin *ministerium*, meaning "instrument or tool employed in the exercise of a craft or skill." This relates *master* and *minister* and explains confusing uses of both words.

Gilbert, Allan H. Belphoebe's Misdeeming of Timias, PMLA, 62 (1947), 622-43.   2072

Skeptical discussion of the attempts to interpret the passages in FQ on relations between Timias-Amoret-Belphoebe (IV, vii, 35-47; viii, 1-18) as an allegory of relations between Sir Walter Ralegh-Elizabeth Throckmorton-Queen Elizabeth (see 458, 965, 2069). Reminds us that "the critic of *The Faerie Queene* must not forget that romantic action is the life of the poem. Though Timias may be Sir Walter Ralegh for many verses or for few or for none at all, he is continuously akin to Lancelot, a hero of chivalrous romance."

Green, Charles H. Sir John Salisbury as Spenser's Timias, TxSE, 31 (1952), 27-34. 2073

Believes Sir John Salisbury's disgrace and reconciliation with Elizabeth are allegorized in Sp's story of Timias and Belphoebe (FQ, IV, vii and viii), as well as in Robert Chester's Love's Martyr (1601).

Henley, Pauline. Spenser's "Stony Aubrian," TLS, Nov. 28, 1936, p. 996. 2074

Identifies Sp's river (FQ, IV, xi, 41) with the Bray-Dargle. See 2082.

Hieatt, A. Kent. Scudamour's Practice of *Maistrye* upon Amoret, PMLA, 77, (1962), 509-10; repr. in 756. 2075

Absolves Amoret of blame placed upon her by Roche (2049) for confusing marriage with adulterous love. Scudamour is to blame for abduction of Amoret from Temple of Venus (FQ, IV, x), exerting his "mastery" over her, in the Chaucerian sense.

Huckabay, Calvin. The Structure of Book IV of *The Faerie Queene*, SN, 27 (1955), 53-64. 2076

Sees the Friendship of Book IV as a Christian virtue rather than a pagan or secular one. The structure of the book parallels that of Book I: in the first half the forces inimical to the virtue receive chief emphasis, while in the second half the forces supporting the virtue gather strength; this movement culminates in the triumph of Concord, as Book I does in the triumph of Holiness. Emphasizes the role of Arthur: "If Book IV has a hero, it is Prince Arthur."

Mills, Laurens J. One Soul in Bodies Twain: Friendship in Tudor Literature and Stuart Drama. Bloomington, Ind.: Principia Press, 1937. 470pp. 2077

Discusses FQ, IV, pp. 226-38. In his treatment of friendship Sp "represents a return to pure Aristotelianism and other philosophical and ethical views," i.e., "he takes the cosmic view of love and friendship."

Nesselhof, John Morrison. Spenser's Book of Friendship: An Aspect of Charity. DA, 15 (1955), 2212. Princeton University, 1955. 152 pp. 2078

Relates Bk. IV of FQ to the "Christian tradition of friendship" and to the mode of Christian allegory which permitted theological interpretation. "Friendship, as Spenser uses it, may be equated with Christian love or charity in all its many forms. Using this premise, the study concludes with an over-all discussion of the thematic unity of the entire book."

Orange, Linwood E. Spenser's *The Faerie Queene*, Book Four, IX, xxx, 5-9, Expl, 17 (1959), No. 22. 2079

On the punning metaphor in the passage.

Parsons, Coleman O. Spenser's Braying Tiger, N&Q, 16 (1969), 21-4. 2080

Spenser's description of the tiger in FQ, IV, x, 46 conveys "the beauty, urgency, and horror of sexual power." For Sp, "bray" may mean "resound," "cry out," "gasp out," "utter," "give forth," depending on modifiers and context. Tigers, however, were not well known either to the ancients or the Elizabethans; the name was given to many large felines. Sp's is perhaps the first noteworthy delineation of a tiger in English literature. [SpN, Vol. 1, No. 2 (1970), 6.]

Smith, Charles G. Spenser's Theory of Friendship. Baltimore: Johns Hopkins Press, 1935. 74pp. 2081

Listed in Atkinson, p. 102.

Smith, Roland M. Spenser's "Stony Aubrian," MLN, 59 (1944), 1-5.   2082

Identifies the "stony Aubrian" (FQ, IV, xi, 41) with the Arlo in Ireland. See 2074.

Staton, Walter F., Jr. Raleigh and the Amyas-Aemylia Episode, SEL, 5 (1965), 105-14.   2083

Episode (FQ, IV, ix) serves dual purpose: establishes love of friend as more important than love of woman, and mildly rebukes Raleigh's pursuit of Queen Elizabeth.

Steadman, John M. The "Inharmonious Blacksmith": Spenser and the Pythagoras Legend, PMLA, 79 (1964), 664-5.   2084

The "sixe strong groomes" whose hammers disturb Scudamour's rest at House of Care (FQ, IV, v, 32-46) derive from legend that Pythagoras discovered harmony by investigations at a blacksmith's forge. "Transformed into a figure of discord, the Pythagorean forge becomes an image of Scudamour's alienation from Amoret and Britomart through Atè's slanders." Revises Steadman's earlier interpretation (2085).

Steadman, John M. Spenser's House of Care: A Reinterpretation, SRen, 7 (1960), 207-24.   2085

Experience of Scudamore in FQ, IV, v, 32-46. Care's attributes reflect conventional conceptions of care or jealousy; the forge, associated with Vulcan and Tubalcain, lends itself readily to theme of jealousy. Also, "forge" means "fabricate," and forge and bellows were medieval symbols of wrath and jealousy. Sp may have been influenced by Varchi's commentary on Della Casa's sonnet on jealousy. Hammer symbol derives from a con-

temporary Italian metaphor for jealousy. The six apprentice blacksmiths may derive from Origen's homily on the sons of Cain. The cock and owl which help disturb Scudamore's sleep symbolize ill thoughts and jealousy, respectively. See 2084.

Stillwell, Gardiner. Chaucer in Tartary, RES, 24 (1948), 177-88.   2086

Unfortunate that Sp, Milton, and Warton have been chief guides in reading Squire's Tale. Milton worst offender in taking it seriously (Il Penseroso, ll. 109-115), and Warton in History of English Poetry influenced by Milton. Sp wrote delightful continuation of Canacee-Cambalo theme (FQ, IV, ii), naturally "quite un-Chaucerian." Theme "is grist for Spenser's very romantic mill," but unsuited to Chaucer's genius. Suggests Chaucer realized this and so left Squire's Tale unfinished.

Uhlig, Claus. Ouroboros-Symbolik bei Spenser, GRM, 19 (1969), 1-23.   2087

Proposes a reorientation of Sp research: the poet's mythopoetic activity "is to be understood in terms of an ability to use a wealth of traditional symbols . . . in ways precisely appropriate to his work, as, for instance, in the great allegorical centres of The Faerie Queene." As a hermaphrodite, the Venus of Bk. IV symbolizes the completeness of worldly love alone and not "the contrast between heavenly and earthly Venus." As encircled by a snake "she also points to the cyclical character of natural life (as displayed explicitly in Garden of Adonis)." Traces the snake with tail in mouth—the Ouroboros—with reference to (1) the period of existence of the cosmos, and (2) the origin of the familiar Boethian contrast between endlessness and eternity. [SpN, Vol. 1, No. 2 (1970), 14.]

Woodring, Carl. On Looking into Keats's Voyagers, KSJ, 14 (1965), 15-22. 2088

The "many western islands" are not the isles of Greece but Pacific islands. Reference to FQ, IV, xii, 22, and Sp's praise of "the warlike Amazons as prologue to chiding the English for the mildness of their rivalry with Spain."

Allen, Don Cameron. A Note on Spenser's Orology, MLN, 61 (1946), 555-6.
2089

The throwing down of mountains (FQ, V, ii, 38) may reflect the belief that at one time the earth was a smooth ball.

Allen, Don Cameron. Spenser's Radigund, MLN, 67 (1952), 120-2. 2090

The Amazon Queen in FQ, V, iv-v and vii is probably patterned after Rhodogune, daughter of Artaxerxes II and wife of Orontes. Sp's description is similar to the portrayals of this Rhodogune by Plutarch and Philostratus.

Anderson, Judith H. Aspects of Allegory in *Piers Plowman* and *The Faerie Queene*. DA, 26 (1966), 4622A. Yale University, 1965. 240 pp. 2091

Uses analogies from intellectual history to define and describe various kinds of persons in both poems. Directs particular attention to FQ, V, because comparison of Piers Plowman with that book is especially fruitful. Bk. V is "the historical culmination of the allegorical concerns, emphases, and problems evident in *Piers Plowman.*"

Anderson, Judith H. "Nor Man It Is": The Knight of Justice in Book V of Spenser's *Faerie Queene*, PMLA, 85 (1970), 65-77. 2092

"Artegall's experiences in Book V reflect both the historic and symbolic poles in the poem: hence they mirror a strain and a more general duality in the techniques and concerns of the Book." [MLA Abstracts, I (1970), 28.]

Aptekar, Jane. Icons of Justice: Iconography & Thematic Imagery in Book V of "The Faerie Queene." New York: Columbia University Press, 1969. 278 pp. 2093

Interprets the iconography of Justice in Bk. V of FQ by correlating thirty-six emblems and pictures with Sp's verbal renditions of these images, and explains their significance in the allegory. Classifies thematic imagery in three divisions: (1) presentation of justice in terms of orthodox Elizabethan concepts; (2) force and fraud; and (3) the Hercules myth. In (1) the monarch resembles God in his role as arbiter and enforcer of justice. In (2) advocates of illicit force are enemies of justice. In (3) are Sp's metaphorical characters based on the Hercules myth. [DA, 28 (1967), 617A.] Rev: R. O. Iredale, RES, 21 (1970), 488; J. Mazzaro, Criticism, 12 (1970), 155; P. Thomson, MLR, 66 (1971), 177; K. Williams, JEGP, 70 (1971), 536; B. E. C. Davis, SN, 43 (1971), 307.

Bache, William B. Spenser and Deloney, N&Q, N. S. 1 (1954), 232-3. 2094

In portraying the attempted murder of Britomart by Dolon (FQ, V, vi), Sp may be drawing on an account, also used by Deloney in the story of Old Cole in Thomas of Reading (written 1597-1600), of a contemporary or traditional crime. Such use of familiar occurrences may have enhanced Sp's popularity in his own time.

Bennett, Josephine W. The Allegory of Sir Artegall in *The Faerie Queene*, V, xi-xii, SP, 37 (1940), 177-200.   2095

Argues for late revision of the last two cantos of Book V, to permit the identification of Sir Artegall with Sir John Norris and of "Good Sir Sergis" with Sir Henry Wallop.

Bieman, Elizabeth. Britomart in Book V of *The Faerie Queene*, UTQ, 37 (1968), 156-74.   2096

Britomart, Sp's "most fully-drawn human figure," is glorified in Temple of Isis. When Artegall falls to Radigund, Britomart must visit the temple before she can rescue him. There she learns both proper restraining effect which mercy exercises upon justice (when Isis subdues crocodile) and (when she accepts crocodile's advances) the properly subordinate role which woman plays in an orderly society: "she is confirmed in readiness to put down what is wrong in woman, to redeem what is good in man. In short, to conquer Radigund for Artegall." In the battle she demonstrates what Artegall has lacked, the ability to be governed by reason and to reject "false woman's wiles." Britomart is victorious because she has "already overcome her internal Radigund by accepting the crocodile within the temple."

Daly, John P., S. J. "Talus" in Spenser's *Faerie Queene*, N&Q, N. S. 7 (1960), 49.   2097

The iron flail of Talus represents "muskets, calivers, cannon, and culverins," firearms adopted recently by English soldiers. Talus symbolizes English soldiers.

Davidson, Clifford. The Idol of Isis Church, SP, 66 (1969), 70-86.   2098

Artegall's Justice, devoid of love and mercy, resembles Mosaic law in its strictness but it cannot perfect society. Hence Talus (Mosaic law) cannot free Artegall from Radigund (FQ, V, v); Britomart's justice, nourished at Isis Church, includes love, mercy, and equity; hence she can free Artegall (V, vii) who learns the lesson and is prepared for Mercilla's court (V, ix).

Dunseath, T. K. Spenser's Allegory of Justice in Book Five of "The Faerie Queene." Princeton: Princeton University Press, 1968. 244 pp.   2099

Emphasizes organic wholeness and thematic integrity of book and its relevance to rest of the poem. Analyzes characters of Artegall and Britomart in commentary on their behavior in Bks. III, IV, and V, i-vii. Demonstrates that myth of Hercules is structural basis of whole of Bk. V. Defends Artegall, a developing character, whose supposed imperfections derive from his status as a public figure, and rejects unqualified praise of Britomart. Chaps.: Introduction, Character and Theme, Humility and Wisdom, Desire and Love, Justice and Peace. [Diss., Johns Hopkins University, 1962.]

Rev: B. E. C. Davis, RES, 20 (1969), 488; Carol V. Kaske, JEGP, 69 (1970), 172; W. J. B. Owen, RenQ, 23 (1970), 323; A. C. Hamilton, CLS, 8 (1971), 163. See 1302.

Fisch, Harold. *Antony and Cleopatra: The Limits of Mythology*, ShS, 23 (1970), 59-67.   2100

Two main characters merge into mythological grouping of greatest significance for Shakespeare's purpose: Isis-Osiris-Set triangle, with Octavius Caesar in a sense functioning as Set (or Typhon). Shakespeare could have known myth from Plutarch's Of Isis and Osiris, since Plutarch's Lives is chief source for play. "He could also have read an account of the appearance of Isis and Osiris in Spenser" [FQ, V, vii, 2-22].

Gilbert, Allan H. A Poem Wrongly Attributed to Sidney, MLN, 57 (1942), 364. 2101

Feuillerat's edition of Sidney's Works (II, 342) contains a stanza from FQ (V, v, 25).

Gillcrist, T. J. Spenser and Reason in the Conclusion of "Salisbury Plain," ELN, 7 (1969), 11-8. 2102

Compares and contrasts final stanzas of Wordsworth's Salisbury Plain with Bk. V of FQ. Concludes that Wordsworth is advocating not actual revolution but doctrinal warfare against the principle of divinely ordained inequality.

Graziani, René. Elizabeth at Isis Church, PMLA, 79 (1964), 376-89. 2103

Britomart's night at Isis Church (FQ, V, vii) can be read as both moral and topical allegory. Topical reading, deriving from priest's interpretation in moral terms of Britomart's dream, identifies her with Queen Elizabeth and allegorizes political situation leading up to execution of Mary, Queen of Scots, including the L'Aubespine assassination plot.

Graziani, René. Philip II's "Impressa" and Spenser's Souldan, JWCI, 27 (1964), 322-4. 2104

The Souldan (FQ, V, viii) represents Philip II of Spain. Sp was familiar with Philip's *impresa*, invented sometime before 1566, showing Philip as a god driving a chariot across heavens and land, representing Philip's belief that it was his mission to spread Christian faith across pagan world. Sp sees Philip's claim as fraudulent, characterizes him in Souldan.

Hall, Louis Brewer, ed. De Casibus Illustrium Virorum, by Giovanni Boccaccio. Gainesville, Fla.: Scholars' Facsimiles & Reprints, 1962. 242 pp. 2105

Reduced facsimile of 2nd ed., Paris, ca. 1520. Intro. cites influence of De Casibus on Elizabethan drama, Sidney's Defence of Poesy, and FQ, V.

Hulbert, Viola B. The Belge Episode in *The Faerie Queene*, SP, 36 (1939), 124-46. 2106

Defends Sp's allegorical portrayal of Leicester's campaign in the Low Countries in FQ, V, x and xi because, although it may be a distortion of history, it is not inconsistent with contemporary views of the campaign. Sp's account conforms to and reflects the view of Leicester himself, of the Queen, and of the Dudley faction at court.

Hulbert, Viola B. Spenser's Talus Again, PQ, 15 (1936), 413. 2107

Refers to John W. Draper's note on Sp's source for Talus, Spenser's Talus Again, ibid., pp. 215-7 (listed in Atkinson, p. 87), pointing out that his suggestion and information are in Alfred B. Gough's ed. of FQ, V (Oxford, 1918), p. 171.

Iredale, Roger O. Book Five of Spenser's *Faerie Queene:* Justice and her Enemies and the Coherency of the Imagery. Doctoral diss., University of Reading, 1959. ITGBI, 9 (1958-1959), Item 154. 2108

Relates Bk. V to the general background of ideas available to Sp when he wrote it. This book "seems, far more than the other books of *The Faerie Queene* to be devoted to a systematic treatment of the virtue around which it is supposed to be constructed—justice." Three episodes given particular attention: "Artegall's argument with the philosopher-giant, the reception of the two knights at Mercilla's court, and the visit of Britomart to the temple of Isis." First of these concerns "the nature of justice and its relationship to the harmony of the universe." The Mercilla episode shows how she deals out justice and mercy to her subjects. "The Isis episode, the allegorical centre of the whole book, sums up in mythological terms all the themes which Spenser has presented."

Iredale, Roger O. Giants and Tyrants in Book Five of *The Faerie Queene*, RES, 17 (1966), 373-81.   2109

Giants and tyrants in Bk. V of FQ can be traced to classical literature, but Sp uses them to represent Roman Catholics in political allegory.

Isler, Alan D. Sidney, Shakespeare, and the "Slain-Notslain" UTQ, 37 (1968), 175-85.   2110

Revolt of the rabble and their slaughter in Bk. II of Sidney's Arcadia was meant to be read as comedy; this technique allowed the rabble to be "slain—not—slain," a situation precluding sympathy in the reader. Offers analogies with mob scenes in Shakespeare and with Talus' massacre of the multitude in Bk. V of FQ. Sp, like Sidney, seems to be offering some humor in his description of the slaughter (V, ii, 51-3; V, vii, 35).

Kahin, Helen Andrews. Controversial Literature about Women: A Survey of the Literature of this Type with Special Reference to the Writings of the English Renaissance. Doctoral diss., University of Washington, 1934. UWAT, 2 (1937), 575-8.   2111

Concludes that under the beneficent influence of Elizabeth the literary discussion of women, which had drawn from the Neoplatonism of Renaissance Italy, attained new vitality.

Kawanishi, Susumu. Simplicity and Complexity in *The Faerie Queene:* An Analysis of The Temple of Isis, SELit, 49 (1972), 17-29.   2112

Episode at Temple of Isis is "allegorical core" which illustrates Sp's varied methods. Change of Isis from equity to "clemence," and of crocodile from malign force to Artegall and Justice (in Britomart's dream) is new vision of justice that causes reader to re-define this virtue. Sp's ability to show justice working on different planes comes from his belief in order and unity of universe. [SpN, Vol. 4, No. 3 (1973), 7]

Knight, W. Nicholas. The Narrative Unity of Book V of *The Faerie Queene:* "That Part of Justice Which Is Equity," RES, 21 (1970), 267-94.   2113

Elizabethan principles of equity provide a framework for the analysis of Bk. V. "Thus as Artegall gains familiarity with procedures in equity under the successive tutelage of the several female figures, he overcomes his vindictive use of the law, and, without falling victim to ineffectual pity, applies the notions of compassion, *misericordia*, and moderation to his judicial discretion." [MLA Abstracts, I (1970), 28-9.]

Langenfelt, Gösta. "The Noble Savage" until Shakespeare, ES, 36 (1955), 222-7.   2114

Cites Sp on Golden Age (FQ, V, Proem). He may have known what Montaigne and Boccaccio said on this theme, and of course he knew the classics (pp. 226-7).

Lievsay, John L. An Immediate Source for *Faerie Queene*, Book V, Proem MLN, 59 (1944), 469-72.   2115

Cites parallels with Loys Le Roy's Of the Interchangeable Course, or Variety of Things in the Whole World

(London, 1594), a translation by Robert Ashley.

Lopach, John A. Educative Allegory: Poet and Reader in *The Faerie Queene*, V. DAI, 30 (1970), 4951A. University of Notre Dame, 1969. 433 pp.   2116

The reader, through the relationship with the poet precipitated by "educative allegory," is himself assimilated to the status of poet. This process occurs in stages "which can be explained by paradigms such as the four degrees of the Neo-Platonic virtues, the traditional threefold soul and its four pre-rational and rational cognitive powers, and the three standard topics by which Renaissance thinkers analyzed Justice—the virtue which is Spenser's subject in Book V." Traces process in which poet "educates" reader toward a full, reflective understanding of Justice in Bk. V.

Lowers, James K. Mirrors for Rebels: A Study of Polemical Literature Relating to the Northern Rebellion 1569. Berkeley: University of California Press, 1953. 130 pp.   2117

Sp in FQ, Bk. V, and Samuel Daniel in Civil Wars introduced same arguments against civil disobedience used by government polemists in ballads, tracts, and pamphlets relating to Northern Rebellion of Catholics in 1569. In five episodes of Bk. V Sp stresses belief royal power derives from God, in two appeals to law of nature to discredit agitators, in three inveighs against traitors, in five warns that no disobedient subject deserves clemency. In three of the episodes he refers to the Northern Rebellion (pp. 80-7).

McNeir, Waldo F. The Behaviour of Brigadore: *The Faerie Queene*, V, 3, 33-34, N&Q, N. S. 1 (1954), 103-4.   2118

Suggests that Sp takes ideas from Ariosto and Montaigne for the actions of Brigadore toward strangers; from Elizabethan horsemanship and Sidney for Guyon's controlling Brigadore by gentle means; and from an incident in Heliodorus' Ethiopian History for Brigadore's response to Guyon. Sp thus combines suggestions from his reading with his own experience to produce an original and dramatic effect.

Male, Roy R., Jr. Toward *The Waste Land:* The Theme of *The Blithedale Romance*, CE, 16 (1955), 277-83, 295.   2119

Both Hollingsworth in Hawthorne's novel and Robert Penn Warren's Willie Stark in All The King's Men, whose original name was Willie Talos, owe something to Sp's "blank-eyed groom, the brutal servant of justice," i.e., Talus, FQ, V.

Milligan, Burton. Spenser's Malengin and the Roguebook Hooker, PQ, 19 (1940), 147-8.   2120

Malengin in FQ, V, ix is endowed with characteristics of the lowest Elizabethan rogue, the hooker.

Murphy, Mallie John. Hamlet's "Sledded Polack," N&Q, N. S. 3 (1956), 509.   2121

Argues for the unemended "studded pollax," citing a parallel usage in FQ, V, xii, 14.

Neill, Kerby. Spenser on the Regiment of Women: A Note on *The Faerie Queene*, V, v, 25, SP, 34 (1937), 134-7.   2122

Sp's attack on the rule of women, an apparent incongruity in a poem glorifying Queen Elizabeth, refers to the lively issue of Mary Stuart's right to the succession.

Nelson, Herbert B. Amidas v. Bracidas, MLQ, 1 (1940), 393-9.   2123

Discusses maritime law in relation to Artegall's award of a treasure chest cast up by the sea to Bracidas (FQ, V, iv). Justice is done by ignoring the law and applying the principles of equity.

Nelson, William. Queen Elizabeth, Spenser's Mercilla, and a Rusty Sword, RN, 18 (1965), 113-7.   2124

Mercilla's rusty sword (FQ, V, ix, 30) praises power that preserves peace and alludes to Queen Elizabeth's own rusty sword mentioned by Sir John Harington in letter dated October 9, 1601, and by Elizabeth herself in poem she wrote about 1570.

Northrop, Douglas A. The Historical Background of the Concept of Justice in Book V of Edmund Spenser's *The Faerie Queene*. Doctoral diss., University of Chicago, 1966. 253 pp.
2125

Chap. I treats historical allegory in each episode of Bk. V, then looks to Elizabethan scene for parallels. Chap. II deals with treatises and apologetics justifying events which historical allegory has presented. Chap. III, Aristotle's treatment of justice, most likely source of Sp's concept of it. Chap. IV considers complex relationships among events alluded to and ideal of justice they construct, and relates Sp's concept of justice to structure of Bk. V. Three Appendixes on supporters of Artegall in administering justice, Sp's political position, and effectiveness of Sp's allegory (pp. 226-45). Selected bibliography (pp. 246-53).

Northrop, Douglas A. Spenser's Defence of Elizabeth, UTQ, 38 (1969), 277-94.
2126

Sp's praise of Elizabeth in FQ, V arose especially from the need for polemic literature to combat the Spanish-Catholic menace. Bk. V illustrates the queen's justice through the high courts, martial law, her just claim to sovereignty, her protection

of the loyal and persecution (tempered by mercy) of the disloyal, and her foreign relations.

Phillips, James E. Renaissance Concepts of Justice and the Structure of *The Faerie Queene*, Book V, HLQ, 34 (1970), 103-20; repr. in 756.   2127

Legend of Justice disappoints readers because they fail to find controlling structural pattern in consistent narrative. Controlling pattern is found in rhetorical principles of Invention and Disposition which determined method of analyzing an idea. First six episodes (i-iv) exemplify Justice Absolute, central section (v-viii) deals with Equity, last six episodes (ix-xii) present in historical allegories Elizabethan concept of Mercy. These three "points" or "places"—Justice Absolute, Equity, and Mercy—used by Renaissance theorists in developing their idea of Justice. [MLA Abstracts, I (1970), 29.]

Phillips, James E., Jr. The Background of Spenser's Attitude toward Women Rulers, HLQ, 5 (1941), 5-32.   2128

The Renaissance controversy over government by women continued long after the death of John Knox, and after the publication of both parts of FQ. The issues were the ability of women to govern (law of nature) and the right of women to govern (laws of God and man). The Catholic supporters of Mary Stuart and the Anglican spokesmen for Elizabeth defended the right and ability of women to govern. Opposed to them were representatives of the Genevan ideal, with Calvin and Bullinger moderate and others more extreme. Evidence to show that Sp was familiar with the controversy and that his own attitude corresponded closely with that of the more moderate Genevans will be presented in a later article; see ibid., pp. 211-34 (2129).

Phillips, James E., Jr. The Woman Ruler in Spenser's *Faerie Queene*, HLQ, 5 (1942), 211-34.   2129

See ibid., pp. 5-32 (2128), for the earlier part of this study. The characterization of Radigund and her government (FQ, V, iv, v, and vii) shows that Sp shared the views of those who emphasized the evils of female rule. That, however, does not make him an uncompromising anti-feminist. Britomart, who overthrows Radigund and her Amazonian system, is the woman called and especially endowed by God; thus a happy exception to the general principle is admitted in the case of Queen Elizabeth.

Phillips, James Emerson. Images of a Queen: Mary Stuart in Sixteenth-Century Literature. Berkeley: University of California Press, 1964. 336 pp.   2130

Important skirmish in "the battle of the books on Mary Stuart" was "the case of James's well-known complaint against the treatment accorded 'himself and his mother deceased' in Canto ix, Book V, of Edmund Spenser's *Faerie Queene*." James tried to have Sp punished for "the highly unflattering and practically unveiled account of his mother in the trial of Duessa before Mercilla." But Sp was not punished. "And, significantly, once [James] . . . was secure on the throne of England, he allowed the portrait of Mary that had at first so offended him to appear in all the editions of Spenser's work published during his reign" (pp. 201-3). For other references to this matter, see Index.

Simmons, J. L. Shakespeare's Julius Caesar: The Roman Actor and the Man, TSE, 16 (1968), 1-28.   2131

Suggests that Cassius's argument to Brutus in Act I, scene ii echoes the egalitarian argument of Sp's Giant of the scales (FQ, V, ii, 30-38).

Smith, Roland M. Spenser's Tale of the Two Sons of Milesio, MLQ, 3 (1942), 547-57.   2132

On FQ, V, iv, 4-20. The quarrel of the two brothers over the treasure chest, which has been supposed to have an English and Roman background, may be based on a hypothetical law case of Ireland.

Steadman, John M. Spenser and the *Virgilius* Legend: Another Talus Parallel, MLN, 73 (1958), 412-3.   2133

A copper horseman with an iron flail, who suppresses wrongdoers, appears in the Lyf of Virgilius (Antwerp, 1518).

Wagner, Geoffrey. Talus, ELH, 17 (1950), 79-86.   2134

Argues against the interpretation of Talus as "a blind instrument of a certain kind of justice, and—as such—a caricature of Grey's harsh regime in Ireland" (p. 79). Believes it was Sp's purpose to "vindicate Lord Grey in Artegall, and that he did this in his allegory by showing that it was the method (Talus) not the man at fault, and that the man, indeed, in many ways, was at the mercy of the method" (p. 85).

Wright, Celeste Turner. The Amazons in Elizabethan Literature, SP, 37 (1940), 433-56.   2135

While the Amazons are praised for physical beauty and virtue, they are condemned for their tyrannical nature, cruelty, and warlike disposition. Sp's Radigund (FQ, V, iv-v, and vii) is a good example of these divergent qualities.

Anderson, Judith H. "Come, Let's Away to Prison": Fortune and Freedom in *The Faerie Queene*, Book VI, JNT, 2 (1972), 133-7.   2136

Cantos preceding appearance of the hermit in FQ, VI, v and of Meliboe in VI, ix seem to show fortune subject in some degree to human wishes. Cannibal episode (VI, viii), and destruction of Meliboe's pastoral world (VI, x-xi) show reassertion of uncontrollable and irrational aspect of fortune. Colin Clout on Mt. Acidale signifies the happy union of fortune and human wishes. [SpN, Vol. 4, No. 1 (1973), 7.]

Atkinson, Dorothy F. The Pastorella Episode in *The Faerie Queene*, PMLA, 59 (1944), 361-72.   2137

Finds the basis of this episode (VI, ix-xii) in The Mirrour of Knighthood (1583-85). Does not discount influence of Sidney's *Arcadia* and other possible sources.

Berger, Harry, Jr. A Secret Discipline: *The Faerie Queene*, Book VI, in Form and Convention in the Poetry of Edmund Spenser, ed. William Nelson, pp. 35-75. New York: Columbia University Press, 1961. 188 pp.   2138

Interprets the seeming collapse of the FQ project at end of Bk. VI. Bks. V and VI reflect "the problems of the Renaissance poet trying to make sense of the world around him," trying also to continue his interior journey through Faerie Land amid increasing distractions. This development culminates in Colin's vision on Mt.

Acidale. The poet, as in Sidney's theory, creates a "second nature" and withdraws into it, sees that his creation is good, is in contact with that Idea from which he himself originated: a symbolic intuition of the real. The poet can then accept what he cannot transform, i.e., the brute facts of the "first nature," the world about him. After delighting in the power and freedom of art, the poet can accept the dissolution of his vision. And the poem can return to the Blatant Beast and to its own dissolution.

Bondanella, Julia M. and Peter E. The Deterioration of the Heroic and Pastoral Ideals in Spenser's Calidore and Pastorella Episode: Book VI, Cantos IX-XII, ErasmusR, 1 (1970), 11-7. 2139

The episode is remarkable in that it shows a failure "of the chivalric order to protect the pastoral order when it is threatened by outside forces." The episode shows "a tragic rejection" by Sp "of the possibility of attaining either ideal in this life."

Culp, Dorothy Woodward. Courtesy and Fortune's Chance in Book 6 of *The Faerie Queene*, MP, 68 (1971), 254-9.
          2140

Narrative of Bk. VI reveals courtesy is "a virtue governing relationships with others, especially those in need." Other properties of courtesy reflected in narrative motifs constituting basic structure. "The motif of the interrupted moment of repose underlies the entire book." This motif emphasizes role of fortune, as in Greek romance more than in chivalric romance; "fortune's chance" important in Aethiopica, in Daphnis and Chloe, and in Clitophon and Leucippe. Examines motif of interrupted moment of repose in stories of three pairs of lovers: Aladine and Priscilla, Calepine and Serena, Calidore and Pastorella. See 2141.

Culp, Dorothy Woodward. The Bands of Civility: A Study of Spenser's Theory of Courtesy. DA, 28 (1967), 1392A. Columbia University, 1967. 260 pp.
2141

In FQ, VI, Sp draws together (1) qualities vaguely associated with courtesy in Renaissance conduct books and (2) "duties that form part of justice as a general moral virtue toward others," and delineates thereby a comprehensive area of action toward others. Also, Sp explains in episodes of Bk. VI the relation between natural inclination to seek good of others and ability to know what duties are appropriate in each situation. Duties of courtesy are directly exemplified; but discourtesy is presented metaphorically through romantic narrative, which conveys the disdain which is willing to use or even destroy others to achieve its own end. Further, Sp demonstrates through romance patterns that all men are subject to misfortune and are therefore dependent on the courtesy of others. See 1327, 2140.

Evans, Maurice. Courtesy and the Fall of Man, ES, 46 (1965), 209-20.   2142

Sp's conception of courtesy in Bk. VI of FQ is based on Christian ideal of mercy. Courtesy exists to repair ruin of fallen and mutable world. Calidore is a Christ-figure; his rescue of Pastorella central to entire poem.

Finley, Thomas Peter. The "Faire Patterne": An Analysis of Book Six of Edmund Spenser's Faerie Queene. DAI,

33 (1972), 2324A. University of Washington, 1972. 193 pp.   2143

Sp in creating pattern for Bk. VI disinclines his reader from the very modes he had encouraged earlier in the poem by attacking allegorical modes of thinking and belittling hero's role. By this process he discovers a path of virtue for his reader, teaching him to reject allegorical modes of thought which yearn for permanence in a changing world, for scapegoats, and for simple heroic solutions to complex situations. Sp directs his reader away from such desires by concept of " 'cherrying.' That concept is based on the idea of borrow and return of unseizable essences." Calidore's ambiguous victory over Blatant Beast is contrasted with the "joining joy" caused by recovery of a foundling, which "describes that concept [cherrying] admirably. . . . Spenser terms that joining joy a 'perfect forme,' and the reader can see in it the completion of the 'faire patterne' " which Sp sought in Proem to Bk. VI.

Fukuda, Shôhachi. Calidore no Vision: Spenser no reisetsukan (Calidore's Vision: Spenser's Idea of Courtesy), Critica, 14 (1968), 2-20.   2144

Geller, Lila. The Acidalian Vision: Spenser's Graces in Book VI of The Faerie Queene, RES, 23 (1972), 267-77. 2145

Sp raises concept of courtesy to the rank of the virtues of other books by suggesting through graces at Mt. Acidale that nobility, a gift of God, is subject to special providence that can lift a humble maiden (4th grace) to the rank of a grace. Extensive use of theosophic lore introduced into Sp criticism by Wind (1211).

Heltzel, Virgil B. Haly Heron: Elizabethan Essayist and Euphuist, HLQ, 16 (1952), 1-21.   2146

Heron's A Newe Discourse of

Morall Philosophie (1579) is a sort of courtesy book for courtiers. Scholars "have been puzzled by Spenser's inclusion of courtesy among his twelve private virtues of the *Faerie Queene*." In the first chapter, Of Humilitie, Heron says a controversy is going on among contemporary poets as to whether courtesy is the right name for the virtue of *comitas*; in any event, it "ought chiefly to be fostered, and dayly practised" (pp. 13-4).

Herron, Dale Susan. The "Triall of True Curtesie": Book VI of *The Faerie Queene*. DAI, 30 (1970), 2968A-9A. Northwestern University, 1969. 231 pp.   2147

FQ, VI is divided into three sections corresponding to three levels of experience. The first, cantos i-viii, provides stories of human failings and weaknesses which are displayed even in Calidore himself. The second, cantos ix-x, includes Calidore's vision of the Graces and the abduction of Pastorella by the brigands, which help to revitalize and resolve the knight's spirit. The third, cantos xi-xii, presents the rejuvenated knight in correlation with Hercules as he performs heroic deeds such as rescuing Pastorella and shackling the Blatant Beast.

Hill, R. F. Colin Clout's Courtesy, MLR, 57 (1962), 492-503; repr. in 756. 2148

In FQ, VI, ix-xii, the Calidore-Pastorella episode, particularly Colin's vision, is key to concept of courtesy. Courtesy, "the outward expression of inner grace," must transcend those hypocritical shows which are generally found in worldly and courtly relations. The pastoral rejection of the worldly provides a natural setting for this process. See 1306.

Hotson, Leslie. The Blatant Beast, in Studies in Honor of T. W. Baldwin, pp.

34-7. Urbana, Ill.: University of Illinois Press, 1958. 276pp.   2149

Demonstrates that Sp's *blatant* (short "a") or *blattant* has nothing in common with the *blatant* (long "a") in use today.

Javitch, Daniel. Rival Arts of Conduct in Elizabethan England: Guazzo's *Civile Conversation* and Castiglione's *Courtier*, YIS, 1 (1971), 178-98.   2150

Partly intended as a corrective to 1523, which is praised. Maintains that Castiglione's ideal of courtliness and Guazzo's ideal of civility were equally influential notions in Elizabethan life, contradictory but not mutually exclusive. Sp hints in opening stanza of FQ, VI "that courtesy is a virtue which reconciles Castiglione's courtliness with Guazzo's civility." Hopes to show at another time how Sp's idea of courtesy represents Elizabethan conflation of both Italian codes. See 2151.

Javitch, Daniel Golbert. Spenser and the Arts of Conduct: A Thematic Background to Book VI of *The Faerie Queene*. Doctoral Diss., Harvard University, 1970. 234 pp.   2151

Introduction (pp. 2-15) says historians of conduct-book tradition, notably Ruth Kelso in The Doctrine of the English Gentleman in the Sixteenth Century (1929), have formulated over-simplified "doctrine" inoperative in Sp's FQ, ignoring progressive modification of values. Spenserian scholars have adopted simplistic view. Chapters on three books influential in later Tudor England. Castiglione's Il Cortegiano (1528) idealized courtly conduct. Philibert de Vienne's Le Philosophe de Court (1547) satirized it. Guazzo's La Civile Conversatione (1574) provided a rival art of conduct. Chap. IV, Spenser's Ideal of Courtesy: *The Faerie Queene*, Book VI (pp. 174-225), discusses Sp's use of all three traditions, ideology and characters reflecting his stubborn idealism and conservatism, increasing disaffection with realities of Elizabeth's court, and adoption of gentlemanly ideal incompatible with FQ, I-III. "By reconciling Castiglione's aesthetic code with Guazzo's civic imperatives, he satisfies the two impulses of his poetry." See 2150.

Knowles, A. Sidney, Jr. Spenser's Natural Man, in RenP 1958, 1959, 1960, ed. George Walton Williams and Peter G. Phialas, pp. 3-11. Southeastern Renaissance Conference, 1961. 110pp.   2152

A paper presented in 1958. The natural world of FQ "is a two-sided world—one side can produce the 'salvage nation' which nearly slays Serena [FQ, VI, viii] . . .; the other side discloses the 'gentle salvage' [FQ, VI, iv] . . . ."

Lerner, Laurence. Sir Calidore's Holiday (Pastoral in *The Faerie Queene*), ESA, 13 (1970), 303-15.   2153

In FQ, Sp creates a tension between (1) the heroic elements and (2) the less pervasive pastoral elements, which depict an assault on the "hierarchical and courtly values of Elizabethan society." This tension is most successfully exploited in the incident at Mt. Acidale (VI, x).

Maxwell, J. C. The Truancy of Calidore, ELH, 19 (1952), 143-9.   2154

In trying "to work simultaneously with the antithesis: 'fidelity of quest versus life of retirement' and 'court versus country'," Sp fails to keep the first terms distinct. Confusion of the allegory in Book VI reveals, not a permanent reaction against formal allegory on the poet's part, but difficulty of assimilating Courtesy into the FQ pattern of conflict and quest.

Mortensen, Peter. The Structure of Spenser's *Faerie Queene*, Book VI: Primi-

tivism, Chivalry, and Greek Romance. DA, 27 (1967), 3015A. University of Oregon, 1966. 234 pp.   2155

Unlike such urban-oriented conduct books as Castiglione's Courtier, action of Bk. VI is displayed against a wilderness or pastoral setting, and includes Salvage Man, cannibals, and brigands. "Courtesy is both a spiritual or natural and a civil or artful virtue in the *Faerie Queene*," and Bk. VI explores these through primitivism and chivalry. Cultural primitivism used to explore spiritual quality of courtesy or discourtesy on which nurture or civil war works; "the virtue of courtesy treats the relationship between nature and nurture." Chivalry is a metaphor for "civil discipline of courtesy," human reflection of a divinely ordered universe. FQ, VI, has 3 sections, first chivalric, other two romantic and pastoral as well. Romance tradition brought together chivalry and pastoralism and explored nature and art. Bk. VI analyzes both nature and art of courtesy, finds they are "complementary and mutually enhancing."

Neely, Carol Thomas. Speaking True: Shakespeare's Use of the Elements of Pastoral Romance. DAI, 30 (1970), 3433A-4A. Yale University, 1969. 226 pp.   2156

In Chap. 1 examines elements central to genre: characteristic story and structure, two communities, landscape, and lovers. Reconciliation of conflicting elements is important theme and major structural problem of genre. Argues that Sidney's two Arcadias and Sp's FQ, Bk. VI, are structurally and thematically unresolved. Neither characters in works nor works themselves achieve integration. Shakespeare explored possibilities of genre in The Two Gentlemen of Verona, Love's Labor's Lost, Midsummer Night's Dream, and As You

Like It, achieved full integration and culmination of Renaissance pastoral romance in The Winter's Tale.

Nestrick, William V. The Virtuous and Gentle Discipline of Gentlemen and Poets, ELH, 29 (1962), 357-71.   2157

Bk. VI of FQ traces development of conflict between freedom and discipline on three levels. (1) Persona's attitude toward this conflict is characterized by the poet's struggle to discipline himself to work within rigid allegorical structure to which he is committed. (2) Dramatization of this conflict is operative in encounter between Calidore and Colin. (3) Conflict is resolved on allegorical level by reconciling nature of true courtesy with means by which it is nurtured.

Neuse, Richard. Book VI as Conclusion to The Faerie Queene, ELH, 35 (1968), 329-53; repr. in 644 and 756.   2158

The disillusionment apparent in Bk. VI rounds off and completes a development in the earlier books. The failure of Calidore to achieve true courtesy dramatizes Sp's conviction that the "potential ideal which his epic was designed to embody has been defeated by a world hopelessly antagonistic to its realization." Thus Sp's epic enterprise has reached its limits.

Staton, Walter F., Jr. Italian Pastorals and the Conclusion of the Serena Story, SEL, 6 (1966), 35-42.   2159

Focuses on FQ, VI, viii. More important than analogue in Achilles Tatius's Clitophon and Leucippe for story of intended sacrifice of Serena by the cannibals and her rescue are intermediary sources such as Sannazaro's Arcadia, Agostino Beccari's Il Sacrificio, Guarini's Il Pastor Fido, Tasso's Aminta, and Antonio Ongara's Alceo, which contribute many details. Point of cannibal episode is to have Serena recognize that true courtesy overrides formal courtesy, and her silence because of her nakedness when Calepine rescues her is unbecoming.

Tayler, Edward William. Nature and Art in Renaissance Literature, New York: Columbia University Press, 1964. 225 pp.   2160

Traces emergence in classical and medieval times of distinction between Art and Nature, opposing views on relative goodness of the two, and opposing views on Nature and the natural. Sp's attitude best set forth in FQ, VI, where dance of graces (canto x) images gifts of Nature perfected by Art. Bk. VI full of contrasts between brutish and benign Nature. Courtesy depends both on gifts of Nature and discipline of Art; Nature and Art themselves both ambiguous, both capable of fostering brutishness or courtesy (pp. 102-20). [DA, 21 (1961), 2279-80.]
Rev: S.K. Heninger, Jr., RN, 18 (1964), 338; Anne Paolucci, CL, 18 (1966), 87; Dean Frye, ShakS, 2 (1966), 296.

Thompson, Phyllis Josephine. Archetypal Elements in The Faerie Queene with Special Reference to Book Six. DA, 26 (1966), 3964A. University of North Carolina at Chapel Hill, 1965. 263 pp.   2161

Jungian reading of FQ, VI. FQ closer to Dante's symbolic allegory than to personification-allegory of Roman de la Rose. Sp uses doubling method: Calidore, Calepine, and Colin Clout all facets of hero-archetype. Their feminine counterparts (anima aspects of heroes), Pastorella, Serena, and Fourth Grace, parallel motifs in Hercules, Orpheus, and Proserpina myths. Wise Old Man archetype illustrated through Meliboe and especially through Salvage Man (natural guidance) and the Hermit (supernatural guidance). Cannibals and robbers are shadow archetype. Blatant Beast a negative aspect of the Great Mother, bringing spiritual stagnation and death. Three categories of archetypal imagery: ordinary psychic experience represented by the forest, morally neutral; brigands' cave presents Hades, dwelling of an evil shadow; Mt. Acidale shows paradise, the memory of lost innocence. Quest plot projects search of soul for God, wholeness through integration of unconscious with conscious.

Tonkin, Humphrey. Spenser's Courteous Pastoral: Book VI of the *Faerie Queene*. Oxford: Clarendon Press, 1972. 329 pp.   2162

The Poetry of Reconciliation (pp. 1-29) introduces FQ in context of Tudor culture, containing twin symbols of Quest and Garden, pastoral pulling against movement; and treats particular qualities of Bk. VI hinted in Proem: poet's voice, levels of ideality and reality, metaphor of flower. Following chaps. analyze Bk. VI in detail: Calidore's Courtesy (cantos i-iii), Forest Folk (cantos iii-vii), Nature Subverted (cantos vii-viii), and The Flower of Courtesy (cantos ix-xii). Next four chaps. link Bk. VI to ideas of Elizabethan period: Courtesy, Nature, Art and Grace, and Courtesy Redefined. Final chap., Pastoral and Myth, reconciles differences between them. "Book VI is the longing and impassioned cry of the idealist faced with the personal problems of day-to-day living in a vicious and none too rewarding world." Book is heavily documented. [Doctoral diss., Harvard University, 1966.]

Rev: A. Kent Hieatt. SpN, 3, No. 3 (1972), 4; R. A. Foakes, English, 21 (1972), 107.

Tung, Mason. Spenser's Graces and Costalius' Pegma, EM, 23 (1972), 9-14.
                                     2163

Supports 1611 reading of "froward" in description of dance of Graces (FQ, VI, x, 24, 7) with precedent for reversal of traditional movement of dance in Costalius's Christianizing of it. See treatment of Graces in Wind (1211).

Voss, Anthony Eden. The Search for Words: The Theme of Language in Four Renaissance Poems. DAI, 28 (1968), 3690A-1A. University of Washington, 1967. 170 pp.   2164

Four essays exploring poetic and verbal self-consciousness in Astrophel and Stella, FQ, VI, Troilus and Cressida, and The Anniversaries. Chap. I examines implications of the linguistic medium. Remaining chapters consider the individual poems. Sp in FQ, VI, "while recognizing how much courtesy and poetry have in common, must eventually dismiss courtesy or accept a limited view of his own poetic function."

Wade, Clyde G. Comedy in Book VI of *The Faerie Queene*, ArlQ, 2 (1970), 90-104.   2165

Disagrees with Arnold Williams's opinion (2166) that comedy in Bk. VI of FQ is of satiric sort. Pastoral episodes (cantos ix-xii) provoke laughter not satiric but joyful because comedy is festive. It derives from myth and Saturnalia; folk rituals of England provide equivalent of materials Aristophanes found in fertility myths. But Pastorella-Calidore relationship surpasses "anything in older comic traditions." Bk. VI is "a comedy of love." [MLA Abstracts, I (1971), 43.] See 1720.

Williams, Arnold. Flower on a Lowly Stalk: The Sixth Book of the Faerie Queene. East Lansing: Michigan State University Press, 1967. 144 pp.   2166

Analyzes "the whole book from end to end several times successively, once for the narrative line, once for the narrative pattern, once for the thematic line, and so on. Naturally, this procedure involves a good bit of repetition" (p. viii). Chap. I, Narrative: Narrative Line, Pattern, Mode; Chap. II, Theme: Thematic Line, Name and Character, Premise and Anti-Premise; Chap. III, Affect: Sentence, Word, and Stanza, Image and Metaphor, Comedy, Picture and Dream. Concludes that Bk. VI "lacks many of the features often regarded as characteristic of Spenser," e.g., personification and myth. Reason for lack is theme of courtesy, "a lowly virtue." Most important effect of "the de-emphasis of the most visible bearers of allegory is the emergence into full importance of the narrative mode and pattern."

Rev: Kathleen Williams, RenQ, 21 (1968), 489.

Williams, Kathleen. Courtesy and Pastoral in *The Faerie Queene*, Book VI, RES, 13 (1962), 337-46.   2167

"Natural" courtesy" (which encompasses order, love, human devotion, eternal joy and supernatural benevolence) best portrayed through "naturalness" of pastoral as presented in Calidore episode (FQ, VI, ix-xii). See 1741.

THE FAERIE QUEENE: BOOK VII

Allen, Don Cameron. On the Closing Lines of *The Faerie Queene*, MLN, 64 (1949), 93-4.   2168

Defends the unemended "Sabaoths sight." Sp's conclusion may be a prayer for admission to heaven: that the God of ultimate repose (Sabbath) may grant him a "God's eye view" of the Hosts (Sabbaoth) as He sees them.

Barker, William. Three Essays on the Rhetorical Tradition. DAI, 29 (1969), 2700A. Brandeis University, 1968. 151 pp.   2169

First two essays discuss ancient and Renaissance rhetorical traditions. Third examines Sidney's Old Arcadia against this background. From classical theorists Renaissance inherited an ambivalent attitude toward rhetoric: faith in words and fear of their deceptiveness; all learning is vanity, yet principles of rhetoric are vital to political order. Comedy of Old Arcadia is that the characters, however rhetorically brilliant in addressing one another, do not know, as narrator and reader do, that "a Logos beyond words is ordering their world." Grand forensic display at end is presided over by a model Aristotelian judge; yet even he can not see the truth, and the resolution comes through Providence. This parallels conclusion of Sp's Mutabilitie Cantos, where the elaborate argument is settled by an appeal to truth beyond the scope of argument.

Blissett, William. "Spenser's Mutabilitie," in Essays in English Literature from the Renaissance to the Victorian Age Presented to A. S. P. Woodhouse, 1964, ed. Millar MacLure and F. W. Watt, pp. 26-42; repr. in 756. Toronto: University of Toronto Press, 1964. 339 pp.   2170

Regards Cantos of Mutability as "retrospective commentary" on whole FQ, as well as affiliated with SC, Complaints, Daph, and View. At various levels of allegory Mutability embodies vain presumption, Marlovian overreacher, destructive change. Analyzes progress of cantos: strident intruder in palace of Cynthia, akin to "malcontent" type; ironic victor in argument with Jove, as woman akin to Erasmus's Folly; relaxed mythological digression; appeal to Nature, related to goddess in Garden of Adonis and Temple of Venus, with processional pageant of seasons, its order implicitly refuting Mutability's claim. Nature's decision calm and joyful, not escape into eternity but acceptance of both worlds, Mutability's and Gloriana's.

Chapman, Raymond. Fortune and Mutability in Elizabethan Literature, CamJ, 5 (1952), 374-80, 382.   2171

Discussion of various attitudes toward the relative importance—cosmic and human—of Fortune, Nature, and Mutability in Sp (Mutability Cantos), Shakespeare, and other Elizabethan writers.

Danby, John F. Shakespeare's Doctrine of Nature: A Study of *King Lear*. London: Faber and Faber, 1961. 234 pp.   2172

Repr. of 1949 ed. In chapter on The Malignant Nature of Hobbes, Edmund and the Wicked Daughters, quotes FQ, VII, viii, 5-6 (Nature is a goddess who may have either a woman's head or a lion's) as illustrating ambivalent attitude toward nature prevalent in Renaissance, and close to malignant nature of Edmund. In View, Sp agrees with Edmund's disbelief in astrology (pp. 35-8).

Edwards, Jean M. Spenser and his Philosophy, CamJ, 4 (1951), 622-8.   2173

On Sp's treatment in the Mutability Cantos of the problems of change, time, eternity, and the destiny of the creation.

Fish, Stanley E. Nature as Concept and Character in the "Mutabilitie Cantos," CLAJ, 6 (1963), 210-5.   2174

Neither Jove nor Mutabilitie but Nature has the dominant role in the Cantos. Mutabilitie's claims equate motion with decay, but Nature suggests movement toward perfection. Nature decides "neither for Jove nor Mutabilitie but for a God of whose existence she is the sole manifestation."

Friedland, Louis S. Spenser's Sabaoth's Rest, MLQ, 17 (1956), 199-203.   2175

Does not believe Sp was equivocating in closing lines of FQ. They are fundamental to an understanding of Sp's Christian-Platonist faith and philosophy. "The concept of the Sabbath as 'a figure of the blest Sabaoth of eternity' is entertained by Spenser in its twofold aspect: the Christian hope and the Platonist (and Neo-Platonist) idealistic vision."

Gleckner, Robert F. Blake's Seasons, SEL, 5 (1965), 533-51.   2176

Studies relation of Blake's Poetical Sketches (1783) to Sp, Milton, and 18th-century predecessors. His seasonal poems probably derive from Sp's procession of seasons preceding months in pageant of FQ, VII, vii, 28-31; but Blake is more innovator than imitator, e.g., all his seasons are male figures.

Goodman, R. A Reconsideration of the Poetry of Edmund Spenser, with Special Reference to the Mutability Theme. Doctoral diss., University of Nottingham, 1953. ITGBI, 3 (1952-53), 8.
2177

First part reviews Sp criticism from his own day to our own century. Second part re-examines FQ as a Renaissance heroic poem, finds Ariosto's Orlando Furioso Sp's model, concludes that "neither on the plane of its direct meaning nor of its allegorical meaning can it be maintained that The Faerie Queene has a satisfactory artistic unity." Third part seeks to establish a new critical view of FQ. "Using the sensuous quality of his verse as a starting point, and moving from there to a consideration of his love of beauty, which is linked to the important mutability theme, a critical revaluation of Spenser's poetry is suggested which ... shows his development and achievement as a poetic thinker."

Harris, Victor. All Coherence Gone. Chicago: University of Chicago Press, 1949. 255pp.   2178

World's decay as a poetic image traced from Sp to Donne, pp. 118-29. Sp first English poet of Renaissance to use "the concept that the world grows old and weary," in Complaints and in Mutability Cantos. In latter, conflict between change and permanence resolved by balance of generation and corruption, a common argument used earlier by LeRoy and later by Hakewill. "Temperamentally [Spenser] belongs with those who look backward instead of forward" (pp. 119-20). See also Index.

Hawkins, Sherman. Mutabilitie and the Cycle of the Months, in Form and Convention in the Poetry of Edmund Spenser, ed. William Nelson, pp. 76-102. New York: Columbia University Press, 1961. 188pp.   2179

Repr. in 649. Nature's verdict in silencing Mutabilitie is not merely an emotional expression of Sp's desire for permanence but an application of the concept of constancy as a directed motion toward a divinely appointed end. This demonstrated in Mutabilitie Cantos through controlled variety of tone, and especially through directed transience of the cycle of the twelve months. Role of Faunus in relation to Diana shown to parallel that of Mutabilitie to celestial Cynthia and other planetary gods.

Holland, Joanne Field. The Cantos of Mutabilitie and the Form of *The Faerie Queene*, ELH, 35 (1968), 21-31; repr. in 644.   2180

Views various actions of FQ as both a progression in time through the great cycle from eternity to eternity cited in the Mutabilitie Cantos, and a collection of simultaneous events. Most important relationships in the poem are independent of temporal sequence, are "relationships of parallelism and contrast, an association of types and antitypes with one another out of sequence, out of time." The good characters are not only allies but are parts of each other, and so are the bad characters. Characters are also members of "two single perennial and recurrent natures," redeemers or enemies of the Golden Age which was and will be, but which is, in this life, always still to be fulfilled or redeemed.

Jones, Buford. Hawthorne's Coverdale and Spenser's Allegory of Mutability, AL, 39 (1967), 215-9.   2181

Miles Coverdale, narrator of The Blithedale Romance, reveals once more Hawthorne's attachment to Sp and FQ in particular. In his thoughts on mutability, Coverdale "imagined his reappearance before the community in terms of an allegoric figure from" FQ, VII, vii. Also, general setting of The Blithedale Romance shows Sp's influence. But Hawthorne's character is not allowed the hope of eventual immutability that Sp presents.

Kahin, Helen Andrews. Spenser and the School of Alanus, ELH, 8 (1941), 257-72.   2182

Opposes Greenlaw's thesis (SP, 20 (1923), 216-43) that Sp's philosophy of nature, which connects ultimately with the ancient cult of Cybele, rests directly on the Complaint of Nature of Alanus de Insulis. Proposes Lydgate as a link between Sp and Alanus.

Kermode, Frank, ed. The Winter's Tale, in The Complete Signet Classic Shakespeare, gen. ed. Sylvan Barnet. New York: Harcourt Brace Jovanovich, 1972. 1776 pp.   2183

Intro. (pp. 1495-1500). Most important clue to nature of Shakespearean romance in The Winter's Tale is "the greatest works in prose and verse of the period, Sidney's *Arcadia* and Spenser's *Faerie Queene*." Shakespeare used them both, especially Sp. "Marina is his Florimel, Perdita his Pastorella." Like Sp, Shakespeare was concerned with Time as "destroyer and renewer, that which ruins the work of men but is the father of truth. . . . Time only seems to change things because it must renew their truth." Quotes FQ, VII, vii, 48, 2-7. This is the philosophy of The Winter's Tale and of Sp's Mutability Cantos.

Koller, Kathrine. Two Elizabethan Expressions of the Idea of Mutability, SP, 35 (1938), 228-37.   2184

Robert Ashley's translation of Louis LeRoy's Of the Interchangeable

Course or Variety of Things in the Whole World (1594); and John Norden's English poem, Vicissitudo Rerum (1600). Norden plagiarized Ashley's translation but ignored the message of progress in change found in LeRoy's work; he expressed the popular belief in the fatal power of change to produce decay. Mutability Cantos are best expression of melancholy Elizabethan awareness of transitory character of life.

Litchfield, Florence Le Duc. The Treatment of the Theme of Mutability in the Literature of the English Renaissance: A Study of the Problem of Change between 1558 and 1660. Doctoral diss., University of Minnesota, 1935. UMST, 1 (1939), 164-8.   2185

Theme of mutability, as old as literature itself, received its finest treatment in English literature between 1558 and 1660. Surveys medieval heritage and general background of problem in social, political, and economic changes which mark Renaissance itself. Sp importantly related to conclusions of thesis in several ways. He was touched by both native and Continental antiquarianism. He refutes relativistic and materialistic arguments in Cantos of Mutability, explaining motion and mutation within framework of a divine plan. In Garden of Adonis episode (FQ, III, vi) he adopts idea that both matter and form are eternal. Like Sir John Davies, he is primarily a Platonist, his Platonic idealism representing a gradual spiritual development.

Owen, Lewis J. Mutable in Eternity: Spenser's Despair and the Multiple Forms of Mutabilitie, JMRS, 2 (1972), 49-68.   2186

Although last two stanzas of Mutabilitie Cantos seem unprepared for in the depth of their disenchantment, they have been anticipated to some

degree by Nature's failure to answer fully Mutabilitie's claim that superlunary regions are subject to change. Sp was probably aware of the "new astronomy," and in his own treatment of the planets represents them as changeable mythological deities. Also, Diana's verdict in the Faunus episode corrupts the purity and sweetness of Arlo, anticipating corruption of supposed perfection of the heavens. Sp retreats at beginning of canto viii from imperfect trinity of Cynthia (Heaven)-Diana (Earth)-Proserpine (Hades) to perfect, unified trinity of God. [SpN, Vol. 3, No. 3 (1972), 10-11.]

Pellegrini, Angelo M. Bruno, Sidney, and Spenser, SP, 40 (1943), 128-44.   2187

Denies Bruno's influence on Sidney as stated by Frances A. Yates in *A Study of Love's Labour's Lost*, 1936; and on Sp's Garden of Adonis (FQ, III, vi) as stated by Ronald B. Levinson in Spenser and Bruno, PMLA, 43 (1928), 675-81. As for the Mutability Cantos, in Bruno's Lo Spaccio della Bestia Trionfante, Fortuna is charged, defends herself, and prevails as Mutability does. But this does not bring Sp any closer to Bruno's conception of change. His "whole doctrine . . . has little in common with Spenser's conception of Mutability."

Ringler, Richard N. The Faunus Episode, MP, 63 (1965), 12-9; repr. in 756.
                    2188

Episode is "a comic inversion of all the more serious matters by which it is surrounded." In addition, episode repeatedly rejects possibility of Ovidian metamorphoses. It "not only complements but advances the main argument, which is an analysis of the mechanism and scope of mutability."

Ringler, Richard Newman. Spenser's Mutabilitie Cantos. Doctoral diss., Harvard University, 1961. 624 pp.   2189

A detailed exegesis of the Cantos. Takes into account mythology, philology, cosmology, law, rhetoric, Sp's classical and Continental sources (among them Homer, Ovid, Lucian, Hesiod, Du Bartas, and Du Bellay), thus emphasizing the principle of "reinforcement"—use of one detail to evoke myriad of related contexts and relationships without limiting development of the poem to one literary source. Concludes that Cantos are a "vast literary mobile" unified by politico-legal framework, quality of diction, and fact that all incidents, from the Faunus episode to the Pageant of Times, treat some aspect of change. Appendices on Date of Composition and Relation to The Faerie Queene, Rejected Analogues, and The Mutabilitie Cantos and William Basse's Urania.

Shroeder, John. Miles Coverdale as Actaeon, as Faunus, and as October: With Some Consequences, PLL, 2 (1966), 126-39.   2190

Hawthorne's Coverdale may have evolved from Sp's treatment of the three characters in the Mutabilitie Cantos. Sees further parallels between Zenobia and Mutabilitie and the overall themes of The Blithedale Romance and the Cantos.

Stampfer, Judah L. The Cantos of Mutability: Spenser's Last Testament of Faith, UTQ, 21 (1952), 140-56.   2191

Proposes that these cantos were written shortly before the poet's death and form an independent poem

which makes a final integration of his secular and religious ideals. Suggests also that the myth of Faunus and Molanna (FQ, VII, vi, 38-55) refers to Sp's recent experiences in Ireland. Comments on the employment of allegory throughout FQ.

Stockton, Richard Engle. The Christian Content of Edmund Spenser's "Mutability" Cantos. DA, 14 (1954), 1732. Princeton University, 1954. 129 pp.
                                   2192

"The poet intends to show, by means of a *pourquoi* story, how Mutability is the very agent of Divine Providence (or even of Christ Himself), and instead of bringing about men's decay, brings about their salvation."

Waller, G. F. Transition in Renaissance Ideas of Time and Place of Giordano Bruno, Neophil, 55 (1971), 3-15.   2193

Bruno's ideas draw on Lucretius and Epicurus, and also Cusa, but look ahead to immanentist philosophies. His God subject to mutability, world of time not transcended. Nevertheless, interesting parallels between Bruno's 'Spaccio and Sp's Mutability Cantos. [SpN, Vol. 2, No. 2 (1971), 10.]

Woodworth, Mary K. The Mutability Cantos and the Succession, PMLA, 59 (1944), 985-1002.   2194

Identifies the titaness with Arabella Stuart, whose history, including the plots to promote her as heir to the throne, is recounted.

Adams, Marjorie. Ronsard and Spenser: The Commentary, RenP, pp. 25-9. A selection of papers presented at The Renaissance Meeting in the Southeastern States Duke University April 23-24, 1954. Columbia, S. C.: University of South Carolina, 1954. 92pp.　　2195

Similarities between Marc-Antoine Muret's commentary on Ronsard's Les Amours I (1553, 2nd ed.) and E. K.'s on Sp's SC. Both follow the same pattern, defending innovations of the poet, anticipating envious detractors, pointing out need of a gloss to unlock poet's secret meaning, appealing to learned audience.

Allen, Don Cameron. The Renaissance Antiquarian and Allegorical Interpretation, in Medieval and Renaissance Studies: Proceedings of the Southeastern Institute of Medieval and Renaissance Studies, Summer 1968, ed. John L. Lievsay, pp. 3-20. Chapel Hill: University of North Carolina Press, 1970. 183 pp.　　2196

Story of Thomalin, boy birdcatcher in March eclogue of SC who is shot in the heel by Cupid's arrow (an action identified by E. K., in a gloss, as emasculation), derives from Bion's second eclogue via Ronsard's "Un enfant dedans un bocage." In another branch of same legend, bird is not Cupid but a symbol of knowledge which the boy seeks. This second branch of the legend, used by antiquary Fortunato Liceti to explain an ancient gem depicting Cupid as a birdcatcher, an allegorical reading which typifies 17th-century antiquaries' habit of applying to classical art-objects the medieval and Renaissance custom of reading classical texts allegorically. See 2197, 2302.

Allen, Don Cameron. Three Poems on Eros, CL, 8 (1956), 177-93.　　2197

A critique of Spitzer's Spenser, Shepheardes Calendar, March 11. 61-114, and the Variorum Edition, SP, 47 (1950), 494-505 (see 2302). Maintains that Sp's poem draws on the whole line of Eros poems from Bion to Ronsard; it abandons the simple charm of Bion, and draws more heavily on the Renaissance tradition which culminates in Ronsard. The March eclogue, seen in the context of the whole SC, "is at once a gloss on the malady of Colin-Spenser and an apologia for his recantation of love." See 463, 2196.

Alpers, Paul. The Eclogue Tradition and the Nature of Pastoral, CE, 34 (1972), 352-71.　　2198

Eclogue tradition, from Virgil to Milton, shows pastoral not concerned with projection of imaginary worlds, either "soft" or "hard." Pastoral poets concerned with extent to which shepherd's song can reconcile man to realities of his situation. Disagrees with Isabel G. MacCaffrey's allegorical reading of SC (2259), because it sees human fulfillment in terms of transcendence of natural world. Speakers and singers of poem accept their bondage to earth. Sp takes seriously pastoral of youth and spring, and also pastoral of age and winter. Later eclogues present coming to terms with reality, not merely negative disillusionment. Colin hangs pipe on tree in December as traditional act of old shepherd who submits to nature of things. [SpN, Vol. 4, No. 2 (1973), 8.]

Arthur, James. The Arte of English Posie [sic], Baconiana, 27, No. 109 (1943), 191-2.   2199

Comment on article by R. L. Eagle, The Authorship of *The Arte of English Poesie* (1589), ibid., No. 106, pp. 38-41. Says The Arte of English Poesie "is, under a slightly altered name, the same book, the eventual publication of which was announced ten years earlier. I mean *The English Poete*, by 'Immerito' (Spenser? Bacon?)," mentioned by E. K. in Argument of October eclogue of SC.

Austin, Warren B. Gabriel Harvey's "Lost" *Ode* on Ramus, MLN, 61 (1946), 242-7.   2200

Harvey's Ode Natalitia (1575), mentioned by E. K. in the gloss to September of SC, exists in a unique copy in Cambridge University Library.

Bates, Paul A. Elizabethan Amorous Pastorals. Doctoral diss., University of Kansas, 1955. 215 pp. DDDAU, 1954-55, No. 22.   2201

Traces the development of pastoral and establishment of its themes from classical times to Renaissance. "Spenser took up the plaintive note introduced by Googe and made it central. He replaced Virgil's homosexual triangle with a homosexual-heterosexual triangle, treating boy-love for the first time in Renaissance English poetry without invidious comment. He made the role of shepherd as poet and as lover especially prominent. Spenser wrote the first invitation to love in English, and he introduced the pane-gyric in the form of an elaborate blazon in praise of Elizabeth. Finally, by writing a series of eclogues of the highest literary quality he firmly established the principle, already well-known in critical writings, that the young poet should begin with pastoral. He had followed Virgil, and he became, like Virgil, a model for aspiring poets." Discusses Lodge, Lyly, Greene, Fraunce, Barnfield, Shakespeare's sonnets, Drummond, Browne, Wither, Drayton, and others.

Bennett, Josephine W. St. Bridget, Queen Elizabeth, and *Amadis of Gaul*, ELH, 10 (1943), 26-34.   2202

The reference to "S. Brigets bowre" in the July eclogue of SC (l. 43) is to the royal palace at Greenwich.

Berger, Harry, Jr. Mode and Diction in *The Shepheardes Calender*, MP, 67 (1969), 140-9.   2203

E.K.'s three types of eclogue in SC defined in terms of two relations to ideal paradise: recreative belong to those contented within pastoral; plaintive to those like Colin and moral pastors seeking reprehensible escapism; marked stylistic difference between bumbling rhetoric of moral pastors and Colin's highly wrought rhetoric. Above these three is "meta-recreative" position of poet himself. Sp reconstructs innocence of young poet more concerned with medium than world's problems. Integration of natural language of pastors, oriented toward society, and Colin's figured rhetoric, oriented toward art, will lead to mature poetry. [SpN, Vol. 1, No. 2 (1970), 11-2.]

Blenerhasset, Thomas. A Revelation of the True Minerva (1582). Introduction by Josephine Waters Bennett. New York: SF&R, 1941.   2204

First imitation of SC to appear in print. The nature of this imitation discussed, pp. x-xiii. See 2296.

Botting, Ronald B. The Making of The Shepheardes Calender, RSSCW, 5 (1937), 43-61.   2205

Most of the eclogues of SC were written as separate pieces. Here considers the individual eclogues and the way they were welded into a unified group.

Breedlove, Mary Louise. *The Bucolicum Carmen* of Petrarch and its Relations to the *Shepheardes Calender* of Spenser: an Edition with Introduction, Translation, Commentary, and Notes. Doctoral diss., University of Texas, 1941. DDAAU, 1940-41, No. 8.   2206

Text based on edition of Domenico Rossetti (Milan, 1829), "which goes back to the *editio princeps* (Cologne, 1473)." Short essay introduces each eclogue and points to Spenserian analogues. Notes amplify introductions and explain intricate allegory. Primary purpose is to make Petrarch's difficult Latin accessible to English readers; secondary purpose is to compare Petrarch's pastoral series with Sp's. "The analogies between the poets are particularly striking in the field of ecclesiastical satire, for which purpose Petrarch was first to use the bucolic and in which Spenser followed suit."

Bristol, Michael D. Structural Patterns in Two Elizabethan Pastorals, SEL, 10 (1970), 33-48.   2207

Structure of SC and Drayton's Shepheards Garland based on scheme of reciprocal pairing in Virgil's Bucolics. Each eclogue offset by contrasting or complementary one of same type. Offsetting or matching pairs form symmetrical pattern receding from central point. Concentric plan disrupts calendar scheme of SC. Sequence moves from frustration in January, February, and March through agony of Colin in June to vision of wasteland in closing eclogues. Sp dwells on consequences of artistic failure; Drayton explores possibilities of artistic achievement. SC is ironic, Shepheards Garland mythic. [MLA Abstracts, I (1970), 28.] See 2208.

Bristol, Michael David. Structural and Thematic Patterns in Michael Drayton's *The Shepheards Garland.* DA, 28 (1967), 1046A-7A. Princeton University, 1966. 192 pp.   2208

Traces Renaissance theories of pastoral, including E. K.'s in the apparatus to SC, to Servius Grammaticus's early commentary on Virgil's Bucolics. Argues that both the Garland and SC belong to a genre, the formal sequence of pastoral eclogues, modeled on Virgil. In both the Garland and SC the structure is "based on a pattern of reciprocal pairing and symmetrical placing found in Virgil's *Bucolics.*" Drayton's structural program is closer to Virgil's than Sp's is. See 2207.

Brown, James Neil. "Hence with the Nightingale Will I Take Part": A Virgilian Orphic Allusion in Spenser's "Avgvst," Thoth, 13 (1972-73), 13-18.   2209

Reference to "the Nightingale" in August of SC is Orphic allusion, helps understand character of Colin Clout and nature of his tragedy. Sp's description of Colin's condition (ll. 173-82) resembles Virgil's description in fourth Georgic of Orpheus' condition after loss of his love, compares him to nightingale. Sp, imitating Virgil, makes Colin a prematurely failed Orpheus, poet who abandoned civilizing function and retired to "augment" his woe. Both Orpheus and Colin seen as poets able to command forces of nature but unable to control own passions. August in SC important stage in Colin's disintegration. [SpN, Vol. 4, No. 2 (1973), 8.]

Brown, James Neil. Stasis and Art in *The Shepheardes Calender*, MSE, 3 (1971), 7-16. 2210

"The whole action and movement" of SC "is concerned with revealing the poet's superiority to—and possible transcendence of—the static pastoral environment in which he is trapped." Various kinds of stasis result from irreconcilable views of shepherds paired in February, March, May, July, and September. Meanwhile, in spite of Colin Clout's despair, samples of his art in April, June, and August clear the way for him to break the bonds of the pastoral world in November, in which he ascends with Dido to Elysian Fields and "enjoys an otherworldly vision unattainable in the microcosmic temporal pastoral world." In December he dies a sacrificial death as Sp's pastoral persona, enabling the poet to be reborn in the "high heroic form" of FQ.

Brown, Richard Kennedy. *The Shepheardes Calender*, 1579-1611. A Bibliographical Survey. DA, 22 (1961), 858. Fordham University, 1961. 223 pp. 2211

Attempts to determine, through various kinds of evidence, what stands between the author's holograph and the text of each edition. Analyzes four categories of variants: spelling, punctuation, substantive, and typographic. Concludes that only the spelling variants give evidence of any generally recognized standard of usage; that little heed was paid at the time to standards of punctuation; and that the correctors and compositors were careful and intelligent.

Bühler, Curt F. Two Renaissance Epitaphs, RN, 8 (1955), 9-11. 2212

Pierpont Morgan Library MS 691 contains epitaph of Edward de Court-eney, third Earl of Devon (d. 1419). It is a variant of verses quoted by Tristram Risdon in the Survey of Devon (1605-1630); and, as Rudolf Gottfried notes, ibid., p. 118, it appears in SC in the gloss on l. 69 of May.

Cain, Thomas H. The Strategy of Praise in Spenser's "Aprill," SEL, 8 (1968), 45-58. 2213

In April eclogue of SC, Colin's encomium of Elizabeth in two parallel sections: in the first, modeled after Aphthonius's Progymnasmata, Eliza is praised as static icon with Colin as poet-artificer (*poeta*); in the second, static praise evolving into a mobile coronation tableau, stanzas parallel those of first section. Colin becomes visionary persona (*vates*). Colin, like Orpheus, is able to control the world through song.

Cameron, Kenneth N. Cyril Tourneur and *The Tranformed Metamorphosis*, RES, 16 (1940), 18-24. 2214

Interprets the poem as an allegorical tribute to Sir Christopher Heydon. Pan in Tourneur's allegory signifies the Church of England, "in view of Spenser's similar use of 'Pan' in *The Shepheardes Calender* (May Eclogue)" (pp. 19, 22).

Carpenter, Nan Cooke. Spenser and Timotheus: a Musical Gloss on E. K.'s Gloss, PMLA, 71 (1956), 1141-51. 2215

Suggests that E. K.'s knowledge of the myth of Timotheus and Alexander, recounted in gloss to October, l. 27, derives from his reading of musical theorists associated with French Pléiade. One inference from this is that E. K. was a real person, of scholarly temperament and habits, different from Sp. See 2247, 2254, 2255, and 2306.

Collinson, Patrick. The Elizabethan Puritan Movement. Berkeley: University of California Press, 1967. 528 pp.   2216

Only one reference to Sp, in connection with troubled times in Elizabethan church in late 1570's and deprivation of Edmund Grindal, Archbishop of Canterbury, as "Leicester's servant and the poet of his party," who pronounced Grindal's epitaph in SC, "which is itself a veiled pastoral allegory of these events" (pp. 191 ff.). Detailed ecclesiastical history with information about John Aylmer, Edmund Grindal, Thomas Cooper, John Piers, John Young, and other bishops in religious setting of SC.

Cullen, Patrick. Imitation and Metamorphosis: The Golden-Age Eclogue in Spenser, Milton, and Marvell, PMLA, 84, (1969), 1559-70.   2217

Golden Age eclogue represented by Virgil's Eclogue 4 becomes part of pastoral convention in Renaissance. Motifs of nature's harmony, Earthly Paradise, eternal spring, return of peace. April in Sp's SC transforms the genre. Elisa's world is golden age in contrast with iron age of Thenot, Piers, and Diggon Davie. She replaces disorder with order. Colin has failed in mission as poet, but Elisa fulfills her mission as song and harmony. She represents divine artist and divinely anointed ruler; thus art and politics are extensions of cosmic order. Elisa is image of fertility, goddess of love; like Britomart, she reconciles love and virginity. Arrival of Graces signifies ordering of both art and society. In similar manner shows that On the Morning of Christ's Nativity and The Picture of Little T.C. in a Prospect of Flowers are original on pattern of messianic eclogue. [SpN, Vol. 1, No. 2 (1970), 11.] See 2218.

Cullen, Patrick. Spenser, Marvell, and Renaissance Pastoral. Cambridge, Mass.: Harvard University Press, 1970. 212 pp.   2218

Two main strands in Renaissance pastoral: "Arcadian," multivalent, idealistic; and "Mantuanesque," rigid, satiric. Moral eclogues in SC (February, May, July, September, and October) present Arcadian and Mantuanesque perspectives in conflict, showing limitations of both. Rustic debates are comic, leavening conflict. Treatment of Colin's one-sided love of Rosalind has both tragic and comic perspectives. "Colin is a figure of tragic paradox and contradiction," failure in both private and public roles. Elisa in April eclogue is symbol of ideal, golden age, in Sp's "pastoral world of questions and doubts." Eclogues organized into three groups: January to June (spring's triumph over winter), May, June, July (overlapping, transitional), July to December (Dido triumphs in November, Colin perishes in December). Section on Marvell: The Christian Lyrics: Pastoral and Anti-Pastoral; and the Amorous Pastorals (pp. 151-202). [DA, 28 (1968), 3139-40A.] See 2217.

Rev: Rosalie Colie, JEGP, 70 (1971), 538; W. F. McNeir, SpN, 4, No. 3 (1972), 1; A.D. Nuttall, RES, 23 (1972), 480; Isabel G. MacCaffrey, MP, 70 (1972), 161. See 954.

Dipple, Elizabeth. The "Fore-Conceit" of Sidney's Eclogue, LM, 1 (1967), 1-47.   2219

Eclogues in Sidney's Arcadia have been underestimated because they had to compete with "Spenser's great eclogue accomplishment" in SC (1579), witness Hallett Smith's discussion of pastoral poetry (see 1091) (p. 6). As in eclogue tradition established by Virgil and continued by Mantuan and Sp, singers of songs in Arcadia are not rustic innocents but educated men (pp. 9-10).

Driskill, Linda Lorane Phillips. Cyclic Structure in Renaissance Pastoral Poetry. DAI, 31 (1970), 2872A-3A. Rice University, 1970. 406 pp.   2219A

Analysis, interpretation, and comparison of Sp's SC, Drayton's Idea the Shepheards Garland, and Milton's Lycidas. Chaps. II-VI on SC. World view unifies SC, cosmic order presented gradually by tracing historical development of ideas of order and evil. Studies relation of "complex linear order to semantic structure," relations between eclogues and cyclic structure of series, temporal perspectives of various speakers in poem, and Sp's use of calendar form. In Chap. VIII compares structure of Shepheards Garland and Lycidas to that of SC. At end summarizes conclusions about structure and genre.

Durr, Robert Allen. Spenser's Calendar of Christian Time, ELH, 24 (1957), 269-95.   2220

Agrees with Hamilton, The Argument of Spenser's Shepheardes Calender, ibid., 23 (1956), 171-82 (see 2238), that SC has unity of design and subject, but denies that the argument is the rejection of the pastoral life for a life of action in the world. Maintains that the governing subject is the contrast "between the humble children of God and the proud partisans of Lucifer, between the life of the eternal spirit and the death of the transient flesh." The work is grounded in religious, not secular, concerns.

Editor. The Shepherd's Calendar. April Aeglogue, Baconiana, 28, No. 110 (1944), 30-1.   2221

Rebuts Edward D. Johnson's arti-

cle, ibid., 27, No. 109 (1943), 184-8, for making Rosalind in SC Marguerite de Valois. See 2253.

Enkvist, Nils Eric. The Seasons of the Year: Chapters on a Motif from *Beowulf* to the *Shepherd's Calendar*. Societas Scientiarum Fennica, Commentationes Humanorum Litterarum, 22. Helsingfors: University of Helsingfors, 1957. 219 pp.   2222

SC, pp. 171-8. Sp's poem contains little in the way of nature description that is new or reflects personal observation. Its descriptions of the seasons derive from the tradition of such descriptions in Old English and Middle English literature (the major study of this book), and from the older pastoral tradition.

Ettin, Andrew Vogel. Style and Ethics in the Pastoral Eclogues of Vergil and Spenser. DAI, 33 (1972), 1140-A. Washington University, 1972. 235 pp.   2223

Pastoral poetry defines characteristics of favored place, or state of mind. Explores troubles that disrupt tranquility, testing possibility of ideal existence. Vergil and Sp use these thematic characteristics of pastoral in combination with an educative style, which draws reader into poetic world. Sp might have recognized extra-literary lessons Vergil could teach. Vergil's Eclogues create mythic sense of values that save or destroy humanity. Destructive force most often is all-consuming love. Reader becomes central character. Studies techniques inducing reader to accept poet's values. SC similarly directed toward ethical understanding, rather than aesthetic appreciation. January and December set pattern of cycle. In both Colin laments lost love, foresees own death. Love has led him to abandon poetry, engrossed in own problems. We perceive practical and spiritual values of world forgotten, understand what will make life worth living.

Faas, Klaus Egbert. Schein und Sein in der frühelisabethanischen Lyrik and Prosa (1550-1590). Doc. diss., University of Munich, 1965.   2224

Tries to show increasing complexity in treatment of appearance-reality problem in early Elizabethan poetry and prose, caused by growing skepticism toward accepted ideas and institutions. Sees this development in language and descriptive techniques, particularly in increasing use of antithesis and *amplificatio*. Of Sp's works, deals only with SC. FQ as well as Sidney's Arcadia too individual in style and complex in form to be typical, so they are not considered.

Friedland, Louis S. A Source of Spenser's "The Oake and the Briar," PQ, 33 (1954), 222-4.   2225

Cites an analogue of the fable in February in one of the entertainments devised by George Gascoigne for Queen Elizabeth on her memorable visit to Kenilworth Castle in 1575. This is a probable source.

Friedland, Louis S. Spenser's Fable of "The Oake and the Brere," SAB, 16 (1941), 52-7.   2226

Answers Rosenzweig, ibid., 15 (1940), 103-9 (see 2293), denying that the fable in February is based on a passage in Ascham's Scholemaster and has an allegorical meaning.

Friedland, Louis S. Spenser's "Wrenock," SAB, 18 (1943), 41-7.   2227

Rejects previous identifications of Colin Clout's tutor in poetry (December, ll. 37-42), says Sp had no particular person in mind.

Fujii, Haruhiko. "Bokujin no koyomi" no kanka (Otium in *The Shepeardes Calender*), Eigo-bungaku-sekai, 6, No. 1 (April, 1971), 24-7.   2228

Fujii, Haruhiko. Lycidas and Spenser's Pastorals, Hiroshima Studies in English Language and Literature, 19 (1972), 34-50.   2229

Fujii, Haruhiko. Time and Colin Clout, the Shepherd, English Criticism in Japan: Essays by Younger Japanese Scholars on English and American Literature, ed. Earl Miner, pp. 19-29. Tokyo: University of Tokyo Press, n. d.   2230

Originally published in Japanese: Bokujin Colin Clout no jikan kankaku, Kikan-eibungaku, 3 (1966), 171-83.

Galway, Margaret. Spenser's Rosalind, TLS, July 19, 1947, p. 372.   2231

The name "Rosalind" was intended to convey all the ladies, from the Queen downwards, whom Sp wished to address. Finds anagrams in the name.

Gilbert, Allan H. The Embleme for December in *The Shepheardes Calender*, MLN, 63 (1948), 181-2.   2232

Suggests that the emblem for December, missing in the early editions, is the "Merce non mercede" printed by mistake after the gloss and the envoy instead of at the end of the eclogue where it should have been. See 2314.

Gleissner, Friedrich. Die Eklogendichtung von Barclay bis Pope in ihrer Abhängigkeit von griechischen, lateinischen und heimischen Vorbildern. Doctoral diss., University of Vienna, 1936. 134 pp. VdD, p. 69.   2233

Briefly sketches development of classical pastoral form by Theocritus, Bion, Moschus, and Virgil. Then surveys English pastoral poetry from Barclay early in 16th century to Pope early in 18th century, devoting a few pages to each of twenty-three poets. Sp had only two predecessors in the genre, Barclay and Googe. Perfunctory treatment of parallels between SC and eclogues of Theocritus, Virgil, and Mantuan (pp. 25-9), but notes Sp's influence on most later pastoralists, e.g., Peele, Drayton (pp. 32-52), Breton, Browne (pp. 58-66), Wither (pp. 67-75), Fairfax, Phineas Fletcher (pp. 81-97), Basse (pp. 102-8), and Pope (pp. 116-28).

Godshalk, William Leigh. "Ripeness is All," N&Q, 14 (1967), 145.   2234

Although Shakespeare's "Ripeness is all" may have been drawn from Cicero, E. K.'s gloss on emblem to November in SC is more pertinent commentary.

Goldgar, Bertrand A., ed. Literary Criticism of Alexander Pope. Lincoln: University of Nebraska Press, 1965. 181 pp.   2235

Intro. (pp. ix-xxxv) explains motivation and irony of Guardian No. 40 (April 27, 1713). A Discourse on Pastoral Poetry (1704), written when Pope was sixteen, with his qualified praise of Sp's SC and condemnation of his use of "country phrases . . . entirely obsolete or spoken only by people of the lowest condition" (pp. 93-7). The Guardian No. 40, Monday, April 27, 1713, with Pope's ironic praise of Ambrose Philips as "the eldest born of Spenser and our only true Arcadian" (pp. 98-104).

Graziani, René. Verses by E.K., N&Q, 16 (1969), 21.   2236

"E.K." who contributed Latin verses (quoted) to book by Everard Digby on swimming may be "E.K." of SC. Considers Edward Kirke of Caius College, Cambridge, most likely person to have written gratulatory lines. [SpN, Vol. 1, No. 1 (1970), 11.]

Greig, C. Margaret. The Identity of E. K. of the Shepheardes Calender, N&Q, 197 (1952), 332-4.   2237

Suggests Richard Mulcaster.

Hamilton, A. C. The Argument of Spenser's Shepheardes Calender, ELH, 23 (1956), 171-82.   2238

Rebuts the position that SC lacks unity of form and content. The argument is the rejection of the pastoral life for the dedicated life in the world. Sp's calling is that of the heroic poet who serves the Queen by inspiring her people to virtuous action. In terms of the Fall and Nativity, man, by rejecting the snare of the pastoral Paradise, may escape death; by embracing the dedicated life of service he may achieve rebirth. See 2220.

Hard, Frederick. E.K.'s Reference to Painting: Some Seventeenth Century Adaptations, ELH, 7 (1940), 121-9.
     2239

Deals with E. K.'s remarks in his letter to Harvey prefixed to SC. They seem to point to a style of painting he has seen, having no classical authority in Plutarch or Horace. Believes E.K.'s commentary found its way into later treatises on the art of painting, such as Junius's The Painting of the Ancients (1638) and Sir William Sanderson's Graphics (1658).

Heninger, S. K., Jr. The Implications of Form for The Shepheardes Calender, SRen, 9 (1962), 309-21.   2240

Sp employs the calendar form in a new way in SC, form derived from Pythagorean tetrad, later employed by Christian writers, and popularized in the hexaemera. Sp combines it with pastoral eclogue, creating dichotomy between macrocosm of pastoral world and microcosm represented by cyclic unity of calendar form.

Hoffman, Nancy. The Landscape of Man: Spenser's Shepheardes Calendar and the Renaissance Pastoral Lyric. Doctoral diss., University of California, Berkeley, 1971.   2241

Sp's originality in SC in viewing nature not as geographical place but as manifestation of qualities of human life. All nature becomes source of moral and psychological landscape. Mantuan, Barclay, and Marot follow Virgil and make nature a geographical place. In June, Sp's *locus amoenus* a state of mind rather than a site. Sp invites reader's participation as he orders pastoral convention to explore human responses to love, death, and faith. Rejects religious allegory in accord with doctrinal flexibility. In 17th century, England's Helicon, Herrick, Donne, Carew, and Marvell modulate pastoral as it becomes highly self-conscious and metaphysical.

Holborne, Anthony. Complete Works. Ed. Masakata Kanazawa. 2 vols. Cambridge, Mass.: Harvard University Press, 1967.   2242

In Vol. I, Music for Lute & Bandora, ed. gives tablature of and transcribes into staff notation Holborne's Lute Galliard No. 13, "Heigh Ho Holiday," possible tune for Perigot's and Willye's roundelay in August of SC (pp. 122, 223). See 530, 632, 844.

Holden, William P. Anti-Puritan Satire, 1572-1642. YSE, 126. New Haven: Yale University Press, 1954. 165pp.
                                           2243

Sp, pp. 86-93. He is impatient with both the extremes of the left and the corruptions of the right. He "speaks as the reforming Anglican on the ordering of the church and the teaching of the people." See 959, 1177, 1194, 1549, 1800.

Huckabay, Calvin, and Everett H. Emerson. The Fable of the Oak and the Briar, N&Q, N. S. 1 (1954), 102-3.
                                           2244

The fable is meant to show the relationship between the new poetry and the old. Sp adopted new forms and vocabulary, but his poetic tradition depended upon Greek and Roman literature. The new poetry, the Briar, is dependent upon ancient traditions, the Oak. This is consonant with Sp's literary theory, and so the fable is of greater significance than if it were either a political or religious allegory.

Hulbert, Viola B. Diggon Davie, JEGP, 41 (1942), 349-67.   2245

The dialect spoken by Diggon Davie in the September eclogue is that spoken by Welshmen. Identifies the "farre country" from which he comes with Wales, and him with Richard Davies, Bishop of St. David's, 1561-1582. See 2263.

Hume, Anthea. Spenser, Puritanism, and the "Maye" Eclogue, RES, 20 (1969), 155-67.   2246

External and internal evidence suggest Sp supported moderate Puritanism when writing SC, printed by Puritan printer. In May eclogue Fox could be secret papist leading simple Christians (Kid) into superstition with "knacks" and "trifles." Points out several key words in Puritan debate. Sp committed to primitive simplicity.

Hutton, James. Spenser's "Shepherd's Calendar," TLS, May 11, 1951, p. 293.
                                           2247

Cites other occurences of the anecdote concerning Alexander and music (October, gloss on l. 27) in various authors, 1491-1558. See 2215, 2254, 2255, and 2306.

Jablon, Barry Peter. *Politics and the Pastoral:* A Study of the Tudor and Stuart Pastoral Eclogue as a Vehicle for Political Expression. DA, 28 (1968), 4133A. University of California, Berkeley, 1967. 203 pp.   2248

The pastoral eclogue was used as a vehicle for political allegory until the eighteenth century. Surprisingly, political and religious biases remained the same in nearly all eclogues in England between 1558 and 1642; the pastoral remained fixed in allegiance to conservative authoritarianism. Milton's Lycidas was the only revolutionary eclogue. The relation of the eclogue to political affairs was so close that Sp's SC cannot be understood at all without a knowledge of its political content.

Jenkins, Raymond. A Note on E.K., SP, 45 (1948), 76-9.   2249

Reiterates thesis that Sp is E.K. (see 2250, 2251). Holds Mitchner's objections, ibid., 42 (1945), 183-90 (see 2280) to Starnes's argument that Sp is E. K., ibid., 41 (1944), 181-200 (see 2304) inadequate.

Jenkins, Raymond. Who is E. K.? SAB, 19 (1944), 147-60.   2250

Part 1 of a series (see 2251). Amasses old and new arguments to prove that Sp was E. K. Believes "E.K.'s" glosses are part of a publicity campaign devised by Sp and Harvey to advertise themselves. Similar "hoaxes" in Harvey's Letter-Book and in the Sp-Harvey correspondence are in the same category as the "E.K." writings.

Jenkins, Raymond. Who is E.K.? SAB, 20 (1945), 22-38, 82-94.   2251

Parts 2 and 3 of the series begun in SAB, 19 (1944), 147-60 (see 2250). Continues the presentation of old and new arguments that Sp was E. K. Suggests that the disguise or mask of E. K. would have been useful to Sp for various reasons.

Jernigan, John Charles. The Sestina in Provence, Italy, France, and England (1180-1600). DAI, 31 (1971), 6554-5A. Indiana University, 1970. 290 pp.   2252

First sestina written by Arnaut Daniel, not serious love poem but comic sexual satire based on elaborate

series of puns. Examines sestinas of Dante (1) and Petrarch (9). Most of Petrarch's imitators wrote banal sestinas. Pontus de Tyard introduced form to France. Sir Philip Sidney introduced form to England in his Arcadia. Also examines sestinas by Barnabe Barnes and Sp—in August of SC. Sestina was integral part of Petrarchism, poetic movement which swept Europe from 1180 [sic] to 1600.

Johnson, Edward D. The Shepheardes Calender, Baconiana, 27, No. 109 (1943), 184-8.   2253

"Proves" that Francis Bacon, son of Queen Elizabeth and the Earl of Leicester, wrote SC. See 2221.

Johnson, S. F. Spenser's "Shepherd's Calendar," TLS, March 30, 1951, p. 197.   2254

Two early versions of the story, related in E. K.'s gloss on October, 1.27, telling the effects of music on Alexander: in Castiglione's Il Cortegiano (1528), and in John Case's The Praise of Musicke (1586). See 2215, 2247, 2255, and 2306.

Johnson, S. F. Spenser's "Shepherd's Calendar," TLS, Sept. 7, 1951, p. 565.   2255

Following leads of Frances A. Yates, has traced the story of Alexander and music (October, gloss on l. 27) to Basil the Great's homily Ad Adolescentes (4th century A.D.), and believes this is the source of the Renaissance version. See 2215, 2247, 2254, and 2306.

Jones, Francis Whitney. "Base Begot With Blame": The Uses of Language and Convention in The Shepheardes Calender. DAI, 32 (1972), 6429-A. University of North Carolina at Chapel Hill, 1971. 150 pp.   2256

Dual theme of SC is uses of language and convention. Imitation is central aspect of Sp's poetic theory: Virgil for classical tradition, Chaucer for English, and Marot for European. In recreative eclogues Virgil is poet of early love, in moral eclogues Chaucer of moral purpose, in plaintive eclogues Marot is rhetorician skilled in language but incapable of major work. In plaintive eclogues (January, June, November) Colin Clout overcomes self-centered despair and achieves new world-view, but in December too old to write epic poem. October, last moral eclogue, presents epic poet as ideal orator, but neither Cuddie nor Colin Clout can fulfill role. Recreative eclogues deal with adolescent love. SC "is not only about growing old, but it is also about growing up." As a whole it deals with expanding world-view attained with development from adolescence to manhood.

Koller, Kathrine. Abraham Fraunce and Edmund Spenser, ELH, 7 (1940), 108-20.   2257

Fraunce closely connected with Sidney circle of serious literati. Constant allusions to Sp and his poetry, especially SC, by Fraunce show taste of this group and importance they placed on Sp's poetry before publication of FQ. Fraunce's unpublished Shepheardes Logike contains his first use of SC for illustrations of style and models of reasoning. Lawiers Logike (1588) has 97 direct quotations from SC to illustrate terms of dialectics and forms of syllogisms. The Arcadian Rhetorike (1588) pays tribute to Sp as author of SC and FQ. This high evaluation of SC shared by George Whetstone, William Webbe, and Henry Peacham, the Elder. In his poetry Fraunce "follows in theory and practice the literary precepts laid down by Sidney and Spenser."

Larrabee, Stephen A. Bydding Base ("October" 5), MLN, 51 (1936), 535-6.   2258

The phrase does not refer to the game of Prisoners' Base but to the challenge to a competition in verse.

MacCaffrey, Isabel G. Allegory and Pastoral in The Shepheardes Calender, ELH, 36 (1969), 88-109; repr. in 644 and 756.   2259

Sp of FQ evident in SC: complex use of allegory and iconography, develops a form which unifies variety; makes setting a controlling metaphor. In various eclogues explores meaning of human life in contexts of nature, contemporary affairs, and cosmos. Calendrical organization gives cyclical ground plan, this intersected by vertical or linear images such as ladder of poetic inspiration or love. Colin fails to realize own human nature fully, but changes from an "innocent" who equates nature with his plight (January) to man experienced enough to realize separation of man from nature (December). In October and November the poetry takes flight from suffering to joy; here imagination is power—unable to conquer natural death, heal love's wounds, or restore innocence, yet able to open transnatural realm to man. [SpN, Vol. 1, No. 1 (1970), 5-6.]

McCormick, Sister Mary Martin, P.B.V.M. A Critical Edition of Abraham Fraunce's "The Sheapheardes Logike" and "Twooe General Discourses." DAI, 29 (1968), 1211-A. St. Louis University, 1968. 243 pp.   2260

Based on microfilmed copy of only known, never before edited, manuscript, Additional Manuscript 34361, now in British Museum, Fraunce's use of 500 illustrative lines from Sp's SC follows Ramist principles connecting poetry and logic. Choice of Sp's poem to illustrate workings of logic gives The Sheapheardes Logike unique value, since date of the manuscript (ca. 1581-1583) approximates publication date of SC (1579), and Fraunce used this first edition or a manuscript from which it was set; variants are copyist's errors.

McCoy, Dorothy Schuchman. Tradition and Convention: A Study of Periphrasis in English Pastoral Poetry from 1557-1715. The Hague: Mouton, 1965. 289 pp.   2261

In Renaissance pastoral, freedom from rigid prescriptions of mode and language was possible, and to certain extent achieved, without abandonment of rules. Studies periphrasis with a purpose in Sidney's Arcadia and Sp's SC. Sp's use of periphrasis at service of decorum, in vital Renaissance sense, and it helped maintain allegory. E. K. justifies "vehement figures" such as periphrasis on grounds of decorum. Sp maintains level of diction he thinks appropriate to topics of eclogues. In 18th century "decorum has entirely lost any applicable literary meaning," resulting in periphrase without purpose, and narrowed perceptions govern conventional usages of style in pastoral. [Diss., University of Pittsburgh, 1962.]

McLane, Paul E. The Death of a Queen: Spenser's Dido as Elizabeth, HLQ, 18 (1954), 1-11.   2262

Develops Mary Parmenter's suggestion, ELH, 3 (1936), 190-217 (see 2287), that November eclogue signifies the figurative death of Elizabeth, who in 1579 was "dead" to the Dudley-Sidney group because of her plan to marry Alençon. Rejects previous identifications of Dido as Ambrosia Sidney, Susan Watts, and an illegitmate daughter of Leicester. Holds it was possible for November to

have been written after Elizabeth's involvement with Alençon. Lobbin is Leicester and the "greate shephearde," Henry VIII. Notes parallels with April.

McLane, Paul E. Diggon Davie Again, JEGP, 46 (1947), 144-9.   2263

Supports Hulbert's suggestion, ibid., 41 (1942), 349-67 (see 2245), that Diggon Davie in September eclogue is Richard Davies, Bishop of St. David's.

McLane, Paul E. James VI in the Shepheardes Calender, HLQ, 16 (1953), 273-85.   2264

Supports Mary Parmenter's view, ELH, 3 (1936), 190-217 (see 2287), that the Kid in May eclogue is young King James of Scotland; the Papist Fox, James's French counsin, Esmé Stuart; and the Goat, James Buchanan, James's tutor. Sp had knowledge of Scottish affairs, the events allegorized happened in time to get into SC, dialectical usages in May are best explained by this interpretation, and parallels with Esmé Stuart's escapades are too close to be accidental.

McLane, Paul E. Piers of Spenser's Shepheardes Calender. Dr. John Piers, Bishop of Salisbury, MLQ, 9 (1948), 3-9.   2265

When Sp was secretary to Bishop John Young, he probably met Bishop John Piers. Sp's Piers is in May and October eclogues.

McLane, Paul E. A Re-interpretation of Spenser's Shepheardes Calender, Doctoral diss., University of Washington, 1943. DDAAU, 1942-43, No. 10. UWAT, 8 (1944), 97.   2266

Identifies Piers, Thomalin, Diggon Davie, and other characters in SC with prelates associated with Dr. John Young, Bishop of Rochester, whose secretary Sp was in 1578, and with Earl of Leicester. Discusses ecclesiastical matter in eclogues in relation to political and religious events, and Sp's intentions in choosing pastoral form. Argues in last chapter against general belief that Sp composed eclogues over long period of time, advancing theory entire poem was written within the year preceding publication.

McLane, Paul E. Spenser and the Primitive Church, ELN, 1 (1963), 6-11. 2267

Although Sp attacked English Church and favored Catholic in MHT, View, and SC, his call for a renewed Primitive Church meant revival of "ascetic and monastic" ideals in priesthood, not a change in doctrine. Bulk of discussion from SC.

McLane, Paul E. Spenser's Cuddie: Edward Dyer, JEGP, 54 (1955), 230-40. 2268

Presents admittedly inconclusive evidence that Cuddie in February, August, and October eclogues of SC is Sp's friend Sir Edward Dyer. Stresses importance of studying the poem in its historical context.

McLane, Paul E. Spenser's Double Audience in the Shepheardes Calender, N&Q, N. S. 6 (1959), 249-50. 2269

Criticizes J. W. Saunders' position in The Facade of Morality, ELH, 19 (1952), 81-114 (see 1064). It is not necessary to posit two distinct audiences to explain Sp's variety in subject matter and poetic procedures; these are accounted for by Sp's experiences and the history of the pastoral form.

McLane, Paul E. Spenser's Morrell and Thomalin, PMLA, 62 (1947), 936-49. 2270

Accepts the view that Morrell is John Aylmer, Bishop of London, and gives new reasons for this identification. Thomalin is not one of the Puritan divines, for this would have been inappropriate in the July eclogue with its praise of Archbishop Grindal, who was not favorable to the Puritans. Suggests that Thomalin is Thomas Cooper, Bishop of Lincoln.

McLane, Paul E. Spenser's Oak and Briar, SP, 52 (1955), 463-77. 2271

In February eclogue. The Oak represents Leicester, a stalwart statesman cut down by Elizabeth, the gardener, because of malicious complaints of Earl of Oxford, the bragging and spiteful Briar. General theme of fable is "an attack on the Queen's policy of capricious ingratitude towards elder statesmen," including Thomas Walsingham and Henry Sidney.

McLane, Paul E. Spenser's Political and Religious Position in the Shepheardes Calender, JEGP, 49 (1950), 324-32. 2272

SC, intentionally or not, revealed Sp's position on the side of Leicester, Sidney, and others who opposed the Alençon marriage. Far from being a Puritan, Sp was a "political" Protestant whose dominant sympathies lay with the bishops against "rapacious courtiers." He had no wish for further religious reform.

McLane, Paul E. Spenser's Shepheardes Calender: A Study in Elizabethan Allegory. Notre Dame, Ind.: University of Notre Dame Press, 1961; repr. 1970. 370 pp. 2273

Deals with political, religious, and personal allegory. Political allegory relates to crisis created 1579 by projected marriage of Queen Elizabeth with Duke of Alençon, opposed by party of Earl of Leicester. Sp's Rosalind represents Queen Elizabeth; in November eclogue Sp laments death of Queen as Dido. In fable of Oak and Briar in February, Oak is Earl of Leicester and Briar is Earl of Oxford. In fable of Fox and Kid in May, Papist

Fox is Duc d'Aubigny and Kid is King James of Scotland (pp. 13-91). In religious allegory Algrind (May and July) is Edmund Grindal, Archbishop of Canterbury, 1576-1583. Roffyn (September) is John Young, Bishop of Rochester. Piers (May) is John Piers, Bishop of Salisbury. Thomalin (July) is Thomas Cooper, Bishop of Lincoln. Diggon Davie (September) is Richard Davies, Bishop of St. David's (pp. 95-234). In personal allegory Hobbinol is Gabriel Harvey. Cuddie is Edward Dyer. E.K. is Fulke Greville (pp. 237-95). SC is dramatic poem, unity discoverable in its allegory (pp. 299-333).

Rev: Joan Grundy, MLR, 57 (1962), 409; William Blissett, RN, 15 (1962), 238; John T. Shawcross, SCN, 20 (1962), 28.

McLane, Paul E. Spenser's Thomalin, PMLA, 64 (1949), 599.   2274

Further evidence supporting his contention, ibid., 62 (1947), 936-49 (see 2270), that Thomalin in March and July eclogues is Thomas Cooper, Bishop of Lincoln. Specifically, "a" means "of"; hence, Thom-of-Lin(coln).

Maxwell, J. C. An Echo of Spenser in "The White Doe of Rylstone," N&Q, 17, (1970), 380.   2275

Lines 35-36 of February in SC are echoed in lines 11-13 of Wordsworth's The White Doe of Rylstone. Spenserian "shepherd groom" also used. [SpN, Vol. 2, No. 1 (1971), 9.]

Melchiori, Giorgio. Pope in Arcady: The Theme of Et in Arcadia Ego in his Pastorals, EM, 14 (1963), 83-93.   2276

While establishing that in his pastorals Pope was already showing his lifelong concern with fact of death, attributes seasonal plan of the pastorals to influence of SC.

Merivale, Patricia. Pan the Goat-God: His Myth in Modern Times. Cambridge, Mass.: Harvard University Press, 1969. 286 pp.   2277

Discusses references to Pan under various aspects in April, May, June, July, September, November, and December of SC. " . . . well into the seventeenth century, the situation is this: Orphic Pan belongs only to scholars; the shaggy Pan of sex and terror is likely to be replaced by a satyr; Plutarchan Pan has perhaps been found by Spenser [Death of Pan in May eclogue], but has only demonstrably been found by E.K. [in the gloss on May]. Spenser, at any rate, always gives some intellectual content to his Pans; his successors use chiefly the brief, stereotyped, emptily decorative pastoral allusion, a mere device (like Warner's title, Pan His Syrinx or Pipe) for bringing in Virgilian or other pastoral associations" (pp. 19-24). Only Spenserian Pan outside SC is in FQ, II, ix, 40 (p. 244, note 54). For other references to Sp, see Index.

Miller, Milton. A Masterpiece if Any: An Interpretation of Spenser's Shepheardes Calender. Doctoral diss., University of Wisconsin, 1954. UWSDD, 16 (1956), 550-1. DDAAU, 1954-55, No. 22. 2278

Opposes traditional view of SC as disunified, takes it to be "a solidly and complexly built structural unit." Unity resides in thematic development and dramatic continuity. Sp "speaks" in the poem and its unity must be sought in the poem as a whole. It is critical and cheerless, pointing ahead to 17th century uncertainty; it also looks back to continuing Christian tradition of contempt of the world. Two principal themes: discord, reflected in seasonal motif; and the Christian paradox of humility and aspiration. The latter is the crux of the poem and the basis of its positive values. Colin Clout, the central figure, attains spiritual maturity, moving from physical love to spiritual love, from pride and self-seeking to humility (lowliness) and spiritual aspiration.

Millican, C. Bowie. The Northern Dialect of *The Shepheardes Calender*, ELH, 6 (1939), 211-3. 2279

In a visitation of 1562 the pronunciation of the pupils at the Merchant Taylors' School was criticized, and the defect was attributed to the fact that most of the ushers were "Northren men borne." Notes possible influence of this situation on the young Sp.

Mitchner, Robert W. Spenser and E.K.: An Answer, SP, 42 (1945), 183-90. 2280

In opposition to Starnes, ibid., 41 (1944), 181-200 (see 2304). Parallels from other contemporary writers make those between E.K.'s commentary and Sp's acknowledged writings less significant. If there are errors in mythology common to E.K. and Sp, similar errors can be found in other Elizabethan works. Also, if E.K. and Sp were working together closely, they would naturally use common sources. See 2249.

Mohl, Ruth. Studies in Spenser, Milton and the Theory of Monarchy. New York: Ungar, 1962. 144 pp. 2281

Repr. of 1949 ed. Two of six essays deal with Sp. In The Glosses Concerning Sp's Rosalinde (pp. 1-14) identifies her with Mary Sidney. In Sp's Diggon Davie (pp. 15-30) identifies him with Philip Sidney.

Montgomerie, William. Sporting Kid (The Solution of the "Kidde in Aesop" Problem), L&L, 36 (1943), 18-24. 2282

The "Kidde" allusion in Nashe's Preface to Greene's Menaphon (1589) is not to Aesop, but rather to the May eclogue of Sp's SC.

Münster, Adolf. Spensers "Shepheardes Calender" und die Einflüsse der antiken bukolischen Dichtung. Doctoral diss., University of Vienna, 1953. 199pp. OeB, 14 (July 15, 1956), 8. 2283

Introduction sketches development of pastoral from Theocritus to Renaissance (pp. 3-12). Main part of study points out in detail classical conventions and themes in each of Sp's twelve eclogues. Those receiving most detailed treatment: January—related to Theocritus, Bion, and Virgil (pp. 19-32); April—related to Theocritus, Virgil, and Calpurnius (pp. 51-73); June—related to Virgil and others (pp. 81-102); August—related to Theocritus, Virgil, Calpurnius, Nemesianus, and Renaissance pastoralists (pp. 106-27); November—related to Theocritus, Bion, Moschus, Virgil, and Nemesianus while admitting commonness of elegy in Renaissance pastoral and immediate debt to Marot (pp. 140-78); December—related to classical pastoral poets behind Marot, immediate source (pp. 178-92).

Murrin, Michael Joseph. Mantuan and the English Eclogue. DA, 26 (1965), 2188-89. Yale University, 1965. 177 pp. 2284

In the sixteenth century there were two kinds of eclogue: (1) the idealized type modelled after Virgil, (2) the moral and satirical type modelled after Mantuan. The only common interest shared by the types was the interest in love, each type evaluating it differently. Barclay, Googe, Turberville and Sp exhibit the attitudes of Mantuan; but Sp did not adopt the social solution to the problem of passion proposed by Mantuan. Turberville made the most significant change in the type by adding archaic diction.

Sp went further in this direction. By the closing decade of the century, the neoclassic Virgilian eclogue replaced the Mantuan type.

Nicolet, William. Another Note on E. K. AN&Q, 2 (1964), 153-4.   2285

E. K. may be Gabriel Harvey. See 2286.

Nicolet, William Pattangall. Edmund Spenser's *Shepheardes Calender:* An Interpretation. DA, 25 (1965), 4704. Brown University, 1964. 270 pp.   2286

SC is a "semi-autobiographical 'portrait of the artist' in which Spenser reveals his state of mind during the period preceding the writing of the *Faerie Queene.*" Chap. I: reviews scholarship on E. K. and the attempts to identify him. Concludes that E. K. is Sp or someone very close to him. Chap. II: E. K.'s technique of glossing. Chap. III: the identity of key personages, especially Rosalind, who is Sp's first wife and also a Platonic mistress who fails to inspire Colin to climb the Platonic ladder. Chap. IV: interpretation of individual eclogues, concluding that all except March reveal Colin's disenchantment with the world. Colin, however, is a temporary stage from which Sp the author has already emerged. Chap. V concludes that the poem, though not wholly successful and unified, nonetheless does have thematic unity, and relates to Sp as Portrait of the Artist and Lycidas relate to Joyce and Milton. See 2285.

Parmenter, Mary. Spenser [sic] *Twelve Aeglogves Proportionable to the Twelve Monethes,* ELH, 3 (1936), 190-217.
                                            2287

Evidence to show that in various ways Sp's 12 eclogues in SC are "truly 'proportioned to the state of the xij monethes,' as stated on the

title page and in the introduction, while at the same time the life of Colin Clout is 'proportioned' to the scheme of the four seasons."

Prescott, Anne Lake. The Reception of Marot, Ronsard and Du Bartas in Renaissance England. DA, 28 (1967), 1406A-7A. Columbia University, 1967. 245 pp.   2288

The English knew Marot fairly well (psalms, pastorals, lyrics, and epigrams), but despite Sp's debts to his eclogues, English references to Marot show little admiration. Nor were English much impressed by Ronsard, although they knew him as a famous love poet, especially in highly rhetorical sonnets to Cassandre; they tended to ignore his serious work and later love poetry. With Du Bartas case very different. Enormously popular, not so much because of perfervid style (some eccentricity lost in translation) and old fashioned content, but simply because his piety was easy to understand. Religous poetry easier to discuss and admire than "the subtle qualities of tone and style in Marot and Ronsard."

Provost, Foster. Pope's Pastorals: An Exercise in Poetical Technique, in Contributions to the Humanities, 1954, pp. 25-37. LSUSHS, 5. Baton Rouge, La.: Louisiana State University Press, 1955. 54pp.   2289

Shows, among other things, influence of SC on Pope's pastoral poetry.

Reamer, Owen J. Spenser's Debt to Marot—Re-examined, TSLL, 10 (1969), 504-27.   2290

Line-by-line comparison of December in SC with Marot's Eglogue Au Roy. Sp neither translated nor paraphrased. Borrowed overall plan of organization and details of Robin's pastoral life applied to Colin's. Intents of two poets different: Marot wanted royal patronage, Sp individual hero whose life-story would form framework for calendar. Sp is imitator with originality. [SpN, Vol. 2, No. 1 (1971), 7.]

Roberts, Warren E. Spenser's Fable of the Oak and the Briar, SFQ, 14 (1950), 150-4.   2291

Finds an analogue of the fable in February of SC in the first story of The Seven Sages of Rome.

Rosenmeyer, Thomas G. The Green Cabinet: Theocritus and the European Pastoral Lyric. Berkeley: University of California Press, 1969. 351 pp.   2292

"Green cabinet" in December of SC; Sp found *"vert cabinet"* in Marot's Eglogue au Roy (p. vii). Sp tries to "capture the earthy feel of the countryside" (p. 18). Sannazaro first used variety of lyric forms in pastoral, followed by Pléiade, who influenced Sp (p. 93). Courtesy in Renaissance became restricted to upper class; hence "awareness of hierarchy" in Sp's pastorals (p. 103). Sp's November, in tradition of pastoral lament, emphasizes "the restorative character of *otium*" (pp. 113-4). Refers to Renaissance flower catalogues, as in Sp's April (p. 197). Despite moral eclogues in SC, relatively free of allegory (pp. 272-3). For other references to SC, and to CCCHA and FQ, see Index.

Rosenzweig, Sidney. Ascham's *Scholemaster* and Spenser's February Eclogue, SAB, 15 (1940), 103-9.   2293

Finds a source for the fable of the Oak and the Briar in Ascham's Scholemaster. Just as Ascham had reversed the usual roles of the Oak and the Briar, so does Sp. The case rests chiefly on verbal parallels. See 2226.

Røstvig, Maren-Sofie. II. *The Shepeardes Calender*—a Structural Analysis, RMS (University of Nottingham), 13 (1969), 49-75.   2294

SC received by contemporaries as great poem because allegory of return of man to God, and of Time from Creation into Eternity. Its inspiration derives from Psalter as interpreted (numerologically and otherwise) by late classical, medieval, and Renaissance theologians. Colin's willing acceptance of death in December is Christian poet's answer to pagan ethics. In Platonic thought time a moving image of eternity and of human history. In SC pattern of (1) state of Nature in eclogues 1-4; (2) reign of law in eclogues 5-8; (3) state of Grace in eclogues 9-12. Pontus de Tyard composed "loix musicales" to operation of Plato's numerical formula (proceeding to square and cube of 2 and 3) in process of Creation and in proportions of human frame. Uses this formula in explaining structure of SC. [SpN, Vol. 1, No. 2 (1970), 12.]

Sasek, Lawrence A., ed. The Poems of William Smith. Baton Rouge: Louisiana State University Press, 1970. 107 pp.   2295

In Intro. (pp. 3-31) discusses Smith's links through his poems with Sp and Countess of Pembroke, two dedicatory sonnets of Chloris (1596) addressed to "Collin Cloute," Smith's low reputation with editors and critics, pastoralism of sonnet sequence, its careful craftsmanship, extensive use of mythology, imitation of SC and Lodge's Phillis; and A newyeares' Guifte made upon certen Flowers, nine short poems in British Museum Add. MS 35, 186, dedicated to Countess of Pembroke. Final evaluation rates Smith "a good minor poet in the age of Shakespeare, Spenser, and

Donne . . . no mean accomplishment."
See 233, 2515.

Schulze, Ivan L. Blenerhasset's *A Revelation*, Spenser's *Shepheardes Calender*, and the Kenilworth Pageants, ELH, 11 (1944), 85-91.   2296

Blenerhasset's A Revelation of the True Minerva, written to win the favor of Leicester and the earliest imitation of SC, is indebted to the Kenilworth pageants of 1575 as well as to Sp. See 2204.

Simeone, William E. A Letter from Sir Richard Fanshawe to John Evelyn, N&Q, 196 (1951), 315-6.   2297

The letter is dated Dec. 27, 1653. It praises Evelyn's translation of Lucretius, and speaks favorably of Bathurst's Latin translation of SC. See 2311.

Sledd, James. "Chamfred Browes" in Spenser's February Eclogue, N&Q, 188 (1945), 34.   2298

Suggests that the phrase may have come from Apuleius's Metamorphoses through Cooper's Thesaurus.

Soens, Lewis, ed. Sir Philip Sidney's Defense of Poesy. Lincoln: University of Nebraska Press, 1970. 95 pp.   2299

In Introduction: Sp and others in Sidney circle concerned with moral uses of poetry; Sp's critical work The English Poet lost, but can infer from SC and E. K.'s glosses, especially in February, March, April, and October, that Sp shared Sidney's views; their mutual Protestant Neo-Platonism; Sidney's idea of imitation, Sp, and Tasso's critical theory; Sidney praises model authors "almost as if they were manifestations of an Idea . . . and Spenser, Worthiness itself"; that poetry enables us to walk in golden world is "a concept of poetry which Spenser might have used to help envisage his great work of building a

Zion in England" (pp. ix-xxxvii). Qualified praise of SC in Defense of Poesy (p. 46). For references to Sp in Supplementary Notes, see Index.

Spevack-Husmann, Helga. The Mighty Pan: Miltons Mythologische Vergleiche. Muenster: Archendorff, 1963. 150 pp.
2300

In Milton's syncretic tradition myth and Christianity intermingled: Christ-Phoebus, Christ-Hercules and Samson-Hercules, Christ-Pan (pp. 76-90). Sp identifies Christ with Pan five times in May, July, and September of SC, as E. K. points out in glosses on these eclogues. Marvell sings of "our Pan" in pastoral Clorinda and Damon. So Milton places "mighty Pan" among shepherds in Nativity Ode. As Sp eulogizes Elizabeth in April of SC, so Milton eulogizes his friend Edward King in Lycidas (pp. 90-4).

Spitzer, Leo. Essays on English and American Literature. Ed. Anna Hatcher. Princeton: Princeton University Press, 1962. 290 pp.   2301

Chap. X (pp. 180-92) is repr. of 2302. See 2196, 2197.

Spitzer, Leo. Spenser, *Shepheardes Calendar, March*, ll. 61-114, and the Variorum Edition, SP, 47 (1950), 494-505.
2302

Comments in Variorum fail to recognize truly classical effect of Willy's discovery of Cupid. It is a poetic depiction of puberty, of the adolescent blundering unaware into Love. Feels that March shows direct influence of Bion, without mediation of Ronsard. See 2196, 2197.

Starnes, D. T. E. K.'s Classical Allusions Reconsidered, SP, 39 (1942), 143-59.
2303

E. K.'s classical allusions in the glosses to SC are not based on first-hand classical sources, but on secondary sources in standard Elizabethan reference books, particularly dictionaries.

Starnes, D. T. Spenser and E. K., SP, 41 (1944), 181-200.   2304

Bases his conclusions on similarities of diction, imagery, mythological allusions, and other stylistic qualities in E. K. and Sp, finding that commentator and poet must be the same person. Stresses the presence in the "E. K." passages of images which recur in Sp's later poems, and certain departures from the traditional versions of well-known myths in both "E. K.'s" glosses and Sp's poems. See 2249, 2250.

Staton, Walter F., Jr. Spenser's "April" Lay as a Dramatic Chorus, SP, 59 (1962), 111-8.   2305

Colin's "April" lay in SC was inspired by classical dramatic choruses in Ronsard's Bergerie. This can be demonstrated both poetically, as in the similarity of meter and tone, and circumstantially, since both works were intended for courtly entertainment.

Steadman, John M. Timotheus in Dryden, E. K., and Gafori, TLS, Dec. 16, 1960, p. 819.   2306

On the Timotheus tradition of inciting deeds of destruction through music. Cites Dryden's Alexander's Feast, October eclogue of SC (gloss on l. 27), and De Harmonia Musicorum Instrumentorum (Bk. IV, chapter 8) by Franchino Gafori. Gafori is link in Timotheus tradition between Sp and Dryden. See 2215, 2247, 2254, and 2255.

Stein, Harold. Spenser and William Turner, MLN, 51 (1936), 345-51. 2307

Concludes, from an examination of Turner's tracts, such as The Hunting and finding Out of the Romish Fox

(1543) and The Hunting of The Romish Wolf (1554; reprinted as The Hunting of the Fox and the Wolf, ca. 1561), that Sp's foxes and wolves in the September eclogue are not simply the High Church party and the Roman Catholics, respectively, but pretending Anglicans with Romish beliefs and Roman Catholics in both belief and profession.

Steinberg, Theodore Louis. In Tempe or The Dales of Arcady: A Reading of Spenser's The Shepheardes Calender. DAI, 32 (1972), 5752-A. University of Illinois at Urbana-Champaign, 1971. 338 pp.   2308

Four introductory chaps.: review of previous criticism; pastoral tradition adapted to make pastoral world a microcosm, use of calendar-scheme, relationship between Art and Nature; language; role of E. K., "Spenser under the persona of a literary critic" whose theories, opposed to theories Sp presents in poetry itself, should be read ironically. Rest of study examines each eclogue in terms of Colin Clout's dilemma, worldly involvement and love. Elisa in "April" is Song. "October" contains various literary theories, all of them inadequate. At poem's end Colin still confused, but "his ultimate recovery appears imminent."

Stewart, Bain T. A Borrowing from Spenser by Phineas Fletcher, MLN, 56 (1941), 273-4.   2309

Fletcher's Third Piscatory Eclogue is a rendering, in piscatory terms, of Sp's January eclogue.

Stillinger, Jack. A Note on the Printing of E. K.'s Glosses, SB, 14 (1961), 203-5.
                                         2310

Urges that the original, disarranged order of E. K.'s glosses be retained in scholarly editions. These "errors" of order would not have disturbed early readers, and certain peculiarities "offer possible evidence of revision in the poems" between 10 April and 5 December, 1579. Points out new disorder in the Variorum reordering of the notes.

Strathmann, Ernest A. *Lycidas* and the Translation of "May," MLN, 52 (1937), 398-400.   2311

"Lycidas" is the name for Piers, the Protestant pastor, in Theodore Bathurst's Latin translation of SC. Milton may have known this work. See 2297.

Strong, Roy C. Portraits of Queen Elizabeth I. Oxford: Clarendon Press, 1963. 23 plates. 173 pp.   2312

Part I, production of portraits, style, delineation, use, theory, Elizabethan legend; Part II, catalogue of portraits. Woodcut 14 (p. 124) illustration to April eclogue of SC, in which "Elizabeth is hymned as Venus-Virgo crowned with flowers and attended by Graces, Muses, and other nymphs."

Swallow, Alan. The Pentameter Lines in Skelton and Wyatt, MP, 48 (1950), 1-11.   2313

Defends Skelton and Wyatt as metrists. Concludes: "Unlike the condition at Spenser's time, the iambic pentameter was not firmly established; rather, the metrical practice which preceded Skelton and Wyatt dictated, if anything, a very loose metrical structure. So Skelton and the young Wyatt were following a tradition of metrics, though in a different manner from that of Spenser; Skelton and Wyatt moved toward a full acceptance of the iambic pattern, whereas Spenser, in the eclogues, moved away from the iambic toward the older tradition for immediate purposes in those poems"—i.e., in order to adapt the versification to the rustic speakers in SC.

Syford, Constance M. *"Merce non mercede,"* MLN, 63 (1948), 435-6.   2314

Objects to Gilbert's suggestion, ibid., pp. 181-2 (see 2232). The emblem for December may have been printed at the end of the book because it was meant to serve an additional purpose as Sp's own envoy.

Thompson, John. The Founding of English Metre. New York: Columbia University Press, 1961. 181 pp.   2315

Traces "the development of the iambic line in English from Tottel's *Miscellany* to *Astrophel and Stella.*" Line developed from "vigorous ... beginning through a dull stretch to a ... triumphant realization." Theory of metre makes use of structural linguistics. In Introduction defines terms and illustrates metrical system used (pp. 1-14). Chap. on SC: new in its variety and freedom of metre in stanza forms, metrical patterns, and placing of words in relation to patterns. Many irregularities, radical experiments. Analyzes four-beat line of February, May, September; "common" and "romance" measures of July and March; songs of August, April, November; pentameter lines in various eclogues (pp. 81-127). Sp and classical metres (pp. 128-38). See 2539.

Tillotson, Kathleen. The Language of Drayton's *Shepheards Garland*, RES, 13 (1937), 272-81.   2316

"The influence of the *Shepheards Calender* is more clearly apparent in Michael Drayton's *Idea The Shepheards Garland* (1593) than in any other Elizabethan poem." Studies effect of this influence on Drayton's archaisms, which, like Sp's, are derived from Chaucer and contemporary rustic dialect; but more are derived from Sp himself. Many of the "artificial elements" disappeared in

Drayton's revisions of 1606 and 1619.

White, Beatrice. "Chevisaunce" as a Flower Name, RES, 21 (1945), 317-9.
2317

Cites E. K.'s gloss on May, l. 92, "spoyle, or bootie," and suggests that in the flower passage of April Sp was thinking of all the flowers worked into a completed nosegay. Thus "chevisaunce" is not used in April as the name of a flower, but more generally in the sense of both "flowery spoils" and "completed nosegay."

Williams, Glanmor. Bywyd ac Amserau'r Esgob Richard Davies. Cardiff, 1953. 139pp.
2318

Life and Times of Bishop Richard Davies. Accepts and confirms identification of Diggon Davie in September with Bishop Davies, as held by Hulbert (see 2245) and McLane (see 2263). Opening paragraph: "Our purpose here will be to seek to gather the reasons of the two American scholars for believing this [that Bishop Davies is Diggon Davie], and to support them with further evidence."

Williams, Glanmor. Richard Davies, Esgob Tyddewi, a'r "Shepheardes Calender," Llên Cymru, 2, No. 4 (1953), 232-6.
2319

Richard Davies, Bishop of St. David's, and SC. On the identification of Diggon Davie in September with Bishop Davies. See 2245, 2263, 2318.

Williams, Raymond. Pastoral and Counter-Pastoral, CritQ, 10 (1968), 277-90.
2320

In discussing realistic pastoral poetry in Crabbe's The Village as opposed to earlier pastoral traditions, mentions Sp's SC. Pastoral metaphor in May, July, and September eclogues is that of the good shepherd as a Christ figure or an ideal pastor set against corruption of the church.

Wilson, Harold S. Gabriel Harvey, TLS, Mar. 9, 1946, p. 115.
2321

Harvey's authorship of the Ode Natalitia, suggested by C. E. Sayle in Early English Printed Books in the University Library, Cambridge (1475-1640), I, 310, "is confirmed by E. K.'s laudatory notice of Harvey's writings in the 'glosse' to the September eclogue of Spenser's 'Shepheardes Calender' (1579)."

Wrenn, C. L. On Re-Reading Spenser's Shepheardes Calender, E&S, 29 (1943), 30-49.
2322

First discusses the poetic qualities of three passages: the flower passage in April, the fable of the Fox and the Kid in May, and the concluding lines of the poem; then examines the language of the poem, especially Sp's archaisms and dialect words.

OTHER MINOR POEMS

Ahrends, Günter. Liebe, Schönheit und Tugend als Strukturelemente in Sidneys *Astrophel and Stella* und in Spensers *Amoretti.* Doc. diss., University of Bonn, 1966. 321 pp.   2323

Relates content of Sp's cycle to form. Analyzes in detail sonnets in which themes of love, beauty, and virtue are paramount, and shows they connect with each other in a pattern. [YWES, 57 (1966), 175.]

Allen, Don Cameron. On Spenser's *Muiopotmos*, SP, 53 (1956), 141-58. 2324

The butterfly is the rational soul, which through the weakness of the senses can wander into the web of impiety. Sees here a fusion of the Psyche and Ariadne myths, and a parallel with Red Cross's meeting with Orgoglio (FQ, I, vii). See 463.

Anderson, Judith H. "Nat worth a boterflye": *Muiopotmos* and *The Nun's Priest's Tale*, JMRS, 1 (1971), 89-106.   2325

Chaucer's Nun's Priest's Tale, of which Sp must have been conscious though not imitating it, points up by contrast characteristics in Muiop which relate it to Calvinistic thought. Nun's Priest's Tale offers vision, serious and comic, of imagined world which has moral norm (life of the widow), moral imperative to reader (to "see" relation between folly and vulnerability), and cosmic structure. Sp's poem presents world less secure and more hostile to butterfly Clarion. Chauntecleer (names of mock-heroes may be related) remains more rooster than hero. Clarion's role broadened beyond mock-heroic to manipulate reader's point of view "from insect to man to God." Hostility of world to butterfly (read psyche here) localized in Aragnoll's hatred. That takes shape in myth of an innocent, Astery, and myth of a demonic Arachne. In tapestry context Arachne's fault is limited vision unable to see what butterfly in Athena's border represents. Calvin's sense of beauty in natural world and corruption which blights it accords with tone of poem. [SpN, Vol. 3, No. 1 (1972), 4-5.]

Andreasen, N. J. C. John Donne: Conservative Revolutionary. Princeton: Princeton University Press, 1967. 249 pp.   2326

Donne's greatest originality appears in "affirmative love poems" like The good-morrow and A Valediction: forbidding mourning. These poems express Platonic love, but are not Platonic poems. Need only compare them with Sp's 4 Hymns and Amor "in order to see how Donne has revolutionized artificial conventions and become fully Donnean" (pp. 195-6). For a few other references to Sp, see Index.

Austin, Warren B. Spenser's Sonnet to Harvey, MLN, 62 (1947), 20-3.   2327

Suggests that the sonnet printed at the end of Foure Letters (1592) was written by Sp in praise of a collection of satirical poems which Harvey had in preparation as early as 1580, but which he never published.

Baldensperger, Fernand, trans. D'Edmond Spenser à Alan Seeger: cent petits poèmes anglais traduits en vers francais. HSCL, 13. Cambridge, Mass: Harvard University Press, 1938. 94 pp.   2328

Amor 34, 37, 39, and 82.

Bartenschlager, Klaus. The Situation of the Speaker in the Poem. Wyatt, Sidney, Spenser. A Historical and Typological Study. Doc. diss., University of Munich, 1970. 125 pp. EASG, 2 (1970), 26-8.   2329

Bulk of dissertation analyzes speaker's situation in Wyatt's songs, continental Petrarchan tradition, Sidney's Astrophil and Stella, and Sp's Amor. Wyatt's sonnets show almost no use of the speaker's situation; in contrast, his songs, close to English courtly lyric, develop situative element. Sidney's individual style explained by his theory of mimetic representation as poetic form. His sonnets show formal affinity with Latin love poetry, develop significant situations. "Spenser's Amoretti, for all the detail of incident they contain, make no use of incident to transform it into a situation in which the living person of a lover would become visible."

Beall, Chandler B. A Tasso Imitation in Spenser, MLQ, 3 (1942), 559-60. 2330

Amoretti, 30. The conceit of fire kindled by ice was also used by Tasso, though not invented by him.

Bennett, Josephine W. A Bibliographical Note on Mother Hubberds Tale, ELH, 4 (1937), 60-1.   2331

The poem is mentioned in a book list of 1596.

Benson, Robert C. Elizabeth as Beatrice: A Reading of Spenser's Amoretti, SCB, 32 (1972), 184-8.   2332

In at least first 60 sonnets of Amor, Elizabeth has symbolic significance similar to that of Dante's Beatrice. As a result of the Fall, man needs "new methods" to approach God; Dante's Beatrice is one of these "new methods"; Sp's Elizabeth is another. Poet's surrender of self is climax of Amor, beginning in #60 and ending with 68. Easter sonnet confirms reading of Elizabeth as type of Beatrice. Sonnets 69-88 disappointing. Lady of Sp's sonnets has symbolic significance she cannot bear without vision of God similar to one Dante is granted at end of Divine Comedy.

Berger, Harry. Spenser's "Prothalamion": An Interpretation, EIC, 15 (1965), 363-80; repr. in 756.   2333

Ten stanzas of Proth fall into three parts: two stanzas referring to poet, one in praise of Essex, and seven celebrating double marriage. First and third parts unified through theme that in spite of recalcitrance of this world, man can control and reorganize his "inward environment." Praise of Essex, though it represents patron-seeking, also indicates need for accommodating oneself to facts of existence.

Berlin, Normand. Chaucer's The Book of the Duchess and Spenser's Daphnaida: A Contrast, SN, 38 (1966), 282-9. 2334

Sp in Daph tried to create an elegy in imitation of The Book of the Duchess. He did not succeed since his view of life differed from Chaucer's.

Bizzarri, Edoardo. L'Influenza Italiana sugli "Amoretti" di E. Spenser, Rom, 6 (1942), 626-37.   2335

Deals with influence of Petrarch, Tebaldeo, Bembo, and Tasso. An appendix (pp. 634-7) lists Italian sources and analogues of 36 sonnets in Amor previously pointed out, and adds 9 others noted for the first time.

Bludau, Diethild. Humanismus und Allegorie in Spensers Sonnetten, Anglia, 74 (1956), 292-332.   2336

It is Sp's medieval emphasis on the universal moral idea rather than on distinctive, subjective emotional response which makes Amor so un-Petrarchan. This emphasis is what gives unity to the seeming chaos of these sonnets.

Bondanella, Peter E., and Julia Conaway Bondanella. Two Kinds of Renaissance Love: Spenser's "Astrophel" and Ronsard's "Adonis," ES, 52 (1971), 311-8.   2337

Sp's elegy influenced by Ronsard's, but two poems describe different kinds of love. Ronsard's deals with *amor ferino* or sensual love, emphasizes Adonis's physical beauty, focuses on Venus, shows lovers as sexual athletes. Sp's deals with *amor umano* or more noble love not based on sense of touch, emphasizes Adonis's courtly and pastoral virtues; lovers are metamorphosed into single flower, so remain united after death. [SpN, Vol. 2, No. 3 (1971), 7.]

Bottin, Ronald B. A New Spenserian Rhyme Scheme? JEGP, 36 (1937), 384-6.   2338

Notes "pattern" in CCCHA with important variation in the second line of each quatrain.

Boyette, Purvis Elton. Milton and the Sacred Fire: Sex Symbolism in Paradise Lost. DA, 27 (1967), 3420A. Vanderbilt University, 1966. 369 pp.   2339

Examines "the male-female principle as a symbolic expression of creative generation." At conclusion of Chap. I, which develops the philosophical and theological contexts, briefly discusses 4 Hymns as "philosophical poems which develop the Neoplatonic distinctions between earthly and spiritual love."

Brewer, Wilmon. Sonnets and Sestinas. Boston: Cornhill, 1937. 245 pp.   2340

Chapter on The History of the Sonnet, pp. 93-178, relates Sp to the European tradition.

Briggs, Sarah W. The English Reflective Elegy. Doctoral diss., Cornell University, 1940. CUAT, 1940, pp. 22-5. 2341

"A study of the reflective elegy shows . . . that the elegiac development almost without exception follows a definite plan: (1) lament, which is threnodic in tone, (2) praise of the dead, which may be lyrical, and (3) the final consolation which is the result of reflection."

Britten, Benjamin. Spring Symphony. New York: Boosey & Hawkes, 1950.
                                    2342

For soprano, alto, and tenor soloists, mixed chorus, boys' choir, and orchestra. Sp included among several poets.

Bryan, Robert A. Poets, Poetry, and Mercury in Spenser's Prosopopoia: Mother Hubberd's Tale, Costerus, 5 (1972), 27-33.   2343

In concentrating on identity of ape and fox in allegory of MHT, critics have neglected other aspects of poem. Unnoticed is important role that poets and poetry play in each part. "Read in this light, *Mother Hubberd's Tale* is about the poet as cleanser, as priest, and as shepherd in society; the poem is an exemplum of how good poetry can reorder a society fallen into chaos." Shows that in Renaissance iconography Mercury, who rouses lion and urges corrective action, was represented as a teacher. Short step for Sp, "with his syncretic imagination, to move Mercury from teacher to poet."

Bullitt, John M. The Use of Rhyme Link in the Sonnets of Sidney, Drayton, and Spenser, JEGP, 49 (1950), 14-32. 2344

Finds that the method used by Sir

Denys Bray to discover "linkage" between Shakespeare's sonnets (see Atkinson, p. 210) reveals equally striking "linkage" between sonnets not meant to be related.

Burgess, Robert M. The Sonnet—A Cosmopolitan Literary Form—in the Renaissance, in Proceedings of the IVth Congress of the International Comparative Literature Association, ed. François Jost, I, 169-84. 2 vols. The Hague: Mouton, 1966. 1459 pp.   2345

Sp blended Platonism, Puritanism, and patriotism in his works and is England's finest poet before Shakespeare. Began poetic career by making translations of poems by Marot and Du Bellay. Later became member of the loosely organized group of writers called the Areopagus which was devoted to the introduction of classical meters into English poetry. Eightynine sonnets of his Amoretti (1595) constitute one of the best sonnet sequences of Elizabethan age. Isolated sources of his sonnets have been traced to Petrarch, Bembo, Tasso, and Desportes.

Burke, Charles B. Keats and Spenser, PQ, 17 (1938), 223-4.   2346

The last four lines of Keats's Bards of Passion and of Mirth are paralleled in RT, ll. 337-43.

Camden, Carroll. Spenser's "Little Fish that Men Call Remora," RIP, 44 (1957), 1-12.   2347

Accounts of the remora (VWV, ix, 10) in Stephen Batman, Cardan, Laurence Andrewe, Holland's Plutarch, Donne, Jonson, and others.

Carpenter, Nan Cooke. Spenser's "Epithalamion" as Inspiration for Milton's "L'Allegro" and "Il Penseroso," N&Q, N. S. 3 (1956), 289-92.   2348

Points out resemblances in cyclic form, classical imagery, individual

images (tower, fairy folk, moon), and—most important—musical background, technique, and overtones.

Casady, Edwin. The Neo-Platonic Ladder in Spenser's Amoretti, in Renaissance Studies in Honor of Hardin Craig, pp. 92-103. Stanford, Cal.: Stanford University Press, 1941. Also in PQ, 20 (1941), 284-95.   2349

In producing his sonnet sequence, Sp selected from the sonnets he had previously written those he found could be used for his present purpose, ordered them as best he could, and then wrote such additional sonnets as were necessary to make the sequence a consistent study of the lover climbing the Neo-Platonic ladder.

Cirillo, Albert R. Spenser's Epithalamion: The Harmonious Universe of Love, SEL, 8 (1968), 19-34.   2350

Sp's Epith presents poet's resolution of amatory situation: "a duly consecrated Christian marriage in which progeny are the hope of a bright eternity." Poem's key concept is harmony, which expands through the verse, the marriage, and all of nature. This restores balance of musica humana and musica mundana which was lost in the Fall, but is "restorable in a love that looks beyond the cessation of temporal joys" to the divine harmony.

Clemen, Wolfgang. Spensers Epithalamion: Zum Problem der künstlerischen Wertmasstäbe. Munich: Bayerische Akademie der Wissenschaften, Philosophische—Historische Klasse, 8 (1964). 52 pp.   2351

See 2352. Gives modernized text of Epith from Philip Henderson's The Shepherd's Calendar and Other Poems (pp. 42-52; see 317).

Clemen, Wolfgang. The Uniqueness of Spenser's Epithalamion, in The Poetic

Tradition: Essays on Greek, Latin, and English Poetry, ed. Don Cameron Allen and Henry T. Rowell, pp. 81-98; repr. in 756. Baltimore: Johns Hopkins Press, 1968. 142 pp.   2352

Uniqueness is twofold: it is culmination of Elizabethan lyric poetry, and Sp's most perfect work. Previous long poems of the day lack sustained energy. Sp's use of the bride as central figure, poet as director of events, refrains, motifs of singing and rejoicing, imagery of light—unify the poem. Outer form corresponds to inner experience. Skillful use of time draws the reader into the poem. Sp is simultaneously "traditional and original, typical and personal, private and public." Poem concludes by drawing in metaphysical and spiritual motifs which lend new dignity to marriage. Most stimulating of all is the poem's inclusiveness, embracing a wide variety of traditions, motifs, and contrasts.

Clements, Robert J. Iconography on the Nature and Inspiration of Poetry in Renaissance Emblem Literature, PMLA, 70 (1955), 781-804.   2353

Most popular symbol for the poet in Renaissance, as in classic times, was the swan. "One of Spenser's 'naked emblems' in the Ruines of Time utilizes the swan motiv exactly as it had appeared in Alciati and Whitney" (pp. 784-9).

Clements, Robert J. Poetry and Philosophy in the Renaissance, CLS, 8 (1971), 1-20.   2354

Medieval oppositon to poetry eventually overcome during Renaissance. New genre arose, "philosophical poem." Sp's 4 Hymns mentioned in passing. [SpN, Vol. 2, No. 2 (1971), 11.]

Clinard, Turner Norman. A Critical History of the Pre-Elizabethan Sonnet.

DA, 16 (1956), 1139. Vanderbilt University, 1956. 331 pp.   2355

Giacomo da Lentino, Guinizelli, Dante, Petrarch; problems and practices of Wyatt, Surrey, Grimald, and "uncertain authors" of Tottel's Miscellany (1557). Background for Sp's Amor.

Comito, Terry. The Lady in a Landscape and the Poetics of Elizabethan Pastoral, UTQ, 41 (1972), 200-18.   2356

In defining poet as maker of golden worlds in Apologie for Poesy, Sidney suggests poet's freedom lies not in dispensing with nature but tying it to human concerns. This ambivalent view of poet implicit in myth animating many Elizabethan pastorals: lady in landscape who inhabits scene and transcends it. In Arcadia Sidney's Platonism is balanced between claim to freedom from nature's order and devotion to sensuous immediacy of things: between philosophy and history, idea and image. In CCCHA pastoral landscape is measured by concerns of "real" world. Poem makes us aware of distance between England and Ireland: between visionary presence and things which evoke it. Closed landscape around Colin limits freedom Sidney claimed for poet. Wanderers in Arcadia find similar duplicity in its landscape: retreat and prison, promise and denial. [SpN, Vol. 3, No. 2 (1972), 7-8.]

Cope, Jackson I. Jonson's Reading of Spenser: The Genesis of a Poem, EM, 10 (1959), 61-6.   2357

Jonson's Epistle to Elizabeth Countesse of Rutland was adapted from themes and tropes encountered while browsing through Sp's Complaints, in MHT, RT, and VB. "Reading Spenser's worst book, he fired it in his mind and turned it to a new poem."

Corbett, Edward P. J. Rhetorical Analyses of Literary Works. New York: Oxford University Press, 1969. 272 pp.
2358

Introduction (pp. xi-xxviii) explains that rhetorical mode of analysis deals with relationship between the Work and the Audience. Reprints essays by modern critics that have appeared elsewhere, under four headings: Argument, Arrangement, Audience, and Style. Under Style is selection from 2454.

Court, Franklin E. The Theme and Structure of Spenser's *Muiopotmos*, SEL, 10 (1970), 1-15.   2359

No reason to interpret poem allegorically. It belongs to convention of tragedy arising from *hubris*, attempt of mortal to equal or surpass a god. Divides poem into twelve sections that outline such a plot. Finds it tightly structured. [SpN, Vol. 1, No. 3 (1970), 12.]

Crowder, Richard. "Phoenix Spencer": A Note on Anne Bradstreet, NEQ, 17 (1944), 310.   2360

Three elegies for Sir Philip Sidney printed in The Phoenix Nest (1593), and again in Sp's Astro (1595), but again unidentified, ascribed by "later scholarship" to Matthew Roydon, Walter Raleigh, and Fulke Greville. Anne Bradstreet in her elegy for Sidney in The Tenth Muse (1650) must have assumed these two were by Sp: "And *Phoneix Spencer* doth unto his life, / His death present in sable to his wife." Perhaps she learned better before her death in 1672, for the couplet was omitted in her Poems (1678).

Cruttwell, Patrick. The Love Poetry of John Donne: Pedantique Weedes or Fresh Invention? in Metaphysical Poetry, Stratford-upon-Avon Studies 11,

ed. D. J. Palmer and Malcolm Bradbury, pp. 11-39. London: Edward Arnold, 1970. 280 pp.   2361

Emphasizing contrast between Donne and earlier Elizabethan poets, quotes Sp and Donne "on the same theme, and that the theme of Petrarchan adoration—Spenser's home ground, one might say": lines from HHOL and part of Donne's The Undertaking. "The change is from a concept of poetry as something chanting, bardic, and pulpit-rhetorical, to something talking, man-to-man, and dramatic." See 611.

Cummings, Peter M. Spenser's *Amoretti* as an Allegory of Love, TSLL, 12 (1970), 163-79.   2362

Rather than as autobiographical record, Amor may be read more profitably as allegory of love in which particular man and woman become exempla of Man and Woman. First sonnet hints that account of love to follow is less ephemeral than a particular courtship. Second introduces theme of "unquiet thought" and "troubled wits" running through the sequence, inviting reader to participate in restless mental processes of poet-lover, his often contradictory succession of attitudes. Idealistic vision of lady qualified by criticism of her flaws, and poet resists role of abject lover. Thus both are brought together on level of ordinary humanity. Imaginative resolutions, as in Easter sonnet (68), suggesting reconciliation of spirit and flesh, prove temporary. Sequence ends in irresolution. Brief Anacreontic poems at end serve as coda; allegorically, they reflect larger structure of sequence. [SpN, Vol. 4, No. 2 (1973), 7-8.]

Davis, William V. Edmund Spenser's "Epithalamion," AN&Q, 7 (1969), 84-5.   2363

References to "fish-tending nymphs" in stanza 4 of Epith and to planet Venus in stanza 16 combine pagan and Christian imagery which "represents in a very subtle way the marriage theme with which Spenser is dealing." See 2398.

Donow, Herbert S. Concordance and Stylistic Analysis of Six Elizabethan Sonnet Sequences, CHum, 3 (1969), 205-8.   2364

Describes procedures in preparing a concordance to sonnet sequences of Shakespeare, Sp, Sidney, Daniel, and Drayton (Idea's Mirror and later Idea). Object to produce "a tool for an analysis of sonnet style." Has explored relationship between word-length and rhythm, and three categories of words in sonnet: function words, context-oriented words, and genre-oriented words. Only Shakespeare available in modern spelling, so has modernized spelling in other sequences. Concordance complete for 7,357 lines of poetry in six sonnet sequences examined. See 2365.

Donow, Herbert S. A Concordance to the Sonnet Sequences of Daniel, Drayton, Shakespeare, Sidney, and Spenser. Carbondale: Southern Illinois University Press, 1969, 772 pp.   2365

Computerized concordance based on assumptions that style is measurable pattern of words and sonnet sequences are much alike. Elizabethan sonneteers worked in tight convention. Appendix gives number of occurrences of each word in each sequence and lists words in descending order of frequency. [SpN, Vol. 2, No. 2 (1971), 2.] See 2364.

Dunlop, Alexander. Calendar Symbolism in the "Amoretti," N&Q, 16 (1969), 24-6.   2366

Association of Epith with June 11, marriage day in poem, may be related to calendrical framework in Amor. Sp's sonnet sequence progresses from Jan. 1, New Year's Day (No. 4), to beginning of Lent, Ash Wednesday (No. 22), to March 25, Lady Day (No. 62), to Easter (No. 68). [SpN, Vol. 1, No. 2 (1970), 7.] See 2369, 2367, 2398.

Dunlop, Alexander. The Unity of Spenser's *Amoretti*, in Silent Poetry: Essays in Numerological Analysis, ed. Alastair Fowler, pp. 153-69. New York: Barnes & Noble, 1970. 260 pp.   2367

Secular and church calendar symbolism unify the sequence. Development parallels workings of love described in HHOL, progression from desire to higher form of love. "Clearly, Spenser saw the religious and the amatory elements not as two levels of meaning, but as inseparable aspects of the same story. . . . Within the calendrical, numerological, liturgical, and thematic bounds" of sequence, finds three groups: (1) in 1-21 lover active in conventional courtship, positive and negative attitudes alternating; (2) in 22-68 tone and theme correspond to Lenten season; (3) in 69-89 lover moves toward fulfillment, but in last 6 sonnets "the lover is plunged back into suffering." Reunion and fulfillment in marriage in Epith. See 681, 2366.

Dyson, Sir George. Sweet Thames Run Softly. London: Novello, 1954.   2368

Cantata for baritone solo, chorus, and orchestra.

Eade, J. C. The Pattern in the Astronomy of Spenser's *Epithalamion*, RES, 23 (1972), 173-8.   2369

Investigates possibility (see 2366, 2398) that stanzas of Epith correspond to "unequal hours of day and night" (at 52 degrees North, on marriage day, day 84 minutes and night 36 minutes), points out planetary allusions in poem reflect positions of heavenly bodies on given date. Astronomical conditions required to provide correspondences with poem occurred only two other times in fifty years before and after 1594. [SpN, Vol. 3, No. 2 (1972), 8.]

Editors. Spenser's *Prothalamion*, Expl 1 (1943), No. 36.   2370

A defense of unity of Proth on grounds that, although swan image is dropped after eighth stanza, it is echoed in later parts of poem when the ladies' "gentle knights" are likened to Castor and Pollux, children of Leda and Jovian swan. "In relating both his ladies and his knights to the Leda and the swan myth Spenser successfully conveys an impression of the godlike passion represented in the espousal."

Elcock, W. D. English Indifference to Du Bellay's "Regrets," MLR, 46 (1951), 175-84.   2371

Sp was the first of Du Bellay's English admirers, translating his Antiquités de Rome in VB and RR. Other Elizabethans used his Olive, as Sp did in Amor. Resemblance in situation and mood between Du Bellay of Les Regrets and Sp of MHT, and in particular, of CCCHA. But Sp's descriptions of the evils of court life are more conventional, more medieval (pp. 176-80).

Entzensberger, Christian. Sonett und Poetik: Die Aussagen der elisabethanischen Sonettzyklen über das Dichten im Vergleich mit der zeitgenössichen Dichtungslehre. Doc. diss., University of Munich, 1962.   2372

Esplin, Ross Stolworthy. The Emerging Legend of Sir Philip Sidney, 1586-1652. DAI, 31 (1970), 2341A. University of Utah, 1970. 336 pp.   2373

Contributing to idealized legend of

Sidney were balladists, historians, and biographers. Most important were poems by Lodowick Bryskett, Matthew Roydon, Fulke Greville, Walter Ralegh, and Sp—poems grouped around Sp's Astro, which glorified Sidney in pastoral terms and expressed personal sorrow. Fulke Greville's long-delayed biography (1652) was crowning point of Sidney legend, attributing to him all that was good. This legendary Sidney lives today.

French, Roberts W. A Note on Spenser and Milton, N&Q, 17 (1970), 412. 2374

Probable source for metaphor in L'Allegro, ll. 121-122 (Ladies "whose bright eyes / Rain influence") is Epith, l. 416 ("happy influence upon us rain"). [SpN, Vol. 2, No. 2 (1971), 9.]   2374

Friedland, Louis S. A Dubious Spenser Quotation, N&Q, 185 (1943), 141.   2375

Whittier in his essay The Beautiful erroneously attributed a quatrain to Sp. The editor identifies the lines as belonging to Matthew Roydon in An Elegie, which he contributed anonymously to Sp's Astro.

Friedland, Louis S. The Illustrations in *The Theatre for Worldlings*, HLQ, 19 (1956), 107-20.   2376

Refutes the idea that the copperplates for the Dutch original of Van der Noot's work were by Marcus Gheeraerts, and presents evidence for attributing them to Lucas de Heere.

Gaertner, Adelheid. Die englische Epithalamienliteratur im siebzehnten Jahrhundert und ihre Vorbilder. Doctoral diss., University of Erlangen, 1935. JdH, 52 (1937), 192. Coburg: A. Rossteutscher, 1936. 100pp.   2377

Notes resemblances and differences between Sp's Epith and epithalamia of Donne, Jonson, Thomas Heywood,

Wither, Drayton, Phineas Fletcher, Christopher Brooke, Herrick, Randolph, and several Restoration poets.

Goldman, Lloyd Nathaniel. Attitudes Toward the Mistress in Five Elizabethan Sonnet Sequences. DA, 25 (1965), 6590A-1A. University of Illinois, 1964. 297 pp.   2378

While sequences of Sidney, Daniel, Drayton, Shakespeare, and Sp are all unified works of art, all rely on traditional Petrarchan conceits. Two basic understandings of the writer's role as writer are evident: Sidney, Shakespeare, and Drayton logically examine the attitudes of their personae; but Daniel and Sp employ their sonnets as emblems. Each writer, except Drayton, uses the "Diana-Venus" complex, i.e., awareness of classical mythology that accounts for feeling of attraction-repulsion toward the lady. Sidney and Sp conceive this complex in terms of Diana and Venus; Daniel, in terms of Minerva and Venus. Sidney analyzes love in light of Christian Agape and pagan Eros; Daniel, as an unattainable ideal state; Drayton presents maturation of the lover; Shakespeare interprets illicit love in light of scholastic principles; Sp portrays romantic love as a prelude to wedded love.

Gordon, D. J. The Imagery of Ben Jonson's *The Masque of Blackness* and *The Masque of Beautie*, JWCI, 6 (1943), 122-41.   2379

Finds possible source of Jonson's puzzling note in Masque of Blacknesse (1605) on Love being awakened by Clotho in HHOL, ll. 107-9. His Dignitas in Masque of Beautie (1608) closely resembles Sp's Sapience in HOHB, ll. 183-96.

Gottfried, Rudolf. The "G. W. Senior" and "G. W. I." of Spenser's *Amoretti*, MLQ, 3 (1942), 543-6.   2380

The two sonnets prefixed to Amor are by Geoffrey Whitney, Senior, and his son. See 2496.

Greene, David Mason. Mediaeval Backgrounds of the Elizabethan Emblem-Book. Doctoral diss., University of California at Berkeley, 1958. DA, 18 (1958), 99.   2381

Much misapprehension exists about origins of emblem-book. Origins not esoteric. Themes of 16th century emblem-books were those found in popular literature of Middle Ages: bestiaries, mythographies, fable-books, encyclopedias. Same themes were prominent in medieval art. In 15th century, works like Jean Mielot's recension of Christine de Pisan's L'Epitre d'Othea provided models, both in form and content, for emblem-book. Geoffrey Whitney's A Choice of Emblems (1586), first English emblem-book, borrowed extensively from Continental predecessors.

Greene, Thomas M. Spenser and the Epithalamic Convention, CL, 9 (1957), 215-28; repr. in 649.   2382

Sketches the history of the genre stemming from Sappho's fragments and Catullus 61. Describes or names examples in medieval Latin, neo-Latin, French, Italian, and English poetry. No significant English examples before Sp, but genre has complicated history in 17th century. Synthesizes chief characteristics or requirements of Renaissance epithalamion, i.e., the convention received by Sp. Points out Sp's modifications of this convention. Finds him original in combining roles of bridegroom and poet-spokesman, as well as in other innovations, mostly successful. Provides several insights in analysis of Sp's Epith.

Griem, Eberhard. Die elisabethanische Epoche, in Epochen der englischen

Lyrik, ed. Karl Heinz Göller, pp. 79-99. Düsseldorf: Bagel, 1971.   2383

Grundy, Joan. Shakespeare's Sonnets and the Elizabethan Sonneteers, ShS, 15 (1962), 41-9.   2384

Keats, in sonnet addressed to Sp: The flower must drink the nature of the soil, / Before it can put forth its blossoming. This expresses Shakespeare's relation to fellow-sonneteers, although he adapted conventions of Renaissance sonnet sequence to own talent. Gives examples of Spenserian conceits he used: Amor 45, l. 1; 17, ll. 13-14; 85, ll. 1-2—mirror, picture, and monument closely linked. Shakespeare's "poetic" similar to that of Daniel, Sp, and especially Sidney; but he gave it new philosophical and critical depth.

Halio, Jay L. "Prothalamion," "Ulysses," and Intention in Poetry, CE, 22 (1961), 390-4.   2385

A split intention in poetry can be artistic or inartistic. Sp uses the marriage theme in Proth to gain patronage of Earl of Essex by a flattering reference to a wedding held at the Earl's house, but poem fails artistically. Tennyson, on other hand, divides his intention between quest for experience and desire for rest in "Ulysses" and succeeds artistically.

Harbage, Alfred. Love's Labor's Lost and the Early Shakespeare, in Shakespeare Without Words and Other Essays, pp. 117-42. Cambridge, Mass.: Harvard University Press, 1972, 229 pp.   2386

Also in PQ, 41 (1962). Argues that Love's Labor's Lost was written for Chapel Children 1588-1589, thus accounting in part for Shakespeare's activity during "lost years." Suggests "our pleasant Willy . . . that same gentle Spirit" in Sp's TM is Shakespeare; "if anyone in his times was equipped to recognize Shakespeare's talents promptly, and to recognize their essential quality, it was Edmund Spenser." Possibly Shakespeare is Aetion in CCCHA (pp. 139-42).

Hardison, O. B., Jr. "Amoretti and the Dolce Stil Novo," ELR, 2 (1972), 208-16.   2387

Sp's Amor not disunified. Contrasting images of saintly lady and "cruel fair" from stil novo tradition. Sonnets span January to Easter in 1594, sequence a symmetrical triptych: first panel, 1-21, introduces conflicts of early courtship; central panel, 22-68, reconciles earlier impulses in ideal of married love; third panel, 69 to end, explores implications of what poet has learned. Sp's originality shows in contrast with Petrarch's Canzoniere, in which motifs of Laura cruel when living and angelicata after death remain irreconcilable. Amor almost alone among Renaissance cycles in celebrating love as benign life force. [SpN, Vol. 3, No. 3 (1972), 11.]

Harris, Brice. The Ape in Mother Hubberds Tale, HLQ, 4 (1941), 191-203.   2388

Identifies the ape in the second part of the poem with Robert Cecil, son of Lord Burghley, who is represented by the fox. See 2425.

Harris, Brice. The Butterfly in Spenser's Muiopotmos, JEGP, 43 (1944), 302-16.   2389

Identifies Clarion the Butterfly with Robert Devereux, Earl of Essex, and interprets the poem as an allegory of Essex's life from childhood up to 1590. The theme of the poem is the conflict between Essex and Burghley, expressing Sp's fear that Burghley would crush Essex.

Harrison, Thomas P., Jr. Flower Lore in Spenser and Shakespeare: Two Notes, MLQ, 7 (1946), 175-8.   2390

Henry Lyte's Newe Herball (1578) suggested as source of Sp's fanciful flower called Starlight, Penthia, and Astrophel in Astro, ll. 183 ff.

Harrison, Thomas P., Jr. Turner and Spenser's *Mother Hubberds Tale*, JEGP, 49 (1950), 464-9.   2391

Shows similarities in the use of animal images between Sp's poem and William Turner's Spirituall Physik (1555).

Hartung, George. A Note on Keats' "To Autumn," N&Q, 196 (1951), 143. 2392

Keats' ode possibly indebted to CCCHA. Close parallels cited in diction and imagery.

Hasan, Masoodul. English Epithalamic Verse of the Earlier Seventeenth Century, IJES, 8 (1967), 10-24.   2393

Discusses style and theme. Sp as an influence upon the 17th-century tradition.

Heltzel, Virgil B. The Arcadian Hero, PQ, 41 (1962), 173-80.   2394

Believes Pyrocles and Musidorus in Sidney's Arcadia portray ideal of gentility that Sidney himself exemplified in person and conduct. "What features of the man and gentleman impressed his friends?" Although Sp was never intimately acquainted with Sidney, impression he formed of first patron survived as lasting memory when years later in Astro he recalled his hero's "comely shape" and beauty of mind and face. These possessed by heroes of Arcadia. Pamphilius a breaker of women's hearts, "like Sidney's opposite, Spenser's superficial courtier" [in CCCHA], but nevertheless had attractive charm. "With Sidney, as with Spenser, friendship is a virtue"—in Bk. IV of FQ. Pyrocles and Musidorus have noble qualities of Sidney himself.

Hendrickson, G. L. Elizabethan Quantitative Hexameters, PQ, 28 (1949), 237-60.   2395

On the quantitative verse techniques of Sidney, Harvey, and Stanyhurst. Draws heavily on Harvey's remarks and hexameters addressed to Sp in Three Proper and Wittie Familiar Letters.

Heyen, William. Narration in Spenser's "Epithalamion," BSUF, 6 (1965), 51-4.   2396

Extends Greene's discussion (2382) of narrative speaker in Epith, whom Greene cites as first instance of fusion of bridegroom and poet-speaker in a wedding poem. Traces creation of mood of impatience in first 16 stanzas, artful delays leading to consummation, and prayerful peace with which poem closes.

Hieatt, A. Kent. The Daughters of Horus: Order in the Stanzas of *Epithalamion*, in Form and Convention in the Poetry of Edmund Spenser, ed. William Nelson, pp. 103-21. New York: Columbia University Press, 1961. 188 pp.   2397

Elaborates the theory, introduced in Short Time's Endless Monument (2398), that first twelve stanzas of the poem are made to match, stanza by stanza, with following twelve. Compares two sets of matching stanzas, 1 and 13 and 3 and 15. Points out numerous parallels and antitheses in each set.

Hieatt, A. Kent. Short Time's Endless Monument: The Symbolism of the Numbers in Edmund Spenser's *Epithalamion*. Port Washington: Kennikat, 1972. 118 pp.   2398

Repr. of 1960 ed. Presents and interprets unexplained variations in stanza, rhyme, and metrical pattern. The length of stanzas and lines corresponds to hours in the day, days in the year, degrees of sun's daily and yearly apparent movement around the earth. The 365 "long" lines symbolize sun's yearly progress. The twenty-four stanzas represent twelve daylight and twelve dark hours in the day. Gives text of poem, following Variorum edition, with glosses. See 2397.

Hill, Elizabeth A. K. The Sacred Epithalamion: A Study of the Song of Songs in Seventeenth-Century English Poetry. DA, 27 (1966), 457A. Columbia University, 1966. 150 pp.   2399

Traces tradition of commentary on Song of Songs from Origen through Bernard of Clairvaux, St. Teresa of Avila, and St. John of the Cross, to Reformation and post-Tridentine commentators; then surveys use of the text and the tradition in Donne, Beaumont, Herbert, Milton, Vaughan, Traherne, Crashaw, Quarles, Carew, Marvell, Habington. Sp among those who used traditional material judiciously and integrated it with their own visions.

Hill, Elliott M. Flattery in Spenser's *Fowre Hymnes*, WVUPP, 15 (1966), 22-35.   2400

Sp, in 4 Hymns, strongly flattered Queen Elizabeth in hope of securing a quick and generous reward for writing FQ.

Hill, W. Speed. Order and Joy in Spenser's "Epithalamion," SHR, 6 (1972), 81-90.   2401

Need to account for success of Epith with readers. Poem orchestrates set of Renaissance antinomies into concord: warfare of sexes resolved in mutual triumph; usury of anxiety summed up in delight; sexual union and social contract; individual intimacy and cosmic formality; fragile uniqueness of the day and its transcendence; comfort but also danger of

isolation in Ireland. Stasis and movement balanced in stanzas related to both sonnet and FQ stanza, which link together in continuity and pause in separate lyrics. [SpN, Vol. 3, No. 3 (1972), 12.]

Hinely, Jan Lawson. The Sonnet Sequence in Elizabethan Poetry. DA, 27 (1967), 3011A. Ohio State University, 1966. 306 pp.   2402

Studies Petrarchan sonnet sequence, its contribution to English poetry, and its relation to "shift in poetic sensibility" of 1590's. Petrarch created the love convention and sonnet sequence, poetry of self-analysis and self-expression. In England only Sidney, Sp, and Shakespeare were able to utilize tradition to create true sonnet sequence. In Amor speaker is stylized representative of poet, but Sp emphasizes narrative, dramatic, and meditative possibilities over the expressive because he wished to create an ideal pattern of reciprocal love. In Shakespeare, expressiveness reaches its acme, poet and persona are interchangeable. Once sonnet tradition succeeded in producing a distinctive lyric voice it was no longer needed, and lost favor; but its poetic achievement was assimilated into lyric current of 1590's, especially in Donne.

Hinnant, Charles H. Marvell's Gallery of Art, RenQ, 24 (1971), 26-37.   2403

Marvell adapted Italian pictorial traditions in his amatory poems. Sp mentioned. [SpN, Vol. 2, No. 3 (1971), 8.]

Hoffman, Arthur W. Spenser and *The Rape of the Lock*, PQ, 49 (1970), 530-46.   2404

Tillotson's Twickenham ed. of The Rape of the Lock notes six Spenserian parallels. "Strong parallels" cited here with Epith and Proth. Analyzes effects produced. Pope's poem not first occasional poem connected with Petre family (the Baron was seventh Lord Petre). William Petre, later second Lord Petre, was one of bridegrooms of Proth. Picture of Belinda much closer to Sp's brides than more modern picture, which also echoes Sp, Eliot's "Thamesdaughters" in the Waste Land. [SpN, Vol. 2, No. 2 (1971), 8-9] See 1629.

Hotson, Leslie. Mr. W. H. New York: Knopf, 1965. 328 pp.   2405

"Important digression" on early tributes to Shakespeare as poet of Sonnets, two by Sp in TM ("that same gentle Spirit," ll. 217-222) and CCCHA (Aetion, ll. 444-447), by Gabriel Harvey in Sonnet 10 of his Foure Letters (1592), and by John Davies in Orchestra ("before June 1594") (pp. 193-200). For other references to Sp, see Index.

Hotson, Leslie. Shakespeare's Motley: New York: Oxford University Press, 1952. 133pp.   2406

Defends the view that Sp's "gentle spirit" (TM, l. 217) and Aetion (CCCHA, l. 444) refer to Shakespeare (pp. 25-32). Based on theory that Shakespeare's sonnets were written 1586-89.

Hughes, Merritt Y. Milton and the Symbol of Light, SEL, 4 (1964), 1-33. 2407

A close-packed essay. Traces evolution in modern criticism of interpretation of Paradise Lost in terms of its dark / light imagery. Recognition followed that imagery is structurally important. Proem to Bk. III now regarded as a theophany, and meaning of "Celestial light" (Paradise Lost, III, 51) much discussed. Also, who are Urania and her sister Wisdom (VII, Proem)? Sp's Sapience in HOHB, of syncretic Christian-Neo-platonist derivation, may be key to meaning (see 2410). Discusses Rabbinical critics on

problem, "the Christology of Robert Fludd's pseudo-scientific theory of the nature of light," hexameral writers, Tasso's exordium to the *Mondo Creato*, Richard Hooker's view of Tertullian's image in Against Praxias, and much more. Immediate source of Proem to Bk. III in Milton's "life-long fondness for the praise of light which led his imagination constantly toward images clustering around that subject." See 2408.

Hughes, Merritt Y. Ten Perspectives on Milton. New Haven: Yale University Press, 1965. 291 pp.   2408

Fourth essay is repr. of 2407.

Hunter, G.K. The Dramatic Technique of Shakespeare's Sonnets, EIC, 3 (1953), 152-64.   2409

Lyric, narrative, metaphysical exercises not what Shakespeare's sonnets are, and biographical approach misses fact Shakespeare's sonnets were written by a dramatist. In sonnets with "the authentic Shakespearean note," e.g., 89 and 86, brilliance of language so vivid that reader "supplies from his imagination a complete dramatic situation." Compares treatment of theme of absence in Sonnet 97 and Amor 88. "Spenser's image has the charm of an idyll; Shakespeare's generates in the reader a reaction more proper to drama."

Hunter, William B., Jr. Milton's Urania, SEL, 4 (1964), 35-42.   2410

Discusses scholarship on Sp's Uranian Venus in HOHB, parallel between Neoplatonic trinity of One-Mind-Soul and Christian Trinity of Father-Son-Spirit, concludes that Milton in invocations which begin Bks. I, III, VII, and IX of Paradise Lost is "praying for help from the Heavenly Spirit, that is, from this virtue and power of the Father as they are manifested in the Son, whom he addresses variously as Holy Light, as Spirit, and as Urania." See 2407.

Hutton, James. Cupid and the Bee, PMLA, 56 (1941), 1036-57.   2411

Notes many translations and imitations deriving ultimately from Theocritus 19 or the similar poem by Anacreon. Discusses (pp. 1047-51) Sp's 6-stanza poem ending Amor, "the most elaborate treatment of the theme that we have encountered." Finds versions of Tasso, Ronsard, and possibly Watson immediately behind Sp's handling of the theme.

Hutton, James. Spenser's "Adamantine Chains": A Cosmological Metaphor, in The Classical Tradition: Literary and Historical Studies in Honor of Harry Caplan, ed. Luitpold Wallach, pp. 572-94. Ithaca: Cornell University Press, 1966. 606 pp.   2412

Sp's use of "Adamantine Chains" in HHOL (l. 89) is metaphor for love which binds and unites discordant elements of nature. This follows Plato, who, in the Timaeus, "explains the union of the elements as a proportion with extremes and means and calls it metaphorically a 'bond.'"

Hyman, Lawrence W. Structure and Meaning in Spenser's *Epithalamion*, TSL, 3 (1958), 37-42.   2413

Shows how Sp uses the same imagery in different contexts with different connotations to maintain the continuity between "the innocence of virginity and the sexuality of marriage."

Izard, Thomas C. George Whetstone, Mid-Elizabethan Gentleman of Letters CUSECL, 158. New York: Columbia University Press, 1942. 297pp.   2414

Whetstone's elegy on Francis Russell, second Earl of Bedford, A Mirror of Treue Honnour and Christian Nobilitie (1585), is dedicated to the boy Edward Russell, third Earl of Bedford, who is spoken of by Sp in TM (ll. 267-73) in the section on the Bedford family (pp. 244-7).

Jack, Ronald D. S. Imitation in the Scottish Sonnet, CL, 20 (1968), 313-28.   2415

James's sonneteers relied mainly on Scottish and French sources; move to London (1603) saw bias shifting to English or Italian. William Alexander, Earl of Stirling, leader of Scottish poets in London, had always imitated English poets. His Aurora echoes Daniel's Delia and Sp's Amor. See 2450.

Jayne, Sears. Ficino and the Platonism of the English Renaissance, CL, 4 (1952), 214-38.   2416

Modifies usual view that Ficino was responsible for the Platonism of the English Renaissance. In the main it derives from Italian popularizers of Ficino's doctrine, or at third hand from the French poets (p. 236). Though direct influence was relatively small, three writers of scholarly prose—Colet, Ralegh, and Burton—and two philosophical poets—Sp and Chapman—knew him directly. Sp's poetry of idealized love and beauty, as in Amor and 4 Hymns, belongs to highest and rarest kind of English Platonic poetry, that which "reflects still deeper probing . . . into the sources of the theory of Platonic love, beyond the popular *trattati* to Pico, Benivieni, and Ficino himself."

Jenkins, Raymond. Rosalind in *Colin Clouts Come Home Againe*, MLN, 67 (1952), 1-5.   2417

The Rosalind of CCCHA can not be the first Mrs. Spenser, and must be Elizabeth Boyle, Sp's second wife.

John, Lisle Cecil. The Elizabethan Sonnet Sequences: Studies in Conventional

Conceits. New York: Columbia University Press, 1938; repr. Russell and Russell, 1964. 278pp.   2418

Numerous references to Sp. Publication of Amor and general quality of Sp's sonnets (pp. 22-3); Ovidian tradition and Cupid (pp. 50-2, 61); Alexandrian or Anacreontic tradition and Cupid (pp. 67-9, 77); melancholy effects of love (pp. 81, 91); temple within the heart (pp. 102-3); wasting in despair (pp. 106, 108-9); absence (pp. 110, 112); animal comparisons (pp. 116-7, 119); "mirror" conceit (p. 124); "eternizing" conceit (pp. 132-3); Sp's sonnet lady (pp. 148-9, 151, 154, 158-9, 160-4); Table of Conceits (pp. 195-200). See also Index.

Johnson, E. D. *Virgil's Gnat*, Baconiana, 27 (1943), 46-8.   2419

Bacon wrote VG.

Johnson, William C. Rhyme and Repetition in Spenser's *Amoretti*, XUS, 9 (1970), 15-25.   2420

In Amor rhyme words used for varied forms of word play, such as homonymic repetitions. Sound patterns create interrelationships between parts of a verse. Rhyme-echo unifies the whole sequence of sonnets. Last three sonnets link with first three through echo and antithesis.

Johnson, William C. Spenser's *Amoretti* VI, Expl, 29 (1971), Item 38.   2421

Sonnet takes its form from sermon and is network of etymological puns using key word "abide." [SpN, Vol. 2, No. 1 (1971), 8.]

Johnson, William C. Spenser's Sonnet Diction, NM, 71 (1970), 157-67.   2422

Sp enlarged his poetic vocabularies in various genres to achieve "expressive and flexible" vehicles for ideas. His diction in Amor more lyrical and modern than usually recognized.

Words "remote" in poetic sense, but not archaic. Remote diction suited to Christian relationship developed in sequence. When Sp alters a word he usually lengthens it; his music not clipped. [SpN, Vol. 1, No. 3 (1970), 13.]

Johnson, William Clarence. "Vowd to Eternity": A Study of Spenser's *Amoretti*. DAI, 30 (1969), 3909-A. University of Iowa, 1969. 291 pp. 2423

Sp's Amor (1595) closer to Renaissance sonnet "sequence" than any other series of prolific decade. As *einzelsonetten* and as sequence work exhibits technical mastery. Examination reveals properties which tie groups of sonnets (and whole sequence) together. Larger patterns reveal emblematic segment of cosmic love and cosmic time. Nature and man set in corresponding movements: as Spring comes forth, so does renewed man; as each planet moves toward completion of year, so does man (metaphysical planet). Explication shows Sp's multi-faceted calender schemes: cosmic year, fiscal year, and Church year. Concludes various amatory and religious parallels concerned with two courtships: poet-lover for lady, penitent Christian for Christ. Amor (Love) of sonnets becomes "the harmony of that which is physical with that which is ideal, exemplified by the Christ-lady to whom, and for whom, these sonnets are 'vowd to eternity'."

Judson, A. C. *Amoretti*, Sonnet I, MLN, 58 (1943), 548-50.   2424

The sonnet written on a blank leaf of the Rosenbach copy of the first issue of FQ is not in Sp's handwriting. See 145.

Judson, A. C. Mother Hubberd's Ape, MLN, 63 (1948), 145-9.   2425

Reviews the various opinions as to

the identity of the Ape. The most likely candidate is Simier, and the Fox is Burghley. Replies to objections that have been raised to this theory. See 2388.

Kehler, Dorothea. *Paradise Lost*, X, 860-862, MiltonN, 2 (1968), 45.   2426

Proposes that in composing Paradise Lost, X, 860-862, Milton used as his source the refrain of Sp's Epith. Passage helps to heighten sense of loss of innocence after the fall and contrasts discord of Adam and Eve with marital harmony.

Kellogg, Robert. Thought's Astonishment and the Dark Conceit of Spenser's *Amoretti*, in RenP 1965, ed. George Walton Williams and Peter G. Phialas, pp. 3-13. Southeastern Renaissance Conference, 1966. 63 pp. Repr. in 649.   2427

It is anachronisitic to take Amor as autobiographical or as realistic fiction; like Dante's and Chaucer's references to themselves, Sp's allusions to himself here and elsewhere are not personal but allusions to the poet as public figure. Amor and Renaissance lyric in general closer to allegory than to realism. In Amor, Sp is expressing his philosophy of love through convenient vehicle of sonnet sequence. Sp's contribution to Renaissance love lyric does not rest on quality of "his own personal experience as religious worshipper, lover and poet," but on his imaginative assertion that "in the highest civilization the three persons are ideally one."

Kernan, Alvin. The Cankered Muse: Satire of the English Renaissance. YSE, 142. New Haven: Yale University Press, 1959. 261pp.   2428

Decorum of satire required a low style, as Sp points out in MHT, ll. 43-4 (p. 58). Contrasts Sp's more "seemly" diction in MHT with

Marston's (p. 100, note 8). In connection with Elizabethan association of satire with satyr, cites Sp's satyrs and Satyrane, a half-satyr (FQ, I, vi), as confirming "the established image of the satyr personality" (pp. 91-2).

Kernan, Alvin B., ed. Modern Shakespeare Criticism: Essays on Style, Dramaturgy, and the Major Plays. New York: Harcourt, Brace, 1970. 447 pp.   2429

Includes Patrick Cruttwell's Shakespeare's Sonnets and the 1590's (pp. 110-40), from The Shakespearean Moment (611). Cruttwell, citing Sp's Amor, "uses Shakespeare's sonnet sequence to trace in the poetry and plays of the time the gradual movement from conventional subject matter and style to a much more complex view of reality and the human condition." (p. v).

Kliewer, Warren. "Prothalamion" as a Pictorial Poem, Descant, 5 (1961), 25-32.   2430

Pictorial quality in Proth not decorative but based on structure. Structure is determined by poem's organization, understood in terms of space rather than time or events. Such structure gives poem a tone of emotional objectivity, and is a poetic experiment to show relation of things in space.

Knight, G. Wilson. The Christian Renaissance. New York: Norton, 1962. 356 pp.   2431

Defends his symbolic Shakespearian criticism by reference to "Spenser and his extravagant use of symbolism, allegory and metaphysical speculation" (p. 5). Dithyrambic commentary on Epith: "So Spenser creates his paradise on earth" (pp. 89-90). "What is the relation of human beauty to worth?" Sp in HHOB (ll. 120-140) and Epith (l. 186) sees through to the soul (p. 293).

Knoll, Robert E. Spenser and the Voyage of the Imagination, WHR, 13 (1959), 249-55.   2432

The hypothetical influence of Titian's Rape of Europa on Sp's description of this rape in Muiop (ll. 277-96) may have been accomplished through Sidney, if he brought home a copy of the painting from Venice.

Kostić, Veselin. Spenser's *Amoretti* and Tasso's Lyrical Poetry, RMS, 3 (1959), 51-77.   2433

Analytical comparison of Sp's sonnets which rely on Tasso with their originals. Finds less integral Platonism in Sp than in Tasso, more dramatic imagery, less compactness of meaning, "a tendency towards stronger colouring and over-emphasis," less unity of structure.

Kristeller, Paul Oskar. The Platonic Academy of Florence, RN, 14 (1961), 147-59.   2434

Florentine humanism mainly "a rhetorical and poetical culture," philosophical speculation in work of Marsilio Ficino and colleagues of Platonic Academy. Ficino's complex and unique kind of Platonism influential in many areas of Renaissance thought. His fundamental concept is "contemplation," which "all human beings must aim at in order to attain not only true knowledge but also moral perfection." Shows this idea is "key" to Ficino's contributions to "the theory of the immortality of the soul and the theory of Platonic love." Background of Sp's 4 Hymns and some other poems.

Lascelles, Mary. The Rider on the Winged Horse, in Elizabethan and Jacobean Studies Presented to Frank Percy Wilson, pp. 173-98. Oxford: Clarendon Press, 1959; repr. Folcroft, Pa.: Folcroft Press, 1969. 359 pp.   2435

A study of myth which associates the poet with the winged horse Pegasus, especially Sp's use of it in RT (ll. 421-427, and 645-658) and Milton's in Paradise Lost, VII, 1-20. Hesiod first associated Pegasus with Bellerophon. Traces expansion of myth in classical, medieval, and Renaissance literature. E. K.'s gloss on April eclogue of SC quite different from Sp's interweaving in two passages in RT, "this great, uneven poem," of themes of fame, Pegasus, and Sidney. Idea of Sidney runs, "like a twisted thread of black and gold, through the variously coloured web" of RT.

Leishman, J. B. Themes and Variations in Shakespeare's Sonnets. London: Hutchinson, 1961. 254 pp.   2436

In chap. on Shakespeare and his English predecessors relates themes in Sp's VB, VP, RT, RR, TM, and Amor to themes in Shakespeare's sonnets. "Temperamentally and spiritually Spenser was, I think, nearer to Petrarch and to the poets of the *dolce stil nuovo* and the *cor gentil* than to Ronsard" (pp. 70-8).

Lever, J. W. The Elizabethan Love Sonnet. London: Methuen, 1956. 282pp.   2437

Chapter V, Spenser, pp. 92-138. Amor is an attempt to blend two different collections of sonnets, with 18 of them belonging to an earlier phase. Remaining 71 are the core. In these the conception of love comes from Platonic doctrines in Book 4 of Castiglione's Il Cortegiano. Discusses the influence of Desportes and Tasso in some detail. Sp's imagery, diction, and verse-form are distinctive but not admirable. The sequence as a whole is conceptual, not dramatic. Sp imposed on his sonnets "a preconceived interpretation of life" that invalidated "the traditional virtues of the sonnet-sequence." See 2451.

Levý, Jiří. On the Relations of Language and Stanza Pattern in the English Sonnet, in Worte und Werte: Bruno Markwardt zum 60. Geburtstag, ed. Gustav Erdmann and Alfons Eichstaedt, pp. 214-31. Berlin: Walter de Gruyter, 1961. 498 pp.   2438

Detailed analysis of prosodic tendencies in English sonnet patterns from Thomas Wyatt to G. M. Hopkins. Sonnet, when transferred from Italian (Romance language) into English (Germanic language), undergoes transformations determined by two agents: literary tradition and form of language. Difficulties of French rhyme-scheme may account for Sp's unrhymed first version of Du Bellay's sonnets in Theatre (p. 219). Italian or French forms perfected only by English poets who tended toward "antithetical construction of lines," such as Sidney and Sp (pp. 224-5). Enclosed rhymes of Italian and French poets changed to alternate rhymes in, e.g., autonomous Spenserian stanza (pp. 226-7).

Leyburn, Ellen Douglass. Satiric Allegory: Mirror of Man. YSE, 130. New Haven: Yale University Press, 1956. 142pp.   2439

MHT not successful animal satire. We cannot believe in Fox and Ape as convincing animal characters, because they "stand for actual individuals at Elizabeth's court, although scholars dispute about the identification of the Ape." Sp was too personally engaged in final episode and feels too deeply about abuses of court "to achieve artistic detachment and the indirection of allegory." George Orwell's Animal Farm more effective social satire than MHT (pp. 66-8).

Locke, Louis G., William M. Gibson, and George Arms, eds. Introduction to Literature. Rev. ed. New York: Rinehart, 1952. 749pp.   2440

First published 1948. Vol. 2 of Readings for Liberal Education. Amor 72, and defense of it by W. B. C. Watkins (reprinted from 1179) against William Van O'Connor's strictures (see 2475) (pp. 19-21).

Lord, John B. Apposite Grammatical Patterns in Spenser's *Epithalamion*, PCP, 3 (1968), 73-7.   2441

Of the 23 refrains Sp used in Epith, 17 are distinct variations. These are designed to correspond to poem's development through the wedding day.

Lynskey, Winifred. A Critic in Action: Mr. Ransom, CE, 5 (1944), 239-49.
2442

Objections to John Crowe Ransom's argument (Shakespeare at Sonnets, in The World's Body, pp. 270-303; see 1021) that Amor 56 is structurally a perfect example of what the English sonnet should be, in contrast to the defective structure of most of Shakespeare's sonnets (pp. 243-6).

McAvoy, William C. A Review of 1968's Contributions to English Renaissance Textual Studies, Manuscripta, 14 (1970), 131-60.   2443

Reviews briefly textual studies of works produced between 1475 and 1642, excluding Shakespeare. Notices S.P. Zitner's edition of Mutabilitie Cantos (453), and praises the "brilliant introduction."

McCown, Gary Mason. The Epithalamium in the English Renaissance. DAI, 29 (1969), 2220A-1A. University of North Carolina at Chapel Hill, 1968. 595 pp.
2444

Discusses structure, imagery, and themes of Catullus' semidramatic 61, amoebean 62, and epical 64. Medieval attempts to convert the pagan genre to religious worship failed. Revival in Renaissance was first in neo-Latin, then in Italian and French. Marriage was regarded as sacrament, ethical compact, and sexual event or political one. With Sidney's *Arcadia*, epithalamium comes to England. Davies, Sp, and Chapman promulgated Christian humanist ideas about marriage. In Stuart wedding masques, ethical emphasis is replaced by personal compliments. Donne introduces new realism. Baroque poets follow events of wedding day as in Sp, but they celebrate sexual consummation as central event, not solemnization of nuptials. Basis of Cavalier poems is wit, and spiritual significance of marriage is ignored. Restoration poets praise gross sensuality or the folly of matrimony.

McNeir, Waldo F. An Apology for Spenser's "Amoretti," NS, 14 (1965), 1-9; repr. in 756.   2445

Sp's sonnet cycle is "original in conception, well organized collectively and individually, metrically dexterous, and dramatic in method." Conception novel in portrayal of normal love affair leading to marriage. Organization is through events occurring in time. Meter is related to meaning through anti-normative metrical feet. Finally, Sp makes cycle dramatic by speaking, in his own voice, with increasing intimacy as affair progresses, and by balancing external drama of pursuit and flight with internal drama "of a middle-aged widower who has found a woman he wants to marry."

McNeir, Waldo F. Spenser's "pleasing Alcon," EA, 9 (1956), 136-40.   2446

CCCHA, ll. 394-5. "On balance, there is some likelihood that Spenser's 'pleasing Alcon' is Robert Greene."

McPeek, James A. S. Catullus in Strange and Distant Britain. HSCL, 15. Cambridge, Mass.: Harvard University Press, 1939. 411pp.   2447

Amor 76 and 77 rely on Carmen ii, Amor 39 and 17 on Carmen li (pp. 64-5, 107-8). Full discussion of Epith in relation to the marriage songs of Catullus, Du Bellay, and Buttet (pp. 159-84) was published earlier as The Major Sources of Spenser's *Epithalamion*, JEGP, 35 (1936), 183-213 (listed in Atkinson, p. 133). See also notes to this section (pp. 341-52).

Mahoney, John L. Platonism as a Unifying Element in Spenser's *Fowre Hymes*, BFLS, 41 (1963), 211-9. 2448

4 Hymns are a unified, carefully constructed poem in four parts and not four separate and different treatments of love and beauty or a retraction of Sp's praise of earthly love. The unifying factor is the philosophy of love in the Symposium and Ficino's commentary on it. See 650.

Main, W. W. Spenser's "Epithalamion," N&Q, 196 (1951), 545.   2449

Stork (l. 345) may mean white stork or stork pigeon. Since the bird is referred to as evil, belief that a white bird is a sign of death may explain Sp's usage.

Markland, Murray F. A Note on Spenser and the Scottish Sonneteers, SSL, 1 (1963), 136-40.   2450

Sp first published sonnets in his characteristic form in 1590, 17 dedicatory sonnets accompanying FQ, I-III. Six years earlier (1584) James VI of Scotland had published The Essayes of a Prentise, in the Divine Art of Poesie, which contains 20 "Spenserian" sonnets. Considers question of priority, discusses differences between Sp's Amor and sonnets of Scottish poets, concludes that they developed same sonnet form independently. See 2415.

Martz, Louis L. The *Amoretti:* "Most Goodly Temperature," in Form and Convention in the Poetry of Edmund Spenser, ed. William Nelson, pp. 146-68. New York: Columbia University Press, 1961. 188 pp.   2451

Repr. in 649. Takes issue with J. W. Lever's belief (see 2437) that Amor attempts unsuccessfully to combine two collections of sonnets incompatible with each other, shows the cruel "Tyrannesse" and the intelligent, witty, and beautiful lady are the same. Critics have taken the sequence too solemnly. "The series is frequently touched with . . . humor, parody, and comedy; it is a light touch, but it is, I think, sovereign." Lover's assured attitude present throughout series; lady knows what she is doing. Finds in Amor "most goodly temperature . . . signifying . . . a due mingling, fit proportion, proper combination, symmetry, a regulating power, an organizing principle."

Mayhead, Robin. Understanding Literature. Cambridge: Cambridge University Press, 1965. 189pp.   2452

Using two Proth stanzas as example, discusses Sp's poetics and compares them to Donne's (pp. 136-142, 181).

Meyer, Sam. The Figures of Rhetoric in Spenser's *Colin Clout*, PMLA, 79 (1964), 206-18.   2453

Discusses three functions of rhetorical figures in CCCHA. They (1) organize material and provide a framework, (2) maintain a consistent stylistic level, and (3) provide emotional tension. Density of the figures, occurring approximately one in every three lines, appropriate to discipline expected of a Renaissance poem. See 2454.

Meyer, Sam. An Interpretation of Edmund Spenser's *Colin Clout*. Notre Dame, Ind.: University of Notre Dame Press, 1969. 218 pp.   2454

Chap. II, Figures of Rhetoric (pp. 7-32), finds CCCHA employing arsenal of linguistic patterns named in rhetorical manuals of Renaissance. Chap. III, Diction and Versification (pp. 33-59), demonstrates "careful and imaginative employment of language and prosody." Chap. IV, Imagery (pp. 60-112), examines imagery as aspect of style embracing character, situation, and action. Chap. V, Tone and Feeling (pp. 113-41), analyzes interaction of ten persons in group, Colin's discourse directed to immediate audience (interior) and to "the Polite readership of the court" (exterior). Chap. VI, Use of Personal Material (pp. 142-71), draws attention to repeated use of pseudonym Colin, in works spanning Sp's poetic career. Chap. VII, Unity (pp. 172-203), concludes that "elaboration of all the elements—subject, style, and tone—gives the poem a comprehensive consistency." [Diss., Loyola University of Chicago, 1960.]

Rev: French Fogle, SEL, 11 (1971), 351; B.E.C. Davis, RES, 21 (1970), 486. See 954, 2453, 2455.

Meyer, Sam. Spenser's *Colin Clout*: The Poem and the Book, PBSA, 56 (1962), 397-413.   2455

Printing history of 17th-century editions of CCCHA suggests that textual changes made in the Variorum are relatively insignificant for a critical, aesthetic evaluation of the poem. See 2454.

Milgate, W. A Difficult Allusion in Donne and Spenser, N&Q, 13 (1966), 12-4.   2456

Donne refers three times to ability of mouse to destroy elephant by crawling up its trunk into its brain. Contrary to common belief, this idea not in ancient or medieval animal lore. Idea that elephant can thwart mouse by sleeping with its trunk knotted first appears in work of Garcia de Orta (1563), translated from Portugese into Latin by Charles de l'Escluze (1567). Mentions other literary allusions to this piece of elephant lore. Some passages in de Orta's work source of stanza viii in Sp's VWV.

Miller, Paul W. The Decline of the English Epithalamion, TSLL, 12 (1970), 405-16.   2457

Vitality of epithalamic genre confined to period 1594-1635, during which eight distinguished epithalamia were written: Sp's Epith (1594), Donne's Epithalamion made at Lincolnes Inne (ca. 1594), Phineas Fletcher's Epithalamium (ca. 1610), Donne's Epithalamion, Or Marriage Song on the Lady Elizabeth, and Count Palatine (1613), his Somerset Epithalamion (1613), Herrick's A Nuptiall Song, or Epithalamie, on Sir Clipseby Crew and his Lady (1625), Jonson's Weston Epithalamion (1632), and Crashaw's Epithalamium (ca. 1635). Since then "no English epithalamion of great distinction has been composed." Decline reflects decline of marriage myth that gave rise to genre, and growth of antimythic, secular, rationalistic view of marriage. Finds traces of decline scarcely evident in Sp's Epith, prominent in Crashaw's Epithalamium.

Milligan, Burton. The Counterfeit Soldier in Mother Hubberd's Tale, N&Q, 176 (1939), 421-2.   2458

Adds Awdeley's Fraternity of Vacabondes (1561) to contemporary descriptions of roguery with which Sp may have been familiar.

Mönch, Walter. Das Sonett: Gestalt und Geschichte. Heidelberg: F. H. Kerle Verlag, 1955. 341pp.   2459

Distinguishes three basic types of sonnet: Italian, French, and English; analyzes various rhyme schemes (pp. 15-23). Discusses sonnet structure and themes (pp. 33-51). The sonnet in 16th century France (pp. 116-28). The sonnet in England (pp. 129-34); Sp, Sidney, and Shakespeare (pp. 135-9). Emphasizes Neoplatonism of Amor.

Moreau, Joseph. Introduction à la lecture des *Hymnes* de Spenser, RTP, 97 (1964), 65-83.   2460

Prof. Ellrodt (650) not a trained philosopher familiar with tangled threads of Platonism, Neoplatonism, Renaissance Neoplatonism, Christian Platonism, Petrarch's reaction against medieval Aristotelianism, Platonic and Ptolemaic cosmogony, and Ficino's adaptation of Platonism and Neo-platonism to Christianity. Briefly discusses all of these in relation to Sp's 4 Hymns. Conclusion: last two hymns celebrating heavenly love and heavenly beauty do not exalt earthly love and earthly beauty dealt with in first two hymns; last two hymns are a retraction, a palinode. Dante, through mediation of Beatrice, achieved transcendence. "Puritan austerity cannot see a beloved woman as an initiatrix into the contemplation and the love of the divine."

Mounts, Charles E. Colin Clout: Priest of Cupid and Venus, HPCS, 3 (1963), 33-44.   2461

Sp's expression in CCCHA of an extravagantly phrased personal religion of earthly love and beauty may have antagonized an influential part of his audience. See 2462.

Mounts, Charles E. The Evolution of Spenser's Attitude toward Cupid and Venus, HPCS, 4 (1964), 1-9.   2462

Continues discussion in 2461.

Mounts, Charles E. The Ralegh-Essex Rivalry and *Mother Hubberds Tale,* MLN, 65 (1950), 509-13.   2463

Reads ll. 615-30 of MHT as an allusion to the Ralegh-Essex rivalry immediately after the Portugal expedition of 1589. Sp's irony shows him partial to his patron, Ralegh.

Mounts, Charles E. Two Rosalinds in *Colin Clouts Come Home Againe,* N&Q, N. S. 2 (1955), 283-4.   2464

Accepts the opinion of Jenkins, MLN, 67 (1952), 1-5 (see 2417), that the loved one celebrated in the poem is Elizabeth Boyle; but feels that l. 940 refers to Sp's dead wife.

Muir, Kenneth. *Locrine* and *Selimus,* TLS, Aug. 12, 1944, p. 391.   2465

In Selimus the apparent borrowing from Sp's Complaints is actually borrowing from Locrine, whose author uses Sp as a source.

Mulryan, John. The Function of Ritual in the Marriage Songs of Catullus, Spenser and Ronsard, IllQ, 35 (1972), 50-64.   2466

Ritual is mechanical organization of worship. Literature varies a stock of common themes; ritual in principle invariable. Epithalamium draws on ritual, social importance of marriage as assurance of stability demanding ritual. Traces ritualistic modes of celebration, propitiation, and efficacy in Catullus 61, Sp's Epith, and Ronsard's Epithalame. All three poets communicate sense of the numinous. As ritual rises above routine, so each poem rises above ritual. [SpN, 4, No. 1 (1973), 8.]

Mulryan, John. Spenser as Mythologist: A Study of the Nativities of Cupid and Christ in the *Fowre Hymnes,* MLS, 1 (1971), 13-6.   2467

Sp applies to nativity of Christ ac-

counts of Cupid's nativity in Plato's Symposium, Marsilio Ficino's Commentary on the Symposium, and Natalis Comes' Mythologia. Sp uses Christ story as myth, not history, gives vision of Christ as new Eros. [SpN, Vol. 2, No. 3 (1971), 7.]

Neuse, Richard. The Triumph Over Hasty Accidents: A Note on the Symbolic Mode of the *Epithalamion,* MLR, 61 (1966), 163-74; repr. in 756.   2468

Function of the envoy or tornata in Epith is to signal a climax in progression from sonnet to wedding song, "from romantic to conjugal love." This movement from Amor to Epith is a movement from "aesthetic time" to "real time" through symbolic devices of night, sun, and numbers.

Noot, Jan Van Der. Theatre for Worldlings. Bibliographical note by William A. Jackson. Introduction by Louis S. Friedland. New York: SF&R, 1939. 107 numbered pp.   2469

Sp's connection with the work discussed in Introduction, pp. iii-viii.

Norton, Dan S. The Background of Spenser's Prothalamion. DA, 12 (1952), 428. Princeton University, 1940. 256 pp.   2470

Proth is last poem Sp published. "It is the final affirmation of his mature talents." In it "he masters a new verse form, first attempted in the *Epithalamion.* His interest in the technique of verse is as fresh and strong in his last work as it had been in the experiments of the *Shepheardes Calender,* and this of course is why he makes such excellent music." Little criticism has dealt with Proth in and for itself. Many critics have dismissed it with general praise, some have fallen back on an inexact comparison of it to Epith. "However, the purpose of this essay is not to quarrel with other critics or to attack their judgments of value. Its aim is toward an understanding of the *Prothalamion* as a poetic and social product of its times."

Norton, Dan S. The Bibliography of Spenser's *Prothalamion*, JEGP, 43 (1944), 349-53.   2471

On the basis of a collation of early editions of the poem, rejects Edward Marsh's proposed emendation of "birdes" for "brides" in l. 176.

Norton, Dan S. Queen Elizabeth's "Brydale Day," MLQ, 5 (1944), 149-54.   2472

Interpretation of stanza 9 of Proth (ll. 155-161) as an allusion to Queen Elizabeth's Accession Day (November 17) and her spiritual marriage to England—"Vpon the Brydale day, which is not long." Sp's "conceit expresses a mystical paradox which he had developed allegorically in the *Faerie Queene* and which is a part of his countrymen's conception of their virgin sovereign."

Norton, Dan S. The Tradition of Prothalamia, in English Studies in Honor of James Southall Wilson, pp. 223-41. UVS, 4. Charlottesville, Va.: University of Virginia Press, 1951. 298pp.   2473

"Prothalamion" means "betrothal hymn." Nine English prothalamia have been identified, but only seven are extant, those by Lydgate, Dunbar, Bizzarri (in Latin), Sp, Shakespeare (in As You Like It), Thomas Carew, and the anonymous poet who wrote one for Elizabeth Stuart's betrothal in 1613. Analyzes each poem.

O'Connell, Michael. *Astrophel:* Spenser's Double Elegy, SEL, 11 (1971), 27-35.   2474

Ronsard's Adonis principal source of Astro, Sp's pastoral elegy for Sidney, but tone very different. Stella of Astro not lady behind Sidney's sonnet sequence, but represents inspiration behind Sidney's poetry. Flower into which lovers are transformed symbolic of Sidney's poetry and links two parts of elegy together. Flower consoles shepherd poet who sings first part but not Astrophel's sister, who finds Christian consolation in Lay, second part. Double elegy thus implies solace for those who loved Sidney as poet and for those who loved him as brother, husband, or friend.

O'Connor, William Van. Tension and Structure of Poetry, SR, 51 (1943), 555-73.   2475

Unfavorable comparison of Amor 72 with poems by Herrick and Stevens. The difference between them "is the distinction between the poetry of exploration and the poetry of exposition." Herrick and Stevens "work through" the intellectual and emotional problem, while Sp "does not *earn* his attitude"—it is preconceived. Sp's sonnet fails because "the basic structure of the lyric [i.e., the necessary three parts, as explained earlier, pp. 556-7] is ignored" (pp. 557-61). See 2440.

Ordeman, D. Thomas. How Many Rhyme Schemes has the Sonnet? CE, 1 (1939), 171-3.   2476

Mathematical cogitations on the number of possible arrangements in the Italian and Elizabethan sonnet; "51,300 arrangements are possible without destroying the sonnet as a recognizable form." Sp's rhyme scheme in Amor cited as one variation.

Orwen, William R. Spenser and Leicester, SP, 42 (1945), 191-7.   2477

Interprets Muiop as a political allegory of the defeat of the Spanish Armada, which Sp credits to the distinguished service of Leicester (Clarion), whose downfall was caused by the opposition of Burghley (Arag-noll).

Orwen, William R. Spenser and the Serpent of Division, SP, 38 (1941), 198-210.   2478

Interprets RT, which he dates 1590, as Sp's warning against the civil strife which might follow the death of Queen Elizabeth.

Orwen, William R. Spenser's "Stemmata Dudleiana," N&Q, 190 (1946), 9-11.   2479

Speculates on the nature of this lost Latin work known through two passages in Harvey-Sp correspondence. It must have been a genealogy in praise of the Dudley family, like Harvey's Gratulationes (1578).

Osborne, Harold. Aesthetics and Criticism. London: Routledge, 1955. 341pp.   2480

In Chapter VIII, Transcendentalism, cites Sp's HOHB in section 2, Art as a Revelation of the Transcendant. "English poetry in particular has been deeply coloured by the belief that the natural world is but a shadow and reflection of a higher reality" (pp. 188-99).

Osgood, Charles G. Epithalamion and Prothalamion: 'and theyr eccho ring', MLN, 76 (1961), 205-8.   2481

Frequent borrowings from Proth and Epith in wedding songs of early 17th century indicate Sp responsible for popularity of genre.

Palmer, Herbert. The English Sonnet, PoR, 48 (1957), 215-8; 49 (1958), 26-8, 84-7.   2482

Appreciative survey of form from Wyatt to present. Spenserian sonnet, "a sort of combination or interlacing of the Shakespearean and Petrarchan forms," discussed. Quotes Amor 30 as "especially striking in declamation,"

but meter of ninth line is faulty (pp. 217-8).

Pearson, Lu Emily. Elizabethan Love Conventions. New York: Barnes and Noble, 1967. 365 pp.   2483

Repr. of 1933 ed. Chap. II, Petrarchanism in Elizabethan England, has section on Amor which refers to Platonic doctrine in sonnets, as in 4 Hymns, and calls Amor 72 "but the prelude to those marvelous hymns of love," Proth and Epith (pp. 158-75).

Pebworth, Ted-Larry. The Net for the Soul: A Renaissance Conceit and the Song of Songs, RomN, 13 (1971), 159-64.   2484

Conceit describing beloved's hair as net for the soul, from Song of Solomon 7:5, transmitted by Petrarch to Tasso, Ariosto, Sidney, Sp, and others. Used in other Semitic wedding songs. Appears in The Arabian Nights at least six times. [SpN, Vol. 4, No. 2 (1973), 8.]

Peterson, Douglas. The English Lyric from Wyatt to Donne: A History of the Plain and Eloquent Styles. Princeton: Princeton University Press, 1967. 391 pp.   2485

Thesis: development of English lyric in 16th century continues medieval tradition of plain style and secular treatment of love, these more important than domestication of Petrarchan sonnet in ornate style and turn to themes of divine love (pp. 3-8). Plain style poets: Wyatt in nonsonnet lyrics, poets in Tottel's Miscellany, Googe, Gascoigne, Donne, Jonson, Greville, Ralegh; ornate style poets: Surrey, Sidney, Daniel, Lodge, Sp, Griffin, Giles Fletcher, Chapman. Sp in Amor used old conceits and tired neo-Platonism. Notable for Christian-Platonic synthesis. Difference between sacred and profane love in 4 Hymns assumed in Amor. Few

sonnets reason from premises to conclusion. Rarely any wit suggestive of
Shakespeare or Donne. Sidney and Sp
established norms of sugared style.
Shakespeare's sonnets exception, best
achieved in eloquent tradition (pp.
201-11). [Diss., Stanford University,
1958.]
    Rev: A. B. Friedman, ELN, 5 (1967),
136; M. P. Gallagher, EIC, 18 (1968),
444; W. Maynard, RES, 19 (1968),
427; D. L. Guss, Criticism, 10 (1968),
81; H. M. Richmond, CL, 22 (1970),
81.

Pettet, E. C. Sidney and the Cult of Romantic Love, English, 6 (1947), 232-40.
                                    2486

    Despite the conventionality of
Astrophel and Stella, Sidney is "less
completely representative of the late
romantic attitude to love than Spenser." This attitude with marriage as
the natural consummation is deci-
sively expressed in Amor, Epith,
Proth, and FQ, Books III and IV—as
C. S. Lewis has shown in The Allegory of Love (see 1513). Sp is the
great exponent of earthly love as a
form of Divine Love. Quotes Amor
61. "This Spenserian, late romantic
note is absent from Sidney's sonnets." Recurrent mood of doubt also
dissociates Sidney from Neoplatonism
of late romantic attitude. He is not a
precursor of the revolt led by Donne
against Neoplatonic thought; "but he
was no orthodox romantic poet like
Spenser either." Three important features of Sidney's style contrast with
Sp's: its intellectuality, realism, and
flexibility.

Petti, Anthony G. Beasts and Politics in
Elizabethan literature, E&S, 16 (1963),
68-90.   2487

    Poems in Sp's Complaints volume
(1591) are best allegories on contemporary political figures of Queen Elizabeth's court circle: MHT, Muiop,

RT, and VG. Book was licensed for
publication, but "it was quickly recalled, and with good reason" (pp.
68, 76, 84-6). Discusses use of beast
fables by Churchyard, Nashe, Shakespeare, and others.

Petti, Anthony G. The Fox, the Ape, the
Humble-Bee and the Goose, Neophil,
44 (1960), 208-15.   2488

    On Love's Labor's Lost, III, i, 83
ff., and Troilus and Cressida, V, x, 41
ff. The fox is Lord Burghley (William
Cecil); the ape, Robert Cecil; the
humble-bee, the Earl of Essex; the
goose, Walter Ralegh. Supports argument for identifications in Love's
Labor's Lost by taking fox and ape in
MHT to be the two Cecils, father and
son. See 2388, 2425.

Petti, Anthony. Political Satire in *Pierce
Penilesse His Supplication to the Divill,*
Neophil, 45 (1961), 139-50.   2489

    In order to prove that "divill" and
fox in Nashe's Pierce Penilesse (1592)
are William Cecil, Lord Burghley, and
his son Robert Cecil, refers to Sp's
satire on two Cecils as ape and fox in
MHT (see 2388). Nashe derived some
ideas from Sp.

Piper, William Bowman. The Heroic
Couplet. Cleveland: Case Western Reserve University Press, 1969. 454 pp.
                                    2490

    History of heroic couplet runs from
Chaucer to present day. Falls into
three nearly equal periods, "only the
second of which offers significant rewards to historical study." In first
period, 1385-1585, Chaucer only
great practitioner of form. In second
period, 1585-1785, nearly every poet
used heroic couplet in some of poetry, and it became staple after 1660.
But before then favorite measure of
Waller and Denham, Donne and Jonson. Third period, "since romantic
poets degraded and rejected it," unin-

teresting (pp. 3-5). Sp's MHT written in stiffer version of Chaucer's couplets, but Sp not good at it, his verse "a compromise between his satiric intention and his Chaucerian discipleship" (pp. 173-4). Sp's couplets mentioned, usually unfavorably, in connection with couplets of other poets of second period: Joshua Sylvester, Michael Drayton, Joseph Hall, John Marston, Sir John Beaumont, and George Wither. See Index.

Piper, William Bowman. Spenser's "Lyke as a Huntsman," CE, 22 (1961), 405.
2491

In Amor 67, Sp transforms the familiar analogy of the lover as huntsman into a "bemused contemplation" of the paradoxical mystery of female timidity and desire to be caught.

Pope-Hennessy, John. Nicholas Hilliard and Mannerist Art Theory, JWCI, 6 (1943), 89-100.   2492

Hilliard's Arte of Limning (written not later than 1603) expounds "an anti-realistic representational technique." His miniatures are "the physical embodiment of certain aspects of Elizabethan aesthetic thought." Quotes Amor 17 as an example of this thought.

Potter, James Lain. The Development of Sonnet Patterns in the Sixteenth Century. Doctoral diss., Harvard University, 1954. HRDP, 1953-1954, p. 14; DDAAU, 1953-54, No. 21.   2493

In Italy and France sonnet was usually divided into octave and sestet; final rimed couplet as separate unit of thought was rare. In Tottel's Miscellany (1557), which introduced sonnet to England, both Wyatt and Surrey stressed final couplet as sense-unit; and Surrey devised English or Shakespearian rime scheme (abab cdcd efef gg). Sidney's Astrophel and Stella (1591) began the vogue. "It is linked with the period that preceded it part-

ly through the work of Spenser, which began in 1569 and was climaxed by his Amoretti of 1594. Almost all of his sonnets were English in form; a number were Shakespearian, but in the dedications to the Faerie Queene of 1590, and in the Amoretti, he employed a scheme of his own, abab bcbc cdcdee. Usually, his sonnets are smooth, coherent, and polished." Reaction against sonneteering began with Chapman's Coronet for his Mistresse Philosophie, " a direct attack on love-sonnets." Traces the decline. "The number and variety of unusual sonnet-patterns point to a convention of experimentation that existed side by side with that which established the Shakespearian scheme and the final sense-couplet as the norm."

Praz, Mario. Ricerche Anglo-Italiane. Storia e Letteratura, 7. Rome: Istituto Grafico Tiberino, 1944.   2494

In Petrarca e gli Emblematisti (pp. 305-19), mentions Sp's connection with Petrarch's Standomi un giorno through Marot's French version.

Price, Fanny. A Line in Spenser, N&Q, 184 (1943), 341.   2495

On Canon T. A. Lacey's discussion in Wayfarer's Essays (1934) of Leigh Hunt's statement that Sp's line, Playing alone carlesse on her heavenlie virginals (Iambicum Trimetrum, 1.6), is the perfect expression in poetry of the andante movement in music.

Prior, Roger. The Life of George Wilkins, ShS, 25 (1972), 137-52.   2496

Supports suggestion that "G.W. Senior" and "G.W.I." who wrote the two sonnets prefixed to Sp's Amor (1595) were George Wilkins, Senior, and his son George Wilkins, Junior, author of The Painfull Adventures of Pericles Prince of Tyre (1608), novel based on Pericles, the play. See 2380.

Quitslund, Jon A. Spenser's Image of Sapience, SRen, 16 (1969), 181-213.
2497

Idea of Sapience in ll. 183-287 of HOHB would affect our understanding of 4 Hymns if critics could agree on meaning. Most critics think Platonic doctrines in HHOB and HHOL replaced by Christian doctrines in HOHB and HOHL, interpret Sapience in strictly Christian terms; cites Ellrodt (650), Lewis (879), Joseph Moreau (1460), Kellogg and Steele (333), Welsford (2551). Proposes alternative view of Sp's conception of Wisdom derived from Christian tradition stemming from Old Testament, Apocrypha, and St. Augustine; Platonic one from Ficino, Pico, and Leone Ebreo; and Jewish one from Kabbala. Thus Sp's syncretic vision of wisdom recognizes diversity of truth; 4 Hymns "are the product of an accommodating and unifying intelligence, open to many influences. Sapience epitomizes the unity in diversity which is the mark of Spenser's genius."

Raizis, M. Byron. The Epithalamion Tradition and John Donne, WSUSB, 62 (1966), 3-15.
2498

In addition to Donne's three epithalamia, discusses Sp's Epith, and mentions Herrick's Epithalamie to Sir Thomas Southwell and his Ladie.

Rees, Christine. The Metamorphosis of Daphne in Sixteenth- and Seventeenth-Century English Poetry, MLR, 66 (1971), 251-63.
2499

In Amor 28 and 29 Sp presents two interpretations of Daphne's transformation. In 28 treats it as gods' punishment for pride. In 29 willing to cede the laurel to his lady as symbol of both conquest and poetry. Two treatments indicate shifting love relationship and ambiguities of lover's attitudes [SpN, Vol. 2, No. 3 (1971), 7.]

Reese, Robert Winter. The Influence of the *Song of Songs* on Elizabethan Literature. Doctoral diss., University of Washington, 1940. UWAT, 5 (1941), 93-5.
2500

In four parts: interpretations of Canticum Canticorum, symbolism and imagery of poem, metrical translations and paraphrases, its influence on Elizabethan sonnets and pastoral poetry. Sp's sonnets, among others, show influence of Song of Songs.

Reichert, John Frederick. Formal Logic and English Renaissance Poetry. DA, 24 (1963), 1174-5. Stanford University, 1963. 233 pp.
2501

Examines importance of logical structure in sonnets and lyrics of Sidney, Daniel, Sp, Shakespeare, Herbert, and Donne. Critics have thought that "Spenser's interlocking rhyme scheme" breaks down "the traditional units of the sonnet, the quatrains and couplet. But . . . Spenser had at least as strong a sense of the logical and grammatical integrity of the parts of the sonnet as any of his contemporaries. He achieves a complex symmetry through the careful arrangement of the parts of arguments, moving, for example, from a proposition to be proved, to an analogy, to another analogy and proposition, and ending with an application of his conclusions to his own situation."

Rice, Eugene F., Jr. The Renaissance Idea of Wisdom. HHM, 37. Cambridge, Mass.: Harvard University Press, 1958. 220pp.
2502

Chapter 3, The Wisdom of Renaissance Platonism, pp. 58-92. Marsilio Ficino, Pico della Mirandola, Florentine Neo-Platonism, doctrine of Ideas, wisdom as a knowledge of divine things. Mystical union with Wisdom and ecstasy produced by this vision "has been described beautifully in Spenser's celebration of Sapience in

An Hymne of Heavenly Beautie" (pp. 67-8).

Richmond, H. M. The School of Love: The Evolution of the Stuart Love Lyric. Princeton: Princeton University Press, 1964. 338 pp.   2503

Stable forms and motifs in love lyric show evolution of sensibility between antiquity and Renaissance. Sappho's description of her love symptoms, standard theme, resembles descriptions by Theocritus, Catullus, Dante, Petrarch, Ronsard, Sidney, and Sp (pp. 3-12). Discusses all of these. Petrarch lacks vividness but adds logical analysis. Ronsard falls back on physiological data of pagans. Sp neater but even less inventive in Amor 3. Sidney in Astrophel and Stella 54 worthy of comparison with Catullus, tongue-tied but argumentative, speaker individualized (pp. 37-46). Sp adjusts sex to "the socially more viable institution of marriage" (pp. 96-7, 239-40). For other references to Sp, see Index.

Ricks, Don M. Convention and Structure in Edmund Spenser's *Amoretti*, PUASAL, 44 (1967), 438-50.   2504

Discusses narrative, thematic, and figurative patterning in Sp's sonnet sequence, finding steady advance from Petrarchistic physical longings to Platonic ideational satisfactions. Makes much of change in line 5 [sic, for line 6] from "having" (35) to "seeing" (83), earlier verb suggesting "physical possession and even carnality," later verb connoting "the lover's new-found enlightenment and understanding."

Ricks, Don M. Persona and Process in Spenser's "Amoretti," Ariel, 3 (1972), 5-15.   2505

Amor unique in Elizabethan love poetry in exploring not a state, but a process—courtship. Sequence suggests narrative by non-narrative techniques: tonal modulation; repetition of motifs such as pain leading to joy; progression of image patterns from war to peace, predatory animals to the deer; ship in storm to ship in port; manipulation of time scheme. Lady of Amor a person, not figment of poet's mind. We see Elizabeth Boyle waiting serenely for poet-lover to mature. Lover, through exposure to the "particular beauty of one body," in Bembo's words, in time outgrows mouthing of Neo-Platonic platitudes, able to see lady's steadfastness as justifiable self-assurance instead of cruel pride. He merits her acceptance. [SpN, Vol. 4, No. 1 (1973), 9.]

Righetti, Angelo. Le Due Versione Spenseriane della Canzone CCCXXIII del Petrarca, ACF, 5 (1966), 115-22. 2506

Considers VP a mature revision of Epigrams (Theatre), almost a retranslation of the Petrarchan canzone (Rime, 323). Sp's maturity in second version shown in relative perfection of the form and especially in seventh stanza, which in VP expands Petrarchan "congedo" into a typically Spenserian reflection on vanity and evanescence of the world which anticipates final stanzas of Mutabilitie Cantos.

Rix, Herbert D. Spenser's Rhetoric and the "Doleful Lay," MLN, 53 (1938), 261-5.   2507

Evidence supporting Sp's authorship of Lay on the basis of the rhetorical figures in the poem, which agree with his practice in other works.

Rollinson, Philip. The Renaissance of the Literary Hymn, RenP 1968, 11-20.   2508

Sp's 4 Hymns cannot be fully understood without recognition of classical and neo-classical tradition of genre. See 2510.

Rollinson, Philip B. A Generic View of Spenser's *Four Hymns*, SP, 68 (1971), 292-304. 2509

Behind Sp's 4 Hymns is classical and Renaissance tradition of literary hymn. Pairing of Sp's poems has esthetic dimension. Earthly hymns show influence of Callimachus, Prudentius, and Michele Marullo; heavenly pair, of Vida and Scaliger. See 2510.

Rollinson, Philip Bruce. Spenser's *Four Hymns* and the Tradition of the Literary Hymn. DAI, 29 (1969), 3586A. University of Virginia, 1968. 164 pp. 2510

Literary hymn originated in Greece. Callimachus imitated Homeric hymn using rhetorical elaboration and mythological erudition. Horace and Catullus imitated Greek lyric hymn; Prudentius christianized it. In 15th century Michele Marullo introduced pagan hymn into neo-Latin literature. Vida and Scaliger opposed him. Ronsard's Hymns show influence of Marullo and Callimachus. Chapman imitated long philosophical hymn in The Shadow of Night. Sp's first two Hymns celebrate earthly love and beauty in manner of Marullo, also follow Callimachus in creation of fictional situation. Sp's originality in role of Petrarchan poet-lover. Last two hymns celebrate heavenly love and beauty, endorsed by Vida and Scaliger. See 2508, 2509.

Rubbra, Edmund. Amoretti. 2nd series. London: J. Williams, 1942. 2511

Voice and string quartet, or piano.

Saito, Takeshi. Spenser's Four Anthems, Rising Generation, 93 (1947), No. 8. 2512

Sandison, Helen E. "Eglantine of Meliflure," TLS, July 6, 1962, p. 493. 2513

Eglantine of Meliflure, as used by Sp in CCCHA, stands for Queen Elizabeth. Meliflure is the Tower of Mireflore, Greenwich Palace, where she was born and where she often resided in summer.

Sandison, Helen E. "The Vanytyes of Sir Arthur Gorges Youthe," PMLA, 61 (1946), 109-13. 2514

A preliminary report on Egerton MS 3165, which contains the "sweet layes of love" of Sir Arthur Gorges ("Alcyon") that Sp praised in CCCHA, ll. 384-91.

Sasek, Lawrence A. William Smith and *The Shepheardes Calender*, PQ, 39 (1960), 251-3. 2515

Smith's sonnet sequence Chloris (1596) owes much to SC, far more than to Amor. Smith is one of the earliest followers of Sp, and he acknowledges his discipleship in referring to Colin Clout as "the Patron of my maiden verse" (sonnet 49). See 233, 2295.

Satterthwaite, Alfred W. Moral Vision in Spenser, DuBellay, and Ronsard, CL, 9 (1957), 136-49. 2516

Discusses Sp's world of uncertainty and mutability, with special emphasis on Visions. Stresses Du Bellay's influence and minimizes Ronsard's.

Satterthwaite, Alfred W. A Re-examination of Spenser's Translations of the "Sonets" from *A Theatre for Worldlings*, PQ, 38 (1959), 509-15. 2517

Does not think Sp translated the last four sonnets. Too many end-stopped lines, too few run-on lines, and meaning is often obscure. Lack of external evidence limits critical examination to "statistical analysis of the language and punctuation." Such analysis shows departure from strict line-for-line translation, as well as over-punctuation and mis-translation.

Schön, Hilda. Catulls Epithalamion und seine englischen Nachahmer bis 1660. Doctoral diss., University of Vienna, 1940. 131pp. Anglia, 71 (1953), 508.
2518

Two short introductory chapters deal with recent studies of Catullus and the work of the Latin poet. Chapter 3, The English Imitators of Catullus, mentions primitive epithalamists: John of Garland, George Buchanan, John Leland. First English epithalamion in English is Sidney's Wedding of Thyris and Kala in Bk. III of Arcadia. Sp's Epithalamion Thamesis, written about 1580, appeared later in FQ (IV, xi). Sp's Epith owes something to all three of Catullus's epithalamia, especially his carmen 61; points out parallels, emphasizing Sp's free transformations (pp. 21-30). Remainder of study considers epithalamia of Chapman, Jonson, Henry Peacham, Donne, Phineas Fletcher, Christopher Brooke, Samuel Sheppard, and Herrick.

Sheehan, James Clement. Form and Tradition in English Epithalamion, 1595-1641. DAI, 32 (1972), 3964-A. University of Michigan, 1971. 199 pp.   2519

Julius Caesar Scaliger divided epithalamion into 4 types: lyric, marriage debate, Ovidian epyllion, and mixed form, recommending lyric type modeled on Catullus' Carmen 61. Sp closely imitated this poem and French epithalamia, but planned Amor and Epith as "mixed" wedding poem. He "began a rich and varied tradition of classical wedding poetry in seventeenth-century England." Discusses epithalamia by Donne, Jonson, Carew, Phineas Fletcher, "even Herrick," Suckling, and others.

Siegel, Paul N. The Petrarchan Sonneteers and Neo-Platonic Love, SP, 42 (1945), 164-82.   2520

Divides writers of Elizabethan sonnet-cycles into two groups: the Petrarchists, including Watson, Barnes, Lodge, Constable, and Percy, whose love is sensuous; and the Neo-Platonists, Sp and Sidney, whose love is spiritual. In Astrophel and Stella reason triumphs over passion. Only in Sp's Amor is "the entire sequence . . . suffused with the pale golden glow of neo-Platonic idealism," and "no other sonnet-cycle gives this effect."

Silverman, Edward Barry. Poetic Synthesis in Adonais. DA, 27 (1967), 2162A. Northwestern University, 1966. 169 pp.   2521

"Treats the structure and development of Adonais through an investigation of its literary background." The chief source is not Bion's Lament for Adonis but Sp's Astrophel, a relationship not hitherto recognized because H. J. Todd printed the last third as Lay. Both poems (Sp's and Shelley's) are, for two-thirds of their length, pastoral narratives based on the Aphrodite-Adonis myth; the rest in each case is a Platonic consolation. Notes parallels in details, and further explains both poems by reference to Garden of Adonis (FQ, III, vi) and 4 Hymns.

Smart, George K. English Non-dramatic Blank Verse in the Sixteenth Century, Anglia, 61 (1937), 370-97.   2522

Considers Sp's blank verse translation of Du Bellay's Songe in Theatre better than any preceding blank verse.

Smith, Hallett. The Use of Conventions in Spenser's Minor Poems, in Form and Convention in the Poetry of Edmund Spenser, ed. William Nelson, pp. 122-45. New York: Columbia University Press, 1961. 188 pp.   2523

Sp in Muiop combines in a delicate jeu d'esprit elements from Ovid's Metamorphoses, Chaucerian tradition of mock-heroic in Sir Thopas and Nun's Priest's Tale, and VG. Daph is in tradition of love-vision-elegy, for which Chaucer's Book of the Duchess was model; also looks back to elegy on Dido in November eclogue of SC, using refrain to heighten lyrical effect. Structure is very formal: seven plaints, each of seven stanzas seven lines long. Preliminary sketches for Epith in April eclogue of SC, and in tempting of Redcrosse by False Una (FQ, I, i, 48) and marriage of Una and Redcrosse (FQ, I, xii). Cites 2382 on epithalamic tradition, emphasizes formal structure. Proth in tradition of river poems (cf. FQ, IV, xi), modifies convention by introducing elements of dream vision and complaint, also contemporary allusions. Sp felt "the personal element in poetry . . . is expressed most vividly when it is embedded in a convention."

Smith, J. Norton. Spenser's *Prothalamion:* A New Genre, RES, N. S. 10 (1959), 173-8.   2524

Proth is a genre invented to accommodate the theme of universal and personal criticism in addition to the theme of marriage.

Smith, Roland M. Spenser and Milton: An Early Analogue, MLN, 60 (1945), 394-8.   2525

Similarities between Sp's Latin verse-letter to Harvey in Two Other Very Commendable Letters (1580) and Milton's sonnet, How soon hath time the subtle thief of youth, addressed to an unidentified friend who may be Thomas Young, his tutor at Cambridge. Sp's tutor at Cambridge was named Young. Milton may have had Sp's letter in mind when he wrote his sonnet.

Snare, Gerald. The Muses on Poetry: Spenser's *The Teares of the Muses*, TSE, 17 (1969), 31-52.   2526

Accepts date about 1590 for TM, and C. S. Lewis's suggestion (see 878) poem reflects elitist views of Sidney-Sp coterie. Documents from classical and Renaissance sources idea that ignorance and barbarism are enemies of Muses, and hence of wisdom and learning. Eight of Nine Muses complain that wisdom and learning have fallen into disrepute, with evil results for poetry. Comments on numerological structure of TM. Sp's vision poetic, philosophical, and religious. "Spenser's view is manifestly not our own. Our Muses would not be inclined to weep over the poetic achievement of Renaissance England. His would." See 2527.

Snare, Gerald Howard. Spenser's *The Teares of the Muses* and the Poetry of the Initiate. DAI, 29 (1969), 3111A. University of California, Los Angeles, 1968. 223 pp.   2527

Sp's Muses do not weep for decline of poetry in modern sense, but because of prevailing ignorance and blindness of men. Sidney circle believed in exclusiveness of poetry, as did coteries of France and Pico della Mirandola. Since poetry can be written only by those initiated into higher realms of knowledge, ignorance in world meant decline of poetry. Sp chose Muses as speakers in his poem because he shared conception of exclusiveness of poetry. Muses represent all realms of knowledge, inspire chosen few, allow only initiates to share arcane learning they can give. Numerological construction of the poem part of deliberate obscurity initiates use. Sp believed exclusive poetry had magical power to bring about new golden age; therefore, complaints of Muses understandably grave. See 2526.

Sowton, Ian. Hidden Persuaders as a Means of Literary Grace: Sixteenth-

Century Poetics and Rhetoric in England, UTQ, 32 (1962), 55-69.　2528

Applies commonplaces of Renaissance rhetoric to analysis of Sp's 4 Hymns and Sir John Davies' Orchestra (1596), two philosophical poems published in same year. Suggests that especially for philosophical poetry application of rhetorical principles exemplified in Thomas Wilson's Arte of Rhetorique (1553) "provided not only stylistic decorations but also structural principles and actual procedures for the conduct of persuasive argument in verse. In *Fowre Hymnes* and *Orchestra* persuasion was one of the chief artistic ends; to this end both Spenser and Davies adopted rhetoric and rendered it completely natural to their artifice."

Spencer, Theodore. The Elizabethan Malcontent, in J. Q. Adams Memorial Studies, pp. 523-35. Washington, D. C.: Folger Shakespeare Library, 1948. Also in Theodore Spencer: Selected Essays, ed. Alan C. Purves, pp. 139-50. New Brunswick: Rutgers University Press, 1966. 368 pp.　2529

An attempt to answer question whether early 17th century was more pessimistic than preceding generation; decides that it was. One feature of both late 16th and early 17th century society that produced malcontents was the life of the court and the profession of the courtier. Quotes Sp's description of court in CCCHA (pp. 531-2).

Spitzer, Leo. Essays in English and American Literature, ed. Anne Hatcher. Princeton: Princeton University Press, 1962. 290 pp.　2530

Includes 2302. See 2196, 2197.

Stageberg, Norman C. The Aesthetic of the Petrarchan Sonnet, JAAC, 7 (1948), 132-7.　2531

Attributes longevity of Petrarchan

sonnet to (1) its control of experience, in terms of Gestalt psychology; and (2) aesthetic pleasure it affords in its system of equipollence. As test of theory, quotes among other examples Sp's first unrhymed "sonnet" in Theatre. This is "without rime but does follow the Petrarchan pattern of stops."

Starnes, D. T. Spenser—and Keats's "Ode to Psyche," N&Q, 192 (1947), 341-2.　2532

Parallels between Epith and the Psyche ode; ll. 50-54 and 58-64, on building a temple for Psyche in the mind, are adapted from Amor 22.

Steen, John. On Spenser's Epithalamion, Spectrum, 5 (1961), 31-7.　2533

Sp, sensing danger of his presumption in creating a poem, alludes to Orpheus and Phaethon, both of whom failed in their tasks. Imperative verbs are signals both of poet's creativity and his prayerful humility. Indicatives are often in emphatic form, emphasizing poet's creative action and energy of his creation. When forced to use simple indicatives, Sp magnifies his action by adding "now." Coming of night in stanza 17 magnifies action by connecting it with universal order, a connection also emphasized by connecting lady's eyes with stars and her journey with the sun, and by associating God and nature with the marriage. After creating the day the poet takes his sabbath and rests.

Stevenson, W. H. The Spaciousness of Spenser's *Epithalamion*, REL, 5 (1964), 61-9.　2534

Chief aspects of Epith, controlled with consummate technique, are theme, pace, and organization. Theme is simple and obvious, pace slow but measured, and organization chronological, treating a series of chosen moments and passing over gaps. Sp succeeds because his plan enables him to do what he is best at.

Stewart, Jack F. Spenser's *Amoretti* LXXIX, 10, Expli, 27 (1969), Item 74. 2535

Metaphor "heavenly seed" carries multiple meanings when examined for Petrarchan, Neoplatonic, Platonic, Catholic, Anglican, and figural ramifications. [SpN, Vol. 2, No. 1 (1971), 8.]

Stewart, James T. Renaissance Psychology and the Ladder of Love in Castiglione and Spenser, JEGP, 56 (1957), 225-30. 2536

"Castiglione influenced strongly all four of Spenser's hymns, and ... in both writers there exists a close relationship between the ladder of love and the principles of Renaissance psychology." As the lover rises from the level of sensation to the level of understanding, he goes through intermediate stages of imagination aided by memory, reason, and will. Finds an unbroken progression in 4 Hymns.

Story, G. M., and Helen Gardner, eds. The Sonnets of William Alabaster. London: Oxford University Press, 1959. 65 pp. 2537

Appendix cites early references to Alabaster as a poet, including Sp's in CCCHA (ll. 400-405) as "knowen yet to few" in spite of Eleseis, which he made for Cynthia.

Taylor, Eric F. *The Knight's Tale:* A New Source for Spenser's *Muiopotmos*, in RenP 1965, ed. George Walton Williams and Peter G. Phialas, pp. 57-63. Southeastern Renaissance Conference, 1966. 63 pp. 2538

Finds verbal and conceptual parallels in the plights of Arcite and Clarion.

Thompson, John. The Iambic Line from Wyatt to Sidney. DA, 18 (1958), 1040. Columbia University, 1957. 260 pp. 2539

Develops a theory of meter based on structural linguistics and applies it. Discusses SC and Sp's four kinds of metrical experiments; these poems "are incoherent and had no issue." See 2315.

Thomson, J. A. K. Classical Influences on English Poetry. London: Allen and Unwin, 1951. 271pp. 2540

Finds in a strong parallel between Bion's Epitaph for Adonis and Astro evidence of Sp's independence of Virgil in his pastoral poetry (pp. 180-1). For other Sp references, see Index.

Thornton, R. K. R. A New Source for Browning's "Love Among the Ruins," N&Q, 15 (1968), 178-9. 2541

Browning's poem may have been influenced by Sp's RR and RT.

Tilley, Edmond Allen. Phonemic Differentiation Analyses of Poems by Sir Thomas Wyatt and Others. DAI, 33 (1972), 1697A. University of Iowa, 1972. 159 pp. 2542

Analysis of 14 sonnets and 10 strambotti of Wyatt on basis of phonemic difference (PD). Five sonnets by Petrarch, Surrey, Sp, Shakespeare, and Wilfred Owen "are distinguished from the Wyatt sonnets in terms of their PD representations."

Tillyard, E. M. W. Reality and Fantasy in Elizabethan Literature, Sprache und Literatur Englands und Amerikas: LAC, 2 (1956), 69-81. 2543

In asserting that it is a fusion of realism and fantasy that gives the age its special character, cites CCCHA with its whimsical rendering of the actual happenings of Sp's visit to London in 1589-90.

Trimpi, Wesley. Ben Jonson's Poems: A Study of the Plain Style. Stanford: Stanford University Press, 1962. 292 pp.   2544

Classical genres using plain style, aside from comedy, are epistle, epigram, and satire (pp. 136 ff.). Outside these genres is Jonson's Celebration of Charis, group of ten short lyrics in tradition of *discorso* or *questione d' amore* of court of love, expressing Neoplatonic rather than anti-Petrarchan attitudes, "and Jonson's sequence seems more a version and an evaluation of the first two of Spenser's Fowre Hymnes than of a conventional Petrarchan sonnet cycle." See Index for references to Sp in analysis of Celebration of Charis (pp. 209-37).

Tufte, Virginia J. "High Wedlock Then be Honored": Rhetoric and the Epithalamium, PCP, 1 (1966), 32-41.   2545

Discusses importance of the rhetoricians in formulating the epithalamic tradition, and "the role of the rhetoricians in enhancing the status of the epithalamium and providing guidelines for English Renaissance poems." Respect for Julius Caesar Scaliger made his Poetices libri septem (1561) "widely influential." Sp thoroughly versed in epithalamic tradition, yet "probably less indebted to the rhetoricians than are most of his colleagues." Experimented with the form in Epithalamion Thamesis, wrote "the masterpiece among English nuptial poems, the *Epithalamion* for his own marriage." Epith reflects narrative epithalamium tradition of the classics, with nature imagery and mythological persons, and Christian epithalamium tradition with Biblical imagery and "devices of tribute to a saint." See 1149.

Van Dorsten, J. A. The Radical Arts: First Decade of an Elizabethan Renais-

sance. Leiden: University Press, 1970. 146 pp.   2546

Understanding of new learning, importance of Dutch refugees in England, new art, and new letters in 1560's necessary to understand flowering of Renaissance in last two decades of Elizabeth I's reign. Evidence of new letters: Thomas Jeney's translation of Ronsard's Discours (1568), and Sp's translations in Theatre (1569). Discusses cultural context of Van der Noot's Dutch version, Het Theatre (1568). Compares eleventh poem in Theatre and sonnet 4 of VB, finds former superior (pp. 75-85). For other references to Sp, see Index.

Vere Hodge, H. S. The Odes of Dante. Oxford: Clarendon Press, 1963. 269 pp.   2547

In Proth and Epith long and short lines alternate at intervals. This technique is found in Dante's odes, e.g., nos. 6 and 9 (p. 9).

Watson, Sara Ruth. An Interpretation of Milton's "Haemony," N&Q, 178 (1940), 260-1.   2548

Believes Sp's reference to "Haemony" in Astro (1.3) and passage on "That hearbe of some, Starlight . . . cald . . . / Of others *Penthia*" (ll. 179-98) came together in Milton's mind. His "creation of the herb Haemony thus leaned heavily upon Spenser." In fact, "the whole passage in 'Comus,' descriptive of the plant, is a tribute to Spenser whom Milton regarded as his master."

Weathers, Winston. Art and Renaissance: The Archetype of Tension, UTDEMS, 4 (1968), 18-23.   2549

Discusses the Renaissance concept of the emergence of order from chaos and its use in literary works. Mentions, in this context, Sp's 4 Hymns. [AES, 16 (1973), Item 2212]

Wells, William. "To Make a Milde Construction": The Significance of the Opening Stanzas of *Muiopotmos*, SP, 42 (1945), 544-54.   2550

The poem is not a mere *jeu d'esprit*, or an allegory of some personal or political conflict at court, but rather "a harmony of the medieval tragedy and the classical mock-heroic." It is appropriately included in the Complaints volume because "it is a 'complaint,' and in its narrative emphasizes once more Spenser's view of the tickle trustless state of vain world's glory."

Welsford, Enid, ed. Spenser: Fowre Hymns, Epithalamion: A Study of Edmund Spenser's Doctrine of Love. New York: Barnes and Noble, 1967. 215 pp.   2551

In Introduction to poems (pp. 1-91) says different treatments of love in 4 Hymns and Epith "suggested their inclusion in one volume." Section on intellectual background discusses treatments of mystical love by Plato and Plotinus; of romantic love by troubadour poets, Cavalcanti, Dante, and Petrarch; of Neo-Platonic and Christianized love by Ficino, Pico, Bembo, Castiglione, and Bruno; influence of Protestantism. Analyzes 4 Hymns in relation to intellectual background. In first two hymns SP "is speaking primarily as a 'Petrarchan' lover (human Eros-love), in the last two as a devout Christian (divine Agape-love)." Both ideas of love "are shown to be good and true." Analyzes Epith, contrasting it with 4 Hymns (pp. 93-139). Notes on Introduction (pp. 140-88). In Appendix II, Number Symbolism in Epithalamion, praises while finding fault with Hieatt's discovery (2398; pp. 191-206). Bibliography (pp. 207-10).
Rev: Raymond Southall, RES, 19 (1968), 426; Sears Jayne, RenQ, 23 (1970), 321.

Wickert, Max A. Structure and Ceremony in Spenser's *Epithalamion*, ELH, 35 (1968), 135-57.   2552

A numerological reading which adjusts Hieatt's proposal of congruity between the first and second halves of the poem to a proposal of symmetry. Draws on astrological lore and the theory of correspondences. See 2398.

Wiersma, Stanley M. Spenser's Statement of the Christian Hope: A Reading of the *Prothalamion*, Universitas (Wayne State U.), 4 (1966), 107-16.   2553

Wilcher, Robert. Details from the Natural Histories in Marvell's Poetry, N&Q, 15 (1968), 101-2.   2554

Attempts to elucidate some of Marvell's allusions to nature-lore. Marvell's fox-badger allusion in line 122 of The Loyal Scot is in Gesner's Historie of Foure-Footed Beastes (1607) and Sp's RT, ll. 216-7.

Williams, Arnold. The Two Matters: Classical and Christian in the Renaissance, SP, 38 (1941), 158-64.   2555

Notes Sp's mingling of pagan and Christian elements in 4 Hymns.

Williams, Ralph Vaughan. Epithalamion. London: Oxford University Press. 1957.   2556

Cantata for baritone solo, chorus, and small orchestra.

Wine, M. L. Spenser's "Sweete Themmes": Of Time and the River, SEL, 2 (1962), 111-7.   2556A

Refrain of Proth, "Sweet Themmes runne softly, till I end my Song," signifies duality of mutability and permanence. The "Song" embodies permanence which transcends mutability of the wedding day and its joys. Refrain satisfies poem on poetic, allegorical, and biographical levels.

Winters, Yvor. Forms of Discovery: Critical & Historical Essays on the Forms of the Short Poem in English. Denver: Swallow, 1967. 377 pp.   2557

Sidney and Sp representative of late 16th-century Petrarchan school (pp. 1-3). Describes them as "poets of transition who modified a well-established tradition and who enabled their successors to improve that tradition. They are not the originators of English lyric poetry . . . they are inferior to their predecessors and to their successors equally." Calls Sp's Epith "the only one of his poems that appears in any measure to justify his reputation." Attacks Sp's sonnets and FQ as inept and vigorless (pp. 28-30). See 1213.

Woodward, Daniel H. Some Themes in Spenser's "Prothalamion," ELH, 29 (1962), 34-46.   2558

Not a "cold and mechanical set piece," Proth is a microcosm of Sp's total poetry encompassing themes of time, beauty, virtue, passion, fruition, and social responsibility, and demonstrating his central concern with union of real and ideal in all areas of human life.

Yuasa, Nobuyuki. A Study of Metaphor in Spenser's Amoretti, SELit, 37 (1961), 163-86.   2559

Calls approach "purely historical," starting with assumption that Sp was committed to old-fashioned allegorical style (simile-prone) in FQ, and in Amor had to come to terms with new sonnet style (metaphor-prone). Reconciliation of metaphor and simile his problem in Amor. Uses Christine Brook-Rose's A Grammar of Metaphor (London, 1958) to analyze noun metaphors in Amor, classified according to grammatical construction as Simple Replacement of tenor by vehicle (most common, rarely used by more innovative Donne), which gave Sp "a handy point of contact with traditional allegory"; Pointing Formulae (rare in Amor, liked by Donne); The Copula (most radical form of noun-metaphor, used sparingly by Sp, often by Donne); and Genitive Link (used to reconcile metaphor with traditional simile). Analyzes verb and adjective metaphors. Discusses other aspects of Amor. Concludes that Sp's "reconciliatory attitude toward the old form and the new form" is "the underlying pattern of his poetry." Ends by comparing Sp to Botticelli; both stand "midway between the Medieval Gothic and the High Renaissance."

Zivley, Sherry. Hawthorne's "The Artist of the Beautiful" and Spenser's "Muiopotmos," PQ, 48 (1969), 134-7.   2560

Parallels suggest reason Hawthorne chose butterfly as image of the beautiful. [SpN, Vol. 1, No. 2 (1970), 6.]

PROSE

Baker, Donald. The Accuracy of Spenser's *Letter to Raleigh*, MLN, 76 (1961), 103-4.   **2561**

Agrees with A. C. Hamilton's note (1413) that the Letter, despite its inconsistencies, is an important statement of Sp's poetic intention in FQ, but denies that the lack of correspondence between the "symbolic pageant" and the actual events of Bk. II can be disregarded.

Borinski, Ludwig. Shakespeare's Comic Prose, ShS, 8 (1955), 57-68.   **2562**

In first section of this packed study, General Characteristics of Shakespeare's Prose, notes Shakespeare's lack of redundancy, main feature of old style and characteristic of Sp and Hooker. Adds, "his metaphors are ... transitional between the unintellectual, visual art of the earlier Renaissance (as it persists, for example, in Spenser) and the new intellectuality of the seventeenth century."

Campion, Edmund. A Historie of Ireland (1571). Introduction by Rudolf Gottfried. New York: SF&R, 1940. 139pp.   **2563**

Reproduces first edition published in The Historie of Ireland, ed. by Sir James Ware, Dublin, 1633. Campion's influence on Sp's View and comparison of the two works, pp. v-vi. See 440.

Crinò, Anna Maria. La Relazione Barducci-Ubaldini sull' Impresa d'Irlanda, 1579-1581, EM, 19 (1968), 339-67.   **2564**

Prints a section of British Museum

MS Yelverton 48082 (740E), account of military expedition to Ireland which ended with surrender and execution of Spanish garrison at Smerwick; account casts doubt on reliability of Sp's defense of Lord Grey, commander of the English force, in View. Irenius, claiming to have been an eye-witness, defends Grey against charge that in executing the Spaniards he violated his terms with them; Grey, Irenius asserts, had demanded unconditional surrender. MS account describes ransoming of 30 members of expedition (point not mentioned by Irenius) and cites as a beneficiary of the ransom Grey's "segretario." If Sp was the "segretario" and account is true, Sp was not disinterested observer and Irenius's assertions come under question.

Cronin, Anne. The Sources of Keating's Forus Feasa ar Éirinn: I. The Printed Sources, Éigse: A Journal of Irish Studies, 4 (1944), 235-79.   **2565**

Keating's History of Ireland was written about 1634. His animadversions on Sp's View, pp. 241-3.

Cronin, Anne. Sources of Keating's Forus Feasa ar Éirinn: 2. Manuscript Sources—Chapter I, Éigse: A Journal of Irish Studies, 5 (1946), 122-35.   **2566**

Scota, pp. 133-4; see Sp's View, 1304, 1703-16, in Variorum edition of Spenser's Prose Works, and commentary, pp. 318, 335-6.

Dean, Leonard F. Bodin's *Methodus* in England before 1625, SP, 39 (1942), 160-6.   **2567**

Knowledge or use of Bodin's Methodus ad facilem historiarum cognitionem (1566) by William Harrison, Holinshed, Sidney, Harvey, Nashe, Sp, and others.

Dunn, Catherine Mary. A Survey of the Experiments in Quantitative Verse in the English Renaissance. DA, 28 (1967), 193A. University of California, Los Angeles, 1967. 355 pp. 2568

After beginnings of "measured" verse movement in Italy and France, English phase of movement began when Ascham attacked "rude barbarous ryming" and urged poets to write "reformed" poetry based on classical meters. First sign of activity in Sp-Harvey correspondence 1579-1580. Sp scans by Latin rules, Harvey advocates taking accent into account. Sidney, following Latin method, most successful in quality and metrical variety. Discusses quantitative verse of Abraham Fraunce, poets of Sidney-Pembroke circle, and others; most of them inept. Last significant quantitative poet Thomas Campion, opposed by Samuel Daniel. Claims some positive results in English poetry from quantitative experiments.

Edwards, R. Dudley. Ireland, Elizabeth I and the Counter-Reformation, in Elizabethan Government and Society: Essays Presented to Sir John Neale, ed. S. T. Bindoff, and others, pp. 315-39. London: Athlone Press, 1961. 423 pp. 2569

Incidental comments on Sp's View, his participation in Irish affairs, and his attitude toward Irish customs (pp. 328-9, 330, 338).

Edwards, Robert Dudley. Church and State in Tudor Ireland: A History of Penal Laws Against Irish Catholics, 1534-1603. Dublin: Talbot Press, [1935?]. 352pp. 2570

View used as source for handicaps of Established Church (p. 206), low quality of Irish-born Anglican clergy (p. 214), Sp's opposition to religious persecution of Irish (p. 236), work of Catholic missionaries (p. 242), Smerwick massacre (pp. 260-1). Valuable bibliography for Sp's Ireland, pp. 313-32.

Falls, Cyril. Elizabeth's Irish Wars. London: Methuen, 1950. 362pp. 2571

Sp cited on itinerant Irish herdsmen (p. 17); on kerne's long lock of hair, known as a "glibb," obnoxious to the English (p. 70); as Lord Grey's secretary (p. 135); as witness of Smerwick massacre (pp. 142-4); on destitution of Irish after failure of Desmond's rebellion (p. 153); his grant of Kilcolman (p. 170); his escape during Tyrone's rebellion, and the burning of Kilcolman (p. 224); as bearer of report from Norris to England (p. 226).

Flower, Desmond. The Pursuit of Poetry: A Book of Letters about Poetry Written by English Poets, 1550-1930. London: Cassell, 1939. 310pp. 2572

Biographical note on Sp (pp. 1-2); Sp's letter to Harvey of April, 1580 (pp. 2-5); Southey's reference to FQ in letter of 1803 to John May (p. 93).

Gottfried, Rudolf. The Date of Spenser's View. MLN, 52 (1937), 176-80. 2573

Argues for 1596 or early in 1597.

Gottfried, Rudolf. The Debt of Fynes Moryson to Spenser's View, PQ, 17 (1938), 297-307. 2574

Moryson in 1600 became secretary to Sir Charles Blount, lord-deputy of Ireland. The Itinerary was published in three parts in 1617. Part of a fourth part printed in 1903 in Charles Hughes' Shakespeare's Europe reveals the debt to Sp's work.

Gottfried, Rudolf. The Early Development of the Section on Ireland in

Camden's *Britannia*, ELH, 10 (1943), 117-30. 2575

Mentions Sp's praise of Camden, and his use of edition of Britannia of 1590 or 1594 in View.

Gottfried, Rudolf. Irish Geography in Spenser's *View*, ELH, 6 (1939), 114-37. 2576

Ireland was for Sp "a country partly of familiar knowledge, partly of written report, and partly of contemporary hearsay" (p. 114). His knowledge of Ulster was derived in all three ways; references to Connaught "seem to reveal a more direct familiarity with their subject"; his first-hand knowledge of Leinster geography was greater than of either Ulster or Connaught; he knew Munster best. Map of Sp's Ireland inserted.

Gottfried, Rudolf. Spenser and Stanyhurst, TLS, Oct. 31, 1936, p. 887. 2577

Sp's unfair and inaccurate attack on Stanyhurst in View shows the haste with which the work was thrown together.

Gottfried, Rudolf. Spenser as an Historian in Prose, TWA, 30 (1937), 317-29. 2578

Sp's sense of history as revealed in View compared with that of Milton. Sp's outlook is colored by his antiquarianism, and he sometimes accepted his sources of information without examination.

Gottfried, Rudolf. Spenser's *View* and Essex, PMLA, 52 (1937), 645-51. 2579

Supports opinion that Sp's View was intended as a compliment to Essex. See 2580.

Heffner, Ray. Spenser's *View of Ireland:* Some Observations, MLQ, 3 (1942), 507-15. 2580

The work has been studied as a lit-erary production rather than as a political treatise; consequently, it has often been misinterpreted. Sp chiefly denounces kerns and outlaws. He did not advocate the extermination of the Irish. In his observations on religion he argued for reform in Ireland with moderation and without force. The View may have been written at Essex's request. See 2579.

Hulbert, Viola B. Spenser's Relation to Certain Documents on Ireland, MP, 34 (1937), 345-53. 2581

Reasons for doubting Sp's authorship of three documents (*A Briefe Note of Ireland*, "To the Queene," and "Certaine points to be considered of in the recouery of the Realme of Ireland") to which Grosart in his life of Sp attached much significance. Rejects them because of differences between the three documents and View.

Hull, Vernam. Edmund Spenser's *Monashul*, PMLA, 56 (1941), 578-9. 2582

On the variant spellings in the editions of Sp's View, and a suggestion based on a knowledge of Irish as to how these could have occurred.

Jameson, Thomas H. The "Machiavellianism" of Gabriel Harvey, PMLA, 56 (1941), 645-56. 2583

Has little direct bearing on Sp; but see note 17, p. 647, and cf. Variorum Commentary on View, ll. 5272-9, and Appendix I, p. 460, l. 499.

Johnson, Francis S. Gabriel Harvey's *Three Letters:* A First Issue of his *Foure Letters*, Library, 5th Series, 1 (1946), 134-6. 2584

Explanation suggested earlier (Library, 4th Series, 15 (1934), 212-23), on basis of bibliographical peculiarities of first edition of Foure Letters and certaine Sonnets, that three letters were intended and during printing of volume Harvey decided to add fourth letter, confirmed by Owen D. Young copy now in Berg Collection in New York Public Library. This copy, therefore, is a first issue of the first edition of Harvey's Foure Letters.

Kliger, Samuel. Spenser's Irish Tract and Tribal Democracy, SAQ, 49 (1950), 490-7.   2585

Argues that View is based on Jean Bodin's precept that any imperialist policy was doomed to failure if it failed to adapt laws to the peculiar needs of subject peoples as determined by race and climate. In calling on the government to adjust its approach to the situation at hand, Sp anticipated the principle of compromise ultimately arrived at in 17th century struggles between King and Parliament.

Kuhn, Ursula. English Literary Terms in Poetological Texts of the Sixteenth Century. Doc. diss., University of Muenster, 1972. 1072 pp. EASG, 4 (1972), 48.   2586

Designed as reference book or dictionary. Gives views of 15 authors important in development of 16th century literary criticism. Most entries have numerous cross-references. Excludes authors concerned only with rhetoric. Only prose contributions considered, "apart from short passages in verse included in the original texts." Authors included: Roger Ascham, Thomas Elyot, George Gascoigne, Stephen Gosson, Gabriel Harvey, E. K., Thomas Lodge, Thomas Nashe, George Puttenham, Philip Sidney, Edmund Spenser, Richard Stanyhurst, William Webbe, George Whetstone, Richard Wills.

Low, Anthony. "Plato, and His Equall Xenophon": A Note on Milton's Apology for "Smectymnuus," MiltonN, 4 (1970), 20-2.   2587

"Equal" means equal in worth, supported by Milton's valuing Sp more than Scotus and Aquinas (Areopagitica), and by Sp's valuing Xenophon as highly as Plato in Letter to Raleigh. For both Milton and Sp, Xenophon teaching "by ensample" worthy to stand with Plato teaching "by rule." See 2598. [SpN, Vol. 2, No. 1 (1971), 8.]

McGuire, James Kevin. Spenser's *View of Ireland* and Sixteenth Century Gaelic Civilization. DA, 18 (1958), 100. Fordham University, 1958.   2588

Describes Irish political and social organization in the age of Sp, and Irish achievement in literature. Examines View and questions Sp's credibility as an authority on Ireland. The first or "antiquarian" half of treatise is more engaging; in second half Sp is "a stern reformer." He relied on English sources and was influenced by official English view of Irish as rebellious savages. Rudolf Gottfried's edition of View in Spenser Variorum (see 413) "relied most heavily on English sources and English historians, who naturally presented a one-sided picture of sixteenth-century Ireland." Admits "the unquestioned excellence of his editorial accomplishment," but hopes "future editors and commentators will give to the evidence 'from the opposite point of view' the weight it deserves in estimating Spenser's hitherto unchallenged stature as an authority on Elizabethan Ireland."

Marjarum, E. Wayne. Wordsworth's View on the State of Ireland, PMLA, 55 (1940), 608-11.   2589

Wordsworth's letter addressed in 1829 to the Bishop of London opposing reform legislation was chiefly indebted to Sp's View. Evidence shows that his familiarity with this work was of much earlier date.

Ó Domhnaill, Sean. Warfare in Sixteenth Century Ireland, IHS, 5 (1946-47), 29-54. 2590

"Burning and desolating the territory of the enemy was a marked feature of a century of war in Ireland.... Edmund Spenser ... who was an eye-witness, paints an appalling picture of the desolation that was wrought in Munster in the great war of Desmond." Quotes View (p. 45).

Ong, Walter J. Spenser's *View* and the Tradition of the "Wild" Irish, MLQ, 3 (1942), 561-71. 2591

Accounts for Sp's qualified antagonism to the Irish by placing him in the tradition of earlier historians: Holinshed, Campion, Sylvester Cambrensis. The Irishman was portrayed as a man of natural ability but lacking in art.

Orwen, William R. Spenser and Gosson, MLN, 52 (1937), 574-6. 2592

Despite Sp's statement to Harvey in the first of Two Other Very Commendable Letters (1580), Gosson apparently obtained Sidney's patronage.

Park, Ben Allen. The Quantitative Experiments of the Renaissance and After as a Problem in Comparative Metrics. DA, 29 (1968), 905A. University of Oklahoma, 1968. 152 pp. 2593

Traces history of quantitative verse movement in Italy, France, Spain, England, and Germany. Nowhere did poets, although "endowed with energy, purpose, and ability," succeed in establishing system of versification which is "unambiguously quantitative." Offers theoretical explanation that "verse systems are complexly related to the phonology of the languages in which they are found."

Phillips, James E. George Buchanan and the Sidney Circle, HLQ, 12 (1948), 23-55. 2594

"Buchanan shared the friendship, attitudes, and ideals of the men who looked to Sidney and Leicester for leadership." Sp was one of these. In View he draws on Buchanan's Rerum Scoticarum Historia (1582), praises his scholarship, and agrees with him in rejecting the legend of Brut. Offers other suggestions of agreement in thought between Sp and the Scottish humanist.

Quinn, David Beers. The Elizabethans and the Irish. Illus. with 25 Plates. Ithaca: Cornell University Press, 1966. 204 pp. 2595

Sp's View repeatedly cited as source in chaps. titled The Curious Eye (pp. 20-33), The Irish Polity Characterized (pp. 34-57), Ireland as Arcadia (pp. 58-61; FQ, VII, vi, 38, 54-55 quoted), A Way of Life Anatomized (pp. 62-90), The Irish Brought to Life (pp. 91-105; FQ, V, xii, 14 quoted), and Horror Story (pp. 123-42).

Raab, Felix. The English Face of Machiavelli: A Changing Interpretation, 1500-1700. London: Routledge & Kegan Paul, 1964. 306 pp. 2596

The horror which greeted The Prince was a natural reaction to Machiavelli's indifference to the assumption of a relationship between the will of God and political behavior. Yet men did not fail to learn from Machiavelli. Sp in View cites him on a point of worldly wisdom. It was left to Bacon, in a new century, to disregard as "unreal" the "finger of God" doctrine, and to later generations to accept politics as secular. [YWES, 45 (1964), 205.]

Ringler, William. Master Drant's Rules, PQ, 29 (1950), 70-4. 2597

Sp's reference in his correspondence with Harvey to Drant's rules for writing English quantitative verse is vague. Sidney left in manuscript three statements on subject that throw light on his eleven poems of this sort. Quotes these statements. A "Nota," heretofore unprinted, in best manuscript of original Arcadia, St. John's College Cambridge 308, gives Sidney's version of "Maister Drants Rules." See 201.

Sasek, Lawrence A. "Plato, and His Equall Xenophon," ELN, 7 (1969), 260-2.
2598

Milton's elevation of Xenophon in his Apology for Smectymnuus is best glossed by reference to Sp's placing Xenophon above Plato as a teacher in Letter to Raleigh. Milton formed high estimate of Xeonophon "out of respect for the poetic method of teaching 'by ensample'." See 2587.

Seymour-Smith, Martin. Poets Through Their Letters: From the Tudors to Coleridge. New York: Holt, Rinehart and Winston, 1969. 464 pp.   2599

Thumbnail sketch of Sp's life and works. Sp's letter to Gabriel Harvey of 5 October 1579, with remarks on "Areopagus" and debate over English prosody, Harvey's "extremely tedious" reply, and Sp's continuation of discussion in letter written April 1580, chiefly interesting because of first mention of FQ and other (lost) works (pp. 64-77). Sp's letter to Raleigh prefixed to first three books of FQ (1590), ostensibly explaining his intent, with remarks on various views of relation of letter to poem, and own view of letter's usefulness (pp. 77-83).

Smith, Roland M. Hamlet Said "Pajock," JEGP, 44 (1945), 292-5.   2600

Convincing demonstration that modern editors are right in retaining pajock (Hamlet, III, ii, 300), which occurs earlier in Sp's View as patchock. The word is Irish. Offers suggestions on some other Irish words in Sp and Shakespeare and their connotations.

Smith, Roland M. The Irish Background of Spenser's View, JEGP, 42 (1943), 499-515.   2601

Sp was not a military expert, some of his knowledge of Ireland coming from military men or from his reading. Authors unfamiliar with the native Irish literature or with the social conditions of Elizabethan Ireland have given erroneous impressions of View. Discusses Irish words and place-names in the work. Much needs to be done before a definitive critical edition can be undertaken.

Smith, Roland M. More Irish Words in Spenser, MLN, 59 (1944), 472-7. 2602

Shows that "Spenser knew more about the Irish and their language than most of his fellow Undertakers, and that some of his opinions were held by reputable Irishmen in Spenser's day and later.

Smith, Roland M. Spenser, Holinshed, and the Leabhar Gabhála, JEGP, 43 (1944), 390-401.   2603

The relation of Sp's View to the Leabhar Gabhála through the Miniugud redaction and the Tudor chroniclers.

Smith, Roland M. Spenser's Scholarly Script and "Right Writing," in Studies in Honor of T. W. Baldwin, pp. 66-111. Urbana: University of Illinois Press, 1958. 276pp.   2604

With plates. Catalogues the known and suspected holographs extant. Assesses their value as guides to Sp's spelling and, hence, as glosses on uncertain words in his works. Discusses pronunciation, diction, and Irish words.

Smith, Roland M. Three Obscure English Proverbs, MLN, 65 (1950), 441-7. 2605

"Life is a pilgrimage" recognized as proverbial by Sp in translation of

Axiochus; and cf. Daph, ll. 372-3. Accepts Sp as translator of 1592 Axiochus (p. 447, note 35). See 417, 658, 2608.

Snare, Gerald. Satire, Logic, and Rhetoric in Harvey's Earthquake Letter to Spenser, TSE, 18 (1970), 17-33.   2606

In Foure Letters of 1592 Harvey gives reasons for publishing his earthquake letter to Sp in Three Proper and wittie familiar Letters of 1580. He was offended by false methods used in numerous pamphlets proclaiming God's judgment expressed in earthquake of April 1580, and wished to expose them. Did so by directly attacking Cambridge doctors and parodying their methods of scientific inquiry in first part of letter, then observing rules of Ramistic logic and rhetoric in second part, demonstrating proper method of scientific investigation. [SpN, Vol. 2, No. 1 (1971), 7.]

Stephenson, Edward A. Some Stylistic Links between Spenser and E. K., in RenP 1956, pp. 66-71. Columbia, S. C.: University of South Carolina, 1956. 112pp.   2607

Compares E. K.'s prose style in prefaces to SC and Sp's in letter to Ralegh, finds both write "Attic" style—unbalanced, asymmetrical sentences which average 47.16 words per sentence for Sp and 49.85 words per sentence for E. K. Supports Starnes's view (see 2304) that E. K. is a pseudonym for Sp.

Swan, Marshall W. S. The *Sweet Speech* and Spenser's (?) *Axiochus*, ELH, 11 (1944), 161-81.   2608

Offers evidence that Anthony Munday and not Sp was the translator of the Axiochus of Plato and the author of the Sweet Speech or Oration spoken at the Tryumphe at Whitehall, both of which were discovered by F. M. Padelford in 1931. Believes the two works were published under Sp's name by an unprincipled publisher because Sp's work was selling well. See 417, 658, 2605.

INDEX

INDEX

Auld, Ina Bell, 482.
Ault, Norman, 249, 250.
Ausonius, Decimus Magnus, 1901.
Austen, John, 400, 401.
Austin, Warren B., 2200, 2327.
Austin, William, 1904, 1986.
Awad, Louis, 483.
Awdeley, John, 2458.
Axiochus (translation attributed to Sp),
    413, 417, 658, 915, 2605, 2608.
Aylmer, John, Bishop of London, 2216,
    2270.
Aziz, Paul Douglas, 484.

B

Babb, Lawrence, 485.
Bache, William B., 2094.
Bacon, Sir Francis, 120, 178, 505, 638,
    708, 719, 790, 845, 953, 992, 1044,
    1178, 1511, 1577, 1596, 1739, 1821,
    1994, 2199, 2253, 2419, 2596.
Bacon, Roger, 992.
Bacquet, Paul, 486.
Bagwell, Richard, 487.
Bahr, Howard W., 488, 1999.
Baine, Rodney M., 1176.
Baker, Carlos Heard, 489, 1245, 1246.
Baker, Donald, 2561.
Baker, Herschel, 375, 490, 1410.
Baker, William Price, 2000.
Bald, R. C., 491.
Baldensperger, Fernand, 7, 2328.
Baldwin, Charles S., 492.
Baldwin, R. G., 493.
Baldwin, T. W., 1247, 1248, 1249, 1730,
    2149.
Bale, John Christian, 494, 926.
Ball, John, 170.
Banks, Theodore H., 123.
Barber, Richard, 1250.
Barclay, Alexander, 880, 2233, 2241,
    2284.
Baretti, J. M., 1771.

Barfield, Owen, 495.
Barkan, Leonard, 1251.
Barker, Arthur E., 496.
Barker, Sir Ernest, 277, 497.
Barker, William, 2169.
Barnes, Barnaby, 2252, 2520.
Barnes, T. R., 498.
Barnet, Sylvan, 2183.
Barnfield, Richard, 731, 821, 939, 1539,
    2201.
Barnhart, Clarence L., 499.
Barnum, Priscilla H. 1252.
Barrows, Herbert, 395.
Bartenschlager, Klaus, 2329.
Bartholomaeus Anglicus, 480, 767, 940,
    1894.
Bartlett, Ruth, 1253.
Bartlett, W. H., 151.
Basil the Great, St., 2255.
Baskervill, Charles Read, 500.
Basse, William, 557, 731, 2189, 2233.
Bassi, 1468.
Bate, Walter Jackson, 501.
Bates, Paul A. 2201.
Bateson, F. W., 8, 24, 502.
Bathurst, Theodore, 2297, 2311.
Batman, Stephen, 480, 1789, 1821,
    1894, 1948, 2347.
Battenhouse, R. W., 1217.
Bauer, Robert J., 1772.
Baugh, Albert C., 251, 544, 1080.
Baxter, Charles, 1894.
Baybak, Michael, 681, 756, 1254.
Bayley, Peter C., 252, 253, 503, 504,
    639.
Baynes, Pauline, 439.
Beach, D. M., 505.
Beall, C. B., 2330.
Beardsley, Monroe C., 1209, 1826.
Beattie, James, 1075, 1728.
Beaty, Jerome, 506.
Beaty, John O. 805.
Beaumont and Fletcher, 617, 677, 1376.
Beaumont, Sir John, 2490.
Beaumont, Joseph, 1118, 2399.
Beccari, Agostino, 2159.

Browning, I. R., 1900, 1921.
Browning, Robert, 736, 981, 2541.
Brumble, Herbert David, 1291.
Bruno, Giordano, 214, 910, 992, 1049, 1834, 2187, 2193, 2551.
Bruser, Fredelle, 1292, 1901.
Bryan, Robert A., 1593, 1785, 1786, 2343.
Bryant, J. A., 550.
Bryce, John Cameron, 551.
Bryskett, Lodowick, 131, 173, 295, 1523, 2373.
Buchan, A. M., 2064.
Buchan, John, 552.
Buchanan, Edith, 1293.
Buchanan, George, 2518, 2594.
Buchanan, James, 2264.
Buchloh, Paul Gerhard, 553.
Buchwald, Emilie, 1294.
Buck, Katherine M., 1902.
Buckler, William E., 246, 247.
Bühler, Curt F., 2212.
Bullett, Gerald, 264.
Bullinger, Henry, 1838, 1881, 2128.
Bullitt, John M., 2344.
Bullock, A., 1383.
Bullough, Geoffrey, 554, 836, 1010, 1295, 1903.
Bunker, Cameran F., 782.
Bunyan, John, 525, 593, 619, 666, 687, 695, 760, 1107, 1265, 1279, 1422, 1429, 1441, 1543, 1638, 1674, 1784, 1789, 1864.
Buonarotti, Michelangelo, 578, 630, 986, 1211.
Burckhardt, Jacob, 564.
Burden, Dennis H., 555.
Burgess, Robert M., 2345.
Burghley, William Cecil, Lord, 238, 823, 957, 1050, 1129, 2388, 2389, 2425, 2477, 2488, 2489.
Burgholzer, Carolyn, 1296.
Burke, Charles B., 1297, 1787, 2346.
Burke, Joseph, 1788.
Burns, Robert, 624, 704, 789.
Burrow, J. A., 1650.

Burton, Robert, 1202, 1224, 2000, 2416.
Bush, Douglas, 349, 556-566, 1033, 1100, 1298.
Bush, Sargent, 1299.
Bushnell, Nelson S., 265.
Butler, Charles, 803.
Butler, Christopher, 567, 681.
Butler, P. R., 568.
Butler, Samuel, 577, 1059.
Butt, John, 569, 1023.
Buttet, Marc-Claude de, 2447.
Buxton, John, 570, 571, 572.
Byron, George Gordon, Lord, 526, 624, 668, 736, 789, 805, 903, 1001, 1107, 1215.

C

Cabbala, 576, 1577, 2497.
Cabeen, D. C., 88.
Caesar, Gaius Julius, 762, 1965.
Cain, Thomas H., 573, 2213.
Cairncross, A. A., 136.
Calderwood, James L., 266.
Calepine, Friar Ambrosius, 1109.
Callimachus, 2509, 2510.
Calpurnius, Titus, 2283.
Calvin, John, 989, 1549, 1680, 1971, 2128.
Calvinism, 566, 575, 584, 606, 785, 910, 959, 989, 1085, 1177, 1194, 1380, 1453, 1460, 1549, 1550, 1840, 2325.
Cambrensis, Sylvester, 2591.
Cambridge Platonists, 497, 578, 1821.
Cambridge, William Owen, 1070.
Camden, Carroll, 1904, 2347.
Camden, William, 119, 173, 613, 654, 762, 975, 976, 2575.
Cameron, Kenneth N., 2214.
Camões, Luisvaz de, 728, 787, 1284, 1383, 1554.
Campbell, Lily B., 574, 836, 1300.
Campbell, Oscar James, 267.
Campbell, Thomas, 736.
Campion, Edmund, 185, 282, 704, 991, 2563, 2591.

Hesiod, 1370, 1596, 1780, 1870, 2189, 2435.

Heuer, Hermann, 70.

Heydon, Sir Christopher, 2214.

Heydorn, Marianne, 785.

Heyen, William, 2396.

Heylyn, Peter, 609, 1191.

Heywood, John, 918.

Heywood, Thomas, 940, 1788, 2377.

Hibbard, Addison, 322.

Hibbard, G. R., 786.

Hibernicus, 2032.

Hieatt, A. Kent, 323, 324, 681, 756, 833, 960, 1014, 1015, 1049, 1254, 1310, 1373, 1930, 1931, 2075, 2162, 2397, 2398, 2551, 2552.

Hieatt, Charles W., 1650.

Hieatt, Constance, B., 323, 1432.

Higashinaka, Itsuyo, 1433.

Higgins, Dennis Vincent, 1821.

Highet, Gilbert, 787.

Hill, Christopher, 788.

Hill, Elizabeth A. K., 2399.

Hill, Elliott M., 2400.

Hill, Iris Tillman, 2027.

Hill, John M., 1434.

Hill, R. F., 756, 1088, 1435, 1646, 1741, 2148.

Hill, W. Speed, 2401.

Hilliard, Nicholas, 2492.

Hillyer, Robert, 789.

Hinely, Jan Lawson, 2402.

Hines, William H., 430.

Hinman, Robert B., 790.

Hinnant, Charles H., 2403.

Hippisley, J. H., 791.

Histories of Sp Criticism, 116, 603, 613, 621, 666, 947, 1190, 1191, 1296, 1676, 1719, 2177.

Hobbes, Thomas, 790, 1079, 2172.

Hobsbaum, Philip, 325, 792.

Hoffman, Arthur W., 355, 1436, 2404.

Hoffman, Daniel, 1822.

Hoffman, Nancy, 2241.

Hoffmann, Ernest Theodore Wilhelm, 1812.

Hogan, Frank, 473.

Hogan, Patrick G., Jr., 163, 1437.

Holborne, Anthony, 2242.

Holden, William P., 2243.

Holinshed, Raphael, 185, 762, 951, 1761, 2591, 2603.

Holland, Joan Nina Field, 644, 793, 2180.

Holland, Philemon, 2347.

Hollander, John, 794, 1932.

Holleran, James V., 1438, 1439, 1440, 1933.

Holloway, J., 1923, 1934.

Holme, Randle, 479.

Holmes, U.T., Jr., 1152.

Holzknecht, K. J., 346.

Homer, 560, 699, 728, 826, 1060, 1067, 1103, 1226, 1334, 1337, 1349, 1408, 1430, 1538, 1735, 1886, 2189.

Honey, William Bowyer, 326.

Honig, Edwin, 327, 1441, 1442, 1443.

Honor and Fame, 459, 485, 511, 519, 1317, 1333, 1401, 1538, 1635, 1747, 1958, 1973.

Hook, Julius Nicholas, 795, 796.

Hooker, Richard, 68, 575, 576, 845, 1333, 1443, 1532, 2000, 2407, 2562.

Hoopes, Robert, 756, 1444, 1753, 1935, 1978.

Hopkins, G. M., 542, 1469, 2438.

Hopkins, Kenneth, 328, 797.

Hopper, Vincent F., 1936.

Horace (Quintus Horatius Flaccus), 302, 1126, 1349, 1901, 2239, 2510.

Hornstein, Lillian Herlands, 70, 1445.

Horton, Ronald Arthur, 1446.

Hortus conclusus, 601, 667, 693, 697, 1118, 1260, 1383, 1483, 1558.

Hotson, Leslie, 798, 1447, 2159, 2405, 2406.

Hough, Graham, 349, 649, 1147, 1267, 1448, 1448A, 1449, 1450, 1480, 1937.

Houghton, Walter E. 395.

Housman, A. E., 422, 1290, 1951.

Wolkenfeld, Suzanne, 1890.
Wood, Paul Spencer, 451.
Woodford, Samuel, 1466.
Woodhouse, A. S. P., 218, 349, 468, 644,
  756, 891, 1217, 1380, 1411, 1641,
  1750, 1751, 1752, 1753, 1754, 1755,
  1935.
Woodhouse, Richard, 1101.
Woodring, Carl, 2088.
Woodruff, Bertram L., 1891.
Woodward, Daniel H., 2558.
Woodward, Frank L., 1994.
Woodworth, Mary K., 2194.
Woolf, Virginia Stephen, 649, 1756,
  1757.
Wordsworth, Dorothy, 945.
Wordsworth, William, 495, 528, 561,
  592, 620, 668, 736, 801, 903, 904,
  931, 945, 983, 1001, 1107, 1166,
  1215, 1218, 1225, 1330, 1532, 1575,
  1578, 1682, 1758, 1792, 1819, 1892,
  1985, 2102, 2275.
Worthington, John, 613.
Wraight, A. D., 239.
Wrenn, C. L., 1218, 2322.
Wright, Andrew, 3.
Wright, Austin, 546.
Wright, Carol Von Pressentin, 1759.
Wright, Celeste Turner, 240, 2135.
Wright, G. W., 139.
Wright, John, 1219.
Wright, Lloyd Allen, 1760.
Wright, Nathalia, 1995.
Wright, Thomas E., 131.
Wurnig, Gertraud, 1761.
Wurtsbaugh, Jewel, 116, 1296.
Wyatt, A. J., 1220.
Wyatt, Thomas, 124, 325, 498, 527, 572,
  592, 669, 742, 801, 817, 853, 918,
  922, 930, 981, 988, 1006, 1019, 1071,
  1105, 1117, 1139, 1186, 1924, 2313,
  2329, 2355, 2438, 2482, 2485, 2493,
  2542.
Wybarne, Joseph, 1338.
Wycliffe, John, 366.
Wynthorne, Thomas, 721.

X

Xenophon, 761, 2587, 2598.

Y

Yates, Frances A., 1057, 1221, 1762,
  1996, 2187, 2255.
Yeats, William Butler, 467, 498, 533,
  545, 660, 662, 700, 764, 884, 885,
  1017, 1024, 1102, 1119, 1676, 1822.
Young (Yong), Bartholomew, 843, 1522.
Young, Edward, 736.
Young, John, Bishop of Rochester, 169,
  175, 1129, 1953, 2216, 2265, 2266,
  2273.
Young, John Jacob, 1763.
Young, Karl, 281.
Young, Owen D., 2584.
Young, Stark, 1033.
Young, Thomas, 2525.
Yuasa, Nobuyuki, 1222, 2559.

Z

"Z. I.," translator of The Historie of
  George Castriot (1596), 233, 234.
Zacha, Richard Bane, 1764.
Zanco, Aurelio, 1223.
Zandvoort, R. W., 1449.
Zaturenska, Marya, 307.
Zeigler, Lee Woodward, 1597.
Zesmer, David Mordecai, 1224.
Zillmar, Laurence J., 452.
Zimmerman, Dorothy Wynne, 1225.
Zitner, Sheldon P., 453, 1226, 1447,
  1474, 2443.
Zivley, Sherry, 2560.
Zocca, Louis R., 1765.
Zodiac and zodiacal cycle, 599, 1367,
  2398.